D1601149

PUBLICATIONS OF RUSSELL SAGE FOUNDATION

Indicators of Social Change

Concepts and Measurements

Edited by
Eleanor Bernert Sheldon
and
Wilbert E. Moore

Russell Sage Foundation
New York · 1968

RUSSELL SAGE FOUNDATION
230 PARK AVENUE
NEW YORK, N.Y. 10017

© 1968

RUSSELL SAGE FOUNDATION. ALL RIGHTS RESERVED.
Printed in the United States
of America

Library of Congress Catalog Card Number: 68–54407
Standard Book Number: 87154–771–6

CONNECTICUT PRINTERS, INCORPORATED
HARTFORD, CONNECTICUT

First Printing: November 1968
Second Printing: April 1971
Third Printing: July 1972

THE CONTRIBUTORS

DANIEL BELL — Professor of Sociology
Columbia University

N. J. DEMERATH III — Associate Professor of Sociology
University of Wisconsin

BEVERLY DUNCAN — Research Associate
Population Studies Center
University of Michigan

OTIS DUDLEY DUNCAN — Professor of Sociology and
Associate Director
Population Studies Center
University of Michigan

PHILIP H. ENNIS — Professor of Sociology
Wesleyan University

WILLIAM J. GOODE — Professor of Sociology
Columbia University

STANLEY LEBERGOTT — Professor of Economics
Wesleyan University

IDA C. MERRIAM — Assistant Commissioner for Research
and Statistics
Social Security Administration

JOYCE M. MITCHELL — Associate Professor of Political Science
University of Oregon

WILLIAM C. MITCHELL — Professor of Political Science
University of Oregon

WILBERT E. MOORE — Sociologist
Russell Sage Foundation

IWAO M. MORIYAMA
Director
Office of Health Statistics Analysis
National Center for Health Statistics
U.S. Public Health Service

MILTON MOSS
Assistant Director
National Economic Accounts
Office of Statistical Standards
U.S. Bureau of the Budget

A. W. SAMETZ
Professor of Finance and
Research Director
Institute of Finance
Graduate School of Business
Administration
New York University

ELEANOR BERNERT SHELDON
Sociologist and Executive Associate
Russell Sage Foundation

CONRAD TAEUBER
Associate Director
U.S. Bureau of the Census

CONTENTS

I. Introduction

II. The Demographic Base

III. Structural Features

I. INTRODUCTION

1. MONITORING SOCIAL CHANGE IN AMERICAN SOCIETY

Eleanor Bernert Sheldon and Wilbert E. Moore

THE NOTION that far-reaching change is taking place in the structure of American society is now rather commonplace. However vague our understanding of the basic functioning of our society, we do know that the growth and urbanization of the population, the rising technicality and bureaucratization of work, the general upgrading in standards of living, the spread and increasingly higher attainment levels of education, and the heightened self-awareness and rise of minority groups have created serious social strains. Concomitantly, national concern for the prospects of our society has increased and extended beyond strictly economic considerations—in civil rights legislation, large-scale support of education, programs to alleviate inequalities, medicare, and many other efforts.

Recent social change is such a prevalent and disturbing feature of contemporary life that both specialists and laymen have begun to analyze and question its antecedents and its consequences. The contemporary resurgence of attention to social change may be attributed partly to "the threatening newness of the world,"[1] partly to the many criticisms that social scientists have neglected these problems, and perhaps partly to the enlarged body of descriptive data about our society. For the social scientist, and particularly for the sociologist, an interest in social change represents a return to a major preoccupation of the founders of the discipline, which began more than a century ago. That interest was almost lost among the great majority of sociologists, as both theorists and methodologists addressed themselves to cross-sectional interdependence rather than to sequential links through time. The recent revival of interest may have been provoked as much by practical concerns in reducing the social costs of headlong change, in deliberate social intervention and program evaluation, as by strictly theoretical developments.

3

It is especially for those who have undertaken responsibility for bringing about publicly approved changes that the notion of "social indicators" is appealing. Such indicators would give a reading both on the current state of some segment of the social universe and on past and future trends, whether progressive or regressive, according to some normative criteria. The notion of social indicators leads directly to the idea of "monitoring" social change. If an indicator can be found that will stand for a set of correlated changes, and if intervention can be introduced (whether on the prime, indicative, variable or on one of its systemic components), then the program administrator may have been provided a powerful analytical and policy tool.

The indicators explored in this volume are *not* designed for program evaluation, although various authors, at our invitation, have noted some practical or policy-oriented implications of the trends discerned and dissected. The volume is heavily weighted toward the scholarly, or analytic, side of the balance between theoretical and practical concerns focusing on large-scale structural change. It asks the primary question: What is changing? Underlying any answer to this question is some theory or model of society, however vague, explicit or implicit.

The chapters in this volume provide the major categories by which we have identified the component parts of a functional system—that society undergoing change. We have proposed four major rubrics for examining structural changes in American society and its constituent features:[2] (1) the demographic base, giving an indication of aggregative population trends, its changing composition and distribution across the nation's surface; (2) major structural components of the society, examining the functionally distinct ways in which a society produces goods, organizes its knowledge and technology, reproduces itself, and maintains order; (3) distributive features of the society, looking at how the products of society—people, goods, services, knowledge, values, and order—are allocated across the several sectors of the American population; (4) aggregative features of the society, suggesting how the system as a whole changes with respect to its inequalities and variable opportunities and in terms of its social welfare.

Our approach does not constitute a theoretical model of American society, for such a model would incorporate the functional and sequential links among the segments. We anticipate, however, that the contents of these chapters may guide us and others in the construction of such models.

MAJOR STRUCTURAL CHANGE AND
ITS MEASUREMENT

The term "social structure" has not been accorded a uniform and consensual meaning in the scholarly literature of the social sciences. The uses of the term range from the very inclusive concept of any *pattern of action or relationship*—say, modes of acknowledging introductions to strangers, traffic flows in central business districts, or forms of religious ritual—to the very restricted concept of *social differentiation,* particularly with respect to status inequalities. It is also possible to view structures as *social systems*—complete with values, norms, and motivated actors playing prescribed roles—or, at another extreme, as a set of *statistical categories*—the age structure of a population, the occupational structure of the labor force.[3]

Social change, too, is a term that may cover a wide range of phenomena:

> Social change is the significant alteration of social structures (that is, patterns of action and interaction), including consequences and manifestations of such structures embodied in norms (rules of conduct), values, and cultural products or symbols.[4]

In this introductory essay and in the subjects discussed in this volume, we shall limit our view of structural change to the central functional features of a society's operation. Thus, changes in the way people earn a living, in the size and kinship composition of households, in the forms of maintaining political order are prime candidates for attention. The emergence of leadership patterns in task-oriented small groups, the effects of succession to office on administrative organization, or seasonal variations in air travel, though examples of change, are not of present concern.

Some Theories of Change

Despite general neglect of social change in sociological analysis, that neglect has not been total or totally lacking in attempts at explanatory generalization. We shall briefly examine some of these attempts.

Evolution and Revolution. The once-popular extension of evolutionary theory to social interpretation had almost dwindled away, only to undergo a recent revival on the part of those seeking explanation of long-term change. The notion of evolution seems to have some explanatory value in accounting for cultural diversity in terms of selective adaptation. It also may have some explanatory value for part of the *general* course of human experience in terms of long-term cultural accumulation and of increasing social differentiation. For evolutionary theory to be sensible, even as a metaphor, a source of variability must be identified, for otherwise the notion of selection makes no sense. Here the concept of *innovation* is appropriate and, given the purposive and problem-solving proclivities of social man, some innovations may be deliberate and not merely accidental discoveries or inventions.

Nevertheless, evolutionary theory has poor predictive power, and is especially poorly fitted to predict large-scale and rapid change. Although evolution and revolution are often placed in sharp contrast, in many instances the explanation of revolution turns out to be a kind of evolutionary theory. Thus in Marxist or neo-Marxist views, revolution is seen as a necessary consequence of antecedent conditions and events, an unfolding of inescapable sequences. But revolution, of course, does emphasize discontinuity in short-term and large-scale transitions.

Both evolutionary and revolutionary theory are, in effect, *special* theories of structural change. They each account for a portion of such changes, but taken together their total contribution to our understanding (read: capacity to predict) is small. Not all significant structural changes are either gradually accumulative and exemplary of evolution or sharply discontinuous with precedent and exemplary of revolution. Without other explanatory principles we should be in dire straits indeed.

Alternative Prime Movers. Still other simplifying solutions to apparent complexity and instability are available. It has occurred to one or another scholar to find the basic, or ultimate, or long-run, or "in-the-last-analysis" source of change in a particular segment of social functions. Persuasive cases can be presented for several prime movers.

The view that economic changes are primary in the alteration of other social arrangements was scarcely invented by Marx, and since Marx's time has been espoused by interpreters not otherwise Marxist in orientation. The argument here is one or another minor variant of the view that social change is interest-based, and that unequal economic power will yield changes in production systems and allocation of benefits, which, in turn, will have wider ramifications. It is not necessary to the theory of economic primacy that the aggregate consequences must be intended, perhaps by anyone. The distribution and use of scarce productive resources is so essential for a variety of other shared and collective goals that the assumption of a kind of economic primacy has served well as a first approximation to the explanation of social change in newly developing countries. The heuristic value of a theory does not, of course, validate it as an unchallenged principle.

A very popular variant of economic primacy is the view that technology leads all else. Certainly in the contemporary world we can witness the institutionalization of rationality (including efficiency), the organized support for deliberate improvements in techniques ranging from production of goods to the control of crimes. Yet it is precisely this purposive element that undermines the theory, for this means that some extensions of knowledge will get major attention, and others minor support or none. A modern society "selects" its technology from a universe of alternative possibilities by virtue of deliberate decisions in resource allocation, not through the consequences of mindless or accidental technical innovations.

Both for advanced industrial societies and, especially, for nations seeking to gain admittance to that rather select circle, a fair case can be made out for the leading position of the polity as a prime mover of change, in the form of the organized national state. One theory of modern history would maintain that the few nations initiating the first Industrial Revolution did so largely under decentralized and private sponsorship, with permissive positions taken by political organs supplemented by occasional positive intervention. The argument continues, however, that late-comers cannot tolerate either gradualness or wasteful competition, with the result that the polity is uniquely equipped to mobilize resources for planned achievement of individual and collective goals. There is a clear tone of authenticity to this argument, but it is still partial, for it relates only to "new nations." There is in fact a secular trend toward increasing governmental participation in the economy in *all* contemporary societies, not only in newly modernizing countries. The particular reasons for governmental guidance may differ, and do. But simplification has been pushed too far, and one must hope to have a change-model that will specify the forms and degrees of political initiative to be expected under varying conditions—and some of those conditions will be variable in terms of historical time and in terms of problems that may be peculiar to each country.

Other explanatory principles have claimed adherents, though less conspicuously. At least since Malthus, a kind of demographic determinism has been a somewhat defensible position. Demographic change may be viewed as the aggregated consequences of individually motivated actions and of primarily environmental determinants of morbidity and mortality. No recent theorist has argued that population trends claim exclusive attention, but theorists who neglect demographic dimensions stand on extremely unfirm ground.

Finally, we dare not neglect the claims of ideological determinism. The classic example of the (largely implicit or unintended) structural consequences of an ideological position is that of Max Weber's interpretation of the primary importance of Protestantism in the rise of capitalism.[5] No one would seriously argue that Protestantism is now a sufficient or even a necessary condition for economic modernization. But a persuasive case can be made for functional equivalents of Protestantism as an ideological determinant of structural change. Communism as a quasi-religious movement, and nationalism in its many manifestations, provide examples of explicit rationalizations for current sacrifice in view of future benefits, for the collectivity if not for the individual.

Typologies. Somewhere between the identification of a unique universal principle of structural change and the nihilist position that "everything depends on particular circumstances of time and place," there may be some tenable positions. One is the resort to typologies. Thus, it may well be that generalizations about social sequences can be most readily upheld if limited to, say, either highly developed or to newly developing economies. Each of those categories may need further subdivision. Indeed, if there are not sharp discontinuities in the defining or identifying criteria, scalar ordering may be preferable to the use of types. This would yield propositions of "The more . . . the more," type (which are still essentially cross-sectional), and possibly such propositions as, "The faster the rate of change in X, the greater the probability of dissonance in Y," and even the form, "If X is changing at velocity V_1, Y will change at velocity V_2."

Backing off from the most general level of theorizing by resort to typologies or even cases may be a necessary concession to complexity poorly comprehended. Yet that alone is not enough. One must also have resort to observation.

Quantitative observation and analysis have only recently become fairly general in the "less developed" social sciences, such as political science and sociology. And even so, with the conspicuous exception of sociological demography, little attention has been given to sequential as distinct from cross-sectional or correlational analysis.[6] Yet such observation seems essential if we are to predict (and possibly alter) social trends, to identify leads and lags, to distinguish proximate causes from proximate effects.

A Note on Measurement

The measurement of social change shares with other targets for measurement a congeries of statistical hazards. The first of these rests in the relation between numbers and meaning. Statistical analysis deals with numbers produced by certain operations and conclusions, based on numbers relating to both the processes producing them and to the explanatory context from which they derive and to which they refer. No item of information, no measure or series of measures, is self-explanatory. For example:

> When we speak of "observing" business cycles we use figurative language. For, like other concepts, business cycles can be seen only "in the mind's eye." What we literally observe is not a congeries of economic activities rising and falling in unison, but changes in readings taken from many recording instruments of varying reliability. These readings have to be decomposed for our purposes; then one set of components must be put together in a new fashion. The whole procedure seems far removed from what actually happens in the world where men strive for their livings.[7]

The aggregation and decomposition of such "observations" are recorded in columns of figures, each of which is as abstracted from reality and as divorced from its particular matrix of meaning as the processes that produced it.

Duncan points to many simple cautions in interpreting time-series data: (1) Large relative gains come easier from a low starting point than from one approaching a ceiling; (2) absolute differences often give an opposite impression from that conveyed by relative differences; (3) quantities in a time series often require standardization before any interpretation can be ventured.[8]

The volume we are here introducing is concerned with the changing quantities (and implicitly the changing qualities) of American life. The authors of the several chapters are uniformly concerned with quantitative demonstration. Yet it would be silly indeed to suppose that they have at hand the reliable quantities necessary for testing leads and lags, let alone a grand probability matrix of sequential changes.

Problems of Statistical Systems. In the United States and in other advanced industrial societies, a great flow of numbers representing forms of social behavior is available from public or private sources. For traffic densities or some forms of market transactions the information may be virtually instantaneous, and summaries (totals or averages) may appear perhaps on an hourly basis. Other information is assembled and codified less frequently.

Many of the bits of information available to the observer have been collected for reasons other than his own. They are often statistics that are a by-product of control-mechanisms for an administrative process: how many dollars were spent in a stipulated time period for how many recipients of a particular publicly supported welfare program? The causes of welfare-payment needs, or the consequences of one or another solution to those needs, or even the over-all magnitude of the identified "problem population" may receive little attention, if any at all.

Problems of Additivity. The great advantage enjoyed by economists in dealing with market transactions and other forms of economic activity has been the availability of a common unit of measurement—money. By translation into monetary terms, one can indeed add apples and oranges, horses and jet-plane trips, public welfare benefits and private savings. Of course, not all economic indicators are additive, and one must be cautious before excluding economists from the penance-box for sinful aspirants to social measurement. The production of kilowatt-hours per capita, or ton-miles of overland freight, or portland-cement production, or freight-car loadings comprise quantities that are changeful and no more additive than crime rates, divorce and separation rates, the "birth" rate of new voluntary associations, and the average educational attainment of the adult population.

There are always available at least partial solutions to problems of adding unlike quantities, particularly in trend analysis. One such solution is the use of index numbers, pegged to a common temporal base, allowing the observer to sort out differential rates of change, and, perhaps, some clues to temporal priorities—which changes lead and which lag.

Additionally, high correlations among some subset of measured observations originally thought to warrant individual inspection may permit the reduction of the series to a more limited number of indicators. We thus return to an earlier theme, the appeal of simplifying reduction of the great big buzzing confusion of social events. In the current state of the theory and art of social diagnosis, it would appear that such simplifying indicators must be established by inductive generalization, not by deductive derivation from established laws.

Problems of Frequency. If we grant the need for a better observational base for plotting, and predicting the course of structural change, does this mean in realistic terms an empty and pious vote for perfection never attainable? Since all of science deals with successive approximations to verity, the counsel of perfection would be a counsel of despair.

The current state of analysis of social change gives no cause for the particular worry that its students are likely to complete their task and be thereafter unemployable because obsolete.

Take, for example, the practical (and theoretical) problem of the frequency with which observations of current state should be made, in order to detect and then generalize about the rates at which component structures change, and the sequences of change among the components.

Theory gives us little help here. There are notions commonly stated to the general effect that values are slow to change and practical techniques relatively fast, but exceptions and clarifications can be adduced to make that formulation either suspect or false.

There is simply no *a priori* basis for determining the frequency of observation of any aspect of social behavior or function. Such a premise would require precisely what we lack—rates of change and their shape over various periods of time.

Some observations can be made almost continuously, we have noted, as they usually derive from some administrative mechanism—market prices, birth and death registrations, passenger miles in domestic and international travel. Other observations may be readily made frequently (say, monthly) because of administrative rules (which may have little intellectual justification)—crime reports, hospital admissions, recipients of welfare payments or services of various kinds.

Short of a continuous and universal surveillance system, there is likely to be no ideal solution to the problem of observational frequency. (On technical grounds, constant and massive inputs would overload any analytical system, quite apart from the ethical issues involved in surveillance, to which we are not insensitive.)

We are impressed with the importance of approaching this problem *empirically,* in the strict and original meaning of the term—that is, attempting to achieve the maximum feasible frequency of observation, and then relenting when this produces scant evidence of short-term fluctuations. Where the reasons for short-term fluctuations are obscure (and we thus, conventionally, give our ignorance the neutral designation of "chance"), those fluctuations may hide underlying trends.

The temporal order of events, of major structural change, has perhaps suffered from too much observation of concurrent relations and too little observation over longer periods of time. The latter is inherently more difficult, if for no other reason than the fact that observers also move through time, and are not immortal. But that is a detail, and scarcely an argument against the cumulative knowledge available to a continuing scientific community.

A CHANGING AMERICAN SOCIETY

It is perhaps not possible—and surely not desirable—to attempt a summarization of the wealth of materials detailed in the chapters that follow. We may attempt, however, to review briefly some large-scale changes that have occurred in the basic structural, distributive, and aggregative features of American society.

Structural Changes

Two primary transformations characterize the nation's population: growth and urbanization, or as more dramatically expressed, explosion and implosion.[9] Between the first (1790) and the latest (1960) decennial census the population of the United States increased from fewer than 4 million to more than 180 million. We are now a nation in excess of 200 million persons. Also at the earlier date, 95 per cent of the population lived in rural areas; by 1960 70 per cent of the American people resided in urban places. About three out of five persons in this nation now live in metropolitan areas. While the population has become increasingly concentrated in urban and metropolitan areas, decentralization has occurred—with rising proportions of residents living in the suburban ring and a declining percentage in the central city.

Along with these sweeping changes occurred the westward movement and settlement of the continent, the growth and redistribution of the Negro population (to the North and West and from rural to urban living), the assimilation of the foreign-born, the decline of large families and households, the virtual eradication of illiteracy and the rise in educational attainment. (See the chapters by Taeuber, Goode, and Beverly Duncan.)

Economic growth over the past century has been great, but, as Sametz notes in his chapter, it is difficult to compare data for 1867 with those for 1967. However, since "structural change is the essence of secular change" (p. 77), it must be accounted for. Sametz outlines a method—adjusting the Gross National Product upward to allow for the increase in quality of output and of leisure and downward to allow for the market effects of the commercialization of domestic activities and the social costs of an urbanizing-industrializing society.

American society has also completed the transformation from an essentially agricultural to an industrial economy, and then to the now emergent "postindustrial" society.[10] (A postindustrial society is one in which more than half of the economic activity is devoted to services, whether measured by value of product or by distribution of the labor force.) As the nation's working force moved from predominantly farm to manufacturing to service occupations, we observe a decline in the role of the entrepreneur and small-scale business enterprise and an increase in the concentration and bureaucratization of work (see the chapters by Taeuber and Lebergott). Per capita output is three to four times greater than a century ago and about 50 per cent greater today than at the end of World War II, as is noted by Sametz. A rising obsolescence in workers' skills has accompanied the increasing productivity, with about 80 per cent of manufacturing workers being displaced by machines. The hours worked each week had fallen rapidly since the turn of the century but that decline ceased by 1929, remaining stable since the 1930's. Union organization and federal wage-hour legislation have done little to cut prevailing factory hours. The tendency to exchange more income for more leisure was apparently checked by the mid-1930's. Since then, productivity gains have been taken mostly in money rather than in leisure (a circumstance noted by Lebergott and Ennis). Evidence that a shorter work-week is at least optional can be found, but national averages obscure the extent to which options are exercised between income and greater leisure.

Increasing productivity has resulted, of course, from rapid advances in technology, a rapid accretion of knowledge, and a startling change in the character of knowledge. The impact of these changes has been felt not only in the economic sphere—rise in output, an extended division of labor, and the increasing scale and concentration of enterprise—but also in ever finer distinctions of social differentiation and psychic differentiation, noted in the chapter by Bell. The world has become more open, more available; there is a greater eagerness for experience and change; a child of today not only faces a radical rupture with the past, but he must also be trained for an unknown future. The family as a social institution combining primary socialization, economic, welfare, recreational, and other functions has been sundered. There ensued a distribution and sharing of these functions by other institutions—thereby producing further structural change. Meanwhile, the family is not about to disappear, as some of its previously less notable functions become prominent—adult sexuality and personality formation, initial socialization, and social placement of infants and the young.

The shift from an agricultural to an industrial to a postindustrial economy and society, with an increasing focus on a service economy, is highlighted by a rising preeminence of the professional and technical class; the centrality of theoretical knowledge as a source of innovation and policy formulation in the society; and the creation of new ways of formulating and solving problems. (See chapter by Bell.) Knowledge has become necessary for the existence of society, living by innovation and growth, and by seeking to anticipate the future. The need for planning and an awareness of the nature of innovation has brought about the centrality of theoretical knowledge—"the primacy of theory over empiricism, and the codification of knowledge into abstract systems of symbols that can be utilized and illuminate many different and varied circumstances" (p. 155). This has given rise to a new "intellectual technology" (linear programming, systems analysis, information theory, decision theory, and the like) which, when linked to the computer, produce a powerful tool for analysis, experiment, and policy formulation.

The intellectual system, once and perhaps still currently the guardian of tradition and values, has provided one of the integrative functions of our society. In the future as the primary source of innovation and thereby bearer of change, it begins (haltingly) to replace the economy in carrying out the adaptive functions of the society. Education as the purveyor and distributor of knowledge is becoming the major determinant of the stratification system. For better or for worse, our society is beginning to place almost exclusive reliance on educational attainment as the sorting mechanism for adult occupational position.

In viewing the political system of the nation as a functional element of this wider—and changing—society we find that it represents a paradox of stability and change. Even in the midst of the rapid and perhaps bewildering social and economic change, the United States "has managed to create and preserve one of the most stable sets of formal political structure ever known," according to the chapter by the Mitchells. This nation possesses the oldest operative written constitution, the oldest continuous two-party system, and the oldest recurrent set of peaceful elections in history. Though the original document still defines the basic formal structure of government, its adaptation to change has been considerable, with the addition of fifteen amendments subsequent to the Constitution and original Bill of Rights and with most important changes brought about by judicial interpretation and implementation. The fundamental aspects of the Constitution, with a federal distribution of power, a separation of power among the several offices of the state, and a federal bill of rights, still hold force.

Though once a "nation," we have now become a "national society" —with political institutions more responsive to needs throughout the nation—seeking national solutions to private problems, and to state and local inequities (see the chapters by Bell and the Mitchells). Legislative and judicial changes have brought the enlargement of federal spending and regulatory powers, rationalized by the commerce, tax, and welfare clauses of the Constitution.

The sphere of protective rights has enlarged—responsive to the impact of growth, urbanization, the increasing role of the mass media, the greater mobility of the population. Economic, social, and military contacts with other nations have transformed the military and foreign policy powers of the executive and legislative branches.

Political life has become both more centralized and decentralized— with greater national and greater state activities, both doing more in specifying problems and implementing decisions. The result has been a proliferation of offices, administrative units, boards, commissions, and the like, across many levels and different geographic jurisdictions. Forms of public and private cooperation have become increasingly widespread. Yet it remains true that in one of the most open and democratic societies the world has yet known, political participation engages no more than two-thirds of the relevant electorates, as the Mitchells note.

If voting is taken as a measure of political effectiveness, the American record is not exemplary. Even in closely contested national elections, the proportion of the qualified electorate that actually votes rarely exceeds 60 to 65 per cent. It might of course be argued that apathy is a privilege in a relatively secure and relatively balanced nation, or conversely that the political process fails to present voters with meaningful choices.

The increasingly interdependent industrial and commercial activities —another feature of a "national society"—has been accompanied by a concentration and bureaucratization of policy-making. National public regulation of the economy has been irrevocably established. Social security, civil rights, medicare, and labor legislation not only bring national regulation, but encourage national protest and complaint—and an increasing bureaucratization of interest groups.

Family and religious variables seem to be somewhat more recalcitrant than the demographic, economic, political, and technological measures to an ordering in accord with some logical scheme of interdependencies, as Goode notes reluctantly in his chapter. Nonetheless, the American family has undergone fundamental change over the years, though its basic stability is apparent. Marriage remains virtually universal for adults of this nation (two-thirds of the nation's women are married by age twenty-five, over 90 per cent by age thirty, and in excess of 95 per cent for women thirty to forty-four years old). As noted earlier, however, family functioning has changed in interaction with the changing economy, urbanization, universal education, and the increasing liberty of married women to make choices concerning economic participation. Also since colonial times, reductions in age of marriage, the diminishing size of the family, reductions in the time span of childbearing and child rearing obligations, declining mortality, and gains in expectation of life have continued to produce an increase in the labor force participation of women, an increase in the span of years husband and wife have together after the last child has left home, and a change in demand for new forms of housing and recreation.

Family change has not been without its disruptions, however. Though offset by an increasing propensity to marry (and remarry), there has been an increase in divorce and an upward trend in illegitimacy. Though most children under eighteen years of age live with both parents, about 15 per cent do not. These proportions have remained constant for at least the past two decades. We must note that national averages may conceal as much as they reveal. For example, several trends otherwise observable tend to cancel out in averages relating to household composition: (1) Early marriage (a secular trend downward now coasting off) will remove some, now unknown, proportion of young couples from parental families. (2) These data do not let us know the precise effects of increasing divorce rates, elsewhere noted in this introductory chapter and this volume. Minor children of divorced parents will usually live with their mothers, some of whom do not remarry. (3) It is probably true—but we do not know for certain —that the increasing urbanization of American Negroes has *increased* the number of children recorded by census-takers (and possibly, in some proximate ratio, the actual number of children) who are living in a one-parent family (normally, that parent being the mother). We see here a trend that is not a trend, but rather a combination of rather disparate trends. Aggregation conceals, and disaggregation reveals.

Data on family change are seriously deficient even for long-term trend charting and certainly for causal interpretation (see the chapter by Goode). If generalizations about the family appear to rest on shaky foundations, we must note that conclusions concerning religious change in America are devoid of firm empirical evidence. The extensive analysis by Demerath remains avowedly inconclusive. Suggestive, however, are the following: the data seem to indicate that the rate of formal religious participation rose in the last century, though it is possible that there has been a recent proportional decline in participation, particularly since the early 1960's; religious belief is losing in both orthodoxy and saliency, though the "death of God" thesis is scarcely acknowledged among the lay citizenry; church organization has become increasingly differentiated and bureaucratized; ecumenism is perhaps the most distinctive feature of modern American religion. The changing nature of religion may be less important to American society today than it was a century ago. ". . . [T]raditional religion is increasingly autonomous but decreasingly relevant. No longer is religion inextricably woven into a close-knit institutional fabric so that it must act and react in conjunction with economic, educational, political and other agencies." (p. 434)

Distributive and Aggregative Changes

The economic growth of the nation has been an equalizing factor; all groups shared in the general gains, resulting in an undeniable upgrading in level of living. These trends are examined in the chapters by Moss and by Merriam. Though the rewards of economic growth over the decades have not been equitably distributed, increasing productivity and modern technology have made possible increased consumption of goods and services at all levels and thereby a less concentrated distribution of the national gains. However, in the years since the 1950's growing unemployment hit hardest among those with lowest income and the younger workers—ending a trend toward lesser inequality.

An unmistakable upward trend in production, productivity, and in the flow of goods and services to the consumer is attested by the following, based mainly on the materials analyzed in the chapter by Moss. The Gross National Product, in dollars of constant purchasing power, has increased eightfold since the turn of the century. This growth has been accomplished with declining man effort; product per man-hour worked has more than quadrupled over this same period. The volume of goods and services purchased (in constant prices) has paralleled the increase in GNP, while consumption per capita more closely parallels the growth in productivity. Personal consumption expenditures, though fluctuating in times of war and depression, comprise approximately 63 percent of the GNP.

This abundance has provided more for everyone, though not equally for all: There has been a narrowing of income differentials among occupation groups and a decline in the share of aggregate income going to the top 20 per cent; an increasing difference between income to men and to women, reflecting in part the increasing proportion of women who work less than full time; rising incomes have accrued more to the white population than to the nonwhite, to earners outside the South more than to earners in the South, to those in the middle-age range than to the younger or the old. Again, these trends and differentials are examined both by Moss and by Merriam.

The risk of being disadvantaged amidst abundance is greater for some population groups than for others. In 1966 about 30 million persons, or 15 per cent of the population, were living in households below the poverty line (using the Social Security Administration definition). The incidence was 12 per cent for whites and 41 per cent for nonwhites. Among the aged it was 54 per cent for whites and 77 per cent for nonwhites. In terms of numbers, however, far more poor persons are white than nonwhite, are young than are old. "Any social policy that is successful in reducing inequality and low incomes will affect larger numbers of whites, of families headed by men and younger family heads than it will nonwhites, families headed by women or aged family heads simply because of their greater number in the total population and in the lowest income groups." (Merriam, p. 757)

In low-income families expenditures for current consumption are appreciably higher than their money receipts, implying the use of assets or credit, the receipt of public or private assistance, gifts, and insurance benefits. In these low-consumption classes food expenditures varied from 27 per cent to 34 per cent of total consumption as compared with 24 per cent for all nonfarm families. A third of the families with incomes below the poverty line lived in housing that was dilapidated or lacked plumbing, totaling approximately 6 million families.

At any level of income consumption entails choice—vocation, location of job, size of family, selection of goods and services, and the allocation of income and time. Affecting the significance of choice, while at the same time reducing the range of choices, have been some developments referred to earlier as characterizing the emergent postindustrial society.

1. The problem of personal choice has been complicated by the increasing expense and time required for developing specialized knowledge in a service economy, and in an increasing obsolescence of occupations over shorter periods of time; the decrease in working time and the lengthening of life expectancy complicate decision and timing in

the accumulation of possessions, in the use of credit, and in financial investment for future use.

2. Concomitantly the increase in government activity (the emergence of a national society) has reduced the range of individual discretion. The proportion of personal income subject to discretionary use, though increasing with affluence, has been eroded by increases in taxes, by increases in many areas of consumption that tend to become "necessities," and by transfer in income provided by public expenditures.

At most income levels and certainly as income levels rise higher, choices become an important issue of personal, family, and social improvement. These choices involve the allocation of income and time among various goods, services, and investments, and between consumption and investment. For the society choices must be made as to how much of the total effort and resources go to private and to public goods and services.

Leisure, health, and education are among those aspects of life that intersect with both personal and public discretionary behavior; and each is differentially distributed among the various social groupings of the population.

Despite the ambiguities involved in distinguishing leisure from other major categories of living and in assigning activities and numbers to one or another categories, leisure time and expenditures for leisure have increased since the turn of the century. However, as Ennis notes, leisure time and dollars are unequally expended by various social groupings, and leisure activities and resources are differentially clustered in the nation. Executive and professional workers expend fewer leisure hours than do white-collar and labor groups, though there is a discernible increase in recreational expenditures as both income and educational levels rise. Apart from weakness in the data, the apparent discrepancy may be attributed, in part, to different types of leisure activities among the various groups. It might be argued that those with higher income can afford leisure activities of higher quality (if that can be inferred from higher cost), but choose a lesser quantity.

Substantial reductions in mortality rates in the past sixty or more years as reflected by increasing life expectancy at birth and by a decline in death rates suggest a remarkable improvement in the health of the nation. As shown by Moriyama, expectation of life at birth has increased from about forty-seven years at the turn of the century to over seventy years today. These gains, however, have not been shared equally by the American people. Length of life for nonwhites was below that for whites as we entered the twentieth century; and though longevity has shown a steady increase, it is still below that of the white population. Longevity in the South remains below that of the North and West, with color differentials accounting for the major portion of the gap.

Improvements in length of life, infant mortality, and other indicators of health began to level off by the 1950's, as did reductions in inequalities. Significant gains in the future health status of the nation hinge on a reduction of these inequities, and more important, on breakthroughs in the prevention of major chronic diseases (heart disease, cancer, and stroke) in the older population, and accidents, congenital defects, and other diseases of early infancy in the younger population.

Trends in the output and distribution of schooling in America show patterns similar to those for income, consumption, and health. The discussion by Beverly Duncan shows that three trends are clear on the output since 1900: (1) a threefold increase in the annual number of school years; (2) a one-third increase in the per capita years of schooling; and (3) an increase of about 5.5 years in the average duration of schooling. Also observed are a growing equality in the distribution of education among members of successive generations and a diffusion of near-universal school attendance from age eleven to both younger and older ages. There has been a decreasing handicap associated with being Negro and being male. Social background (as indexed by family size, education of family head, occupation of family head, ethnic status, public or parochial schooling, presence of both parents in family, region and rural-urban residence) has been and remains significant in its effect on education. Educational attainment is negatively related to family size and positively associated with education and occupational status of family head. The association of education with the family variable is retained even after allowance is made for ethnic status, types of school attended, and place of residence. Despite all attempts at equalization of educational opportunity, the type of family into which a child is born is a major determinant of educational achievement or its relative lack.

The nation's increasing output in goods and services, in consumption levels, health, education and leisure has been attested to by utilizing both a variety of concepts and by many measures pertaining to those concepts. Similarly, we have been able to point out that inequalities in the distribution of our society's outputs have been diminishing since the turn of the century, though perhaps levelling off in the 1950's to date. We seek an answer to still another question: Has there been change in the extent to which achievement in our society depends upon one's level of social origin? Has there been a change in the "rigidity" of the stratification system, in the relationship between origin status and achieved status, in the degree to which a son's occupational status depends upon that of his father? Duncan's very careful analysis of available indicators provides a partial answer to this question: At least for white males the data suggest that no change has occurred in the rigidity of stratification in America between 1910 and 1950, and the same is probably true through 1966.

Recommendations for Future Developments

Any compilation of data or any time series represents only a sampling of the information that could have been collected. These data themselves indicate which data are considered important, which can be useful in meeting the nation's problems. "All record-keeping is an implicit assertion that it would be costly to do without this information, and that additional facts would cost more than they would be worth. . . . Both social scientists and political leaders are increasingly coming to understand that a much wider range of information is needed for *practical* purposes, simply because the sociopolitical structure has become (or is thought to be) much more complex and is guided at so many points by conscious decisions that need to be based upon adequate information. As any organization becomes more complex, and multiform in its output, far more kinds of information are needed . . ." (Goode, p. 334).

This growing reliance on statistical data for policy decisions is creating an increased demand for data which can be used for projection and prediction. This calls, in part, for firmer evidence of past trends and the factors underlying these trends, as Taeuber has noted. The ensuing chapters confirm both of these proper concerns. As these chapters attest and as pointed out by Taeuber, data that have already been collected are not fully utilized and might well be given more adequate attention before mounting new collections and surveys.

Beverly Duncan, for example, notes, as a top priority in gauging the past and future trend of education, that a more judicious arrangement of data collected under existing statistical programs would provide much of the sought-after material. Collected data might be reassembled in order to examine the progression of successive birth cohorts through the school system. "The pressing need is not the collection of new items, but a new tabulation format for old items. Records now on file which include information about enrollment status, grades of school completed, and birth year . . . must be re-examined with a view to compiling as complete an account as is possible on the progress of successive birth cohorts through the school system. As additional records including these items accumulate, the series for each birth cohort can be extended forward in time or made more detailed with respect to the past." (p. 670)

In addition to exploiting already collected data, more frequent collection, greater speed in availability, more detailed tabulations, and greater attention to future descriptive and analytic needs are recommended by several contributors. The most serious gap at present, cited by many of our authors, is the absence of longitudinal data. The largest bulk of currently available information consists of discrete occurrences and events. Trends are deduced when comparable observations are taken at different time periods, as in two censuses. Observations made on a cohort of individuals or families followed over a long period of time are called for by contributors seeking family change data, consumption choice information, and poverty and welfare changes. It is recognized that longitudinal studies are expensive and require a long-term research commitment; the attempts to compress real time into cross-sectional analyses—for example, by age differences—provide major hazards in interpretation.

Periodically repeated surveys, rigorously planned and designed with respect to standardized concepts, scales, and survey techniques are recommended for an assessment of measuring the influence of social background on schooling while that schooling is taking place rather than retrospectively. Similarly, repeated surveys (perhaps with ten-year intervals) could provide data for examining any real change in degree of social stratification, or in correlations between variables implicated in the process of stratification. Thus Otis Dudley Duncan places a high priority on the replication of the Occupational Changes in a Generation survey in 1972.

Concern with social policy is necessarily related to economic stability, to projecting education and training requirements, to anticipating the market for skill and the job prospects for the Negro, the unskilled, the teenager. Such concerns are intensified by estimates of the inundation of technology and automation. Lebergott addresses these matters in calling for data consistency between employment and labor force statistics and those on output, capital consumption, sales and investments; greater utilization of Bureau of Labor Statistics wage rate surveys; a widening of information on reports to the Internal Revenue Service; a linkage between household and establishment reporting and more intensive research aimed at disentangling the net contribution of various psychological and social factors (intelligence, motivation, family background, etc.) to income differentials.

Analytical sophistication and adequate temporal series, however, do not provide all the necessary materials for charting the course of change, or for attempted intervention in that course in terms of policy. The answers to informational questions rarely can be better than the sense of the questions or the reliability of the source of information. Information on cause of death is notoriously inaccurate, because the reporting official (normally a physician) gives the proximate but not the underlying cause. It may be that the underlying cause is nonmedical—driving a car recklessly—but in other instances the underlying cause is a distinct medical pathology not reported. Moreover, the records exempt a very important proximate cause—therapy itself. Some substantial proportion of decedents are the victims of medical and surgical procedures used to deal with other diagnosed ailments. To argue that the patients would have died anyway is indubitably accurate for the long run and probably accurate in the short run for most patients, but one cannot be confident of the detailed accuracy of a statistical system that leaves out such an obvious observational category.

The answers are, of course, not likely to be better than the questions asked. And the rationale for those questions may be theoretical or practical (and the two may or may not coincide). We asked, until recently, about mortality rates, and occasionally about morbidity rates (for classifiable diseases), but as Moriyama notes, not about ill health operationally defined as incapacity for normal and expected role performance. We have asked, for decades, about the relationship of the members of a household to its "head," but those data until recently were thinly reported, only by age and sex, and not in terms of the kinship composition of living units. (Demographers were primarily interested in number of children per primary family as an indicator of fertility trends and differentials, and secondarily in the extent of multigenerational doubling. Anthropologists and sociologists had not "come on strong" as an interest group concerned with the census as a source of information on American kinship. They were concerned with tribal societies or with relatively uninformed theory about the destruction of the extended family in urban industrial societies.) We have been reluctant to have public officials ask anything about religion or religiosity, for constitutional reasons, but other inquiries have done little better—partly, perhaps, because secular social scientists found the whole range of phenomena more than faintly embarrassing.

All these several and collective failings are regrettable, and the volume at hand represents a considered effort to make amends. To pretend that all is now well would be ridiculous. To pretend that we are no better off would be almost equally foolish.

We are grateful beyond (readily quantifiable) measure for what our learned colleagues have contributed here. It is, of course, their book. We present it now with pride, and not a little fear. For if the book is our colleagues', the initiative was ours, and for that we are accountable.

NOTES

1. Goode, W. J., Chapter 7, p. 296 in this volume.
2. Sheldon, Eleanor Bernert, and Wilbert E. Moore, "Toward the Measurement of Social Change: Implications for Progress," in *Economic Progress and Social Welfare,* Goodman, Leonard, editor, Columbia University Press, New York, 1966, pp. 185–212.
3. See Moore, Wilbert E., "Social Structure and Behavior," in *Order and Change: Essays in Comparative Sociology,* John Wiley, New York, 1967, pp. 171–233.
4. Moore, Wilbert E., "Social Change," in Sills, David L., editor, *International Encyclopedia of the Social Sciences,* The Macmillan Company and Free Press, New York, 1968, vol. 14, pp. 365–375; excerpt from p. 366.
5. Weber, Max, *The Protestant Ethic and the Spirit of Capitalism,* Parsons, Talcott, translator, Allen & Unwin, London, 1930.
6. Moore, Wilbert E., "Toward a System of Sequences," in McKinney, John C., and Edward A. Tiryakian, editors, *Theoretical Sociology: Perspectives and Developments,* Appleton-Century-Crofts, New York, in press (1969).
7. Burns, Arthur F., and Wesley C. Mitchell, *Measuring Business Cycles,* New York, National Bureau of Economic Research, 1946, p. 14; as cited in Wallis, W. Allen, and Harry V. Roberts, *Statistics: A New Approach,* The Free Press, Glencoe, Ill., 1956, p. 131.
8. Duncan, Otis Dudley, "Discrimination Against Negroes," *The Annals of the American Academy of Political and Social Science,* Philadelphia, vol. 371, May, 1967, pp. 85–103.
9. Hauser, Philip M., in *National Growth and its Distribution,* U.S. Department of Agriculture in cooperation with the Departments of Commerce, HEW, HUD, Labor and Transportation, Symposium on Communities of Tomorrow, December 11–12, 1967, Washington, April, 1968, p. 70.
10. Bell, Daniel, "Notes on the Post-Industrial Society (II)," *The Public Interest,* no. 7, Spring, 1967, pp. 102–118.

II. THE DEMOGRAPHIC BASE

2. POPULATION: TRENDS AND CHARACTERISTICS

Conrad Taeuber

POPULATION TRENDS SINCE 1790

GROWTH AND change have long characterized the population trends in the United States.[1] Statistical data clearly document the growth of the nation, the settlement of the entire country, the westward migration, the increasing urbanization, and the concentration in metropolitan areas. They reflect the assimilation of the foreign-born, the movement of a large number of Negroes from the rural South to the urban areas of South, North, and West, and the current position in which the Negro population has a higher percentage of urban residents than the white population. They show that the population has increased its proportion of adults and older people, as family size has declined from that of colonial days. The proportion of persons who do not marry has declined; nearly everyone marries, usually at a relatively early age. The nuclear family, consisting at most of two generations, i.e., parents and children, has become the predominant pattern. There has recently been a substantial increase in the number of one-person households, as older people, and young adults also, have found it possible to maintain their own homes rather than living with relatives. The boarding house has largely disappeared.

Birth rates have fluctuated, with a long-term decline which continued through the depression years of the 1930's, an increase following World War II, and a subsequent decline. Increased length of life reflects primarily the reduction in infant and childhood mortality and relatively little improvement in the length of life for persons who have already survived to advanced ages.

Illiteracy has largely disappeared and high school graduation has become the norm, with increasing proportions going on to college and even to postgraduate studies. The relative growth of white-collar occupations and the corresponding decline of unskilled labor is clearly reflected, as is the increase in personal and family incomes. The income trends are influenced in part by a growing participation of married

27

women in the labor force. For them, too, the emphasis has shifted from household and unskilled tasks to service, clerical, and professional occupations.

The rate of total growth was more than 30 per cent per decade between 1790 and 1860. From 1860 through 1910, with heavy inflows of immigrants who came primarily from Europe, the rate of growth was between 20 and 27 per cent per decade. Since 1910 it has been between 14 and 18 per cent, except during the 1930's when the rate dropped to an all-time low of 7.2 per cent for the decade. The rate in the 1960's has been somewhat lower than that of the 1950's. The numbers involved have grown, as the base to which these percentages are applied has grown. With a population of more than 200 million, even a 1 per cent increase per year means a net addition of at least 2 million persons annually (Figures 1 and 2).

Westward Movement

As the population has grown, the areas of settlement have extended across the continent. The director of the 1890 census commented that settlement had then reached the point at which there no longer was any large frontier area. The center of population reflects the westward movement, with relatively little variation north and south (Figure 3). In little more than one hundred years, California moved into first place in numbers of people, displacing New York, which had long held that position. Rapid rates of growth have characterized the southwestern states and Florida, a consequence of the movement of industry and of retirees to favorable climates (Figure 4).

Urbanization

In 1790 the population was predominantly rural; only about 5 per cent were classified as urban. The urban sector grew far more rapidly and the 1960 census found that 70 per cent of the population was urban. Nearly two-thirds of the people lived in Standard Metropolitan Statistical Areas (SMSA), i.e., cities of 50,000 or over, the counties in which they are located, and adjoining counties which meet stated criteria of economic and social integration with the central city. In 1790 no city had as many as 100,000 people; by 1960 there were 132 such cities. The census of 1900 found three cities with 1 million persons or more; the 1960 census reported five such cities. City boundaries in many cases are relatively fixed, but settlement patterns do not necessarily observe the corporate municipal limits. Taking into account the city and its adjoining densely settled area, there were 16 "urbanized

FIGURE 1.   POPULATION OF THE UNITED STATES
AND REGIONS, 1790–1960

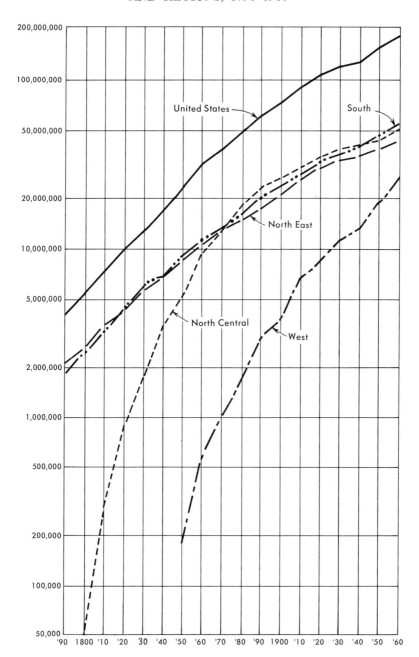

SOURCE: U.S. Bureau of the Census

FIGURE 2. TOTAL POPULATION INCREASE, AND
PERCENTAGE OF INCREASE, 1790–1960

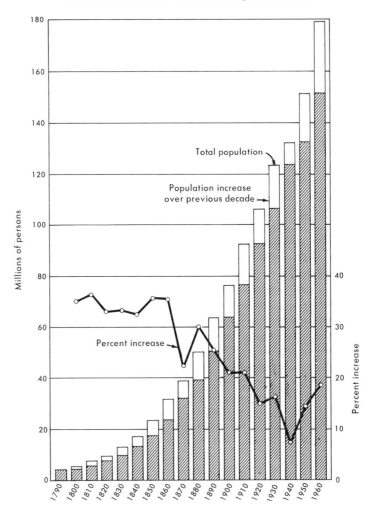

SOURCE: U.S. Bureau of the Census

areas" of 1 million or more inhabitants in 1960. The census in that
year recognized as urban some 10 million persons who did not live in
places of 2,500 or over, but in distinctly urban areas in the vicinity
of the larger cities (Table 1).

Although there has been significant decentralization of population

FIGURE 3. CENTER OF POPULATION FOR CONTERMINOUS UNITED STATES, 1790–1960

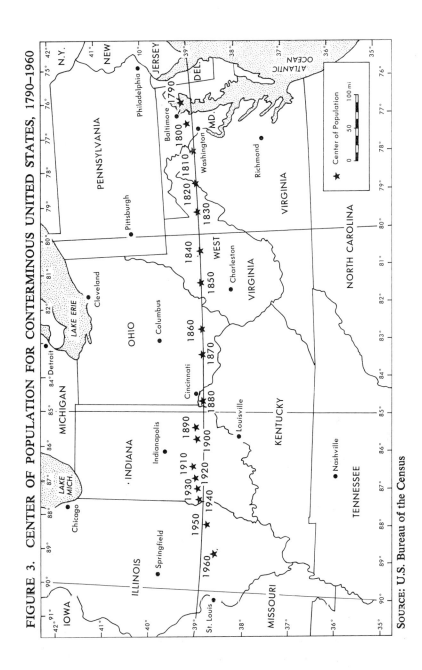

SOURCE: U.S. Bureau of the Census

31

FIGURE 4.   PERCENTAGE DISTRIBUTION OF THE
POPULATION OF THE UNITED STATES,
BY REGIONS, 1790–1960

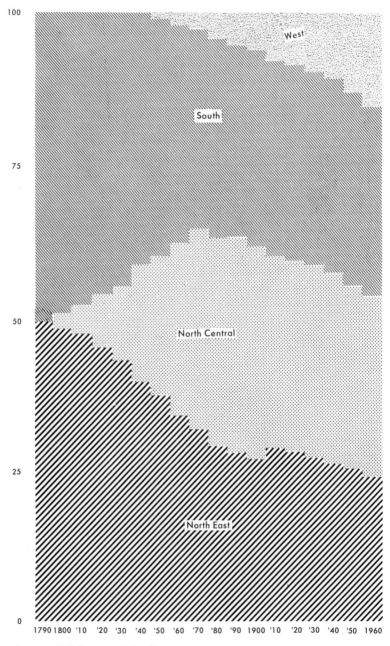

SOURCE: U.S. Bureau of the Census

TABLE 1.   POPULATION IN PLACES BY SIZE, 1790–1960

Size of place	1790	1850	1900	1950	1960
			(*in thousands*)		
Urban territory	202	3,544	30,160	96,468	124,699
Places of:					
Under 5,000	44	316	2,899	7,107	8,270
5,000 to 25,000	96	1,157	7,542	20,070	27,348
25,000 to 100,000	62	896	5,510	17,766	28,787
100,000 to 250,000	—	659	3,272	9,727	11,652
250,000 to 500,000	—	—	2,861	8,242	10,766
500,000 to 1,000,000	—	516	1,645	9,187	11,111
1,000,000+	—	—	6,429	17,404	17,484
Other urban	—	—	—	7,344	9,851

SOURCE: U.S. Bureau of the Census, *U.S. Census of Population: 1960*, vol. I, part 1, Table 7.

TABLE 2.   URBAN AND RURAL POPULATION, CONTERMINOUS UNITED STATES, 1790–1960

Year	Urban	Rural
	(*percentages*)	
1790	5.1	94.9
1850	15.3	84.7
1900	39.7	60.3
1950	64.0[a]	36.0
1960	69.9[a]	30.1

[a] Current urban definition. Under the definition used prior to 1950 the urban percentage would have been 59.6 in 1950 and 63.1 in 1960.

SOURCE: See Table 1.

within the metropolitan areas, in 1960 nearly 70 per cent of the total population was concentrated in slightly less than 1 per cent of the land area. In recent years more than four-fifths of the national growth has occurred in the metropolitan areas. In large sections of the agricultural areas of the Middle West and the South there has long been a decline in population, as the modernization of agriculture and of transportation have altered the basis on which the earlier pattern of settlement was based. With approximately half the counties losing population in the 1950's, the density of settlement in large areas was declining (Table 2).

Growth and Migration of Negro Population

The growth and redistribution of the Negro population has been the subject of much attention. In recent years the Negro population has been growing more rapidly than the white population, after a long period during which the rate of growth of the two groups was approximately equal. At present 11.1 per cent of the population is Negro, not much different from the percentage of 11.6 in 1900, but substantially below that of 1860 when 14 per cent of the total population was Negro. At the time of the Revolutionary War the percentage had been even higher. In 1900 about 90 per cent of the Negroes were living in the South; by 1960 the share of the South was only about 60 per cent (Table 3).

TABLE 3.   NEGRO POPULATION FOR THE UNITED STATES AND REGIONS, 1900–1960[a]

Year	Total	North	South	West
	(thousands)			
1900	8,834	881	7,923	30
1920	10,463	1,472	8,912	79
1940	12,866	2,790	9,905	171
1950	15,042	4,246	10,225	571
1960	18,872	6,475	11,312	1,086

[a] Data for 1900 to 1950 exclude Alaska and Hawaii.

SOURCE: U.S. Bureau of Census, U.S. Census of Population: 1960, vol. I, Characteristics of the Population, part 1; and Historical Statistics of the United States, Colonial Times to 1957.

More than four-fifths of those not living in the South were in the northern states. The Negro population in the North and West was predominantly an urban population and in the South the shift from rural to urban living had proceeded rapidly (Table 4). By 1960 Negroes had a larger share of their population in urban areas, especially the largest cities, than did the white population.

TABLE 4.   NEGRO POPULATION IN METROPOLITAN AREAS FOR THE UNITED STATES AND REGIONS, 1900–1960

Year	Total	North	South	West
	(thousands)			
1900	2,352	582	1,750	20
1920	3,547	1,203	2,291	54
1940	5,840	2,474	3,219	147
1950	8,360	3,886	3,953	520
1960	12,198	6,010	5,186	1,002

SOURCE: U.S. Bureau of the Census, U.S. Census of Population: 1960, vol. III, Selected Area Reports, Standard Metropolitan Statistical Areas, PC(3)-1D.

Assimilation of Foreign-Born

Historically immigration has played a major role in the development of the American population. But although the number of the foreign-born, in 1960, about 9 million, was not much different from the number of the foreign-born in 1890, the proportion of the white population which was foreign-born in 1960 was little more than a third of the proportion in 1890. There has also been a continuing decline in the proportion of the white population which was native-born of foreign or mixed parentage, and a corresponding increase in the proportion which was native-born of native parentage. By 1960 approximately four-fifths of the white population was classified as native-born of native parentage. Virtually all the Negroes and a large share of other nonwhites were also native-born of native parentage. In recent years the concern over the assimilation of the foreign-born was concentrated on a few relatively small groups rather than on the very large numbers involved at the beginning of the century (Table 5).

Decline in Large Households

Large families and households were the rule in early colonial times. Birth rates were high and the average age of the population was relatively low. In 1790 about one-third of all households, including servants, slaves, and other persons not related to the head, consisted of seven persons or more; by 1960 only one household in twenty was of this size. Few households contained persons not related to the head, and the one- or two-generation family had become the predominant household unit. The economy of colonial America had little room for a household consisting of only one person. In the present urban society, which has provisions for income maintenance, especially Social Security, it has become possible for many persons to live alone, and the number and proportion of one-person households has increased rapidly, especially in recent years (Table 6).

The decline in the relative number of large households is primarily the result of the long-term decline in birth rates, which has led to a decline in the proportions of the population consisting of young children and a corresponding increase in the proportion of adults. In 1790 the average age of white males was seventeen years; and although such figures were not collected for females, their average age was probably the same. There was little change by 1820, but after that the average age increased; and by 1950 half the white population was over thirty years of age. There was some decline during the 1950's reflecting the increase in births during that decade, and in 1960 the average for the

TABLE 5. NATIVITY COMPOSITION OF THE WHITE
POPULATION, 1890–1960

	1890	1900	1920	1940	1960
Total	*55,101,258*	*66,809,196*	*94,820,915*	*118,701,558*	*158,460,699*
Native of native parentage	34,475,716	40,949,362	58,421,957	84,124,840	125,444,612
Native of foreign or mixed parentage	11,503,675	15,646,017	22,686,204	23,157,580	23,736,768
Foreign-born	9,121,867	10,213,817	13,712,754	11,419,138	9,279,319
Percentage distribution total	*100.0*	*100.0*	*100.0*	*100.0*	*100.0*
Native of native parentage	62.6	61.3	61.6	70.9	79.2
Native of foreign or mixed parentage	20.9	23.4	23.9	19.5	15.0
Foreign-born	16.6	15.3	14.5	9.6	5.9

SOURCE: U.S. Bureau of the Census, *U.S. Census of Population: 1960*, vol. II, *Subject Reports, Nativity and Parentage*, PC(2)-1A; and *Sixteenth Census of the United States* [1940], vol. IV, *Nativity and Parentage of the White Population*.

TABLE 6. DISTRIBUTION OF HOUSEHOLDS BY SIZE,
1790–1960

Number of persons	1790	1890	1900	1950	1960
			(percentages)		
Total	100.0	100.0	100.0	100.0	100.0
One	3.7	3.6	5.1	9.3	13.3
Two	7.8	13.2	15.0	28.1	28.1
Three	11.7	16.7	17.6	22.8	18.9
Four	13.8	16.8	16.9	18.4	17.2
Five	13.9	15.1	14.2	10.4	11.1
Six	13.2	11.6	10.9	5.3	5.9
Seven or more	35.8	23.0	20.4	5.8	5.5

SOURCE for 1790–1950 data: Glick, Paul C., *American Families,* U.S. Bureau of the Census, 1957, p. 22, Table 14.

SOURCE for 1960 data: *U.S. Census of Population: 1960,* vol. II, Final Report PC(2)-4A, *Families,* Table 24.

white population was 28.8 years. The high birth rates of the nonwhite population are reflected in a lower average age of the population; in 1960 the average for the nonwhite population was about 7.5 years below that of the white population (Table 7).

TABLE 7. MEDIAN AGE OF THE POPULATION,
BY COLOR, 1820–1960

Year	Total	White	Nonwhite
1820	16.7	16.5	17.2
1850	18.9	19.2	17.4
1900	22.9	23.4	19.7
1950	30.2	30.8	26.1
1960	27.8	28.8	21.3

SOURCE: U.S. Bureau of the Census, *Sixteenth Census of the United States [1940],* vol. IV, part 1, Table III; and *U.S. Census of Population: 1960,* vol. I, part 1, Table 47.

Increase in Educational Attainment

The long-term American commitment to universal education is clearly reflected in the decline of illiteracy and in the increase in educational attainment. As recently as 1870, 11.5 per cent of the white population was reported as illiterate. By 1940, the last year for which census figures are available, this had dropped to 2 per cent. Education for

Negroes had received relatively little attention while slavery was in effect, but by 1940 illiteracy among Negroes had declined to 11.5 per cent. As the older generation dies, the proportion continues to drop (Table 8).

TABLE 8.   ILLITERATE POPULATION, BY COLOR, 1870–1940

Year	Total	White	Nonwhite
	(percentages)		
1870	20.0	11.5	79.9
1900	10.7	6.2	44.5
1920	6.0	4.0	23.0
1940	2.9	2.0	11.5

SOURCE: U.S. Bureau of the Census, *Historical Statistics of the United States, Colonial Times to 1957*, p. 214.

The change is clearly shown by figures on the educational attainment of persons who have recently been exposed to the school system. For both the white and the Negro population in 1960, half the persons twenty-five to twenty-nine years old had completed twelve or more years of school. The white persons of this age reported half a year more of schooling than the nonwhite. These figures reflect years of school completed. A complete interpretation of their significance would need to take into account the wide variations in the educational content of the same number of years of exposure to the schools (Table 9).

TABLE 9.   MEDIAN YEARS OF SCHOOL COMPLETED FOR PERSONS 25–29 YEARS OF AGE, BY COLOR, 1940–1967

Year	Total	White	Nonwhite
1940	10.3	10.7	7.0
1950	12.1	12.2	8.7
1960	12.3	12.3	10.8
1967	12.5	12.6	12.1

SOURCE: U.S. Bureau of the Census, 1967 Current Population Survey (unpublished figures).

Changing Occupational Patterns

Rising educational levels have been a prerequisite to the changing pattern of occupational attachments of the American people. The modernization of agriculture has led to a decline in the proportion of the workers engaged in that branch of the economy from more than 40 per cent in 1900 to 6.4 per cent in 1960. There have been some further declines since 1960. The most rapid increase has come in the number and proportion of white-collar workers, especially professional and technical workers. These are the groups expected to increase most rapidly in the future. Conversely, the relative demand for unskilled manual workers of all types has declined, and is expected to decline further (Table 10).

TABLE 10.   BROAD OCCUPATION GROUPS OF MEN,
1900–1967

Occupation groups	1900	1920	1940	1960	1967
	(thousands)[a]				
Total occupation reported	23,711	33,569	39,168	43,531	47,507
White-collar workers	4,166	7,176	10,434	15,413	18,647
Manual and service workers	9,664	16,172	20,247	24,422	25,822
Farm workers	9,880	10,221	8,487	3,696	3,041
Percent distribution total	100.0	100.0	100.0	100.0	100.0
White-collar workers	17.6	21.4	26.6	35.4	39.3
Manual and service workers	40.8	48.2	51.7	56.1	54.4
Farm workers	41.7	30.4	21.7	8.5	6.4

[a] Parts may not total because of rounding.

SOURCE, 1900 to 1940: *Occupational Trends in the United States 1900 to 1950,* Tables 1 and 2. This represents the economically active civilian population.
1960: *U.S. Census of Population: 1960,* vol. I, *Detailed Characteristics, United States Summary,* Table 201. This represents the experienced civilian labor force.
1967: *Employment and Earnings May 1967,* Tables A-16 and A-26. This represents employed persons.

SOURCES AND LIMITATIONS OF DATA

A "census of population" is one of the oldest statistical undertakings in the world. Governments have long recognized the need to know with a reasonable degree of accuracy how many persons are located in the areas for which they are responsible and how that number changes from time to time. The distribution of the population within a designated area is equally important to them, and population counts have been made for small and large units of areas.

Mere headcounts, however, do not supply the range of information that is needed. They may give an indication of the amount of food that is required, though even such a computation must take into account the different requirements according to age, sex, and level of bodily activity. Mere headcounts fail to supply essential information which is basic to any form of governmental planning or action.

Decennial Census

The United States Census was initiated to provide an equitable basis for representation in the House of Representatives. The procedure recognized that the states were of unequal size at the time the Constitution was adopted and, therefore, were entitled to different numbers of legislative representatives. Moreover, it was recognized that in the future the states would grow at uneven rates and that the number of representatives from a state would need to be altered from time to time. Furthermore, there was a great likelihood that new states would be carved out of the largely unknown frontier lands to the West and that they would demand their appropriate share in the membership of the House of Representatives. It was determined to have a census of the population within three years after the first meeting of Congress, and then one within every ten years thereafter. This provision has been carried out regularly, and the nineteenth Decennial Census is scheduled to be taken in April, 1970.

Representation was to be based on the rule of one-man-one-vote, except that Indians not taxed were to be omitted from the count; and in computing the base for representation, the whole number of free persons, including those bound to service for a term of years, was to be added to three-fifths of all other persons.

To meet this requirement the first census had to make a distinction between the free and the slave population, which was included in every census until slavery was abolished. However, even a new government could not be content with a count limited to the distinction between slave and free persons. An interest in military manpower was recognized; consequently a distinction was made according to sex, and for the male persons according to age. Therefore, the first census included some basic characteristics of the population; namely, sex, color, and age. They are still included in the census as essential to any population count in the United States.

The persons responsible for the first census discussed at length the role of this enumeration in supplying needed information on a broader scale than had originally been proposed. The debate continued when the results became available, and government officials and members of the scientific community recommended that the enumeration be expanded in the future to provide needed intelligence about the nation. The history of the United States census is one of change and adaptation to the conditions and requirements for information. Eventually a number of inquiries were split off as separate censuses, manufactures and agriculture. Business and housing censuses were added in the twentieth century. The collection of statistics on births and deaths as part of the census was abandoned, and instead a system of registration of these events was introduced.

The establishment of programs to deal with the problems of the Great Depression led to the development of a number of sources of periodic reports of current information. These resulted in the Current Population Survey, which in 1967 involved monthly interviews at about 50,000 addresses and which is a source of a considerable volume of current demographic information for the nation as a whole and for its major regions.

The decennial census provides data on the size and characteristics of the population in all parts of the country, in each of the 50 states, each of the 5,445 places of 2,500 or more, and each of the 14,345 places of less than 2,500, as well as the population of each of the 3,134 counties and their 37,867 subdivisions. Insofar as they maintain comparable boundaries from census to census it is possible to derive rates of change of growth or decline for each ten-year period.

Small Area Data

For many purposes cities and minor civil divisions are rather large areas and there has been a growing demand for information for smaller areas. The need for statistical information for such areas has led to the establishment of census tracts. These tracts have relatively fixed boundaries and an average population of approximately 4,000 persons. They were first established in a few cities in 1910. The number of cities with census tracts has increased over the years, and the plan for the 1970 census provides for census tracts in each of the Standard Metropolitan Statistical Areas. The Census of Housing called for some limited statistics by city blocks. Population counts were provided by city blocks in 1960 for each block in cities of 50,000 and over and for a few smaller places. The plan for 1970 calls for population counts by blocks not only in these larger cities, but in the densely built-up adjoining areas as well, and possibly for blocks in cities with populations between 25,000 and 50,000. The information to be available for these small area units is the total population by color. Additional information could, however, be supplied for individual blocks or for combinations of blocks.

The decennial census is the only source of comprehensive information on the numbers and characteristics of the population of each of the areas in the United States. Such information becomes available for the years ending with "0." For other years there is no such information which is nationwide in scope and comparable from one area to another. Although there may be very dramatic changes in the population of many areas from year to year, these are not reflected in official statistics other than at the time of the census.

Special Censuses and Estimates

The information gap which exists by virtue of the maintenance of the tradition of censuses at ten-year intervals is partially filled in a variety of ways. National estimates of the population are prepared on a monthly basis. Estimates of the population of states by broad age groups are now prepared annually by the Bureau of the Census, which also provides annual estimates of the population of some seventy Standard Metropolitan Statistical Areas and their component counties. Some experimental work has been undertaken to test the possibility of using the records of the Internal Revenue Service as a basis for preparing annual estimates of the population of each county. By using the number of exemptions claimed on the returns from each county, it is expected that it will be possible to develop annual or biennial estimates of the change in numbers from a census base. Exploratory work is now under way and there is hope that the system can be operative for use following the 1970 census.

Estimates of population numbers and of population change for areas smaller than states are prepared by a large number of agencies and by a variety of methods. There is no comprehensive source for comparable estimates and no agreement on methods which are broadly acceptable. Methods range from fairly simple arithmetic or geometric projections of some recent decennial changes to elaborate combinations, including regression equations based on a number of indicators. The major problem is the lack of information about the volume of migration. An increase in the number of housing units, measured directly or through such indicators as water or electricity connections, or mail delivery stops, may be seriously in error as a result of a change in the rate of vacancies or even a small change in the average number of persons per household. School enrollments may serve as a useful indicator of population change, but this is subject to some limitations as well.[2]

Only two states are now taking their own censuses, a practice which at one time involved a number of states. Massachusetts takes a statewide census for the years ending in "5"; Kansas takes a statewide census every year.

A number of states have established offices which prepare estimates as needed for administrative purposes. In the state of Washington annual estimates are made for each place and each county in the state. In California the State Finance Office prepares estimates or conducts censuses of localities on request. These become official population figures as of the designated time. However, these estimates are prepared only for communities which request the service, generally because they believe they have increased in size and are, therefore, entitled to a greater share of state funds. Similar procedures operate in other states as well.

To meet the need for official population counts, the Bureau of the Census conducts special censuses at the request and expense of the local communities. Between 1950 and 1960 there were over 1,500 such censuses including 40 million persons, and between 1960 and mid-1967 there were 1,350 more, including 26 million persons. The fact that most of these censuses are taken for administrative purposes, such as allocation of tax funds, redistricting for legislative purposes, or establishing eligibility for some benefit, limits their value as indicators of change. Only very rarely will a community which is believed to have lost population be included in such a census. These censuses clearly have only limited value for a general analysis of population change.

Information on current trends in the size and distribution of the population is of very uneven quality. For the nation as a whole it is possible to prepare estimates which correspond very closely to the total census count. Estimates for state totals are available annually on a basis which corresponds reasonably well with the census counts, but in both 1950 and 1960 there were a few states for which the estimate prepared prior to the census was uncomfortably far from the figure reported by the census. In 1960 there were three states for which the estimate differed by 5 per cent or more from the state count, although the average deviation was only 2.6 per cent.

It is difficult to secure generally acceptable figures on the growth or decline of areas such as a region of a state, a declining large city, or its rapidly growing suburbs, or about functional groupings of such areas. Much of the information about broad trends in the distribution of the population since the year of the census must be based on scattered observations and incomplete and frequently inadequate indicators of the changes which are occurring. For the nation as a whole it is possible to generalize concerning developments such as the relative growth rates of central cities and their outlying suburban areas, and the increasing concentration of Negroes in our larger cities. To apply such generalizations to small groups of cities or metropolitan areas is a very tenuous practice. Statements concerning trends in largely agricultural counties, or in a region such as Appalachia, for a time removed from the decennial census, must rely on ad hoc estimates or population counts.

Because of the absence of comprehensive information on population trends for individual cities or other small areas, very little can be known about current trends in the population of subareas such as the poverty areas in major cities, the growth or decline of suburban areas, the increase of population in urban areas outside the metropolitan areas, or the decline in rural areas. The emergence of problems in any area often leads to the development of data to serve as a basis for remedial action. But at the present time the information on changes in the number of residents, or their characteristics, or changes in the ethnic composition of a population is based essentially on the data from the most recent census, plus some indicators, which may be entirely inadequate. The failure to note that out-migration has removed a large share of the younger population, has, for example, led to overestimates of the number of persons per household and, thus, to a failure to appreciate the possible extent of population decline. Similarly, a rapid increase in the number of children of a given ethnic group in the schools has at times led to an overestimate of the growth of the ethnic group in relation to the total population.

The concepts of "urban" and "rural" play an important role in much research and governmental policy. Providing current figures on the changes in the rural and urban population is particularly difficult because of the way in which the boundary between the two is established. The census has traditionally based its definition of rural and urban on the population of incorporated places. Later it was recognized that some clustered settlements had not found it necessary or desirable to seek corporate status. The census identified certain nucleated settlements as unincorporated places and treated them like those which had full corporate status. The rapid growth of suburban settlements on the outskirts of our larger cities led to new problems of classification, for much of this settlement occurred outside the corporate limits of any place. To classify a densely settled area within the commuting range of a large city as rural simply because it had not adopted a particular form of government was not consistent with the purpose of such a classification. In the 1950 census, the Bureau established a category known as urbanized areas. The urbanized area included a central city of 50,000 or more inhabitants and the adjoining settled area which met the stated criteria of density of settlement and contiguity, whether separately incorporated or not. The establishment of urbanized areas called for a reclassification of about 6 million persons who would have been classified as rural under the previous rules. The concept was retained in the 1960 census, though there were some minor modifications in the procedures used for identifying the urbanized areas outside the central cities.

Maintaining comparability of the statistics in the light of rapidly changing conditions is difficult even for the censuses. In 1960, there were more than 12 million persons in the urban population who would have been classified as rural under the definition in use prior to 1950. Moreover, there were about 1 million persons who were reclassified as urban because the places in which they lived had grown beyond the 2,500 dividing line between 1950 and 1960.

Statistics on the rate of change in the urban and rural populations are available only at the time of the census. There is no way in which sample surveys can now take into account the changing boundaries between rural and urban because individual places grow beyond the 2,500 dividing line and settlements which qualify as urban are continually springing up in areas previously classified as rural.

An area classification which has gained wide acceptance is that of the Standard Metropolitan Statistical Area. SMSA's were established by the Bureau of the Budget to provide some standardization in the definition of areas surrounding the major metropolitan areas, with the expectation that governmental agencies reporting for such areas would use the same geographic units. SMSA's consist of counties, except in New England where the town is used as the basic unit. An SMSA includes a city of 50,000 or more, the county in which the city is located, and adjoining counties which meet specified criteria of metropolitan character and of economic and social integration with the central city. The primary criterion is that of commuting from the counties to the central city. Twin cities, i.e., adjoining cities with a combined population of 50,000 or over, may serve as the central city if they constitute a single community for general economic and social purposes and if the smaller of the two has at least 15,000 inhabitants. Since the SMSA's consist of counties, except in New England, and since the constituent units have boundaries which are essentially stable, statistics of change in the population which can be developed for counties are also available for SMSA's. The program to provide annual estimates of the larger SMSA's takes advantage of this circumstance.

To meet some needs for consideration of closely related SMSA's, two Standard Consolidated Areas (SCA), New York and Chicago, were recognized in 1960. These included adjoining SMSA's which were closely related to the central cities involved. It seems likely that additional SCA's will need to be recognized in the future if the present restrictive commuting criterion is to be maintained for SMSA's. Census and current statistics which can be developed for SMSA's, as well as other groupings of SMSA's, obviously can be developed for SCA's also.

DEFINITIONS OF INCLUDED POPULATION

From its beginning the United States census has counted persons as residents of their usual place of abode, which is generally construed to be the place where they live and sleep most of the time. It is recognized that this is not necessarily the place of legal or voting residence, although for the great majority the place so identified would be the same as the place of usual residence. It has also been necessary to adopt some special rules to take care of special situations. Persons with no fixed place of abode are counted where they are found. Persons in the Armed Forces quartered in military installations are counted where their installation is located. College students are counted as residents of the communities in which they reside while attending college. Inmates of institutions, who ordinarily live there for long periods of time, are counted as inhabitants of the place in which the institution is located. Patients in general hospitals who ordinarily remain for short periods of time are counted at their usual place of residence.

For operational reasons college students who are not maintaining their own homes are counted in the parental home in the Current Population Survey. Suggestions have been made from time to time that they should be allocated to their parental homes at the time of the census also, but no feasible procedure has been found. The present treatment in the census affects the interpretations to be made of family and personal income distributions. It also affects the interpretations to be placed on income in relation to household size and composition.

Since the onset of World War II the growth of the Armed Forces has made it necessary to develop explicit rules for their treatment in the preparation of population estimates. Estimates are prepared for the civilian population and the total population including Armed Forces. Estimates of the total population of the United States ordinarily include Armed Forces stationed overseas, and separate estimates are also prepared for the population resident in the United States, excluding Armed Forces overseas. Estimates are also prepared separately for the total population and for the civilian population.

For the country as a whole there is essentially no difference between the population counted as of their place of usual residence, and the population actually present. For individual places there can be significant differences, depending on the season of the year when the count or estimate is made. There may be substantial differences also in the population of states, if the date of the estimate or count happens to fall at a time when large numbers of persons are congregated in certain states, for example, during vacation periods.

The rule of residence places considerable emphasis on the place where a person sleeps—it provides in effect a count of the night-time population. For some purposes a count of the daytime population is needed. Some estimates of daytime population have been prepared, taking into account the places where people work, go to school, do their shopping, and have their homes. There is no program for preparing such estimates regularly or for specified classes of cities.

Accuracy of Enumeration

When Secretary of State Thomas Jefferson transmitted the results of the first census, he commented that the returns were far short of the truth, and in some of the copies he inserted presumed corrections in red ink. Whether he was simply voicing the disappointment of many that the reported numbers were not as large as had been expected, or whether there was indeed a substantial undercount cannot now be established. It is significant that questions as to the completeness of the enumeration should have been raised then, as they have for subsequent censuses. Some major corrections were made in the returns from the census of 1870, when it became apparent that the enumeration had omitted a substantial number of persons.

In more recent years the Bureau itself has sought to develop estimates of the underenumeration which may have occurred.[3] The first correction factor which was made available was that for the under-enumeration of children under five years of age. In connection with both the 1950 and 1960 censuses, intensive efforts were made to secure measures of the possible underenumeration or overenumeration in the census, and also to secure measures of the accuracy with which certain items of information were reported. The results of these studies have been published, thus providing important guides to users of the statistics and giving information of value in planning for improvements in subsequent censuses.

The studies have shown that the major problem is one of underenumeration, rather than duplicate counting or other overenumeration. The underenumeration is greater for some population groups than for others, and is particularly concentrated in certain age, sex, and color groups. Underenumeration is greatest in metropolitan and in rural areas. It is somewhat less in the medium-sized and smaller cities. The underenumeration of young children is in large part a function of the underenumeration of young adults, the parents of these children. Definitive estimates of the amount or rate of underenumeration are difficult to establish. The groups which appear to have the largest degree of underenumeration are also the groups which are most difficult to reach by the alternative, more intensive, and more expensive methods which have been used in the reenumeration. A major conclusion is that a great deal of work remains to be done before anyone can say with assurance what the degree of underenumeration is. It is clear that if such a statement could be made, the techniques for correcting the situation would be indicated, and then the question would be only whether the possible improvement would be worth the additional effort and cost.

The Bureau of the Census has concluded that a reasonable estimate of the underenumeration in the 1950 and 1960 censuses is 3.6 and 3.1 per cent respectively.[4]

DATA ON POPULATION CHARACTERISTICS

Age and Sex

From the beginning of the United States census, information has been collected and published giving the age, sex, and color or race of the population. Age detail has varied over time, and with growing use of the data there has been an increase in the amount of detail provided in the tables. Some data are reported by single years of age. Errors in age reporting have been noted, and efforts have been made to reduce the preference for ages in multiples of five or ten. Asking for year of birth, rather than for age, appears to have resulted in more precise reporting. Year of birth is not entirely free of the tendency to report in round numbers; 1900 as a year of birth apparently was somewhat over-reported in the 1960 census. Age reporting for the older population continues to be affected by some biases, as well as response errors. Efforts to demonstrate eligibility for Social Security may have played a role in recent years, and adversely affected the correctness of reporting of age—or year of birth—but the tendency to overreport high ages was present before the Social Security legislation was in effect. The reports for centenarians have not been considered of adequate quality to warrant detailed tabulation.

The information by age and sex has served as the basis for the computation of widely used ratios. The sex ratio for the total population and for specified age groups reflects changes in the population due to mortality and migration and provides a useful indicator of major social changes. The ratio of persons below working age plus those above working age to those of working age (the dependency ratio) is frequently used, though it is recognized that many persons of working age may be economically dependent and many persons outside these ages may be economically independent. Fertility ratios (ratios of children under five per thousand women of childbearing age), are a useful indicator of recent fertility, though they are based on children who survived to the time of the census and are, thus, affected by differences in mortality, as well as fertility. They are readily computed and provide a simple indicator of differences among areas and groups in the population. Combined with life table values they provide a basis for estimating the rate at which a population is replacing itself.

Other replacement ratios may be readily computed. If labor force ages are taken as twenty to sixty-four, it is a relatively simple procedure to estimate how many persons in those age groups will die or reach the upper age limit of that group during the next ten years, in relation to the number of persons ten to nineteen who will reach their twentieth birthday during the same time period. Such computations for the population living on farms have shown for many years that even if the work force in agriculture were to remain stable, a substantial proportion of the boys and girls growing up on farms would need to seek employment in nonagricultural occupations.

Race

Prior to the 1960 census, enumerators were instructed not to ask a question about color or race, but to make their own judgments and record them. Since enumerators ordinarily are residents of the area in which they conduct their census activity, the classification tended to be in terms of the one which was recognized locally. The shift to greater reliance on self-enumeration in 1960 did not seriously affect the comparability of the Negro-white data, despite fears in some quarters that self-enumeration might lead to a substantial amount of misreporting in relation to the reporting of previous censuses. In describing the statistics on race in the census reports, the Bureau says: "The concept of race, as it has been used by the Bureau of the Census, is derived from that which is commonly accepted by the general public. It does not, therefore, reflect clear-cut definitions of biological stock, and several categories obviously refer to national origin."[5] The basic distinction is between white and nonwhite, and nonwhite is divided into Negro, American Indian, Japanese, Chinese, Filipino, Korean, Asian Indian, and Malayan races. In 1960, Negroes constituted 92 per cent of the total nonwhite.

Late in the nineteenth century the census tried for a time to make a finer distinction among persons with some Negro ancestry, and to identify full-blooded Negroes, mulattos, quadroons, and octoroons. But it was recognized that a census enumeration is not the vehicle for making this type of biological distinction, which would be difficult under any circumstances.

Although the census classification is frequently criticized because it is not a clear-cut biological classification, it has provided a useful basis for distinguishing the social and economic characteristics of groups in the society and the conditions under which they live. Some efforts have been made to use the statistics to secure estimates of "passing," but these have met with little success.

Ethnic Origins

The major role of immigration in the growth of the country has led to a continuing interest in statistics on immigrants and on the ethnic origins of the population. The census identifies persons of foreign birth by country of origin, and persons born in this country with a parent who was born abroad according to the country of the parent's origin. In this way it is possible to identify first- and second-generation immigrants. The same procedure is used to identify persons of Puerto Rican stock, even though technically Puerto Ricans who come to the mainland are not immigrants. The classification of the two generations of foreign stock has shown significant differences between them and provided important clues to assimilation to the dominant American patterns. No such information is available concerning the third or later generations.

With the declining numbers and proportions of persons of foreign stock the question has been raised whether it would be possible to identify their descendants and to find whether there are persistent differences in the degree of assimilation. An effort to do this through a question asking people about their mother tongue has not been productive. Mother tongue was asked only of the foreign-born in 1960, and was useful primarily in dealing with the ethnic groups in areas of origin where there had been numerous boundary changes. Some students are urging that an effort be made to identify the ethnic origins of the native-born of native parentage, but there is no agreement on the methods that might be used or the utility of the results. Questions on ethnic origin or identification are standard items in the census statistics of a number of countries, including Canada. Substantial biases have been encountered where such questions have been used to identify groups which would be the subjects of special action. Even where no special action is indicated, it is likely that the responses would be subject to considerable bias.

One group of native-born of native parentage which is identified according to ethnic origin in the census statistics is the group in the southwestern states known as "Mexicans," "Spanish Americans," or "Mexican Americans." They include persons born in Mexico and their native-born children who are also identified through the questions regarding country of origin. In addition, they include the descendants of the persons living in the areas which formerly were a part of Mexico but became part of the United States in 1845–1853. These persons are found chiefly in five states: Arizona, California, Colorado, New Mexico, and Texas. In those five states white persons of Spanish surname are identified with the use of a list of surnames which are identified as of Spanish origin. Such a classification is dependent in part on the correctness of the original list of names which are accepted as of Spanish origin. Persons who have changed their names, including women who have married outside the group, are not identified with the group. The admittedly rough classification of this ethnic group apparently has met a major need for statistics and has provided a basis for indicating the geographic and social and economic mobility of persons so identified. Unless the procedure is extended to other states, no information is available on the migration of these groups away from the five southwestern states.

One important index of assimilation is the extent to which immigrants have acquired citizenship. This item was included in censuses from 1890 to 1950 and in some earlier censuses.

Immigration

One of the oldest series of statistics relating to immigration is collected for administrative purposes by the Immigration and Naturalization Service. Consequently it tends to stress the legal basis for admission rather than the usual demographic variables. As Hutchinson[6] has pointed out, emphasis is on aliens who cross the border rather than on citizens and more on alien admissions than on departures. The Immigration and Naturalization Service is not required by law to collect statistics on all entries and departures, but only for specified classes. Changes in the laws governing immigration have led to changes in the emphasis of the statistics. Throughout, the primary interest has been on the immigrant alien. Statistics on departures are far less complete, a condition which is not unique to the United States. The provisions of the present law lead to the omission of certain persons who cross the national borders, including parolees, members of the Armed Forces, members of NATO country forces who enter under orders, persons entering as nonimmigrants such as students, returning resident aliens, certain travelers from Canada, and certain persons crossing from Mexico. Aliens entering illegally without inspection are, of course, not included in the statistics. The number of deportees does not provide a clue to the number who have entered illegally. Aliens who enter the United States via one of the islands may be counted when they first came to the island, but not again when they came to the mainland.

Different provisions in earlier laws led to different inclusions and exclusions. Despite these changes, which affect the comparability of the data over a considerable period of years, the immigration statistics have been used for many analyses and they have been invaluable sources for a study of one of the major aspects of the development of the American population.

Religious Preference

Although religious preference or affiliation is believed to exercise a major role in many aspects of social behavior, it cannot be established from official statistics.[7] No decennial census has asked individuals to report their religion. With few exceptions, sample surveys by government agencies have omitted this item, and it is only rarely found in other statistical reports issued by government agencies. The propriety of having a government agency ask a question about religion is a subject of considerable controversy. Although a statistical inquiry on religion is not specifically mentioned in those sections of the Constitution which deal with freedom of religion or the establishment of a religious test for office, some objections to the collection of such information are based on appeals to the doctrine of separation of church and state.

Information about the social and economic characteristics of members of the several religious groups or on the correlation between religion and various elements of social behavior must come entirely from small-scale private surveys. Some religious organizations have conducted or sponsored such surveys of their own groups, but these provide no time series nor do they yield much information which would permit comparisons with other groups.

Statistics of religious organizations are published by the religious organizations and in the *Yearbook of American Churches,* issued by the National Council of Churches of Christ in the United States of America.

For a period of years the Census Bureau collected some information about religious organizations in connection with the decennial census. From 1906 to 1936 there was a decennial Census of Religious Bodies. This is the only periodic census specified in the basic census law which is permissive; i.e., the Secretary is authorized but not required to take such a census. This census was based on replies to questionnaires submitted by local religious organizations, reporting on the number of members, size, and qualifications of their staffs, activities, and funds. It provided no information on the characteristics of the individual members of the groups.

Education

Education has been a major value in American life. For many years the census included a question on literacy in which the individual was asked to report whether he was able to read and write. As educational levels of the population increased and illiteracy declined, this question lost its significance. Since 1940, it has been replaced by a series of questions on school enrollment and educational attainment, in the form of the highest number of years of school completed. Information on the characteristics of persons enrolled in school is regularly available in the census and in annual sample surveys. The highest grade of school completed is also reported for the entire population beginning with persons of school age. The available series reflect the increasing school enrollment of children beyond the compulsory school attendance ages, the characteristics of dropouts, i.e., persons of school age who are not in school but have not finished high school, the increasing number of college graduates and their location, occupations, income, marital status, and family size as well as other characteristics. Enrollment in kindergartens and in other preschool activities has also been reflected in these statistics, which are available by sex, color, or race, and for small as well as larger areas. In recent years particular attention has also been given to the characteristics of the families of the children of school age and their enrollment in school, as well as their school attainment. Indicators of advancement or retardation in relation to the norms for the age group are readily calculated from the available data. These can, in turn, be related to the characteristics of the school children and their parents.

Economic Activity

The economic activity of the population is reported in considerable detail. Participation in the labor force is reported in the census and also in *Employment and Earnings and Monthly Report on the Labor Force,* now published by the Department of Labor. These same sources report also whether persons are employed or unemployed, and the occupation and industry if employed, or the former occupation and industry if not currently employed. Labor force participation rates by age and sex reflect the ages at which young people move into the labor force as well as the ages at which older persons withdraw from economic activity. Employment and unemployment rates are available for younger and older workers, for married men and others, for women who are heads of households, and for women with young children, and by color or race, educational attainment, and place of residence.

The long series of reports on the occupations of workers reflects clearly the declining role of the unskilled and semiskilled and the rise of the white-collar occupations. They provide a basis for an analysis of the changing occupational attachment of white and Negro workers, and of men and women. They also provide information on the occupations which are followed by young workers in contrast to those of older workers. The role of education, race, and occupational attachment in relation to income can be traced. Any discrimination in occupations in relation to race or national origin can be inferred from the available data.

Persons who are working are classified as self-employed, employees of private employers, employees in government service, or unpaid family workers. The decline of the self-employed and the corresponding increase in wage and salary earners is clearly mirrored in these statistics over a period of years. With the decline in the number of the self-employed and with the growing coverage of pension plans there has been a continuing decline in the percentage of older persons who are reported as employed. For self-employed persons in such activities as farming, retail trade, and the professions, there is frequently a possibility of continuing work long after the normal retirement age by arranging the work input in accordance with declining capacities. The employee, on the other hand, is more likely to face an abrupt end to his economic activity during his senior years, as is clearly reflected in the rapid decline of labor force participation rates after age sixty.

The reports on economic activity are based on the labor force concept, i.e., on the activity during the week preceding the interview. Prior to 1940 the classification was in terms of the usual occupation of the individual, a concept less precise than that relating to current activity. Current labor force participation is affected by seasonal factors, which may result in some understatement of occupations which are not fully manned at the time of the census. The monthly report on the labor force, however, provides estimates for each month for broad occupational groups.

No effective means has been found to measure underemployment, particularly that of the self-employed. Persons working part-time for economic reasons are distinguished from those working part-time for personal or other reasons, and a distinction is also made between those who were working part-time regularly or temporarily. Persons who are working part-time for economic reasons are distinguished from other part-time workers. In addition, persons working part of the year are shown separately from those working throughout the year. But there is little or no information on the persons who, though apparently working full-time, are actually not fully and productively employed. The Census of Agriculture provides some clues to the number of such persons who reported that they did little or no work off the farm, but whose farms supplied far less product than would constitute appropriate wages for a year's work. But little is known about the characteristics of such persons or of their counterparts in nonagricultural activities.

Information about persons not in the labor force is available, and their characteristics can be compared with those of persons who are in the labor force. Information about the labor reserve is provided through tabulations showing the occupations of persons who worked at some time during the preceding ten years. Reasons for withdrawal or failure to enter the labor force must, however, be inferred from the characteristics of the individuals involved.

Relatively little information is available on the gross changes in employment from month to month or year to year, the shifts from employment to unemployment and vice versa, and the shifts from job to job. Some longitudinal studies have recently been started to follow selected groups of workers over a period of years, and there is the possibility of some limited information of this type from a sample maintained by the Social Security Administration. But little information has been developed about the demographic characteristics of a cross-section of the population in relation to occupational and labor force changes, and there is no comprehensive series on occupational shifts of individuals during their lifetime. A considerable amount of information is available from a special survey conducted in March, 1962, by the Bureau of the Census, called the Occupational Changes in a Generation (OCG) survey.

Income and Expenditures

Beginning in 1940 the Census Bureau collected information on annual incomes of individuals and of families. Although the initial effort met with some opposition, which continues to some extent, this item of information has proved so valuable that there has been a continuing effort to refine and improve the income reporting both in the census and in the Current Population Surveys. The information is restricted to money income. No account is taken of home-produced food, which is of almost no importance except for the farm population and which is rapidly declining there as well. No account is taken of other noncash forms of income, such as the rental value of an owned home, or fringe benefits which are not reflected in the wages or salary payments before taxes or other deductions. Wage and salary payments are reported with a high degree of accuracy; reports for self-employment income or for transfer payments leave a good deal to be desired. Nevertheless, the information on individual and family income in relation to demographic characteristics has become well established as a major item of current and census information.

Detailed tabulations of the characteristics of families at various income levels have provided much information about the number of families, adults, and children who are living below the poverty level. The classification by race, age of head, education, occupation, and place of residence has supplied essential information for programs aimed at improvement of the conditions under which the American people live. The income levels of young people and senior citizens have been examined in detail as bases for programs designed to assist these groups in particular. Business groups have found information about the income levels of the types of families of considerable importance for general planning.

The role of households as consumption units has led to a demand for information on the characteristics of households, including the reporting of income. Some surveys have endeavored to identify spending units as the appropriate groupings for which to report income and expenditures, but this involves a degree of refinement which has not appeared feasible in censuses or in surveys related to the censuses.

Consumer expenditure surveys provide a wealth of information about buying patterns of the several groups in the population. Such surveys are undertaken at approximately ten-year intervals. Although they provide detailed information on purchasing and consumption, relatively little use has been made of this material in relation to demographic variables.

Internal Migration

The volume and direction of internal migration can be inferred from the decennial population changes of the states. The speed with which the western states were settled was clearly the result of migration to the frontier. Simple procedures make it possible to separate the volume of change in the decade between censuses into two components—natural increase and migration. However, it has not been possible in all instances to separate the effects of internal and international migration.

Beginning in 1850 the census included a question asking for the state of birth of the native-born, along with the country of birth of the foreign-born. A comparison of the state of birth and the state of residence provided an indication of the volume and direction of internal migration. The fact that this measure yielded information for only two points in the individual's lifetime—birth and the time of the census—deprived it of some precision, for it failed to take account of moves that were made between the two observation points. The person who had moved out and returned to his state of birth would be counted as a nonmigrant. Nevertheless, it was possible from the series of reports of the several censuses to secure a picture of the exchange of population among the states, and to discern some clear patterns of the direction of movement.

The census of 1940 included for the first time a question on place of residence at a previous date, in this case 1935. From this it was possible to secure information about migration during a relatively short time period. This inquiry provides a basis for measuring the increasingly important volume of migration among metropolitan areas. Because it was felt that the dislocations due to World War II would unduly affect the statistics if the question were to be repeated in the same form, the 1950 census limited the period covered to a single year. In 1960 the question was again placed on a five-year basis.

Professor Dorothy Thomas and her colleagues at the University of Pennsylvania have developed estimates of migration to and from each state for the years 1870 to 1950.[8] This has been done separately for age and sex groups, for the white and Negro populations, and for native-born and foreign-born persons.

One new item has been added through the census publications comparing the state of birth with the state of residence five years previously as reported in the 1960 census. The comparison of recent and lifetime migration has added important new information on the currents of migration.

Some special surveys have attempted to trace all the residential changes in the course of a person's lifetime. In some instances special attention has been given to the place where the individual spent his early years, and particular attention was placed on rearing in urban or rural environment, and in some instances whether the rural environment was that of a farm residence.

The migration from farms has been a dominant element in internal migration; between 1920 and 1960 the net movement off the farm amounted to about 32 million persons. This figure is based on an annual series prepared jointly by the Department of Agriculture and the Census Bureau and it includes estimates of the changes in the farm population with particular emphasis on the movement to and from farms. The series has continually shown that although the net movement was off the farm, there was a substantial amount of movement to farms as well. Few data have shown so dramatically that migration involves a continuing interchange of population and that the net movement may represent only a small fraction of the total amount of movement. The migration from farms has been the subject of many special studies, conducted by the Bureau of the Census, the Department of Agriculture, and others.

Beginning in 1948, the Census Bureau has issued annual estimates of the number of persons who moved and the extent to which the move involved crossing the lines of the county, or the state. More recently a distinction has been made between contiguous and other states. In one instance an effort was made to relate the moves to reasons for moving, such as those related to jobs or service in the Armed Forces, and those related to housing, changes in marital status, health, or other factors.

Most of the information on migration has dealt with individuals, with considerable emphasis on such characteristics as age, sex, and color, and in some instances marital status, educational level, employment status, occupation and industry and income. There is, however, little information on the extent to which families move as units, which appears to be an increasingly important element in the total volume of migration. At present the scope can only be inferred from the age and sex composition of the migrants. With the increasing frequency of transfers of employees by large employers, including the federal government, and with the major role played by the Armed Forces, the absence of information concerning the movement of family units represents an important gap in the information on internal migration. Little is known about the extent to which families are left behind when the chief earner moves and then follow him after he has found a suitable job.

Commuting is not a new form of behavior, but it had not called forth any significant statistics until the 1960 census provided information comparing place of residence and place of work, along with the means of transportation used in getting to work. The Bureau of the Census has been under considerable pressure to provide similar information in the future, but to relate it to smaller geographic areas, including detail for parts of the major cities, for example, the central business districts. Such information would also be useful in improving the current estimates of daytime population for various areas.

Families and Households

Information on the number of persons and on their characteristics is of primary importance for many purposes. For other purposes attention is focused on the social groups in which persons function. Families and households represent two major groupings which affect many aspects of life from the bearing and rearing of children to the consumption of goods. Much social policy concerns itself with the family or the household. The welfare of children and the aged is intimately related to the welfare of the family units of which they are parts, and provisions for their assistance are intimately related to the family structure.

In census statistics, a family consists of two or more related persons who are living together; a household consists of all persons, whether related or not, who share common living quarters. A household, but not a family, may consist of only one person. All persons are classified as living in households or in group quarters. Group quarters include institutions, lodging and boarding houses, military and other types of barracks, college dormitories, fraternity or sorority houses, hospitals, homes for nurses, convents, monasteries, ships, and similar living arrangements. Statistics on the number, size, and other characteristics of families are available on an annual basis and are given in considerable detail in Census Bureau reports.

A distinction is made between primary families, i.e., a family which includes the head of the household; secondary families which are members of the household but not related to the head (for example, a domestic servant and her child living as members of the household); and subfamilies which are families living in a household and related to, but not including, the head of the household (for example, the married son and his wife, or the widowed daughter and her child).

Families are also subdivided into three types: husband-wife families, families with other male head, and families with a female head. When husband and wife are both present, census practice designates the husband as the head. In the statistics for the United States no distinction is made between consensual unions and legal marriage. Married couples are classified as to whether they have their own households, or whether they are sharing housing accommodations with relatives or nonrelatives. The number of families sharing housing accommodations gives a measure of "doubling up" of family groups. As a consequence of wartime housing shortages, the percentage of couples without their own households rose to 8.7 per cent in 1947. Since then it has dropped to 1.8 per cent, which may be nearly a minimal figure for all practical purposes. Some family groups find it desirable to share housing accommodations for economic reasons; others do so to facilitate the care of children, aged persons, or invalids, or for other reasons, which are not related to the general availability of housing accommodations.

An additional distinction is that of unrelated individuals. An unrelated individual is a person (other than an inmate of an institution) who is not living with any relatives. If he is a household head living alone or with nonrelatives only, he is identified as a "primary" individual. Other unrelated individuals are identified as "secondary" individuals.

The designation of the head is a key element in the classification of households. The designation is left to the respondents, except that in a household consisting of a married couple, with or without children, the man is designated as the head. In the case of a household which includes two generations of related adults there may occasionally be some question as to which one should be given priority for purposes of classification of the head. Special tabulations of the census data have shown that in such cases the chief economic provider of the household is generally designated as the head. With the decline in the number and proportion of subfamilies the ambiguity in the classification of the head loses most of its numerical significance. One of the reports of the 1960 census shows that 90 per cent of the family heads were the chief income recipients in the family.

Families are further classified by the presence and numbers of children of preschool and school ages. When this classification is presented according to the age and sex of the head, the information gains considerable significance for school and welfare programs. Other classifications by the age of members and their relationship to the head of the household provide information on the number and characteristics of multigeneration families and changes in their number and relative importance.

Such tabulations have provided information on the life cycle of families, i.e., the progression from the state of a newly married couple without children, to the couple with infants, then school-age children, teen-age children, followed by the departure of the children to establish their own households and the eventual "empty nest" when all the children have left home. With the recent trends toward early marriage and childbearing, a smaller number of children per family, earlier departure of the grown children from the parental roof, and some increases in the expectation of life at adult ages, there has been a substantial increase in the number of couples in the age bracket when the children have left home. The long-term change in this respect is illustrated by a comparison of conditions at present with those of the 1890's. In the earlier years, one of the parents—usually the father—had died by the time the youngest child married and left home. Under present-day conditions, the couple can look forward to an average of twelve to thirteen years together after the youngest child has married and left home. This change has major consequences for family organization, and many aspects of consumption and social behavior.

Changing patterns of age at marriage, and the number and spacing of children, have also played an important role in the increasing participation of women in the labor force. The presence of small children in the home is a major deterrent to the labor force participation of women; but because many women are relatively young when the youngest child grows beyond the period of intensive care, they are receptive to the possibility of re-entry into the labor force. Statistics on the labor force participation of mothers, by the age of their children, the presence of a husband, and the income of the family are regularly available.

The statistical series shows clearly the decline in the number of households which include boarders and lodgers and the decline in the number of persons of this status. For recent years it is possible also to show the extent to which older persons are living with their children, or maintaining their own households. The disappearance of the "maiden aunt" who played a large role in helping meet family responsibilities in an earlier day is clearly reflected in statistics on the presence of relatives of the head among the members of the household.

The rapid increase in the number of one-person households is primarily the consequence of the increased possibility of economic support for the older person who wishes to maintain an independent household rather than living with the children. The living arrangements of older citizens have become the subject of a great deal of attention, and a substantial body of data on this subject is available, both in the periodic censuses and in current statistics.

The concentration on the nuclear family and on the household as the group of persons sharing common living quarters, has resulted in relative neglect of the extended family in its modern manifestation. Only scattered studies have endeavored to portray the extent to which the ability of older persons to maintain their own households is contingent upon mutual aid from relatives who maintain separate households. Some information is available on the extent of and sources of financial support, but relatively little attention has been given to the role of relatives in other households. Scattered studies have shown that relatives play an important part in the life of many families and households, although the more traditional extended family has virtually disappeared from the American scene. But in this field there is a large gap in our statistical information.

The stability of family units has long been a matter of considerable concern. Census and current statistics provide information on the number of persons who at the time of the census are single, married, widowed, or divorced. They also provide information on the number of married persons who are maintaining separate homes because of marital discord or other reasons. To a lesser extent, information is becoming available on the extent to which persons whose marriages have been broken by death or divorce have established new families, and the probabilities that a person who is divorced or widowed will remarry.

Although the events which lead to a change in marital status due to marriage or divorce involve legal recording, the statistical reporting of these events leaves many gaps. The current reporting of marriages is not yet complete for the entire United States, and the gaps in the reporting of divorces are even greater. The recording of marriage and divorce actions has been viewed primarily as an administrative and legal requirement, and the statistical aspects have not received the attention which is needed to provide essential knowledge about these events. Death reporting is virtually complete, but the statistics of deaths have given relatively little attention to the marital status of the deceased.

The growth in the number of households is of major importance to many sectors of the society. A prospective increase in the number of households calls for an increase in the number of housing units; conversely, a housing shortage leads to doubling up, i.e., a reduction in the rate of new household formation. The household is the unit for the consumption of some major items, including housing, and "big ticket" items such as refrigerators, kitchen stoves, television sets, automobiles, heating and air conditioning equipment, and many others. An important gap in the statistics now available relates to the processes of household formation and dissolution. Information is lacking on the frequency with which marriage, divorce, separation, or death leads to a change in the number of households. The marriage of a young couple may lead to a net addition in the number of households if both have been living in the parental home; it may lead to a decrease in the number of households if both have been maintaining separate households, or the numerical effect is nil if one of them has been maintaining an independent household while the other has been living in the parental home. A death does not necessarily result in the reduction of the number of households, for the surviving partner may elect to continue the household. The lack of information on the relationships of the events and the change in the number of households has led at times to unsupported conclusions and to misjudgments about the consequences of demographic developments on the demand for housing. Only recently has there been a systematic effort to develop the statistics which would clearly reflect the changes in relation to marital status and their effects on the number of households, fertility, and family structure.

Mechanical tabulating equipment was designed to deal with individual units, but did not provide for relatively simple means of relating an individual to the family unit to which he belongs. More recent developments have facilitated such comparisons with the result that there is now a substantially improved capability to provide statistics in which the individual is related to the characteristics of the family of which he is a member. No doubt in the near future these capabilities will be much more fully utilized than has been the case up to the present time.

Births, Deaths, Marriages, and Divorces

Statistics on births, deaths, marriages, and divorces are by-products of the civil registration of these events. This registration is a function of the states (in some instances of counties or towns within the states). State agencies assemble these reports and issue the statistics, and copies of documents are made available to the federal government for the preparation of current national statistics. Provisional statistics are available by states with a time lag of about two months. The assembly of the individual certificates from the large number of local registrars is necessarily a time-consuming process and consequently the publication of detailed reports has a considerably longer time lag.

The registration of vital events is a responsibility of the states, and in the past not all states have given the same degree of attention to this function. A consequence is that the historical series for some states are of very limited use, while those for other states can effectively be carried back for a considerable period of years. Massachusetts has supplied such reports since 1851. Some records in that state go back to 1639 when the General Court ordered "that there be records kept of all wills, administrations, and inventories, as also of every marriage, birth and death of every person within this jurisdiction."

By 1833 only five cities in the United States registered births and deaths routinely—Boston, New York, Philadelphia, Baltimore, and New Orleans. Massachusetts adopted a state registration law in 1842 and strengthened it in 1844, when it provided for central filing, standard forms, fees, and penalties, and specified types of information including causes of death, and lodged responsibility with designated officials.

Government and private agencies, including especially the American Public Health Association and the American Medical Association, consistently urged improvement in the reporting of these events, but progress was slow. In 1880 the Census Bureau had established a registration area for deaths. This area consisted of only two states, Massachusetts and New Jersey, and of the District of Columbia and several large cities with efficient registration systems. By 1900, eight other states had been admitted. The birth registration area was established in 1914, including ten states and the District of Columbia. In 1903 Congress adopted a joint resolution requesting the state authorities to cooperate with the Census Bureau in securing a uniform system of birth and death registration. By 1907 a model bill was submitted to the states with the endorsement of many organizations.

The entry of the United States into World War I provided a notable stimulus to securing current health and mortality statistics. As a wartime measure weekly telegraphic reports of deaths and infants' deaths were reported for cities of 100,000 and over.

Pressure for a registration area for births and deaths continued, and in 1933 the area was completed with admission of Texas to the birth registration area.

Because of the growth of the area for which data were collected and tabulated, a national series of geographically comparable data prior to 1933 can be obtained only by estimation. Registration of at least 90 per cent of the events was one of the requirements for admission to the registration area. The early years after completion of the areas were devoted to strengthening the system of registration. But only in 1959 did the National Center for Health Statistics discontinue publishing the birth rate both as reported and as adjusted for underregistration.

The compilation of central statistics on marriage and divorce has not had the same degree of attention which the states gave to births and deaths. At the beginning of 1967 only 38 states and the District of Columbia were included in the marriage registration area and only 22 states in the divorce registration area.

Statistics dealing with mortality include not only the general level of mortality, but provide information on causes of deaths as well as on the frequency of deaths which in themselves are important indicators of levels of living. The over-all decline of infant mortality to about one-fourth its level fifty years ago and the reduction of the maternal mortality rate during that same time to about one-twentieth its earlier level reflect important social changes. The virtual elimination of the infectious diseases which at one time were responsible for numerous deaths among children likewise reflect important changes in control of disease, as does the near-elimination of deaths from tuberculosis or of typhoid and paratyphoid fever. The simultaneous increase in death rates due to cardiovascular-renal diseases, malignant neoplasms, and the sharp increase in death rates due to motor vehicle accidents, are indicative of other major changes in living.

An important summary measure is the expectation of life at various ages. The expectation of life at birth is one of the most commonly cited, but expectation of survival at various attained ages are also important. The major increases in expectation of life at birth are primarily the result of reductions in infant and childhood mortality, and only secondarily to an extension of life once an advanced age has been reached. National values are available only for the period during which reasonably complete registration of deaths has been achieved. Data for some states are available for a much longer period of time; in the case of Massachusetts such figures are available since 1850.

Such rates, as well as the underlying death rates, are available by sex, by color, and for each of the states on a regular basis. They are also available for some cities. Very limited data are available to show the differentials among the socioeconomic groups.

The computation of survival rates has been extended to a part of the life span, and also to computations of the length of working life, or of school life. Replacement rates of the working-age population have also been computed for the total population and for the farm population. In the latter case the computations have been used to indicate the "surplus" manpower growing up on farms in relation to the numbers needed to replace farm operators as they died or reached retirement age.

Fertility

In the absence of birth registration, use has been made of the census counts of children and of women of childbearing age to develop ratios of young children to women in childbearing age back to 1800. Such estimates are available for the country as a whole and for the nine geographic divisions recognized by the census. Since 1910 they have also been prepared for the rural and urban populations of each of the geographic divisions. The ratios in turn have been used to develop estimates of birth rates by color and age of mother for the census years back to 1800.

The number of births per thousand of the population, and the more specific rate of births per thousand women of childbearing age provide the major information on the current level of births and fertility. What effect a given rate of fertility has on the growth of the population is shown by the gross reproduction rate, i.e., the number of daughters a hypothetical cohort of 1,000 women entering the childbearing period would have if during their lifetime they were subjected to the age-specific birth rates observed at the stated time, and if none of them were to die before reaching the end of the childbearing period. If mortality is taken into account, the net reproduction rate is derived. Such rates have been computed back to 1910, by color. With declining infant and maternal mortality rates, there is relatively little difference between these two measures of fertility, but in the early years of the twentieth century the gross reproduction rate was about one-third higher than the net rate and thus overstated the potential growth resulting from a given level of fertility.

Statistics of births can be related to the age and color or race of the mother, the number of children she has previously had, and a number of economic and social factors, to derive meaningful measures of the social and economic factors which are related to the trend of fertility. Because the major variable in current population trends is fertility and because fertility is increasingly subject to voluntary control, population trends are subject to considerable variations in response to changes in social and economic conditions. There have been some major changes in the past fifty years, especially since the end of World War II. The concern with understanding these fluctuations and interpreting their significance for future population trends has led to considerable elaboration of methods of identifying the significant elements in current trends. Attention has been focused on the number of children born to a cohort, i.e., group of women born in a specified period, and particularly on the number of children women of a given cohort have had by the end of their childbearing period. This has, in turn, given rise also to a concern with the spacing of children, recognizing that changes in current birth rates may occur because women are having their children earlier or later in life or at shorter or longer intervals. Such changes may or may not be related to the number of children which women will eventually have, and, therefore, attention has been given to the number of children which women of given cohorts have had during their lifetime. Information on the number of children ever born permits an analysis of fertility over a considerable time span. The women who were sixty-five to sixty-nine years old in 1910 had completed their childbearing by 1890. The births they reported reflect fertility prior to that date.

This indicator, however, is not very sensitive, for it becomes necessary to wait until the end of the childbearing period for any given cohort before it can be determined that there has been a significant change in the lifetime pattern of childbearing. To arrive at an earlier indication of changes, Whelpton initiated a sample survey in which women were asked to state the number of children they expected to have during their lifetime and also during the next years.[9] Similar surveys have been repeated by private research organizations at five-year intervals. The National Center for Health Statistics is now collecting such information routinely from a sample of women who have recently given birth to a child; there is continuing pressure to have these questions asked of a sample of the population at regular intervals, on the assumption that this information would provide an early and sensitive indicator of changes in the attitudes of the potential mothers and perhaps also of the potential fathers. Such information has not been collected over a sufficiently long period of time to provide any clear basis for evaluation of its effectiveness in interpreting changes within a short period of time, but recently there have been some serious challenges to the validity of some of the underlying assumptions of such statistics. This field requires a great deal more study before full use can be made of the responses secured.

A child born to a mother who is not currently married suffers a number of legal and social disadvantages and, therefore, an effort is made to identify whether a birth is to be classified as legitimate or not. In some jurisdictions this information is regarded as confidential, and special arrangements are made to secure the statistics which show the number and proportion of illegitimate live births. Such statistics are now generally available for individual areas as well as for the nation, and are given separately by color and by age of mother.

Although data showing the variations of births during the year are available, relatively little analysis has been made of seasonal variations in birth rates.

Information on family planning, the extent and effectiveness of the use of contraceptives, and the methods used are available only from relatively small-scale surveys which have been done by private organizations. There are no official series available on these subjects, and the official series on the manufacture or shipment of various contraceptives are limited in scope and of very recent origin.

Figures on abortions are at best guesses though there is little doubt that the numbers are relatively large. Similarly, there are no official or other comprehensive figures on the number of sterilizations performed or the number of sterilized persons.

Census inquiries about the date of marriage and the date of birth of the first child have also provided estimates of the frequency of premarital conceptions, as well as on the variations in the interval between marriage and birth of the first child. Information on the timing of the births of the children of a mother is used to secure estimates of the time interval between successive births, and to derive time series for these intervals.

In summary, a review of the available demographic statistics shows that while some information can be obtained at ten-year intervals for the entire period of the nation's history, much of the information now available was developed relatively recently. As the nation's need for demographic statistics has grown, steps have been taken to meet the demand. Small-scale national surveys have been developed to provide some data for the years between the censuses. The census itself has continued to be on a decennial basis, though there are indications that it may be shifted to a five-year basis after 1970. Data for small areas are generally available only from the censuses. Sample surveys of a size to permit estimates for individual SMSA's or major cities, or areas of equivalent population size, have not been developed on any comprehensive basis.

The rapid expansion of municipal and metropolitan area planning has created an administrative need for more current statistics for individual areas. Electronic computers make it possible to visualize the use of indicators of population trends which can be extracted from administrative records to provide important information for intercensal years. The more effective use of such computers has already had an important effect in the more complete utilization of the data which are collected through the governmental agencies which deal with demographic information. The analyst of demographic matters in the near future will have vastly more information at his disposal, just as the contemporary analyst finds vastly more information than was available to his predecessors.

SOME FUTURE DATA NEEDS

More frequent data collection and greater speed of publication, more detailed tabulations, greater attention to the "determinants and consequences" of demographic developments, and more orientation to future developments are major demands being placed on the data collection agencies.

When the United States census was first established, it was to be taken once in ten years. As the recognized needs for data grew, and the population of the country increased, the tabulations often appeared so late that they were of little more than historical interest. The application of punch card techniques in the 1890 census, and of electronic data processing in 1960 were efforts to meet the need for more rapid tabulation of the data collected in the census. At the time of writing the chances that Congress will approve the taking of a census of population every five instead of every ten years appear better than at any time in the preceding thirty years.

Electronic data processing and related developments in printing promise significant reductions in the time required to process the data. Greater speed has also been called for in the compilation of the current data on births and deaths, and a number of methods have been developed to meet these needs. The rapid rate of population change has led to consideration of a program of quinquennial censuses, supplemented by large-scale sample surveys, possibly at biennial intervals. These surveys would provide data for major metropolitan areas, as well as for states and geographic regions. Annual figures on gross population changes for small areas can be based on a variety of indicators developed from administrative records, for example, Social Security and income tax reports. Where changes in housing units, water or power connections, or residential telephones can be supplemented by surveys to ascertain the changes in the number of persons per unit observed (such as persons per household), useful local estimates of gross population changes can be developed. The use of electronic data equipment has opened the door to more powerful procedures utilizing such indicators, and taking advantage of the recorded number of births and deaths. Such work needs to be pursued much more actively than heretofore if many administrative and research needs are to be met.

Greater detail in data collection and tabulation is an urgent requirement; and here, too, the newer data processing equipment promises to give substantial assistance. The census makes a unique contribution by providing data for very small areas on a uniform basis. More and more the demand is for statistics for small areas, partly because of the analytic uses to be made of such data for ecological relationships, and partly because the small areas can be used as building blocks to construct areas which are meaningful in analytic terms. For administrative purposes it continues to be necessary to provide data for units with recognized political boundaries, but increasingly there is a need for data for functional areal units. These may be defined quite differently for different purposes; therefore, flexibility is required in the tabulation program and in the procedures for making data available to users.

The basic items to be included in series of demographic data are generally agreed upon. The needs for detailed subdivisions or for auxiliary data have varied over time and new needs will arise from time to time. As new techniques are developed, new data requirements grow up; for example, the data required for cohort analysis of fertility. A serious gap at present is the absence of longitudinal data. Most of the information available consists of observations of discrete events. Trends may be deduced when two comparable observations are taken at time intervals, as in two decennial censuses. However, this cannot substitute for the observations which might be made if a cohort of individuals or families could be followed over a long period of time.

Greater detail is needed in regard to subject matter. Both census data and the current vital statistics reports cover such large masses of data that substantial and detailed cross tabulations are possible. This facilitates isolation of the factors considered most significant. Techniques need to be developed to facilitate the more detailed tabulations which microanalytic methods require, and this calls for closer cooperation between the data producers and analysts. In large measure, the data which have been collected have not been fully utilized; and many field surveys have been undertaken without adequate attention to the related data already available. Improved channels of communication regarding both needs and availabilities of data are needed. New and flexible methods to increase the accessibility of the data which are assembled will fill a part of the need. The reduction of the time interval between collection and availability of data will enhance their utility for analytic studies.

Family structure and family relations are intimately related to demographic events and are affected by them. To cite only one illustration: the combination of early marriage, the concentration of childbearing within a few years after marriage, and some increase in longevity has led to a relatively long period of joint survivorship of the original couple after the children have left home. This situation is in sharp contrast to an earlier one in which the responsibility of childrearing extended beyond the death of one of the marriage partners. Obviously such a change has important demographic, social, and economic consequences. Identifying and measuring such interrelationships will require some new efforts in data collection and tabulation.

Demographic data have tended to be limited to "hard" data, recording specific individuals or events. Strenuous, and generally successful, efforts have been made to clarify definitions of such events as stillbirths, or a condition such as unemployment, but much less work has been done to measure the relevant social and psychological factors in population. Although efforts to relate such factors to fertility changes have not yielded the results hoped for, the future will see more attention to psychological and social factors in relation to fertility as well as other demographic elements.

American social science has developed relatively little information on the interrelationships among economic, social, and demographic developments. The failure to predict the postwar changes in birth rates is only one of several examples which might be cited. Equally significant is the relative absence of systematic analyses of the costs of rapid population growth; of the factors which account for the observed differentials in fertility or mortality, or of the effects of population growth or decline on the level of public services and the means of supporting them. The role of internal migration in current problems of urban development has been relatively neglected. The effect of migration on the demand for housing, educational, health, and other facilities has not received adequate attention. The efforts to develop simulation models of demographic phenomena have revealed a need for far more detailed information on interrelationships than has been available. For many purposes demographic variables have been treated as independent. While this has simplified the manipulation of the data, it has rarely led to the insights which research workers or policy makers require.

There are frequent calls for the development of a population policy for the United States. The research community may soon need to supply the analyses needed before such a policy can be successfully developed. A list of gaps could be readily compiled. Three illustrations will indicate the range:

1. The demographic effects of guaranteed family incomes can only be guessed.
2. Information is lacking on the interplay of social and economic factors which bear on the effect of marriage, death, and divorce on the number and characteristics of households. A marriage may lead to an addition of one to the number of households, no change, or a diminution of one in the number of households. A divorce may increase the number of households, and death frequently has no effect on the number of households.
3. In the analysis of the situation of immigrant stocks considerable attention was paid to the distinction between first and second generations. Similar data concerning rural-urban migrants within the United States would shed considerable light on some matters of current social interest.

The growing reliance on statistical data as a basis for action is creating an increased demand for data which can be used for projection and prediction. In part this calls for firmer evidence of past trends and the factors underlying these trends. In part the need is for more insight into the interrelationship between demographic trends and the elements in the society which influence and are influenced by them. It has been argued also that more attention must be given to measurement of the intentions of the persons involved and their forecasts of their own behavior.

The time span involved may be only a few years into the future or a period of a generation or even a century. Planning to meet future needs for public or private services is gaining increasing attention and the ability to project future demographic developments takes on a practical urgency which is relatively new. Shifts in age composition, in migration, in the racial composition of the population, in birth rates, mortality, and length of life all are relevant in such considerations. Decisions concerning data collection and presentation will increasingly deal with the relevance of a particular datum to the future.

Meeting future needs will require more effective utilization of data already available. Administrative records, such as those of the Social Security and Internal Revenue systems, have already been utilized to provide data on income distributions and on population shifts. Undoubtedly current surveys, such as the Current Population Survey, with the records accumulated over a period of time can be utilized more fully. The possibility of matching records from two or more sources, and thus providing new information has only begun to be tapped. Some steps have been taken to make micro-data available in a form which permits detailed cross tabulations to meet special purposes.

There are also significant developments in regard to procedures for data retrieval. The role of electronic data processing in facilitating the more effective exploitation of data which have been collected is rapidly growing. Newly recognized needs will lead to the collection of new data, more effective use of data already being collected, and more effective use of the instruments for data collection which have already been developed.

NOTES

1. For the most recent decennial census statistics, see U.S. Bureau of the Census, *U.S. Census of Population: 1960,* Washington. The final reports were published in three volumes. Volume I, *Characteristics of the Population,* Series PC (1), issued in four sections, contains separate reports for the entire United States,

each state, and other areas. Volume II, *Special Reports,* Series PC (2), contains 31 reports on subjects such as ethnic origin and race, migration, education, employment, and so on. Volume III, *Selected Area Reports,* Series PC (3), contains reports by states, Standard Metropolitan Statistical Areas, size of place, and social and economic characteristics of Americans overseas.

Subsequent Census Bureau data are available primarily through the series of *Current Population Reports.*

For historical data, see U.S. Bureau of the Census, *Historical Statistics of the United States from Colonial Times to 1957,* revised edition; and *Statistical Abstract of the United States,* published annually.

2. U.S. Bureau of the Census, "Inventory of State and Local Agencies Preparing Population Estimates: Survey of 1965," *Current Population Reports,* Series P-25, No. 328, Washington, 1966.
3. U.S. Bureau of the Census, *Evaluation and Research Programs of the United States Census of Population and Housing, 1960,* Series ER-60, Nos. 1–7; and *Postenumeration Survey: 1950,* An Evaluation Study of the 1950 Census of Population and Housing, Technical Paper No. 4.
4. Siegel, Jacob S., Leon Pritzker, and N. D. Rothwell, *Procedural Difficulties in Taking Past Censuses in Predominately Negro, Puerto Rican, and Mexican Areas,* presented at the Conference on Social Statistics and the City, June 22–23, 1967, sponsored by the Joint Center for Urban Studies of the Massachusetts Institute of Technology and Harvard University.
5. U.S. Bureau of the Census, *U.S. Census of Population: 1960,* vol. I, *Characteristics of the Population,* part 1, *U.S. Summary,* p. xli.
6. Hutchinson, E. P., *Our Statistics of International Migration: Comparability and Completeness for Demographic Use,* A Report to the Committee on Population Statistics of the Population Association of America, July, 1965.
7. [See Chapter 8 on religion for further discussion.—Ed.]
8. Lee, Everett S., *et al.,* under the direction of Simon Kuznets and Dorothy S. Thomas, *Population Redistribution and Economic Growth, United States, 1870–1950,* The American Philosophical Society, Philadelphia, 1957.
9. Whelpton, Pascal K., Arthur A. Campbell, and John Patterson, *Fertility and Family Planning in the United States,* Princeton University Press, Princeton, N.J., 1966.

III. STRUCTURAL FEATURES

3. PRODUCTION OF GOODS AND SERVICES

The Measurement of Economic Growth

A. W. Sametz

ALTHOUGH THE "national income and product accounts" for the U.S. are among the best known and reputable economic series, they are not very useful to measure economic growth or welfare. The accounts do, of course, serve the purpose for which they were designed: to measure the current state of the nation, uncover the proximate causes of economic fluctuations, and suggest countercyclical policies. Keynesian economics—essentially a theory of aggregate demand—required, indeed specified, the Gross National Product (GNP) array we have so successfully used for short-run explanation and policy making.

But change in GNP over long periods of time is not a good measure of economic growth or welfare. One cannot ignore—as one can for cyclical problems—price and population changes, nor can one assume that the *composition* of inputs (or costs) or of output is relatively unchanged. Worse, one cannot even assume unchanged tastes or constant social priorities. In short, since structural change is the essence of secular change, it must be accounted for.

Although it is permissible to interpret an increase in GNP from 1966 of 8 per cent as a rough index of real growth or improvement, it is not possible to take the trebling of GNP in a generation (1947–1966) seriously. Further, it is obvious folly to take the 65-fold increase in GNP over the century since the Civil War as an indication that the nation has "grown" that fast, much less that the nation or the average American is 65 (or even 22) times "better off" today than in 1867. (See Table 1.) The problems of comparing the national output of the U.S. in 1966 with the U.S. in 1867 are just as formidable as comparing U.S. output in 1967 with the output of India in 1967; indeed, for all practical purposes the U.S. in 1867 is "another country."[1]

It is relatively easy to make 1929 or 1946 data comparable to those of 1967 once we have designed a format for 1967 output data that produces the arrangement we need to measure economic advance. What is

77

TABLE 1. PER CAPITA GROSS NATIONAL PRODUCT IN THE UNITED STATES FOR VARIOUS PERIODS, 1869–1966, AND CHANGE RATIOS

	1869–1879 and 1939–1948	1929–1966	1947–1966	1965–1966	1869–1966
GNP, in billions of dollars	7 to 155	103 to 739	231 to 739	681 to 739	11 to 739
Change ratio	(22×)	(7×)	(3×)	(1.08×)	(65×)
Real GNP, in billions of dollars	10.5 to 128	204 to 648	310 to 648	615 to 648	25 to 648
Change ratio	(12×)	(3×)	(2×)	(1.05×)	(26×)
Real GNP per capita Real GNP / Population	$\dfrac{10.5 \text{ to } 128}{43.5} \quad 138$	$\dfrac{204 \text{ to } 648}{122} \quad 197$	$\dfrac{310 \text{ to } 648}{144} \quad 197$		$\dfrac{310 \text{ to } 648}{43.5} \quad 197$
		(in dollars)			
	$240 to 930	$1,671 to 3,280	$2,150 to 3,280	—	$575 to 3,250
Change ratio	(4×)	(2×)	(1.5×)	—	(5.5×)

required is price and population deflation and quality and leisure "inflation" of the data, in addition to an allowance for the sharply increased role of government in the economy. But to measure the change since the Civil War is much more difficult, for the whole process of industrialization has to be "costed" out. That is, the output data have to be deflated for industrialization's side effects: its "nonpriced" costs such as pollution, and for its previously nonpriced (i.e., nonmarketed) output of a "domestic" or handicraft system.

Although the process of making 1867, 1929, and 1966 comparable for the purpose of measuring social change may appear to some so conjectural as to be useless for historical purposes, it serves an important current purpose. Our principal concern is to develop a *new set of accounts* for use in analysis of problems in growth and development and for measuring changes in economic welfare. As always, facing up to a problem means devising a framework suitable to its analysis, which in turn suggests the basic data needed (in conjunction with explicit value judgments) to come to policy conclusions. If nothing else, the backward look suggests the data blanks that require filling-in if future growth is to be evaluated in welfare terms more successfully, to say nothing of being created in accordance with our desires. To measure growth of output of goods and services successfully is not merely to contribute to the *measurement* of social welfare but also to the *achievement* of that welfare as well.

REAL PER CAPITA GNP

Everyone agrees that output time series should be price-deflated, and many agree that output series should be converted to per capita form for growth or welfare measurement. But accurate price deflation is as difficult to do (over long periods of time) as it is universally agreed that it ought to be done; population deflation, on the other hand, is easy to execute but sometimes difficult to justify.

To say roughly that "output" has "increased" since the Civil War fourfold or fivefold rather than 22- or 65-fold does not violate common sense or other intuitions about the change in national well-being over the span of one hundred years. In that sense, the change in real output per capita is the proper measure to use for gauging economic growth.

Although intuitively we assume correctly that a country whose output doubles while its population is not growing is "better off" than a country whose output *and* population double, the important "scale" issue is thereby neglected. Population increase has both benefits and costs. Population increase lowers current per capita output; but because of lagged increases in the *working* population, it leads to increased *future* aggregate output, perhaps in exponential fashion, if economies of scale in production are achieved thereby. And for some purposes, e.g., war, mere size may be critical. Beyond some critical mass, it is appropriate to "deflate" output data for population increase, if one is trying to measure standards of living and individual material welfare. This is especially true in a society in which hours of work (but not real income) are falling, and in a society in which there is by definition no labor shortage and in which the social costs of "congestion" are rising. (We shall return to these matters later.)

On the other hand, no case can be made that price increases (unlike population income) ought to be counted. The problem is, however, that our methods of price deflation cut the rate of real output advance excessively, for the indexes do not allow sufficiently for the improvement of quality in products and have difficulty with the introduction of new (presumably superior) products. This is, of course, not a trivial matter for such changes are an important implicit aspect of economic growth.

Adjusting GNP for population and price change is surely essential to the measurement of economic advance; but the reduction in the growth rate as we shift to real per capita output is too great. We must also allow for the quality improvements that are not reflected in the price data and for the reduced inputs (effort) expended for a given unit of output.

ALLOWING FOR THE INCREASE IN THE QUALITY OF OUTPUT AND OF INPUT

Assume two countries with equal rates of per capita output increase; but in *A* the average working day is six hours and shrinking faster than in *B* where it is eight hours. Surely the individual in *A* is better off. Whether one says that *A* has more productive inputs (more output per unit input) or that in *A* one has the same amount of goods but more *leisure,* the conclusion is that economic progress is better measured by real per capita output *per unit of input*. The economic welfare of the individual is surely advanced whether he makes the effort and takes the goods or chooses leisure. We can measure the additional advance by the reduction in hours worked over time multiplied by the real wage (i.e., real output) foregone.

The typical real per capita output measure also underestimates the rate of advance because the price index by which the output data are deflated tends to overestimate price rises. The deflator makes no allowance for quality improvements (not marked by cost increases and hence price increases), and only tardy and partial allowance for new products. While there are more conceptual problems in rectifying the "population" deflator (for lessened work time) than in modifying the "price" deflator, the actual measurement of the allowance for leisure is less difficult (though difficult enough!) than the allowance for product change and improvement.

Quality

Fortunately the quality problem is restricted largely to consumer durables and some consumer services such as medical care where technological change has been rapid. Quality changes in capital goods are automatically reflected in future output, and quality changes in consumer nondurables ("necessities") tend to be reflected in cost increases. Furthermore, by varying the index sample and weights, the Bureau of Labor Statistics (BLS) tries to take account of some quality changes.

For purposes of our rough long-run measure of output change, my guess (which I would defend only very weakly) is that half the price rise since 1929 and one-fourth of that for 1869–1929 should be restored to the growth index to allow for increased quality of output. The customary estimate that quality improvement has been large enough to offset all the normal annual rate of increase (1.0 to 1.5 per cent)[2] in the Consumer Price Index (CPI) has been rejected because for our purposes we should allow for the historical episodes of abnormal price rise and the secular shift to nonnecessities consumer spending. On the other hand, the allowance should be greater than zero. Everyone agrees that the evidence of consumer shifts to new or better products means that consumer satisfaction is increased thereby and that this increased welfare is not reflected in an output index that is deflated by the conventional method.

The seriousness of the need and an operational technique for quality weighting of price indexes has been explored in some depth by Zvi Griliches. His technique as applied to the auto industry might well be applied to all goods and services for which quality change is significant. The auto is considered a bundle of different "quality" combinations (horsepower, weight, length, engine, etc.) whose price in various years is found by cross-section price specification regressions to be the sum of a "priced" series of such qualities; this price is then compared with the list prices of cars for selected years. For example, over the period 1947–1961 the new auto component of CPI rose 39 per cent, but the "quality" index rose by 25 to 50 per cent, "indicating little or no rise in the real price of new automobiles."[3] Since the auto makes up almost 3 per cent of the CPI, that index over this short period was too high by over 5 per cent due to the auto adjustment alone. This method is applicable, despite difficult methodological problems, to other consumer durables and services, say for a medical cure for appendicitis. Quality can and must be measured in measuring economic change; as a precaution, the pure quantity or cost-oriented index should be run side by side with that index as amended for quality or "utility" changes.[4]

Questions of possible quality deterioration (not reflected in lower price) are not pertinent at this point. If the revised product is chosen in preference to the old product, given identical prices, it is an "improved" product, despite the scholar's disdain. And although the consumer might have gained more if, instead of higher horsepower at the same cost, he had chosen the old low horsepower at reduced cost, this choice is the scholar's, not the consumer's. Insofar as a real problem is raised here, it involves not quality loss but side effects or public costs not counted in the producer's sales price. Higher horsepower may add to air pollution, etc.

Leisure

The increase in leisure over time can be added to the measure of economic growth by computing the goods and services that *could* have been produced (but voluntarily were not) if those hours had been worked instead. We assume, and here conceptual problems abound, that it is the average rather than the marginal product that is foregone, that the issue of whether the choice of leisure is totally voluntary or not is unimportant, and that the question of increased efficiency per hour of the reduced hours is implicitly taken care of by our measurement technique. Temporarily putting aside conceptual problems, we take the decline in working hours below standard to be worth the average real wage foregone.[5]

The maximum work week standard is assumed to be 78 hours so that the 67 hours standard work week of the 1870's provided 11 hours of leisure. The value of this leisure is found by taking 11/67 or 16 per cent of the value of national output attributable to labor (80 per cent of the real total output). Thus for the 1870's the value of leisure was .16 × 80/100 ($9.4 billion) or $1.2 billion. Thus the real national output of those times including the value of leisure taken was $10.6 billion not $9.4 billion, or one-eighth greater. On this crude base we have evaluated by a parallel methodology the value of the increased leisure taken over the last century.

Leisure taken increased 3.5-fold since 1869; as the standard work week fell from 67 to 40 hours, leisure hours (to be valued and added to output) rose from 11 to 38 per week. The additions to output involved are substantial. (See Table 2.)

TABLE 2. VALUE OF LEISURE AS A CORRECTION TO
CALCULATED NET NATIONAL PRODUCT,
UNITED STATES, 1869–1966

	Real NNP	Real value of leisure	Leisure over NNP	Total
	(billions of dollars)			
1869–1878	$ 9.4	$ 1.2	1/8	$ 10.6
1929	97.0	60.0	3/5	157.0
1947	150.0	108.0	7/10	258.0
1966	315.0	240.0	3/4	555.0

Crude as these data may be, comparisons of the leisure-adjusted data are surely more appropriate for measuring economic progress than the unadjusted data. Note that the slowing up of the reduction in hours worked since 1947 means that adding in the leisure component reduces the rate of advance of current years over the past. The opposite effect is the consequence of the quality adjustment which restores more of the price deflation for recent years than earlier years.

Evaluating the revised rates of economic advance:

1. Between 1869 and 1948 (Kuznets' data) the quality improvement factor raises the real per capita output growth from fourfold to fivefold; and the leisure adjustment raises it further to sixfold.
2. In the postwar period between 1947 and 1966 (Commerce data) the advance was not 1.5 but twofold in doubly adjusted real output per capita, *all* owing to quality improvement.
3. Since 1929 we figure that "individual economic welfare" has risen not two times but three times.
4. Very roughly, over the whole period 1869–1966, an elevenfold increase—twice the real but unadjusted data—is the suggested number.

TABLE 3. "ADJUSTED" REAL PER CAPITA GROSS
NATIONAL PRODUCT PER UNIT OF INPUT AND CHANGE
RATIOS, UNITED STATES, VARIOUS PERIODS, 1869–1966

	1869–1878 and 1939–1948	1929–1966	1947–1966	1869–1966
	(billions of dollars)			
Quality adjusted real GNP	$10.5 to 157	204 to 870	310 to 817	25 to 850
Change ratio	(15×)	(4.5×)	(2 2/3×)	(34×)
Adjusted real per capita		(dollars)		
GNP	$240 to 1,140	1,671 to 4,416	2,150 to 4,150	575 to 4,310
Change ratio	(5×)	(2.5×)	(2×)	(7.5×)
Adjusted real per capital GNP per unit of input				
GNP	$ 12 to 235	326 to 1,525	527 to 1,429	28 to 1,480
Population	43.5 138	122 197	144 197	43.5 197
	(dollars)			
	$280 to 1,700	$2,670 to 7,900	$3,650 to 7,200	$650 to 7,500
Change ratio	(6×)	(3×)	(2×)	(11×)

At this point, once more, one intuitively begins to doubt not the
method but the results, especially the longer-run results. It does not
seem plausible that the average citizen is eleven times economically
better off today than in the post-Civil War period; nor even that he is
three times as well off as in 1929. Although the "unadjusted" real data
provide more plausible answers, the adjustments are analytically essential; the problem is that we have neglected two other major structural
changes of the industrialization process in the economic system, which
tend to pull in the opposite direction. Adjusting for the increased quality and leisure made possible by the process of industrialization swells
apparent total output; but we must also adjust downward for the market and ill-fare effects of the commercialization of domestic activities
and the social costs of an urbanizing-industrializing society.

ALLOWING FOR THE FALL IN NONMARKET "SALES" AND THE RISE OF "INDUSTRIALIZATION" COSTS

Principles

First, we have not allowed for the fact that over time an increasing
proportion of total output is marketed and is therefore counted, although it is not *additional* output. This we will call the "market" adjust-

ment. There is also a "cost" adjustment to be made, for an industrializing economy incurs social costs of production (side effects) that should be deducted from GNP, and some spending that is traditionally included in GNP is really cost or intermediate product and should be removed from output data.

The "market" effects are one consequence of the structural shifts typical of an economy moving from an agricultural, handicraft society to an industrialized urban society. In general, it is the commercializing of economic activities formerly carried on within the household that inflates GNP insofar as there is no increase in such activity but simply a relabeling of the activity from an unrecorded household activity to a recorded business transaction. For example, home (farm) growing and processing of food, domestic-bound personal care and recreation, and farm investment expenditures largely were not part of nineteenth-century GNP. Even today the housewife's unrecorded labor causes GNP to be underestimated, but this gap is much less important for recent than for earlier periods.

On the other hand, the so-called "occupational" costs (e.g., the extra costs of getting to work and the extra costs of "delivery" or distribution of goods) increase with urbanization and industrialization, and in any case become recorded commercial transactions and thus enter GNP. In any statistic intended to measure the growth of economic well-being, only additional want-satisfying goods and services should be included and not the additional costs of making them available. These costs are in effect intermediate products and should be deducted from GNP when the latter is used as a measure of growth or welfare rather than as a measure of aggregate expenditures. Note that these "occupational" costs are private, out-of-pocket expenditures; the issue of *social* costs (e.g., pollution) is quite a separate and more difficult matter because of the lack of actual expenditures as a measure. But both sets of costs do arise in consequence of the industrialization-urbanization process, both are offsets to the advantages of those processes, and both should be accounted for by a deduction from recorded GNP.

Before turning to social costs—the most difficult of all the variables in our model to measure—let us consider the other major source of "intermediate goods" that we must delete from an output measure of progress. Only government expenditures for direct services for final consumers such as health, education, recreation, and welfare, or public investment in buildings, and dams and highways, etc. should be counted in GNP; most other government expenditures are intermediate products.

Because the bulk of government expenditures is not part of "welfare" output, and because government expenditures as a proportion of GNP have risen steadily since 1869, another adjustment should be made to reduce the huge apparent gap between real output per capita today compared with various earlier dates. The great increases in government spending (and employment) over the past century can in good part be considered as "costs" of industrialization and urbanization or as "costs" of maintaining the basic social framework *within* which final production takes place. The flow of economic goods and services to individuals from the economy is a flow of output "produced and secured under conditions of internal peace, external safety and legal protection of specific rights and can not include these very conditions as services. . . . (The social framework) is a pre-condition of such service, not a service in itself."[6]

Removing all government services to society at large (including defense or war expenditures on men and equipment) from the government sector of GNP, leaving only that spending which provides services directly to consumers (collective consumption) or public investment, removes three-quarters of government spending in 1966 but only half of government spending in the 1870's. Since government spending constitutes 20 per cent of the official NNP for 1966 and only 5 per cent of NNP for 1869–1878, it is clear that for welfare purposes, our adjustment reduces government spending to a narrow range of 2.5 per cent to 5 per cent over the whole period. (Note that 1967 complaints of public squalor vis-à-vis private affluence call for increases in collective consumption and production—an increase in the component we have not excluded from government spending.)

Measurement

Most of the techiques for making preindustrial and industrial economies comparable have been developed in the comparative systems literature, where, for example, Chinese and American standards of living are contrasted. Colin Clark's "international units" and the expression of consumer goods in terms of the "effort required (hours worked) to obtain them" are attempts to avoid the obviously absurd comparison of a $37 per capita annual real output of the average Chinese vs. the $1,500 of the average American (for the 1931–1936 period). The gap was greatly narrowed by adding the nonmarketed output to the preindustrial society's totals, etc., and subtracting the varied "costs" from the industrial society's total; for example, doubling the Chinese number to $75 and halving the U.S. number to $750, reduced the apparent fortyfold difference to a more plausible tenfold.[7]

The Market Effect

Housewives' services and other "domestic" production, which are excluded from the current GNP as well as 1869 GNP, are a significant omission today and a disabling omission from the earlier totals. It has been customary to estimate that in recent years housewives' services had a value of about one-quarter of GNP. We estimate that recorded GNP of 1869–1878 should be *doubled* to allow for domestic production. This estimate is based on reasoning that the proportion would necessarily rise back through time because of the very definition of a handicraft or domestic system and on recent estimates of housewives' services as a proportion of GNP for the benchmark years 1929, 1947, and 1965 of 45 per cent, 25 per cent, and 21 per cent respectively.[8] If housewives' services were still almost half of GNP in 1929 when the industrialization process had proceeded so far, surely all extramarket domestic activities were 100 per cent of GNP in the 1870's. (If anything, this is likely to be an underestimate.)

Costs of Industrialization

Nongovernmental. The "inflated costs of urban civilization" were estimated for 1929 to be 20 to 30 per cent of consumer outlay or about one-fifth of GNP.[9] For the last decade these "intermediate" costs probably rose to two-fifths of GNP, for the rural urban shift has proceeded apace. As recently as 1930, one of three Americans lived on a farm; in 1947 the figure fell to one in seven and by the 1960's to one in fourteen. We will use 30 per cent of GNP as our estimate for the 1947 benchmark year and to avoid a zero cost for the 1870's we will assume a token 5 per cent of GNP to be deducted for the 1870's for the farm to city costs.

Governmental. There has been an unmistakable increase in the proportion of total spending accounted for by government over the last century. But there has been no proportional increase at all in the final product part of that spending. (In this sense there has been no *advance* in collective consumption and production since the 1870's.)

Total government spending to GNP was 4.5 per cent in the 1870's, 9 per cent in 1929, 17 per cent in 1946 and 20 per cent in 1966.[10] But if we remove spending on defense and civil functions, leaving only government spending on education, health, highways, and the like, the trend disappears.

For example, in 1966 of the total government expenditures for goods and services of $196 billion, HEW plus transportation and housing expenditures summed to $50 billion or one-quarter of total government spending. (Defense constituted over one-half of the total, and civil government and the like took up the rest.) For 1947 we estimate that one-third and for 1929 two-fifths of all government spending was *not* intermediate product. For the years prior to 1929, indirect evidence is needed because detailed breakdowns of the types of government spending are not available. It is known, however, that between 1900 and 1965 state and local expenditures declined secularly as a percentage of all government expenditures from two-thirds to one-third; it is also clear that a higher proportion of state and local expenditures (we assume 0.5) should be retained as final output than for federal expenditures (we assume 0.2). A fairly steady 70 per cent of federal expenditures seem always to consist of defense and war-related expenditures. For 1900 it seems likely that, as in 1929, about two-fifths of government expenditures should be held in our final output results.

Federal expenditures	$.33 \times 20\% = 0.066$	
State and local expenditures	$.67 \times 50\% = 0.335$	
Total	0.40	

But for 1870, we would raise the proportion to 50 per cent on the basis that only about 10 per cent of total government spending was federal.[11]

Roughly, then, the contribution of government for output growth purposes is *not* between 4.4 per cent of GNP in 1870 and 20 per cent in 1966 but between 2.2 per cent and 5 per cent. We remove from apparent GNP 2.2 per cent in the early period and 15 per cent of today's 20 per cent. This is the "cost" of urbanization, etc., that is included in the government spending totals. (For 1947 we remove 11.4 per cent of GNP and for 1929, 5.4 per cent.)[12]

But now let us pull all our "market and cost" deductions together to see the effect on per capita real output comparisons over time.

Output per capita is three to four times greater than a century ago and about 50 per cent greater today than in either 1929 or 1947. Of course the *aggregate* economic size of the economy increased at a far faster pace, growing 18-fold in a century and doubling in total output since 1947. But these total figures are not indications of economic welfare but rather of national power or total monetary transactions or aggregate demand, etc.

These welfare results are intuitively appealing. They say that we are, on the average, twice as well off materially as our grandparents (1914) who in turn were about twice as well as their grandparents (1865).

TABLE 4. "WELFARE" GROSS NATIONAL PRODUCT IN THE UNITED STATES, VARIOUS PERIODS, 1869–1966, AND CHANGE RATIOS

	1869	1949	1929	1966	1947	1966	1870	1966
			(billions of dollars)					
Doubly adjusted real GNP (quality and leisure)[a]	12	235	326	1,525	527	1,429	28	1,498
Addition for nonmarket activities[b]	+12	+59	+147	+320	+132	+300	+28	+315
Deductions for "costs" of GNP								
Nongovernmental[c]	−0.6	−71	−65	−610	−158	−572	−1.4	−599
Governmental[d]	−0.3	−27	−18	−229	−60	−214	−0.6	−225
Net change	+11.1	−39	+64	−519	−86	−486	+26.	−509
Welfare GNP	23	196	390	1,006	441	943	54	989
(Magnitude of growth)		(8.5×)		(2.5×)		(2+×)		(18×)
GNP	23	196	390	1,006	441	943	54	989
Population	43.5	138	122	197	144	197	43.5	197
Welfare GNP per capita (in dollars)	$528	$1,420	$3,197	$5,107	$3,063	$4,787	$1,241	$5,020
(Magnitude of growth)		(2 2/3 ×)		(1 3/5 ×)		(1.5×)		(4×)

a From Table 3.

b 100 per cent of GNP for 1869, 45 per cent for 1929, 25 per cent for 1947, and 21 per cent for 1966 (to add to GNP the decreasing proportion of total output that is not marketed or otherwise counted as an economy develops).

c −5 per cent of GNP for 1869, −20 per cent for 1929, −30 per cent for 1947 and −40 per cent for 1966 (to reduce GNP by the increasing occupational costs of an industrializing and urbanizing society).

d −2.2 per cent of GNP for 1869, −5.4 per cent for 1929, −11.4 per cent for 1947 and −15 per cent for 1966 (to remove intermediate products from the government's contribution to GNP, leaving only government expenditures for direct services to final consumers).

89

DEVELOPING THE "WELFARE OUTPUT" INDICATOR

To get these results required laborious digging into data designed for other purposes and some fairly wild surmises. If the basic approach provides a reasonable approximation of economic progress and welfare, we should begin to collect and arrange data in such a way as to make the "welfare output" indicator less of a guess. And many of the times series required could be reworked for the past from existing work sheets.

The minimum requirement is:

1. An index of quality improvement parallel to the consumer price index—a "quality of goods reflator."
2. A measure of the amount and value of change in leisure time—a "quantity of work deflator."
3. *Revisions and additions to GNP series*
    a. Development of imputed values for crucial nonmarket economic activities.
    b. Reworking of the government account to remove "intermediary" or "necessary evil" social expenditures, assigning the remainder to consumption and investment.
    c. Revision of private sectors to remove "costs" from consumption just as we remove "maintenance" from investment.
    d. The end product to be final consumption and investment regardless of originating sector and whether market priced or not.

This is not an impossible bill of particulars. Work is underway in all categories:

1. Z. Griliches' work on quality has been noted. P. Dhrymes and E. F. Denison, among others, are also at work on the problem.[13]
2. G. Becker's work is leading up to an evaluation of (the opportunity costs) of leisure.[14]
3. a. The 1967 *Annual Report* of the NBER reports much work underway here under the direction of John Kendrick. However no provision has been made for studies of the nineteenth-century domestic economy to develop imputed output data.
    b. and c. I know of no work since Kuznets' on historical social costs or side effects. However there has been a great burst of "benefits-cost" analysis of such nonmarket-priced social costs

as water (air, noise, etc.) pollution, traffic congestion, and the like.[15] As this analysis is currently applied, additions to empirical estimates of the costs of industrialization will be developed.[16]

    d. Kendrick's research group is also finding that investment ("all outlays that enhance future output . . . producing capacity") really constitutes one-half of GNP, not the official one-sixth when household and government investment in HEW, R & D etc. are included.[17]

Although our output indicator 1869–1966 takes no direct account of these particular social costs, by removing occupational costs from the consumer and business accounts and intermediate product from the government accounts, most of the social costs were allowed for. Moreover, there are probably unrecorded social advantages of size and industrialization comparable to the unrecorded social costs of pollution, etc. Probably too, over time social costs like pollution affect consumer (intermediate) expenditures—water meter fees—and business (intermediate) expenditures—water filtration costs, etc. Finally, as we develop social cost accounting, these imputed social costs are converted into net out-of-pocket expenditures.

Thus, at least our *future* welfare indicator—real per capita output per unit of input—could be truly net of all costs masquerading as product and gross of nonpriced but real social costs. Social cost accounting is an essential supplement to the national output accounts (even if the latter are recast as specified) for measuring economic progress.

Note that government's role as *regulator* is at least as important as its role as spender (or employer); and if one removes national defense expenditures, much more so. In specifying social cost allocation and income distribution, it controls major welfare determinants that do not appear in official GNP or BLS statistics.[18]

SOCIAL WELFARE AND HAPPINESS

It should be explicitly noted that after all the trials of arriving at the net output index, we will have only succeeded in specifying the measurable *part* of economic welfare. Nor have we said anything about its achievement, much less of *social* welfare or happiness.

Supplementary Indicators

In addition to the net output indicator—a flow index—stock indexes would be useful; for (as Kenneth Boulding has stressed[19]), it is not clear whether economic welfare is better measured by, for example, the act of eating or the state of being well fed.

An "Index of Absolutes" (average per capita) including life expectancy, caloric and protein intake, square footage of shelter, years of schooling, etc.

An "Index of Consumer Wealth" including stocks of housing and cars plus financial assets such as deposits, securities, and insurance and pension funds.

Achievement: Indicators as Targets

It is not at all clear that the index of real output per capita can be expected automatically to double by say, 2000—the pace indicated by past behavior. It is not that the index determining variables is inadequate or inappropriate but that structural shifts in the economy are likely to inhibit net output.

The two most noted structural changes in process on the consumption side are the shift toward collective consumption and toward services. On the production side the two major shifts in process are toward collective (social) costing and simultaneously toward automated and toward "domestic" (do-it-yourself) production.

The difficulties in measuring and implementing collective consumption and production in a traditionally market-oriented economy are evident; it is likely for some time to come to be as inefficiently done as it is essential to do.[20] The result will be sluggish output increases but more inclusive and therefore surging input (cost) increases. Likewise, the shift to services is a shift toward less productive activity in the sense of output per unit of input obtained in that sector; this is of course even more true for nonmarket or home-produced services than of services bought in the market. Net output growth is more dependent than ever on "the advance of knowledge"—technological change, advances in education, and more widely applied organizational skills—to offset these output depressants.[21] But this paper is not intended to explain or to predict economic advance but simply to provide viable means for its measurement.

Note too that the structural shifts foreseen will make it as inherently difficult to use our indicator to measure future economic progress as it was to extend it backward through time, still another reason to design supplementary indicators as well. However, if the components of the indicator are the appropriate ones (as we believe they are) and if there is an effective demand for such an indicator, the requisite data can be specified and collected and processed. In this sense it ought to be easier to create the future than to recreate the past.

The transitional difficulties accompanying these great structural changes in process perhaps are implicit in the sluggish increase of leisure—the fall in the rate of decline of hours worked—of recent years. Of course, this sluggishness is generally attributable to the fact that at current levels, reduction in hours are not matched (simply through reduced fatigue, etc.) by increased productivity per hour worked; historically, leisure has not been taken at the expense of levels of living. The recent real increase in social costs as well as the increased consciousness of the need to account for them, in addition to the lesser productivity of labor in the growing service sector may be holding down that part of economic advance measured by increased leisure.

Social Welfare

While it has not been assumed that the output index is any more than a partial indicator of social welfare, and no disclaimers on that account are necessary, it may be that the output indicator is of less significance for future than for past social welfare levels. This may be true simply because beyond certain levels of real per capita income (and output), the additional satisfactions are more psychological than physiological, and are more dependent on relative than absolute living levels and on collective or joint than private decisions.

As a consequence, social welfare or happiness may not be increased by increases in output per capita even if shared proportionally. For example, a 10 per cent increase in real income to everyone—say to the $10,000 income group as well as to the $25,000 income group—may lead to increased envy that more than offsets the effects of the material gains on felt welfare.[22] Moreover, additional satisfactions at higher real income levels seem to be more easily achieved through the quality of work than the quantity of income. This may not be observed in our leisure component for it depends more on the nature of the job than the hours worked.[23] Finally, insofar as future individual satisfaction is increasingly dependent on achievements in social costing and collective production and consumption, we are increasingly less dependent on established principles of economic efficiency than on the vaguer, more experimental principles of political "efficiency."

My personal judgment is that, first, the advance of knowledge will more than suffice to offset the external diseconomies we are confronting, just as it offset the depletion of natural resources; second, that the increasing role of government in economic affairs will introduce representative social decision-making without sacrificing allocational efficiency; and third, that increasing equality of income and opportunity will make it more reasonable to imply increased social welfare from increases in the output indicator.

I suspect that academics (except perhaps economists) will either not agree with this analysis and judgment or will not like it. Academics tend, as Lecht does, to inquire after "the aspirations of knowledgeable people" rather than the representative spender or voter in selecting targets. Moreover recent (and expected) economic tendencies, i.e., economic "progress," bodes ill to the newly prestiged (and well-paid) average professor. Professorial hours are not really reducible; the professor is not interested in the increased quality (or quantity) of gadgets or mass-produced goods but in personal and other services whose cost is rising (quality falling); he tends not to see the costs of industrialization and urbanization as necessary (and costable) evils but simply as evils; he sighs about the "quality of life" as do the poverty-stricken but for quite different (and unsentimental) reasons. Before quoting Thoreau approvingly that the "mass of men lead lives of quiet desperation," academics should realize that he wrote that in 1854 in the pre-industrial era and that today we are (hopefully) moving into a postindustrial era. Unfortunately, a "Great Society" seems to be prerequisite to a "Good Society."

NOTES

1. It will be apparent to anyone at all conversant with the problems of measuring economic growth how greatly I am dependent on the work of Simon Kuznets. While I have not footnoted in detail, his numbers and techniques are utilized at every turn. It is more than graciousness that impels me to say that without his work this paper could not have been written. All crucial numbers used, with the exception of those from the official income and product accounts, are cited.
2. "It is not at all improbable that correctly measured there has been no real rise in the general price level (as of 1961) since 1952." Adelman, I., and Z. Griliches, "On an Index of Quality Change," *Journal of the American Statistical Association,* September, 1961, p. 545. The CPI showed an 11.5 per cent increase over the decade 1952–1961.
3. Griliches, Z., "Notes on the Measurement of Price and Quality Change," in *Models of Income Determination,* National Bureau of Economic Research, 1964, Table 8, p. 397.
4. Other methods allowing for quality changes may be developed based on

such clear physical standards as caloric content (food), durability (auto tires), etc. Griliches suggests that new products can be valued as a service flow to be compared to the price or cost of achieving the same level of service at a prior time.

5. See Kuznets' Table 7 in "Long-Term Changes in the National Incomes of the U.S.A. since 1870," in *Income and Wealth,* vol. 2, Cambridge, Bowes & Bowes, 1952, p. 65.

6. Kuznets, S., "Government Product and National Income," in *Income and Wealth,* vol. I, Cambridge, Bowes & Bowes, 1951, pp. 193–194.

7. Kuznets, S., "National Income and Industrial Structure," in *Economic Change,* Norton, New York, 1953, pp. 145ff.

8. Kendrick, J. W., in *Annual Report,* National Bureau of Economic Research, New York, June, 1967, Table II, p. 11. (Kuznets' estimate for 1947 in "National Income and Economic Welfare," in *Economic Change, op. cit.,* p. 195).

9. Kuznets, "National Income and Economic Welfare," *op. cit.,* p. 196.

10. See Kuznets in "Long-Term Changes . . . ," *op. cit.,* Table 14, p. 89.

11. "In fact the ratio of federal spending to GNP was as low as ½ of 1% during extended periods of America's early history." Herber, B. P., *Modern Public Finance,* R. D. Irwin, Homewood, Ill., 1967, p. 121.

    With all government expenditures comprising 4.4 per cent of GNP in 1869–1878, we assume that 1/9 of 4.4 or 5 per cent comprised federal expenditures. Then adding $1/9 \times 20$ per cent $+ 8/9 \times 50$ per cent we get 47 per cent. And half of 4.4 per cent = 2.2 per cent.

12. 1929: 9% of GNP $\times$ 3/5 excluded = $-$ 5.4% GNP.
    1947: 17% of GNP $\times$ 2/3 excluded = -11.4% GNP.

13. Dhrymes, P., "On the Measurement of Price and Quality Changes in Some Consumer Capital Goods," *American Economic Review,* May, 1967, pp. 501–518; Denison, E. F., *Why Growth Rates Differ,* Brookings Institution, Washington, 1967.

14. Becker, G., "A Theory of the Allocation of Time," *Economic Journal,* September, 1965.

15. See, e.g., Smith, S. C., and E. N. Castle, *Economics and Public Policy in Water Resource Development,* Iowa State University Press, Ames, Iowa, 1964.

16. L. A. Lecht's work, *Goals, Priorities and Dollars,* The Free Press, New York, 1966, is of little use for it specifies no priorities and simply lists the costs of overcoming social disutilities of all varieties.

17. Kendrick, J. W., *op. cit.,* pp. 11–12.

18. Failure to stress this accounts for the fact that much of Eli Ginzberg *et al., The Pluralistic Economy,* McGraw-Hill, New York, 1965, seems outdated or beside the point. Perhaps the expected surge in collective consumption will alter this impression, say, by 1972.

19. Boulding, Kenneth, "The Economics of the Coming Spaceship Earth," in Jarrett, H., editor, *Environmental Quality in a Growing Economy,* Johns Hopkins Press, Baltimore, 1966, pp. 3–14.

20. Criticism of the market system's ends (as limited) should not obscure the great efficiency of the market system's means! (Would intellectuals object to mass persuasive advertising of the benefits of [taxes for] education expenditures or a mass campaign against smoking or other pollution?)

21. E. F. Denison has stressed these "intangible" investment components, not merely the quantity of capital goods, as an increasing source of economic growth. See his *The Sources of Economic Growth in the U.S.,* Committee for Economic Development, New York, 1962.

22. Although everyone gains materially and no one loses, one cannot say that social welfare has increased. (See Mishan, E. J., "A Survey of Welfare Economics," *The Economic Journal,* June, 1960, pp. 251ff.)
23. See Abramowitz, M., "The Welfare Interpretation of Secular Trends in National Income and Product," in *The Allocation of Economic Resources,* Stanford, Stanford University Press, 1959, p. 20.

4. LABOR FORCE AND EMPLOYMENT TRENDS

Stanley Lebergott

EVERY FORCEFUL change in American society and the American economy has had its impact on the pattern of labor supply and use. Variations in supply and utilization have, in turn, induced changes in the economy, for employees are both the producers and the consumers of the nation's output. To review that entire set of relationships is clearly impossible. This chapter, therefore, focuses on some of the more striking changes in labor supply and employment since 1900.

The first section is addressed to the role of the family. Since family income goals turn out to be determinative in shaping labor supply, this section also considers the contribution of the major components in that supply and reviews some consequential changes in the labor market. During these decades the role of the traditional entrepreneur dwindled while business concentration increased, creating a new era in labor relations. New ways of controlling labor input had to be established, and in the second section we review some of the labor alternatives chosen. In the third section we turn to variations in employment by industry and by occupation associated with the new pattern of final demands and the new array of costs that marked the first half of the twentieth century. The fourth section goes on to consider the extent to which these various changes did or did not produce a new era of mechanization and automation. The concluding section proposes a set of changes to be made in existing data collections in order to support more judicious government policy choices and more careful governmental and private administration in the decades ahead.

PATTERNS OF LABOR FORCE SUPPLY

The Role of the Family

The work of a nation is done by individuals, but individuals alone do not determine the nation's work patterns. To understand the dramatic changes in the pattern of U.S. labor force supply since 1900, we must turn to that island of primitive communism—the family. In American society decisions made within the family determine who will seek work, for how long, and where. Family members allocate labor and income among themselves by personal criteria, with little reference to private market allocation procedure. The children alone do not decide whether they will work. The wife alone does not choose between a part-time and a full-time job. Or when to quit the labor force. Family pressures for income and other goals enter into all these decisions.

Of course, these choices are constrained by the expectations of the larger society: fathers in most social classes go to work, children go to school, mothers keep house, and so on. But most American families live above a coarse subsistence level. Hence a significant share of labor is provided by men and women busily working to add optional items to the family expenditure level. Faster junking of automobiles, homes with greater privacy for family members, added television sets, money for retirement years—all of these are options. However, they are options that can be achieved only by extra work on the part of family members. Hence the labor supply is ultimately fixed by family expenditure horizons, or, if you will, the associated income horizons.

It is easy to explain why most adult males work. But to explain work patterns in a society well above subsistence levels we must look to the role of income horizons. Data in Table 1 on sources of family income, put together from surveys scattered over two-thirds of a century, tell us something about those horizons. They report an unsuspected constancy.

Apparently families set their income horizon at 25 per cent more than the head of the family earns, the husband earning approximately 80 per cent of the total family income. So it was in 1901, when unemployment and real income were low. So it was a third of a century later, in the midst of our most extended depression. And so it was in the piping warlike days of 1965. As real hourly wages of husbands rose from 1901 to 1935–1936, other family members adjusted their own participation so that they continued to add 25 per cent to the husband's income. As wages continued to rise over the next thirty years, and unemployment to fall, there was again an adjustment to 25 per cent. Since wage rates for women and teenagers had also been rising, it is clear that the historic increase in female labor force participation was not required to yield the same real income. But income horizons had shifted. And the family continued to seek 25 per cent more in-

TABLE 1.   PERCENTAGE OF INCOME OF URBAN
FAMILIES CONTRIBUTED BY HUSBAND,
SELECTED YEARS, 1900–1965

Year	Percentage
1900	80
1935–1936	82
1960	80
1965	81

SOURCES: 1900: Estimated from data for 1901 in U.S. Commissioner of Labor, *Annual Report*, 1904, pp. 362, 366.

1935–1936: ratios for particular sampling areas, as shown in the Bureau of Labor Statistics–Bureau of Human Nutrition and Home Economics Consumer Purchases Volumes, weighted by the appropriate distribution of nonfarm families from National Resources Committee, *Consumer Incomes in the United States*, 1938, Table 24B.

1960: Census of Population, *Sources and Structure of Family Income*, p. 158. The data refer to urban husband-wife families.

1965: Bureau of the Census, *Current Population Reports,* series P-60, no. 51, "Income in 1965 of Families and Persons in the United States." For nonfarm families, male head, married wife present, the median family income was $7,436 (p. 19) of which the head's income was $6,026 (p. 32), or 81 per cent. Of 39,419 wives, 19,816 had a median income of $1,789 or an average of $872 per family, leaving $538 contributed by children and other family members.

come than the husband provided, despite his higher wage rates and despite his overtime work. A moralist or philosopher could probably explain why the American family always seeks more than the husband's income. But it would require a more protean analyst to explain why the family income horizon apparently kept moving throughout two-thirds of a century to a point 25 per cent beyond the income that the husband could provide.

The Labor Supply Context

The simple facts of labor supply in the U.S. can readily be summarized in about 50,000 time series. We shall not make that summary here. They are conveniently analyzed in perhaps a hundred key monographic studies. We shall not review them here either. Instead, let us refer to only two facts:[1]

Some 60 per cent of the U.S. population aged sixteen and older is in the labor force.

The proportion for males has been running about double that for females—80 per cent to 40 per cent.

The nation has arrived at these proportions as a resultant of tradition and the subtle interplay of family relationships. That the proportion for males is not closer to 90 per cent reflects the extent to which society and the structure of the economy make it possible for the individual to quit the labor force for some years of retirement (uneasy or untroubled) before he dies, as well as to postpone his entry into the labor force. That the proportion for females is so much lower reflects the arrangement whereby male dominance in society is achieved (in exchange for? in addition to?) a greater rate of employment outside the home. (We conventionally do not count unpaid employment inside the home as being labor force activity, whether one deals with child rearing, or do-it-yourself home maintenance.) The labor force measures in use since 1940 do include unpaid work in a family enterprise such as farm or store when it exceeds 15 hours a week. They do not include the housewife's usual activities, largely because to do so would yield a near tautology: i.e., virtually all healthy persons in the prime ages would always be in the labor force.

The entrepreneur who bids for labor cannot alter many of these preferences. His offers of wages and working conditions must elicit labor supply within the boundaries of this social structure and slowly moving system of values. As a result, the rise in output is bounded by many factors: The extent to which women can be induced to leave their role at home for work outside. The extent to which men can be induced to forego education in order to begin work earlier in life. The degree to which workers can be induced to give up more tantalizing activities in order to continue working into later years, or take a second job.

Society also has to reckon with the converse—namely, the reluctance of workers to leave the labor force when the demand for their work slackens. Under some conditions slackening demand leads to a relatively happy withdrawal from the labor force (women leaving at the end of World War II). But under other, less happy, conditions, the withdrawal has been labeled "disguised unemployment." Where the labor force does not dwindle along with demands, the result is a rising unemployment rate and growing social concern.

Advertising and Government Action

Since the twentieth century began its unpredictable course, two titanic forces have been shaping U.S. labor supply—one to expand, the other to restrict it. Advertising, in sight and sound, has been the expansionist force, constantly persuading the consumer to buy new goods and new versions of old goods. Desire may spring eternal in the consumer. But the ubiquitous salesman stimulates and focuses it. The consumer, however, is a worker in another hat. Typically the new commodity he learns to desire can be acquired only by work. (One may agree with Conrad that "Thieving is a form of human industry . . . undertaken for the same reason as work in the potteries." In any event it is a rarely used alternative. Embezzling, forgery, and other activities are best undertaken as complementary activities to working. Drawing down assets is no solution, since saving goals usually require that they be replenished.) Hence the consumer who wants to reify his desires and expand his real expenditures must seek additional work. Thus by making more goods more desirable to more people, advertisers have been increasing the national labor supply.

Opposed to these market forces have been government actions constricting the supply of labor. Immigration, which had been adding more than a million a year to the population before 1914, was cut sharply. Rising education requirements blocked youngsters from entering the labor force at age six or ten. The initiation of government old-age pensions induced older workers to quit at sixty-five rather than to try to work until seventy or later.

Trends for Major Groups. The over-all results of these opposed pressures have been something of a draw. The proportion of the U.S. population in the labor force changed hardly at all between 1900 and 1966: 56 per cent of all Americans fourteen and over were in the labor force in 1900, and 58 per cent in 1966.[2] But this apparent stability was the compensated resultant of many differing trends. For the opposed forces of restrictionism and expansion noted above worked differently on each of the key age-sex groups.

For men in the central age groups work has always been a normal responsibility. This responsibility has diminished hardly at all over the years. Some 96 per cent of men in the twenty-five to forty-four age group were in the labor force in 1900—and in 1966 as well.[3]

But the hours worked each week by these men has fallen rapidly since 1900. A reasonable indicator of this change is the weekly hours worked in factories (Table 2).

The swoop downward from 1900 to 1929 stands out. But so does the sudden halt, and the grand stability since the 1930's. Union organization during the 1930's and federal wage-hour legislation together did little to cut prevailing factory hours. The tendency to exchange more income for more leisure was apparently checked by the end of the mid-1930's. Workers thenceforth took productivity gains

TABLE 2.   AVERAGE HOURS WORKED PER WEEK
IN FACTORIES, SELECTED YEARS, 1900–1967

Year	Hours
1900	59
1929	44
1940	38
1967	41

SOURCES: For 1900 Rees gives a daily average of 9.89 hours in manufacturing. (Albert Rees, *Real Wages in Manufacturing 1890–1914,* National Bureau of Economic Research, Princeton University Press, Princeton, N.J., 1961, p. 33.)
1929, 1940, 1967: *Economic Report of the President, January 1968,* p. 245.

almost wholly in money rather than partly in leisure. It is irrelevant to our present purpose to note that coffee breaks and the like have probably proliferated. The worker's 40-hour presence on factory premises is required. Additional hours have not (as in earlier decades) been traded for less income. Declines in trade, and in private industry as a whole, are not to the point, for they reflect the increase in part-time employment by women.

The second pressure forcing down male labor input was concentrated in the older ages (Table 3).

TABLE 3.   MALE LABOR FORCE PARTICIPATION RATES,
BY AGE, AND FOR WIDOWERS, 1900, 1930, AND 1966

Year	Age 60–64	65–69	65	Widowers
1900			68	77
1930	87	76	58	
1966	76	41	25	32

SOURCES: 1900–1930: Estimates made for developing the annual series in Lebergott, Stanley, *Manpower in Economic Growth; The American Record Since 1800,* McGraw-Hill, New York, 1964, pp. 393, 402. Cf. 1900 Census, *Occupations,* p. cxviii; 1930 Census, *Occupations,* p. 115.
1960ff.: Bureau of Labor Statistics, Special Labor Force Report No. 80, *Marital and Family Characteristics of Workers, March, 1966,* April, 1967, p. A–6.

The effect of rising incomes is mildly apparent in the sixty to sixty-four age group for 1930 to 1960. Additional data for the fifty-five to sixty-four interval suggest an equally mild decline from 1900 to 1930. But such declines are surely trivial when matched against those in the over-sixty-five group. The permission offered by a nest egg saved during the affluence of the 1920's was a mild inducement to reduce the over-sixty-five rate by 1930. But much more formidable was the inducement of the Social Security Act, offering a pension to those over sixty-five, but denying (or whittling down) that pension if any work were performed (or, more accurately, reported). The availability of a more limited pension prior to age sixty-five appears to have exercised nothing like the full pension effect. The attractions are seen in another dimension in the corresponding rate decline for widowers. (Interestingly enough, the rate for widows—about 30 per cent— hardly fell. The labor market impact of the Act was confined to those most customarily in the labor force—the men.)

TABLE 4.   LABOR FORCE PARTICIPATION RATES
FOR CHILDREN, BY AGE, 1900–1965

Year	Age 10–13	Age 14–15
1900	12.1	30.9
1920	4.4	17.5
1930	2.4	9.2
1940	n.a.	5.2
1950	7.9	20.8
1960	n.a.	17.5
1965	n.a.	16.8

SOURCES: 1900: 1900 Census, *Population*, Part II, p. 2; and *Occupations*, p. clxii.

1920–1950: Lebergott, Stanley, "Labor Force and Employment, 1800–1960" in Conference on Research in Income & Wealth, *Output Employment and Productivity in the United States after 1800*, p. 148.

1960: Bureau of Labor Statistics, Special Labor Force Report No. 14, *Labor Force and Employment in 1960*, April, 1961, Table B–1.

1965: Bureau of Labor Statistics, Special Labor Force Report No. 69, *Labor Force and Employment in 1965*, 1966, Table B–1.

For children the (much less certain) data (Table 4) suggest two massive forces—one of decline, immediately followed by one of increase. The decline to 1940 reflects the debilitation of the traditional source of jobs for children, farming. The data also reflect the way in which school attendance laws and rising incomes conspired to drive children from (certainly) useful and (probably) unhappy work to (probably) useful and (certainly) unhappy study.

But with the epoch of World War II rates for children reversed sharply. There is no reason to believe that any of the above factors had changed after the war. Nor must we assume that the desire of children for spending money in a more affluent period was greater than in earlier days. What was happening was a lagged adjustment by employers, who increasingly offered part-time work to school children as an alternative to buying expensive overtime from adult workers. In 1900 few children had part-time jobs: less than 1 per cent of urban children aged ten to sixteen went both to school and to work. But by 1966 the comparable figure ran to more than 10 per cent.[4]

If we turn now to the data for women, in Table 5, the unmistakable trend is toward similarity of rates.

TABLE 5.　FEMALE LABOR FORCE PARTICIPATION RATES, BY COLOR AND MARITAL STATUS, SELECTED YEARS, 1890–1966

Year	White			Nonwhite		
	Total	Single	Married	Total	Single	Married
1890	12.1	35.2	2.5	39.5	56.4	22.5
1940[a]	26.9	47.9	14.6	43.2	45.1	33.5
1951[a]	31.5	50.5	24.3	41.1	41.3	36.0
1960[a]	34.1	45.5	29.6	41.2	33.6	40.8
1966[a]	36.5	41.9	35.0	44.1	32.7	49.4

[a] March

SOURCES: 1890–1960: Lebergott, Stanley, *Manpower in Economic Growth, op. cit.*, p. 519.

1966: Bureau of Labor Statistics, Special Labor Force Report No. 80, *Marital and Family Characteristics of Workers, March 1966, pp.* A-5–A-7.

The worker rates for married nonwhite women had been nearly ten times that of white women in 1890. But by 1966 they were not even twice as great. Rates for single women, white or nonwhite, had vastly exceeded those for married women in 1890; by 1966 the differences were far more modest. The most substantial force for change was the rising rate for married women—a rise by a factor of over 2 for nonwhite women, by a factor of over 13 for white women. The decline in number of babies had provided time and energy that could be used for work outside the home. But that exodus would not have taken place without a preference for indirection and the division of labor. Thus bread was no longer baked at home; women worked at something else and used the money to buy bread. (Some 22 per cent of urban families bought no bread in 1900, with the proportion for families of Swedish nativity, 28 per cent; Italian, 39 per cent; Russian, 35 per cent.[5] By 1966 these differences had disappeared.) No less significant, of course, were the decisions to purchase laundry services, washing machines, other household conveniences designed to transform housework. The presence of children and household responsibilities once gave married women a far different relation to the labor market than single women—as the 1890 rates testify. But for white women such differences had been wiped out by the 1950's. And the differences for white women bid fair to disappear by the 1960's. Raising children and keeping house are no longer a straightforward alternative to work in the labor force.

Some Consequences

Given the delayed entrance of men into the labor force, their shorter scheduled work week while in it, and their earlier retirement, one might infer a flight from labor to leisure. But no such inference is necessarily warranted. Factory and business scheduled hours have declined. But it does not follow that the hours worked by individuals have declined. For the central age group, males twenty-five to forty-four, data for 1965 report that:

40.1 per cent worked overtime (on a given job);
 8.2 per cent additional workers had two or more jobs (and they averaged 39 hours in their primary job, 13 or more on their secondary ones).[6]

Moreover, we may note that:[7]

37.2 per cent of these men had working wives
11.8 per cent additional workers had other family members in the labor force (but not working wives).

We may add these four figures together with only limited error to conclude that nearly every family in the central age groups was busy making some extra effort to earn income—extra beyond a regular job held down by the husband. Half did so by additional work of the husband; half by wives or children working. (Some attempted both.) By such efforts family incomes have reached their present heights. One might be tempted to infer that such increases in family labor supply have tended to drive down wage rates, and hence have merely provided the family with the same income that the husband might otherwise have made by himself. However, since employers have a spectrum of possible inputs, such additional work may merely have substituted for machinery or for expanded immigration.

One shift in consumption patterns appears related. In 1900 about a fourth of urban families took in boarders and lodgers; less than 5 per cent do so today.[8] Expanded incomes from work therefore have not been used merely to adorn the home with artifacts. They have made it more private. Since attention is usually given to the increased concentration of our population in cities, to its exposure to the mass media, and to the resultant decline in privacy, this important contrary tendency is worth noting.

What conclusions can we draw? The rising labor force participation of women has been one of the most significant aspects of manpower change since 1900. The incomes that women now bring into the family compensate in part for the declining participation of children, who begin work later. While the head of the household now has a vastly shorter scheduled work week than in 1900, if one reckons in the amount of overtime being worked and the number of second jobs, it is not clear how much his actual work week has fallen. If we reckon in the rising wage rates for men, the probable decline in the average hours they worked, the changes in child and female worker rates, the entire process appears to have resulted in other family members now adding about the same proportion of income to the husband's earnings as in 1900.

The margin does not imply feast or frustration. Family goals may be far beyond income receipt. But the exchange of family leisure for money was a self-limiting process, with a similar proportion of income actually achieved at widely different dates.

STATUS CHANGES IN THE LABOR MARKET

The Decline of the Entrepreneur

The Farmers. What changes transformed the economy of 1900 into that of today? Foremost, surely, was the shift away from farming. More than half our 1900 labor force engaged in the classic pursuits of radical innocence. But today fewer than three Americans in a hundred grow cotton or raise pigs.[9] What brought so spectacular a decline? Was the rural way of life doomed because the rural birth rate failed to replace farmers and farm laborers? Hardly, for rural areas still remain the great breeding sources, supplying population to farm and city slum, to Southeast and Far West.

Two advances cut the rural labor force.

(1) Most potent was the advance in farm productivity. Gaining more sluggishly than nonfarm productivity from 1900 until the late 1930's, farm productivity really began moving ahead after World War II (Table 6).

TABLE 6. CHANGES IN FARM AND NONFARM
PRODUCTIVITY, SELECTED YEARS, 1900–1967

Year	Output per man-hour (1929 = 100)	
	Farm	Nonfarm
1900	88	54
1935	107	111
1947	146	146
1967	502	250

SOURCES: U.S. Census Bureau, *Long-Term Economic Growth, 1860–1965*, p. 191; *Economic Report of the President*, 1968, p. 248.

Its spurt after 1935 baffled conservative premises, and frustrated liberal policies. The premise that no government interference could improve private efficiency was confronted daily by a farm program demonstrating that with proper incentive, interference could do just that. But the "liberal" policy adopted to help the poor farmer and to keep him on the land offered powerful incentives that made large farms engulf smaller ones, and benefited the poorest farmers least of all—unless pushing them off the land really benefited them. In any event the shifts under the AAA helped farm productivity keep steady pace with nonfarm productivity for the first time since 1900.

(2) Close complement was the ever-gaining competitive advantage of city industries. They were efficient—able to market ever-increasing quantities of goods, hence able to pay rising wages. And they were attractive—housed where the range of churches for worship and of establishments for sin drew population away from farm work and farm ways. Particularly important for the labor force was the range of job alternatives industry offered workers. Thus the average downstate Illinois worker in 1960 could choose among 2,000 employers by spending a quarter for commuting. But the average Chicago worker (with the same quarter for gas or bus transport) could choose among 100,000.[10]

In the wake of World War II the attractions of urban living drew farm residents into urban areas around the world, from Moscow to Abadan and from Mississippi to Maine. Productivity gains on farms suddenly began to outpace those in industry, despite the enormous spate of business investment. Hence we conclude that both the advance in farm productivity and the growing attractiveness of city jobs conspired to cut the farm labor force:

— relatively, since 1900
— absolutely, since 1906
— spectacularly, since 1949.[11]

Did an expanding market for food products compensate for these factors? Quite the contrary. Americans actually consumed less protein per capita, and less food energy, in 1967 than in 1900. Their increased fruit and vegetable consumption (and mild gains in meat consumption) did not remotely compensate for the vast declines in consumption of bread and potatoes.[12] U.S. production of fiber fared even more miserably. The onslaught of Dupont de Nemours and its followers on the cotton market proved irremediable. Our foreign markets offered neither consolation nor compensation. Cotton was not particularly competitive in those markets. U.S. wheat could be exported only by a complicated giveaway program. And even our formidable success in propagating the cigarette habit added little to U.S. labor requirements.

It remains only to emphasize the consequent change: in 1900, a nation still dominated by rural traditions, run by rurally chosen legislatures, heavily involved in farming; in the 1960's, a nation solidly urban in its work and orientation. In 1900 Americans could still meaningfully feel a common bond with the peasants who constituted most of the population of other nations. In large measure they too made their living as farmers. Today the American labor force retains only the most peripheral commitment to farming. Links with the hundred new nations of the world must be made on behalf of urban-oriented citizens. Over 90 per cent of those in our labor force work at nonfarm jobs; over 75 per cent of them do not even have parents who worked on farms.[13] And today's city governments, with the same urban perspectives, are trying to solve the problems created when millions of farm-bred workers migrate to cities, bringing farm habits and farm mores with them.

The Self-Employed. As the farm sector dwindled, the urban world expanded—immense, complex, bursting with opportunities. But that world had little room for the entrepreneur, the traditional creator of opportunities and innovations. In 1900, as Table 7 reports, approximately 13 million persons were involved in running family businesses, and approximately 13 million also worked as employees. The ratio helped distinguish American from European orientations. Europe had entered the twentieth century holding on to feudal remnants and a clearly structured class system. The United States, with its one-to-one ratio between the independent and the hired worker groups, still man-

TABLE 7.   LABOR FORCE AND TYPE OF EMPLOYMENT, SELECTED YEARS, 1900–1966

Type of employment	1900	1941	1960	1966
	(in millions)			
Civilian labor force	28.4	55.9	70.6	75.8
Self-employed and unpaid	12.7	12.8	10.9	9.5
Unpaid family workers	3.0	2.0	1.7	1.3
Self-employed	9.7	10.8	9.2	8.2
Farm	5.8	5.2	2.8	2.1
Service	1.1	1.6	2.2	
Trade	1.3	2.3	2.4	
Construction	.5	.5	.8	
Manufacture	.4	.3	.4	
Other	.4	.5	.6	
Employees	12.5	35.5	53.4	
Domestic service	1.8	2.1	2.5	2.5
Unemployed	1.4	5.6	3.9	2.9
Armed Forces	.1	1.6	2.5	3.1

SOURCES: 1900–1960: Tables A3, A4, A7 in Lebergott, Stanley, *Manpower in Economic Growth;* 1966: Data for persons aged 16+ from *Manpower Report of the President . . . April 1967,* pp. 201, 213.

aged to retain the self-image of an open society. Its workers could still, not unreasonably, think of advancing their status by becoming entrepreneurs, even if on a small scale. It was more surely a reflection of this belief in opportunity than a testimony to the power of legal injunction and employer actions that less than 4 per cent of the labor force in 1900 was unionized.[14]

Self-employment reached its peak—perhaps not surprisingly—in the Coolidge years, 1926–1927. From that point it declined absolutely, although it had been falling relatively since McKinley's day. And in nonfarm enterprises, the number of employees increased by 30 million from 1926 to 1966—but less than a million entrepreneurs were added to guide their work.[15] In fact, of course, even these entrepreneurs directed few workers. (The additions came almost wholly in trade and service, where they typically supervised some relatives and a few clerks. The scene might be taken from *The Merchant of Yonkers,* or, more fashionably, *Hello Dolly.*)

The demise of independent entrepreneurship coincided with two events: the inexorable accumulation of unemployment in the 1930's, and the swift increase of organized labor force—from 8 per cent at the beginning of the Roosevelt-Truman era (1932) to 26 per cent at its end (1952). By 1967 declines in farm employment had nearly completed the decimation of the total self-employed group. It then reached about 12 per cent[16] (few of whom were employers). That percentage may not exceed the corresponding rate for the Union of Soviet Socialist Republics. Most of the 71 million labor force now took their orders from other employees—corporate officers, foremen and others who possessed power, but not the power (nor the perspective) of the classic independent entrepreneur. The "employing class" was on its way to extinction.

Concentration of Employment

The swift increase in the employee share in the labor force had its deepest impact on that dynamic, critical sector of the economy where goods were made. Factory production had been somewhat equitably shared between independent proprietors and corporations in 1900. But output (and employment) thereafter centered in corporations (Table 8).

TABLE 8.   MANUFACTURING SALES, 1900 AND 1964

	1900	1964
	(in billions)	
Sole proprietors	$3	$ 7
Corporations	8	453

SOURCES: 1900 Census, *Manfactures,* Part 1, p. 503. U.S. Internal Revenue Service, *Business Tax Returns, 1964–1965,* p. 7. Data for "partnerships and firms" in 1900 totaled a further $2.6 billion.

Neither fate nor malignant endeavor accounts for this shift. Increasing returns to scale had appeared throughout the economy: more goods were produced with the same effort and investment as the scale of production increased. But to achieve that larger economy, larger business units were apparently required. And to assemble financing for such units, the corporate form proved more effective (largely because safer) than the sole proprietorship. Hence the growth of the corporation. Hence its taking over of the vast bulk of U.S. output and employment.

Only in part did greater efficiency spring from larger production units. (True, plant size did rise after 1900. But most factory workers, even today, are not employed in those giant plants with over 1,000 workers.) Changes in plant size proved trivial compared to changes in the size of business firms. Larger firms began to dominate the economy. The advancing concentration of employment can be noted most reliably for manufacturing. Between 1900 and 1963, as Table 9 indicates, the proportion of all factory employees in the 185 largest firms rose from 8 per cent to 27 per cent.

TABLE 9.   CONCENTRATION OF MANUFACTURING
EMPLOYMENT, 1900, 1947, AND 1963

	1900	1947	1963
	(in thousands)		
Total employment	5,124	11,918	12,232
In the 185 largest firms	425	(2,035)[a]	(3,000)[a]
Percentage in largest firms	8%	(17%)[a]	(30%)[a]

[a] Estimates

SOURCES: 1900: 1900 Census, *Manfactures*, Part 1, pp. lxxxii, 3. We take the 185 organizations for which data are tabulated as equivalent to the 185 largest. Such an assumption is mildly in error: the Carnegie firm was omitted, as well as a few others who might supersede some of the smaller 185. Hand trades are excluded.

1963: For 1963 the U.S. Census Bureau, *Concentration Ratios in Manufacturing Industry, 1963*, p. 2, gives figures of 28 per cent for the top 150 firms, and 31 per cent for the top 200, from which we interpolate.

1947: The same source gives data on concentration of value added, data which show a ten point rise from 1947 to 1963 for the 150 largest firms—and for the 200 largest as well. We reduce the employment ratio for 1963 by ten points to get a 1947 estimate.

This advance in concentration probably signaled with broad accuracy the greater centralization of employment in the entire economy.[17] (Although small-employer sectors such as trade and service grew at faster rates than did total employment, that most centralized of employers, the government, grew still faster.) Today we reside in neither the early world of small master and humble journeymen, nor in the caricature of "the apogee of monopoly capitalism." Yet Table 9 does suggest a speeding up in concentration after 1947. And one might speculate that by the year 2000 half our labor force will work for the 250 largest businesses and government units.

The Supervision of Labor

Given the growing concentration of employment and the greater role of larger business units, differences in the mode of production appear, What were the corresponding differences in wages and working conditions?

There is no evidence that the competition of 400,000 factory enterprises in 1963 produced a different kind of wage determination than the competition of 450,000 in 1900, even ignoring the labor market competition across industry sectors.[18] But whether the growing concentration of employment in larger firms makes a major difference for wage determination (via pattern bargaining, etc.) is uncertain. The analytic warfare between (1) those who argue for the impacts of market power, unions, and oligopolies on wages; and (2) those who argue for demand forces and the power of competition, has not yet been settled—if ever it will be.

But there are some changes with respect to the labor force to which one can point with more confidence.

Foremen. To control workers in larger plants, in greater firms, employers put together control mechanisms that were weak (or superfluous) when workers and owners labored together. One obvious and standard component was direct hired supervision. It is probably impossible to report the number of persons engaged in supervision. But Table 10 tells us something about that trend. As the number of self-

TABLE 10.   EMPLOYMENT STATUS OF WORKERS
IN MANUFACTURING, 1900, 1940, AND 1960

Status	1900	1940	1960
	(in thousands)		
Self-employed[a]	504	324	383
Foremen[b]	175	293	742
Employees[b]	7,280	10,601	17,530
Foremen per 100 employees	2.40	2.76	4.23

SOURCES: (a): Lebergott, Stanley, *Manpower in Economic Growth,* Table A-7.

(b). 1910, Employees: Gladys Palmer and Ann Ratner, *Industrial and Occupational Trends in National Employment,* 1949, App. III. These data are based on the Population Census, hence comparable with the others shown here. Foremen, 1910 Census, *Occupations,* p. 91.

1940: 1940 Census, *Occupation Characteristics,* Table 9.

1960: 1960 Census, *Occupation by Industry,* pp. 17, 19.

employed, who directed their own businesses, drifted downward over the years, the number of foremen—a fairly clear-cut and indicative category—increased. The ratio of foremen to employees changed little from 1910 (perhaps from 1900) to 1940. But when unions began to spread in the late 1930's, and wage rates spiraled, a sharper cost consciousness was apparently generated. Supervision became markedly closer after 1940, the ratio of foremen to employees rising at five times the rate it did from 1910 to 1940.

Wage Incentives. But there were further alternatives to the urgency that a master could communicate, or the drive that a foreman could command. Some were embodied in another control mechanism—the incentive pay system. That system did not rely on personality to shape worker responses, nor on command and status. Instead it trusted to direct financial stimuli.

Incentive pay schemes are, of course, very old. The men who chased Moby Dick were paid a percentage of the sales value of the catch. And sharecroppers have long been classic examples of workers paid by results.

For manufacturing we have trend data of real reliability (Table 11). What do they report? First, and most obviously, the tide was running toward incentive plans: the proportion of all factory workers under incentive plans rose from 18 per cent in 1890 to 27 per cent in 1958. More than two-thirds of the sectors reported increases. Spectacular ones showed up in the durable goods industries: primary metals from 10 to 46 per cent; stone, clay and glass from 8 to 25 per cent; electrical machinery from 16 to 40 per cent.

TABLE 11.   PERCENTAGE OF FACTORY WORKERS
ON PIECE WORK (1890) OR INCENTIVE PAY (1958)

	1890	1958
All Manufacturing	*17.9*	*27.0*
Tobacco	64.1	30.9
Furniture	54.2	25.0
Apparel	51.3	59.3
Leather	44.0	63.2
Paper boxes[a]	45.3	20.0
Printing	14.6	3.8
Textiles	13.4	39.7
Food	10.4	11.5
Chemicals	5.6	8.8
Lumber	4.1	6.3
Instruments	45.2	29.2
Toys, sporting goods[a]	24.5	24.0
Nonelectrical machinery	21.2	25.9
Fabricated metals	18.6	23.1
Electrical machinery	15.6	40.3
Primary metals	10.1	46.4
Jewelry, silverware[a]	10.0	35.0
Transport equipment	4.6	10.4
Stone, clay, and glass	8.4	25.1

[a] Bureau of Labor Statistics coverage too limited to permit showing two-digit totals for paper or miscellaneous.

SOURCES: 1890: Computed from data in Eleventh Census, *Manufacturing,* Part 1, Table 4.

1958: *Monthly Labor Review,* May, 1960, p. 461.

Second, and no less significant, were spectacular declines in some nondurable industries—tobacco falling from 64 to 31 per cent, printing from 15 to 4 per cent, furniture from 54 to 25 per cent.

What are we to make of this mixed pattern, particularly if we note the fairly trivial changes for a few sectors (e.g., food from 10.4 to 11.5 per cent)? Most sectors, particularly those with a small proportion originally, found increasing scope for incentive plans. Transport equipment and other industries under increasing pressure for higher wage rates found them an effective cost control tactic.

On the other hand, a list of industries that were relatively sluggish in their productivity advance, that generally bombarded the Congress with pleas for tariff protection, would include some that had high incentive percentages to begin with—and then increased them further: leather (44 to 63 per cent), apparel (51 to 59 per cent), textiles (13.4 to 39.7 per cent). And that list would include such other high-ratio industries as knitting (65 per cent), steel (60 per cent), glass (45 per cent). All of which simply suggests that incentive pay schemes proved to be no panacea.

Technology. The third major technique adopted for creating spirit in the labor force and controlling labor costs can be inferred from the fact that tobacco and furniture cut their high 1890 incentive percentages markedly by 1958. Bumping up against the limits of the incentive technique, they shifted the burden of payroll control to machine pacing. By 1958 only 3 per cent of cigarette workers (and 13 per cent of motor vehicle workers) were under incentive schemes. The other 97 per cent (87 per cent) were controlled more effectively by the scheduling inherent in the production line, the pacing of the conveyor belt.

In sum, no industry has found a single, simple control to replace the eye of the master in the small workshop. Some have expanded supervision by foremen. Some have put in piecework schemes. Some have instituted machine pacing of work. Some have combined techniques, their mixture depending on the rate of technical advance, the constraints of materials, and the quality of management.

TRENDS IN THE DISTRIBUTION
OF EMPLOYMENT

Industry

How a nation uses its resources tells a good deal about its national values and purpose. Employment data provide one such set of measures. For example, the number of clergymen rose by 100,000 between

1900 and 1960, while the number of hairdressers rose by 300,000. That fact gives some useful insight into changing market demands for different types of consolation and ministration. However, increases in the efficiency with which labor is used tend to counteract the effects of increasing demands for final products. It is the net calculation of these opposed factors that appears in actual employment trend data.

Public Sector. The more massive shifts are suggested in Table 12. The most blatant increase is that for the armed forces. Guerrilla war-

TABLE 12.   EMPLOYMENT TRENDS, BY INDUSTRY, 1900, 1947, AND 1967

Industry	1900	1947	1967
	(in thousands)		
Armed Forces	124	1,589	3,446
Farm employment			
Family	8,670	6,589	1,996
Employees	2,380	1,677	1,848
Employees in			
Mining	637	955	613
Construction	1,147	1,982	3,264
Manufacturing	5,468	15,545	19,339
Transportation and utility	2,282	4,166	4,262
Trade	2,502	8,955	13,672
Finance	308	1,754	3,228
Service	1,740	5,050	10,071
Government			
Federal civil	239	1,892	2,719
Public education	487	1,499	4,595
State ⎫ (nonschool)	95		1,440
Local ⎭	273		2,863

SOURCES: 1900, 1947: Lebergott, Stanley, *Manpower in Economic Growth, op. cit.,* pp. 514, 517.

1967: Bureau of Labor Statistics, *Employment and Earnings,* March, 1968, Table B-2; and *Economic Report of the President 1968,* pp. 234, 240.

fare in Asia (against Aguinaldo) required a far smaller share of the U.S. labor force than jungle warfare in Asia (against Ho Chi Minh), reckoning in the "military presence" elsewhere as well. Because the nonspecialist knows little about how much deterrence and/or death is created by how many soldiers, we have no productivity adjustment for translating this increased input into anything associated with final demands.

To some extent this problem applies equally to the category with the next largest rate of increase, state governments. Despite the widely held belief that the federal government, on the one hand, and the cities, on the other, have been chipping away at state responsibilities, state employment has risen faster than has employment in the other governments. However, that nearly half the gains in state expenditure over these years went to provide more roads, wider roads, better roads points to a much more tangible set of goals for state employment.[19]

Private Sector. The largest public increase—that for the armed forces—represents an attempt to assure stability. The largest rate of private employment increase was that for insurance, within the finance group, and hence indicates another reaching toward stability, while banking reported the next most vigorous rate of increase. Despite the extension of supermarkets which tend to reduce employment, the proliferation of the national network of stores and of service activities is apparent. The increases for other sectors are more modest.

What of the numerically largest group, manufacturing? Given the mounting tide of goods piled up in houses, attics, basements, front halls, garages, and junk yards, it is somehow difficult to believe that manufacturing's share in total employment did not rise more than Table 12 suggests. But it did not. A zestful rise in productivity had made possible intense accumulation with relatively small gains in employment. But the increases in employment that did take place reported three moving forces in final demand.

(1) Most spectacular was the advent of the automobile and all that is associated with it. Nearly 40 per cent of the increase in consumer demands for factory products from 1900 to the eve of World War II was for the automobile—the car, its tires, gasoline, and parts.[20]

(2) Since 1947 the most vital factor has been the constellation of increased demands for goods consumed by the Defense Department—and the machines to make the missiles, the iron ore to make the machines, and so on. It goes without saying, of course, that had there been no war demand the increases required for the production of more television sets, acromycin, frisbies, and the like—would have forced up total factory employment. But considering that from 1965 to 1967 the rate of factory employment rose by six times the rate from 1947 to 1965, the primacy of defense demands is confirmed.

(3) Less spectacular but wider and more persistent has been the absorptive capacity of the American family for more goods and services. From 1947 to 1960 the real income of the average American

employee rose by about as much as it had over the (near) half century from 1900 to 1947.[21] Yet savings rates increased little and few income recipients—as distinct from social critics—complained of a super-fluity of material goods or undue affluence.

Another view of this experience can be obtained from Table 13.

TABLE 13.   CHANGES IN SOURCES
AND USES OF LABOR: 1900–1960

Sources: (*in thousands*)	
Rise in total labor-force participation	3,650
Decline in farm employment (total)	21,880
Farmers	11,390
Family workers	5,860
Hired workers	3,930
Decline in nonfarm self-employment (total)	3,000
Construction	300
Manufacturing	560
Trade	430
Service	690
Other	1,020
Decline in domestic service	1,890
Total	*29,520*
Increase in uses:	
Armed forces	**2,210**
Unemployment	480
Nonfarm unpaid family workers	200
Nonfarm employees	26,630
Total	*29,520*
Change in number of employees in nonagricultural *establishments:*[a]	
Trade	5,300
Manufacturing	3,250
Production workers	120
Salaried personnel	3,130
Service	2,800
State and local government	2,400
Finance	1,780
Education	1,740
Federal: defense	960
Federal: nondefense	700
Construction	0
Mining	−270
Transport and utilities	−1,620

[a] Not directly comparable with entries above.

SOURCE: Lebergott, Stanley, *Manpower and Economic Growth, op. cit.,* p. 109.

These numbers are derived from a very simple calculation.[22] Had all sectors kept their 1900 places, each increasing over these 60 years by the same percentage as did the U.S. population, there would have been zero sources and zero uses of labor. Insofar as any sector increased less—e.g. farmers—it provided a source of labor for the others. Similarly, a greater rate of increase—e.g., in participation in the labor force, or in the armed forces—constitutes a use of these labor supplies. The table reiterates the decline in farming and self-employment with which we are acquainted, as well as that in domestic service— these sectors contributing major sources of manpower for the rise of an urban working group. The pre-eminent role of the expanding trade network as a user of labor is particularly noteworthy, given the putative efficiency of supermarkets.

One qualification must be added. These figures relate to our usual totals for industry employment. It would be misleading to carry them much further. Thus the decline for transport and utilities does not imply any weakening of demands for employment in transport as an activity. For while railroads and over-the-road trucking firms did not grow at any very marked rate, many other transportation-related activities did expand. Perhaps a million workers were added for the manufacture of autos and gasoline; perhaps a million and a half in selling automobiles; perhaps another million and a half transport workers in laundries, factories, and other industries that bought their own trucks and hired their own drivers.[23]

Occupations

The more pronounced occupational trends are an odd mixture of industry impacts, already noted, and complex shifts within industry. Thus the declining requirements for farm work and the rise in hospital employment has brought the expected corollary changes in the number of farmers and nurses. But the expansion of any industry also involves the continuous substitution of one occupation for another as advantage is taken of new machines, the markets for new products, and the potentials for cutting costs. We can consider only a few central elements in this process (Table 14).

Professional and Technical Workers. More than half the increase in this group reflects occupations not shown in Table 14. These range from personnel managers and public relations men to golf pros, abstract impressionist artists, veterinarians, and funeral directors.

But the numerically largest gains are those shown. From the pro-

TABLE 14. EMPLOYMENT TRENDS, BY OCCUPATION,
1900 AND 1960

Occupation	1900	1960	Change[a]
		(in millions)	
Professional, technical and kindred workers	1.2	7.2	6.0
Teachers			1.4
Engineers and draftsmen			1.0
Nurses			.6
Accountants			.5
Managers, officials, and proprietors	1.7	5.4	3.7
Nonfarm self-employed[b]			2.5
Clerical	0.9	9.3	8.4
Typists, stenographers			2.1
Clerks in trade			0.9
Clerks in finance and insurance			1.0
Clerks in professional service			1.0
Clerks in government			1.2
Sales	1.3	4.7	3.4
In trade			2.2
In insurance and real estate			.3
Craftsmen	3.0	8.7	5.7
Craftsmen in manufacturing			1.5
Craftsmen in transportation			1.0
Craftsmen in construction			.6
Mechanics, not otherwise specified			2.2
Operatives	3.7	11.9	8.2
Manufacturing	2.1	7.5	5.4
Laborers	8.7	4.5	−4.2
Farm	5.1	2.9	−2.2
Manufacturing	1.4	1.0	−0.4
Transportation	.9	.4	−0.5
Service workers	2.6	7.2	4.6
Janitors			.5
Waiters and waitresses			.7
Policemen, guards, firemen			.5
Hairdressers and barbers			.3
Hospital workers			.5
Hotel workers			.2
Domestics			0

[a] Data for individual occupations lack sufficient comparability to do more than show the change.

[b] Data from Lebergott, Stanley, Manpower in Economic Growth, op. cit.

SOURCES: Major group totals from David Kaplan and Claire Casey, Occupational Trends in the United States 1900 to 1950, Bureau of the Census, Washington, 1958, Table 1; and 1960 Census, Occupational Characteristics, Table 1.

For detailed occupation change we have also drawn upon Alba Edwards, Comparative Occupation Statistics for the United States, 1870 to 1940, Bureau of the Census, Washington, 1943, Table 8; and the 1900 Census, Occupations, Table 1.

liferation of children has come that of schools, thence of teachers. From the expansion of incomes has come the ability to buy more medical care, hence jobs for nurses. (The lack of equally significant gains for physicians reflects the relative shift to pills, potions, and a twentyfold increase in chiropractors and healers, not to mention the discovery of medical practice by telephone.) From the burgeoning of a technological society, the demands for improved techniques for shooting men into space or onto the ground, has come the ebullient increase of engineers and draftsmen. And from the insistence on keeping precise cost records for all these activities has come the rise in accountants.

Managers, Officials, and Proprietors. These are the men who run businesses—their own or someone else's. Not all movers and shakers appear under this heading. The expert plumber who runs his own business, as well as the intrepid milliner who creates casual chapeaus in her own shop, may appear as craftsmen. And some drug store proprietors may be reported under a more prestigious professional category of pharmacists. It is on this account that we record the (somewhat noncomparable) figure for self-employed businessmen. Their 2.5 million increase suggests that the growth of organization men in corporate management—included here along with managers for hundreds of thousands of grocery stores, etc.—may be more modest than recent discussion of the new industrial economy might suggest.

Clerical. The growth of the "Paper Economy" is most obvious from the clerical totals. Two million more typists must indeed generate many more pieces of paper—to be moved from basket to basket, and filed into eternity. But the rising numbers of clerks—concentrated in the service and public administration industries—have also added to such proliferation. In any event, we must add those who carry the bills and messages through the mails, the phone operators who help transmit them through the air, and the employees in newspaper morgues and corporate storehouses who file them away to account for the growth of the largest single occupational sector.

Sales. The increase for this group is centered in trade, with a scattering of additional manufacturers sales agents, insurance and real estate agents, etc. Perhaps most striking is an implicit ratio. About 5 million operatives were added in factories. Not all the goods they turned out were sold through retail stores. Hence for every two workers added in factories at least one was added in trade to distribute the goods so produced.

Craftsmen, Operatives, and Laborers. These three groups together are largely responsible for the actual production of most goods and many services as well. It has long been assumed that the declining number of laborers and the rising number of craftsmen and operatives reflect a critical shift toward more highly skilled labor, because places are no longer available for the unskilled and the illiterate. (Confirmation appeared to have been given by the heavy decline for farm labor.) It will be noted, however, that the increase for the craftsmen group was far smaller than that for operatives, both in manufacturing and in all industries as a group. Had employers preferred skill, high training, and expertise, per se, the numbers and/or the wage rates of craftsmen should have increased more substantially than those of operatives.

A central problem in interpreting the population census data for these three occupation groups is that the distinctions among them appear to be—but are not—simple distinctions of skill, training, and scarce abilities. There are reasons to believe that the skill levels, education, and training of many operatives do not differ significantly from the average "laborer." Although effective investigation on this point requires more complex inquiry, it may be possible to define the nature of the problem by asking whether a Maine lobsterman, with his knowledge of the winds, tides, and habits of lobsters, fish, and gulls —now classed as a laborer—is less "skilled" than the woman who picks the lobster apart to pack it in cans—now classed as an operative in food manufacturing. The laborer-operative line is surely a difficult one to draw even with full information; and it is not altogether clear that the housewife respondent, census enumerator, and coder together give us those precise distinctions we think we are observing when we contrast the massive increase of 8.2 million "operatives and kindred workers not elsewhere classified" with the 2 million decline in nonfarm "laborers not elsewhere classified." We need further information on the work and skills of those engaged under each heading before we can draw conclusions about changing requirements for skills and schooling.

Service. "They also serve who only stand and wait"—particularly since much service consists of standing around in a variety of more or less humble and/or graceful attitudes. The data for this group show the large gains for occupations that offer limited amounts of "service" and large amounts of "availability," or physical presence, i.e., guards and policemen, waiters, hospital attendants. The waitress, the hairdresser, the janitor, and hotel chambermaid now provide in institutions services of a kind once provided in the home by the butler, the 'tweenie, the ladies' maid, and so on. This substitution helps explain the total lack of increase in domestic servants per se. Finally, it should be noted that because the consumer has been devoting an ever higher proportion of his income to services, a swifter expansion of service workers is taking place than of laborers or "operatives." So far as skill levels are concerned the service group is a mixed one. Janitors are probably less skilled than most "laborers." Hairdressers are probably more skilled than most "operatives." Hence for drawing inferences about skill trends this expanding group is not particularly comparable with the traditional craftsman-operative-labor groups.

STABILITY AND CHANGE IN THE LABOR MARKET

Automation and Technical Change

Cybernation. Automation. Mechanization. Each generation finds workers being displaced by machines. And in each generation some are stung into reacting as though no human experience resembled today's changes, so that no prior experience with technical change can offer us guidance. Others maunder comfortably along as though it had all happened many times before, in much the same fashion, and hence time alone will find solutions.

Perhaps the most climactic change that ever took place in U.S. technology, in its effects on employment, was the transition from hand to machine methods. Its major impacts were probably centered in the years from 1865 to 1900. If so, the displacements it wrought would have been signaled by an accumulation of unemployment in the late 1890's and early 1900's.

What was that experience? An enormous study by the Commissioner of Labor permits us to come to some estimate for the vast range of manufacturing industry.[24] From its results we can judge that of every 100 workers required by hand methods of production, machine methods made 82 superfluous. Going on from these solid data for manufacturing and making a crude allowance for experience in other industries we may conclude that the displacement ratio for all employment would not have been widely different.[25]

The implied cut in job requirements and rising obsolescence of workers' skills were vast, of course. Machine methods in plow making had made 97 out of 100 workers unnecessary; in brass button manufacture, 88 out of 100; in boots and shoes, 77 out of 100. Even the most lurid discussions of cybernation, automation, and mechanization in recent years have not involved figures as high as these. For example, John Snyder, President of U.S. Industries, stated in 1963 that "automation is eliminating jobs in the United States at the rate of more than 40,000 a week," surely a chilling statement.[26] But what is 40,000 a week in an economy with over 70 millions in the labor force? About 3 per cent a year. How does that 3 per cent compare with the 75 per cent displacement rate in the transition from hand skills to machine work—even calculating that the latter transition took place over a longer period?

If we assume that the hand to machine transition took place mainly between the end of the Civil War and the beginning of the twentieth century, we can contrast two changes:

	1870	1900
Workers required per unit of output		
Hand method	100	—
Machine method	—	25
Workers actually employed	100	238

By 1900 only one-fourth the 1870 employment was required to turn out a given volume of goods; yet the actual number employed had more than doubled.[27] The answer? Clearly, manufacturing output rose steeply—carrying with it an overwhelming increase in the aggregate demand for labor despite lower manpower requirements per unit of output. To what levels of unemployment did the process lead? One answer would treat the entire period from 1866 to 1914 as representing that transition. It would imply that even the apparently cyclical agonies of the 1870's and 1890's themselves arose from more massive displacements taking place beneath them. Hence although immediate shocks were superimposed on them, and on the economy, it is these adjustments that are really to be considered as primarily responsible for the level of unemployment in the entire period. If so, how substantial was that level? The answer, based on a fairly speculative average for 1870–1914, would be: 7 per cent of the labor force.[28] But one may find this view too extensive; and prefer, say, the average for the first decade of the twentieth century. If so, we are dealing with a 4 per cent rate. Neither figure, needless to say, points to a level of unemployment that was trivial so far as the workers involved were concerned. But neither one points to a level of adjustment that differed seriously from the 5 per cent we find in such high employment decades as 1940–1949, or 1950–1959.

Suppose we consider the period 1947–1967. In these twenty years output per manhour rose by 85 per cent. Did employment in manufacturing correspondingly drop by 85 per cent as this pell-mell advance in productivity proceeded? Hardly. In fact it rose, by 25 per cent.[29] Did displaced workers in increasing number end up in the unemployment pool? Hardly. The unemployment rate was virtually unchanged—3.9 per cent in 1947 and 3.8 per cent in 1967.

In the hand-to-machine work transition, and again in the recent decades of automation, the high levels of manufacturing employment, and low levels of unemployment, testify to an adjustment process that is not markedly worse—or better—than what we associate with less stormy times. Does it follow that these transitions are trivial? Or that as our social sensitivity increases we should not deploy increased assistance to those involved? Not at all. The relevant findings are merely these: Substantial labor market changes generally take place in the American economy, and those shifts associated with technical change are neither the most ominous nor the only serious ones. Such technical changes are absorbed into levels of employment that, judged by political reactions, are found generally acceptable, provided the operations of the unemployment insurance system and the employment service are effective.

Labor Market Stability

Societies require an improbable combination of stability and change. Stability, to hold the social fabric together, to prevent the transformation of uncertainty into chaos. Change, to afford the prospect of hope to those who lack it, and the evidence of things seen to those who would move upward in the economic and social scale. The corresponding stabilities in the labor market are linked with satisfaction, rapport—and sloth. The corresponding instabilities, with tension, hatred, waste—and economic advance.

Job Changes. In the American economy the balance is clearly on the side of change. Instability is endemic in our job market. Workers live between the threat of declining incomes and the unsettling hope of greater ones. Job loss associated with technological change is one, but only one, aspect of that variability. Thus 1967 was not associated with any unusual amount of technical change. In that year employment was increased by 1.1 million persons. To accomplish that increase 20.7 million persons were hired.[30] In other words, almost 20 million workers were hired just to compensate for job quitting and layoffs. To emphasize the point one may take the year 1960–1961: employment barely increased; nonetheless, over 20 million hires were made just to compensate for layoffs and quits. Employers must ceaselessly adjust to rising or declining sales, to the changing advantage of using one component or raw material versus another, to the use of different machines, and fewer (or different) workers, etc. The power of pensions, plus that of seniority, does not remotely compensate for the instabilities that these produce in the work process. At the same time it is no less true that in an open society workers who move to a good job will often react by desiring a better job—and achieving that, by seeking a still better job.

Put the above considerations into one question: How steady is the job of an American worker? The answer is roughly the following: during his work life the American man fills twelve different jobs, each for about four years.[31] Not for the American worker the job and place that his father, and his father's father, knew before him. Not even the Horatio Alger hero—who after all rose within one firm.

If we cast back in time we shall find such instability intensifying since the twentieth century began. In 1900 the occupational mix was largely different. May we not infer that job stability also was different? Self-employed farmers (whose median years on the job now run 18.7) then assumed a larger role in 1900 and teachers (a 3.6 year median), a smaller one. If we adjust for such changes in occupational composition of the labor force, we surmise that the typical worker in 1900 had only six jobs in his lifetime.[32] If we assume, as well, somewhat longer jobs in that quieter era, we might well find that today's worker has three times as many jobs in his lifetime as his 1900 predecessor.[33] But either figure would lead to the same inference: job loyalty and stability are markedly less in today's world, despite all the counteracting influences that make for stability. Doesn't it seem likely that doubling the number of jobs a worker holds during his lifetime affects the efficiency and the satisfactions of the labor force? One may read an inference about efficiency from the ubiquitous appearance of seniority provisions and the extension of pension programs in recent years. The inference is that employers prefer stability of employment—presumably because a stabler group of employees has more predictable characteristics; hence can be deployed more efficiently. Such a reading is supported by the fact that turnover rates are much higher in industries with low productivity gains (e.g., textiles and lumber) than in those with high productivity advances (e.g., autos and petroleum). However, such static comparisons tell us noth-

ing certain of the actual direction of impact through time of such turnover.

One can be fairly definite about worker satisfactions, for perhaps
half of the twelve job changes made by the average American worker
in his lifetime are voluntary ones.[34] Such changes need not have been
made: it is generally possible for a worker to retain a job by accepting
lower pay and worse working conditions.[35] The voluntary moves therefore point to choices that the worker expects to be for the better. As
in the choice of marriage partners, or a hazard of numbers at Monte
Carlo, such choices may prove disappointing. But the value to the
worker of having that option may nonetheless be significant and positive.

Strike Rates. One objective indicator of the extent to which the
opportunity to move was associated with greater social stability may
appear in the data on strike rates (Table 15). Most remarkably, the

TABLE 15.   NUMBER AND RATE OF NONFARM WORKERS
INVOLVED IN STRIKES, SELECTED PERIODS, 1900–1966

Years	Employed in nonfarm enterprise	Involved in strikes	Strike ratio
	(in thousands)		
1900–1904	11,506	637	5.5
1925–1929	27,046	311	1.1
1962–1966	52,867	1,412	2.7

SOURCES: Bureau of the Census, *Historical Statistics of the United States,
Colonial Times to 1957,* p. 99; and *Monthly Labor Review,* February, 1967.
    Employed: Lebergott, Stanley, *Manpower in Economic Growth, op. cit.,* p.
513; and Bureau of Labor Statistics, Special Labor Force Report No. 69, *Labor
Force and Employment in 1965,* Tables C-6 and D-2. For 1962–66 we take wage
and salary workers in nonagricultural industries less the number of private household workers. For comparison with 1900 and 1929 the number in domestic service, if available, would have been used.

trend over these high employment years is down. Expanding unionism
may have provided channels for grievances that previously erupted
into strikes. Possibly too the contribution of strike-prone industries to
tension has declined. Such industries have dwindled as employers—
relatively (steel) and absolutely (coal mining). The increase in the
number of jobs between the 1900 generation of workers and today's
suggests some cheerful combination of (1) advancing efficiency—
workers moving more promptly to jobs where they performed more

effectively, or used scarcer talents, and/or (2) improving conditions
of work—fewer occupational hazards, supervision by better foremen,
or higher pay corresponding to the improved utilization of worker
skills. Both 1900 and 1966 were years that occurred in periods of
generally stable high employment. Hence we need not qualify these
statements for involuntary changes arising from disemployment.

DATA DEVELOPMENT

To assess economic and social policy in the decade ahead we shall
certainly need tougher, more solid measures of labor market activity
than we now possess. What are they going to look like? Where are our
present measures foggiest, most misleading? And where are new directions in social change going to bring new needs? We designate below
five areas of advance.

Government Data

The first area for advance turns on the role of government in our
society. Government began to intervene in the economic order with
our very first session of Congress—bounties were set for shipping,
drawbacks for salt, tariffs for cotton, and so on. It is not government
intervention per se that marks our own time. But—particularly since
the Employment Act of 1946 was validated by a Republican Administration's activist policy during the 1953–1954 recession—a larger
commitment has been assumed by government. That commitment is a
guarantee against massive instability of the entire economy—against
major depression or price inflation, and, in practice, against milder
depressions that might burgeon into major ones.

Any commitment to guarantee the performance of the whole economy requires an incredibly complex and consistent working knowledge of how the economy interacts. And we need to know not merely
in a general, end-of-semester-examination sort of way, but in a specific
"manipulate the rediscount rate by ¼ of a point" way, in a "change
the tax rate by 1 per cent" way. For such operations the employment
consequences are one crucial result if not actually *the* hoped-for resultant. And where social goals include providing better jobs for slum
dwellers, improving the skills of nonwhites, training this group and
retraining that, the need for even more precise measures of labor
market consequences of federal policies of many types is even more
intense. From all this it follows that the relevant employment-labor
force statistics must be closely comparable to data on output and capi-

tal consumption, and the like, as well as on sales and investment, and so on. If the data are not comparable, our policy choices, and our subsequent measures of their success or failure, will be loosely linked. Given enough data incomparability, policy could be working reasonably badly, yet our data would not be telling us so; or policy could be working reasonably well, while our data reported unreal costs and untrue consequences. Most Americans committed to intervention would nonetheless want to preserve their political capital, and would not like to see intervention take place more frequently or more precipitously than necessary. Those opposed to intervention would not want more vigorous action than needed.

Hence for both groups we require first of all to maintain a consistency between our labor data and the other measures normally used by the Council of Economic Advisers and the White House for testing where the economy is—and where it is headed. Such consistency is today regrettably unlikely. There is little assurance that consistency prevails between (1) the employment reports made by payroll clerks in the various plants of Company X to the Bureau of Labor Statistics; (2) the investment figures its comptroller reports to the Office of Business Economics; (3) the capital stock figures the vice-president's office reports to the Securities and Exchange Commission; and (4) the shipments figures plant managers report to the Bureau of the Census. In part conceptual differences are involved: one agency wants overseas operations included, another wants them omitted, a third doesn't specify. In part there is no assurance that the reports from the many separate respondents are consistent, additive, without omissions. To the extent that consistency exists it is imposed by the expert judgment of the National Income Division (NID) of the Department of Commerce, which hammers together the employment and earning data, forces them into adjustment with its theoretical model of how data on sales, production, investment, and profits are related.

To project education and training requirements over the next quarter century we must project the moving demand for skills. To do so we must project final demand, for it is the demand for television sets or missiles that ultimately determines the size and pattern of demands for labor. Another element is the contrasting cost of labor and machinery, which goes to determining the rate of automation, the rate, more generally, of capital-labor substitution. Yet our measures of final demand now bear no necessary relationship to measures of labor embodied in that demand, either in the aggregate or—where it really counts—by major product. Nor is the pattern of substituting capital and machinery for labor clear, since our measures of labor input to an industry link in no necessary way to the measures of capital stock and capital service in that industry.

Our concern with social policy may relate to economic stability, to projecting education and training requirements, to anticipating job prospects for the nonwhite, the unskilled, or teenagers. But in all these cases we require consistency between the employment data and those related data on economic activity that must be brought together to achieve sharp policy analyses and sound recommendations.

The first step toward the consistency required for tough policy analysis and proposal rests on a recognition of one fact: Some 1,500 corporate and governmental units account for well over half of output, capital investment, etc. Most such units already report to various agencies of the federal government—on employment to the Bureau of Labor Statistics, on expenses to the Internal Revenue Service, and so on. The series that each agency derives from these reports are now taken over by the National Income Division.

Each agency receiving a report from any of these 1,500 units should send a copy to the NID. The NID should then combine these reports, evaluate their consistency and reasonableness (in concert with the agency if the latter is willing). The NID should then send a combined report and evaluation back to the firm that originated the reports. If this process were continued over several years, we could expect that the firms themselves would begin to send out more consistent and accurate reports.

A further—more difficult—proposal would tie together reporting by these giants in the first place. Consider General Motors. As one of our greatest corporations and largest employers, it will inevitably be included in any sample set up by the BLS to report on current employment, by the Census Bureau to report on current sales, the SEC to report on current investment. Arrangements should be worked out between these agencies and GM so that the scope of the monthly and quarterly reports by GM on one factor—e.g., employment—can correctly be added and compared with those on other closely relevant factors—e.g., investment or capital stock. We could then be confident that one report did not include overseas operations, while others did; that one report did not include central office establishments while the others did; that one set of reports included sales activities while another included, perhaps, only manufacturing activities, etc. To tailor arrangements for 1,500 units will be a burdensome chore for the government agencies. But it will be an investment in data improvement, and can be amortized over the many years that one can anticipate these companies will in fact be reporting. Such companies already are burdened by the reporting tax. They will surely continue to be so burdened given their dominant position in the economy. (In designating the burden on them we do not imply that it is not passed on to the taxpayer via their tax deductions. But since many of them possess some degree of market power, there may be a cost at the expense of shareholders.) It is therefore to their advantage if improving the statistics from company reports helps make government economic policies as intelligent as possible.

Market Skills

To establish the shape of public education over the next quarter century, or to plan Manpower Development Training Act programs for unemployed and dissident Negro teenagers, we must assess trends in the market for skill. Judgments about whether automation is inundating us intensify these strident concerns.

Occupation serves either—depending on your preference—as a precise measure or a widely used proxy for these sets of skills.[36] Moreover, occupation data are the measures most readily available to indicate in what directions the young should be trained and the middle-aged retrained. How sufficient are our present measures of occupation, and how can they be improved?

For measuring occupational composition our most reliable and detailed data appear, perhaps improbably, not in the sources most widely used—but in the Bureau of Labor Statistics surveys of wage rates. To my knowledge this source has, however, never been used for that purpose. These surveys classify all workers in an industry according to standard definitions. They do so in conjunction with the responsible factory officials who hire and pay the workers. No less important, the wage rate reported for them tells us a great deal in the form of a market judgment about their skills. (We would hardly consider a factory worker paid $1 an hour to be skilled even if his title were "machinist.")

It is something of an anomaly that in all the discussions of the rising tide of automation and of the decline in job opportunities for unskilled workers, virtually no use has been made of this sound and relevant source. One reason, of course, is the irregular and limited coverage of the surveys. Another is that they do not go as far back in time as the population census. Nonetheless, though we may have succeeded in ignoring them for the past, we have no equal warrant for avoiding them in the future. Specifically, the future program for these surveys should be organized to yield measures of change in (and substitution among) occupations in key industries. To do so neither major changes in program nor massive costs are necessary.

Occupational Classifications

For many decades judgments on the trend in occupational requirements have depended largely from a single set of data: the occupation reports of the decennial population census. Endless care, continuous elaboration, and a succession of expert dedicated census staff has brought these to a level that is probably above that for any other nation in the world.[37] Had the Census Bureau rested on its laurels we might not be able to say much more about the quality of these data or about future needs. Fortunately, the Census Bureau itself has conducted extensive analysis—unique among survey organizations—of the quality of its own findings. One of its studies tests the reliability of its occupation data by comparing them with those obtained from employers.[38]

These results, summarized in Table 16, suggest massive differences between employer and housewife on respondent classification. One difference is implicit in a figure from that study: 18 per cent of all persons classified by the 1960 population census in a given major occupation group really belonged in another one. That result is itself sufficiently disturbing. Since one may reasonably assume that errors compensated within the major groups, one may infer that a still larger percentage of all persons were incorrectly classified in individual occupations. Perhaps a guess that one-third of all persons were reported in the wrong occupation by the decennial census would not be wildly high.[39]

Consider the differential pattern shown in the table.[40] Some 36 per cent of those whom the census reported as laborers belonged in other occupation groups—some even being professional or technical workers, while many were really craftsmen or operatives. Over a third, therefore, of those whom the census reported as laborers belonged in higher status, higher income groups. The bias for the professional group, at the other end of the status ranks, was by no means as great —19 per cent to the 36 per cent for laborers. However, a uniform status-linked bias is not apparent, for the 7 per cent for service is the smallest of all.

To the occupational distortion must be added that for industry. Errors here range from 40 per cent of the business and repair service group to 8 per cent for public administration. As could be seen if one

TABLE 16.   PERCENTAGE OF PERSONS INCORRECTLY
CLASSIFIED IN MAJOR OCCUPATION
AND INDUSTRY GROUPS, 1960 CENSUS

Group	Percentage
Occupation	
Total	*18*
Laborer	36
Manager and official	28
Craftsmen	25
Professional	19
Clerical	14
Sales	13
Operatives	12
Service	7
Industry	
Total	*14*
Forestry and fisheries	72
Business and repair services	40
Construction	33
Entertainment and recreation	27
Wholesale trade	25
Manufacturing: nondurables	17
Manufacturing: durables	16
Retail trade	14
Transportation, communication, public utilities	9
Public administration	8
Professional and related services	6
Finance, insurance, real estate	2
Personal services	2
Mining	0

SOURCE: U.S. Census Bureau, *The Employer Record Check*, Series ER 60, No. 6, 1965, Tables 2, 4.

were to put together a broader "service" group, the error ratio would decline. One may infer that data shown in census reports for detailed manufacturing industry, as for detailed retail trade categories, would be even more incorrectly designated than the rates for the combined groups indicate.

Much of the discussion of differentials in earnings by occupation, in the contribution of education—via access to occupations—to differentials in income, and so on, must be considered in the light of these data. To call upon compensating errors to save such analyses, based as they are on complex cross-classifications within the major groups, is to put one's trust in a void.

The inferences for changes over time become difficult. In earlier decades there may have been little shame among recent immigrants, and even the second generations, in reporting that family members were laborers, janitors, and servants. For even these tasks were associated with higher incomes, and perhaps more status than in Europe. Today the aspiration for social mobility has led to janitors being reported as building superintendents, operating engineers, and so on; and how many times is even such a qualifying adjective inaudible or unuttered? And how many times is the factory job, the duties of which are unknown to respondent or enumerator, upgraded in the interview process, whereas in earlier years the social stigma was less and the impulse to upgrade weaker?

What can be done for the future? The usual prescriptions for data improvement will not serve here. Better staff? This country has not had a more astute, competent, and dedicated staff at work on such data, and it is doubtful that any other nation has. Improve the training of enumerators? Tried for many years, that technique is on its way out: Plans for the 1970 census call for a further shift toward complete self-enumeration. To expand occupation questions on the proposed self-enumeration forms may help somewhat. But the ignorance and bias of respondents themselves are largely indicated in Table 16, the figures of which relate only to persons using self-enumeration in 1960.

It is time to reconsider the approach. It is time to begin going to the most reliable source of information on industry and occupation—as well as earnings, place of work, and other linked items—the employer.

This suggestion would not be made if the employer were not already reporting annually to the federal government for every worker (on the W-2 form) the sum of taxable wages paid every employee, as well as employer's name, place of business, and identification number. (From the taxable wage figures we now derive our basic information on payrolls as embodied in the national income accounts.)

Something like 87 per cent of all persons in the labor force are employees.[41] Their employers now have a legal obligation to report on wage payments to them, using the W-2 forms. For most social, and for many economic, problems the earnings on the job are fully as important as the fact of the job or the occupation. It is therefore more useful for social policy to have available consistent and more accurate data on all three factors than merely unrelated bits of data. To know that unemployment has been reduced by people taking jobs might have been sufficient information thirty years ago. Social policy today also raises the question of whether the jobs thus filled were low-paid or at rates below those characteristic of the jobs involved. And whether the jobs are mostly deadend ones. Hence we really want consistent data on employment status, occupation, and occupational earnings for individuals. Mere marginal comparisons, in which we cannot associate information for individuals in particular categories, will not suffice in the 1970's.

To take advantage of the massive system of reporting already present in the employer W-2 reports, our aims must be clear. The goal is not to get reports for every person who does any work during the year. Nor to get reports for all full-time workers at once. The goal is to widen the information on the W-2s so as to replace wide-scale census data collection. Initially one can imagine using the employer identification number—already present on the W-2—as a basis for establishing a more accurate industry report than we now get from the housewife.

The census already assigns an industrial classification to most American businesses as part of its program of enterprise surveys—e.g., Census of Manufactures, Census of Business—doing so in collaboration with the Social Security Administration. The employer identification number (on the W-2) provides a direct key to these classification data. Hence the W-2, in principle, provides data on wages paid, industry, and place of work. The primary addition needed is job title.

One alternative would be for the employee simply to provide a copy of the W-2 when he provides the rest of his census information (either to the enumerator or mailed in with his form). Alternatively, the census could take such information from forms received by the Internal Revenue Service. Data could be most sensibly taken from the April 15 filings, which would provide income detail (from the 1040 tax form) and detail on occupation, place of work, and a key to industry classification (from the attached W-2s). Census enumeration could then be restricted to the small proportion of persons not covered by IRS— or, more accurately, the 20 per cent of that small proportion who would fall into the occupation sample.

In sum, the employer can provide more reliable data on occupation than the employed—at low cost. And, perhaps even more important, the employer can provide a nexus of information—industry, occupation, and pay for that job—each fact helping to check and to illuminate the others.

Productivity Measures

Declarations, ringing or hollowly ominous, about the trend in productivity typically come into judging the wisdom of proposed wage increases or tax adjustments. The White House generally settles steel strikes—and it has settled a good many—after making some presumptions as to productivity trends. Proposals for income policy, or for wage-price guide lines, take into account such productivity inferences.[42] But our present productivity figures are produced by combining sets of employment data and output data that have no necessary comparability.

If we are to make reliable estimates about productivity, one direction of advance—complex and unlikely to be taken—is inevitable. And that is to derive employment and output data from the same survey—so that the employment data would be directly comparable with the output data and so that sampling differences between the two sources would not confound matters.

Prime example. Data on retail sales are provided by a sample of firms reporting to the Census Bureau. In the process of estimating retail output these data are deflated by price data secured by the Bureau of Labor Statistics from a second sample of stores. The results are then related to employment data, derived from a third sample of stores, surveyed by another part of the Bureau of Labor Statistics. If instead a single sample of stores were used to collect data on all three aspects, with subsamples for certain detail, we could expect closer comparability of data and hence more reliable figures on productivity than we now achieve. (If one were concerned with more than "labor productivity," the advantages of considering comparable data on capital inputs and cost elements would additionally be worth considering.) Noncomparability of output and employment data similarly plague the construction and service sector measures. As a result the over-all figures on productivity for the U.S. economy are affected.

Because some individuals have more than one job in a week, and because productivity estimates are derived from different sets of surveys (one for manufacturing, another for trade, and so on) the combination of data leads to two over-all productivity series.[43] It is not now clear that the differences between the series arise from desirable conceptual differences, from purely statistical differences, or from both. It is possible to remove the purely statistical differences by integrating the underlying sample surveys. If the Current Population Survey were viewed as a sampling frame for locating establishments to be canvassed in the establishment surveys, one major cause of difference could be removed. Thus the thousands of families who report to the CPS on employment status constitute as well a sample of employees on the payrolls of various establishments. The frequency with which their employers implicitly appear in that sample will be proportionate to their size as employers. Thus a list of establishments in which CPS employees work could constitute a list for the usual employer reporting sample.

One advantage of such a list over the usual one is that it is immediately updated. When a new construction firm goes into business that fact is immediately reflected in the CPS sample. (Even if the firm had no employees, the sole proprietor is himself reported as such in the CPS.) Such immediate representation is an advance over the usual establishment listings, which cannot locate new firms for some, non-regular, time after their opening (except at prohibitive cost).

A second advantage of such an approach, and a greater one, is that it would become immediately possible to compare the employment status of the same individual as he reports it in CPS and as his employer reports it. At present the sometimes marked differences in trend between the (unpublished) CPS industry trends and those of the BLS establishment sample cannot be interpreted with certainty. They may reflect differences in the status of the same individual as reported in different surveys. They may reflect variations in dual jobholding. Or they may report some more complex phenomenon. (As a starting point in evaluating such an alternative, a record of employment status as given in the CPS sample should be compared with the employer records for the same individuals.)

For the longer run a survey of households seems an integral part of our statistical reporting system: it provides wide and efficient coverage of many interrelated characteristics. At the same time the reliability of employer reports on wage rates, payrolls, hours, occupation, and the like seems great. Moreover, the cost of such information from employers is relatively low. If we were committed to both surveys, however, we should be equally committed to a consistency of data. For these sets of data possess no inherent virtues and values. They constitute raw materials for analysis; and accurate analysis requires data consistency and comparability.

Education

More education is a Good Thing. Are there other public policy positions in recent years on which there has been wider agreement? Newly developing nations commit large amounts of resources, and propose to commit still more, for schools. In this country more education has been proposed as the answer to a host of labor market problems. To rehabilitate slum dwellers so that they will be more employable and thereby able to work their way out of poverty. To assist young workers who lack skills. To retrain older workers displaced by fast-moving technology. To provide the cadres of trained workers the nation will need in the years ahead. For these, and many other purposes, education has been offered as the primary answer, if not the only one.[44]

A variety of able studies have argued the contribution of more education—or, more accurately, more schooling—to the advancement of the individual worker and to the growth of national output.[45] Even more casual observation indicates a clear association between years of school attended and personal and national income differentials: the longer the schooling for a given occupation, or worker, the higher the income appears to be. Suppose that we were to observe that the longer the hair of young men in the 1960's the greater their income in the 1980's. It would be unlikely that such a finding would evoke many proposals to abolish barbers or panegyrics on the contribution of long hair to economic growth. It would be recognized that long hair was serving only as a proxy to indicate something else—namely, to distinguish those men who attended college from those who went right to work.

Unfortunately, our belief in the contribution of formal schooling per se is not yet sufficiently founded to make the question of cause and effect wholly irrelevant. When an employer pays higher wages to a worker with more education than those with less, how much is he paying for mere endurance of schooling, and how much for learning plus the complex of intelligence and background for which formal schooling inevitably stands? Mere additional injections of formal schooling may not advantage workers from slums, or in underdeveloped countries, if these other factors dominate the reasons for wage differentials. We know, for example, that sharply different income gains are associated with an additional year of schooling for whites and nonwhites. (But we immediately ask whether that difference may not be a proxy for something else—namely, discrimination.) Few educational theories would find that a year's manual training in production of superfluous book ends and boxes for shoe polish kits will create the same income earning potential for the economy as a year of Virgil. But when we accept the homogenized results of "years of school" we tend to analyze as though a year is a year is a year.

Most critically, we have not begun to reckon with the consequence of the simple fact that while only 7 per cent of seventeen-year-old students in the top half of the IQ distribution fail to reach the senior year of high school, 50 per cent in the bottom half fail to do so.[46] It is an indicator of our ignorance in this area that there has been widespread objection to the arbitrariness in Denison's major study of his stipulating that 40 per cent of the income differentials apparently associated with education really reflect ability, etc.[47] Most of these objections miss the fact that many prior studies have made no allowance whatever for ability differences, whereas this study made a carefully explicit one. But until we have some less arbitrary and more rigorous basis for allowing for the netting of ability differentials, we shall not know the contribution of education per se.

Finally, the sets of expectations of parents, neighbors, and teachers, as well as the attitudes and perspectives of fellow students, may have a serious impact on the development of motivation, persistence, and ability to sustain a task. At present our evidence on this point is only beginning to accumulate.[48]

Even aside from the importance of education per se, its importance for producing income growth, for affecting the flow of persons into different occupations, is considerable. For these various concerns we need to disentangle the contribution of formal schooling to income differences from the net contributions of intelligence, motivation, willingness to accept distant gratifications, range of home neighborhood stimuli, parental backgrounds and impacts, and so on. Such a task may be nearly as impossible as to disentangle the separate contributions of nature and nurture to personality type. Yet valuable studies could be made without reaching toward so formidable a goal. The widening reach of data on measured ability of high school students, of characteristics of schools and teachers, of adults in the communities from which children come, suggest that useful studies could be made even without achieving the ultimate goal. Such studies can enrich our knowledge of the particular contribution of schooling, and particular types of schooling, even if the deeper issues remained unplumbed. They could thereby help toward more intelligent social policy in the United States, toward more effective resource allocation in the developing nations, which have such scanty resources for all purposes.

NOTES

1. *Manpower Report of the President . . . April 1967,* p. 201.
2. Lebergott, Stanley, *Manpower in Economic Growth: The American Record since 1800,* McGraw-Hill, New York, 1964, p. 512. Note that other data cited above relate to age sixteen and older, in accord with the new definition adopted in 1967.
3. 1900 Census, *Occupations,* p. cxviii; Bureau of Labor Statistics, Special

Labor Force Report No. 80, *Marital and Family Characteristics of Workers, March, 1966,* April, 1967, p. A–6.

4. 1900: Commissioner of Labor, *Eighteenth Annual Report,* 1903, p. 253. 1966: Bureau of Labor Statistics, Special Labor Force Report No. 68, p. A–5 reports 16 per cent for those fourteen to fifteen, and 32 per cent for those aged sixteen to seventeen. An estimate for urban ten- to sixteen-year-olds would run to more than 10 per cent, or over 20 times the 1900 rate.

5. U.S. Commissioner of Labor, *Annual Report,* 1903, p. 495.

6. Bureau of Labor Statistics, Special Labor Force Report No. 81, *Overtime Hours and Premium Pay,* May, 1967, Table J, reports 6,949,000 male wage and salary workers working overtime as of May, 1966, or 40.1 per cent. Bureau of Labor Statistics, Special Labor Force Report No. 63, *Multiple Job-holders in May 1965,* February, 1966, reports 1,676,000 males in May, 1965, with two or more jobs, or 8.2 per cent of those employed in the group. Given the broad stability in the dual jobholder percentage we assume that 8.2 per cent applies to May, 1966, as well. Since about 60 per cent of the self-employed worked longer than 40 hours (Bureau of Labor Statistics, Special Labor Force Report No. 69, *Labor Force and Employment in 1965,* Table D–2), the 40.1 per cent for wage earners plus 8.2 per cent should run to over 50 per cent for all males twenty-five to forty-four.

7. Bureau of Labor Statistics, Special Labor Force Report No. 80, *Marital and Family-Characteristics of Workers, March, 1966,* Table B, indicates that 37.2 per cent of all females, married husband present, aged twenty-five to forty-four were in the labor force. Since women tend to be married to men slightly older than themselves, the rate for wives of men twenty-five to forty-four might be 0.5 per cent or so lower. Page A–6 reports 37.2 per cent of females husband present age twenty-five to forty-four in the labor force. To this we apply a ratio of 30.4 per cent to derive 11.8 per cent for other family members, but not working wives. We derive the 30.4 per cent as the ratio of p. A–21 data indicating 35.5 per cent of all wives in the labor force and 10.8 per cent of husband-wife families with no wife but other members in the labor force.

8. U.S. Commissioner of Labor, *Cost of Living and Retail Prices of Food,* 1904, p. 362, reports for a large (but in some respects biased) sample of urban families in 1901, that 23 per cent had income from boarders and lodgers; 9 per cent from working wives; 22 per cent from working children. 1960 Census, *Families,* p. 195, reports just under 4 per cent of all families in urbanized areas as having lodgers.

9. Lebergott, Stanley, *Manpower in Economic Growth,· op. cit.,* p. 512; and Bureau of Labor Statistics, Special Labor Force Report No. 69, *Labor Force and Employment in 1965,* p. A–7.

10. I have derived this estimate in "Tomorrow's Workers" in Sam B. Warner, editor, *Planning for a Nation of Cities,* MIT Press, Cambridge, 1966, p. 125. If one deals, more realistically, with choices for those in particular occupations, the ratio of advantage is still greater.

11. Taken from Lebergott, Stanley, *Manpower in Economic Growth, op. cit.,* p. 512.

12. Consumption data from U.S. Bureau of the Census, *Historical Statistics of the United States, Colonial Times to 1957,* pp. 186–187.

13. Data on parental occupations for males twenty-five to sixty-four as of March, 1962, are from the census survey, "Occupational Changes in a Generation," summarized in Peter Blau and Otis Dudley Duncan, *The American Occupational Structure,* John Wiley, New York, 1967, p. 496.

14. Lewis, Gregg, *Unionism and Relative Wages in the United States,* University of Chicago Press, Chicago, 1963, p. 244.

15. 1900: Lebergott, Stanley, *Manpower in Economic Growth, op. cit.,* p. 513. 1966: *Manpower Report of the President . . . April 1967,* p. 213.
16. Bureau of Labor Statistics, Special Labor Force Report No. 69, *Labor Force and Employment in 1965,* Table C–4.
17. Such a conclusion appears to be at variance with the well-known study by Warren G. Nutter, *The Extent of Enterprise Monopoly in the United States, 1899–1939,* University of Chicago Press, Chicago, 1951, and later work built upon that. The findings of that study are questioned by the writer in the *Review of Economics and Statistics,* November, 1953. Moreover, it deals with national income. When we come to measuring employment concentration the role of government is necessarily greater, for the contribution of government capital is omitted in the income estimate.
18. For 1900 we roughly adjust the 512,254 establishment figure (1900 Census, *Manufactures,* Part 1, p. 503). For 1963 we use the IRS total from *Business Tax Returns, 1964–65,* p. 7.
19. State expenditure data from U.S. Bureau of the Census, *Historical Statistics of the United States, Colonial Times to 1957,* pp. 728–729, deducting educational spending from total state spending. It should be noted that some state spending did not involve direct state employment, money going to highway contractors and other contractors. Nonetheless, the primacy of road activity above other activities seems likely.
20. The total gain was $16 billion (in 1913 prices), of which $7 billion was for autos and related items. Computed from William H. Shaw, *Value of Commodity Output since 1869,* National Bureau of Economic Research, Columbia University Press, New York, 1947, Table I 3. We overstate insofar as the inclusion of all manufactured fuels adds more gasoline than that used in cars and trucks. But we understate by omitting asphalt, pavement materials, etc.
21. Lebergott, Stanley, *Manpower in Economic Growth, op. cit.,* p. 523. We use data for real earnings of employed workers.
22. *Ibid.,* p. 109.
23. *Ibid.,* p. 111.
24. Ratios of hand-to-machine method time requirements were computed from the U.S. Commissioner of Labor, *Thirteenth Annual Report,* 1898 (1899), vol. 1, using the reports on pages 24–76 of this study for units 28 thru 653. These ratios were then weighted, giving a figure of 17.6 per cent. The weights were value-added by individual industry as computed from data in the Ninth Census, *The Statistics of Wealth and Industry,* 1872, pp. 399–405.
25. Data from the same source are available on various agricultural, mining, transport, and construction activities. Trends in output per manhour for agriculture and manufacturing, as estimated by John Kendrick, show an 1869–1900 rise of 57 per cent for manufacturing compared to 44 per cent for agriculture. U.S. Census Bureau, *Long-Term Economic Growth, 1860–1965,* Washington, p. 190.
26. Snyder, John, "Ethical Challenge of the Automation Age" in Connecticut Mutual Life, *Preserving the Individual in an Age of Automation,* 1963, p. 39.
27. Lebergott, Stanley, *Manpower in Economic Growth, op. cit.,* Table A–1.
28. Based on estimates in *ibid.,* pp. 189, 512, 522.
29. Productivity and employment changes computed from data in *Economic Report of the President February 1968,* pp. 240, 248.
30. In 1967 a monthly average of 1,634,000 persons were unemployed 4 weeks and under (*Economic Report of the President, 1968,* p. 238). Multiplying by 12 gives 19.6 million entries to unemployment over the year. Employment rose by 1.1 million from January, 1967 to January, 1968 (Bureau of Labor Statistics, *Employment and Earnings, February, 1968,* p. 34).

31. In 1965 21.4 per cent of the male noninstitutional population aged fourteen to fifteen was in the labor force, 44.6 of the sixteen to seventeen age group, 70 per cent of the eighteen to nineteen-year-olds, and so on. (Bureau of Labor Statistics, Special Labor Force Report No. 69, *Labor Force and Employment in 1965,* Table B–1.) Assuming a zero participation rate below fourteen, we infer that 21.4 per cent entered the labor force beginning at age fourteen, that 44.6 minus 21.4 (or 23.2 per cent) entered at ages sixteen to seventeen, and so on, till the 29 per cent rate for age thirty to thirty-four, taking that as the effective maximum. A problem arises at the other end of the age spectrum because rates for a given year necessarily do not reflect the nonparticipation of those in our beginning-period population who have already died or entered institutions. We pick an arbitrary sixty-five in the light of participation rates and death rates. Hence the average male enters at 18.5, leaves at sixty-five, based on rates in 1965. (Rates for 1900–1964 are much the same.)

    In January, 1966, a labor force survey indicated that males then aged sixty-five to sixty-nine had spent 14.6 years on their current job; those aged sixty to sixty-four had spent 16.5 years, and so on. (Bureau of Labor Statistics, Special Labor Force Report No. 77, *Job Tenure of Workers, January, 1966,* January, 1967, Table A.) Taking 15.5 as the average for men sixty-five years of age, we then estimate the duration figure for men aged 49.5 (i.e., 65 minus 15.5), and so on. Summing these intervals indicates twelve jobs from age 18.5 to sixty-five. Tenure surveys for 1951 and 1963 suggest shorter job durations were probable during peak hiring periods (e.g., World War II and the Korean War), and longer during slow growth. Using the 1966 report for projections assumes something like the 4.5 per cent to 5.5 per cent unemployment that prevailed in the 1960's. (This estimate uses somewhat better procedures, and a more recent survey, than that in Lebergott, Stanley, editor, *Men Without Work,* Prentice-Hall, Englewood Cliffs, N.J., 1964.)

32. Industry medians from Bureau of Labor Statistics, Special Labor Force Report No. 77, *Job Tenure of Workers, January, 1966,* Table D, were weighted by employment data from Lebergott, S. L., *Manpower in Economic Growth, op. cit.,* Tables A–4 and A–5. We stipulate a work life from age fifteen to age sixty-five, assuming that higher death rates in 1900 were offset by a longer period in the work force for those who survived to old age.

33. If one dealt not with the entire labor force but merely that in manufacturing, one might be tempted to qualify this conclusion given the Bureau of Labor Statistics data on labor turnover rates. Cf. the discussion by Arthur Ross, "Do We Have a New Industrial Feudalism?" *American Economic Review,* December, 1958. We find, however, that the very high turnover rates reported by 160 firms to the Metropolitan Life Insurance Company for years prior to 1926 do not appear sufficiently comparable with later data to warrant the belief that quit rates for all employees were as high in those earlier years as these firms reported.

34. The 1966 survey provides a distribution of jobs then held by starting date. We use these to weight the Bureau of Labor Statistics data on layoff and quit rates in manufacturing in the relevant years. The result should tell us something about that proportion of voluntary to involuntary job changes.

35. The exceptions (i.e., where there is tight union control, or absolute employer opposition) appear limited. It is to be remembered we are dealing not with the layoff component but the quit component of job turnover.

36. Recent reconsiderations of occupation categories appear in papers by R. W. Hodge and P. M. Siegel, and by G. G. Cain, W. L. Hansen, and B. A. Weisbrod, each entitled "The Classification of Occupations" in *Proceedings of*

the American Statistical Association—Social Statistics Section, 1966 as well as in J. G. Scoville, "The Development and Relevance of U.S. Occupational Data," *Industrial and Labor Relations Review,* October, 1965.

37. The most comprehensive, adjusted set of materials for 1900–1950 appears in Kaplan, David L., and M. Claire Casey, *Occupational Trends in the United States, 1900 to 1950,* Bureau of the Census Working Paper No. 5, Washington, 1958; while earlier reviews, ranging back somewhat in time, are those by Edwards, Alba, *Comparative Occupation Statistics in the United States, 1870–1940* (1943) and the 1900 Census, *Occupations.*

38. U.S. Bureau of the Census, Evaluation and Research Program of the U.S. Census of Population and Housing, 1960: *The Employer Record Check,* 1965—E.R. 60, No. 6—the source of data used in Table 16. Earlier analyses include the Census Bureau's *Post Enumeration Study: 1950,* Technical Paper No. 4, and work by a census expert, Gertrude Bancroft, *The American Labor Force,* 1958, pp. 172 and *passim.* One must note the precedent set in the earlier basic study of Margaret Bell and Gladys Palmer, *Employment and Unemployment in Philadelphia in 1936 and 1937,* Part II, Appendix A, p. 43 and Katharine Wood in *Social Security Bulletin,* May, 1939.

39. The employer check survey omitted self-employed and unpaid family workers, domestics, farm workers. E.R. 20, No. 5 makes Census-CPS comparisons for all occupation groups. From its findings we may infer that the omitted groups averaged the same error ratio as those included. The progression then would be: for the entire employed group the assignment of some occupation major group by census—99 per cent; for correctness of major group, with eight groups—82 per cent; for correct assignment of specific occupation, with 297 occupations—66 per cent.

40. In Table 16 we utilize only those data from the Evaluation and Research program that relate to the areas in which self-enumeration was utilized, the so-called two-stage areas. We do so because present plans for the 1970 census call for relying still more heavily on self-enumeration. Data for the one-stage areas, in which enumerators were used, suggest that errors for earlier censuses would have been relatively greater. Mildly different results would have been obtained by declaring agreement if the census code were matched by using employers primary *or* secondary job title and primary or secondary job description as well.

41. Bureau of Labor Statistics, Special Labor Force Report No. 69, *Labor Force and Employment in 1965,* Tables A–1, C–4. We include wage earners and unemployed.

42. A recent look at the guide lines appears in Shultz, George P., and Robert Z. Aliber, editors, *Guidelines, Informal Controls, and the Market Place,* University of Chicago Press, Chicago, 1966.

43. Cf., for example, the *Economic Report of the President, February 1968,* p. 248, giving one series on an establishment basis, the other on a labor force basis. The fact that both are presented implies that the trends shown by each series have been, or might be, significantly different.

44. For a discussion on the labor market aspects, cf. *inter alia,* the recent report of the Advisory Council on Vocational Education; Hearings of the Committee on Labor and Public Welfare (90th Congress, First Session) entitled, *Examination of the War on Poverty;* the *Manpower Report of the President, April 1967,* Parts II and III.

45. Much of the recent discussion was sparked by the insightful address of Theodore Schultz, "Investment in Human Capital," *American Economic Review,* March, 1961; while the major analytical study is Gary Becker's *Human Capital,* National Bureau of Economic Research, Columbia University Press, New York, 1964.

46. Computed from data in Folger, John, and Charles Nam, *Education of the American Population*, A 1960 Census Monograph, Washington, 1967, p. 46.
47. Denison, Edward, *The Sources of Economic Growth in the United States*, Committee for Economic Development, New York, 1962, p. 69. Cf. Denison's more recent study, *Why Growth Rates Differ*, Brookings Institution, Washington, 1967, p. 84, where he alludes to evidence from a study by Wolfle and Smith that, he finds, confirms his percentage.
48. The importance of student peers has been emphasized in the major study by James Coleman *et al.*, *Equality of Educational Opportunity*, Government Printing Office, Washington, 1966, pp. 302, 325 and *passim*. Cf., however, Bowles, Samuel, and Henry Levin, "The Determinants of Scholastic Achievement—An Appraisal of some Recent Evidence," *The Journal of Human Resources*, Winter, 1968.

5. THE MEASUREMENT OF KNOWLEDGE AND TECHNOLOGY

Daniel Bell

LET US BEGIN with a parable: all the rest is exegesis.

> ... the Library is composed of an indefinite, perhaps an infinite number of hexagonal galleries, with enormous ventilation shafts in the middle, excluded by very low railings. ...
>
> Everything is there: the minute history of the future, the autobiographies of the archangels, the faithful catalogue of the Library, thousands and thousands of false catalogues, a demonstration of the fallacy of these catalogues, a demonstration of the fallacy of the true catalogue, the Gnostic gospel of Basilides, the commentary on this gospel, the veridical account of your death, a version of each book in all languages, the interpolations of every book in all books.
>
> When it was proclaimed that the Library comprised all books, the first impression was one of extravagant joy. All men felt themselves lords of a secret, intact treasure. There was no personal or universal problem whose eloquent solution did not exist—in some hexagon. The universe was justified, the universe suddenly expanded to the limitless dimension of hope. ...
>
> The uncommon hope was followed, naturally enough, by a deep depression. The certainty that some shelf in some hexagon contained precious books and that these books were inaccessible seemed almost intolerable. A blasphemous sect suggested that all searches be given up and that men everywhere shuffle letters and symbols until they succeeded in composing, by means of an improbable stroke of luck, the canonical books. ...
>
> Other men, inversely, thought that the primary task was to eliminate useless works. They would invade the hexagons, exhibiting credentials which were not always false, skim through a volume with annoyance, and then condemn entire bookshelves to destruction: their ascetic, hygienic fury is responsible for the senseless loss of millions of books. Their name is execrated; but those who mourn the "treasures" destroyed by this frenzy overlook two notorious facts. One: the Library is so enormous that any reduction undertaken by humans is infinitesimal. Two: each book is unique, irreplaceable, but (inasmuch as the Library is total) there are always several hundreds of thousands of imperfect facsimiles—of works which differ only by one letter or one comma. ...
>
> *The Library is limitless and periodic.* If an eternal voyager were to

145

traverse it in any direction, he would find, after many centuries, that the same volumes are repeated in the same disorder (which, repeated, would constitute an order: Order itself). My solitude rejoices in this elegant hope.[1]

Jorge Luis Borges
"The Library of Babel"

THEORETICAL PERSPECTIVE

Modern life is a world of change. Because it brings large numbers of persons into the market place—for goods and services, for culture, for ideas, for political decisions—the modern world is in distinct ways extraordinarily different from all previous cultures, folk and traditional. The vehicles of change are the new technological modes of transportation and communication which break down the isolation of villages and regions, and which make it possible for people to interact with each other. The consequences of change, in breakneck accelerating fashion, are the rapid accretions of knowledge; the new, instrumental use of knowledge; and a startling shift in the character of knowledge itself.

The initial and obvious consequence of such intereaction is economic—the extended division of labor, the development of specialized occupations, and the growth of complementary enterprises. But such interaction, one must remember, leads not only to social differentiation, but to psychic differentiation as well. The world becomes more open, and there is a greater eagerness for experience, a desire for change and novelty, and a more strenuous search for sensation. And this results in the erosion of old creeds and a new syncretism of culture which distinctively sets the rhythm of contemporary life. It is this syncretism—the mingling of all creeds and all styles, the jostling of primitive and classical modes in the "museum without walls," the breakdown of the old conceptions of what is sacred and the loss of specific rituals and established *rites de passage*—which underlies the deracination and restlessness afflicting so many individuals in their search for "meaning" in the contemporary world.

Any discussion of knowledge and technology in this modern society —their nature, their impact, and their measure—has to be put into a context which explains their distinctive new character, and this is the intention of the first section of the chapter.

The Pace of Change

Few men have sought to understand contemporary society so desperately as Henry Adams, a scion of one of the most distinguished families in American life. His grandfather, John Quincy Adams, had been the last representative of the patriciate in politics, and had fallen, finally, before the onslaught of Jacksonian populism. In a mass democracy there was little room, Henry Adams felt, for the natural aristocracy to which he belonged. In order to understand himself and his times, he turned to history.

For forty-five years Henry Adams pondered history. He wrote a massive *History of the United States,* which is today unread; he traveled widely, retracing the steps of Gibbon through Rome. In the end, in that remarkable autobiography written in the third person, *The Education of Henry Adams,* he admitted his failure. "The human mind," he wrote, "has always struggled like a frightened bird to escape the chaos which caged it. . . ." He found himself in the same cage. "Never before had Adams been able to discern the working of law in history, which was the reason of his failure in teaching it; for chaos cannot be taught. . . ."

Yet he would not give up his search for the hidden order of history; and thus it happened, as he wrote, that "after ten years of pursuit, he found himself lying in the Gallery of Machines at the Great Exposition of 1900, his historical neck broken by sudden eruption of forces totally new." It was in the great hall of dynamos that this revelation took place.

In the energy churning from the dynamo, Henry Adams felt he had caught a glimpse of the secret that could unravel the complexities that men had begun to feel about their time. In the nineteenth century, he wrote, society by common accord measured its progress by the output of coal. The ratio of increase in the volume of coal power, he now said exultantly, might serve as a "dynamometer." Between 1840 and 1900, he pointed out, coal output had doubled every ten years; in the form of utilized power, each ton of coal yielded three or four times as much power in 1900 as it had in 1840. The gauge on the dynamometer of history had started out with arithmetical ratios; but new forces emerging around 1900—Adams had in mind the cracking of the world of appearances by the discovery of x-rays and radium—were creating new "supersensual" forces. What all this revealed, he said, was the foundation for a new, social physics, for a dynamic law of history, the fundamental secret of social change—the law of acceleration.

Impossibilities no longer stood in the way, he wrote in the *Education,* with a strange mingling of exultation and dismay.

> One's life had fattened on impossibilities. Before the boy was six years old, he had seen four impossibilities made actual—the ocean steamer, the railway, the electric telegraph and the Daguerrotype. . . . He had seen

the coal output of the United States grow from nothing to three hundred million tons or more. What was far more serious, he had seen the number of minds engaged in pursuing force—the true measure of its attraction—increase from a few score or hundreds in 1838, to many thousands in 1905, trained to a sharpness never before reached, and armed with instruments amounting to a new sense of indefinite power and accuracy while they chase force into hiding places where nature herself had never known it to be. . . . If science were to go on doubling or quadrupling its complexities every ten years, even mathematics would soon succumb to unintelligibility. An average mind [i.e., Adams] had succumbed already . . . it could no longer understand [science] in 1900.[2]

The idea of exponential curves—the acceleration of doubling rates of all kinds—has now become commonplace. We know that the time for circumnavigating the globe decreased exponentially every quarter of a century by a factor of two between Nelly Bly's voyage around the world in 1889 and the first transworld airplane flight in 1928, and by a factor of 10 since then. Derek Price claims (in a problem we will examine later) that the amount of scientific work since Newton has doubled every fifteen years, or presumably about three times in the course of the working life of a scientist.

It is crucial to grasp that such exponential curves not only signify a rapid change in time scales, but more and more quickly transform the character of our knowledge and our lives. Caryl Haskins, the President of the Carnegie Institution of Washington, wrote (in his presidential report of 1965–1966) that as late as 1920, "it was still widely believed that the Milky Way really comprehended our entire universe. Only within the last 10 years have we become fully aware that this galaxy of ours is in fact but one among millions or perhaps billions of such galaxies, lacing the heavens, stretching to distances of which the world of 1920 or even 1950 could have had little conception. . . ."

Only in the past seven years have we become aware of quasars (quasi-stellar radio sources), one of which, identified little more than two years ago, was reckoned to be about two and a half trillion times as luminous as our sun. Such findings have radically altered our ideas about the nature and extent of the universe. In fact, the rate of discovery itself in the three hundred years since Galileo has accelerated so greatly that insights attained only within the past few years have combined and welded together partial visions that required many earlier decades to achieve.

From the outer reaches of astronomy to the biological world within, the same story is repeated. A hundred years ago, the monk Gregor Mendel laid the foundation for the science of genetics. A few years later, a young biochemist named Friedrich Miescher broke down the cytoplasm of living cells with enzymes to discover the basic bonds of the nucleus. It took seventy-five years from Miescher's work to the theoretical proposals of Linus Pauling and Robert Corey in the 1950's about the molecular structure of genes, and from there it was less than a decade before Crick and Watson deciphered the basic genetic code of life itself.

Important as any of these examples may be, the simple and crucial fact which Henry Adams had so poignantly grasped in 1900 was that no longer would any child be able to live in the same kind of world —sociologically and intellectually—as his parents and grandparents had inhabited. For millennia—and this is still true in some sections of the globe, but they are shrinking—children retraced the steps of their parents, were initiated into stable ways and ritualized routines, had a common book of knowledge and morality, and maintained a basic familiarity with place and family. Today, not only does a child face a radical rupture with the past, but he must also be trained for an unknown future. And this task confronts the entire society as well.

The Change of Scale

The second salient fact that distinguishes our time from the past is the "change of scale" in our lives. Consider, first, the matter of numbers. It is startling to recall that when the Constitution which still guides American society was ratified, there were less than four million persons in the thirteen states of the Union. Of these, 750,000 were Negro slaves, outside society. It was a young population—the median age was only sixteen—and at that time fewer than 800,000 males had reached voting age. When George Washington was inaugurated as the first President of the United States, New York City, then the capital of the country, had a population of only 33,000.

Few people lived in cities. About 200,000 persons were settled in what were then called "urban areas"—that is, places with more than 2,500 inhabitants. Living in isolated clumps of small communities, or in sparsely inhabited areas, people rarely traveled great distances, and a visitor from afar was a rarity. Because it was an agricultural world, and artificial illumination came mainly from candles and kerosene lamps, daily life followed the orbit of the sun ("Good day" is, after all, a greeting from agricultural times), and there was little night life in the land. News meant local gossip, and the few news sheets that existed concentrated on parochial events. The ordinary citizen's image of the world and its politics was exceedingly circumscribed.

Consider the present. Today the population of the United States is over 200 million, and more than 110 million persons live in metropolitan areas (that is, within a county containing a city of at least 50,000 residents). Few persons live or work in social isolation. (Sixty per cent of the manufacturing force works in enterprises that employ more than 500 workers each.) Even those who work on farms are tied to the national society by the mass media and the popular culture.

But the most striking difference—and this is the real change of scale between 1798 and today—has to do with the number of persons each one of us *knows* and the number each of us *knows of*—in short, the way in which we *experience* the world. An individual today, on the job, in school, in the neighborhood, in a professional or social milieu, knows immediately hundreds of persons and, if one considers the extraordinary mobility of our lives—geographical, occupational, and social—during a lifetime one comes to know, as acquaintances or friends, several thousand. And through the windows of the mass media, and because of the enlargement of the political world and the multiplication of the dimensions of culture—the number of persons (and places) that one *knows of* accelerates at a steeply exponential rate.

What happens when the world's population begins to experience this leap—in social awareness, contact, and interaction? Consider the quantum jumps in population simply in the past century. It was only in 1859, after thousands of years of social life, that the world achieved a population of one billion persons. The second billion took seventy-five years more (from 1850 to 1925), and the third billion was added only thirty-five years later, in 1960. In all likelihood, a world population of four billion will have been reached by 1980; and, if the present rates continue unchecked, a fifth billion will be added only ten years later, by 1990. As Roger Revell points out, given present birthrates and deathrates, the population increase between 1965 and 2000 will be larger than the entire existing population. Or, to look at the doubling rates in a different light, it is estimated that, of all the people who have ever lived, one-fifth are alive today.

But a change of scale is not simply the original institution writ large. No biological organism or human institution which undergoes a change in size and a consequent change of scale does so without changing its form or shape. It was Galileo, more than three hundred and fifty years ago, who laid down this "general principal of similitude." The great biologist D'Arcy Wentworth Thompson, who described this problem in his classic *On Growth and Form,* put it thus:

[Galileo] said that if we tried building ships, palaces or temples of enormous size, yards, beams and belts would cease to hold together; nor can Nature grow a tree nor construct an animal beyond a certain size while retaining the proportions and employing the materials which suffice in the case of smaller structure. The thing will fall to pieces of its own weight unless we . . . change the relative proportions. . . .[3]

For Galileo, changes in proportion followed a mathematical principle, defined in normal spatial geometry as the square-cube law: as volume increases by cubic function, the surface enclosing it increases only by a square. Social institutions do not follow a fixed spatial law but, although the metaphor is biological, there is a process of *structural differentiation* "whereby *one* unit or organization differentiates into *two* which differ from each other in structure and in function for the system but which together are in certain respects 'functionally equivalent' to the earlier less differentiated unit."[4]

The concept of structural differentiation, as derived from Durkheim and Max Weber, and elaborated by Talcott Parsons and his students, is probably the key sociological concept today in the analysis of crescive social change. It points to the phenomena that as institutions grow in size and in the functions they have to perform, specialized and distinct subsystems are created to deal with these functions. With the growth of specialized subsystems one finds as well new, distinct problems of coordination, hierarchy, and social control.

In a general theory of society the processes of differentiation can be traced far back to early human societies in which, for example, sacerdotal and political functions that were conjoined (the Pharaonic powers of the old Egyptian kingdom) were differentiated into separate religious and political institutions (and this is true symbolically of post-Meiji Japan or even England today). Or the family, which was once the nuclear social institution, combining economic, welfare, recreational, and other functions, was sundered, resulting in a separation between the family and the occupational system, so that the family farm, the family business, or the family trade began to erode.

In contemporary industrial society, it has been the economic institutions which have shown the most marked form of internal differentiation. When firms and communities that were essentially alike began to meet, competition and a "heightened struggle for existence" took place. In the past, such competition often led to—in fact, was the prime cause of—war between communities. In contemporary society, because of the possibilities of economic growth through productivity, rather than through exploitation or plunder, such competition has led to a division of labor and to complementary relationships. In order to meet competition, or to avoid going under, social units (regions, cities, firms) began to specialize, to narrow their activities, and to become complementary to one another. Just as, say, the complex process of supplying goods to larger and larger markets forced the division of trade into wholesale and retail components, so similar processes of differentiation were at work in the specialization of jobs that accompanied the growth of the economy, and of firms, as a whole. Just as one found a differentiation between ownership and management, so one found a differentiation in the tasks of management, so that production, finance, marketing, research, personnel, and the like, each became the subject of new and professionalized vocations.

But what has been so marked and pervasive a feature of economic life now begins to appear in the once simple structures of educational and intellectual life. The growth of a university from 5,000 to 50,000 students is clearly not just a linear increase in size but a massive upheaval in structure as well. Where in the past (and this is still somewhat true of colleges in Oxford and Cambridge) one could find economic investment, administration, admissions, and teaching in the hands of one academic body, now one finds the complex hierarchy of business officials, administrators, deans, institute heads, admissions officers, and teachers existing in new and difficult bureaucratic relationships to one another. Within scientific institutions and academies of research one finds the same processes of differentiation—and strain —at work. If there is anything which, in this sense, marks off the second half of the twentieth century from the first half, it is the extension of the specialization of function from the economic to the intellectual realm.

Structural Change

If the two major processes which have characterized our time are the accelerated pace of change and the change of scale, with a resultant structural differentiation, there also has been emerging a distinct structural change in the "boundary systems" of the society, the coming of what I have called a "postindustrial" society.

Five dimensions of the postindustrial society can be outlined schematically at this point:

1. The creation of a service economy.
2. The pre-eminence of the professional and technical class.

3. The centrality of *theoretical knowledge* as the source of innovation and policy formulation in the society.
4. The possibility of self-sustaining technological growth.
5. The creation of a new "intellectual technology."

Creation of Service Economy. More than twenty-five years ago Colin Clark, in his *Conditions of Economic Progress,* divided the kinds of economy into sectors, the primary being predominantly agricultural; the secondary, manufacturing or industrial; and the tertiary, services. He argued that there was a trajectory along which every nation would pass, once it became industrialized, whereby, because of the sectoral differences in productivity (i.e., the relative reduction of employment in manufacturing) and the demand for health, recreation, and the like as national incomes increased, the greater proportion of the labor force would inevitably move to the service sector. By that criterion, the first and simplest dimension of a postindustrial society is that the majority of the labor force is no longer engaged in agriculture or manufacturing but in services which are defined, residually, as trade, finance, transport, health, recreation, research, education, and government.

Today the overwhelming number of countries in the world (see Table 1) are still dependent on the primary sector: agriculture, mining, fishing, forestry. These are economies based entirely on natural resources. Their productivity is low, and they are subject to wide swings because of the fluctuations of raw-material and primary-product prices; yet in Africa and Asia more than 70 per cent of the populations are in "agrarian economies." In western and northern Europe, Japan, and the Soviet Union, the major portion of the labor force is engaged in industry or the manufacture of products. The United States today is the only nation in the world in which the service sector accounts for more than half the total employment and more than half the gross national product. It is the first service economy, the first nation in which the major portion of the population is engaged neither in agrarian nor in industrial pursuits. It is estimated that today about 55 per cent of the labor force is engaged in services; by 1975 that figure will rise to 60 per cent.[5]

Growth of Professional and Technical Class. The second way of defining a postindustrial society is in the change of occupational pattern i.e., not only *where* people work, but the kind of work they do. The onset of industrialization brought with it a new phenomenon, the semiskilled worker, the man who can be trained easily within a few

TABLE 1.   THE WORLD'S LABOR FORCE BY BROAD ECONOMIC
SECTOR, AND BY CONTINENT AND REGION, 1960

Region	Total labor force (millions)	Percentage distribution by sector		
		Agriculture	Industry	Services
World	1,296	58	19	23
Africa	112	77	9	14
Western Africa	40	80	8	13
Eastern Africa	30	83	7	10
Middle Africa	14	86	6	8
Northern Africa	22	71	10	19
Southern Africa[a]	6	37	29	34
Northern America[a]	77	8	39	53
Latin America	71	48	20	32
Middle America (Mainland)	15	56	18	26
Caribbean	8	53	18	29
Tropical South America	37	52	17	31
Temperate South America[a]	12	25	33	42
Asia	728	71	12	17
East Asia (Mainland)	319	75	10	15
Japan[a]	44	33	28	39
Other East Asia	15	62	12	26
Middle South Asia	239	71	14	15
South-East Asia	90	75	8	17
South-West Asia	20	69	14	17
Europe[a]	191	28	38	34
Western Europe[a]	60	14	45	41
Northern Europe[a]	34	10	45	45
Eastern Europe[a]	49	45	31	24
Southern Europe[a]	47	41	32	27
Oceania[b]	6	23	34	43
Australia and New Zealand	5	12	40	49
Melanesia	1	85	5	10
USSR[a]	111	45	28	27

NOTE: Owing to independent rounding, the sum of the parts may not add up to group totals.
[a] More developed regions.
[b] Excluding Polynesia and Micronesia.
SOURCE: *International Labour Review,* January-February, 1967; I.L.O. estimates based on national censuses and sample surveys.

weeks to do the simple routine operations required in machine work. Within industrial societies, the semiskilled worker has been the single largest occupational category in the labor force. The expansion of the service economy, with its emphasis on trade, finance, education, and government, has naturally brought about a shift to white-collar occupations; and in the United States, by 1956, the number of white-collar workers, for the first time in the history of industrial civilization, out-numbered the blue-collar workers in the occupational structure. Since then the ratio has been widening steadily: today the white-collar workers outnumber the blue-collar by more than five to four.

But the most startling change has been the growth in professional and technical employment—jobs which usually require some college education—at a rate twice that of the average. In 1940, there were 3.9 million such persons in the society; by 1964, the number had risen to 8.6 million; and it is estimated that by 1975 there will be 13.2 mil-lion professional and technical persons, making it the second largest of the eight occupational divisions of the country, exceeded only by semiskilled workers (see Table 2). One further statistical breakdown is necessary to round out the picture—the role of scientists and engi-neers, who form the key group in the postindustrial society. For while the growth rate of the professional and technical class as a whole is twice that of the average labor-force rate, the growth rate of the scientists and engineers is triple that of the working population as a whole. By 1975, for example, the United States may have as many as 650,000 scientists, or twice as many as it had in 1960, and about two million engineers, compared to approximately 850,000 in 1960.

But in identifying a new and emerging social system, it is not only in the extrapolated social trends—such as the creation of a service economy or the expansion of the professional-technical class—that one seeks to understand fundamental social change. It is in some specifically defining characteristic—the ganglion, so to speak, of a social system—which becomes the source of stratification and change in the society. Industrial society is the organization of machines for the production of goods, and in this respect capitalism and socialism are two variants of industrial society. They differ in the relationship to property and the decision centers of investment, but they are both technical civilizations. The postindustrial society, however, is organ-ized around knowledge, and this fact gives rise to new social relation-ships and new structures which have to be organized politically.

Primacy of Theoretical Knowledge. Knowledge has been necessary for the existence of any society. But what is distinctive and new about the postindustrial society is the change in the character of knowl-edge itself. What has now become decisive for the organization of decisions and the control of change is the centrality of *theoretical* knowledge—the primacy of the theory over empiricism, and the codi-

TABLE 2. EMPLOYMENT BY MAJOR OCCUPATION GROUP, 1964, AND PROJECTED REQUIREMENTS, 1975[a]

Major occupation group	1964		1975		Per-centage change, 1964–75
	Number (in millions)	Per cent	Number (in millions)	Per cent	
Total employment	70.4	100.0	88.7	100.0	26
White-collar workers	31.1	44.2	42.8	48.3	38
Professional, technical, and kindred workers	8.6	12.2	13.2	14.9	54
Managers, officials, and proprietors, except farm	7.5	10.6	9.2	10.4	23
Clerical and kindred workers	10.7	15.2	14.6	16.5	37
Sales workers	4.5	6.3	5.8	6.5	30
Blue-collar workers	25.5	36.3	29.9	33.7	17
Craftsmen, foremen, and kindred workers	9.0	12.8	11.4	12.8	27
Operatives and kindred workers	12.9	18.4	14.8	16.7	15
Laborers, except farm and mine	3.6	5.2	3.7	4.2	[b]
Service workers	9.3	13.2	12.5	14.1	35
Farmers and farm managers, laborers, and foremen	4.4	6.3	3.5	3.9	–21

[a] Projections assume a national unemployment rate of 3 per cent in 1975. The choice of 3 per cent unemployment as a basis for these projections does not indicate an endorsement or even a willingness to accept that level of unemployment.

[b] Less than 3 per cent.

NOTE: Because of rounding, sums of individual items may not equal totals.

SOURCE: *Technology and the American Economy*, Report of the National Commission on Technology, Automation, and Economic Progress, vol. 1, Washington, 1966, p. 30; derived from Bureau of Labor Statistics, *America's Industrial and Occupational Manpower Requirements, 1964–75.*

fication of knowledge into abstract systems of symbols that can be utilized to illuminate many different and varied circumstances.

Every modern society now lives by innovation and growth, and by seeking to anticipate the future and to plan ahead. It is this commitment to growth that introduces the need for planning and forecasting into society; and it is the altered awareness of the nature of innovation that makes theoretical knowledge so central. One can see this, first, in the changed relationship of science to technology. In the nineteenth and early twentieth centuries, the great inventions and the industries that derived from them—steel, electric power, telegraph, telephone, and automobiles—were the work of inspired and talented tinkerers, most of whom were indifferent to the fundamental laws underlying their investigations. In this sense, chemistry is the first of the "modern" industries, in that its inventions, the chemically created synthetics, are based on the theoretical properties of the macromolecules which are manipulated to achieve the planned creation of new materials. In a less direct but equally important way, the changing relation between theory and empiricism is reflected in the management of economies. The rise of macroeconomics, and the new codifications of economic theory, now allow governments to intervene in economic matters in order to shape economic growth, redirect the allocation of resources, maintain balances between different sectors, and even, as in the case of Great Britain today, to engineer a controlled recession in order to redeploy resources. In all this the element of conscious policy and planning come to the fore as the heart of the postindustrial society.

Self-Sustaining Technological Growth. With the new devices of technological forecasting, my fourth criterion, the postindustrial societies may be able to achieve a new dimension of societal change, that of self-sustaining technological growth. Modern industrial economies became possible when societies are able to create new institutional mechanisms to build up savings (through banks, insurance companies, equity capital through the stock market, and government loans and taxes) and use these pools of money for investment purposes. The ability to re-invest annually about 10 per cent of the Gross National Product became the basis of what W. W. Rostow has called the "take-off" point for economic growth. But a modern society, in order to avoid stagnation or "maturity" (however that vague word is defined), has to open up new technological frontiers in order to maintain productivity and expansion. The development of new forecasting and "mapping techniques"—to be discussed later in this chapter—make possible a new phase in economic history, the conscious, planned advance of technological change.

Creation of "Intellectual Technology." And last in this catalogue of the new character of the postindustrial society is the emergence of a new "intellectual technology" which by the end of the twentieth century may be as decisive in human affairs as the machine technology has been for the past century and a half. By an "intellectual technology" I mean such varied techniques as linear programming, systems analysis, information theory, decision theory, games, and simulation which, when linked to the computer, allow us to accumulate and manipulate large aggregates of data of a differentiated kind so as to have more complete knowledge of social and economic matters. On more sophisticated levels, we can, through simulation, create "controlled experiments" in the social sciences in order to trace the progressive and regressive consequences of alternative choices of action, and create models, such as econometric and forecasting models of the economy, which can rapidly "solve" the thousands of simultaneous equations necessary for the new planning tools for social policy.

The Emergent Postindustrial Society

The concept of a postindustrial society deals primarily with long-run structural changes in the society. It is not, nor can it be, a comprehensive model of the complete society: it does not deal with basic changes in values (such as the hedonism which now legitimates the spending patterns of an affluent society); it can say little about the nature of political crises, such as our entrapment in Vietnam or the racial disorders which have erupted in recent years; it cannot assess the quality of the national "will" which is so important in the immediate political decisions of a society. However, by positing certain fundamental shifts in the bases of class position and in modes of access to places in the society, and by introducing a new crucial variable, that of "the centrality of theoretical knowledge," it does outline certain problems which a society must now solve. Just as an industrial society has been organized politically and culturally in diverse ways by the USSR, Germany, and Japan, so too the postindustrial society may have diverse political and cultural forms. The character of that society, however, will be shaped by specific political decisions.

The most crucial questions will deal with education, talent, and science policy. The rapid expansion of a professional and technical class, and the increased dependence of the society on scientific manpower, suggest a new and unique dimension in social affairs: i.e., that the economic growth rate of a postindustrial society will be less dependent on money than on "human capital." And this poses new problems in the way of planning. In the past (and in many of the less developed countries), societies stepping onto the escalator of industrialization required huge sums of money capital to develop the economic infrastructure (highways, railroads, canals) necessary for transport and communication, and the basic physical plant of heavy industry. Tomorrow, however, the long-range economic expansion of the society will be limited by shortages in technical and scientific manpower. Such problems are novel. We know, from economic theory, how to raise money capital—by restricting consumption and increasing investment—even though the political mechanisms are not easy to manipulate. But the source of brainpower is limited in part by the genetic distributions of talent and also by cultural disadvantages. The process of identifying and husbanding talent is long and difficult, and it involves the provision of adequate motivation, proper counselling and guidance, a coherent curriculum, and the like. The "time-cycle" in such planning, a period of from fifteen to twenty years, is vastly different from that required in the raising of money capital.

The nature of education itself is bound to change; it will necessarily become for the professional and technical person, a continuing, lifetime affair. Beyond the colleges and graduate schools we will need postdoctoral universities where new knowledge and new techniques can be passed along. Such continuing pressures and ratings inevitably invite increased anxiety. For many persons, the achievement of college was equivalent to reaching a plateau, to "having it made." It was a guarantee of higher pay and higher status in society. With the erosion of that system, with the plateau becoming more of a slope, more psychological strains will be introduced into the society.

In the postindustrial society, the university necessarily achieves a new, central role. It is the place where theoretical knowledge is sought, tested, and codified in a disinterested way, and thus it becomes the source of new knowledge and innovation. It has a new importance as the gatekeeper for the society. With the increasing "professionalization" of occupations, the university becomes the source of all training. Outside the classic professions, one went to a university for a liberal education and then learned "on the job." With old knowledge becoming quickly obsolete, the greater need is a grounding in theory, and only in the university can one acquire the conceptual structures that allow one to organize and reorganize new knowledge for the purpose of instrumental use. Perhaps it is not too much to say that just as the business firm was the key institution of the past hundred and fifty years because, as a marvelous social invention, it was the means of harnessing men and materials for the mass output of goods, so the university, because of its new role as the source of innovation, will become the primary institution in the next fifty years.

The chief question is whether the university is sufficiently adaptive and flexible to undertake the vast new functions that are being thrust upon it so rapidly. In the past, and to some extent in the present, the ideal of the university saw it as the place for humane learning, for maintaining a relation to tradition. Under the weight of the new professional demands, the liberal-arts tradition and function may crumble —to the disadvantage of society. The multiplicity of new demands— for research, for application, for consultation, for training of graduate students, for the custodial and experimental work on government and large science projects—may itself become so huge a burden that a different system, dividing many of the functions between universities and new social forms may be necessary.

In a broader, theoretical frame, if one adopts a Parsonian view of the different functional subsystems of the society, one can say that the intellectual system, as the guardian of tradition and values, has been responsible for one of the main integrative functions of the society. But in the future, as a source of innovation and as a bearer of change, it begins to replace "the economy" in carrying out the "adaptive" functions of the society. The question is whether the intellectual system is capable of carrying such a double burden, of being both integrative and adaptive.

Within a different theoretical framework, one can see education as becoming the chief determinant of the stratification system of the society. Over the long stretch of Western history, the property system has been the chief axis of stratification, and it was maintained by the family and inheritance. Within modern societies, the political system has been a new means for the acquisition of power and privilege. Now the three systems (in simplified model here) become alternative modes, with the skill/education axis as the most important for the vast majority of persons:

Base of Power	Mode of Access
Property	Inheritance
	Entrepreneurial ability
	Condottieri methods
Skill	Education
Political office	Mobilization
	Co-optation

The postindustrial society, necessarily, becomes a "meritocracy," raising various kinds of problems for the society. On the one hand, there is the *traditionalist/modernist* split, with certain older social groups emphasizing individualist and property values against the urban sophisticates; this has been one of the axes of politics in the society in the past forty years. There are, on the other hand, a variety of inherent conflicts between different kinds of skill groups (the military elite versus the intellectual), and a possible conflict between technocratic and political modes of decision-making.

But to the overwhelming extent that a postindustrial society depends upon knowledge and technology, the policies relating to the institutions concerned with their will become the central political questions for the society.

THE DIMENSIONS OF KNOWLEDGE

The Definition of Knowledge

When does one date a social change; when does one identify the onset of a trauma? In the case of knowledge, I will place it arbitrarily in the year 1788. The indicator? As the Prefatory Note to the 11th edition of the Encyclopedia Britannica reveals: "These earliest editions of the Encyclopedia Britannica [1745–1785] . . . like all their predecessors . . . had been put together by one or two men who were still able to take the whole of human knowledge for their province. It was with the Third Edition [1788] that the plan of drawing on specialist learning was first adopted." Thus we know when the unity of knowledge was fragmented. The 1967 edition, it may be noted, had 10,000 "recognized experts" involved in its preparation.

What does one mean by knowledge? An *encyclo-paedia* means the whole circle, and one can take everything known (recorded or stated) as the province of the definition. For the purposes of this chapter, I shall define knowledge *as a set of organized statements, setting forth a reasoned judgment or an experimental result, which is transmitted to others through some communication medium in some systematic form.* Thus, I distinguish knowledge from news and from entertainment. Knowledge consists of new judgments (research and scholarship) or new presentations of older judgments (text and educational).

This definition is broader than some established philosphical efforts. Thus Max Scheler distinguished three classes of knowledge: *Herrschaftswissen, Bildungswissen,* and *Erlösungswissen* or, knowledge for the sake of action or control, knowledge for the sake of nonmaterial culture, and knowledge for the sake of salvation; in Fritz Machlup's translation as instrumental knowledge, intellectual knowledge, and spiritual knowledge.

My definition is narrower, however, than Machlup's own comprehensive classification, which argues that "an objective interpretation to *what* is known will be less satisfactory than a subjective interpretation according to the meaning which the knower attaches to the known, that is *who* knows and *why* and *what for.*[6] Using then "the subjective meaning of the known to the *knower* as the criterion," Machlup distinguishes five types of knowledge:

(1) Practical knowledge: useful in a man's work, his decisions, and actions; can be subdivided, according to his activities, into:
   a) Professional knowledge
   b) Business knowledge
   c) Workman's knowledge
   d) Political knowledge
   e) Household knowledge
   f) Other practical knowledge
(2) Intellectual knowledge: Satisfying a man's intellectual curiosity, regarded as part of liberal education, humanistic and scientific learning, general culture; acquired as a rule in active concentration with an appreciation of the existence of open problems and cultural values.
(3) Small-talk and pastime knowledge; Satisfying the non-intellectual curiosity or his desire for light entertainment and emotional stimulation, including local gossip, news of crimes and accidents, light novels, stories, jokes, games, etc.; acquired as a rule in passive relaxation from "serious" pursuits; apt to dull his sensitiveness.
(4) Spiritual knowledge: related to his religious knowledge of God and of the ways to the salvation of the soul.
(5) Unwanted knowledge: outside his interests, usually accidentally acquired, aimlessly retained.[7]

Robert Lane, who has put forth the idea of "a knowledge society," seeks to establish an epistemological foundation for his conception. Like Machlup, Lane includes both the "known" and the "state of knowing," but he also seeks to emphasize the increased self-consciousness about society which such knowledge provides. Lane writes:

As a first approximation to a definition, the knowledgeable society is one in which, more than in other societies, its members: (a) inquire into the basis of their beliefs about man, nature and society; (b) are guided (perhaps unconsciously) by objective standards of veridical truth, and, at upper levels of education, follow scientific rules of evidence and inference in inquiry; (c) devote considerable resources to this inquiry and thus have a large store of knowledge; (d) collect, organize and interpret their knowledge in a constant effort to extract meaning from it for the purposes at hand; (e) employ this knowledge to illuminate (and perhaps modify) their values and goals as well as to advance them. Just as the "democratic" society has a foundation in governmental and interpersonal relations, and the "affluent society" a foundation in economics, so the knowledgeable society has its roots in epistemology and the logic of inquiry.[8]

Definitions of this kind are neither right nor wrong; they are, rather, boundaries of usage. An effort to deal with comprehensive societal change would need to take these definitions into account. For the purposes of social policy, however—the need to determine the allocation of societal resources for some specified purpose of social utility—I have formulated a restricted definition. Knowledge, then, is that which is objectively known, an *intellectual property,* attached to a name or a group of names and certified by copyright or some other form of social recognition (e.g., publication). This knowledge is paid for—in the time spent in writing and research; in the monetary compensation by the communication and educational media. It is subject to a judgment by the market, by administrative or political decisions of superiors, or by peers as to the worth of the result, and as to its claim on social resources, where such claims are made. Thus knowledge is part of the social overhead investment of society; it is a coherent statement, presented in a book, article (or even a computer program), written down or recorded at some point for transmission, and subject to some rough count. Such a utilitarian definition, needless to say, shuns the relevant questions of a "sociology of knowledge": the social setting of ideas, their interconnections, their relation to some structural foundation, and the like. Any evaluation of the specific character of particular sets of knowledge would, of course, have to take up such questions; these, however, are outside my purview here.[9]

The Measurement of Knowledge

Patterns of Growth. In recent years we have become accustomed to the statement that the "amount" of knowledge is increasing at an exponential rate. The first rough count—the first flag of warning on the growth of knowledge as a coming storage and retrieval problem—came in 1944 when Fremont Rider, Wesleyan University librarian, calculated that American research libraries were, on the average, doubling in size every sixteen years. Taking ten representative colleges, Rider showed that between 1831 (when each college had on the average about 7,000 books in its library) and 1938, their holdings had doubled every twenty-two years; taking comparable growth figures of larger American universities from 1831, the doubling rate was about sixteen years.[10] Rider chose Yale as an example of what the problem would be like in the future:

> It appears that, along in the early part of the eighteenth century, the Yale library possessed somewhere around 1,000 volumes. If it had continued from this start to double every sixteen years it should, in 1938,

have grown to about 2,600,000 volumes. In 1938, it actually did have 2,748,000 volumes, i.e., an amazingly close correspondence with the "standard" rate of growth. . . . It takes but a few moments' computation to work out that the Yale University library in 1849 occupied approximately 1¼ miles of shelving, and that its card catalog—if it then had a card catalog—would have occupied approximately 160 card drawers. In 1938 its 2,748,000 volumes occupied perhaps eighty miles of shelving, and its card catalog of all sorts in all locations must have occupied a total of somewhere around ten thousand drawers. To service this library required in 1938 a staff of over two hundred person, of whom probably half were catalogers.[11]

Rider speculated—whimsically, it seemed at the time—what would happen if the Yale Library continued to grow "at a rate no greater than the most conservative rate" at which library holdings have been growing. In the year 2040, he estimated the Yale Library will have

approximately 200,000,000 volumes, which will occupy over 6,000 miles of shelves. Its card catalog file—if it then has a card catalog—will consist of nearly three-quarters of a million catalog drawers, which will of themselves occupy not less than eight acres of floor space. New material will be coming in at the rate of 12,000,000 volumes a year; and the cataloging of this new material will require a cataloging staff of over six thousand persons.[12]

Rider's findings on the growth of American research libraries were generalized by Derek Price to include almost the entire range of scientific knowledge. In *Science Since Babylon,* the first of his book publications to deal with this problem,[13] Price sought to chart the growth of the scientific journal and the learned paper as the two major indicators of knowledge. The scientific journal and the learned paper were innovations of the scientific revolution of the late seventeenth century. They allowed for the relatively rapid communication of new ideas to the growing circle of persons interested in science. The earliest surviving journal was the *Philosophical Transactions of the Royal Society of London,* first published in 1665, followed by some three or four similar journals published by other national academies in Europe. Thereafter, the number of journals increased, reaching a total of about one hundred by the beginning of the nineteenth century, one thousand by mid-century, and some ten thousand by 1900. Price concludes:

If we make . . . a count extending in time range from 1665 to the present day, it is immediately obvious that the enormous increase in the population of scientific periodicals has proceeded from unity to the order of a hundred thousand with an extraordinary regularity seldom seen in any man-made or natural statistic. It is apparent to a high order of accuracy, that the number has increased by a factor of ten during every half-century starting from a state in 1750 when there were about ten scientific journals in the world.[14]

In subsequent publications, Price has defended the counting of papers as a relevant indicator of scientific knowledge. In a paper published in 1965, he wrote:

> To the scientist himself, the publication represents something mysteriously powerful, eternal, an open archive of the Literature into which he is reading his findings. Only in very rare and special instances does one have to consider pure scientific work in which there is no end product of literature. These would include pathological cases such as that of Henry Cavendish, who researched diligently but did not publish the bulk of his findings, which were therefore lost for a century until they were disinterred by Clerk Maxwell only a few years after the valuable results had been discovered independently by others. Is unpublished work like this, or work that is suppressed and unpublished because it is a national secret, a contribution to science? I find, in general, that it is fair enough to say it is not. Science is not science that communication lacks! . . .
>
> Our definition holds, then, that science is that which is published in scientific journals, papers, reports and books. In short it is that which is embodied in the Literature. Conveniently enough, this Literature is far easier to define, delimit and count than anything else one might deal with. Because of its central function for scientists, it has been subjected to centuries of systematization by indexes, classifications, journals of abstracts and retrieval systems. . . . All such literature can be, and in very many cases has actually been counted, classified, and followed through the years as a time series. The chief component of the Research Literature, for example, can be defined as the papers published in the scientific serials included in the *World List of Scientific Periodicals*—a familiar tool of all reference librarians.[15]

By 1830, when it became obvious, with about three hundred journals being published in the world, that the cultivated man of science could no longer keep abreast of new knowledge, a new device appeared, the abstract journal, which summarized each article so that the interested individual could then decide which article to consult in full. But, as Price points out, the number of abstract journals has also increased, following the same trajectory, multiplying by a factor of ten every half-century. Thus, by 1950 the number of abstract journals had attained a "critical magnitude" of about three hundred.

Out of these figures, Price has sought to draw a "law of exponential increase." He considers that the most remarkable conclusion is that the number of new journals has grown exponentially rather than linearly. "The constant involved is actually about fifteen years for a doubling, corresponding to a power of ten in fifty years and a factor of a thousand in a century and a half. . . ."

If this is true, it is remarkable that not only do we find such a rapid growth but that the particular curve should be exponential, the mathematical consequence of having a quantity that increases in such a way that the bigger it is the faster it grows. "Why should it be," asks Price, "that journals appear to breed more journals at a rate proportional to their population at any one time instead of at any particular constant rate?" It must follow, he says, "that there is something about scientific discoveries or the papers by which they are published that makes them act in this way. It seems as if each advance generates a new series of advances at a reasonably constant birth rate, so that the number of births is strictly proportional to the size of the population of discoveries at any given time."[16]

This "law of exponential increase," which applies to the number of scientific journals, is also "obeyed," Price argues, by the actual number of scientific papers in those journals. Taking the papers recorded in the *Physics Abstracts* from 1918 to the present day, the total number, he claims, has followed an exponential growth curve, the accuracy of which does not vary by more than 1 per cent of the total. At the beginning of the 1960's, there were about 180,000 physics papers recorded in those volumes, and the number has steadily doubled at a rate even faster than once every fifteen years. On the basis of about thirty such analyses since 1951, Price concludes that "it seems beyond reasonable doubt that the literature in any normal, growing field of science increases exponentially, with a doubling in an interval ranging from about ten to about fifteen years."[17]

A recent study of mathematical publications by Kenneth O. May[18] confirms the general pattern sketched by Price for physics, but finds that "the rate of growth for mathematics is only *half* that found by Price." The doubling intervals cited by Price "correspond to an annual increase of from about 7 to 5 per cent, whereas we have found for mathematics, an annual increase of about 2.5 per cent and doubling about every 28 years."

The difference arises from the choice of a starting point. As May points out: "Before jumping to the conclusion that mathematics has a different growth rate than other sciences, note that although Price speaks of 'the literature' as though he were referring to the total literature his data are actually for the literature in each field after a certain time, in each case the beginning of an abstracting service: 1900 for physics, 1908 for chemistry, 1927 for biology, and 1940 for mathematics."

Professor May, in his inquiry, went back to 1868, to the *Jahrbuch über die Fortschritte der Mathematik*, tracing the growth through 1940 and from 1941 to 1965 in the *Mathematical Reviews*. He also points out that in mathematics, by successively ignoring the literature prior to 1900, 1920, and 1940, one could achieve a series of growth curves similar to Price's higher findings. "It appears likely," May concludes, "that if Price and others took into account the literature prior to their statistical series, they would obtain substantially lower growth rates. This analysis supports the conjecture that the over-all total scientific literature has been accumulating at a rate of about 2.5 per cent per year, doubling about four times a century."

Limits of Growth. Any growth which is exponential must at some point level off, or we would reach a point of absurdity. Published figures on the electrical industry, for example, show that if we start with a single man, circa 1750—the time of Franklin's experiments with lightning—the exponential increase would bring us to two hundred thousand persons employed in 1925 and an even million by 1955; at that rate, the entire working population would be employed in this one field by 1990.[19] At some point, necessarily, there is a saturation. In the measurement of the growth of knowledge, as in other fields which have shown similar patterns, the questions revolve around the definition of that saturated state and the estimation of its arrival date.

The pattern which has been described, the approach to some ceiling, is a sigmoid or S-shaped curve in which the rate below and above its middle is often quite symmetrical. Because this is so, it lends itself easily to prediction, since one assumes that the rate above the midpoint will match that below and then level off. It is, in fact, the beauty of this curve which—if one looks at the literature—has seduced many statisticians into almost believing that it is the "philosopher's stone" for the charting of human behavior.

The phenomenon of saturation, as applied to a general law of human population, was first proposed in the 1830's by the statistician Adolphe Quetelet, the formulator of social physics, in his reflections on Malthus. A typical population grows slowly from an asymptotic minimum, multiplies quickly, and draws slowly to an ill-defined asymptotic maximum, the curve passing through a point of inflection to become S-shaped. A mathematical colleague of Quetelet's, P. F. Verhulst, in 1838 sought to give a mathematical shape to the same general conclusions, to find a *"fonction retardatrice"* which would turn the Malthusian curve of geometrical progression into the S-shaped or, as he called it, the logistic curve, which would constitute the true "law of population," and indicate the limit above which the population was not likely to grow.[20]

Verhulst was making a number of assumptions: that the rate of increase cannot be constant; that the rate must be some function, a linear one, of the population for the time being; and that once the rate begins to fall, or saturation sets in, it will fall more as the population begins to grow. Thus the growth factor and the retardation factor are proportional to one another so that, because of the "symmetry" of the curve, one can project or forecast the future.[21]

In 1924, the mathematical biologist Raymond Pearl came across Verhulst's papers and formulated the Verhulst-Pearl law. In seeking to draw an S-shaped population growth curve, Pearl stated that the rate of growth will depend upon the population at the time, and on "the still unutilized reserves of population-support" existing in the available land. Pearl had earlier formulated equations to describe the population growth of fruit flies in a closed environment, and in 1925 on the basis of similar equations, he predicted an American population in 1950 of 148.7 million and in 1960 of 159.2 million. The 1950 prediction came within 3 million persons of the actual count, but the 1960 prediction was already off by more than 25 million. Pearl's estimate of an upper limit of 197 million in the population of the United States has already been surpassed within this decade, and the population seems to be heading toward the 300 million mark by the year 2000.

The key problem in the use of S-curve analysis is that it works only within some "closed system," based on either fixed resources or physical laws or some concept of an absolute. In other words, the "ceiling conditions" force the levelling off of the curve. We do not have a "closed system" in human populations, or society, thus there is always a risk in using such curves for purposes of prediction. Yet there is some value in considering such a model as a "baseline" or fiction against which to test a social reality. The late Louis Ridenour, the former chief scientist of the Air Force, who was the first person to comment on the Fremont Rider data (in a 1951 paper printed in *Bibliography in an Age of Science*), pointed out that the phenomenon of the doubling rates of university libraries could be found as well in the assets of life insurance companies, the number of long-distance telephone messages and radio-telephone conversations, the time for circumnavigating the globe, the gross weight of aircraft in common use, airline-passenger miles flown, passenger-car registrations, and so forth. Ridenour, assuming the exponential law to be empirically established, argued, in fact, that there was a "law of social change" paralleling the "autocatalytic processes" such as chemical reaction or cell growth which are found in chemistry and biology. In seeking to establish an explanation, Ridenour argued that the rate of public acceptance of a new product or service (such as long-distance telephoning or airline travel) will be proportional to the number of people who are familiar with it through exposure. *Since at some point there has to be a saturation,* Ridenour, like Verhulst, proposed a differential equation to indicate the rate of slowdown when the curve would begin to reach an absolute upper limit.[22]

The difficulty with Ridenour's proposed "law of social change" is that such curves are plotted only for single variables and presume a saturation. But what may be true of beanstalks, or yeast, or fruit flies, or similar organisms whose logistic growths have been neatly plotted in *fixed* ecological environments may not hold for social situations where decisions may be postponed (as in the case of births) or where substitutions are possible (as in the case of bus or subway transit for passenger cars), so that the growths do not develop in some fixed, "immanent" way. It is for this reason that the use of logistic curves may be deceptive.

Yet one advantage of this technique remains: by the use of mathematical language, one can often discern identical underlying structures in highly diverse phenomena. One may not think of people marrying and having children as the same kind of phenomenon as replacing capital equipment in a plant, but Richard Stone, the Cambridge, England economist, finds an exact mathematical analogy between the two. Stone discerns an equally striking analogy between epidemics in a population and the demand for education.[23] In charting the demand for education, the simple extrapolation of past trends is clearly unacceptable, for as we have seen, at some point there is a "system break," and a jump in the trend. (If one had projected the demand for American universities on the basis of the trends in the 1950 decade, one would have assumed that only by 1975 would 40 per cent of the age eighteen to twenty-two cohort be in college; actually that figure was reached in 1965.) Stone suggests that higher education can be regarded as an "epidemic process." "At each stage, the number who catch the infection and decide to go to a university depends partly on the numbers who have gone and so are available to be infected." In time, the "contagion" spreads until everyone susceptible to it is infected. The pattern is definable by a differential equation whose product, again, is the S-shaped or logistic curve.

To the extent that one can use logistic-curve analysis, even as baselines rather than for actual forecasts, a number of difficult problems present themselves, for at crucial points in the trajectory of the S-curve, "critical magnitudes" are reached and the logistic curve "reacts" to the approaching ceiling conditions in different ways. Pearl and Ridenour posited a simple saturation and a levelling off. In *Science Since Babylon,* Derek Price seemed to accept the same simplistic view:

> It is a property of the symmetrical sigmoid curve that its transition from small values to saturated ones is accomplished during the central portion in a period of time corresponding to only the middle five or six doubling periods (more exactly 5.8), independent of the exact size of the ceiling involved. . . . For science in the United States, the accurate growth figures show that only about thirty years must elapse between the period when some few percent of difficulty is felt and the time when that trouble has become so acute that it cannot possibly be satisfied. . . . We are already, roughly speaking, about halfway up the manpower ceiling.[24]

Two years later, however, Price had begun to change his mind. It seems that the knowledge curves were not simple S-shaped or logistic curves. Under the influence of the writings of Gerald Holton, the Harvard physicist, Price sought to identify more differentiated modes of change. In rather exuberantly hypostasized language, Price now wrote:

> . . . growths that have long been exponential seem not to relish the idea of being flattened. Before they reach a mid-point they begin to twist and turn, and, like impish spirits, change their shapes and definitions so as not to be exterminated against that terrible ceiling. Or, in less anthropomorphic terms, the cybernetic phenomenon of hunting sets in and the curve begins to oscillate wildly. The newly felt constriction produces restorative reaction, but the restored growth first wildly overshoots the mark and then plunges to greater depths than before. If the reaction is successful, its value usually seems to lie in so transforming what is being measured that it takes a new lease on life and rises with a new vigor until, at last, it must meet its doom.
>
> One therefore finds two variants of the traditional logistic curve that are more frequent than the plain S-shaped curve. In both cases the variant sets in some time during the inflection, presumably at a time when the privations of the loss of exponential growth become unbearable. If a slight change of definition of the thing that is being measured can be

so allowed as to count a new phenomenon on equal terms with the old, the new logistic curve rises phoenixlike on the ashes of the old, a phenomenon first adequately recognized by Holton and felicitously called by him 'escalation.' Alternatively, if the changed conditions do not admit a new exponential growth, there will be violent fluctuations persisting until the statistic becomes so ill-defined as to be uncountable, or in some cases the fluctuations decline logarithmically to a stable maximum. At times death may even follow this attainment of maturity, so that instead of a stable maximum there is a slow decline back to zero, or a sudden change of definition making it impossible to measure the index and terminating the curve abruptly in midair.[25]

So much, then, for the symmetry of the sigmoid curve! Price proposes: "Now that we know something about the pathological afterlife of a logistic curve, and that such things occur in practice in several branches of science and technology, let us reopen the question of the growth curve of science as a whole."[26]

What Price finally tells is that after the "breakdown" of the exponential growth of knowledge, the curve (after tightening its sinews for a jump!), may move "either toward escalation or toward violent fluctuation." But in which direction we do not know. So where are we then? The idea of "escalation," or the renewal of an upward curve, may have some meaning where there is a deterministic path, following some physical laws, and in this sense it has found a place in technological forecasting, where it appears under the rubric of "envelope curve" forecasting. But to talk of "violent fluctuations" provides little help in charting measurable changes, for such fluctuations have no determinate pattern. We find, in sum, that the "gross" measures of scientific knowledge, plotted as growth curves, are, so far at least, of little help, other than as metaphors, or as a means of alerting us generally to the problems we may have to face in the future because of such growths. To plan for social policy on the basis of such plotted curves would be highly misleading. To deal with such questions, we have to turn to less "exact" but sociologically more meaningful observations on the patterns of the development of knowledge.

The Differentiation of Knowledge

The idea of exponentiality, the idea that scientific knowledge accumulates "linearly" in some compound fashion, has obscured the fact that the more typical, and important, pattern is for the development of "branching" or the creation of new and numerous subdivisions or specialties within fields rather than just growth.

Contrary to the nineteenth-century image of science as a bounded or exhaustible field of knowledge whose dimensions would eventually be fully explored, we now assume an openness to knowledge which is marked by variegated forms of differentiation. Each advance opens up, sometimes rapidly, sometimes slowly, new fields which, in turn, sprout their own branches. Thus, to take the illustration cited by Gerald Holton, the field of "shock waves" initiated in 1848 by the British mathematician and physicist G. C. Stokes and the astronomer J. Challis, with their theoretical equations of motion in gases, led not only to significant contributions in mathematics and physics along this general line (by Mach, and later by von Neumann and Bethe, among others), but to the branching off of shock tube, aerodynamics, detonations, and magnetohydrodynamics, as four distinct fields. The latter field, developed in 1942 by Alfven, plays a fundamental part in both basic and applied fusion research.[27]

Sometimes a stasis is reached and it seems that a field has been explored as far as possible, and then some new discoveries suddenly create a series of new "spurts." In 1895, Röntgen seemed to have exhausted all the major aspects of x-rays, but in 1912 the discovery of x-ray diffraction in crystals by von Laue, Friedrich, and Knipping transformed two separate fields, that of x-rays and crystallography. Similarly the discovery in 1934 of artificial radioactivity by the Joliot-Curies created a qualitative change which gave rise, in one branching point to the work of Hahn and Strassman, which Lise Meitner successfully interpreted as the splitting of the uranium atom, and in another branch to Enrico Fermi's work on the increased radioactivity of metals bombarded with slow neutrons, work which led directly to controlled atomic fission and the bomb.

Much of the phenomenon of branching derives not simply from the "immanent" logic of intellectual development, but from the social organization of science itself. In the nineteenth century, science was a small but worthy profession for individuals in its own right. But in the twentieth century, the way in which scientists have come to organize and coordinate their individual research "into a fast-growing commonwealth of learning," as Holton puts it, has spurred individuals to develop their own work, subsequently, with their own teams. Holton illustrates this phenomenon with a drawing of a "tree" and its "branches," which traces, among other things, the work of Nobel laureate I. I. Rabi. In 1929 at Columbia Rabi made a "breakthrough" in pure physics—sending molecular beams through a magnetic field —which gave rise to branching in several different directions, in optics, solid state masers, atomic structures, and a half-dozen other fields.

Rabi not only developed the original molecular beam techniques—the "trunk" of the "tree"—but he also stimulated a group of productive associates and students to originate new questions, to move into neighboring parts of the same field, and to provoke a rapid branching into several new areas, some of which then developed new branches of their own.[28]

One can find some indicators of the extraordinary proliferation of fields in the breakdown of specializations listed in the National Register of Scientific and Technical Personnel, a government-sponsored inventory of all persons with competence in scientific work. (The National Register is a cooperative undertaking of the National Science Foundation with the major professional scientific societies in the country.) The Register began shortly after World War II, with about 54 specializations in the sciences; twenty years later there were over 900 distinct scientific and technical specializations listed. To a considerable extent, the proliferation of fields arises out of a system of reclassifications as more and more fine distinctions are made; but in many instances, the increase is due to the creation of new specializations and branchings. In physics, for example, the 1954 roster listed ten distinct subfields with seventy-four specializations; in 1968, there were twelve fields with a hundred and fifty-four specializations. In 1954, for example, "Theoretical Physics" (Quantum) was listed as a distinct field, with subspecializations headed as nuclear, atomic, solids, field; in 1968 the field was no longer listed as such and a more differentiated classification had appeared. In 1954, however, solid state physics was broken down into eight subspecializations; in 1968 there were twenty-seven subspecializations under the solid state classification, a proliferation which was the consequence of the additional "branching" of the field.

None of the scientific societies which are responsible for the maintenance of the rosters have made any studies of the basis of the reclassification or addition of fields. A consistent monitoring of each field might reveal some useful and significant indicators of the rates of change in the development of fields of knowledge.

THE MEASUREMENT OF TECHNOLOGICAL CHANGE

Modernity and Technological Change

The claim of being "new" is the distinctive hallmark of modernity, yet many of these claims represent not so much a specifically new aspect of human experience as a change of scale of the phenomenon. The syncretism of culture was already a distinctive feature of the age of Constantine, with its mingling of the Greek and Asiatic mystery religions. The bifurcation of sensibility is as old, if not older, than Plato's separation of the rational from the spirited. But the revolutions in transportation and communication which have banded together the world society into one great *Oikoumenē* (ecumene) have meant the breakdown of older, parochial cultures and the overflowing of all the world's traditions of art, music, and literature into a new, universal container, accessible to all and obligatory upon all. This very enlargement of horizon, this mingling of the arts, this search for the "new," whether as a voyage of discovery or as a snobbish effort to differentiate oneself from others, is itself the creation of a new kind of modernity.

At the heart of the issue is the meaning of the idea of culture. When one speaks of a "classical culture" or a "Catholic culture" (almost in the sense of a "bacterial culture"—a breeding of distinctly identifiable strains), one thinks of a long-linked set of beliefs, traditions, rituals, and injunctions, which in the course of its history has achieved something of a homogeneous style. But modernity is, distinctively, a break with the past *as* past, catapulting it into the present.

Mass society contains "the tradition of the new," in Harold Rosenberg's phrase. Under such conditions, not even an avant-garde is possible, for it is by its very nature a rejection of a specific tradition. Modernity castrates an avant-garde by quickly accepting it, just as it accepts, with equal flexibility, elements from the Western past, the Oriental past (and present) in its omnium-gatherum of culture. The old concept of culture is based on continuity, the modern on variety; the old value was tradition, the contemporary ideal is syncretism.

If there is a radical gap between the present and the past, it lies in the nature of technology and the ways it has transformed social relationships and our ways of looking at the world. To be arbitrary, we can list five ways by which technology wreaked these transformations:

1. By producing more goods at less cost, technology has been the chief engine of raising the living standards of the world. The achievement of technology, the late Joseph Schumpeter was fond of saying, was that it brought the price of silk stockings within the reach of every shopgirl, as well as of a queen. But technology has not only been the means of raising levels of living, it has been the chief mechanism of reducing inequality within Western society. In France, writes Jean

Fourastié, "the Chief Justice of the Court of Accounts . . . earned in 1948 not more than four and a half times as much as his office boy *by hour of work,* although the difference between these two positions was of the order of 50 to 1 in 1800." The simple reason for this, as Fourastié points out, is the cheapening of goods and the rise of real wages of the working class in western life.[29]

2. Technology has created a new class, hitherto unknown in society, of the engineer and the technician, men who are divorced from the site of work but who constitute a "planning staff" for the operations of the work process.

3. Technology has created a new definition of rationality, a new mode of thought, which emphasizes functional relations and the quantitative. Its criteria of performance are those of efficiency and optimization, that is, a utilization of resources in terms of least cost and least effort. This new definition of functional rationality has its carry-over in new modes of education in which the quantitative techniques of engineering and economics now jostle the older modes of speculation, tradition, and reason.

4. The revolutions in transportation and communication, as a consequence of technology, have created new economic interdependencies and new social interactions. New networks of social relationships have been formed (pre-eminently the shift from kinship to occupation and professional ties); new densities, physical and social, become the matrix of human action.

5. Esthetic perceptions, particularly of space and time, have been radically altered. The ancients had no concept of "speed" and motion in the way these are perceived today: nor was there a synoptic conception of height—the view from the air—which provides a different standard of assessing a landscape or a cityscape. It is in art, especially in painting, that such a radical change of sensibility has taken place.[30]

Measures of Economic Change

It is with the economy that we are first concerned because technology is the foundation of industrial society. Economic innovation and change are directly dependent upon new technology. Yet the awareness of this fact is relatively recent. The founding fathers of contemporary economics were preoccupied with a "dismal science" because of their belief that capital accumulation could not continue indefinitely. These conclusions were based on three assumptions: the law of diminishing returns, the Malthusian principle of population in which an increase in real wages would simply lead to faster population growth, and, implicitly, an invariant state of technology. This was the basis of Ricardian economics.[31]

Even Marx, in this sense a post-Ricardian economist, came to a pessimistic conclusion. Though he was far more sensitive to the revolutionary role of machinery than his contemporaries, Marx felt that the chief consequence of the substitution of machinery for labor would be the centralization of capital, at the expense of other capitalists, and the increased exploitation of labor (through worse conditions or longer working days) as more backward capitalists sought to meet competition. Arguing from a labor theory of value, Marx felt that the expansion of the "organic composition of capital" could lead only to a decline in the average rate of profit and the continuing impoverishment of labor.

Yet this earlier pessimism has been belied. Real wages have risen consistently in the past hundred years; the increase in the per capita income in the United States has averaged more than 2 per cent a year since 1870. How did the classical economists err so badly? As Professor Lave writes: "Had Ricardo been asked whether increased productivity were possible, he would probably have answered that productivity would increase if capital per worker, including land per worker, were increased."[32] But he could not give a quantitative formulation of this effect. The standard capital-output ratios (known as the Cobb-Douglas function) which typically have been used assume that output will rise 1 per cent for every 3 per cent of capital increase, holding labor constant. Between 1909 and 1949, the capital per man-hour employed in the private nonfarm sector of the U.S. economy rose by 31.5 per cent. On this basis, the increase in goods (per capita output) should have been about 10 per cent. But the startling fact is that during this period, with a capital input of 31.5 per cent, output per man-hour rose not 10 per cent but 104.6 per cent. In short, there was an increase in productivity of 90 per cent that is unexplained by the increase in capital per worker. The explanation, simple in conception but complex in detail and proof, was supplied by Robert M. Solow in a now classical (or should one say neo-classical?) article, namely, *technological change*.[33] Technology, as we now know, is the basis of increased productivity, and productivity has been the transforming fact of economic life in a way which no classical economist could imagine.

The simple answer, however, begs a complex question. What is technological change? One can say that technological progress consists of all the better methods and organization that improve the efficiency (i.e., the utilization) of both old capital and new. But this can be many things. It can be a machine that will forge car engines, replacing old hand-casting methods. It can be a physical technique, such as building a ramp to move stones up a pyramid. It can be a simple sociological technique such as a rough division of labor in the construction of a shoe or a sophisticated technique of industrial engineering such as time and motion studies. It can be a logical analysis embodied in operations research or a mathematical formula such as linear programming which specifies new queuing tables or the production schedules in which orders are to be filled. Clearly, all of these are incommensurate. How do we combine all these different things under one rubric and seek a measurement?

What makes the problem all the more vexing is that we are repeatedly told that we are living in a time of "constantly accelerating rate of technological change" which is creating new and "explosive" social problems. Now no one can deny that a good deal of technological change has taken place since World War II: atomic energy, electronic computers, jet engines are three of the more spectacular introductions of new products and processes. But the difficulty with the publicistic (and political) argument is that the word "rate" implies a measurement, and that somehow the changes that are being introduced now can be measured, say, against the introduction of the steam engine, the railroad, the telephone, the dynamo, and similar technological devices of the nineteenth century. How does one distinguish the change wrought by electricity from that created by atomic energy? We cannot. Both are "revolutionary" innovations. But there is no way of matching their effects in a comparable way. More than that, many social changes are occurring simultaneously, and writers often lump these together as part of the idea of rapid technological change.

The question of what constitutes *the* accelerating revolution of our time can be left to other writers and other places. Clearly, it is in part technological. But it is also political in that, for the first time, broadly speaking, we are seeing the inclusion of the vast masses of people into society, a process which involves the redefinition of social, civil, and political rights. It is sociological in that it portends a vast shift in sensibility and in mores: in sexual attitudes, definitions of achievement, social ties and responsibilities, and the like. It is cultural, as we have already noted. If we are to restrict ourselves to the technological dimension, and ask about the measurement of change, we have to, first, return to the realm where its values (beginning first in the monetary sense) are expressed—to economics.

For the economist, a technological change is a change in the "production function."[34] Simply stated, the production function is a relationship between inputs and outputs which shows, at any point in time, the *maximum* output rate which can be obtained from the given amounts of the factors of production. In the simplest cases, the factors of production are assumed to be capital and labor, and the production function would show the most effective combination (the optimal proportions) of factors at given costs.[35] Increases in real income per man-hour are a function of both relative increases in capital and the more efficient utilization of resources. Classical economic theory emphasized that the higher levels of real income are generated by increasing the capital stock. But real wages might also be increased by an upward shift in the production function as a result of research which leads to better combinations of resources, new techniques, and so on. In fact, we assume today that technological change, rather than capital stock, is the more effective determinant of higher real wages. Solow, for example, in his 1957 paper created an "aggregate production function" (which has been criticized for its assumptions of homogeneity and high elasticity of substitution of capital for labor and capital for capital), which sought to separate the increase in productivity as caused by growth in capital from that due to technological change. He found that in the period from 1909 to 1949 that the capital increase accounted for approximately 12.5 per cent of increased productivity, while technological change accounted for 88 per cent.[36]

In the broader context, we have to move from production functions to the measures of productivity computed in regular time-series. Conventionally, the gross measurement of technological change is the year-by-year change in the output per man-hour of labor, or what economists call a partial productivity index. It is arrived at by dividing the market value of goods and services produced during a given year (in the economy as a whole, or in a particular industry) by the number of man-hours it has taken to produce them. Productivity so defined in no way identifies whether the increased efficiency has been brought about by new machinery or by a better skilled labor force, or even by a speed-up of work done on the job. Still, if we are to consider the question whether technological change has been vastly accelerating in recent years and at what rate, this is the only consistent measure we have.

The most comprehensive study of labor productivity in recent years, by John W. Kendrick,[37] draws the following conclusions: First, during 1889–1957, the nation's real output per man-hour of work has been rising at an average rate of between 2 and 2.5 per cent. These gains have been widely diffused resulting in a rapid increase in real hourly earnings and a decline in working hours of between 20 and 30 per cent since the turn of the century. According to Kendrick, there was a break before and after World War I. During 1889–1919, output per man-hour rose at an average rate of 1.6 per cent; during 1920–1957, it grew at an average rate of 2.3 per cent per year. The reasons for this increase are by no means clear. Kendrick suggests that it may have been due to the spread of scientific management, the expansion of college and graduate work in business administration, the spread of organized research and development, and the change in immigration policy. A similar picture is obtained if one uses the "total" productivity index for computations. The total productivity index, developed by Evsey Domar, relates changes both in labor and capital inputs rather than in labor inputs alone. Kendrick, using this index, estimated that during 1889–1957, total productivity for the entire domestic economy increased by 1.7 per cent and that in the period following World War I, this rose to 2.1 per cent.

In these measures, the usual assumption is that technological change is essentially "organizational," i.e., that technological progress consists of better methods and organization that improve the efficiency of both old capital and new. If one tries to measure that aspect of change which is due directly to machinery, rather than just to methods (i.e., time and motion studies, linear programming, etc.), these changes must be capital-embodied if they are to be utilized. For example, the introductions of the continuous wide strip mill in the steel industry and the diesel locomotive in railroads necessitate large capital investments, and we can thus "factor out" those proportions of productivity due to machinery. In a study based on capital-embodied change, published in 1959, Solow estimated that the rate of technological change in the private economy during 1919–1953 was 2.5 per cent per year.[38]

Most of the analytical and specialized estimates stop at a period of ten years ago. Has there been a recent increase? In the early 1960's, the seemingly persistent high unemployment rates (averaging about 6 per cent) gave rise to fears that a rapid increase in automation (which necessarily would be reflected in an accelerating rate of productivity) was responsible for the unemployment. A number of economic writers prophesied so dazzling a rate of increase that the economy would be unable to absorb the new production without making a sharp separation between income and work.

In 1965, President Johnson appointed a National Commission on

Technology, Automation and Economic Progress to report on the question, and after a year of study, the Commission concluded that the arguments had been greatly exaggerated. The report stated: "In the 35 years before the end of the Second World War, output per man-hour in the private economy rose at a trend rate of 2 per cent a year. But this period includes the depression decade of the 1930's. Between 1947 and 1965 productivity in the private economy rose at a trend rate of about 3.2 per cent a year, or an increase of more than 50 per cent. If agriculture is excluded, the contrast is less sharp, with the rate of increase 2 per cent a year before the war and 2.5 per cent after."[39]

If one moves to the more refined indexes, Kendrick and Sato found that the average annual rate of increase of *total* productivity in the private domestic economy during the 1948–1960 period was 2.14 per cent as compared with a rate of 2.08 per cent for the larger 1919–1960 period. Richard Nelson, assuming that technological change was organizational, estimated the average rate of technological change as 1.9 per cent in 1929–1947; as 2.9 per cent in 1947–1954 and 2.1 per cent in 1954–1960. Thus, while there is some evidence that the rate of technological change has been higher since World War II, the difference is much smaller than that indicated by the behavior of output per man-hour.[40]

As the President's Automation Commission concluded:

> Our study of the evidence has impressed us with the inadequacy of the basis for any sweeping pronouncements about the speed of scientific and technological progress. . . . Our broad conclusion is that the pace of technological change has increased in recent decades and may increase in the future, but a sharp break in the continuity of technical progress has not occurred, nor [since most major technological discoveries which will have a significant economic impact within the next decade are already in a readily identifiable stage of commercial development] is it likely to occur in the next decade.[41]

The Forecasting of Technology

Even though it is difficult to demonstrate that the "rate" of technological change has leaped ahead substantially in the past decades, it is undeniable that something substantially *new* about technology has been introduced into economic and social history. It is the changed relationship between science and technology, and the incorporation of science through the institutionalization of research into the ongoing structure of the economy, and, in the U.S., as a normal part of business organization. Two things, therefore, are new: the systematic develop-ment of research and the creation of new science-based industries.

Classical economists, even as late as John Stuart Mill, held that population and land were the limiting variables on economic growth and that eventually a prudent economy would end in a "stationary state."[42] Marx, to the contrary, saw that the dynamic of capitalist so-ciety was, necessarily, accumulation but that monopoly would inevita-bly slow down the rate of growth and that the system itself might even break down because of its "contradictions." Several generations of post-Marxian economists have, in turn, expected a new state of "eco-nomic maturity" based either on the exhaustion of markets and in-vestment opportunities in new lands (the theme of imperialism), the slowdown of population growth (a favorite theme of economic pessi-mists of the 1930's, *vide,* Alvin Hansen,[43]) or the ending of new tech-nological advances as the "long waves" of business activity because of the waning impetus of the railroad, electricity, and the automobile.

The bogey of "economic maturity" today is largely dispelled. And the principal reason is the openness of technology. In his *Capitalism, Socialism and Democracy,* published in 1942, Joseph Schumpeter wrote: "We are now in the downgrade of a wave of enterprise that created the electrical power plant, the electrical industry, the electri-fied farm and home and the motorcar. We find all that very marvelous, and we cannot for our lives see where opportunities of comparable importance are to come from."

Though Schumpeter was pessimistic about the future of capitalism (because of the bureaucratization of enterprise and the hostility of the intellectual), he did have a clear view of the promise of technology. Thus he added: "As a matter of fact, however, the promise held out by the chemical industry alone is much greater than what was possible to anticipate in, say, 1880. . . . Technological possibilities are an un-charted sea . . . there is no reason to expect slackening of the rate of output through exhaustion of technological possibilities."[44]

In the quarter of a century since Schumpeter made those prophetic remarks, two changes have occurred. One has been the systematic joining of science to invention, principally through the organization of research and development efforts. The second, more recent, change has been the effort to "chart the sea" of technology by creating new techniques of technological forecasting which will lay out the future areas of development and which will allow industry, or society, to plan ahead systematically in terms of capital possibilities, needs, and products. This new fusion of science with innovation, and the possibility of systematic and organized technological growth, I regard as one of the underpinnings of the "postindustrial society."

Earlier inventions and innovations were not tied to scientific research. As Nelson, Peck, and Kalachek have observed:

> Compare Watt's utilization of the theory of latent heat in his invention of the separate condensing chamber for steam engines, or Marconi's exploitation of developments in electromagnetism with Carothers' work which led to nylon, Shockley's work which led to the transistor, or recent technological advances in drugs and military aircraft. In the earlier cases the scientific research that created the breakthrough was completely autonomous to the inventive effort. In the later cases, much of the underlying scientific knowledge was won in the course of efforts specifically aimed at providing the basic understanding and data needed to achieve further technological advances. Carothers' basic research at Du Pont which led to nylon was financed by management in the hope that improvements in the understanding of long polymers would lead to important or new improved chemical products. Shockley's Bell Telephone Laboratories project was undertaken in the belief that improved knowledge of semiconductors would lead to better electrical devices.[45]

But, they continue, the new industries of the 1970's—the polymers and plastics, electronics and optics, chemicals and synthetics, aerospace and communications—are all integrally science-based.

> The science-based technologies and industries have a great advantage in achieving major advances in products and processes. Research aimed at opening up new possibilities *has substituted both for chance development* in the relevant sciences, *and* for the classical major inventive effort aimed at *cracking open a problem through direct attack*. The post World War II explosion of major advances in electronics, aircraft, missiles, chemicals, and medicines, reflects the maturing of the science base in these industries, as well as the large volume of resources they employ to advance technology. Many of the products of the science-based industries are the materials used by other industries, and their improvement has led to rapid productivity growth in many sectors of the economy. The more important new consumer goods have come either directly from these industries or through incorporation into new products by other industries of the materials and components created by the science-based sector.[46]

The role of "research and development" as a component of scientific and economic activity will be discussed in the third section, on structural dimensions of knowledge and technology. In this discussion of the measurement of knowledge and technology, we can turn to the new kinds of knowledge represented by technological forecasting.

Three factors distinguish the prediction of today from that of the past: (1) the awareness of the complex differentiation of society and the need, therefore, to define the different kinds of systems and their interrelations; (2) the development of new techniques, primarily statistical and often mathematical, which facilitate the ordering and analysis of data so as to uncover the different rates of change which obtain in different sectors of society; and (3) the sheer quantity of empirical data which allow one to see the detailed components of sectors and to plot their trends in consistent time-series.

The simplest and perhaps most important advantage is the sheer amount of statistical data. In 1790, it was debated in the English Parliament whether the population of England was increasing or decreasing. Different people, speaking from limited experiential evidence, presented completely contradictory arguments. The issue was resolved only by the first modern census. An important corollary is the number of competent persons who can work with the data. As J. J. Spengler said, tongue not altogether in cheek, "Not only can economists devote to the population question more attention than they gave it in the past eighty years when they devoted only about 1 to 1½ percent of their articles to population, but there are many more economists to do the job. Today more economists are practicing than lived and died in the past four thousand years, and their number is growing even faster than the world's population."[47]

In simple terms, the more data you have (look at the total number of entries needed to build up a picture of the national product accounts), the easier it is to chart the behavior of variables and to make forecasts. Most, if not all, of our basic economic and social projections today are built around the concept of Gross National Product. Yet it is startling to realize how recent are the government gathering and publication of such macroeconomic data, going back only to Franklin D. Roosevelt's budget message in 1944. And systematic technological forecasting is still in its infancy. As Erich Jantsch writes, in a comprehensive survey of technological forecasting for the Organisation for Economic Cooperation and Development (OECD),

> The bulk of technological forecasting today is done without the explicit use of special techniques. . . . The need for formal techniques was not felt until a few years ago. While the beginning of systematic technological forecasting can be situated at around 1950, with forerunners since 1945, the existence of a more widespread interest in special techniques first made itself felt about a decade later, in 1960, with forerunners already experimenting in the late 1950's. Now, in the mid-1960's,

a noticeable interest is developing in more elaborate multi-level techniques and integrated models that are amenable to computer programing.[48]

Most technological forecasting is still made on the basis of what an imaginative engineer or writer can dream up as possible. In 1892, a German engineer, Plessner, forecast technological developments (supercritical steam and metal vapor turbines) and functional capabilities (television and voice-operated typewriters) which were—and to some extent still are—far in the future. Arthur C. Clarke, who has made some of the more speculative forecasts in his serious science fiction, has argued that anything that is theoretically possible will be achieved, despite the technical difficulties, if it is desired greatly enough. "Fantastic" ideas, he says, have been achieved in the past and only by assuming that they will continue to be achieved do we have any hope of anticipating the future.[49] Much of this kind of expectation is "poetry," because little attention is paid to constraints, especially economic ones. Fantasy may be indispensable but only if it is disciplined by technique. With his usual gift for paradox, Marshall McLuhan has said that the improvement of intuition is a highly technical matter.

Much of the early impetus to disciplined technological forecasting came in the recognition of its necessity by the military and was pioneered by Theodor von Karman, the eminent Cal Tech scientist in the field of aerodynamics. His report in 1944 on the future of aircraft propulsion is often referred to as the first modern technological forecast.[50] Von Karman later initiated the concentrated technological forecasting, at five-year intervals, of the U.S. Air Force and the technological forecasting in NATO. His innovations were fairly simple. As described by Jantsch: Von Karman looked at basic potentialities and limitations, at functional capabilities and key parameters, rather than trying to describe in precise terms the functional technological systems of the future; he emphasized the evaluation of alternative combinations of future basic technologies—i.e., the assessment of alternative technological options; and he sought to place his forecasts in a well-defined time-frame of fifteen to twenty years.

In this respect, as James Brian Quinn has pointed out, technological forecasts are quite similar to market or economic forecasts. No sophisticated manager would expect a market forecast to predict the precise size or characteristics of individual markets with decimal accuracy. One could reasonably expect the market analyst to estimate the most likely or "expected" size of a market and to evaluate the probabilities and implications of other sizes. In the same sense, as Mr. Quinn has put it,

> Except in immediate direct extrapolations of present techniques, it is futile for the forecaster to predict the precise nature and form of the technology which will dominate a future application. But he can make "range forecasts" of the performance characteristics a given use is likely to demand in the future. He can make probability statements about what performance characteristics a particular class of technology will be able to provide by certain future dates. And he can analyze the potential implications of having these technical-economic capacities available by projected dates.[51]

The "leap forward" in the past decade has been due, in great measure, to the work of Ralph C. Lenz Jr., who is in the Aeronautical Systems Division of the Air Force Systems Command at the Wright-Patterson Air Force Base in Ohio. Lenz's small monograph, *Technological Forecasting,* based on a Master's thesis done ten years before at MIT, is the work most frequently cited for its classification and ordering of technological forecasting techniques.[52] Lenz divided the types of forecasting into *extrapolation, growth analogies, trend correlation,* and *dynamic forecasting* (i.e., modeling), and sought to indicate the applications of each type either singly or in combination. Erich Jantsch, in his OECD survey, listed 100 distinguishable techniques (though many of these are only variations in the choice of certain statistical or mathematical methods), which he has grouped into *intuitive, explorative, normative,* and *feedback* techniques.

Of those broad approaches which have demonstrated the most promise, and on which the greatest amount of relevant work seems to have been done, four will be illustrated here: S-curves and envelope curves (*extrapolation*); the Delphi technique (*intuitive*); morphological designs and relevance tree methods (*matrices and contexts*); and the study of *diffusion times,* or the predictions of the rates of change in the introduction of new technologies that have already been developed.

Extrapolation. The foundation of all forecasting is some form of extrapolation, the effort to read some continuing tendency from the past into a determinate future. The most common, and deceptive, technique is the straight projection of a past trend plotted on a line or curve. Linear projections represent the extension of a regular time series—population, or productivity, or expenditures—at a constant rate. The technique has its obvious difficulties. Sometimes there are "system breaks." If one had computed agricultural productivity from the mid-1930's for the next twenty-five years at the rate which it had followed for the previous twenty-five, the index (using 1910 as a base) would in 1960 have been about 135 or 140, instead of its actual figure of 400. The mechanization of agriculture was accelerated by wartime demand, which was the "exogenous" variable. In a different sense, if the rate of expenditures on "research and development" for the past twenty years were projected in linear fashion for the next twenty, this would mean, as many persons have pointed out jovially, that by then, most of the Gross National Product would be devoted to that enterprise.

Most of economic forecasting is still based on linear projections because the rates of change in the economy seem to be of that order. In other areas, such as population or knowledge or sudden demand, where the growth seems to be exponential, various writers, from Verhulst to Price, have sought to apply S-shaped or logistic curves. The difficulty with these curves, as we have seen, is either that they presume a fixed environment, so that one can sketch the move to saturation, or that in an open environment they become erratic. Recently, however, particularly in the field of technological forecasting, writers have been attracted to the idea of "escalation," that is, as each curve in a single trajectory levels off, a new curve "takes off" following a similar upward pattern.

The notion of "escalation" has been taken up in recent years by Buckminister Fuller, Ralph Lenz, and Robert U. Ayres to become the most striking, if not the most fashionable, mode of technological forecasting under the name of "envelope curve" extrapolation.[53] In this technique, the best performance of the parameters of any *particular* invention (say, the speed of aircraft) or a *class* of technology, is plotted over a long period of time until one reaches the maximum limit of performance—which is called the *envelope*. There is an assumption here of a final fixed limit, either because it is an *intrinsic* theoretical limit (e.g., 17,000 miles an hour, the point at which the increase of speed in flight sends a vehicle into atmospheric orbit), or because it is an *extrinsic* presumed stipulation (e.g., a figure of a trillion GNP by 1975). Having stipulated a final saturation, then one plots previous escalations, and presumed *new* intermediate escalations by the *tangents* along the "backs" of the individual curves. In effect, envelope curves are huge S-curves, made up of many smaller ones, whose successive decreases in the rate of growth occur as the curve approaches upper limits of intrinsic or extrinsic possibilities.

In other words, for any class of technology, one has to know, or assume, the absolute finite limits, and then estimate a regular rate of growth toward that limit. The fact that, *at the moment,* the engineering possibilities of moving beyond the present do not exist is in and of itself no barrier. It is assumed that the engineering breakthrough will occur.

Envelope-curve analysis, as Donald Schon points out, is not, strictly speaking, a forecast of invention, but rather the presumed effects of *sequential* inventions on some technological parameters.[54] It assumes that since there is some intrinsic logic in the parameter—e.g., the efficiency of external combustion energy conversion systems, the rate of increase of operating energy in high-energy physics particle accelerators, in aircraft power trend, or speed trend curves (see Figure 1)—there will necessarily be an immanent development of the parameter. It also assumes that some invention inevitably will come along which will send the curve shooting up along the big S. Thus, a large envelope curve of the efficiency of external combustion systems indicated the role of a gas turbine, though a National Academy of Science Committee many years ago proclaimed that the turbine could not be produced because of a heavy weight-to-power ratio.

Robert U. Ayres of the Hudson Institute, who has been the most enthusiastic proponent of envelope curve extrapolation, has argued that the technique works, even when one extrapolates beyond the current "state-of-the-art" in any particular field, because the rate of invention which has characterized the system in the past may be expected to continue until the "absolute" theoretical limits (velocity of light, absolute zero temperature, temperature at which molecular bonds break up) are reached for any particular parameter. One therefore should not judge the existing performance capacity of a parameter (e.g., operating energy in a particle accelerator) by the limits of a *particular* kind of component, but should look at the broad "macrovariable" in an historical context. By aggregating the particular types one can see its possible growth in a "piggy-back" jump which takes off from the previous envelope point.

Ayres points to the "self-reinforcing" nature of these curves in the progress of modern computers measured in terms of a composite variable, high-speed memory capacity (in bits), divided by add-time (in seconds). Computer manufacturers try to increase the number of bits and decrease the add-time. Someone charged with setting the technical performance specifications for a corporation's next generation of electronic computers doesn't want to aim too low, lest he be surpassed by a competitor, nor set too high a goal and fail. The envelope curve, argues Ayres, can tell him the best range within which such extension

FIGURE 1. SPEED TREND CURVE

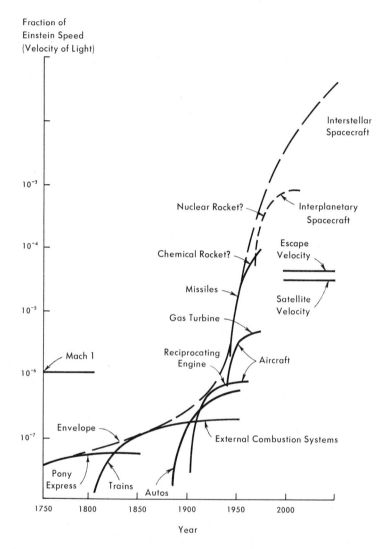

SOURCE: Courtesy Robert U. Ayres, Hudson Institute

can take place. On a curve plotted to show the development of computers from 1940, two points fall noticeably *above* the envelope. These correspond to IBM's "Stretch" and the Philco "2000," both of which were unsuccessful efforts to outpace the rest of the industry. To this extent, the envelope curve can set program objectives.

Technological forecasters have claimed that in most instances it is useful to extrapolate from such envelope curves in terms of continued logarithmic growth, and to deviate from this assumption only when persuasive reasons are found for doing so. For example, forecasts adhering to the existing trend at any time after 1930 would have produced a more accurate forecast about the maximum speed of aircraft than those based on the existing technological limitations. The singular point about envelope curve extrapolation is that it cannot deal with individual technologies but with performance characteristics of "macrovariables." Ayres remarks that the more disaggregative (component-oriented) the analysis, the more it is likely to be biased intrinsically on the conservative side. In fact, it is almost normal for the maximum progress projected on the basis of analysis of components to be, in effect, the lower limit on actual progress, because it assumes no new innovations will come to change the technology. By dealing with a single *class* of technology, upper limits of growth can be readily stated for envelope curves, although these cannot be given for *individual* techniques, since these are subject to innovation, substitutability, and escalation.

Macrovariables have their obvious limits as well.[55] Thus in the plotting of the maximum energy curve in a thermal power plant since 1700 (see Figure 2), the curve has escalated in typical fashion from 1 or 2 per cent to about 44 per cent where it stands today. Increases have occurred rather sharply, and have been of the order of 50 per cent each time, but at steadily decreasing intervals. Ayres predicts, on this basis, a maximum operating efficiency of 55–60 per cent around 1980. In view of the long lead time of a commercial power plant, many persons might doubt this prediction. But since efficiencies of this magnitude are feasible by several means (fuel cells, gas turbines, magnetohydrodynamics) which are being explored, such a forecast may be realizable. However, increases after 1980 would pose a question for the curve since only one improvement factor of 1.5 would bring efficiencies up to 90 per cent and improvement beyond that at the same rate is clearly impossible.

It is important to understand the central logic of envelope curve projections. The basis on which Raymond Pearl, for example, developed his logistic curves was the fixing of a theoretical "upper limit" or saturation point, and having specified that point and knowing the initial climbing rate, he could then specify the trajectory of the S-curve and plot its intermediate points. This does work where there is a fixed environment. Pearl erred in his statement of saturation in his population projections, so that, while for a short period his projections of

FIGURE 2.   EFFICIENCY OF EXTERNAL COMBUSTION
ENERGY CONVERSION SYSTEMS

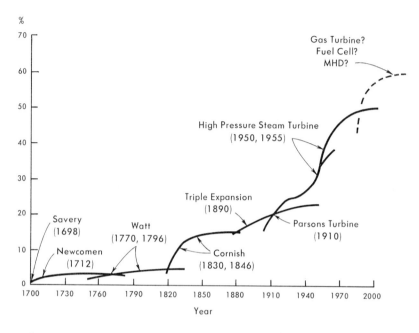

SOURCE: From *Energy for Man* by Hans Thirring, copyright by Indiana University Press 1958, published by Harper & Row Torchbooks. Reproduced by permission of Indiana University Press and George C. Harrap and Company.

the rates of increase seemed to hold, at a later period they began to diverge markedly from the actual rates. Human population growth did not follow an immanent development; nor is there, *pace* Malthus, a fixed upper limit of resources.

What the envelope curve projections assume is that, for any class of technology, there are somewhere a set of fixed limits (such as the absolute velocity of light). Then having stipulated that outer point, they seek to estimate the intermediate trajectory of the technological development as a series of escalated S-curves moving toward that upper limit.

The weakness in the theory is, in part, the problem of any forecasting, namely, the choice of parameters and the estimation of their place in the curve, relative to the present at which successive leveling-offs will occur, and relative to the presumed final limit, whether intrinsic or extrinsic. More generally, when one takes performance characteristics of variables (such as aircraft speed) there is no developed theory why progress *should* occur in this fashion other than the argument that certain engineering parameters tend to grow logarithmically, or the crucial assumption that *some* invention will be forthcoming to produce the next escalation. As to the latter point, forecasters come more and more to rely on the observation, first made by William F. Ogburn, and refined considerably by Robert K. Merton, that invention is a "multiple" or simultaneous affair. Because invention is, increasingly, an impersonal social process and not dependent on the genius of individual inventors, such inventions are responses to social need and economic demand. But there may be little reason to assume that such inventions will appear "on schedule."

Intuitive Technique. In most "common-sense" forecasting, the simplest procedure is to ask the expert, presumably the man who knows most and best about a field. The problem, of course, is who is an expert, how to determine the test of reliability for his forecasts, and, if experts differ, how to choose among them. To deal with this problem of "the epistemology of the inexact sciences," Olaf Helmer, a mathematician at the RAND Corporation, devised the "Delphi technique" as an orderly, planned, methodological procedure in the elicitation and use of expert opinion. The rudiments of the procedure are simple: it involves the successive questioning individually of a large panel of experts in any particular field and the arrival by confrontations at some range, or consensus, of opinion in later rounds. Together with Theodore Gordon, Helmer conducted a long-range forecasting study at RAND to test the efficacy of the method.[56]

In the RAND forecasting study, six broad areas were selected for investigations—scientific breakthroughs, population growth, automation, space progress, probability and prevention of war, and future weapons systems—and a panel of experts was formed for each of the six areas. Professionally there were twenty engineers, seventeen physical scientists, fourteen logicians and mathematicians, twelve economists, nine social scientists, five writers, four operations analysts, and one military officer. In all, about eighty-two experts participated, forty-two of them RAND staff members or consultants.

In the panel on inventions and scientific breakthroughs individuals were asked by letter to list those innovations which appeared urgently needed and realizable in the next fifty years. A total of forty-nine possibilities were named. In the second round, again by letter, the panel was asked to estimate the fifty-fifty probability of the realization of each of the items within a specified time period. From the results, the median year and quartile range for each item was established. (Thus it was predicted that economically useful desalination of sea water would come between 1965 and 1980, with 1970 as the median year, that controlled thermonuclear power would be available between 1978 to 2000, with 1985 as the median year.) In this second round the investigators found a considerable consensus for ten breakthroughs. They selected seventeen of the remaining thirty-nine for further probing. In a third round, the experts were asked to consider the probable time of these seventeen breakthroughs; if the individual opinion fell outside the range established by the middle 50 per cent of the previous responses, the expert was asked to justify his answer. In the fourth round, the range of times was narrowed even further and thirty-one items were included in the final list on which reasonable consensus had been obtained and majority and minority opinions were stated.

Laborious as all this may be, the panel technique was adopted for a double reason: it eliminated or lessened undue influence that would result from face-to-face discussion (e.g., the bandwagon effects of majority opinion, embarrassment in abandoning a publicly expressed opinion, etc.) and it allowed a feedback, through successive rounds, which gave the respondents time to reconsider an opinion and to reassert or establish new probabilities for their choices.

With what "state of confidence" can we accept the method and these predictions? The major difficulty lies not in any single prediction but in the lack of defined contexts. Each prediction is made as a single instance, isolated from the others, though all participants easily recognize that the realization of any one prediction is not only dependent on many others but, even more, is dependent on the state of the nation itself. The implicit premise underlying all these predictions is that the context of the U.S. and the world will not change. But the social systems and the relationships between them are bound to change, and these changes, more than the technical feasibility of any of the individual breakthroughs, will determine the possibility of these breakthroughs being realized. In short, if forecasting is to advance, it has to be within a system context which specifies the major social, political, and economic relationships that will obtain at any given time. In the RAND use of the Delphi technique, what we are given is a set of possibilities, but the way in which these possibilities are combined depends upon the system in which they are embedded. And the art— or science—of forecasting can be extended only when we are able to advance in the creation of models of the social system itself.

Matrices and Contexts. The effort to provide an "orderly way" of looking at possibilities underlies most of the work now going on under the headings of "morphological research" and "relevance trees." In principle these amount to a systematic effort to explore all possible solutions of a large-scale problem. What is novel is the means of ordering and the use of mathematical techniques to assign values to the different parameters of the problem.

The morphological method was developed by Fritz Zwicky, a Swiss astronomer working at Mount Wilson and Mount Palomar observatories while he was engaged in rocket research at the Aerojet Engineering Corporation in California. In 1961, a Society for Morphological Research was formed in Pasadena, California, with Zwicky as its president. As Erich Jantsch comments rather wryly, in his OECD report on technological forecasting, "It appears that Zwicky's stubborn 'campaign' for his method, has somewhat obscured his message. Everybody knows of Zwicky, but very few have acquainted themselves with his method."[57]

The method is concerned with exploring the complete range of the solutions of a given problem. For instance, writes Zwicky in a 1962 monograph on propulsive power, "we may wish to study the morphological character of all modes of motion, or of all possible propulsive power plants, telescopes, pumps, communication, detection devices, etc. . . . It will be found that the task of formulating the initial statement or definition of the problem is far more exacting than most investigators . . . are inclined to think. In fact one is hard put to find in the existing literature satisfactory definitions of even well-known devices like pumps, stationary power plants, telescopes, and so on."[58] In the case of telescopes, some of these parameters are the location, the nature of the aperture, the recording device, the nature of the changes to which the light is subjected to from aperture to recording device, the motion of the telescope, the sequences of operations, etc. Each parameter has a number of independent irreducible values (e.g., motion may be in three directions) and these are placed in matrices in which all possible chains are linked to construct an N-dimension space or a "morphological box." Performance values of all derived solutions become the basis for the determination (on the basis of technical efficiency and cost) of particularly desirable solutions.

In his early work on rocket research and jet engines, a morphological box setting forth the different combinations of eleven classes of variables, each class with its own range of possibilities (e.g., propellants would be the class and gaseous liquid and solid state would be the possibilities; motion the class and translatory, rotatory, and oscillatory as the possibilities) produced a total of 25,344 possible kinds of engines. A previous evaluation, in 1943, on the basis of fewer parameters, derived 576 possibilities which included, however, the then-secret German pulse-jet powered aerial V-1 bomb and V-2 rocket, at a time when Professor Lindemann, Churchill's scientific advisor, failed to recognize the potential of the V-2, even when he was shown photographs, because he rejected the idea of liquid propellants.

As Jantsch has observed, "the full-scale application of [the morphological scheme] as it has been practiced by Zwicky in rocket and jet fuel development, apparently has had considerable success and was decisive in producing an unbiased approach in the early stages." The idea of morphological charts, as Jantsch points out, is used by a number of companies to block out, or even to "block," possible future inventions by trying to patent, in a rather abstract way, combinations of basic parameters. ("For example, one could observe a 'rush' for patents which would fit into hitherto unpatented fields of a coolant/ moderator chart of nuclear reactors.") [59]

The need to relate forecasting to specific objectives at different levels has given rise to the idea of "relevance trees," sometimes called "reliance trees" or simply "decision trees." The concept of a relevance tree was first proposed by Churchman and Ackoff in 1957 [60] and is also an "ordering device," like a company organization chart, for the mapping out of the program elements of a task and relating these to specific objectives. What is novel again is the effort to provide weights and scores to the different functional subsystems to see which patterned combinations provide the best payoffs.

While the "relevance tree" itself is simply a mapping device, the forecasting arises in the effort to deal with the unfolding of problems, and new technologies over a five-, ten-, or fifteen-year sequence. North American Aviation's Autonetics division in Anaheim, California, has a "tree" called SCORE (Select Concrete Objectives for Research Emphasis) to relate objectives five to fifteen years ahead to specific strategies. And the most prominent example of a "decision tree" is that of the Planning-Program-Budgeting System (PPBS) used by the Defense Department. In the Pentagon system the decision-making process begins with broad policies laid down by the Administration. A Joint Strategic Objectives Plan (JSOP) prepared by the Joint Chiefs of Staff relates force requirements to major missions within a five-year time-frame, taking into account long-range points of view and exploratory forecasts. The JSOP goes down to the "subdivision" level of the decision tree and contains formal proposals for changes over the next five-year period. Cost assessments are made of program elements (e.g., a Polaris system), on a five-year basis for development, eight years for operational use. The detailed cost structure is represented on a "Program Element Summary Data" sheet, which is programmed on computers, and the totality of these sheets represents the "Five-Year Force Structure. and Financial Program" which is approved by the Secretary of Defense.

Norbert Wiener once defined a system as "organized complexity." But when one has, as in the NASA Tree, 301 tasks, 195 systems, 786 subsystems, 687 functional elements, the job of keeping track of these, of evaluating performance, of calculating the effect of new technologies in one system on all the others, is quite obviously an awesome one. What these matrices and morphology schemes attempt to do, then, is to provide some charts for these trackings.

Diffusion Times. Paul Samuelson has made the fundamental observation that the output that can be obtained from a given stock of factors "depends on the state of technology" existing at the time.[61] Some knowledge of the direction and spread of technologies therefore is crucial for the survival of any enterprise. But the important point is that technological forecasting rarely predicts, or can predict, specific inventions. Inventions, like political events, are subject to surprise, and often represent an imaginative "breakthrough" by the investigator. No one predicted the transistor by Shockley or the laser by Townes. Most technological forecasts *assume* invention—and this is the crucial point—and then go on to predict the rate of extension through new escalations as in the case of the envelope curves, or the rate of diffusion, as the new invention spreads throughout an industry. Our chief *economic* method of doing technological forecasting is the rate of diffusion.

What is true is that the rate at which technology has diffused through our economy has accelerated somewhat in the past seventy-five years, and this is one of the measures of the popular conception of the increase in the rate of change. A study by Frank Lynn for the President's Commission on Automation reported:

• The average lapsed time between the initial discovery of a new technological innovation and the recognition of its commercial potential decreased from thirty years for technological innovations introduced during the early part of this century (1880–1919), to sixteen years for innovations introduced during the post-World War I period and to nine years for the post-World War II period.

• The time required to translate a basic technical discovery into a commercial product or process decreased from seven to five years during the sixty to seventy years time period investigated.[62]

In effect, the "incubation" time for new products has decreased drastically, principally because of the growth of research and development; although the marketing time, while shorter, has not decreased so substantially. But what does stand out is the conclusion, stated "with reasonable confidence," that "those technological innovations which will have a significant impact on our economy and society during the next five years have already been introduced as commercial products and those technological innovations that will have a significant social and economic impact during the 1970–75 period are now in a readily identifiable state of commercial development." It is on this basis that social and technological planning is possible.

Although that is a general conclusion, innovation and diffusion do vary considerably by sector and industry. In 1961, Edwin Mansfield studied how rapidly the use of twelve innovations spread from enterprise to enterprise in four industries—bituminous coal, iron and steel, brewing, and railroads.[63] From the date of the first successful commercial application, it took twenty years or more for all major firms to install centralized traffic control, car retarders, by-product coke ovens and continuous annealing. Only in the case of the pallet-loading machine, tin container, and continuous mining did it take ten years or less for their installations by all the major firms. In his study Lynn concluded that the rate of diffusion for technological innovations for consumer applications is nearly twice as fast as for those with industrial applications.

These studies have been ex post facto. Some efforts have been made to forecast the rate and direction of diffusion of technology. Everett M. Rogers, in his *Diffusion of Innovations*,[64] uses historical diffusion curves (dollar volume and number of units in use are the measure) plotted against time in order to identify characteristic curve shapes. Mansfield has constructed a simple model[65] built largely around one central idea—that the probability that a firm will introduce a new technique increases with the proportion of firms already using it and the profitability of doing so, but decreases with the size of the investment required. So far, these are all experimental.

With the question of diffusion one passes over from technology to economic and social forecasting, for the spread of a new invention or product clearly depends not only on its technical efficiency, but on its cost, its appeals to consumers, its special costs, by-products, and the like; the introduction of any new inventions thus depends upon the constraints of the economy, the policies of government, and the values and social attitudes of the customers.

Technology, in a sense, is a "game against nature," in which man's effort to wrest the secrets from nature comes up largely against the character of physical laws and man's ingenuity in mapping those hidden paths. But economic and social life is a "game between persons" in which forecasting has to deal with variable strategies, dispositions, and expectations, as individuals seek, either cooperatively or antagonistically, to increase individual advantage.

All of this takes place within social limits—which is the task of the forecaster to define. No large-scale society changes with the flick of a wrist or the twist of a rhetorical phrase. There are the constraints of nature (weather and resources), established customs, habits and institutions, and simply the "recalcitrance" of large numbers. Those who made, for example, sweeping predictions about the radical impact of automation, based on a few spectacular examples, forgot the simple fact that even when a new industry, such as data processing or numerical control, is introduced, the impact of industries with sales mounting quickly even to several billion dollars is small in comparison to an economy which annually will generate $800 billion in goods.

The outer limit of a society is its economic growth rate, and theorists such as Robert M. Solow of MIT (whose development of an economic growth model, now called, with heavy responsibility, the Ricardo-Marx-Solow model, is one of the accomplishments of contemporary economics) have argued, actually, that each economy has its "natural" growth which is compounded of the rate of population increase and the rate of technological progress (the latter being defined as the rate of productivity, the rate of new inventions, the improvement in quality of organization, education, etc.).[66] Because of existing institutional arrangements (patterns of capital mobilization and spending, proportions of income used by consumers, etc.) and the large magnitudes of manpower, resources, and GNP in a society, even the revolutionary introduction of new technologies (such as in agriculture) will not increase the total productivity rate markedly. Some societies have a higher growth rate than others because of a later start and the effort to catch up. For short periods, advanced economies can speed up their growth rate within limits, but a shift in the "production function" to a greater utilization of capital leads later to replacement costs, lower marginal efficiency, and a flattening out of the rise until the "natural" rate again is resumed. According to studies of Edward Denison, for example, the "natural" rate of growth of the U.S. economy, for reasons of institutional arrangements and technology, is about 3 per cent a year.[67] Eventually—in logic, at least, though perhaps not in sociologic—to the extent that technology, as a part of the common fund of knowledge, is available to all societies, the rate of increase of all economies may eventually tend to even out. But within any appreciable frame of time, the limit which frames the forecasts of any economist or sociologist, is the growth rate of an economy—for this determines what is available for social use—and this is the baseline for any social forecasting.

THE STRUCTURE OF THE KNOWLEDGE SOCIETY

The "postindustrial society," it is clear, is a knowledge society in a double sense: first, the sources of innovation are increasingly derivative from research and development (and more directly, there is a new relation between science and technology because of the centrality of *theoretical* knowledge); and second, the "weight" of the society— measured by a larger proportion of Gross National Product and a larger share of employment—is increasingly in the knowledge field.

Fritz Machlup, in his heroic effort to compute the proportion of GNP devoted to the production and distribution of knowledge, estimated that in 1958 about 29 per cent of the existing GNP, or $136,436 million, was spent for knowledge.[68] This total was distributed as shown in Table 3.

The definitions Machlup employs, however, are broad indeed. Education, for example, includes education in the home, on the job, and in the church. Communication media include all commercial printing, stationery, and office supplies. Information machines include musical instruments, signalling devices, and typewriters. Information services include monies spent for securities brokers, real-estate agents, and the like. To that extent, the figure of 29 per cent of GNP, which has been widely quoted, is quite misleading. Especially because of student attacks on Clark Kerr, who used this figure in *The Uses of the University*,[69] the phrases "knowledge industry" and "knowledge factory" have assumed a derogatory connotation. Any meaningful figure about the "knowledge society" would be much smaller. The calculation would have to be restricted largely to research (the development side of R & D has been devoted largely to missiles and space and is disproportionate to the total), to higher education, and to the production of

TABLE 3. DISTRIBUTION OF PROPORTION OF GROSS
NATIONAL PRODUCT SPENT ON KNOWLEDGE, 1958

Type of knowledge and source of expenditures	Amount in millions of dollars	Percentage
Education	60,194	44.1
Research and development	10,990	8.1
Communication media	38,369	28.1
Information machines	8,922	6.5
Information services (incomplete)	17,961	13.2
Total	136,436	100.0
Expenditures made by:		
Government	37,968	27.8
Business	42,198	30.9
Consumers	56,270	41.3
Total	136,436	100.0

SOURCE: Machlup, Fritz, *The Production and Distribution of Knowledge in the United States,* Princeton University Press, Princeton, N.J., 1962, pp. 360–361.

knowledge, as I have defined it, as an "intellectual property," which involves valid new knowledge and its dissemination. Within the purview of this limited essay, it was not possible to compute such a figure. Some more delimited indicators can be seen in the tables provided in the following subsections.

Dimensions of the Knowledge Class

In the Republic of Plato, knowledge was vouchsafed only to one class, the philosophers, while the rest of the city was divided between warriors (guardians) and artisans. In the Scientific City of the future there are already foreshadowed three classes: the creative elite of scientists and the top professional administrator (could one call them the "new clerisy," in Coleridge's term?); the middle class of engineers and the professorate; and the proletariat of technicians, junior faculty, and teaching assistants.

The metaphor can be carried too far, yet there is already an extraordinary differentiation within the knowledge society, and the divisions are not always most fruitfully explored along traditional class lines of hierarchy and dominance, important as these may be. There are other sociological differences as well. In the social structure of the knowledge society, there is, for example, the deep and growing split between the technical intelligentsia who are committed to functional rationality and technocratic modes of operation, and the literary intellectuals who have become increasingly apocalyptic, hedonistic, nihilistic, and the like. There are divisions between professional administrators and technical specialists, which sometimes result in dual structures of authority, for example, in hospitals and research laboratories. In the universities, there are divisions between deans and faculty, and in the faculty between research and teaching. In the world of art there are complex relations between museum directors, curators, magazines, critics, dealers, patrons, and artists. The performing arts have different striations. Any further exploration of the knowledge class would have to explore in detail these varying patterns of stratification and differentiation.

Conventionally, in social structure analysis, we begin with population. The gross figures are startling indeed. If one assumes, as does Abraham Moles, that by 1972, 5 per cent of the population of the "advanced" countries and 3 per cent of the total world population will be involved in intellectual work, then the global population of the Scientific City of tomorrow itself would number a hundred million persons![70]

World comparisons are difficult, and the figure just cited was intended to indicate the change in scale which the growth of an intellectual class has produced. Because we have no figures for the past, such comparisons are difficult. One of our tasks, however, is to provide baselines for the future; and here we shall restrict ourselves to U.S. data, and to the census categories which allow us to make some comparisons over time and some projections for the future.

The chief census category with which we are concerned is that of "professional and technical persons." Between 1947 (the baseline after World War II) and 1964, the employment of professional and technical workers in the U.S. more than doubled, rising from about 3.8 million to over 8.5 million workers. By 1975, manpower requirements for this occupational group are expected to rise by more than half, to 13.2 million persons. If one assumes a total labor force at that time of 88.7 million, then the professional and technical group would make up 14.9 per cent of the working population. If one adds in, as well, an estimated 9.2 million managers, officials, and proprietors, then the total group would make up 25.3 per cent of the working population. In effect, one out of every four persons would have had about four years of college—the educational average for the group —and this 25.3 per cent would comprise the educated class of the country.[71]

Of the professional class, teachers make up the single largest group. Employment of public and private school teachers combined increased from about 1.3 million in the 1954–1955 school year to about 2.1 million in 1964–1965. Thus teachers comprised about 25 per cent of all persons classified as professional and technical by the census. In the 1964–1965 academic year, more than half of all teachers were employed in elementary schools, more than a third in secondary schools, and about 10 per cent in colleges and universities. The number of teachers is expected to rise by almost a third during the 1965–1975 decade, reaching almost 2.7 million in the 1974–1975 school year, but given the more rapid rise of other professional and technical groups, the proportion of teachers in this class will fall to about 20 per cent.

Engineering is the second largest professional occupation, exceeded in size only by teaching, though for men it is the largest profession. Employment of engineers increased by more than 80 per cent between 1950 and 1964, rising from an estimated 535,000 to about 975,000, the chief reason being the expansion in this period of the science-based industries such as electronics, space, missiles, scientific instruments, nuclear energy, and computer technology, and the longer time required to develop and produce products because of the increasing complexity of the production processes. About half of all engineers work in manufacturing, another quarter in construction, public utilities, and engineering services. A high number of engineers, about 140,000, are employed by government, half of these by the federal government. Educational institutions employ about 30,000 engineers in research and teaching. The number of engineers is expected to rise by more than 50 per cent between 1964 and 1975, to about 1.5 million; this group would then comprise more than 11 per cent of the total professional and technical class.

Allied to the engineer is the engineering and science technician (excluding draftsmen and surveyors), whose numbers grew from 450,000 in 1960 to 620,000 in mid-1964, making up about 7 per cent of all professional and technical workers. The number of engineering and science technicians is expected to rise by about two-thirds by 1975, bringing the total to more than a million.

The most crucial group, of course, in the knowledge society is scientists, and here the growth rate has been the most marked of all the professional groups. The number of engineers, for example, rose from 217,000 in 1930 to almost a million in 1964; in the same period, the number of scientists increased from 46,000 to 475,000. To put this growth in another context, whereas between 1930 and 1965 the work force increased by about 50 per cent, the number of engineers increased by 370 per cent and that of scientists by 930 per cent. While estimates for 1975 have been difficult to make, a forecast by a team of OECD experts indicates a still rapid increase in the scientific population, strictly defined, for 1970[72] (see Figure 3 and Table 4).

TABLE 4.   FORECASTS OF SKILLED POPULATION AND SCIENTIFIC PERSONNEL

	1963	1970	1975
Population of the United States (in millions)	190	209	227
Work force (millions)	76	86	
Civil employment (millions)	70.3 (1964)		88.7
White collar workers	31.12 (1964)		42.8
(as percentage of civil employment)	(44.2%)		(48%)
Professional and technical	8.5 (1964)		13.2
(as percentage of civil employment)	(12.2%)		14.9
Scientific population (millions)	2.7	4	
(as percentage of active population)	(3.6%)	(4.7%)	
Scientists in the strict sense	0.5 ⎫ 1.43	0.74 ⎫ 2.14	
Engineers	0.93 ⎭	1.4 ⎭	
Technicians	1	1.6	
Science teachers in secondary schools	0.25	0.3	
Doctorate degrees (in thousands)	106	170	
In science	96	153	
In engineering	10	17	

SOURCE: *Reviews of National Science Policy: United States,* Organisation for Economic Co-operation and Development, Paris, 1968, p. 45.

All this growth goes hand in hand with a democratization of higher education on a scale that the world has never seen. No society has ever attempted to provide formal education for the bulk of its youth through age nineteen or twenty (the junior college level) or through age twenty-two, yet this has now become the explicit policy of the United States. Just as in the 1920's a decision was made to provide a secondary school education for every child in the country so, too, in the past two decades, the decision has been made to provide a college education, or at least some years in college, for all capable youths in the country. At first this decision was made spontaneously through education for veterans, and then it spread through the vari-

FIGURE 3.   TREND OF THE POPULATION STRUCTURE,
1930–1975

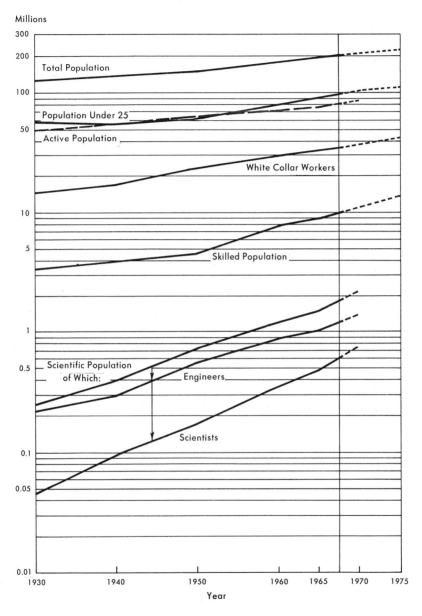

SOURCE: Organisation for Economic Co-operation and Development, *Reviews
of National Science Policy: United States,* Paris, 1968, p. 43.

ous state systems as it became apparent that the new science-based industries would require more technically trained personnel. The change can be seen most graphically in Table 5 showing the consistent rise in the proportion of the population aged eighteen to twenty-one attending college.

TABLE 5.   TOTAL STUDENT BODY AND CORRESPONDING AGE GROUPS 1946–1964

Year	Population 18 to 21	Enrollments	Percentage of enrollments to population
1946	9,403,000	2,078,095	22.1
1947	9,276,000	2,388,226	25.2
1948	9,144,000	2,403,396	26.3
1949	8,990,000	2,444,900	27.2
1950	8,945,000	2,281,298	25.5
1951	8,742,000	2,101,962	24.0
1952	8,542,000	2,134,242	25.0
1953	8,441,000	2,231,054	26.4
1954	8,437,000	2,446,693	29.0
1955	8,508,000	2,653,034	31.2
1956	8,701,000	2,918,212	33.5
1957	8,844,000	3,036,938	34.3
1958	8,959,000	3,226,038	36.0
1959	9,182,000	3,364,861	36.6
1960	9,546,000	3,582,726	37.5
1961	10,246,000	3,860,643	37.7
1962	10,745,000	4,174,936	38.9
1963	11,129,000	4,494,626	40.4
1964	11,286,000	4,950,173	43.9

SOURCE: OECD, *Reviews of National Science Policy: United States,* p. 494.

The OECD survey indicates that the United States has the world's highest percentage of enrollments in this age group, 43.9 per cent for 1964. The table also shows a more rapid growth rate in the second decade than in the first. Total enrollments increased by 145 per cent in the eighteen-year period 1946–1964 and by 104 per cent during the last ten years of the period.

Another statistical series, used by the OECD reporting team, provides a more useful definition than simple enrollment. A series measuring the growth of resident students in degree courses allows the growth in the number of students to be measured over a longer period, from 1869 to the present. Table 6 illustrates the different stages in university expansion.

Since 1879, the U.S. university population has doubled every twenty years. But compared with the corresponding age group, a very fast growth became apparent after World War II and was even more accentuated during the 1950's. This evolution reflects not only the growth in college enrollments, but also the growth of graduates as well, their number doubling since 1950, whereas the number of undergraduates increased by 50 per cent over the same period. Thus, not only is the total number of enrollments growing, but that of the more advanced students is increasing disproportionately.

TABLE 6.   STUDENT POPULATION STUDYING FOR
DEGREES AND CORRESPONDING AGE GROUPS, 1869–1963

Academic year	Student population			In percentage of the population	
	Total	Under-graduate	Graduate	18–21 years	18–24 years
1869–70	52,286	—	—	1.68	1.14
1879–80	115,817	—	—	2.72	1.63
1889–90	156,756	154,374	2,382	3.04	1.78
1899–1900	237,592	231,761	5,831	4.01	2.29
1909–10	355,213	346,060	9,153	5.12	2.89
1919–20	597,880	582,268	15,612	8.09	4.66
1929–30	1,100,737	1,053,482	47,255	12.42	7.20
1939–40	1,494,203	1,388,455	105,748	15.59	9.08
1949–50	2,659,021	2,421,813	237,208	29.58	16.50
1959–60	3,215,544	2,873,724	341,820	34.86	20.49
Intake 1963	4,234,092	3,755,515	478,577	38.05	23.33

SOURCE: OECD, *Reviews of National Science Policy: United States*, p. 52.

The number of degrees has increased in proportion to the number of students, as shown in Table 7. Since 1947, the number of doctorates has tripled, the number of Masters degrees or the equivalent has been multiplied by 2.4, and the number of Bachelor degrees or the equivalent by 1.8.

If one breaks down the degrees by level and discipline, a startling result is disclosed (Table 8). Both in 1954 and 1964 about 72 to 73 per cent of the Bachelor degrees were taken in the social sciences and the humanities, and only 26 to 28 per cent in the natural sciences and mathematics. Yet, for doctorates, the figures are reversed sharply. In both periods, almost 50 per cent of the doctorates were in the natural sciences and mathematics. This figure itself reflects two main factors: first, the average time in achieving a doctorate in the sciences is

TABLE 7. EARNED DEGREES CONFERRED BY
INSTITUTIONS OF HIGHER EDUCATION,
1869–1870 TO 1963–1964

| | Earned degrees conferred | | | |
Year	All degrees	Baccalaureates and first professional	Master's except first professional	Doctorates
1869–70	9,372	9,371	0	1
1879–80	13,829	12,896	879	54
1889–90	16,703	15,539	1,015	149
1899–1900	29,375	27,410	1,583	382
1909–10	39,755	37,199	2,113	443
1919–20	53,516	48,622	4,279	615
1929–30	139,752	122,484	14,969	2,299
1939–40	216,521	186,500	26,731	3,290
1941–42	213,491	185,346	24,648	3,497
1943–44	141,582	125,863	13,414	2,305
1945–46	157,349	136,174	19,209	1,966
1947–48	317,607	271,019	42,400	4,188
1949–50	496,661	432,058	58,183	6,420
1951–52	401,203	329,986	63,534	7,683
1953–54	356,608	290,825	56,788	8,995
1955–56	376,973	308,812	59,258	8,903
1957–58	436,979	362,554	65,487	8,938
1959–60	476,704	392,440	74,435	9,829
1961–62	514,323	417,846	84,855	11,622
1963–64	614,194	498,654	101,050	14,490

NOTE: Beginning in 1959–60, includes Alaska and Hawaii.
SOURCE: OECD, *Reviews of National Science Policy: United States,* p. 54.

considerably shorter than in the social sciences and humanities; and second, the employment opportunities in the sciences are more sharply defined by the possession of a doctorate than in the other fields.

Distribution of Scientific Personnel

The chief resource of the postindustrial society is its scientific personnel. Their distribution, by sector (industry, government, university) and by function (production, research, teaching) forms the start of any coherent science policy on the use of scarce resources in the society.[73] The definitions of such personnel are complicated, particularly in the case of engineers. Many persons are classified as engineers, especially in industry, who have not received formal training or possess a degree from a college; on the other hand, because of their training, many engineers are engaged in managerial activities outside their original specialization. The restrictions are less true of scientists,

TABLE 8. DISTRIBUTION OF DEGREES BY DISCIPLINE, 1954–1964

Disciplines	1954			1964		
	Bachelor and equiva-lent	Master and equiva-lent	Doctor and equiva-lent	Bachelor and equiva-lent	Master and equiva-lent	Doctor and equiva-lent
	(percentages)					
Natural and mathematical sciences as percentage of whole	28.0	21.7	48.1	26.1	27.3	49.7
Mathematics	1.4	1.3	2.8	4.0	3.9	4.2
Engineering	7.9	7.7	6.8	6.9	11.0	12.3
Physics	3.7	4.4	19.4	3.5	4.5	16.9
Biology	3.2	2.8	11.2	4.6	3.3	11.1
Health	8.2	3.0	2.1	5.2	2.3	1.3
Social sciences and humanities	72.0	78.3	51.9	73.9	72.7	50.3
Social sciences	12.1	7.1	12.1	15.7	9.5	12.3
Education	18.6	47.5	16.6	18.0	37.6	14.8
Total number	287,401	58,204	8,840	529,000	111,000	15,300

SOURCE: OECD, *Reviews of National Science Policy: United States*, p. 56.

though some number in recent years have turned to administration and educational innovation. In general, scientific personnel are defined as persons engaging in any scientific work requiring knowledge or training equivalent to at least four years in college and specializing in one of the scientific disciplines. A similar definition applies to engineers.

We draw our first classification from the census. For 1960, the census of skilled personnel showed that there were 335,000 scientists and 822,000 engineers.

We can show three basic classifications: by *discipline,* by *sector,* and by *function,* and, following this, by specialty and function in *industry,* in *universities,* and in *government.*

Figure 4 shows the distribution of engineers and scientists by discipline. It is striking that while the distribution of engineers is fairly even throughout the four major components of engineering (industrial, civil, electrical, and mechanical), the greater proportion of scientists are concentrated in two fields—the biological sciences and chemistry.

Table 9 shows the distribution of engineers and scientists by sector.

FIGURE 4. DISTRIBUTION OF SCIENTISTS AND ENGINEERS IN 1960

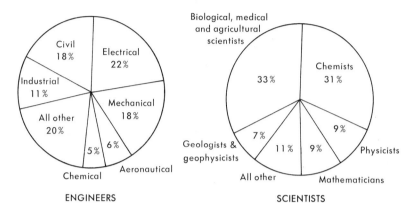

ENGINEERS   SCIENTISTS

SOURCE: OECD, *Reviews of National Science Policy: United States*, p. 207.

The bulk of engineers are still located primarily in manufacturing and secondarily in government; and while the single largest group of scientists are located in manufacturing, the universities and government combined employ the greater number.

TABLE 9. DISTRIBUTION OF SCIENTISTS AND ENGINEERS BY SECTOR, 1960

Sector	Scientists and engineers	Engineers	Scientists
Total	*1,157,300*	*822,000*	*335,300*
Mining	31,600	19,100	12,400
Building and public works	55,100	52,700	2,400
Manufacturing industries	613,500	472,800	140,700
Transport, communications, and other services	61,500	58,800	2,800
Other industries	100,400	82,100	18,200
Government (federal, state, and local)	170,100	109,400	60,700
Colleges and universities	125,100	27,000	98,100

SOURCE: OECD, *Reviews of National Science Policy: United States*, p. 208.

To illustrate the importance of the science-based industries, note the proportion of scientists and engineers to the total employment in each field. For 1962, the percentages were as follows:

Manufacturing	3.0%
All chemicals	10.2%
Pharmaceuticals	16.9%
Electrical engineering	7.8%
Communications	12.3%
Aviation	12.4%
Scientific instruments	17.7%

The crucial question, of course, is what use is made of scientific personnel in each sector. The question of how many scientists, for example, are engaged in basic research compared to applied research (assuming one can draw these lines) can only be answered for smaller, more detailed samples. On the gross census level, we can deal with three main functions: production, research and development, and management and administration. All other functions, including teaching, are grouped as miscellaneous (Table 10).

TABLE 10. DISTRIBUTION OF SCIENTISTS AND ENGINEERS BY FUNCTION, 1960

Personnel	Production	Research and development	Management and administration	Miscellaneous
	(percentages)			
All scientists and engineers	35	34	7	24
Scientists	24	42	4	30
Engineers	41	30	8	21

Source: OECD, *Reviews of National Policy: United States,* p. 210.

A further classification of function is necessary by industry, university, and government to see the existing use of scientists and engineers.

Table 11 shows the distribution specialty and function of scientists and engineers employed in industry. Thirty per cent of the total in industry are engaged in research and development. But 72.1 per cent of the physicists and almost half of the mathematicians and biologists are engaged in research. Yet the number of scientists doing work other than research is far from negligible. By the same token, half the mathematicians and half the chemists in industry are doing something far different from research.

Table 12 on universities uses a different set of figures. The data here are for 1965 and show that in that year higher education as a whole employed 261,000 scientists and engineers or more than twice

TABLE 11. PROPORTIONS OF SCIENTISTS AND ENGINEERS EMPLOYED IN INDUSTRY BY SPECIALTY AND PRINCIPAL FUNCTION, 1962

Employment	Scientists and engineers	Research and development	Management and administration		Technical commerce, sales and maintenance services	Production and operation	Other functions
			R. & D.	Other			
Total	*100*	*30.1*	*5.5*	*12.6*	*10.9*	*34.3*	*6.5*
Engineers	100	27.2	5.1	13.6	10.9	36.9	6.3
Physical sciences	100	44.9	7.6	8.4	8.0	24.6	6.5
Chemists	100	47.4	8.3	7.1	9.5	24.6	3.0
Physicists	100	72.1	12.6	2.8	3.0	7.0	2.4
Metallurgists	100	33.7	6.8	13.7	6.3	37.3	2.3
Geologists and geophysicists	100	6.8	2.3	16.3	2.8	38.1	33.6
Mathematicians	100	48.4	4.6	8.8	10.3	19.0	9.0
Life sciences	100	29.7	5.4	10.9	24.3	19.1	10.5
Medicine	100	17.8	5.0	9.0	44.2	7.8	16.1
Agriculture	100	18.7	5.3	20.0	13.3	27.3	15.4
Biology	100	48.0	5.9	4.7	18.5	20.7	2.2
Other scientists	100	33.4	13.6	10.6	9.3	12.1	21.0

SOURCE: OECD, *Reviews of National Science Policy: United States*, p. 211.

TABLE 12. NUMBER OF SCIENTISTS AND ENGINEERS, BY
EMPLOYMENT STATUS AND BY FIELD AND FULL-TIME
EQUIVALENT NUMBER OF SCIENTISTS AND ENGINEERS,
BY FUNCTION, IN UNIVERSITIES AND COLLEGES, 1965

| Item | Total | Universities and colleges proper | | | Federal contract research centers attached to universities |
		Graduate-degree granting institutions in the sciences and engineering Number	Other institutions	
		(thousands)			
Scientists and engineers, total	261.0	250.0	210.3	39.8	11.0
Employment status					
Full-time	158.9	148.8	118.1	30.6	10.1
Part-time	41.0	40.8	31.9	8.9	.2
Graduate students	61.1	60.4	60.2	.2	.7
Field					
Engineers	37.4	32.4	28.2	4.1	5.1
Physical scientists	67.6	62.4	49.6	12.7	5.2
Life scientists	101.2	100.7	93.6	7.1	.5
Psychologists	12.8	12.7	9.3	3.4	.1
Social scientists	40.8	40.7	29.0	11.7	.1
Other scientists	1.1	1.1	.5	.6	a
Full-time equivalent number of scientists and engineers, total	203.2	192.6	158.5	34.1	10.6
Function					
Teaching	117.7	117.7	85.1	32.6	a
Research and development	65.4	54.9	54.3	.6	10.5
Other activities	20.0	19.9	19.1	.9	.1

a Less than 50.

SOURCE: OECD, *Reviews of National Science Policy: United States*, p. 510.

the number in 1960 (see Table 9). The figures differ in part because
of different counting techniques, that is, the 1960 figure was staff,
while the 1965 figure included all persons employed at research centers
in universities. Despite these differences, the figures reflect the sharp
increase in half a decade in the numbers of scientists and engineers
at universities. In 1965, in full-time equivalent, 61 per cent of the
personnel were engaged in teaching, 29 per cent in research and

development, and 10 per cent in other activities (administration, etc.) Nearly all the personnel in the federal contract research centers attached to universities were doing research work, while only 29 per cent of the 192,600 scientists and engineers who make up the university full-time personnel performed research as their major activity.

Finally we turn to the distribution of scientists and engineers employed in government. In 1962, approximately 144,000 scientists and engineers were employed by the government in federal laboratories or in administrative functions, representing 8 per cent of federal employees. The Department of Defense employed the largest proportion of qualified persons, followed, surprisingly, by the Department of Agriculture. It is highly likely that later figures would show a considerable increase in the Department of Health, Education, and Welfare, reflecting the expansion of research in medicine and the life sciences in the past decade. In addition to direct government employment, one must count as well a total of 17,884 scientists and engineers employed (in 1965) in nonprofit organizations.

These data were drawn primarily from the census, and in a few instances from some special samples. In 1968, the National Science Foundation released the results of its full enumeration of the 242,763 persons listed in the National Register of Scientific and Technical Personnel (NRSTP). As the title of the report indicates, this *is* America's Science Manpower. This group forms the "upper class" in the "Scientific City" of the day.

In terms of general characteristics of scientists, the single largest group are chemists (27 per cent) followed by physicists (12 per cent) and biological scientists (12 per cent). The physical sciences, as a group, account for almost half (47 per cent) of all scientists on the roster. The life sciences account for 16 per cent, the social sciences 15 per cent, and mathematics and statistics 10 per cent.

Only 37 per cent of the group have a Ph.D. An additional 27 per cent have a Master's degree, and 30 per cent have a Bachelor's degree. These proportions can be expected to change over time.

In the area of primary work activity, 31 per cent are engaged in research and development, 20 per cent in management and administration, and only 18 per cent in teaching.

If one looks at the smaller group of Ph.D. holders (Table 13), some further refinements can be observed. Thus, the social sciences have a higher proportion of Ph.D. holders to total registrants than do the physical and natural sciences. For example, 90 per cent of the anthropologists in the register have Ph.D.s, compared to 24 per cent,

TABLE 13. PERCENTAGE OF PH.D. DEGREE HOLDERS TO
TOTAL NRSTP REGISTRANTS, BY FIELD, 1966

Field	Total registrants	Ph.D. degree holder		
		Number	Percentage of total	Percentage
All fields	*242,763*	*90,304*	*37*	*100*
Chemistry	65,917	23,915	36	26
Earth sciences	19,749	4,330	22	5
Meteorology	6,283	668	11	1
Physics	29,130	11,850	41	13
Mathematics	22,806	5,485	24	6
Agricultural sciences	10,038	2,310	23	2
Biological sciences	29,633	15,218	51	17
Psychology	19,027	12,545	66	14
Statistics	3,042	919	30	1
Economics	13,150	5,593	42	6
Sociology	3,640	2,757	76	3
Anthropology	919	830	90	1
Linguistics	1,269	750	59	1
Other fields	18,160	3,134	17	3

SOURCE: *American Science Manpower, 1966,* A Report of the National Register of Scientific and Technical Personnel, National Science Foundation, NSF 68–7, Washington, 1968, p. 25.

say, of the mathematicians or even 42 per cent of the economists. This difference reflects the fact that where employment opportunities are primarily in universities, the greater is the percentage of persons in those fields who hold a Ph.D. One-half (52 per cent) of the doctorate scientists were in the physical and mathematical sciences, one-third were in the life sciences, and 11 per cent were in the social sciences.

In terms of the type of employer (Table 14), more than half (55 per cent) of the "upper class," the doctorate holders, were employed by educational institutions, and only 23 per cent were employed by industry and business, a sharp contrast to the general occupational pattern of the "Scientific City" as a whole.

In terms of primary work activity of the "upper class" (Table 15), one-half (51 per cent) of the doctorate holders were engaged primarily in some phase of research and development (compared to one-third of the "Scientific City"); and 28 per cent of the doctorate holders reported teaching as their primary work activity.

In summary, the major conclusion is that the "elite" of the educated were concentrated primarily in the universities rather than business or government, and that the majority is engaged primarily in research.

TABLE 14.   PERCENTAGE OF PH.D. DEGREE HOLDERS TO
TOTAL NRSTP REGISTRANTS, BY TYPE OF EMPLOYER, 1966

| | | Ph.D. degree holder | | |
Type of employer	Total registrants	Number	Percentage of total registrants	Percentage of Ph.Ds
All registrants	242,763	90,304	37	100
Educational institutions	87,315	49,792	57	55
Federal government	24,689	7,294	30	8
Other government	8,268	2,193	26	2
Military	5,891	751	13	1
Nonprofit organizations	9,813	4,498	46	5
Industry and business	83,990	20,830	25	23
Self-employed	4,914	1,489	30	2
Other	1,309	478	36	—
No report	1,791	551	31	1

SOURCE: *American Science Manpower*, p. 26.

TABLE 15.   PERCENTAGE OF PH.D. DEGREE HOLDERS TO
TOTAL NRSTP REGISTRANTS, BY PRIMARY WORK
ACTIVITY, 1966

| | Ph.D. degree holder | |
Primary work activity	Number	Percentage
All activities	90,304	100
Research and development	35,606	39
Basic research	(22,956)	(25)
Applied research	(11,313)	(12)
Management or administration	17,075	19
Management or administration of research and development	(11,147)	(12)
Teaching	25,520	28
Production and inspection	790	1
Other	5,780	6
No report	3,105	3

SOURCE: *American Science Manpower*, p. 26.

Forecasting Future College Enrollments

The major problem for the postindustrial society will be the adequacy of numbers of trained persons of professional and technical calibre. We assume, and this is unique in human history, a continuing demand into the foreseeable future. The expansion of the science-based industries will require more engineers, chemists, and mathematicians. The needs for social planning—in education, medicine, and urban affairs—will require large numbers of persons trained in the social and biological sciences. As the 1966 *Manpower Report* says:

> Growth in research and development . . . can be expected to demand ever-rising number of experts in many professional and technical disciplines. In addition, greater number of city planners, engineers, and architects will be needed to rebuild and redesign blighted areas of many of our major metropolitan centers. Talents of a wide range of social scientists will be used to redeem human resources in these cities. Many more teachers will be needed. Among other occupations due for major increases are those involving personnel necessary to implement the new medicare program and other programs developed by Federal, State and local government agencies to improve the health of the Nation's citizens.[74]

The question is one of supply. Short-range forecasts are fairly simple. The college graduates of 1972 are already in high schools and one can make rough estimates of the proportion of college-age population who will go on to higher education—though the projections in the past have been notoriously faulty and low. On the basis of estimates by the U.S. Office of Education, the picture for 1974 is shown in Table 16.

TABLE 16.   EDUCATION IN 1974 AND GROWTH RATE, 1964–1974

	1964	1974	Growth rate 1964–1974 in percentage
School population (in millions)	48.1	54.6	13.5
Enrolment in higher education (in millions)	5.0	8.7	74.0
Higher education degrees	655,300	1,148,000	74.0
Baccalaureates and the like	529,000	906,000	72.0
Masters and the like	111,000	210,400	90.0
Doctorates and the like	15,300	31,900	108.0
Science	49.7%	54.0%	—
Social sciences and humanities	50.3%	46.0%	—
University staff	420,000	695,000	65.0
Total education expenditure (in billions of constant 1963–64 dollars)	38.0	60.9	60.0
Total expenditure on higher education (in billions of constant 1963–64 dollars)	11.9	22.5	94.5
Current expenditure per student (in constant 1963–64 dollars)	2,148.0	2,648.0	23.8

SOURCE: OECD, *Reviews of National Science Policy: United States*, p. 58; derived from Department of Health, Education and Welfare, *Projections of Educational Statistics to 1974–1975*, Washington, 1965.

These projections indicate, according to John K. Folger, that "the expanded number of college graduates anticipated in the next decade will be sufficient to maintain the rise in the educational level of each occupation, to replace workers leaving the labor force, and, among women, to provide a modest surplus for further accelerating the rising educational levels of the white collar occupations."[75]

It is estimated that for the period from 1965 to 1970, about 1,650,-000 men will graduate from college, about in balance with estimated requirements for additions and replacements of graduates during the five-year period. For the 1970-to-1975 period, the number of male graduates—2,200,000—will exceed projected requirements by about 200,000 to 250,000 persons.

What is the meaning of the term "more adequate supply"? As Folger concludes, optimistically, "It simply means that there will be more graduates than required to continue the 1940–1960 rate of improvement in the educational level of occupations. Almost none of these graduates is likely to be unemployed, even if the growth of the labor force falls short of the projected figures in the *Manpower Report of the President*. The projections do suggest that educated manpower shortages are not likely to impede the growth of the economy unless the latter grows faster than 4 percent a year."[76]

What of the future beyond 1975? Between 1960 and 1980, the college-age population (18 to 21) will have increased by about 7 million; by the turn of the century it is likely to climb by another 7 million.[77] The crucial question is what proportion of this group will go on to college. Allan M. Cartter and Robert Farrell have made some estimates on higher education to the last third of the century.[78] Table 17 summarizes the historical relationship between the eighteen to twenty-one age group and undergraduate enrollment. The pattern of college attendance has changed markedly in the first two-thirds of the century, for the attendance ratio has risen steadily from about .04 to .40 with only a minor break during war years. (In view of the age dispersion of college students noted in footnote 77, these figures are expressed as attendance *ratios* rather than as percentages of the age group.) The lower half of the table projects five attendance ratios to the year 2000.

Applying various attendance rates to the population projections, Cartter and Farrell give a variety of estimates for future undergraduate enrollments (Table 18).

These are baselines and can be employed as rough indicators, but as Alice Rivlin has remarked: "It does not seem likely that anything

TABLE 17. HISTORICAL AND PROJECTED RELATIONSHIPS OF UNDERGRADUATES TO THE 18–21 AGE GROUP

Year	18–21 Age group (millions)	Ratio of undergraduates to 18–21 age group
1889	5,160	.030
1899	5,931	.039
1909	7,202	.048
1919	7,312	.080
1929	8,901	.118
1935	9,236	.122
1945	9,558	.163
1955	8,508	.276
1960	9,546	.345
1964	11,282	.400

		Projections				
		S_1	S_2	S_3	S_4	S_5
1965	12,282	.400	.416	.387	.412	.416
1970	14,278	.400	.459	.433	.468	.459
1975	16,107	.400	.483	.475	.519	.507
1980	16,790	.400	.483	.527	.566	.560
1985	16,957	.400	.483	.552	.607	.618
1990	18,880	.400	.483	.552	.645	.682
1995	21,570	.400	.483	.552	.679	.753
2000	23,730	.400	.483	.552	.710	.832

NOTE: S_1 assumes a constant ratio at the 1964 level—an unlikely state of affairs, and one already disproved by the early reports of 1965 enrollments. S_2 assumes that the ratio will increase at a constant rate of 2 per cent per year through 1970, then increase at a rate of 1 per cent through 1975, and finally level off at its 1975 level. S_3 is based on Office of Education projections through 1975, then assumes a decline in the rate of increase until a constant ratio is achieved in 1985. S_4 is hyperbolic in form, rising at a constantly declining rate. S_5 assumes a constant 2 per cent per year increase in the attendance ratio after 1965 (a condition which would provide a statistically possible, but improbable, ratio of more than 1.0 by the year 2010).

SOURCE: Cartter, Allan M., and Robert Farrell, "Higher Education in the Last Third of the Century," *The Educational Record,* Spring, 1965, p. 121.

Derived from: Column 1: Historical data from the Bureau of the Census, Projections through 1980 appear in the Bureau of the Census, *Current Population Reports,* Series P-25, No. 286, July 1964 (Series B data). After 1980, data were supplied to the American Council on Education by the Bureau of the Census. Data are as of July of the year indicated.

Column 2: Ratios for 1889–1955 are based on resident degree-credit series presented in U.S. Office of Education, *Biennial Survey of Education, 1957–58,* chap. 4, sec. 1, p. 7. Ratios for 1960 and 1964 are derived from U.S. Office of Education *Opening Fall Enrollment* series and *Enrollment for Advanced Degrees.*

TABLE 18. UNDERGRADUATE DEGREE-CREDIT
ENROLLMENT, FALL 1960 AND PROJECTED
THROUGH FALL 2000

Year	Series 1	Series 2	Series 3	Series 4	Series 5
	(thousands)				
1960	3,296	3,296	3,296	3,296	3,296
1965	4,829	5,021	4,675	4,973	5,021
1970	5,711	6,556	6,182	6,688	6,556
1975	6,443	7,773	7,655	8,366	8,166
1980	6,716	8,103	8,843	9,495	9,397
1985	6,783	8,183	9,367	10,296	10,478
1990	7,552	9,111	10,429	12,176	12,881
1995	8,628	10,410	11,915	14,648	16,249
2000	9,492	11,452	13,108	16,648	19,739

NOTE: Series 1 merely illustrates the effect of the growth in the size of the college-age population, indicating that undergraduate enrollments would grow from 3.3 million in 1960 to approximately 9.5 million by the end of the century even if there were no further change in attendance rates. Series 2 is a conservative estimate, rising to 11.4 millions. The authors hazard the guess that Series 3 and 4 are the more likely indicators of the magnitude of the impending expansion, with undergraduate enrollments rising to 10 million by the late 1980's, and to between 13 and 16 million by the year 2000. Series 5 is probably the outside limit for periods ten or more years ahead.

SOURCE: See Cartter and Farrell, "Higher Education in the Last Third of the Century," p. 122.

useful can be accomplished by fitting more trend curves to the same basic data on enrollment ratios. . . . It is time to begin looking at college enrollment as a dependent variable."[79]

The chief problem, in the past, has been that all projections vastly underestimated the proportion of high school youths who would go on to college, and planning was woefully inadequate. There was no "theory" about who would go to college; there was little expectation that the various states would respond so quickly to the postwar situation and expand the educational plant so rapidly.

If one is to look ahead at the year 2000 and consider the question of whether the supply of educated persons will continue to match the demand, the central fact is that the college population, by and large, is still drawn principally from the middle class. As Martin Trow has remarked: "With all of the expansion of educational opportunities in the United States, there is still a very sizeable body of students who have the ability for college work but never get there. In [a study of the California state system, it was found] that nearly half (47 per cent) of the high school graduates in the top 20 per cent of academic ability whose fathers were manual workers did not go on to college (though some of them may after a period of working or in military service). This compares with 25 per cent of the students in the same ability brackets from middle class homes who did not go on to college."[80]

If there is going to be a continuing expansion of the proportion of high school graduates going on to college, it is clear that in the succeeding decades a larger number will have to be drawn from working-class families. But why do not the children of working-class homes go on to college? The usual assumption has been that the failure is due largely to discriminatory barriers—that working-class children could not afford to go to college, were needed as early wage earners to contribute to the family, and so on. More recently, however, some sociologists have raised the question whether working-class children really want to go on to higher education. As John Porter has posed the issue:

> One of the recurring questions is whether or not mobility values are part of a common values system for the whole society, or whether they are middle-class subcultural values. . . . In the light of the evidence that levels of aspiration and attitudes to education vary so much by class one wonders how it could ever be claimed that, as part of the common value system, all Americans are achievement-oriented or share in a great quest for opportunity. . . . The notion of common values about mobility has serious implications when social policies assume—something like the old instinct theory—that by providing certain opportunities where they did not previously exist, latent mobility aspirations and achievement motives will be triggered and the previously deprived will be brought into the main stream of an upwardly mobile and achievement-oriented society.[81]

Porter is dubious about the proposition and argues that the new stage of major industrial societies (which he calls "postmodern") may find itself facing a shortage of highly trained manpower in consequence of these differences in values. The question is a relevant one and is not resolvable by opinion. If some of the data cited by Trow, however, is relevant, then it seems likely that going to college or not going to college is not the issue for working-class children, but *what kind of college* to go to. A study carried out both in the Midwest and in California on the effect of the availability of public institutions on the proportions of students from working-class families compared to other class groups who attended college showed that while students from professional and other white-collar backgrounds are much more likely to go to college out of town than working-class students, the students from working and lower middle-class homes are about as likely to go to a local public junior college as are boys and girls from wealthier homes.

As Trow reports: "Where there is a local public junior college in the community, half of the boys from lower-class backgrounds went on to college, as compared with only 15% of boys from similar backgrounds living in communities with no local college. The presence of a four year state college (usually somewhat more selective, somewhat less vocational than the junior college) in the community raised college going rates to nearly a third."[82]

If the data cited by Trow can be generalized for the society as a whole, the "gross" problem of vertical upward mobility, and the supply of trained technical manpower, may be negotiated. The differential patterns of attendance do raise, of course, the troublesome question of whether the educational system, divided as it is into a bifurcated "elite" and "mass" pattern, may not itself reinforce the class divisions within the structure of the "Scientific City" itself.

Institutional Structure

The most striking fact about the intellectual institutions of the society—largely the educational system and the organization of basic research—is the high degree of intertwining with the polity. If one thinks of the major institutional sectors of the society as the polity, the economy, the intellectual system, the cultural and entertainment structures, the religious system, and the kinship system, then what is noteworthy is the high degree of dependence of the intellectual system on government. In the economy, there is an indirect political management by government through the control of the levels of money and the rate of growth through fiscal policies, and there is, increasingly, a direct share of purchases of goods by government; yet in the economy there is a high degree of independence of the operating units (corporations and firms), despite many government regulatory agencies. Similarly, the cultural and entertainment structures, despite the regulation of television and radio by government, are largely dependent on the market; and, in the case of serious works, to a small extent on foundations and patronage for support. The religious institutions are almost entirely dependent on private support and the family, except for welfare recipients, exists as an autonomous institution.

Educational institutions depend on the polity because of three factors: first, education has been traditionally a public function, in which the states have had primary responsibility for elementary and secondary education; second, the balance between private and public higher education in which, historically, the greater number of advanced students were educated in private schools (though a large number of the colleges were church-supported) has shifted so that today the larger number of students are in publicly supported institutions of higher learning; and third, the increasing dependence of the entire educational system on federal financing, particularly in higher education. This takes various forms—the dependence of private colleges on the government for student stipends, particularly in graduate work; the increasing use of loans from government for construction of college facilities; and, the dependence of research on the federal government for their monies—to the extent that about three-fourths of all research funds today are supplied by the federal government.

And yet, despite this extraordinary dependency on government, which of course, is not unique to the United States, there is little or no centralized control of the education system. In France, for example, a centralized ministry is responsible for uniform curricula, examinations, and all (except denominational) universities. There is also in the U.S. little organized direction of research and planned allocations, such as, for example, the Academy system provides in the Soviet Union. Instead, we have what is called "administrative pluralism," which is sometimes a euphemism for disorganization and disarray. There is no centralized research budget, or any set of coordinated policies. Responsibilities are distributed throughout the federal departments, in addition to a host of independent agencies such as the Atomic Energy Commission, the National Science Foundation, the Office of Science and Technology, and the like. Alan Pifer has summed up this high degree of decentralization in the organization of education:

> Looking at the "structure" of higher education, [an outside] observer would discover some 2,200 institutions of widely varying types and wildly varying standards. He would find that some of these institutions are publicly controlled, some privately, with some of the latter church-related and some not. He would also find 50 separate state systems of higher education, all different, and with the exception of some regional coordination, not related to each other in such a way as to add up collectively to anything like a national system of education. . . . Our observer would be even more surprised when he looked at the role of the national government in regard to higher education. Here he would discover: that there is no clearly expressed and clearly understood federal role . . . that the federal role in higher education (with the exception of that mandated in the Land-Grant Acts) has over the years

been only a by-product of other federal purposes, such as the support of research or discharge of responsibilities to war veterans or to the disadvantage that only recently has the Federal government begun to support higher education for its own sake and in so doing only on a hesitant, fragmented basis that could best be described as backing into a federal policy. . . . At the present time every federal department except the Post Office and Treasury and at least 16 independent agencies have direct relationships with institutions of higher education and that the Office of Education alone is responsible for administering over 60 separate programs in this area under the authorization of 15 different legislative enactments. Finally, he would find out that there is no single place in the federal government where all this activity is directed or coordinated, or its collective impact on the colleges and universities even assessed—no locus of concern about the health and welfare of higher education *per se*.[83]

This picture, which has become the conventional view of American higher education, fails to indicate the degree of *concentration* of resources—that is, students and research money—in a comparatively *small* number of universities. If we trace the degree of concentration from the abundance of statistics, we find that of the more than 2,000 institutions of higher education in the United States, there are only 154 universities. The largest single group in Fall, 1965, was private liberal arts colleges (699), followed by public and private junior colleges (622), and then by theological schools (207).[84] Attending these 154 universities, however, were nearly one-third of all students in the United States and nearly one-half of all students in four-year degree institutions.

The concentration can be traced by another measure. Between 1940 and 1960 college enrollment increased from 1.4 million to 3.6 million, but institutions which were founded after 1940 accounted for only about 10 per cent of the increase. Thus existing institutions approximately doubled in size. But the large universities accounted for the greatest concentrations of all. In 1964, thirty-five universities, or only 1.6 per cent of the number of all institutions, accounted for more than 20 per cent of student enrollments. A hundred and four schools, or less than 5 per cent of the total, accounted for 40 per cent of the enrollments (Table 19).

Within the university world itself, there is a high degree of concentration. Of the more than 2,000 colleges and universities in the country, 100 carry out more than 93 per cent of the research. And, within this circle, 21 universities carried out 54 per cent of all university research, and 10 universities carried out 38 per cent of university research.[85]

TABLE 19. NUMBER OF INSTITUTIONS OF HIGHER
EDUCATION, BY SIZE OF DEGREE-CREDIT
ENROLLMENT: UNITED STATES AND
OUTLYING AREAS, FALL 1964

Number of students enrolled	Institutions		Enrollment	
	Number	Percent	Number	Percent
Total	2,146	100.0	4,987,867	100.0
Under 200	327	15.2	33,940	.7
200 to 499	418	19.5	144,924	2.9
500 to 999	493	23.0	357,743	7.2
1,000 to 2,499	465	21.7	726,733	14.6
2,500 to 4,999	201	9.4	718,805	14.4
5,000 to 9,999	138	6.4	986,703	19.8
10,000 to 19,999	69	3.2	963,364	19.3
20,000 or more	35	1.6	1,055,655	21.2

SOURCE: *Digest of Educational Statistics, 1966,* U.S. Office of Education, Washington, 1966, p. 80; derived from U.S. Department of Health, Education, and Welfare, Office of Education, "Opening Fall Enrollment in Higher Education, 1964"; and unpublished data.

Given this degree of concentration, one can say that on the "elite" level, there is a "national system" of education and university research, which is characterized by a number of indicators. These are the universities which are most responsive to "national needs," in that such diverse work as the expansion of foreign area training (Russian, Chinese, Latin American studies), oceanography, space, health, urban affairs, are undertaken at these universities; these are the universities which have direct ties with government, often by the loan of personnel not only for high-level administrative jobs but also for such diverse tasks as foreign aid, economic development, technical assistance, and the like; within this university system there is a high degree of mobility and a strengthening of professional ties between key persons.

I have argued elsewhere that the university increasingly becomes the primary institution of the postindustrial society.[86] In the past twenty years, the university—and by "the university" I have in mind the elite group—has taken on a vast number of enlarged functions: in basic research, as a service institution, and the expansion of general education. In one sense, none of the specific functions is new, since the university, when it first undertook the organization of graduate schools, going back to Johns Hopkins and Chicago, had these functions in mind. What is new is the vast change of scale. The majority of research scientists in basic research today are in the universities; the university serves as the source for the specialized intellectual personnel for government and public organizations; even the majority of critics and writers today are employed in the university. The university has become the center of "establishment" culture. The unrest of the students in the mid-1960's is itself a significant sign of protest of the neglect of traditional teaching functions and the attention to the student. But the singular fact is that, lacking any organized Academy system, the government has forced on the university, willy nilly, a vast array of tasks which in other countries are performed outside the university system. It is not the traditional dependence of the educational system on the polity which is the important dimension of the post-war society but the "scientific-administrative complex" which represents an intermingling of government, science and the university unprecedented in American history. While it is often mentioned that in his "farewell speech," President Eisenhower warned against the "military-industrial complex," it is seldom recalled that in the same speech President Eisenhower balanced his sentence with an equal warning against the "scientific-administrative complex" which he felt represented also an undue concentration of influence.

If, as is projected to the end of the century, we may see a doubling of student enrollments in higher education, there is a very significant question whether the existing concentration of elite universities will continue. Much depends upon the source of the student body. If a significant proportion is recruited from the children of working-class parents, it is likely that the greater number will go on to junior colleges. The junior colleges have been the fastest growing segment of the American education scene. In 1930, there were 217 junior colleges; by 1950 the number had jumped to 503; a decade later there were 776; and by 1963 there were 975 junior colleges in the country. The elite private schools, universities, and colleges have begun to limit enrollment, in contrast to the major state universities, such as Wisconsin, Ohio, Minnesota, Michigan, and the California schools, which have expanded enormously. As Jencks and Riesman have noted: "The private sector's share of the market, which had hovered around 50 percent from 1910 to 1950 started falling about 1 percent annually. It was 36 percent in 1964 and is expected to be about 20 percent in 1980. Limiting enrollment had two consequences. One, it raised the ability of the average student, making private colleges relatively more attractive to both students and faculty, and probably indirectly raising the cash value of their degrees. Two, it meant that the philanthropic income did not have to be spread so thin."[87]

Over the years, the number of elite schools has remained comparatively stable (though there have been changes of standing within the group). Whether this will continue is an open question.

Despite the enormous sums spent by the United States government on research (for details, see the next section), there is no central science or research budget in the government, no set of priorities or objectives, no evaluation, no long-range planning as to fields of necessary interest or kinds of manpower to be encouraged. Beginning with the "Manhattan District" which produced the atomic bomb, American research policy has been overwhelmingly "mission-oriented," and each sector of the government—defense, health, atomic energy, space—determines its own missions, the monies being subject to some review by the Budget Bureau and the allocation by Congress. Because of this mission-orientation, there is no system in which existing laboratories or resources belonging to one agency or department is able to put its resources, manpower, and facilities at the service of another. As fresh needs, urgencies, and priorities develop, new research facilities, organizations, and laboratories, and new arrangements with universities are created to meet these fresh tasks. Because needs were often urgently defined, and capacities were unavailable within government, a whole host of "federal contract" devices, with newly established nonprofit corporations and universities was designed in which these tasks were performed outside of government. So scattered and dispersed are the institutional structures of science and research activities of the government that there is no single description extant of its range and structure!

Within the Executive Office of the President, there is the President's Special Assistant for Science and Technology, created in 1957. He serves as chairman of the Office of Science and Technology (OST, created in 1962), the President's Science Advisory Committee (PSAC, 1957), the Federal Council for Science and Technology (FCST, 1959) and as a member of the Defense Science Board of the Department of Defense.

The President's science advisor is supposed to have an over-all view of Federal science policy, but his position is weakened by the fact that almost 90 per cent of the expenditures for research and development are expended by four agencies—defense, atomic energy, space and health—and the science advisor has little say about their activities. The President's Science Advisory Committee is a government agency whose membership is drawn from outside the government. It is a policy advisory body charged with defining necessary new areas of science expenditures, and to assess the balance of science resources between science and technology and military and nonmilitary uses. But on actual political issues, it has had little influence.

Because research budgets are primarily in the hands of the different federal agencies, a multifarious system has developed which varies from agency to agency. The National Aeronautics and Space Agency (NASA) has built a large in-house technical capacity, but much of its development work is contracted with private industry. The Atomic Energy Commission (AEC) has created a large number of national laboratories, but in almost all instances these are managed, under contract, by universities (e.g., the Argonne laboratory at Chicago by the University of Chicago), a consortium of universities (e.g., the Brookhaven laboratory on Long Island) or a private corporation (Oak Ridge, managed by Union Carbide, or Sandia by Western Electric). The Defense Department has a wide variety of devices. Applied research and development may be evaluated by nonprofit corporations, such as RAND, or the Institute of Defense Analysis; exploratory research may be handled on contract with universities, such as the Lincoln Lab at MIT; design work may be handled by nonprofit corporations which have been created by universities, such as MITRE from MIT or the Riverside Institute from Columbia; development work would be handled by nonprofit corporations such as the Aerospace corporation, and production by major corporations such as Lockheed, Boeing, etc. In the health field, there has been a move toward the setting up of government institutes, and the National Institutes of Health, created in 1948, today comprise nine institutes. The National Institutes of Health are responsible for nearly 40 per cent of the total U.S. expenditure on medical research. From the start, NIH was empowered to make research grants as well as operating its own research facilities. At the start, these activities were in equal balance. Since then, the weight of activities has swung largely to research grants; and in 1966, about $912 million was disbursed in contracts and $218 million for in-house operations. (As a measure of the expansion of these activities, in 1950 some $30 million was spent in research and $15 million in direct operations.)

In general, the institutional structure of U.S. science policy until now has been marked by two features: where special tasks are defined, particularly in new fields, applied research and development, new institutional groupings and forms have been created *ad hoc* to meet these missions; in pure and basic research, monies have been given, on a project basis, to individuals who have been able to convince juries or research panels of the worthiness of the project or their competence as researchers.

This double feature of *mission-orientation* and *project grants* has had the unique quality of encouraging a high degree of success, by the concentration on the specific mission and the mobilization of large resources for the tasks, and the encouragement of a high research productivity by individuals who can prove themselves very quickly (compared to the European pattern, where a research man may be "indentured" for a long time to a specific professor). The drawbacks are equally obvious: there is a loss of sustained institution-building, either as an in-house capacity of government, or even in a university since, in most cases, research facilities are provided largely for individuals or small teams, not for the institution. (The university, remarked Clark Kerr wryly, as often as not, has simply been a hotel.) Nor is there the possibility for sustained, long-run research since the project system tends to emphasize specific and identifiable bits of research which can be completed in two or three years.

In the larger, political context, the lack of a unified science policy, or a major Academy or ministerial system, has meant that the "technocratic potential" inherent in the growing influence of science and the nature of technical decision-making is minimized in the American system. Science itself has simply become a constituency, but with no inherent unity other than some major professional associations and the political role of older clique groups who had played influential roles during World War II and shortly after. As a constituency, it is one more claimant on the national resources, like industry, or labor, the farmers, or the poor, although much of its "business" is done with the Executive agencies, rather than with Congress. But power, as regards science policy, has rested with the political and bureaucratic interests of the major agencies—Defense, Atomic Energy and Space —rather than with the scientific community, or even an over-all political policy body for science.

The Allocation of Resources

By common agreement, the "financial" measure of the growth of science and technology has become the expenditures on "research and development" (R & D). Efforts have been made to relate the expenditures of R & D to economic growth, to scientific productivity, to the acceleration of the pace of invention, to the shortening of time between invention and production, and the like. There are analytical problems in each of these alleged relationships. What we can take as the simple indicator, however, is the "commitment" of a country to its scientific and technological potential by the expenditures on R & D, and to a secondary extent on education.

The United States, by devoting 3 per cent of the GNP to research and development has, in the words of the OECD report on science in the United States, "become a symbol for other countries which now regard this as a target to be reached."[88]

Over the past twenty years, R & D expenditures in America have multiplied by 15 times, and the total expenditure on education by six, whereas GNP itself has only tripled. In 1965, the U.S. was spending more than 9 per cent of the total GNP on research and development and education.[89]

While international comparisons in this area are quite risky, a comparison between the U.S. effort and those of western Europe, Canada, and Japan reveal a very large gap, indeed. As a percentage of national product, R & D expenditure amounts to 2.3 per cent in the United Kingdom, which is the country nearest to the "magic" 3 per cent mark, and about 1.5 per cent for the other large industrialized nations. In comparing the number of researchers, relative to population, the U.S. has about four times as many as Germany, France, Belgium or Canada, and more than twice as many as the United Kingdom or Japan (Table 20).

What is striking about the pattern of R & D expenditures is that the federal government supplies most of the funds while the work is performed principally by industry, universities, and the nonprofit organizations. Without the lead of the federal government, there probably would have been little expansion in R & D in the U.S. federal expenditures between 1940 and 1964 grew at the average annual rate of 24.9 per cent. In 1965, a total of $20.5 billion was spent on R & D, of which the federal government financed 64 per cent of the total; industry contributed 32 per cent, universities spent 3.1 per cent; and nonprofit institutions 1 per cent.[90] Yet only 15 per cent of the work was done by the federal government; 70 per cent was performed by industry, 12 per cent by universities (including 3 per cent at federal contract research centers) and 3 per cent by nonprofit institutions. For fundamental research, the federal government still provides about 64 per cent of the funds, but the universities are the principal performers. Of almost $3 billion spent for fundamental research in 1965, 58 per cent was used by universities, 21 per cent by industry, and 7 per cent by nonprofit institutions (Table 21).

TABLE 20. COMPARISON OF THE R & D EFFORT OF THE UNITED STATES WITH THAT OF OTHER WESTERN STATES

State	GNP in billions of dollars 1964	GNP per capita in dollars	Population (in millions) 1964	R & D expenditure			Qualified R & D personnel[a]		
				(In millions of dollars)	As % of GNP	Year	Total	Number per 10,000 population	Year
Germany	103.98	1,774	58.2	1,436	1.4	1964	33,382	6	1964
France	88.12	1,674	48.4	1,299	1.6	1963	32,382	7	1963
Italy	49.58	897	51.1	290	0.6	1963	19,415	4	1963
Belgium	15.44	1,502	9.3	123	0.9	1963	5,536	6	1963
Netherlands	16.86	1,385	12.1	314	1.9	1964	9,227	8	1964
EEC, excluding Luxembourg	273.98		179.6	3,462	1.4	63–64	99,942		63–64
United Kingdom	91.90	1,700	54.2	2,159	2.3	64–65	59,415	11	1965
Sweden	17.47	2,281	7.6	253	1.5	1964	16,425	22	1964
Japan	69.08	622	96.9	892	1.5	1963	114,839	12	1964
Canada	43.54	2,109	19.2	425	1	1963	13,525	7	1963
United States	638.82	3,243	192.1	21,323[b]	3.4	63–64	474,900	25	1965

[a] Full-time equivalent.

[b] Estimated according to OECD standards and not according to those of the NSF.

Source: OECD, Reviews of National Science Policy: United States, p. 32.

TABLE 21. EXPENDITURES OF FUNDAMENTAL RESEARCH, 1965

Origin of funds (millions of dollars)	Performers						Percentage origin of funds
	Federal government	Industry	Universities		Nonprofit organizations	Total	
			Proper	FCRC[a]			
Federal government	424	191	920	198	118	1,851	63.0
			1,118				
Industry		416	25		16	457	16.0
Universities			473			473	16.0
Nonprofit organizations			74		71	145	5.0
Total	*424*	*607*	*1,492*	*198*	*205*	*2,926*	*100.0*
Percentage of performers	14.0	21.0	51	7	7.0	100	
			1,690				
			58.0				

[a] Federal contract research centers.

SOURCE: OECD, *Reviews of National Science Policy: United States*, p. 34.

If we think of R & D not just as contributing to economic growth, or being the engine of science and technology, but in *political* terms, then a very different picture of the U.S. effort emerges, however. It has long been clear that the largest proportion of total R & D expenditures is spent for defense purposes. These direct expenditures (Department of Defense and certain Atomic Energy Commission programs) have fluctuated around 50 per cent from 1953 to 1961, but according to the NSF decreased to 32 per cent in 1965. But much of this offset in proportions was due to relatively increased spending for space, rather than domestic needs, and if, with the OECD report on science policy in the United States, we consider "as a single category" all *expenditures connected with external challenge,* it appears, from Table 22 that this political reason dictates more than 80 per cent of all federal expenditures and more than 60 per cent of the total R & D expenditure. (Since a large proportion of the privately financed industrial R & D is probably also connected with defense, the proportion of the total R & D which is related to the political response to external challenge is undoubtedly higher than 60 per cent.)

Given this pattern, the considerable "lead" of the U.S. over other countries in R & D assumes a different proportion. For the United Kingdom devotes about 33 per cent of its R & D expenditure to military research and defense (including military atomic research); Germany, 17 per cent to atomic, space, and military research; Italy, 21 per cent; Canada, 23 per cent; Japan, 3 per cent; and France, 45 per cent (of which 22 per cent is devoted to atomic research). To this extent it is clear that the driving force of the U.S. government in financing R & D is primarily related to political objective, as is, in fact the proportions spent by the state in any country. The crucial question is whether government support will continue on this magnitude when the political competition is reduced and the external challenges become minimized.

What of the future? Research and development expenditures rose at a compound annual rate of 12.1 per cent, from $5.2 billion in 1953 to about $20.5 billion in 1965. Over the same period, GNP rose by a compounded rate of 5.3 per cent. But the average growth rate in R & D, measured from the survey base year of 1953, has been falling since it peaked at 17.6 per cent in 1953–1956. In the 1964–1965 period, while GNP moved upward to 7.8 per cent, R & D slowed down to a 6.7 per cent increase, the first period in which the percentage increase in research and development was less than that for the economy as a whole.

TABLE 22. RESEARCH AND DEVELOPMENT LINKED
WITH EXTERNAL CHALLENGE, 1954–1967

Fiscal year	Federal R & D expenditure in millions of dollars	R & D expenditure linked with external challenge (millions of dollars)	Column 2 as % of column 1	Column 2 as % of total R & D expenditure
1954	3,147	2,768	87.9	49.4
1955	3,308	2,896	87.5	46.7
1956	3,446	2,947	85.5	35.4
1957	4,462	3,775	84.6	39.5
1958	4,990	4,155	83.2	38.4
1959	5,803	4,766	82.1	38.5
1960	7,738	6,548	84.6	48.1
1961	9,278	7,917	85.3	55.3
1962	10,373	8,711	83.9	55.8
1963	11,988	10,068	83.9	58.1
1964	14,694	12,440	84.7	66.5
1965	14,875	12,580	84.6	62.2
1966	15,963	13,208	82.7	—
1967	16,152	12,941	80.1	—

NOTE: The figures in column 2 are obtained by adding the expenditure of the Departments of Defense, NASA and about 50 per cent of the expenditure of the Atomic Energy Commission which can in the view of most experts, be regarded as "defense-oriented."

SOURCE: OECD, *Reviews of National Science Policy: United States*, p. 38.

Research and development manpower, the most critical component of research, grew faster than the country's civilian labor force
during the decade of 1954–1965, advancing from 237,000 to 504,000
persons, an annual rate of 7.1 per cent compared with the 1.5 per
cent for the labor force as a whole. As a percentage of the labor
force, the number of R & D scientists moved from 0.37 to 0.68 per
cent in that same period. Industry, in 1965, as in the past, was the
largest employer of R & D scientists and engineers, reporting 351,200
in full-time equivalent numbers or around 70 per cent of the 503,600
total. The federal government employed 69,000 professional scientific and engineering personnel or about 14 per cent of the total. The
universities and colleges employed 66,000 R & D scientists and engineers for 13 per cent of the total, 54,900 of them in universities and
colleges proper. Three per cent of the R & D scientists worked in
the other nonprofit sector. This percentage distribution was close to
the pattern of 1958 (Table 23).

TABLE 23.   SCIENTISTS AND ENGINEERS EMPLOYED IN
RESEARCH AND DEVELOPMENT, BY SECTOR,
1954, 1958, 1961, AND 1965

Sector	1954	1958	1961	1965
Total	237,000	356,000	429,600	503,600
Federal government[a]	37,600	50,200	55,100	69,000[b]
Industry[c]	164,100	256,100	312,000	351,200
Universities and colleges[c]	30,000	42,500	51,700	66,000
(Universities and colleges proper)	(25,000)	(33,900)	(42,700)	(54,900)
Other nonprofit institutions[c]	5,300	7,200	10,800	17,400

[a] Numbers of civilian and uniformed military personnel; uniformed scientists
and engineers (Department of Defense) were estimated at 7,000 in 1954, 8,400
in 1958, 9,200 in 1961, and 12,000 in 1965.
[b] Estimate.
[c] Numbers of full-time employees plus the full-time equivalent of part-time
employees. Includes professional R & D personnel employed at federal contract
research centers administered by organizations in the sector.
SOURCE: National Science Foundation.

Research and Development data is classified by the National Science
Foundation into funds allocated for *development, applied research,*
and *basic research.* Development is defined as the design and testing
of specific prototypes and processes to meet a specific functional (e.g.,
defense) or economic requirement. Applied research is defined as

the first pilot steps in translating existing knowledge into applications. And basic research is defined "as primarily motivated by the desire to pursue knowledge for its own sake . . . free from the need to meet immediate objectives and . . . undertake to increase the understanding of natural laws." Whether these distinctions, particularly between basic and applied research, are meaningful is an important theoretical question that needs to be pursued.[91] Inasmuch as these distinctions, however, are used by the National Science Foundation, one can follow certain trend lines and establish future baselines from their data. While the proportion of monies spent for development and applied and basic research have remained relatively constant—about two-thirds of all monies have gone for development and one-third for research—the balance between monies spent for applied and basic research have changed somewhat. In 1965, basic research outlays amounted to 14 per cent of total R & D and applied research about 22 per cent; in the period between 1953 and 1958, the monies spent for basic research were about 9 per cent of the total.

If one examines the distribution between fields, it is seen that of the federal research total of $5.6 billion in 1967, approximately 68 per cent, or $3.8 billion, went to the support of the physical sciences; 25 per cent, or $1.4 billion, to the support of the life sciences; and 7 per cent, or $0.4 billion, to support of the psychological, social, and other sciences (Table 24).

In the past decade, there have been strong increases in money outlays for research. The greatest absolute growth has been in the physical sciences, followed by that of the life sciences. However, the social and psychological sciences, starting from smaller bases, show faster relative gains. From 1956 to 1967 their combined average annual growth rate is 26 per cent and it is expected to be an additional 15 per cent in 1968. These figures contrast with the other sciences whose average annual growth rates have been 20 per cent in the decade. In the next decade it is expected that the major research emphases will be in the atmospheric sciences, marine science and technology, space, biomedical research, and in the social sciences in education and urban affairs.

The distribution of applied research funds among the major science fields is not very different from that for basic research. Funds for applied research are largely concentrated in the physical sciences because this is the area of prime interest to the Department of Defense and NASA. Physical sciences account for 69 per cent of total obligations in 1967, life sciences 23 per cent and the behavioral sciences

TABLE 24. FEDERAL OBLIGATIONS FOR TOTAL
RESEARCH, BY FIELD OF SCIENCE

Field of science	Actual, 1966	Estimates 1967	1968
	(millions of dollars)		
Total	$5,271	$5,623	$6,390
Life sciences	1,290	1,431	1,584
Medical sciences	811	909	1,020
Biological sciences	370	406	441
Agricultural sciences	109	116	124
Psychological sciences	100	107	124
Physical sciences	3,641	3,817	4,382
Physical sciences proper	1,842	1,852	2,040
Engineering sciences	1,677	1,840	2,205
Mathematical sciences	123	124	137
Social sciences	166	178	209
Other sciences	74	90	91

NOTE: Detail may not add to totals because of rounding.
SOURCE: See Table 23.

8 per cent. In basic research, the physical sciences receive 65 per cent of funds, the life sciences 29 per cent and the behavioral sciences 6 per cent.

It is in subdisciplines that important differences exist. Within physical sciences, 46 per cent of the applied research funds were channeled to the engineering sciences in 1967, as compared to only 10 per cent of basic research funds. Within the life sciences, biology accounts for only 2 per cent of the applied research effort; in basic research it represents 16 per cent. The relative distribution of applied research funds by fields of science and discipline has remained stable since 1956: more than 45 per cent of the funding has been for engineering disciplines and approximately 20 per cent for medicine. In the basic research area, significantly higher growth rates are expected for the behavioral and the life sciences (Table 25).

Much of the basic research, of course, is done in universities. In 1966, universities and federal contract centers attached to them spent almost $2 billion dollars for research and development. (The universities spent $1.3 billion; the federal contract centers $640 million.) More than half (55 per cent) went for basic research, two-fifths (39 per cent) for applied research, and only 6 per cent for development. Five agencies—Health Education and Welfare, Defense, the National

TABLE 25. FEDERAL OBLIGATIONS FOR BASIC
RESEARCH, BY FIELD OF SCIENCE

| Field of science | Actual, 1966 | Estimates | |
		1967	1968
	(millions of dollars)		
Total	$1,844	$2,074	$2,331
Life sciences	540	603	670
Psychological sciences	53	58	64
Physical sciences	1,202	1,354	1,530
Physical sciences proper	974	1,094	1,280
Mathematical sciences	60	63	63
Engineering sciences	168	198	187
Social sciences	44	51	59
Other sciences	4	8	8

NOTE: Detail may not add to totals because of rounding.
SOURCE: See Table 23.

Science Foundation, NASA and the Atomic Energy Commission—
provide almost all the funds to universities and colleges. The single
largest sum comes from HEW, more than 40 per cent, primarily from
the National Institutes of Health, and accounts for most of the medical,
life sciences, and behavioral sciences programs. Twenty-two per cent
is spent by the Department of Defense for research projects. Although
the dollar volume of monies spent for research in the universities (exclusive of the federal contract centers) is increasing, the rate of increase
itself has fallen off sharply. In 1966, obligations rose 14 per cent over
the previous year, in 1967 it rose 9 per cent, and the indicated increase
for 1968 is 7 per cent.

It is clear that the governmental expenditures on research and development are leveling off. During the Eisenhower and Kennedy administrations, R & D increased by an average of 15 to 16 per cent a
year. Under President Johnson it has continued to increase but only
at a 3 to 4 per cent annual increase, but as a percentage of the total
federal budget it has begun to decline.

Several other changes are evident as well. Whereas formerly the
bulk of the money was spent by the Pentagon and NASA, in the past
two years there has been a shift to other agencies, particularly HEW.
This itself parallels a shift in the federal budget, which has been interrupted by the Vietnam war, for social expenditures to rise. In 1956,
social expenditures accounted for 15.2 per cent of the federal budget;
in 1968 it is estimated at 29.6 per cent.

These two basic changes pose the clearest challenges. Can the allocative process be one, simply, of immediate responses to urgent definitions, either of defense or even of social needs, because of the "discovery" of pollution, poverty, urban chaos, and other social ills, or will there be an effort to spell out a coordinated set of policies based on some considerations of national goals defined in long-range terms? Is the present system of "administrative pluralism," in which the individual agencies hold power to be maintained or will there be some unified science and educational agencies? Can science and research be funded on largely a project basis, or will there be a consideration of long-run institution building, either as a federal in-house capacity, or in independent institutes and agencies, or in conjunction with the universities themselves? If the research and development effort, in short, has been motivated largely by "external challenge" and the need to expand quickly the science complex of the country to help the defense posture, will there be a similar effort for sustained support of domestic social needs and the long-range interests of science and universities in a postindustrial society?

CODA

This essay has undertaken three tasks: to delineate the fundamental structural trends in the society as they affect knowledge and technology; to analyze some problems in the measurement of knowledge and technology; and to put forth the present and future dimensions of the educated and technical class of the country. These tasks have been large ones, and necessarily many questions have been slighted. Moreover, a number of major questions have been ignored entirely for reasons of space; yet, in any full discussion of knowledge and technology they would have to be included: the changing organizational contexts of knowledge (e.g., the compatibility of hierarchical and bureaucratic work organization with collegial and associational modes of status); the norms of science (e.g., the compatibility of the idea of the autonomy of science with the call for service to national goals); communication patterns within knowledge structures (e.g, the problems of informational retrieval, formal and informal networks of communication, etc.); the revolutionary nature of the new "intellectual technology" (e.g., the role of simulation, systems engineering, and the like linked to the computer).

Much of this essay has been concerned with facts, data, measurement. David Hume, that skeptical Scotsman, once asked of knowledge: "If we take in our hand any volume of divinity or school metaphysics let us ask: Does it contain any abstract reasoning concerning quantity and number? No. Does it contain any experimental reasoning concerning matter of fact and existence? No. Commit it then to the flames: for it contains nothing but sophistry and illusion."

We can observe the skeptic's caution, yet reserve a realm of knowledge for that which cannot be weighed and measured, the realm of values and choice. For the central point about the last third of the twentieth century, call it the postindustrial society, the knowledgeable society, the technetronic age, or the active society, is that it will require more societal guidance, more expertise.[92] To some extent, this is an old technocratic dream which one can find anticipated, in extraordinary fashion, by the French socialist, Henri de Saint-Simon. But the feeling of Saint-Simon was that in such a technocratic society there would be the disappearance of politics since all problems would be decided by the expert and one would obey the competence of a superior just as one obeys the instructions of a doctor, or an orchestra conductor or a ship's captain.[93] It is more likely, however, that the postindustrial society will involve *more* politics than ever before for the very reason that choice becomes conscious and the decision-centers more visible.[94] The nature of a market society is to disperse responsibility and to have "production" decisions guided by the multiple demands of the scattered consumer. But a decision to allocate money in one scientific project rather than another, or to put a road through the ghetto rather than the rich section of town, is made by a political center and, as against a market decision, one can quickly see "whose ox is being gored." Since politics is a compound of interests and values, and those are often diverse, an increased degree of conflict and tension is probably unavoidable in the postindustrial society.

Inasmuch as knowledge and technology have become the central resource of the society, certain political decisions are inescapable. Insofar as the institutions of knowledge lay claim to public resources, some public claim on these institutions is unavoidable.

We are, then, at a number of turning points and the society, and the knowledge community, will have to confront a number of crucial decisions about its intertwined future. To illustrate:

1. *The financing of higher education.* It is clear that the balance in higher education is shifting from the private school to the public college, but that even the private school can no longer continue without substantial public aid; and that in both cases the degree of aid requires a centralized federal effort.[95] But the obvious question, then, is: for

whom and how? Is every type of institution, large and small, public and private, religious and secular, undergraduate, graduate and professional to be helped, regardless of quality? If not, who is to make the decision? And if new schools are to be created, are the decisions to be left largely to the states, with no consideration of regional or national needs? If there is to be public funding, what is to be the public voice?

2. *The evaluation of knowledge.* If public resources are employed what are the ways in which results of research are to be evaluated as the basis for future expenditures, and by whom? If there is a choice, because of the limitation of resources, between expenditures of manpower and money on space and, say, particle accelerators (whose total costs may run to more than a billion dollars), how are these decisions to be made?

3. *The conditions of creativity.* Is knowledge more and more a product of "social cooperation," a collaborative effort whose setting is the laboratory and the team, or the fruits of the individual cogitator working from his own genius? And if this is too rigid, or even false an antinomy, what are the conditions and settings for creativity and productivity?

4. *The transfer of technology.* What are the processes whereby discoveries in the laboratory may be transferred more readily into prototypes and production? In part this is an information problem and raises the question, for example, of the responsibility of the federal government in establishing a comprehensive technology "infusion" program which goes beyond the mere publication of technological findings to an active encouragement of its use by industry; in part, if one sees this as a piece of the larger problem of spreading the findings of technology to the underdeveloped world, a cultural and technical aid program.

5. *The pace of knowledge.* If knowledge and new disciplines are accelerating at a more rapid rate, how can the teaching of these subjects keep apace with these developments? Is there not a need to assess the nature of curriculum in terms of "structures of knowledge" to use Jerome Bruner's phrase, or "conceptual innovation," along the lines I have argued before.[96]

6. *The strains of change.* Insofar as this, like every society, is undergoing multiple revolutions of a diverse yet simultaneous character—the inclusion of disadvantaged groups *into* the society; the growth of interdependence and the creation of national societies; the increasing substitution of political for market decision making; the creation of fully urbanized societies and the erosion of an agricultural popu-

lation; the multiple introductions of technological items, and so on —do we not need more conscious means of "monitoring" social change and the creation of mechanisms for anticipating the future?

Let us return to our parable. The tower of Babel was foretold in *Genesis* at the dawn of human experience. "And the Lord said: 'Behold, they are one people, and they have all one language; and this is what they begin to do; and now nothing will be withholden from them, which they purpose to do. Come, let us go down, and there confound their language, that they may not understand one another's speech.' "

Cast out from the Eden of understanding, the human quest has been for a common tongue and a unity of knowledge, for a set of "first principles" which, in the epistemology of learning, would underlie the modes of experience and the categories of reason and so shape a set of invariant truths. The library of Babel mocks this hubris: like endless space, it is all there and is not all there; and, like Gödel's theorem, knowing it is a contradiction makes it not a contradiction. In the end, said the poet, is the beginning. This is the curvilinear paradox, and necessary humility, in the effort to measure knowledge.

NOTES

1. From "The Library of Babel," by Jorge Luis Borges, translated by James E. Irby, in LABYRINTHS © 1962 by New Directions Publishing Corporation. Reprinted by permission of New Directions Publishing Corporation and Laurence Pollinger Limited.
2. Adams, Henry, *The Education of Henry Adams: An Autobiography,* Boston and New York, Houghton Mifflin, 1918, pp. 494–495.
3. Thompson, D'Arcy, *On Growth and Form,* Cambridge University Press, Cambridge, 1963, vol. I, p. 27.
4. Parsons, Talcott, and Neil J. Smelser, *Economy and Society,* Free Press, London, 1956, pp. 255–256.
5. For data on American employment in the service sector, see Fuchs, Victor, "The Growing Importance of the Service Industries," National Bureau of Economic Research Occasional Paper 96, New York, 1965.
6. Machlup, Fritz, *The Production and Distribution of Knowledge in the United States,* Princeton University Press, Princeton, N.J., 1962, p. 20.
7. *Ibid.,* pp. 21–22.
8. Lane, Robert E., "The Decline of Politics and Ideology in a Knowledgeable Society," *American Sociological Review,* vol. 21, no. 5, October, 1966, p. 650.
9. For a comprehensive paradigm which sets forth the kinds of questions a sociology of knowledge would have to answer, see Merton, Robert K., "The Sociology of Knowledge," in *Social Theory and Social Structure,* rev. ed., Free Press, Glencoe, Ill., 1957, esp. pp. 460–461.

10. Rider, Fremont, *The Scholar and the Future of the Research Library,* Hadham Press, New York, 1944.

11. *Ibid.,* pp. 11–12.

12. *Ibid.*

13. Price, Derek, *Science Since Babylon,* Yale University Press, New Haven, 1961. His first publication on the subject was in the *Archives Internationales d'Histoire des Sciences,* No. 14, 1951. This was extended and republished in more popular form in *Discovery* (London), June, 1956.

14. Price, Derek, *Science Since Babylon, op. cit.,* p. 96.

15. Price, Derek, "The Science of Science," in John R. Platt, editor, *New Views of the Nature of Man,* Chicago, 1965, pp. 47–70, esp. pp. 58–59.

16. Price, Derek, *Science Since Babylon, op. cit.,* pp. 100–101.

17. *Ibid.,* p. 102 *n.*

18. May, Kenneth O., "Quantitative Growth of the Mathematical Literature," *Science,* vol. 154, December 30, 1966, pp. 1672–1673.

19. The example is taken from Price, Derek, *Science Since Babylon, op. cit.,* p. 108.

20. The account here is drawn from Thompson, D'Arcy, *On Growth and Form, op. cit.,* pp. 142–150.

21. "The point where a struggle for existence first sets in, and where *ipso facto* the rate of increase begins to diminish, is called by Verhulst the *normal level* of the population; he chooses it for the origin of his curve, which is so defined as to be symmetrical on either side of this origin. Thus Verhulst's law, and his logistic curve, owe their form and their precision and all their power to forecast the future to certain hypothetical assumption." *Ibid.,* p. 146.

22. See Ridenour, Louis, R. R. Shaw, and A. G. Hill, *Bibliography in an Age of Science,* University of Illinois Press, Urbana, Ill., 1952. Ridenour introduces the mathematical equations on the "law of social change" by saying (p. 34):

    "Since so many aspects of human activity seem to be governed by the same general type of growth curve, it is of interest to inquire whether we can find a rationalization for the empirical law of social change.

    "One is, in fact, immediately accessible. It depends on the seemingly reasonable assumption that the rate of further public acceptance of a new device or service will, at any time, be proportional to the extent to which the device or service is already used. To take a specific example, this assumption claims that the number of people who will buy and register automobiles, per unit time, will depend upon the extent of the opportunity for those who do not own cars to ride in a car that is owned by someone else. The extent of this opportunity will be proportional to the number of automobiles that are already registered."

23. Stone, Richard, "A Model of the Educational System," in *Mathematics in the Social Sciences and Other Essays,* MIT Press, Cambridge, 1966, esp. p. 105.

24. Price, Derek, *Science Since Babylon,* pp. 115–116.

25. Price, Derek, *Big Science, Little Science,* Columbia University Press, New York, 1963, pp. 23–25.

26. *Ibid.,* p. 30.

27. Holton, Gerald, "Scientific Research and Scholarship: Notes Toward the Design of Proper Scales," *Daedalus,* Spring, 1962, pp. 362–399. In this discussion of branching, I have largely followed Holton's account.

28. *Ibid.,* pp. 386–387.

29. Fourastié, Jean, *The Causes of Wealth,* The Free Press of Glencoe, Ill., 1960, chap. I, esp. pp. 30–31.

30. For an elaboration of this point, see Bell, Daniel, "The Disjunction of Cul-

242 INDICATORS OF SOCIAL CHANGE

ture and Social Structure," in Gerald Holton, editor, *Science and Culture,* Houghton Mifflin, Boston, 1965, pp. 236–251.

31. As Ricardo wrote in his *Principles of Political Economy and Taxation:* "With a population pressing against the means of subsistence, the only remedies are either a reduction of people or a more rapid accumulation of capital. In rich countries, where all the fertile land is already cultivated, the latter remedy is neither very practicable nor very desirable, because its effect would be, if pushed very far, to render all classes equally poor." Cited in Lave, Lester B., *Technological Change: Its Conception and Measurement,* Prentice-Hall, Englewood Cliffs, N.J., 1966, p. 3. In the paragraph above, I have followed Lave's formulations.

32. *Ibid.*

33. Solow, Robert M., "Technical Change and the Aggregate Production Function," *Review of Economics and Statistics,* vol. 39, August, 1957.

34. The definition here is based on the paper, "Technological Change: Measurement Determinants and Diffusion" by Edwin Mansfield, prepared for the National Commission on Technology, Automation and Economic Progress, and published in Appendix 1 to the report of the Commission, *Technology and the American Economy,* Washington, 1966.

35. Nelson, Richard R., Merton J. Peck, and Edward D. Kalachek, in their interesting book *Technology, Economic Growth and Public Policy,* The Brookings Institution, Washington, 1967, present a more disaggregated theory of a production function for technological progress. Seeking to designate the kinds and quantities of Research and Development inputs needed to make a design idea operational, they argue that the quantity of resources required depends on three key variables: (1) the magnitude of the advance sought over existing comparable products; (2) the nature of the product field, in particular the size and complexity of the system; and (3) the stock of relevant knowledge that permits new techniques to be derived or deduced, as well as the stock of available materials and components with which designers can work." (p. 23)

36. Recalculations of Solow's model disclosed some errors, and the share of capital in increasing productivity should have been 19 per cent, not 12½ per cent. See Lave, *op. cit.,* p. 34.

37. Kendrick, John, *Productivity Trends in the United States,* National Bureau of Economic Research and Princeton University Press, Princeton, N.J., 1961.

38. Solow, Robert M., "Investment and Technical Change," in *Mathematical Models in the Social Sciences,* ed. by Kenneth J. Arrow, Samuel Karlin, and Patrick Suppes, Stanford University Press, Stanford, 1959.

39. *Technology in the American Economy, op. cit.,* p. 2.

40. The data are cited in Mansfield, "Technological Change," *op. cit.,* p. 105.

41. *Technology in the American Economy,* p. 1. The words in brackets are from page 4 of the report. The Commission attributed the high unemployment rate of the period from 1958–1966 to a low growth rate in the economy, as a result of a lagging aggregate demand, and the doubling of the entry rates of youths into the labor force, as the "baby boom" of the post-World War II period began to reach a crest.

Since some of the conclusions of the Commission's report may be subject to challenge, it may be prudent to "declare one's interest." I was a member of the Commission, participated in the studies, and signed the conclusions. The principal drafter of the sections on the pace of technological change was Professor Robert M. Solow of Massachusetts Institute of Technology.

42. See John Stuart Mill, *Principles of Political Economy,* New York, 1886, vol. II, book IV, chap. VI. As Mill says, so appealingly:

"I cannot . . . regard the stationary state of capital and wealth with the unaffected aversion so generally manifested towards it by political economists of the old school. I am inclined to believe that it would be, on the whole, a very considerable improvement on our present condition. I confess I am not charmed with the ideal of life held out by those who think that the normal state of human beings is that of struggling to get on; that the trampling, crushing, elbowing and treading on each other's heels, which form the existing type of social life, are the most desirable lot of human kind, or anything but the disagreeable symptoms of one of the phases of industrial progress. It may be a necessary stage in the progress of civilization, and those European nations which have hitherto been so fortunate as to be preserved from it, may have it yet to undergo." (p. 328)

43. Hansen, Alvin, *Fiscal Policy and Business Cycles,* W. W. Norton, New York, 1941.
44. Schumpeter, Joseph, *Capitalism, Socialism and Democracy,* Harper & Brothers, New York, 1942, pp. 117–118.
45. Nelson, Peck, and Kolachek, *Technology, Economic Growth and Public Policy, op. cit.,* p. 41.
46. *Ibid.,* p. 43, italics added. For the supporting argument, see chap. 2 as a whole.
47. Spengler, J. J., Presidential Address, *American Economic Review,* May, 1966.
48. Jantsch, Erich, *Technological Forecasting in Perspective,* Organization for Economic Cooperation and Development, Paris, 1967, p. 109.
49. Clarke, Arthur C., *The Promise of Space,* Harper & Row, New York, 1968.
50. Von Karman, Theodor, *Towards New Horizons,* report submitted on behalf of the US Air Force Scientific Advisory Group, November 7, 1944.
51. Quinn, James Brian, "Technological Forecasting," *Harvard Business Review,* April, 1967.
52. Lenz, R. C., Jr., *Technological Forecasting,* Air Force Systems Command, June, 1962.
53. I follow here largely the work of Robert Ayres and draw from a number of memoranda he has prepared for the Hudson Institute.
54. Schon, Donald, "Forecasting and Technological Forecasting" in Bell, Daniel, editor, *Toward the Year 2000: Work in Progress,* special issue of *Daedalus,* 1968, pp. 759–770.
55. If one, in forecasting parameters, seeks to reduce the "margin of error" for particular techniques by grouping the "micro-variables" into larger classes of relationships, there is the logical problem of classification: may not one be arbitrarily selecting items to put together because they form a neat curve? The effort here to simplify may only distort. Most models to be useful —and one sees this in economics—are highly cumbersome, involving hundreds of variables and equations. And yet this complexity is necessary if the predictions are to have a meaningful "purchase" on reality.
56. The exposition of the Delphi technique, as well as the results of the RAND study, are contained in Helmer, Olaf, *Social Technology,* Basic Books, New York, 1966.
57. Jantsch, Erich, *Technological Forecasting, op. cit.,* p. 175.
58. Quoted in *ibid ,* pp 175–176.
59. *Ibid.,* pp. 178–180.
60. Churchman, C. W., R. L. Ackoff, and E. L. Arnoff, *Introduction to Operations Research,* John Wiley, New York, 1957.
61. Samuelson, Paul, *Problems of the American Economy,* Oxford University Press, New York, 1962.
62. See Appendix 1 to *Technology and the American Economy, op. cit.*

63. Mansfield, Edwin, *Econometrica,* October, 1961.
64. Rogers, Everett M., *Diffusion of Innovation,* The Free Press, Glencoe, Ill., 1962.
65. Mansfield, *op. cit.*
66. Solow, Robert M., "Investment and Technical Change," *op. cit.*
67. Denison, Edward, *Sources of Economic Growth,* Committee on Economic Development, New York, 1962.
68. Machlup, Fritz, *Production and Distribution of Knowledge in the United States, op. cit.,* pp. 360–361.
69. Kerr, Clark, *The Uses of the University,* Harper & Row, New York, 1966.
70. Moles, Abraham, "La Cité Scientific dans 1972," *Futuribles,* Paris, 1964.
71. These figures and projections, and those that follow for the subclassifications are taken from "America's Industrial and Occupational Manpower Requirements, 1964–1975," prepared by the Bureau of Labor Statistics for the National Commission on Technology, Automation and Economic Progress, and printed in the appendix to *Technology and the American Economy, op. cit.*
72. *Reviews of National Science Policy: United States,* Organisation for Economic Co-operation and Development, Paris, 1968, pp. 44–45.
73. The statistical material in this section is drawn principally from two reports: the OECD *Review of Science Policies, ibid.;* and *American Science Manpower 1966,* A Report of the National Register of Scientific and Technical Personnel, National Science Foundation NSF 68–7, Washington, 1968.
74. U.S. Department of Labor, *Manpower Report of the President,* Washington, 1967, p. 44.
75. Folger, John K., "The Balance Between Supply and Demand for College Graduates," *The Journal of Human Resources,* vol. II, no. 2, Spring, 1967, p. 163.
76. *Ibid.,* pp. 163–164.
77. The 18–21 age group is not a completely reliable guide for purposes of projection, since about 33 per cent of the present college and university students fall outside this range. According to the 1960 census, the age distribution of undergraduates was as follows:

Under 18	*18–21*	*22–24*	*25–29*	*30 and over*
2.2%	67.7%	13.9%	11.2%	5.0%

Yet for comparative purposes, over time, we use the 18-to-21 age group as a convention."
78. Cartter, Allan M., and Robert Farrell, "Higher Education in the Last Third of the Century," *The Educational Record,* Spring, 1965, p. 121.
79. Rivlin, Alice, "The Demand for Higher Education," in *Microanalysis of Socio-Economic Systems,* New York, 1961, p. 216; cited by Folger, "Balance Between Supply and Demand for College Graduates," *op. cit.,* p. 144.
80. Trow, Martin, "The Democratization of Higher Education in America," *European Journal of Sociology,* vol. III, no. 2, 1962, p. 255.
81. Porter, John, "The Future of Upward Mobility," *American Sociological Review,* vol. 33, no. 1, February, 1968, pp. 12–13.
82. Trow, Martin, "Democratization of Higher Education," *op. cit.,* pp. 255–256.
83. Pifer, Alan, "Toward a Coherent Set of National Policies for Higher Education," address to the Association of American Colleges, January 16, 1968.
84. *Digest of Educational Statistics, 1966,* U.S. Office of Education, Washington, 1966, Table 99, p. 78.

85. The first ten, in order, are: University of California (combined), Massachusetts Institute of Technology, Columbia, University of Michigan, Harvard, University of Illinois, Stanford, University of Chicago, Minnesota, and Cornell.

    The others, not in order, are: Yale, Princeton, Pennsylvania, North Carolina, Wisconsin, Michigan State, Ohio State, New York University, California Institute of Technology, Rochester, and Washington.

86. See Bell, Daniel, *The Reforming of the General Education,* Columbia University Press, New York, 1966, chap. 3; and "Notes on the Post-Industrial Society," *The Public Interest,* nos. 6 and 7, Winter, 1966, and Spring, 1967.

87. Jencks, Christopher, and David Riesman, *The Academic Revolution,* New York, 1968, p. 272.

88. OECD, *Reviews of National Science Policy: United States, op. cit.,* p. 29.

89. The statistical data in this section, unless otherwise noted, have been taken from two reports of the National Science Foundation, *National Patterns of R & D Resources,* Funds & Manpower in the United States (NSF 67–7); and *Federal Funds for Research, Development and Other Scientific Activities,* Fiscal Years 1966, 1967, and 1968. Volume XVI (NSF 67–19).

90. The proportion of public funds in other countries is considerably lower. In 1964, according to the OECD, it was:

Country	Percentage
France	63.3
United Kingdom	56.6
Sweden	47.7
Germany	40.4
Netherlands	40.0
Japan	27.8
Italy	33.1

91. A useful set of questions along this line is posed by Michel D. Reagan, "Basic and Applied Research: A Meaningful Distinction," *Science,* March 17, 1967.

92. A comprehensive effort to provide a conceptual framework in sociological terms for this new, different kind of society has been made by my colleague Amitai Etzioni in *The Active Society,* The Free Press, New York, 1968. Pointing out, quite accurately, that the historic language and received models of sociology, even when emphasizing process, lack a vocabulary to deal with direction and choice, he has attempted the task of providing a scaffolding for the construction of new sociological structures. What I find contradictory about Etzioni's effort is his employment of *consciousness* and *cybernetics* as his key terms. A cybernetic model, even though involving feedback and self-adjustment, is essentially mechanical and closed. Consciousness, and the implication of the enlargement of human vision and control over nature and society, can only operate in an open system.

    The phrase "technetronic age" was coined by my colleague Zbigniew Brzezinski in *Encounter,* January, 1968. I find it useful, but in its emphasis on the new technology, I feel it slights the importance of "theoretical knowledge" which I would regard as central to the new kind of societal guidance that is emerging as a necessary feature of the coming age.

93. A more sophisticated version of this argument is made by Robert Lane in his essay, "The Decline of Politics and Ideology in a Knowledgeable Society," *American Sociological Review,* October, 1966.

94. I have traced this technocratic dream in such writers as Saint-Simon, Cournot, F. W. Taylor, and Veblen, and sought to show its limitations in a politicalized world in an essay presented at the 75th Anniversary celebration

of the California Institute of Technology, October, 1966, reprinted in *Scientific Progress and Human Values,* edited by Edward and Evelyn Hutchings, American Elsevier Co., 1967.

95. See the symposium on "The Financing of Higher Education," in *The Public Interest,* No. 11, Spring, 1968, with contributions by Clark Kerr, David Truman, Martin Meyerson, Charles Hitch, *et al.*

96. See Bell, Daniel, *The Reforming of General Education, op. cit.;* and Bruner, Jerome, *The Process of Education,* Havard University Press, Cambridge, 1960.

6. THE CHANGING POLITICS OF AMERICAN LIFE

Joyce M. and William C. Mitchell

WHILE HISTORIANS have been assiduous in their quest to describe change in the United States, they have not often tried broader and more systematic estimates of *what* changes, at what *rates,* in which *directions,* and *how.* One result has been a confusion about whether the American polity is one of the more stable or less stable in the world. Facts can be found to support both points of view. The safest course and probably the most nearly correct is to say that some elements of American political life have, indeed, changed drastically, while certain others have changed very little, and many others fall variously in between. We hope to distinguish these varying possibilities within a loose formulation of "systems" analysis.

In brief, we view the political system as a functional element of the wider, more inclusive society engaged in a variety of valued activities. In various ways the polity extracts resources from the citizenry and transforms them into differentially valued goods and services. This highly generalized activity is, of course, the product of countless decisions arrived at through such typical processes as conflict, competition, bargaining and authoritative coordination. None of these processes are neat and orderly, although they are understandable and even quite predictable in many regards. In any case, the polity produces public policies which, in turn, involve the mobilization of scarce resources, their allocation among competing ends, the distribution of benefits and opportunities, the allocation of burdens, and the application of regulations and controls to society. Such universal problems are handled through a great variety of processes, which are shaped by both formal governmental and legal institutions and by general social and economic elements in the system. Therefore, issues and public choices can assume particular and often unique form in specific societies; the United States is no exception. Within American history one finds the same recurring problems, but "answered" through somewhat changing processes and with greater variations in the "answers," "solutions," or policies as time passes. In this chapter we hope to provide at least a summary view of what has happened within this broadly formulated conception of our changing political system.

FORMAL POLITICAL STRUCTURES
AND PROCESSES

While attempts to institutionalize formal rules of the political game have often incurred costly results for scores of nations, the United States, even in the midst of a bewildering amount of social and economic change, has managed to create and preserve one of the most stable sets of formal political structures ever known. We have the oldest operative written constitution, the oldest continuous two-party system, and the oldest recurrent set of peaceful elections in history. The constitution under which we now operate has been subject to considerable change in interpretation since 1789, but the original document still defines the basic formal structure for policy-making. The original remarkably brief United States Constitution is still a very general document, with but fifteen amendments subsequent to the original Bill of Rights. Interestingly, the fifty state constitutions are all much longer, more detailed, and subject to more frequent change, including general revisions, than the national document. We began with a formal federal distribution of power, a separation of powers among office-holders, and a federal bill of rights was soon added—all generally following various provisions of state constitutions. These fundamental aspects of the constitution still hold force, whereas Latin American nations which enacted constitutions soon after the United States have not been able to maintain the basic legal prescriptions. They have typically been overridden by dictatorships, coups d'etat, and even by rebellion and revolution. Even the democracies of western Europe have had many more basic legal changes; France since 1789 has had five republics, at least one dictatorship, and a monarchy; while Germany has had a monarchy, two democracies, and a totalitarian dictatorship during this century alone.

The most important American constitutional and legal changes have been brought about by judicial interpretation and application to changing kinds of social, economic, and political challenges. Space prohibits detail, but we can note some very general and significant changes. The great commercial and industrial growth of the country has brought enlargement of federal spending and regulatory powers, rationalized by the commerce, monetary, tax, and welfare clauses of the Constitution. Rapidly changing technology has not only integrated the activities of the nation greatly, but also brought this country into extensive economic, military, and social contacts abroad, which were greatly intensified by two world wars and a prolonged cold war. These have substantially transformed the military and foreign policy powers of the executive branch especially and produced a level of investment, deployment of forces, and international commitments certainly inconceivable in late eighteenth-century terms. Here at home, urbanization, the increasing role of the mass media, greater mobility, leisure time, and organizational means of conducting affairs, have more recently challenged and tended to enlarge the sphere of protective rights—in religious and political belief, labor and political organization, and in the exercise of rights to vote, travel, work, and reside. However, one may note that these vindicated challenges were not easily won, most coming after World War II; and that they were typically a reaction to repressive legislation and official practices which are not always easily erased by a general legal rule.[1]

Growth of Governmental Activity

American political life has become both more centralized and decentralized. In spite of the intentions of many of the Founding Fathers, we have witnessed within our own time a movement toward both greater national and greater state activities. This seems a paradox, but the exercise of power is not always zero-sum, in which the gains at one level are balanced by the losses of other levels. The national government's power to accomplish its ends is very difficult to measure, but qualitatively it appears to have increased at a more rapid rate than has state power during the twentieth century. But local and state governments played a most important relative role in the early nineteenth century, and in many ways remained more significant than the federal government until recent decades. Both units can now do more in the way of defining or specifying problems and issues, resolving and implementing their choices than they could, say, a hundred years ago.[2] If we empirically plotted these changes in activity they might appear as in Figure 1.

We do not have good historical measures of these relationships but such readily observable indicators as population size, density, and industrialization all suggest that earlier Americans simply did not have as pressing a need for national solutions to private problems, nor for state and local aids, as today. We do know, from a variety of state and

FIGURE 1. THE GROWTH OF GOVERNMENTAL ACTIVITY

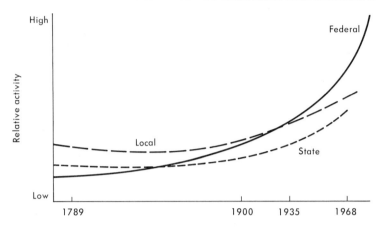

local histories and some observer accounts, that local governments typically took on some assistance for the poor, however meager, and provided law and order; and development of community facilities was primarily a local problem in the earlier years. At least in the North, states also took on some public assistance responsibilities, and were involved in developing public education, a practice encouraged by early federal land policies.[3] We learn that state training of militias soon became spasmodic and laggard in the early nineteenth century, ultimately necessitating an enlarged standing federal force, even before the Civil War.[4] Most notable was the very considerable early nineteenth-century activity of state governments in financing and forming investment groups for banks, turnpikes, canals, river improvements, bridges, and railroads. One scholar has noted that with these efforts, an aggregate funded debt of over $200,000,000 was created, which was "a larger debt than the federal government had ever owed, and the first large funded debt created by the government of any country for purely industrial purposes."[5] In comparison, the federal government contributed about $15 million in its first thirty years to comparable economic development activity, and about $55 million in the next twenty years.[6] But there was probably more sharing of functions across governmental bodies than the formal records show. For example, the federal Corps of Engineers was apparently used extensively by states and localities at least until the mid-1830's, and often the federal government contributed some share to local investment concerns, at least in instances investigated by one scholar.[7] These generalizations need further refinement, as there was undoubtedly much local and regional variation. For example, public investment in canals was apparently greatest in the Northeast, and generally the share of public investment in transport ventures was greater in the later states and communities of the West.[8]

It is difficult also to typify trends in the kinds of cooperative, collective endeavors of the citizenry in earlier days which might be organized privately, but were quite similar to public functions such as neighborhood building bees, volunteer fire fighting, wagon trains, contributions to teachers' salaries, posses, etc. In any case, later governmental agencies and programs assumed many such public activities; and governments experimented with many "mixed" or "quasi-public" bodies, especially for investment and development purposes.

The most direct indicators of the increasing organization of public life, its size and complexity, are the numbers of units and people involved. The scope of the polity is vastly enlarged; today we are a society of 200 million people as contrasted with 3.9 million in 1789. Our nation now covers a contiguous land mass of more than 3.6 million square miles, while the first thirteen states occupied but 888,881 square miles along the Eastern seaboard. There are now fifty states, including two widely separated from the mainland; a variety of overseas dependencies and controlled areas. While this country ranks fourth in the world in both population and area, it is the largest democracy history has known. The fact that a democracy can operate over so large a territory and govern so many people with such a degree of effectiveness is no small tribute to the durability of this system.

Complexity of Governmental Practices

Whereas the Founding Fathers tended to conceive of the political division of powers and functions as something which could be simply and completely segmented, subsequent generations of lawmakers have increasingly viewed the work of government as entailing more exchange and cooperative activities among semiautonomous officials and agencies. The result has been a proliferation of more elective offices, administrative units, boards, commissions and committees, at and across all levels and different geographic jurisdictions. And forms of public-private cooperation have become increasingly widespread. The extent of early shared activities and reciprocities were underestimated by political scientists until recent pioneering studies of federalism initiated by the late Morton Grodzins, and further research in administrative history. An earlier view of our governing system placed a higher significance on the differences, demarcations, and competitive relationships. A likely conclusion is that these cooperative endeavors evolved in highly dispersed, pragmatic fashion, only recently becoming so pervasive and visible as to require a revision of traditional tenets.[9] The forms these cooperative practices have taken demonstrates the inventiveness of politicians and administrators in this country. For example, states engage in a variety of cooperative commissions and authorities, dealing with common resources, transportation, educational, law enforcement, and other problems. These have involved innumerable compacts and agreements, and negotiating, liaison, and informational arrangements. Governments share fiscal resources through grants-in-aid and delegations of legal powers to other levels and agencies. Alternatively, governmental functions have been combined in regulatory commissions; sometimes in interdepartmental and advisory bodies or commissions of inquiry appointed by executive, legislative, or judicial branches; in some congressional committees; and in governmental authorities, boards, and corporations. Public powers are shared with private agents in many advisory committees, consultant, and contract arrangements, and by various inducements for private groups to perform services deemed of public value, such as job retraining, conservation, and various welfare activities.[10]

Formal governmental units often work with private agencies to study social problems and cooperate in seeking solutions. Universities are continuously called upon to assist governments; and private persons and groups frequently serve government as administrators, in effect, while maintaining their private roles. Thus doctors are now an integral part of Medicare programs, and businessmen collect Social Security and income taxes. Farmers participate in the administration of agricultural programs and engage in voting on their own crop restrictions. Insurance companies rate fire departments; and private persons serve in civil defense organizations. These are but a few of the many examples of cooperative and complementary activities in carrying out governmental regulations and services that could be cited. The point is that the political system we have today can be characterized by an extraordinary growth of cooperative behavior and devices, both formal and informal. The growing interdependence of society, with its great variety of problems and responsibilities, has stimulated more complex organizational solutions and more willingness to invent and employ them.

Not that there was an absence of differences and conflicts between governmental branches and levels, and between public authorities and the citizenry. We would hazard the generalization, however, that many areas of persistent discord tend to become regulated either by legal processes, or by cooperative bodies which serve to turn conflict into methods of consultation and negotiation. Thus the court and administrative systems have been increased by special claims units and appeals procedures; boundary disputes are adjudicated; and conflict over jurisdictions (revenue sources, economic regulation, etc.) are ruled upon by higher courts, or by legislative enactment. Policy disputes between major branches of government are also often resolved by the nature of electoral victories and the perceived support elective officials can claim. Thus early nineteenth-century Presidential vetoes of internal improvements became irrelevant with the Republican coalition of North and West; in this century a conservative Supreme Court gave way to urgent New Deal demands for new regulations and programs.[11]

Trends in resistance or noncooperation by citizens with regard to public appeals or rules are much more difficult to estimate. History, however, records some notable occasions: the Whisky Rebellion against alcohol excises; state conventions and resolutions opposing the Alien and Sedition Acts; the nullification controversy, the Dorr rebellion, the "underground" of the abolitionists, the great Civil War and its draft riots, the postwar force acts and occupation of the South, the great evasion of Prohibition, and more recently aired issues of police brutality, underworld syndicates, and citizens' organizing and arming for self-protection or aggression. Systematic appraisal in terms of relative populations involved, or comparable degrees of such practices is a challenge we must leave to the historian. To some extent we will take up this question from another perspective in considering the question of participatory opportunities. One might reason that as laws and administrative and legal procedures proliferate, there is less opportunity for citizen activity to take overt nonlegal forms, except with immense effort, and with an intensity only likely to be exhibited very briefly.[12]

We can also note one kind of countertrend, in response to the great proliferation of units and functions. In this century there have been recurrent moves toward consolidation, encouraged both by improved technologies of coordination and control, and by the desires of various citizens and groups for efficiency, economy, and centralized responsibility.[13] We see this trend especially at the local level in school district consolidations, by city annexations, by areawide or functional authorities across boundaries; and statewide in constitutional revisions and governmental reorganizations.[14] At the federal level, there have been many departmental and agency reorganizations, typically with centralizing results; for example, in the Defense Department (by unifying commands, consolidating service and supply agencies, and centralizing budget, contract, and research decisions), and more recently in new departments grouping similar functions and activities (HEW, HUD, Transportation).

We might try to document some of these general points, briefly. One study of interstate relations estimates almost 200 separately enacted federal grants-in-aid programs between 1803 and 1962. There were very few before the Civil War: an allocation of some proceeds of public land sales for schools and internal improvements, a provision of assistance for state militia, and some minor appropriations for local benefits. There were about eight more from the Civil War to the turn of the century: for agriculture and forests, veterans and the blind. The great increase in grants programs, in number and amounts, occurred in this century, right after World War I, the Great Depression, and today in the 1960's.[15]

At the local level one finds unsystematic evidence of the current cooperative efforts but very little in the way of trend data. For example, one study of 22 cities of over 1000 population in Minnesota, during 1953, reveals a total of 91 different agreements of cooperation in 17 different policy areas ranging from airports to library services. In the Philadelphia metropolitan area alone, the astonishing number of 756 compacts or agreements were counted among eight counties, with 686 separate local units of government. Most of these agreements had to do with school districts and police protection.[16]

In terms of organizational devices, the first major federal regulatory commission came in 1887 (ICC) pursuant to state experimentation with this form. A few years earlier (1883) Congress had set up a Civil Service Commission for general policy and advisory purposes. With the Progressive era five more major boards and commissions were created to handle various aspects of monetary, tariff, shipping, and power (i.e., fuel) policies. New Deal programs brought further regulatory bodies and other forms, including the TVA regional authority experiment, and various business-like lending agencies. In spite of academic criticism of their "mixed" or independent powers, post-World War II decades have witnessed an even greater proliferation of these collegial or independent agencies, covering such matters as atomic energy, public housing and home loans, farm credit, mine safety, labor conciliation, foreign claims, general services, Indian claims, small business, selective service, subversive activities, arms control, tax appeals, education and research, and space exploration. The U.S. Government Organizational Manual for 1967–68 lists 78 more boards, committees, and commissions not formally attached to any one agency, plus 31 multilateral and bilateral organizations in which the United States participates with other nations or international bodies.[17]

It is estimated that only about fifty consultative and advisory committees on which interest groups and citizens have representation, were active just before World War II; today the departments of Agriculture and Defense are said to have as many as the entire government twenty years ago, with one estimate putting the governmental total at probably over two thousand.[18]

As the polity has grown in size and complexity, officialdom has become more specialized and professionalized. This is especially the case with civil servants who now number more than ten million, and who typically satisfy some competitive test for entry into public service. Whether elective officials are more or less professionalized today is more difficult to ascertain, but they deal with issues and problems which are more demanding of technical knowledge than was the case during the earlier years of the nation. In any case, a far greater percentage of the present-day civil service and the elective officials are college-educated.[19] Highly specialized training in public administration, law, and even political techniques are further evidence of a growing concern with professional public service. Casual inspection of career patterns and political longevity among Congressmen suggests that they, too, tend to develop professional careers of being Congressmen. Many more Congressmen of our time have longer continuous terms of service than in the nineteenth century. Earlier Congresses had higher turnover rates resembling, in that respect, those of state legislatures today.[20]

The basic formal structure of the political system, in short, may be said to continue to be formally decentralized, highly segmented, and functionally differentiated, but increasingly complex and more visible (i.e., more capable of public observation). The basic legal structure has been remarkably stable, and countless informal practices have evolved to supplement the workings of the formalized elements. While many detailed changes have occurred, there have been relatively few fundamental alterations or experiments. Totally novel and different systems have not supplanted one another, as has been the experience in many

other lands. Instead, expansion, proliferation, and some concentration
—not always evenly paced—has characterized changes in the American political structure.

POLICY AND POLICY-MAKING

Trends in formal political structures should contribute some clues
about the governing processes they entail—the political methods of resolving issues, rendering public decisions, and producing public policies. The generalizations we offer are best supported for recent years;
we do not have appropriate evidence very far into the past. Historical
materials necessary to test them would be very costly and sometimes
impossible to acquire. We resort to the authority of some distinguished
observers and scholars for "confirmation" of the historical plausibility
of present generalizations. Only the most painstaking research such as
that conducted so imaginatively by Merle Curti and his students on a
Wisconsin county for the period of 1840–80;[21] Charles S. Grant on a
Connecticut frontier town (1732–1800);[22] Oscar and Mary Handlin
on Massachusetts,[23] and Lee Benson on New York state,[24] will supply the necessary links from national to local policy processes. We
should also note the newer contributions—attempting broader empirical tests—made by Robert Brown[25] and Forrest MacDonald[26] in their
critiques of Charles Beard's interpretation of the making of the Constitution, and by many of their contemporary colleagues in history applying new analytic techniques to electoral and political processes. Further
insights on trends in national policy-making are provided by such traditional political science literature as Henry Jones Ford's *The Rise
and Growth of American Politics;*[27] Arthur N. Holcombe's *The Political Parties of Today;*[28] E. E. Schattschneider's *Party Government,*[29]
and the invaluable administrative histories of Leonard D. White.[30]

1789 to the Civil War

We must begin with a clear recognition that policy-making involves
most continuously the few directly involved actors, typically those
in official roles and those with direct and visible stakes in what the
government does. The state of technology in the early years of the
republic confined typical policy-making to active elites with time, resources, or occupational interests in public policy. Seldom would a
matter such as Constitutional ratification bring in a broader electorate
over one single issue, and there, as MacDonald shows, the most effective element of the electorate was the aspiring or prosperous farmer

with strong tax and trade concerns. Beyond this policy sphere were the isolated small farmers of the countryside and frontier, those in more remote small towns and localities, the laboring and serving classes, the migrant elements coming into the cities and moving out to frontiers, the retreating native Indian, the black slaves.

As Ford indicates, the national policy-makers maintained many of the attributes and practices of a fairly exclusive elite. The revolution had taken care of the royalist element with its special ties and authoritative support from the mother country. The revolutionary experience and trials of the confederation brought an expectation of unified statesmanship, and that appeared to be the major premise of the writers of the *Federalist Papers,* as well as the first President. The first national policies involved institution-building in which Washington spent great attention on formal detail, with a rather formalistic process of soliciting individual or written views from his chief officers who were primarily preoccupied with managing affairs in their separate spheres.[31] The chief executive could thus moderate initial differences, and render separate, "impersonal" decisions when consultations or cabinet meetings revealed lack of agreement. In spite of some crises and intense consultations, there was plenty of "looseness" in this very early period, with Presidents frequently returning to their own private matters away from official business. More informal delegation of administrative duties might also have been encouraged because officialdom contained many interpersonal and family ties.[32] There is little suggestion of much pressure or demands from the populace at large directly aimed at the national leadership over general policy issues. The citizenry took action only when directly affected, at places often far from the center of government: veterans agitating for promised bounty lands, spasmodic outbreaks against taxes deemed excessive.

The beginnings of organized competition over general policy began within the President's official family, as with the famous Hamilton-Jefferson disputes. But it was the legislative branch that first enabled organized competition, with the developing roles of committees and the Speaker of the House providing institutional leadership, and with the more autonomous set of relationships among elected representatives. Jefferson is given much credit for his tactical success in organizing an opposition party among political groups in the countryside, to provide an electoral base for concerted opposition at the nation's capital. In any case, party competition was initially likened to treason in a country still used to censorship of the press, where appeals to outside groups looked like subversion against established leadership. The fact that the anti-Federalists did arouse rather widespread turmoil over various Federalist policies, the reactive Alien and Sedition Acts, and the indeterminate electoral outcome of 1800 with its prolonged and bitter resolution in the House of Representatives, indicate the rather tenuous stability of the early republic.

We propose to view this period as essentially an intra-elite competition over policy among factions largely within a dominant social strata. The divisions and concerns were not of continuous vital import to the mass of active citizenry. Matters of work, trade, development, law, order, and citizenship were decentralized by necessity, with states and localities the scene of most public activity.

During this period federal programs were primarily extractive or distributive in impact. Who gave and who got what were national issues insofar as relevant interests were affected. The national policy body for such issues was the Congress; given its basis of representation the "interests" it perceived as affected became identified geographically, especially as the new nation expanded. The older North and South were opposed regarding the benefits of tariffs and internal improvements, but would support higher prices for public lands and thus more public income. The North and Southwest were joined in favoring generous public land disposal and internal improvements but were opposed on the tariff question. Bargaining was facilitated by the specific and visible nature of the impacts of these policy goods, for the different sections, and by the mixed nature of the preferences of each. There were a variety of possible "bargains" in terms of joining in alliances on one issue, or exchanging support across issues, constrained only by the talents and convictions of the sectional leadership in Congress, and by the relative balance of representation as the country grew. The fact that the national policy "goods" were exchangeable to some degree avoided any polarized competition or conflict, and this period shows frequent shifts in winning coalitions. Congress produced many internal improvements bills; some passed, though several were also vetoed by unpersuaded Presidents; there was successive legislation to lower the price of public lands and in other ways liberalize its distribution; some succeeded and some failed; there were periodic changes in tariff rates and coverage, initially upward, and then in alternation.[33] Measured by these variable policy outputs, this was a relatively fluid policy process, encouraged by the exchangeability of the separate policy concerns of major actors. The bulk of enforcement and regulation rested with the states; the bulk of popular concern lay with private matters or local issues, and any general patterns of public conflict at that level are beyond us, at this point.

Civil War to the Present

This fluidity in policy-making was, of course, completely broken by the Civil War and the slavery issue, and the first massive policy of national regulation was underway with Reconstruction. The deeply divisive attitudes engendered in this period will only be mentioned here and left to the immensely detailed documentation of historians. Beyond national policy directed at the South, a new kind of policy pattern emerged from a Republican dominance and the exclusion of the old Southern leadership from national policy-making. One might label it a "cumulative coalition," still based primarily on distributive policies for those outside the South. There was a "breakthrough" in benefits and services, primarily for the farmer, but also nodding to a variety of other organized and economic groups: the Homestead Act, the establishment of the Department of Agriculture, railroad grants, the coal disposal act, land grant colleges, an office of education, and most important, ever higher tariffs. The Republican coalition was predominantly an instrument of Northern commercial and industrial interests which used the tariff as an expanding protective umbrella for any important new claimant in the industrializing North. The support of the farmer of the West was gained by giving land and aiding transportation; then, when these were less of a concern, by specific tariff concessions.[34] The tariff became the major national political issue distinguishing the parties; but competition was impossible until something unsettled this dominant coalition.[35]

The unsettling feature, as is well known, was economic distress. And the distinguishing element was its directness of impact on the farmers, especially in the West and South, then its pervasive influence in other sectors, given increasingly interdependent industrial and commercial patterns. The successive farmer movements have been taken as classic patterns of "grass roots" protest, first organizing for localized and state policy solutions and ultimately merging into a national partisan protest.[36] The Populist Party nationalized the issue but, as recent scholars have pointed out, their movement was aborted in the "critical" electoral period of 1892–1896, when the Republicans reconsolidated their strength, and ended the competitive pattern of shifting balances this rural protest had brought to the Congressional branch at least.[37]

Recent historical studies indicate the next great wave of reform, the Progressive movement, was less "grass roots" than "middle class" (business and professional). It produced some municipal reform, and stimulated various anticorruption crusades that often aligned newer commercial and professional groups against workingmen and their local political party organizations.[38] In contrast, organized labor did not start as a political movement; it kept close to job concerns. Early labor agitation and violence were resolved typically by specific executive or court action, and initial legislation of benefit to labor was typically the product of progressive reform movements, first at the state level. Only with the Great Depression did labor become a distinctly organized element in the new national Democratic coalition, whose voting base was generally a combination of urban ethnic and lower-class economic groups.

Thus the early twentieth-century Progressive era was but an interlude in the long-run pattern of Republican and business dominance, where substantial economic interests worked out compatible policies with a directness of access to policy-makers exposed finally by the muckrakers of the period. Wilson profited from the party division caused by this "middle class" reform movement, and won significant regulatory legislation from the new but rather tenuous coalition of Southern and rural Democrats with urban reformers. The regulations of trade and the monetary system, and the new income tax, were more significant policy products than most of the spasmodic gestures of earlier populist-inspired legislation. National public regulation of the economy was irrevocably established, then reinforced by wartime measures, and impossible to reverse in the subsequent return of Republicanism.

From there we move into the modern era of "bureaucratized politics" emphasized in the rest of this chapter. Trade associations were encouraged by governmental officials to aid in stabilizing the market—by Wilson's wartime policies, then most notably by Herbert Hoover both as Secretary of Commerce and as President, and by New Deal administrators who desired stabilization even as they worried over excessive monopoly. National economic policy-making moved from the competition and bargaining typical of the legislature, to the more frequent negotiation and consultation of executive agencies and commissions. We will elaborate upon this currently more typical policy process in further sections.

We have said nothing about emergent processes in the judicial system, but Hurst's excellent studies indicate that during the nineteenth century the courts performed much of the low-level, pragmatic policy application to particular daily concerns of citizens and merchants, within a broad framework of very general laws passed by legislatures. Bargaining and compromise were as much a feature of this policy process as was conflict in litigation, given the variety of kinds of new problems confronted.[39] With the increasing complexity of interests, special claims courts and procedures were established through the early decades of this century. Hurst thinks it significant that much of the emergent law developed by this specialized litigation has been superseded by the new social welfare programs of state and nation, and by administered protections and guarantees thus afforded.[40]

One final note. We cannot completely lament the demise of grass roots politics, nor of political conflict and competition, even in this highly industrialized, organized, bureaucratized era of policy-making. The national media increasingly dramatize national policy disputes in the post-World War II era, and contending national leadership find these media formidable in Presidential contests, in policy disputes between national leaders, and in dramatizing policy needs through committee investigations and exposés. They appear even to have encouraged a new generation of national protest, at least among the younger generation of Negroes and students protesting discrimination, poverty, and the Vietnam war. We cannot assess at this point whether the more typical bureaucratic politics will be deeply affected by this trend, or continue to function in spite of the intense drama on the outside and in the streets. One cannot deny, in the short run, that the remarkable shift in the party margins of 1964 enabled a rash of innovative and reform legislation for such a brief span of time. But effective policy changes are still delegated primarily to established bureaucratic processes—the schools, the volunteer and professional social work organizations, to particular agencies, and local economic or professional groups. At this point in time it is impossible to predict a major shift from these more continuous, organized, and diffused forms of policy-making within the great institutionalized sectors of national life.[41]

CHANGING POLITICAL ACTIVITIES OF CITIZENS

Because systematic counts and studies of political behavior were not made during the first century of our national existence, we know little about individual and group political activities. Our information is most complete and reliable for only the most recent decades. Nevertheless, some reasonable generalizations seem warranted.

Bureaucratization of Interests

We may note, for example, that increasingly the major actors have become the highly organized associations or interest groups and the political party or campaign organizations. The former, in particular, have become a highly bureaucratized system. The number of interest groups organized for political activity during the early nineteenth century could not have been great, because the smaller, rural population was engaged in a much simpler division of labor. Still, Oscar and Mary Handlin remind us that as the century progressed, there was a considerable proliferation of voluntary associations and rapid development of the corporate device for organizing business activity and interests.[42] Today, we read estimates of organized groups numbering in the vicinity of 200,000[43] with perhaps 57 per cent of the population belonging to one or more associations.[44] At the national level, alone, as many as 7,600 lobbyists have registered with Congress and spent an annual average of about 5 million dollars.[45] In 1950, over 10 million dollars were expended in pursuit of national legislative goals.[46] More recent years have witnessed sharp drops from that officially reported high. As all students of political finance warn us, these figures are undoubtedly very conservative estimates.

The current situation at the state and local levels is much less clear, but scatterings of information are available. For example, California and Florida each have more than 430 registered interest groups.[47]

While the interest group is a major political means of achieving policy and other public ends, it is also clear, at all levels of government, that not all segments of society have been, or are, equally organized into equally powerful organizations. All commentators are agreed today that the business world is by far the most thoroughly organized. Labor and professional interests follow, along with groups composed of public officials and employees. Consumers, religious, ethnic, racial, and general-interest citizen groups are the least well represented, again, at all levels, lacking similar resources to compete effectively with the major producer and service organizations.

Whether interest groups are becoming more or less significant in the American polity is still highly debatable. Zeigler, for example, predicts that as the states become more industrialized and urbanized they will develop stronger, more competitive political parties which, in turn, will diminish the power of interest groups to determine policy outcomes.[48] Others have argued the same thesis, claiming an inverse relationship exists between the power of parties and interest groups. Beer, however, has contended that in Britain both interests and parties are powerful, and that in this country both are essentially weak.[49] Measures of these relationships are not easily devised or agreed upon.

As interests have become more bureaucratized, they have become more distant from their members and more impersonal. Many members do not know their organizations pursue political goals, nor do they participate in regularized ways within the organization. Interest groups are almost universally organized along highly stratified lines in which elites make the choices, constrained primarily by the fear of making major mistakes that might arouse counterelites or the mass membership. Widespread participation in organizational activities, especially the political type, is rare in most groups.

Still another characteristic of interest group politics deserves note: most interest groups pursue particularistic goals and engage in discontinuous political activity, i.e., tend to become politically activated when their concerns are visibly threatened or their goals directly require political protection or advancement. Most routine organizational activities involve internal services and functions for their membership —social and occupational information, and reinforcement of group values and norms. Indeed, most interest groups are relatively small, highly issue-specialized and frequently quite inefficient, ineffective, slow to perceive their interests and often ignorant of what they might be or how they can best be achieved. The efficient mobilization of effective political resources is no mean task so that only the major organizations employ full time professionalized political advisers. The major organizations (AFL-CIO, Chambers of Commerce, AMA, NAM, etc.) have institutionalized political activity, most of it in the form of public relations, internal information, and generalized discussion and debate at conventions. Recent studies emphasize the limited effectiveness of lobbying to influence legislative and executive decisions, as contrasted to crucial elite contacts, a visibly and intensely aroused membership, or the regularized consultations and understandings among public and private bureaucrats.

Many scholars view the role of the political party as "integrating" the body politic in the face of irregular or diversionary interest group activity. Yet the party as a vast and decentralized campaign organization materializes only in Presidential election years, and then to wage a competitive contest. It is sufficient to arouse some sense of citizen "sovereignty" across large segments of the electorate. But other scholars contend that the exclusion—willful or apathetic—from the polls of about one-third of the electorate even in that great contest (and rising to about two-thirds or more in local balloting) is testimony rather to division and alienation. In any case the efficacious and informed activists who regularly attend to politics and derive rewards therefrom are a very small proportion of the adult population. Electoral activity most pervasively touches the electorate through the mass media and the propaganda efforts of highly specialized campaign organizations. Instead of direct contacts, major candidates employ professional pollsters to reveal grass roots sentiment based on very minute samples. Analysts tend to conclude that it is the primary group relationship—at home or on the job—that is most likely to be reinforced or tested by general political discussion and not party solidarity for its own sake. This kind of theory cannot at all be adequately tested against earlier times.

It is not much easier to check the hypothesized integrative influence of the party on official decisions, as an indicator of party efficacy. Legislative voting studies are now turning to the historical dimension, and tend to show great variations over time and issues, from strong party voting to other kinds of divisions based on sections, local concerns, economic, and other interests. There are many problems both of sufficient comparability of issues over time, and of differentiating the party influence on elective officials from the voting coalitions of group and area interests comprising the party. The efficacy of party as a special integrating link for the electorate cannot therefore be identified easily.

What we do realize today, with closer study, is the greater amount of discretion exercised by officials for most decisions, than traditional "pressure" or "influence" theories maintained. There is evidence that this discretion increases as the decision-maker deals more frequently with complex, highly particularized, and less visible kinds of decisions; and that this is ever more the case given the economic, political, and social complexities of the modern policies. Interest groups and economic enterprises apparently had greater influence toward the later nineteenth century, for in spite of minimal organizational technology and resources, there were fewer major policy decisions and they had more direct and visible impacts to those actively concerned. The heyday of interest pressures took place when groups were fewer and less competitive. More recent studies indicate that politicians are, or at least feel, far freer to decide and act.[50] The relative power of interests and officialdom has probably changed most during the past three decades. Many high governmental officials and military officers now have broader scope for initiative and command than corporate captains.[51]

Of continually growing importance is the compulsory bureaucratization of interests. The older version of interest groups emphasized the voluntary association, direct citizen responses to common hopes and ills, and a mustering of freely contributed resources. Today one finds organizational membership increasingly compulsory for one's occupation, whether a labor union or a professional association. The means of interest representation have consequently also become institutionalized and bureaucratized, embodied in such typical forms as advisory commmittees, consultant commissions, formal negotiation conferences, and information-sharing devices. In addition, we have witnessed an extraordinary lateral mobility of high-status persons between governmental, private, and quasi-public positions. And, some of these public figures work for both Democratic and Republican administrations. How much of this may have taken place in earlier history is difficult to say, but it could not have taken this form of modern professionalized politics.

Eli Ginzberg and his associates have pointed out that many newer institutions can no longer be viewed in the old context as "private" concentrations of interests, for they have a "quasi-public" role.[52] They are often tax-sheltered, for example, foundations for charity and research, hospitals, libraries, schools, and churches. Or they do privileged business with government involving public concessions and incentives, for example, much of the defense industry or research and development firms doing contract business with government. And there are the burgeoning public enterprises, especially in such service areas as welfare, health, sanitation, local transportation, and communications, which either enjoy subsidies or monopoly privileges. In these expanding sectors, public and private interests can no longer be as easily separated as was once the case. Again negotiations, consultation, and concession are commonplace, with formal notice or ceremony presenting a consensual picture of the results to the public.

Role of the Citizen

The picture we have sketched thus far plays havoc with the prized traditional role of the individual citizen as portrayed in the civics books. The policy preferences and demands of the citizen can still be voiced but seldom in the direct fashion of personal participation. Politicians look for issues and support, and at least at the national level may be thought of as among the chief initiators of action and policy. While we believe that the American system continues to pay considerable attention to the people, it is an attention resulting from far more impersonal heights than was the case on the frontier or in the village.

Yet, the American citizen of today who has a gripe does not appear to have surrendered completely; how else can we explain the persistent and passionate protests and direct action that our society has witnessed these past ten years? Black citizens especially have confronted authority and made considerable impacts upon it. We may note that as in the past a passionate minority can pursue strategies involving demonstrations, sit-ins, violence through rioting, as well as the traditionally approved political actions, to attain ends or at least gain attention. These alternatives in political action are not new, but the extent of their usage in this country and the methods available are. What may be common with the past is the "marginal status" of the particular group of protestors. Student political activity has never, until recently, been expected or approved. And Negroes have only recently been able to break the bonds which have held them in weak political positions for centuries. Perhaps the next groups to become politically aroused will include the Mexican-Americans, native Indians, and Puerto Ricans. But the pervasive problems of American Negroes are now at a crucial threshold, likely to trigger systematic rebellion and repression, or creative and revolutionary political responses. Few are predicting peaceful negotiations or piecemeal change at this time.

If past experience is indicative of the future, political action may well follow a typical cycle of sporadic individual protests, accommodation or repression by private and some governmental units, increased agitation, increasing amounts of organized effort, formation of formal organizations, negotiation and compromises with more established private organizations and governments, internal divisions and protests by members as the original movements become establishment-oriented, and then routinized bureaucratic participation in political life, as success is taken for granted. This cycle of behavior may not always be completed, but it seems a realistic possibility. An optimistic aspect may be found in the belief in what Alvin W. Gouldner has demanded— the recognition of an "iron law of democracy" to counteract Michels' justly famous generalization.[53] Americans do rebel, protest, and counterorganize against repression, authority, power, and deprivation. We expect they will continue that long tradition and perhaps devise some new tactics in the process.

CHANGING GOVERNMENTAL ACTIVITIES

Policies, Goods, and Services

If the governments of a democratic polity are as important as we maintain, then a concern for their established activities must be a significant part of any investigation into social change. Fortunately, a great deal of quantitative source material now exists which permits fairly precise measurements of such matters as the nature of official activities, their scope, magnitudes, and rates of change. As we shall see, public budgets are invaluable sources for much useful data.

Political outputs, the goods and services produced and distributed by governments, come in a vast profusion of types and quantities. While there is no single authoritative classification of the variety of governmental services, at least two observers have attempted to inventory governmental activities. Chatters and Hoover, in a now dated counting, listed more than 400 broad sets of activities classified into fifteen major groupings.[54] No other organization or institution in the society engages in so many different tasks.

Another useful indicator of the scope of political activity are the legislative records of the numbers of bills introduced for consideration and the number which survive the struggle to become enacted into public law. The historical record is incomplete, but we know that early legislatures sat in session for much shorter periods while contemporary state legislatures sit for months, and Congress is in almost continual session. At the state level, it is now typical for more than 100,000 bills annually to be introduced altogether, while in Congress during each session approximately 18,000 bills are introduced.[55] Of the latter, not more than a thousand are usually enacted, while the state legislatures pass, perhaps, a third of their measures.

Similarly, the work of the court system displays an increasing amount of activity.[56] As recently as 1940, for example, the Supreme Court handled over 900 cases; while in 1964, they disposed of more than 2,100 cases. Various other courts (U.S. Courts of Appeal, U.S. District Courts) have increased their work and services by as much as three times. The U.S. Courts of Appeals handled 2,730 cases in 1945, but in 1965 dealt with 6,766 cases.

Like courts and legislatures, the administrative agencies have also increased the volume of their services. We need not detail this change except to note the steadily increased number of agencies, employees, revenues; and the number of goals, laws, orders, programs, etc., that they are expected to implement. The point is, then, that the sheer volume of governmental activities, whether productive or not, has increased enormously over the history of the nation.

Another measure of governmental activity which in some areas can be direct, precise, and useful, are the resources with which the governments have to operate and perform their tasks. In addition to impressive legal-rational authority to decide and act, governments have command over more resources than any other type of institution in our society. In 1802, the public domain was but 200 million acres of land, while in 1964 it amounted to more than two billion acres. In 1966 the federal government alone owned about 766 million acres and more than 426,000 buildings valued, at cost, as worth more than $24 billion. Total costs of all federally owned land, buildings, and facilities are estimated at more than $66 billion.[57] All this property is put to work with increasing amounts of revenue from taxes and a variety of other sources. In 1965, all governments took in more than $202 billion with which to conduct their activities.[58] Total revenues and expenditures for state and local governments are not available for the years prior to 1900, but estimates for 1913, for example, show governments receiving about $3 billion.[59] This was about 8.8 per cent of the Gross National Product as contrasted with the 25 to 30 per cent that is now taken by all governments.

Whether we measure governmental activity by the cost of its services, the extent to which collectively made decisions replace private choices, or the extent to which society's resources are administered by government, one cannot escape the greatly increased significance of government today. It produces more services, engages in more activities, pays greater costs to produce them, administers more resources, and has supplanted and/or regulated many private marketplace processes and choices with political processes and choices.

Let us look at more budgetary data. First, total governmental budgets have increased enormously. Federal expenditures in 1789–1791 were $4.2 million as contrasted with a predicted $189 billion for 1968.[60] On a per capita basis this was approximately $1 in 1789, and $945 for the proposed budget of 1968. The data for all governments in the early years of the Republic are not available, but by 1902 per capita expenditures of all governments had risen to $21 and by 1966 exceeded $1,126.[61] Even granting price changes and varying levels of efficiency, these are huge increases.

Manifest as the sum totals are, they may not be as interesting as the changing composition of these aggregates. What evidence there is indicates the major early federal budget allocations were devoted to some provisions for internal order, external defense, payment of interest on the public debt, granting veterans' bounties, and financing of roads, ports, and canals. The federal government in 1789–1791 spent more than half its total expenditures on interest payments and much of the remainder on veterans, while defense took about $633,000 from a budget of slightly more than $4.2 million.[62] Contrasting the situation with later years shows that total sums spent on these traditional functions increase greatly but each in varying degrees in proportion to the total federal budget and the Gross National Product. Overall federal spending during the nineteenth century remained a rather stable percentage of the Gross National Product—about 5 per cent as contrasted to about 25 per cent in recent years. Activities which show the greatest gains as increased shares of the federal budget during the twentieth century include defense, international affairs and finance, social welfare, and agriculture.[63] Another study concurs with these earlier estimates but extends them to 1962. It notes that in more recent years foreign aid programs initiated after World War II have declined sharply, as did veterans' programs for awhile; while spending on natural resources and highways stabilized somewhat during the late 1940's and 1950's. On the other hand, research, space exploration, and educational expenditures were greatly accelerated.[64] The Tax Foundation has claimed that the largest single percentage increases within the federal budgets during the period 1947 to 1961 were, as to be expected, in space research and technology (2,025.7 per cent), and education (1,373.4 per cent). Veterans' benefits declined during that period by 26.6 per cent, while housing declined by slightly more than 10 per cent. Expenditures for labor increased by more than 300 per cent while expenditures on health and welfare, commerce, and natural resources all increased by anywhere from 261 per cent (health and welfare) to 289 per cent in the case of commerce.[65]

Along with changing budgetary priorities and activities, there has been a redistribution of the responsibilities for conducting these activities. In 1902, for example, local governments clearly dominated in most domestic functions such as education, highways, public welfare, parks and recreation, natural resources, and police protection.[66] By the 1960's, however, local governments found themselves sharing these activities to a far greater extent with state and federal governments. Local governments, today, predominate primarily in education and law enforcement. The states now act as the senior partner in highways, public welfare, health and hospitals, while the federal government has taken over the greater role in natural resources and non-highway transportation. The federal government has always had exclusive responsibility in national defense, foreign affairs, the postal system, and management of the money supply, and continues predominant in veterans' affairs and agricultural stabilization.

Contributory Factors

These basic facts about changing governmental budget allocations remain unexplained. We can briefly note some of the contributory factors cited by economists and political scientists in explaining the growth of governmental activities and expenditures. Population growth and geographical redistributions of that growth from rural to urban centers are cited as bringing new problems and, therefore, demands for increased services and controls. Dewhurst has claimed that population growth alone for the period of 1913–1950 was responsible for an increase of 6.9 per cent of the total government expenditure.[67] Changing age patterns in the population, with greater proportions of both the young and old, create problems which cannot, apparently, be met successfully without greater governmental assistance. And the move to cities and suburbs has also generated more demands for public services.

Economists also attribute some rise in governmental expenditures to changes in the price level of the things governments purchase. A long-run decline in the purchasing power of the dollar has inflated the budgetary figures beyond what corrected prices would do. Dewhurst has calculated that the actual increase in government expenditures in terms of 1950 dollars, for the period 1913–1950, was 7.2 times rather than 22.4 times as is the case in current dollars.[68] Thus 31.2 per cent of the total expenditure increase during that period could be estimated as due to price level changes alone.[69] One must, therefore, interpret the dramatic dollar changes frequently cited in the newspapers with some care, for the growth of government, while impressive, has not been quite that dramatic.

Adjusting for price and population changes allows a more realistic picture of the degree to which additional and improved public services account for governmental growth. It has been estimated by Dewhurst, for the period 1913–1950, that the expanded scope of governmental activities contributed about 40.9 per cent of the total increases.[70] Increasing services are, then, the single most important factor in the long-term growth of public expenditures, although they may not be for specific short-run periods, as in war and inflationary times.

The remaining 21 per cent of the increase in expenditures can be accounted for, according to Dewhurst, by the combined interaction of population changes, price level alterations, and increased services. The interaction of these three factors, Dewhurst contended, produced their greatest impact during the years 1913 to 1932. Over one-third of the total expenditures growth during this period could be attributed to this multiple cause. During the next ten years (1932–1942) their combined influence dropped to about one-fourth of the total rise in spending, but during the 1942–1950 period it actually became negative.[71]

These many figures and the Dewhurst explanation cover changes in amounts of government spending, but leave open to speculation the qualitative aspects of these activities, that is, what they entailed in other than monetary terms. They must also be assessed in terms of "disappointed" preferences and by the degree to which these activities entailed requirements and controls on the behavior and choices of private persons and groups. We should ask for better measures of how the perceived costs compared to desired benefits when these additions and increases came about for whom and where. We should assess degrees and kinds of change in terms of relative support versus resistance, especially when established levels of programs are substantially shifted. Such changes may benefit certain groups, but they also entail the restriction of other citizens' free choice and behavior. Doing good for one segment of the population can rarely be achieved except as an additional burden on others; that is what makes politics so difficult and policy-advising so treacherous.

Control activities are basic functions of polities, but they are not as easily measured by expenditures or personnel. Scholars seem agreed that the great eras of expanding controls were at the turn of the century and during the New Deal. But controls are enacted at some level nearly every day, and while most are undramatic and affect relatively few, they are nevertheless controls and cost money to implement. Each decade seems to emphasize certain activities to be controlled; during the 1880–1914 period, and again during the 1930's, it was business behavior. During the 1920's and 1950's the concern turned to subversive tendencies and behavior and the lack of patriotism. Policing morality in the areas of sex, liquor, drugs, obscene literature or performances, and so on have always been a potentially powerful object of control in American life, mostly at the local level.

Budgets do not accurately reflect the extent of control activities because lump-sum allocations to civilian bureaucracies do not disclose how much of the monies go into control. In any event, we know that much of the daily work of many bureaucrats is either direct or indirect control. The proliferation of agencies, personnel, and budgetary allocations to these tasks are indicators of the continuing growth of legal restraints in American life.

SOME CHANGING IMPACTS OF THE POLITY ON SOCIETY

In this section we should like to explore the changing impact of the American polity upon the lives of its members—the American people. In brief, we wish to contend that politics and government have an increasing impact on more citizens, more of the time, in more areas of daily life. Measures of these impacts are not as direct and unambiguous as one might prefer, especially for long periods of time. But indicators of several impacts are available, and while they point to "objective" events rather than "subjective" feelings on the part of the citizenry, they clearly support the assumption that government is an increasingly more important factor in the lives of American citizens than it was in the nineteenth century. We may illustrate the general contention in a variety of areas, beginning with the citizen's role in supporting and maintaining the system.

Extraction of Resources

No political system has ever been able to maintain itself and provide services completely on the basis of voluntary contributions from its citizenry. The United States is no exception; it too depends upon mandatory or compulsory contributions. Taxes are, of course, the most commonly used form of such involuntary extractions, although military service, jury duty, fire-fighting, and road work by prisoners are also mandatory means of raising needed manpower. The draft has taken increasing numbers of young men as our wars have become larger enterprises and the role of the United States in world affairs has expanded.

But the best indicators and the ones for which we have good historical data are taxation, governmental indebtedness, governmental units, and public employment. In Table 1, for example, we see the growth in per capita taxation (Column 1) for selected years. The increase in absolute amounts is paralleled, to some extent, by increases in per capita public indebtedness to the citizenry (Column 2). In Column 3 we note the numbers of governmental units and, in Col-

TABLE 1. SELECTED INDICATORS OF THE GROWTH OF
GOVERNMENTAL ACTIVITY

Year	Column 1 Per capita taxation	Column 2 Per capita public indebtedness	Column 3 Number of governmental units	Column 4 Government employees as percentage of total work force
1902	$18	$41	—	—
1913	24	58	—	—
1927	80	281	182,651 (1932)	—
1936	83	416	—	6.9
1940	108	479	155,116 (1942)	9.5
1944	389	1,644	—	9.5
1950	364	1,861	116,743 (1952)	12.4 (1949)
1955	537	1,939	—	11.0
1960	709	1,979	91,736 (1962)	12.0
1965	860	2,151	—	13.3

SOURCES: Columns 1 and 2: *Facts and Figures on Government Finance,* Tax Foundation, Inc., New York, 1967, pp. 23, 25.

Column 3: U.S. Bureau of the Census, *Census of Governments,* vol. 1, "Governmental Organization," Washington, 1962, p. 1.

Column 4: variously computed from U. S. Bureau of the Census, *Statistical Abstract of the United States: 1966,* Washington, 1966, pp. 219, 437; and *Historical Statistics of the United States: Colonial Times to 1957,* Washington, 1960, pp. 70, 709–711.

umn 4, the numbers of governmental employees as a percentage of the total work force. These latter two indicators may also be used as indicators of the possible number of contact points with governments[72] while the first two columns may be interpreted as measures of the growing significance of governmental activity for the individual. Our most general interpretation of these arrays of figures is that governments not only provide more opportunities for citizen contact but also consume larger sums of personal income. Even with price and income adjustments, governments do today command both larger proportions of individual income and larger absolute amounts. The income tax, instituted in 1913, has made this possible, and in so doing made nearly every adult vulnerable to taxation—a contributor to his polity, whether he likes it or not, whether he supports governmental policies and leaders or not.

While the extraction of resources is achieved primarily through taxation in countless ingenious ways, United States governments have also employed many other devices to raise resources and revenues, such as user fees, fines, borrowing, inflation, forced labor as in drafts and prison camps, and volunteered services (air raid wardens, volunteer fire departments). We do not know the relative reliance placed on each of these practices through time, but we have a strong hunch that less emphasis has come to be placed on volunteered activities and more on both compulsory taxation and pricing of individual services. Governments are a major buyer of goods and services; in fact the federal government is the largest single buyer in the United States.[73] But governments are also sellers of goods and services; while not the largest, certainly major ones. It appears governments have become increasingly more active in both areas. Governments have resorted to user fees, or prices, as means of financing many divisible services in addition to the typical generalized or pure public goods it produces through general taxation. Besides the traditional postal charges, there are patent and copyright fees, charges for governmental publications, lease payments for mineral rights and grazing on public lands, park fees, licenses, public utility charges, and that most common of all fees —parking meter charges. As more private goods and services are produced and/or distributed by governments through publicly owned enterprises, we may expect greater use of prices to distribute these goods.

Allocation of Tax Burdens

Over-all measures of governmental absorption of resources are highly useful for many purposes, but the distribution of relative costs or personal contributions may be a more relevant question for an average citizen. Unhappily, historical data on this problem are hard to come by; in fact, highly reliable measures of present-day incidences of burden-sharing and attitudes about it are difficult to find. The complexity of the incidence problems is itself a major obstacle to such information-gathering. Another problem stems from the fact that governments have not really made an attempt to measure actual tax incidence.

A few hypotheses can be advanced on the basis of well-known generalizations of economics, and some historical information. It is clear that as American governments have increased the scope of their activities, they have had to find more lucrative sources of revenue, mostly by higher rates and by extracting taxes from new groups of citizens. More is taken from lower-income recipients and the consumer than was the case in the nineteenth century, primarily through the sales tax and lowered levels of taxable income.

The structure of revenue sources has changed considerably during the history of the nation.[74] Land sales and tariffs contributed the greatest amounts during the very early decades. Customs and excises were the most stable sources of federal government revenue before the Civil War especially. Excises replaced land sales as a major federal revenue source after the Civil War, and in this century income tax returns exceed all other sources, especially after the 1920's. During the nineteenth century state governments relied heavily on borrowing, bank taxes and the general property tax. After that century additional sources were sought, including taxes on insurance companies, corporation franchise taxes, inheritance taxes, and taxes on liquors. The property tax provided and continues to provide basic support for local governments, but state governments now rely to a far greater extent on the general sales tax than they did early in the century. State income taxes were unheard of before 1902; today, almost a quarter of the states' revenues originate in income taxes, and more large cities are now turning to that source. Motor fuel taxes obviously did not exist before 1900; today they make up 16 to 17 per cent of state tax revenues. The property tax, contrary to public opinion, declined in importance as a source of state governmental revenues from a high of 52.6 per cent in 1902 to 2.9 per cent in 1961. The property tax has also declined in importance for local governments, but still provides over half the local governmental revenue. Local governments now rely more heavily upon new excise taxes, sales taxes, and particularly intergovernmental revenues. During the twentieth century, alone, they increased their shares of state revenues almost fivefold (5.7 per cent of the total local revenues to 25.4 per cent). At the same time the federal government has provided more monies to state and local governments.

All these changes in types and importance of tax revenues have distributive significance for citizens, but an importance that is not easily measured since they have mixed or even contradictory consequences. For example, the federal tax system tends to be somewhat more progressive than either the state or local governments; though income taxes for the latter are probably beginning to offset the regressive nature of sales and property taxes. One study concludes that the total tax burden is somewhat progressive for income receivers earning less than $3,000, regressive from $3,000 to $10,000, and progressive above that level.[75] Other investigators with different definitions and measures have concluded that total tax burdens are roughly proportional for incomes up to $10,000 and substantially progressive for incomes above $10,000.[76] The net impact of tax payments and benefits received is a subject about which we should know more, given increasing concern with inequalities in our system.

The Distribution of Benefits

While such well-known governmental publications as the *Statistical Abstract of the United States* and its supplements include considerable data on governmental revenues and expenditures, they rarely contain materials on the distributive outcomes of the expenditure side of budgets.[77] The problems involved in determining incidences of benefits are extremely perplexing, requiring heroic assumptions if progress is to be made. The indivisible nature of many public goods creates almost intractable difficulties. It is also probably true that governments and established groups are reluctant to investigate the unequal distribution of benefits in a society which presumes equality before the law. No administration is apt to relish publicity on the extent to which it provides unequal favors. Scholarly research and general observation, however, suggest considerable inequalities in the distribution of public goods and services and in the official treatment of citizens.

We can do little more than offer some illustrations, since systematic evidence, particularly historical, is sadly missing.[78] We have a strong suspicion that distributive problems are becoming more pervasive and crucial as governments produce and distribute larger shares of the national product. During earlier years of the republic governments simply did not manage and control as many of the national resources as they do today. Governmental activity has always had distributive consequences, but one's status, power, and income were much less often affected crucially by government. Governmental regulations of the economy and promotion of economic effort surely benefited some citizens more than others. The vast sales of cheap public lands to the railroads, in particular, has been well-documented. The public construction of canals and other transportation facilities promoted commerce and aided the businessman directly in his operations. The provision of army protection to certain areas in the settlement of the West was by no means an equal benefit. The taxation of external sources rather than domestic businesses was in effect a subsidy with differential effects. But exactly who received how much of what benefits is difficult to say and would call for a greater research effort.

The materials available for distributive studies are far more plentiful with regard to the twentieth century. In fact, the national government itself has sponsored some justly famous inquiries which were not called "distributive" but, in fact, shed much light on just such problems. Early Congressional and Presidential commission investigations of working conditions, treatment of immigrants, the plight of the poor, the munitions industry, concentration of economic wealth, and later studies of trade and marketing practices, "administered prices," air and water pollution, interest charges, migrant labor conditions, civil rights, and criminal justice make the fact of extensive inequality undeniable. Interestingly, these same inquiries have sometimes served to show the complicity of government itself in maintaining inequality, either as a result of deliberate policies or as unintended consequences.

Perhaps we can illustrate these inequalities with some fairly concrete data. Subsidies of the national government provide a useful example. Table 2 displays some figures on subsidy payments by the

TABLE 2. SUBSIDY PROGRAMS OF THE
U.S. FEDERAL GOVERNMENT, 1955 AND 1965

Group	1955	1965
	(millions of dollars)	
Agriculture	$1,074	$5,600
Business	741	1,466
Labor	269	465

SOURCE: Adapted from U.S. Bureau of the Census, *Statistical Abstract of the United States, 1966*, Washington, 1966, p. 394.

national government for the period of 1955 to 1965. One may note that agricultural groups, comprising less than 10 per cent of the population, received about three times as much in subsidy payments as the other 90 per cent during 1965. Interestingly, agriculture's share has increased considerably since 1955, when it acquired about twice as much as business and labor. Various other studies have strongly suggested that agricultural subsidies are, themselves, unequally divided with large-scale absentee owners receiving far more than the family farm-type operation; that cash grain (wheat, rice) and cotton are highly favored; that cattle feeders are disadvantaged.[79]

The course of social and technological change has produced other distributive results which are interesting because they did not exist on the same scale prior to the present century. We note the vast defense programs of the national government and its domestic policies of intergovernmental aid or grants-in-aid to state and local governmental units as cases in point.

Defense-related expenditures go primarily to private businesses, since the government relies chiefly on contracting out to private industry. In acquiring defense hardware we may observe that some corporations receive much more business than others, that certain states and regions are favored over others, that some cities do better than others. These distributions are subject to change, since the nature of the defense equipment itself changes and requires new materials and different skills in its design and production. Thus there have been some spectacular cases of firms and areas suffering severe losses. In recent years, the greatest number and amounts of prime military contracts have gone to California, New York, Texas, Washington, Pennsylvania, Ohio, and Illinois.[80] The rise of Texas has been notable, while the eastern states and middle-western states have seen business go west. Michigan, in particular, has "suffered," since her preeminence during and shortly after World War II when conventional motorized military equipment was in greater demand. No doubt, further changes may be expected in the distribution of military expenditures as the means of waging war are altered.

These same defense monies, as well as other federal expenditures, are distributed most unequally in terms of regions and income groups, as is clearly indicated in Table 3. Still, there appear to be some compensations taking place for a region through other programs, and an income group may derive relatively little from one program but far more from another. Whether such compensations equalize benefits to any substantial degree depends on the volume of the individual programs. Defense expenditures are far greater than all other programs together. The lower-income regions derive greater shares than the middle-income regions in six of the nine programs and the average-income regions receive more than those of higher income group in six of the nine instances. But defense expenditures are far greater than nondefense, so that high income regions profit much more than Table 3 suggests.

Our last example of governmental distributions pertains to federal grants-in-aid to the state governments. The growing significance of such revenues for the states is illustrated by the fact that in 1902 only $7 million were so allocated, whereas in 1965 more than $11 billion were divided among the states.[81] In per capita terms the rise has been from one of $13.37 to more than $457 in 1965. In aggregate amounts California and New York have done far better during recent years than other states. California leads by a wide margin—having received over $1.3 billion (1965), or about one-seventh of the

TABLE 3.   REGIONAL SHARES OF POPULATION, INCOME, AND SELECTED FEDERAL EXPENDITURE PROGRAMS, 1963 PERCENTAGE DISTRIBUTIONS

Region	Popu-lation	Personal income	Defense	Composite non-defense	NASA	Reclama-tion	High-ways	Veterans	Public assist-ance	Corps of Engi-neers	Educa-tion	Farm sub-sidies
Low income	29.7	22.9	17.8	36.2	21.8	22.4	31.1	32.8	37.1	38.7	45.1	52.9
Southeast	21.7	16.1	11.2	24.6	18.8	—	21.8	23.9	26.2	21.4	34.6	30.9
Southwest	8.0	6.8	6.6	11.6	3.0	22.4	9.3	8.9	10.9	17.3	10.5	22.0
Average income	36.3	37.7	32.1	33.9	15.8	48.2	39.9	35.4	31.9	28.6	28.0	42.5
Rocky Mountain	2.4	2.3	4.2	3.2	.4	35.4	5.8	2.5	2.8	.3	1.8	1.6
Plains	8.3	7.9	6.3	13.8	9.6	12.8	9.5	8.9	8.7	21.1	8.9	31.7
Great Lakes	19.8	21.0	12.6	13.0	3.3	—	19.6	17.2	14.5	5.8	14.2	9.2
New England	5.8	6.5	9.0	3.9	2.5	—	5.0	6.8	5.9	1.4	3.1	
High income	34.0	39.4	50.1	29.9	62.4	29.4	29.0	31.8	31.0	32.7	26.9	4.6
Mideast	21.4	24.6	22.0	12.9	11.8	—	15.1	20.1	15.9	10.1	17.6	.3
Far West	12.6	14.8	28.1	17.0	50.6	29.4	13.9	11.7	15.1	22.6	9.3	4.3

SOURCE: U. S. Economic Growth to 1975: Potentials and Problems, Joint Economic Committee of the 87th Congress, 2nd Session, 1966.

sum total for all states.[82] New York acquired about half the California sum. In redistributive terms, i.e., the ratio of federal taxes to federal grants-in-aid, for each state, Alaska had the most favorable "balance of trade" in 1961, receiving more than four times as much in aid as was paid out in taxes. Delaware had the unfortunate position of paying in about twice as much as her citizens received from the federal government. In total, thirty-three states had favorable balances, while the remaining sixteen experienced losses.[83] Variations in these figures are an annual matter and an important one, since federal grants-in-aid have been increased by more than 140 per cent since 1953. Once again, we expect that the amounts going to the states will continue to increase and that distributive outcomes may also be changed as new demands arise.

These three illustrations of distribution and redistribution by American governments offer but a hint of vast research possibilities inherent in these sorts of data. We hope that governments might attempt a more self-conscious and systematic, continuing survey of the incidences of both burdens and benefits. We encourage historians, in particular, to conduct investigations into these same problems for the nineteenth century. It is most difficult to assess what has been happening in terms of governmental redistribution of income, wealth, status, and power, as even economists disagree about the structure of income through time. Certainly political scientists have not achieved unambiguous measures or reliable data on trend distributions of power. It seems to us that the problem of distribution is a peculiarly good one for combining the skills of historians, economists, and other social scientists.

The discussion, thus far, has emphasized distributions of material goods and services and ignored nonmaterial benefits, particularly status and opportunity. Governmental officials acquire status directly from public office and distribute status gains and losses among citizens. While foreign commentators have informed us of the noticeable equality of condition and treatment among earlier Americans, they were unable to measure differential treatment and, thereby afford us a precise means of comparison. We have the sensitive observations and reflections of de Tocqueville, for the 1820's and the somewhat less imaginative reflections of Lord Bryce for the latter part of the century, plus a myriad of investigations of social stratification during recent decades, but no common yardstick. Whereas de Tocqueville wrote about citizen-governmental relationships, latter-day sociologists have seldom looked at government as a dispenser of status. Occasionally, we learn of the social status of politicians, administrators, and others connected with politics, but seldom of the means and distribution of political status.[84] No confident historical generalizations can be made, yet there are many sorts of indirect indicators which could be more systematically explored. The names of those in public positions may indicate which groups attain these positions, just as the rolls of prisons and welfare agencies suggest which social groups experience other statuses. Those groups or types honored in civic books and legends also point to status differentials in previous periods. For the present, we have much more knowledge about the treatment accorded various citizens by officials in the city halls and state departments, at least. Charges of police brutality may exaggerate the modern case but study of the records are indicating considerable variation in the means of interrogation, penalties, and sentencing by police and court officials. Obvious group discrimination persists. Local governments often make their facilities available to middle-class groups, their businesses and associations, but not to lower-income people. The amount of service, types of service, and the courtesy with which they are accorded vary with the clients and officials.

Distribution of Participatory Opportunities

More or less equalized benefits are not the only objectives in a democracy; indeed, they may not be the principal one for many citizens. Instead, one finds a profound concern for more widespread and more meaningful individual participation in the political process, regardless of distributive policy outcomes. Two aspects of the situation seem important in this regard: access to decision-makers and direct expressions which can affect the decision-making process.

Most citizens in the United States participate in spasmodic, indirect ways in political life. The average citizen seldom writes to or communicates with elective officials, seldom works in or contributes resources to political parties, rarely competes for public office, seldom reads political information on a regular basis, seldom attends public meetings of governmental organizations. Many citizens do not even vote. Some are cynical, alienated, and powerless; and the estimates of these have been placed at about one-third of the population.[85]

In general, we can assert that those who tend to derive the greater shares of the goods and services from society are those who have the greatest access to politicians and public office. And those who acquire the lesser shares have lesser access. Causally, one should state the proposition in reverse. In any event, the activists tend to be those who have middle- and upper-class social status, earn higher incomes, have more education, are Protestant or Jewish, white, and urban. On the other hand, the apathetic, the alienated, tend to be lower class, lower income, less educated, and/or nonwhite. American democracy, particularly at the local and state levels tends to be a middle- and upper-middle class system. At the national levels one finds more attention paid to the interests and values of a wider population and even wider participation in elections, since much greater average percentages of the qualified electorate turn out for Presidential voting (about 60 to 65 per cent) than for state and local offices (seldom exceeding 50 per cent).[86] And, voting, we should point out, is the major if not only form of participation for large numbers of citizens. Lower-status groups must make their influence felt through other channels and in coalitions with dissenting groups within the power structure. Our history indicates that this is a discontinuous but recurrent phenomenon.

Such an unhappy portrayal of American democracy must, however, be qualified. Almond and Verba, in their five-nation study of political cultures, point out that the United States ranks very high, if not always first, in terms of such matters as citizen acceptance of their government, pride in its political institutions, feelings that government officials are courteous, concerned, and fair in their dealings with the individual.[87] This other side of citizen-government relationships must also be taken into account.

Further, we have only partial and contradictory evidence about long-term trends in political participation. Very little systematic evidence has been produced on nonvoting forms of activity for earlier periods. We do have a wealth of historical accounts of petitions, demonstrations, riots, and rebellions with the strong implication that the channels of access were monopolized by higher status groups. Repeated demonstrations and rioting by farmers, various immigrant groups, and the anti-draft riots of the Civil War testify to the importance of noninstitutionalized political action throughout the nineteenth century.

The evidence on voting is much more complete and systematic, but it is still difficult to gather information about voting at the state and local levels during our early history. And the facts can be differently interpreted. Robert Lane, for example, writes as though the proportion of the population voting has increased almost continuously from the Revolution to the present,[88] while Walter Dean Burnham claims that

. . . even the crudest form of statistical analysis makes it abundantly clear that the changes which have occurred in the relative size and shape of the active electorate in this country have not only been quantitatively enormous but have followed a directional course which seems to be unique in the contemporary universe of democratic politics. In the United States these transformations over the past century have involved a devolution, a dissociation from politics as such among a growing segment of the eligible electorate and an apparent deterioration of the bonds of party linkage between electorate and government.[89]

Long-term trends indicate, according to Burnham, that the late nineteeenth-century electorate was larger (proportionally), and more intensely party-oriented than at any time since. Approximately two-thirds of the potential national electorate were what he calls "core" voters. A steep decline set in about 1900 and continued until 1930 when a moderate resurgence took place. The 1930's restored two-party competition to many states outside the South but did not stimulate voter turnouts to equal nineteenth-century levels. Further historical inquiry will assist in clarifying the apparent differences between Lane and Burnham. At present, Burnham can claim the authority of the late V. O. Key, Jr., in support of his position that the voting proportions of the eligible electorate had decreased from 80 per cent in 1896 to 60 per cent in 1956.[90] It is now rising again.

Besides the highly institutionalized processes of voting, citizens may participate by actually "running" for public office. The United States provides an unusual set of opportunities in this regard with more than 530,000 available elective positions, subject to frequent elections. The vast bulk of these offices are not important except for some small arena of discretion; still they do provide an opportunity to participate in and experience political life. The total number of candidates running for these offices has been estimated at not more than 1 per cent of the population.[91] From what we do know, it would seem that there is some ease of access for most of the positions, but as the power and significance of the office increases it becomes less accessible, particularly for less advantaged citizens. The offices of President, Senator, Congressman, and state governor, for example, are largely the prerogatives of the upper-middle and upper classes.[92] Few persons of lowly origins and life manage to attain many of these offices. Political life is costly in terms of energy, time, and money; only those who can afford these costs can offer themselves for election and only those who have some status, education, and experience can hope to win higher offices and/or make a career of public office.

Opportunities to participate in direct decision-making are plentiful, but also stratified along the expected class, religious, and racial lines. Of course, abnormal conditions are not unknown in American history. Racial, ethnic, and class concentrations, especially in cities, have afforded minority members more opportunities to vote for members of their groups, to campaign for, and win, public office. Perhaps we may observe, as did V. O. Key, Jr., that while political activity increases as one goes up the status and income levels, "the chores and debates of politics, however, are by no means the exclusive preserve of any small political caste or class."[93]

Thus far, we have considered voting and other forms of political activity; little has been said about the accessibility of bureaucrats and politicians for the ordinary citizen. Office-holders probably tend to be more formally accessible than most of the citizens realize. Legislatures meet most of the time in public sessions, invite numbers of group representatives as witnesses before their committees, and pay a great deal of attention to the mass media. Most elective politicians spend some portions of each day with constituents and maintain staffs for the explicit purpose of handling their constituents' concerns. But the politicians of yesteryear apparently had far more time in which to write and otherwise communicate with voters. Today's politician is so pressed for time that he meets more people but for briefer periods and employs staff to handle the bulk of the constituent problems. Form letters are the normal response to citizen inquiries and demands. Those who are paid greater attention tend to be more important constituents or direct acquaintances.[94]

As time passes we note a proliferation of highly institutionalized mechanisms for citizen-government contacts. In the past thirty years, countless consultative groups have been created by administrative agencies involving various segments of the population. Most citizens would not ordinarily participate in such groups but it does afford additional representation of preferences.

Demand-making upon the agencies of government is an activity about which we know even less. More likely than not we will discover that some people make more demands than others; that types of demands for public goods and services are partial functions of class, residence, occupation, age, etc. Wealthy people, for example, probably do not frequent the police station very often, while their accountants regularly visit the Internal Revenue Service. Perhaps, too, various groups have different interactions with each level of government— some levels making more regulatory decisions while others tend to act as facilitators of private activities. We do not know the full answers to these questions, either for the past or the present or by level of government. There are, of course, formal records of hearings and cases in courts and regulatory agencies which give some idea of the volume and nature of some control interactions.

The types and extent of various political activities on the part of a citizenry depends upon a variety of factors: the political culture of a nation, formal prescriptions and proscriptions, effective distribution of political power, the flow of political information, and the salience of political matters. The relative weightings of these variables for most of American history are missing; we would like to know how they operated in fixing the range of participatory opportunities at different periods. The state of civil liberties, for example, is a much debated and controversial matter in most eras. Konvitz, for example, maintains that civil liberties have expanded, at least since World War II.[95] Others tell us they have become more restricted, if not by government then by private groups and communities. Some say the huge metropolitan areas have encouraged and permitted more privacy and freedom, while others tell us that freedom existed "among" communities if not always within each during the frontier days. And we know that Americans have experienced several episiodes of varying duration and tension when political expressiveness was severely repressed. While a variety of theories have been advanced to account for repressive movements, all seem to suggest that it has been, at least until recently, cases of groups with declining or marginal statuses, whether rural, small town, small businessmen, the elderly, second-generation Americans, or others who suffer from isolation, declining economic or status fortunes, low educational attainments, and who tend to assume that a rapidly changing society is a threat.[96] The unconventional, whether in belief or behavior, have been the targets: Catholics, Jews, Negroes, communists, atheists, and intellectuals. In more recent times previously victimized groups now act as the aggressors. With communism viewed as a worldwide threat new coalitions of fear and reprisal came to the fore to replace earlier domestic enemies.

Participatory opportunities for such extreme or highly intense oppositions have never been easily institutionalized in American life. On the other hand, passionate minorities have often been able to discourage and repress less intense and more numerous moderate elements. Generally, the range of permissible political deviance is confined by the alternatives of a two-party system, capitalist values, Protestant norms, and middle-class democratic institutions to such an extent that fundamental differences are frequently and effectively eliminated from public discussion. Deviant political values, norms, and policies must normally be couched in a symbolism of religiosity, morality, "states rights," "property," "private enterprise," or "The American Way of Life." Americans, it seems, are a highly ideological people.

While social scientists and historians have documented the history of participation in its particulars, they have not produced sound comparative generalizations. We are left as we began with despairing reminders of low levels of participation and antidemocratic feelings and actions of many citizens in an otherwise democratic system. It is seldom a matter of "bad" men persecuting "good" men, but of men who are sometimes liberal and sometimes less so, who engage in conflict over issues having powerful meaning for them. If we can point to the less attractive side, so too can we remind ourselves of the vast experiment in participation that has characterized American politics.

AN AGENDA FOR RESEARCH

With the resources and techniques now available, there should be far more systematic efforts to measure trends and evaluate them in more reliable form. Indeed, there are impressive institutionalized efforts to do so at such well-known places as the Survey Research Center at Michigan, the Yale Political Data Program, the National Bureau of Economic Research in New York, and the Brookings Institution in Washington, D.C. We think the following tasks should have high priority:

More comprehensive analyses of *electoral behavior,* especially for comparable units at local levels. Far more investigation than at present is required concerning patterns and trends in voter turnout, short-run and secular changes in party choice, and changing patterns of party and candidate competition.

There should be more systematic, continuous counts of "non-legitimate" forms of *political action,* including riots, intimidation of the political behavior of others (and nonlegitimate sanctioning by official persons or groups), evasions or resistance of the laws, brutality and violence between officials and citizenry, and other such efforts at coercion, disruption, evasion, and pressure.[97] These require subtle and often ingenious methods of observation, inference, and reporting, and pose rather difficult problems of avoiding the biases and ethical questions of police-type investigations and reports, or the typical bureaucratic modes of documentation. There should be relevant accounting in terms of *who* does *what, where,* for how *long,* with what *effects,* i.e., relevant and sensitive dimensions of characterizing the actors, the action, the arena, timing, and outcomes. Good examples are contained in the recent Report of the National Advisory Commission on Civil Disorders.

While the attitude survey and opinion polls have become familiar forms of political information, and very useful archival records are kept in such repositories as the Roper Public Opinion Research Center, there are many aspects of *political communication* which need more comprehensive and effective assessment. Sources, channels, volume, and ultimate distribution or reception are most important questions, and there is good communication and psychological theory to provide a useful framework for counting and assessing such data. Relevant dimensions of content will require careful definitions and measures. Economic models of production and exchange will provide useful analogies for a political communications accounting system, and such questions as monopolies and unequal distributions of information are at the heart of much political concern by scholars, officials and citizenry alike.[98]

A great deal of basic conceptualization remains to be done on measuring *policy outputs* of American governments. We do not have political equivalents of national income accounts or measures of the performance of the polity, which are systematic and comparable from one system or level to another. Measures of public budget allocations and numbers of employees for various activities is only a first start, and initial efforts at productivity measures for public programs indicate the magnitude of the task.[99] More attention must also be paid to further definition and measures of public "goods" in terms of their ultimate goals or consequences, such as security, welfare, benefits, burdens, and satisfactions. The task of definition may be eased somewhat, if a variety of indicators or checks were chosen, which could afford more than one kind of alternative appraisal. For example, assessments of welfare might consist of a checklist of individual and communal material goods and comforts, plus the attainment and opportunities for employment, income, education, and so forth. Different analysts may then choose their own set of indicators relevant to their purposes.[100]

More systematic surveys of *citizen-governmental transactions* are needed. Exchange theory provides many relevant categories for assessment in terms of demands made, responses rendered, rewards and costs traded, subsequent interaction, and so forth. Linked to some of the

above indicators, this type of data could illuminate the nature of crucial linkages in the political system. Such concepts as access in group
theory; channels and perceived salience in communication; availability
and accessibility between elites, intermediary groups, and the populace
in elite theory are all relevant for testing by such indicators. In addition to bureaucratic records and newer "time budget" proposals,[101]
periodic surveys of the type employed by the Survey Research Center
at the University of Michigan regarding consumer behavior and political participation could be extended to include questions on the numbers and types of interactions with governmental agencies.

These are very generalized proposals, to be sure. Some would pose
very great difficulties for observation and measurement. But if we are
serious about understanding the broader life of the polity more com-
prehensively and sensitively, we must move beyond the more typical
forms of records and research. And we must pose questions which
have a more direct bearing on change in terms of political action and
its consequences.

NOTES

We wish to thank Miss Kathleen O'Brien, a graduate student at the University
of Oregon, for her most helpful assistance in the preparation of this chapter.

1. Swisher, Carl, *The Growth of Constitutional Power in the United States,*
   University of Chicago Press, Chicago, 1946, gives a somewhat dated summary view. *The Supreme Court in Modern Role* by the same author can
   serve as well as any other recent constitutional commentary for later events,
   New York University Press, New York, revised edition, 1965. For a most
   perceptive analytic explanation of changing law in the social context, see
   Hurst, James Willard, *Law and Social Process in United States History,*
   University of Michigan Law School, Ann Arbor, 1960.
2. Riker, William H., *Federalism: Origin, Operation, Significance,* Little,
   Brown, Boston, 1964, chap. 3; Grodzins, Morton, *The American System;*
   A New View of Government in the United States, Daniel J. Elazar, editor,
   Rand McNally, Chicago, 1966, chap. 2; Green, Constance McLaughlin,
   The Rise of Urban America, Harper & Row, New York, 1965; and Scheiber,
   Harry N., *The Condition of American Federalism: An Historian's View,* a
   study submitted by the Subcommittee on Intergovernmental Relations to
   the Committee on Government Operations, United States Senate, 89th
   Congress, 2d Session, October 15, 1966.
3. Still most relevant for a first-hand comparative description in the early
   nineteenth century is Alexis de Tocqueville's classic *Democracy in America,* Vintage Books, New York, 1945, chaps. V, XIII, XVII. As Tocqueville notes even then, an over-all generalization is made in the face of
   considerable regional variation, especially in the case of the South. Green,
   Constance, *The Rise of Urban America, op. cit.*

4. Riker, William, *Soldiers of the States,* Public Affairs Press, Washington, 1957, chap. III.
5. Callender, G. S., "The Early Transportation and Banking Enterprises of the States in Relation to the Growth of Corporations," *Quarterly Journal of Economics,* vol. XVII, 1902–1903, pp. 111–162, at p. 115; as quoted by White, Leonard D., *The Jeffersonians,* Macmillan, New York, 1956, p. 493. White's set of federal administrative histories generally provide material not only on the federal role, but its relations with states and localities. See also by the same author: *The Federalists,* 1956; *The Jacksonians,* 1954; and *The Republican Era: 1869–1901,* 1958—all by the same publisher. See also Hartz, Louis, *Economic Policy and Democratic Thought: Pennsylvania. 1776–1860,* Harvard University Press, Cambridge, 1948; and Handlin, Oscar and Mary, *Commonwealth; A Study of the Role of Government in the American Economy: Massachusetts. 1774–1861,* New York University Press, New York, 1947.
6. Trescott, Paul B., "Some Historical Aspects of Federal Fiscal Policy, 1790–1956," in *Federal Expenditure Policy for Economic Growth and Stability,* papers submitted by panelists appearing before the Subcommittee on Fiscal Policy, Joint Economic Committee, United States Congress, 85th Congress, 1st session, November 5, 1957, pp. 60–84.
7. Elazar, Daniel T., *The American Partnership,* University of Chicago Press, Chicago, 1962.
8. Cranmer, H. Jerome, "Canal Investment, 1815–1860," in *Trends in the American Economy in the Nineteenth Century,* National Bureau of Economic Research, Princeton University Press, Princeton, N.J., 1960, pp. 547–564; Broude, Henry W., "The Role of the State in American Economic Development, 1820–1890," in Hugh G. Aitken, editor, *The State and Economic Growth,* Social Science Research Council, New York, 1959, pp. 4–25.
9. For the famous "marble cake" analogy, see Grodzins, Morton, "The Federal System," in *Goals for Americans,* The American Assembly, Columbia University, New York, 1960, pp. 265–282.
10. Graves, W. Brooke, *American Intergovernmental Relations; Their Origins, Historical Development and Current Status,* Charles Scribner's Sons, New York, 1964, parts V and VI.
11. After the Civil War vetoes were used more frequently; Cleveland, Franklin Roosevelt, Truman and Eisenhower were "champion scorers." But its incidence seldom substantially affects major policy disputes, and when it does so there appears to be far greater likelihood of an overriding vote by Congress. See Kallenbach, Joseph E., *The American Chief Executive,* Harper & Row, New York, 1966, chap. 11. For a very effective analysis of the very short-run effects of judicial review on legislative policy issues, see Dahl, Robert A., *Pluralist Democracy in the United States: Conflict and Consent,* Rand McNally, Chicago, 1967, chap. 6.
12. Dahl, Robert, *ibid.,* chaps. 10–13. For some kinds of data on conflict trends, see lists on the President's use of troops in the states, and uses of militia in Graves, W. Brooke, *American Intergovernmental Relations, op. cit.,* pp. 412–413.
13. This trend was well under way with the successes of progressive reform, especially at state and local levels; and it is reported in the monumental survey, *Recent Social Trends in the United States,* Report of the President's Research Committee on Social Trends, McGraw-Hill, New York, 1930, especially "Public Administration" by Leonard D. White, pp. 1391–1429, and "The Growth of Government Functions" by Carroll H. Wooddy, pp. 1274–1330.

14. Graves, W. Brooke, *American Intergovernmental Relations, op. cit.,* chaps. XVIII and XXI.
15. *Ibid.,* pp. 932–933; see chaps. XIV through XVI and Appendix A, pp. 932–968.
16. *Ibid.,* pp. 743–747.
17. A detailed early description of federally enacted agencies is Lloyd Short's *The Development of National Administraive Organization in the United States,* The Johns Hopkins Press, Baltimore, 1923; for a shorter and more recent summary, see Woll, Peter, *American Bureaucracy,* W. W. Norton, New York, 1963.
18. Estimates from Powell, Norman John, *Responsible Public Bureaucracy in the United States,* Allyn & Bacon, Boston, 1967, p. 124.
19. White, Leonard D., "Public Administration," in *Recent Social Trends in the United States, op. cit.,* pp. 1414–1421; for data up to the present, see annual reports of the United States Civil Service Commission.
20. Polsby, Nelson W., "The Institutionalization of the U.S. House of Representatives," paper presented at the 1966 Annual Meeting of the American Political Science Association; Matthews, Donald R., *The Social Background of Political Decision-Makers,* Doubleday, Garden City, N.Y., 1954, chap. 3.
21. Curti, Merle, *The Making of an American Community,* Stanford University Press, Stanford, 1959.
22. Grant, Charles S., *Democracy in the Connecticut Frontier Town of Kent,* Columbia University Press, New York, 1961.
23. Handlin, Oscar and Mary F., *Commonwealth Massachusetts: 1774–1861,* New York University Press, New York, 1947.
24. Benson, Lee, *The Concept of Jacksonian Democracy: New York as a Test Case,* Princeton University Press, Princeton, N.J., 1961.
25. Brown, Robert, *Charles Beard and the Constitution,* Princeton University Press, Princeton, N.J., 1956; and *Middle Class Democracy and the Revolution in Massachusetts,* Cornell University Press, Ithaca, 1955.
26. MacDonald, Forrest, *We the People: The Economic Origins of the Constitution,* The University of Chicago Press, Chicago, 1958.
27. Ford, Henry Jones, *The Rise and Growth of American Politics,* Macmillan, London, 1900.
28. Holcombe, Arthur N., *The Political Parties of Today,* Harper & Brothers, New York, 1924.
29. Schattschneider, E. E., *Party Government,* Rinehart, New York, 1942.
30. White, Leonard D., *The Federalists: A Study in Administrative History,* Macmillan, New York, 1948; *The Jeffersonians: A Study in Administrative History, 1801–1829,* Macmillan, New York, 1951; *The Jacksonians: A Study in Administrative History, 1829–1861,* Macmillan, New York, 1954; *The Republican Era: 1869–1901,* Macmillan, New York, 1958.
31. White, Leonard D., *The Federalists: 1789–1801, op. cit.,* p. 27.
32. Aronson, Sidney H., *Status and Kinship in the Higher Civil Service: Standards of Selection in the Administrations of John Adams, Thomas Jefferson, and Andrew Jackson,* Harvard University Press, Cambridge, 1964.
33. Englebert, Ernest A., "Political Parties and Natural Resources Policies: An Historical Evaluation, 1790–1950," *Natural Resources Journal,* vol. I, November, 1961, pp. 224–256. Fainsod, Merle, Lincoln Gordon, and Joseph C. Palamountain, Jr., *Government and the American Economy,* Norton, New York, 1959, chap. 5, pp. 93–126. Still an excellent account and explanation of the role of sectionalism in American politics is Holcombe, Arthur N., *The Political Parties of Today, op. cit.,* chap. IV.

34. Fainsod, Merle, *et al.*, *Government and The American Economy, op. cit.*, chap. 5.
35. On the tariff as a distributive policy, see Schattschneider, E. ·E., *Politics, Pressures and the Tariff*, Prentice-Hall, Englewood Cliffs, N.J., 1935; and for more current analyses, Bauer, Raymond A., Ithiel de Sola Pool, and Lewis Anthony Dexter, *American Business and Public Policy*, Atherton Press, New York, 1964. See also the very perceptive review by Theodore J. Lowi, "American Business, Public Policy, Case-Studies, and Political Theory," *World Politics*, vol. XVI, July, 1964, pp. 677–715. Lowi analyzes the changing patterns in policy processes in terms of the changing kinds of policy outputs, similar to the treatment here.
36. Cf. McConnell, Grant, *The Decline of Agrarian Democracy*, University of California Press, Berkeley, 1953.
37. Key, V. O., Jr., "A Theory of Critical Elections," *Journal of Politics*, vol. 17, February, 1955, pp. 3–18. Schattschneider, E. E., *The Semi-Sovereign People*, Holt, Rinehart & Winston, New York, 1960, chap. V, pp. 78–96, makes the same point but uses the 1896 election for assessing the realignment.
38. Hays, Samuel P., "The Social Analysis of American Political History, 1880–1920," *Political Science Quarterly*, vol. LXXX, 1965, pp. 373–394.
39. Hurst, James Willard, *The Growth of American Law: The Law Makers*, Little, Brown, Boston, 1950; *Law and Social Process in United States History, op. cit.*, chaps. II and IV.
40. *Ibid., The Growth of American Law*, pp. 176–177.
41. For some recent attempts at analyzing the new political economy, see Reagan, Michael D., *The Managed Economy*, Oxford University Press, New York, 63, and Galbraith, John Kenneth, *The New Industrial State*, Houghton Mifflin, Boston, 1967.
42. Handlin, Oscar and Mary, *The Dimensions of Liberty*, Harvard University Press, Cambridge, 1961, chap. V.
43. Truman, David B., *The Governmental Process*, Alfred A. Knopf, New York, 1955, p. 58.
44. Almond, Gabriel, and Sidney Verba, *The Civic Culture*, Princeton University Press, Princeton, N.J., 1963, p. 304.
45. *Congressional Quarterly Almanac, 1965*, Congressional Quarterly, Inc., Washington, 1965, p. 1459.
46. *Congress and the Nation: 1945–1964*, Congressional Quarterly, Inc., Washington, 1965, p. 1586.
47. Zeigler, Harmon, "Interest Groups in the States," in *Politics in American States*, Herbert Jacob and Kenneth N. Vines, editors, Little, Brown, Boston, 1965, p. 110.
48. *Ibid.*, p.. 141–142.
49. Beer, Samuel H., "New Structures of Democracy: Britain and America," in *Democracy in the Mid-Twentieth Century*, William N. Chambers and Robert H. Salisbury, editors, The Washington University Press, St. Louis, 1960, pp. 30–59.
50. Cf. Bauer, Raymond A., Ithiel de Sola Pool, and Lewis Anthony Dexter, *American Business and Public Policy, op. cit.*, chap. 30.
51. Mills, C. Wright, *The Power Elite*, Oxford University Press, New York, 1956, especially chap. 12.
52. Ginzberg, Eli, Dale L. Hiestand, and Beatrice G. Reubens, *The Pluralistic Economy*, McGraw-Hill, New York, 1965, pp. 1–17.
53. Gouldner, Alvin W., "Metaphysical Pathos and the Theory of Bureaucracy," *American Political Science Review*, vol. 49, June, 1955, pp. 496–507.

54. Chatters, Carl H., and Marjorie Leonard Hoover, *An Inventory of Governmental Activities in the United States,* Municipal Finance Officers Association, 1947, as cited in Fabricant, Solomon, *The Trend of Government Activity in the United States Since 1900,* National Bureau of Economic Research, Inc., New York, 1952, p. 47.

55. Dye, Thomas R., *Politics, Economics, and the Public: Policy Outcomes in the American States,* Rand McNally, Chicago, 1966, p. 20. National figures can be found in U.S. Bureau of the Census, *Statistical Abstract of the United States: 1966,* 87th edition, Washington, 1966, p. 690.

56. *Ibid.,* p. 154.

57. *Ibid.,* pp. 196, 199, 395.

58. *Ibid.,* p. 418.

59. *Facts and Figures on Government Finance, 1967,* Tax Foundation, Inc., New York, 1967, p. 17.

60. U.S. Bureau of the Census, *Historical Statistics of the United States, Colonial Times to 1957,* Washington, 1960, p. 711.

61. *Facts and Figures on Government Finance, 1967, op. cit.,* p. 20.

62. *Historical Statistics of the United States, Colonial Times to 1957, op. cit.,* p. 719.

63. Fabricant, Solomon, *The Trend of Governmental Activity, op. cit.,* pp. 62–63.

64. Mosher, Frederick C., and Orville F. Poland, *The Costs of American Governments: Facts, Trends, Myths,* Dodd, Mead, New York, 1964, chap. 7.

65. *Growth of Federal Domestic Spending Programs, 1947–1963,* Tax Foundation, New York, 1962, p. 17.

66. Mosher, Frederick, and Orville Poland, *The Costs of American Governments, op. cit.,* pp. 42–43.

67. Dewhurst, J. Frederic, and associates, *America's Needs and Resources: A New Survey,* The Twentieth Century Fund, New York, 1955, p. 597.

68. *Ibid.,* pp. 590–592.

69. *Ibid.,* p. 597.

70. *Ibid.,* pp. 595–597.

71. *Ibid.,* p. 597.

72. It should also be noted that most governmental employees do not work in Washington, D.C. Of the more than 2.5 million paid civilian federal employees in 1965, only 275,000 work in the nation's capital.

73. In 1929, total governmental purchases of goods and services amounted to 10.2 per cent of the GNP, but in 1964 that proportion had risen to about 21 per cent. See U.S. Department of Commerce, *U.S. Income and Output,* 1958; and U.S. Bureau of the Census, *Statistical Abstract of the United States, 1966,* p. 322.

74. This section is based on Herber, Bernard P., *Modern Public Finance,* Richard D. Irwin, Homewood, Ill., 1967, chap. 7.

75. Gillespie, W. Irwin, "Effects of Public Expenditures on the Distribution of Income," in Richard A. Musgrave, editor, *Essays in Fiscal Federalism,* The Brookings Institution, Washington, 1965, pp. 137, 163–167.

76. *Tax Burdens and Benefits of Government Expenditures by Income Class, 1961 and 1965,* Tax Foundation, New York, 1967, p. 15.

77. At least two exceptions should be noted: The annual *Statistical Abstract of the United States* lists a table of subsidy programs of the federal government, and the Joint Economic Committee of the Congress of the United States has published various materials on the same matter in a Committee Print entitled *Subsidy and Subsidy-Effect Programs of the U.S. Government,* U.S. Government Printing Office, Washington, 1965.

78. There is, however, a wealth of fine, detailed, historical studies of the role of government in promoting economic development during the nineteenth century. See footnotes 5 and 8, for a minute sample of some of these analyses.

79. Gaffney, Mason, "The Benefits of Farm Programs: Incidence, Shifting, and Dissipation," *American Journal of Economics and Sociology,* vol. 26, July, 1967, pp. 237–250.

80. Isard, Walter, and Gerald J. Karaska, *An Atlas on United States Military Contracts,* World Friends Research Center, Philadelphia, 1963, p. 10. See also *Statistical Abstract of the United States, 1966,* Section 9 in particular, for more current materials on defense contracts.

81. *Facts and Figures on Government Finance, 1967, op. cit.,* p. 140.

82. *Ibid.,* p. 170.

83. *Congressional Quarterly,* June, 1962, p. 1108.

84. Mitchell, William C., "The Ambivalent Social Status of the American Politician," *The Western Political Quarterly,* vol. XII, September, 1959, pp. 683–698.

85. Figures on participations were derived from Milbrath, Lester W., *Political Participation,* Rand McNally, Chicago, 1965.

86. Key, V. O., Jr., *Politics, Parties, and Interest Groups,* 4th edition, Thomas Y. Crowell, New York, 1958, pp. 622–628.

87. Almond, Gabriel and Sidney Verba, *The Civic Culture, op. cit.,* pp. 102, 108–109.

88. Lane, Robert E., *Political Life,* The Free Press, Glencoe, Ill., 1959, p. 26.

89. Burnham, Walter Dean, "The Changing Shape of the American Political Universe," *American Political Science Review,* vol. LIX, March, 1965, p. 10.

90. Key, V. O., Jr., *Politics, Parties, and Interest Groups, op. cit.,* p. 624.

91. Milbrath, Lester W., *Political Participation, op. cit.,* p. 21.

92. Matthews, Donald R., *The Social Background of Political Decision-Makers,* Doubleday, Garden City, N.Y., 1954, pp. 23–28.

93. Key, V. O., Jr., *Politics, Parties, and Interest Groups, op. cit.,* p. 643.

94. Litt, Edgar, "Civic Education, Community Norms, and Political Indoctrination," *American Sociological Review,* vol. 28, February, 1963, pp. 69–75.

95. Konvitz, Milton R., *Expanding Liberties: Freedom's Gains in Postwar America,* Viking Press, New York, 1966.

96. Variations on these themes may be found throughout Bell, Daniel, editor, *The Radical Right,* Doubleday, Garden City, N.Y., 1963. See also the fine perceptive study of Joseph Gusfield, *Symbolic Crusade: Status Politics and the American Temperance Movement,* University of Illinois Press, Urbana, 1963. For a sharply different view see Rogin, Michael, *The Intellectual and McCarthy: The Radical Specter,* Massachusetts Institute of Technology Press, Cambridge, 1967.

97. Cf. Feierbend, Ivo K. and Rosalind L., "Aggressive Behaviors within Polities, 1948–1962: A Cross-National Study," *The Journal of Conflict Resolution,* vol. X, September, 1966, pp. 249–271.

98. Some useful insights may be garnered from Machlup, Fritz, *The Production and Distribution of Knowledge in the United States,* Princeton University Press, Princeton, N.J., 1962.

99. See *Measuring Productivity of Federal Government Organizations,* Executive Office of the President, Bureau of the Budget, Washington, 1964, for examples of how productivity measures were attempted for federal agencies.

100. A number of imaginative efforts at assessing benefits are contained in

Dorfman, Robert, editor, *Measuring Benefits of Government Investments,* The Brookings Institution, Washington, 1965.
101. Szalai, Alexander, "Trends in Comparative Time-Budget Research," *The American Behavioral Scientist,* vol. IX, May, 1966, pp. 3–8.

7. THE THEORY AND MEASUREMENT OF FAMILY CHANGE

William J. Goode

IN THE FIELD of the family, analysts have for generations been concerned with the problems of social change. Like sociologists in other subfields, however, they have not been able to overcome the difficulties of achieving precise measurement and fruitful theory. Indeed, one might argue that a preoccupation with one of the major problems of family change—"the impact of industrialization"—has dominated this subfield to the detriment of its adequate theoretical and mensurational development. Consequently, a careful analysis of both types of difficulties, each of which is a function of the other, may help to illuminate the field of social change generally, and serve as a stepping stone to progress in the subfield of family change as well.

The present-day expansion of research in social change is partly a response to an increase in available research grants, and to the enlarged flow of descriptive data about social systems undergoing change. In addition, however, it is a response to the many criticisms that this range of problems has been neglected, indeed that contemporary social theory is not even capable of dealing with it. As in all such developments, both philosophical and scientific factors play a role. In the succeeding discussion, then, we shall first ask: why have social scientists in recent years given increased attention to the study of social change and thus to family change?

More important, since scientific progress is an outcome of the continuing mutual challenge between theoretical problems and measurement tasks, it is fruitful to analyze the difficulties of data gathering by eliciting the main types of theoretical questions to be answered, and determining which kinds of data each requires. In this discussion, we hope to reduce considerably the scope of the larger problem of analyzing social change. Specifically, we hope to show that most questions in family change can be answered by the types of measurement we are already utilizing or developing, and that we can tolerate for some time our failure to solve the most difficult of change questions, i.e., the establishment of *deterministic sequences.*

After devoting much of the chapter to the main types of social change problems, we shall consider the problem of *units.* Which are the kinds of relevant units about which we want information, and what are the difficulties of obtaining the information we want? Finally, we shall look at a few solutions to special problems that are part of the general domain of family change.

RENEWED INTEREST IN THE THEORY OF CHANGE

The contemporary resurgence of concern with social change theory is both salutary and indicative of a confidence based on more than a generation of growing theoretical rigor and technical precision. This current impulse, however, grows less from a clear conception of the potential scientific importance of these problems than from more general human concerns. In part it is an assertion that the world is changing rapidly, perhaps more rapidly than in the past. Social structures, it is further claimed, are not stable, tightly integrated, or harmonious, but are unstable, loosely put together, and torn by dissension. To ignore this profound phenomenon and process is to miss a central fact about societies. Increasingly, we accept a Heraclitean view of the world as flux, rather than as composed of solid building blocks. Since all is change, the analysis of change must be a central concern.

At a more emotional level, most people may welcome progress and improvement in their lives, but the general rapidity of change makes many people uneasy. Some alterations seem to bring losses, not gains. Security of adjustment is partially lost when each day renders obsolescent some old habits. Thus, attention is turned to the threatening newness of the world.

At still another level, the impulse to study social change is part of a slowly crystallizing, increasingly articulate feeling that both the physical and the social worlds are highly contingent, not really completed and fixed. The cosmos that is becoming demands that we create it. This conception is expressed in new philosophies and procedures for attacking problems in such diverse areas as chess playing, architecture, mountain climbing, military tactics and strategy, and statistics. Modern plans embody numerous alternatives in which lability and time play as large a role as strength and fixed positions. Since such contingencies lie in the future, it is necessary to study change over time.

A political impulse is also evident in this increased attention to change, and here especially its relevance for family change is clear. It is a protest against the acceptance of things as they are. Rejecting the idea that roles are fixed, it is an assertion that both physical and social relations *can* be changed. Rejecting the exhortation to accept the world as it already exists, this view expresses a preference for change, a demand that the world be altered because it is not adequate.

A pragmatic assumption can also be discerned in this new concern with change theory. Since social relations are contingent, they can be altered; and if they are to be altered in the direction we prefer, they must be controlled now. If family patterns need not be accepted in their present form, we must experiment now, and shape the future now. To do so requires a charting of time trends and some knowledge of their laws. Without that knowledge, we shall fail to create the future as we want it to be.

Although these forces that press toward a better understanding of social change generally and family change in particular are worth studying, they do not specify *which* problems are worth solving. Such motivations for solving a problem cannot serve as criteria for evaluating the scientific importance of the problem itself. The general area of change analysis contains many types of questions, and they differ in theoretical yield and difficulty of data gathering.

TYPES OF PROBLEMS IN FAMILY CHANGE

Almost all formulations of problems in the theory of family change can be classified under the two traditional classes of idiographic and nomothetic, that is, the analysis of particular events and the search for laws. In turn, these two classes contain the following subtypes:

1. Analyses of particular events (idiographic)
    a. Trends
        (1). The grand evolution of man
        (2). Particular epochs or time spans
    b. Causal interpretations of particular events
2. The search for "laws" of family patterns (nomothetic)
    a. Timeless propositions
    b. Patterned sequences in time
        (1). Evolutionism
        (2). Limited evolution

Because "trends" and "timeless correlations" become important only late in intellectual history, we shall discuss them later in this chapter. In any event, the logical order of classification need not determine the order of exposition. Logically, trends are unique events, whether they encompass all of man's rise from the amoeba or the decline in fertility in Victorian times. Analysis of such occurrences is, then, idiographic. A specific trend, such as the continual rise of the divorce rate in the United States since the Civil War, is not a "law." Clearly, in no prior epoch of the West did that specific trend occur. It is indeed as historically unique as the divorce rate of a particular year. Similarly, the analysis of Milton's plea for the right to divorce, or the legislation on illegitimacy during the French Revolution, is idiographic —They are unique events. (And, like all unique events, they can be classified by their *shared,* nonunique, traits, when we search for "laws.")

Logical order cannot be followed in treating of evolutionary thinking about the family, because the grand rise of man is historically first thought of as a great trend, a spectacular event, unique in history; but it is gradually transformed (as noted later) into a hypothetical *type.* That is, the evolutionary process comes to be seen as a set of *laws:* If there were many appearances of man, they would follow the same sequences. Consequently, although these two forms of evolutionary thought are logically distinct, the idiographic is the ancestor of the nomothetic type, and thus they will be discussed sequentially in this first section.

The first of these need not detain us long, since the great thinkers of the past who mused on the cosmic meaning of man's rise from the primordial slime did not bother to grapple with the difficulty of obtaining relevant data. The earliest philosophers and social commentators were moralists, and treated family relations as part of the fabric of society. Many, and perhaps all who were religious prophets as well, asked man's first social science question. This was a social change query, and often a *family change* inquiry as well: Whence came man, and whither does he go? All or nearly all religions contain an origin myth. One common legend is that the sea and the sun (or moon and sun) cohabited and brought forth a line of gods, who in turn created man. Religious rituals celebrate this origin and describe the appropriate relations among men and women, or human beings and the gods or ancestral figures.

The Adam and Eve myth expresses a nearly universal theme, contrary to the post-Renaissance Western view, that family relations *have* changed since the beginnings of time, and for the worse. The golden age lies in the past. Probably there is no period in any great civilization (other than the modern West) in which moral interpreters announced that family relations had improved since the dawn of man. Instead, they exhorted men, women, and children to return to the ancient ways of virtue.

Such voices have never been stilled. Greek and Roman playwrights frequently selected as themes of comedy some characteristically modern complaints—increasing domination by women, excessive freedom and incivility of children, libertarianism of wives, nostalgia for an older patriarchal system. (Needless to say, the "old system" is never given a specific date in the past.) Many moderns in all countries continue to express the view that if man ever did rise, certainly his family relations have worsened over the past few generations.

Precisely because such analyses are not empirical descriptions of man's great drama, but attempts at moral suasion, each era produces a steady stream of them. To the moralist, each generation is constantly falling away from virtue.

But though this theme never lost all its popularity, Western philosophers gradually came to believe in progress. Perhaps not until the eighteenth century did this new view become dominant. The *philosophes,* like Gibbon, saw mankind as once "betrayed by barbarism and religion . . . expelled from nature's Garden of Eden. The Christian Middle Ages were the unhappy times after the fall and expulsion. . . ."[1] The present was better than the past; the future would be better still.

The "Universal History" of the eighteenth century became for a time the modern vehicle for moralistic commentaries on the great, unique event, man's appearance on earth and his eventual conquest over it. In this view, though perhaps man's family relations had once been natural and innocent (as Rousseau and Godwin argued) and later degraded, husbands, wives, and children were at least finally moving toward a more enlightened system of liberty and rationality.

Patterned Sequences in Time

Evolutionism. Those interpretations were not, however, serious efforts to develop an adequate body of historical and archeological data about man's family patterns. Family relations in the Old Testament might be discussed, but at best the next step would be Greece and Rome, and the sources were always literary. It was not until the nineteenth century, in its preoccupation with one or another version

of evolution as a set of laws, that the problem of data became important.

This later evolutionism, like the cosmic interpretations of man's history, was imbued with the idea of progress. Man, like other "higher"
animals, had risen from lower forms, but had also evolved a family
system that was superior to that of animals. However, the formulation of the problem was (as indicated in our earlier classification of
types of family change problems) transformed qualitatively. For
though the new thinkers also evaluated the total evolutionary process
as *upward,* and agreed that it had occurred only once, it was more
fundamentally seen as a *type,* as a set of laws.

Phrased in a more modern form, social theorists of the nineteenth
century looked for universal evolutionary "laws" of family development, such that if there had been many lines of evolution, or if the
grand process had ever occurred many times, they would all have
followed a similar *form.* Thus, the philosophical problem—the significance of man's hegira—was transmuted into the empirical analysis of
a hypothetical *type.*

From the late eighteenth century to World War I, evolutionism
dominated most analyses of family change. The flood of new data
enhanced the persuasiveness of this biological view, and most social
theorists utilized it. In turn, the new approach created a demand for
new data, especially about "primitive" societies. As the century drew
to a close, actual field observations of such societies became common,
gradually replacing the often curious and sometimes incredible stories
of missionaries or hunters. Unfortunately for the larger theory, the field
data did not always fit a simple evolutionary scheme.

One of the first systematic field workers in anthropology, Lewis
Henry Morgan,[2] created perhaps the first detailed outline of phases in
the evolution of the family. In one form or another his general description was widely mirrored by other writers of the last generation
in the nineteenth century: man rose from the primordial slime to
promiscuous intercourse and then to the intermarriage of brothers
and sisters; thence to "the intermarriage of several sisters, own and
collateral, with each other's husbands in a group"; and then to the
marriage of two individuals but without exclusive cohabitation. Thereafter comes the polygamous and finally the monogamous family, which
is the highest development of modern society.[3] In some versions (for
example, that of Spencer), polyandry precedes polygyny as a definite stage.[4]

We now judge this evolutionary framework to have been a failure, in both the highly speculative writings of Robert Briffault or the cautious analyses of Edward B. Tylor,[5] but it should not be forgotten that these men addressed themselves daringly to the problems of family change. They attempted a grand synthesis of the then known facts of kinship and family behavior. In their attempt to integrate measurement and theory,[6] they made four great assumptions which we do not now accept, but which undoubtedly represent a first approximation to solving the problem of measuring family changes over great time spans:

1. That the family and religious patterns of a society with a low level of technology are closer to, say, Paleolithic man than to modern man; consequently, we can reconstruct the time stages in between by observing contemporary primitive societies;
2. That we can view a "cultural survival" like ritual wife capture as the equivalent of a social "fossil," and thus reconstruct the past;
3. That observable family patterns evolved because they contributed more to the survival of the society than did the patterns which were discarded in the past;
4. That, as in biological evolution, a standard set of sequences could be found, through which all family and kinship systems would pass.

It is fair to say that modern theorizing about family change has not developed a more valid substitute body of theoretical or measurement assumptions, though of course modern skepticism makes us less daring.

The evolutionistic scheme not only organized the expanding body of descriptive facts about family systems, but (unlike prior inquiries into family change) *demanded* that more facts be gathered. They also expressed, as noted, the assumption that evolutionary *laws,* or deterministic sequences, would be discovered if the data could be found.

That framework was generally discarded after World War I, but simple evolutionary assumptions as to the "primitiveness" of primitive societies were general in German anthropology until the end of World War II. The *Kulturkreis* group under the leadership of Fritz Graebner discarded simple evolutionism, but continued to focus on the general problem of change, and specifically the processes of diffusion.[7] American anthropologists also abandoned evolutionism under the influence of Boas, but continued to view their field as a *historical* discipline, dedicated to recording social change. The "functionalist" approach became dominant early in England, and in France by the 1930's, but field workers were always expected to garner what data they could on changes in family patterns. It must, then, be conceded that in this segment of the sociological tradition, problems of family change remained important after the abandonment of the nineteenth-century evolutionistic schema.

The search for a grand evolutionary framework was abandoned in favor of precise descriptions of ongoing family systems, analyses of short-term trends, and diffusion studies, because it was agreed that the available data did not confirm the larger theory. However, almost all such schemata foundered on a deeper problem of measurement and theory: *Most were unifactorial hypotheses.* They asserted or assumed (without testing) that all family change was caused by a single factor, such as race, climate, the survival of the fittest, or "economic" variables. Perhaps the hardiest survivor has been the last of these, in the hands of more or less sophisticated devotees of Marxism.[8] Engels, Kovalevsky, and Kautsky, among others, offered versions of such hypotheses, e.g., that the evolution of the family was determined by changing property relations, that the creation of property from a primitive communism led to the enslavement of women and the treatment of children as economic goods, that women had remained chattels under capitalism, etc.

It is not necessary or useful to expound any of these unifactorial hypotheses in detail. They are all equally vulnerable because they fail to solve the main problems of measurement and theory. Let us consider them.

Their central theoretical difficulty is that they assert that all family (or social) change is caused by factor X. If the critic suggests that other factors (values, temperament, technical skill, etc.) might also contribute, the author responds by claiming that factor X includes these factors as well. Thus, for example, if the critic asserts that values "make a difference," then the economic determinist argues that values are also determined by economic relations. If the critic of a racist theory claims that "cultural level and education" make a difference in family patterns, the unifactorial race theorist proclaims that race determines these, too. In short, factor X causes all the stages in human evolution, all the forms of family behavior, because in fact X *is* everything, and surely everything does in fact cause everything.

That central theoretical difficulty creates the fundamental measurement problem: If the single great factor is everything or, more cautiously, is intermixed with it, how can one *empirically* abstract it, separate it out, in order to ascertain how much weight it has? Moreover, since the factor cannot be measured easily, it is not possible to formulate precise hypotheses of the type, "more (or less) of factor X causes a rise (or fall) in family pattern Y." If a general factor such as climate or economic relations is vaguely involved in family change (as it must be if it is general enough) but no one can measure how much of a change in that factor will actually create which changes in family patterns, then there is no possibility of testing any important hypothesis.

The measurement "solution" utilized by most evolutionistic theorists in their unifactorial analyses was the "shotgun method," i.e., adducing many arbitrarily chosen examples from a wide span of time and space. Unfortunately, they did not have records of actual *change,* but reports from *different* societies at *different* time periods, and had to manufacture the crucial test datum, i.e, the transformation of kin patterns. We have seen their errors, and have become more cautious, but we have not fully solved their problem of measurement.

Limited Evolution. Our scientific knowledge of man's biological (or at least anatomical) background has progressed substantially during the past quarter century, and with it our knowledge of man's gradual mastery of technology since his appearance more than a million years ago. Since both biological and technological evolution seem to have a visible logic of succession, modern social science has not lost the century-old dream that man's social and family patterns might also be fitted into some kind of *patterned sequence, each successive stage necessarily emerging from the previous one.*

Family variables have proved to be especially recalcitrant to any effort to order them in accord with some logical, scientific, or evolutionary pattern. They do not appear to be highly correlated with technology.[9] This failure of fit is at least one good argument that family variables are not merely dependent.

Economic variables, it might be argued, would correlate better with some family evolutionary pattern, but economists have not bothered to work out either a detailed patterned sequence of economies, such that each economic pattern must succeed another type; nor have they agreed upon even a set of variables for *classifying* the possible types of economies, to permit in turn a set of correlations with family types.

But though family analysts were not successful in the past in their endeavor to measure *where* on an evolutionary scale each family system might be placed, the search for regularities of sequence has not been dropped. With the resurgence of inquiries into family change after World War II came a renewed effort to tackle the question, but limiting its scope to *shorter* time spans and *fewer* sets of sequences so that the hypotheses would not again outrun any possible data as they did in earlier evolutionary schemas.

The limitation of *time span* is especially important, because we have no adequate measurement of family relations beyond those that existed prior to written records. The necessary time span for any full-scale evolutionary scheme goes far beyond any possible records, whether of nations or of primitive tribes. Fossil remains at best yield anatomical and technological knowledge, but this is a far cry from reconstructing the role definitions of fathers and mothers, or the process of socialization. Those data are forever lost. Once we have accepted the harsh fact that even the most technologically backward primitive society now in existence has an evolutionary past as distant as that of the population of New York City, we have to abandon reluctantly the notion that we can use such societies as mental time machines.

However, approximations for shorter time periods can be created. Although we can no longer accept Tylor's idea of using "survivals" as social fossils, the persistence of both religious and family patterns even when political and economic structures break down has been noted frequently. Consequently, for at least a modest time span it might be possible to reconstruct the *immediately* past set of successions, and possibly from such reconstructions achieve determinate sequences. To do this for nonliterate societies is fruitful, since thereby a greater range of *variation* is achieved than for Western societies—or for that matter, China or Japan. It is possible to ascertain, for example, that a direct transition from a patrilineal to a matrilineal system very likely never occurs; and that direct borrowing of kinship patterns must be rare, because physically contiguous societies share technology far more than they share family patterns.[10]

In a clever use of this notion, Driver and Massey have used the measure of statistical association among family patterns. They argue that any two kinship traits that succeed one another closely in time ought to be correlated more closely than those which occur at very distant stages from one another, and are not tied as part of a sequence. It must be emphasized that they are forced to use *synchronic* data in the absence of diachronic observations.[11]

According to their hypothesis, developed from Murdock's earlier work, a change in the sexual division of labor ought to take place before an alteration in the rules governing where a couple should live after marriage. These rules in turn should change before rules about land tenure, descent, and kinship terminology, in that order. This is, then, a series of hypotheses that if a change did occur, it would take place in the first set of variables before occurring in the second set, and so on. Having no real time data, and certainly no time data adequate to the problem posed, they inferred that the correlation between any two successive "stages" would show the highest correlations in the data from contemporary primitive societies, while the lowest correlation should be found between variables at the furthest remove from one another in this sequence.

The correlations do support the hypothesized sequences, but do not at all support the idea of unilinear evolution, and later statistical analysis has suggested that alternative models might fit the data somewhat better—specifically, the hypothesis that labor and residence rules both affect land tenure changes yields higher correlations.[12]

Just as dendrochronology and Carbon 14 datings have for the first time yielded some precision to the time estimates of archeologists in their attempts to establish time successions for human skeletons and artifacts, so glottochronology has come to aid (with somewhat less accuracy) in the dating of linguistic changes—and thus alterations in kinship terminology.[13] Of course, kinship terminology does not control family behavior, but rather the reverse. It is nevertheless an *index* of such changes, and linguistic analysis may in the future produce more reliable statements about the succession of kin terminology, and thus role behavior, in societies without written records.

It must be emphasized that the best of these estimates do not carry us far into unrecorded history—though, of course, far into the unrecorded history of some *non*literate societies—and have not helped at all in establishing the sequences of family changes in great civilizations beyond the present records. At present, these latter data go back beyond even possible estimates that could be made from glottochronological analyses of contemporary primitive societies.

Needless to say, the search for such sequences and for better modes of testing them continues. If we could establish a few, we could predict much better the future stages of family patterns in different societies, and could illuminate the present systems much more adequately. In spite of the technical and theoretical difficulties that have been pointed out in the preceding discussion, family analysts will persist in seeking better solutions.

Causal Interpretations of Particular Events

Logically, as noted earlier, the moral or philosophical search for the *meaning* of the unique event, the appearance of man and his peculiar family system, is very different from the nineteenth- and twentieth-century search for general or specific *regularities* or laws of evolution. However, we were forced to treat them in direct sequence (unlike our earlier classification of problems) because the latter grew organically from the former. Now, however, let us return to our first large class of family change problems, the analysis of unique events, and consider the subtype, causal interpretations. This, in turn, contains three different subclasses, all of which have in common an attempt to illuminate a unique occurrence—past, present, or future—through a set of laws, rules, or correlations that are thought to have a wide applicability. The three subclasses are: (1) the interpretation of a past or present event; (2) the prediction of the immediate future; and (3) the attempt to shape or control the future.

Like most historical interpretations, this type of explanation does not aim at achieving regularities of potentially wide validity. Specifically, it does not typically attempt to test a scientific hypothesis by reference to family change data, but instead seeks to apply sociological generalizations in order to understand a historical event (women's suffrage, a sudden rise in the divorce rate, Henry VIII's marriage to Boleyn).

Often, the generalizations utilized are no more than ad hoc comments of a common sense nature (e.g., cousin marriage used to be more common in the rural U.S., because families wanted to retain the land within the kin network). Others aim at more systematic statements. A good example of this type is Marion J. Levy's explanation of the relative failure and success of China and Japan in solving the problems of industrialization.[14] By showing the considerable number of similarities in the social structure of the two countries, and the range of comparable difficulties they faced, Levy was able to argue persuasively that differences in family patterns may have given Japan a sizable advantage in its efforts to modernize.

Many demographers have sought to explain the particular event of the modern population explosion. Kingsley Davis, among others, has pointed out that it is relatively easy to reduce the death rate through measures that do not require great changes in the values and behavior of most of the population.[15] Societies at a low technological level of development as well as more advanced ones are willing to accept many modern medical practices, because all share the wish to stay alive and to keep their children alive. Sanitary engineers and public health officials can also diminish the death rate from malaria, gastro-intestinal diseases, smallpox, and the like by mass measures that require little cooperation from the populace.

By contrast, not only is birth control an individual decision, but until recently each act of sexual intercourse required an individual contraceptive decision. More fundamentally, the socialization process lays heavy stress upon the importance of having children, perhaps because the advantages are not so self-evident as the advantages of simply staying alive, so that a strong motivation to have children remains long after the death rate has dropped. Thus, a society that has survived in part because in a biologically threatening environment its fertility values are strong, begins to be choked by an oversupply of surviving children when the death rate declines.[16]

The conflict between immigrant parents and their native-born American children is another continuing event that is "explained" by referring to the general relationship between the rapidity of social change and conflict between parents and children.[17] The child can be socialized rapidly to the newly emerging or surrounding culture while his parents cannot be. New authorities exist to challenge the rule and judgment of parents. We expect this conflict to be intensified in a time of revolution or any period of rapid social change, and thus we expect it to appear when any ethnic group is being assimilated into another culture. In this case, we apply the general relationship to the special instance of the immigration from European countries to the United States.

Similarly, if we were to compare the courtship pattern of Germany in 1900 with that of the period immediately following World War II, and found in the latter period that newspapers carried advertisements in which women announced their search for a husband or made thinly veiled offers of an apartment for a companion, we might interpret these events as having been caused by a severe shortage of marriageable men. If we found that the age of marriage dropped in Ireland in the latter part of the eighteenth and beginning of the nineteenth centuries, we might interpret this trend as having been "caused" by the introduction of the Irish potato, which could yield sufficient food for a family on soil that formerly could not be exploited easily. In a family system that requires each couple to establish an independent household, the opening of new land or the improvement of agricultural technology is followed by a drop in the age at marriage.[18]

In these examples, the problem of measurement does not loom large. Very broad observational data are sufficient to demonstrate some important structural differences in kinship between Japan and China, and common sense is enough to suggest that they should be of consequence for industrialization. Although birth and death records contain gaps, they are adequate to show the sudden drop in the latter without much change in the former, when modern sanitary technology has been introduced. By contrast, note the difficulty of proving that a great change in contraceptive motivation (as contrasted with the motivation to accept new medical technology) is difficult to engineer because parents expend more socialization energy in inculcating fertility values in their children.

The validity of such interpretations depends on first, the correctness of the general proposition; and second, the appropriateness of applying the general rule to the unique historical case. Note that the problem of *application* is also one of *measurement,* not a matter of simple definition. For example, it would not be easy to prove that the introduction of a new and more productive crop is equivalent to the general expansion of the economy, the opening of frontier lands, or the establishment of new posts in a foreign colony. Each would require separate data in order to show that they are all analogous cases to which the same rule might be applied.

Earlier in this section it was noted that this general class contains three subtypes. These are (1) the interpretation of a past or present event; (2) the prediction of the immediate future; and (3) the attempt to shape or control the immediate future.

In all the subtypes of causal interpretations, general sociological notions or regularities are applied to a concrete case in order to understand it better. Thus, from what we know about the factors that are changing more or less in modern population growth, we can predict with little error that the population of Peru will not react immediately to a substantial reduction in the death rate by an equally great reduction in the birth rate. Or, we might have predicted that the Chinese revolution of 1949 would be followed by a great deal of parent-youth conflict, as indeeed it was.

Similarly, we could "engineer" a reduction in the illegitimacy rate of Jamaica or the U.S. Negro population by creating an economy by which most lower-class men would have steady, well-paying jobs.[19] Less fancifully, we might reduce the family authority of eldest sons in a traditional society by altering the inheritance laws from primogeniture to equal heirship.

In both short-term prediction and social engineering, the assumption *ceteris paribus* is made, i.e., if other concrete factors do not intervene powerfully, the abstract (nomothetic) relation will be observed in reality. In most cases of this type of family change little effort is in fact expended to demonstrate that other possible factors neither cause the observed result nor prevent it from being easily observable. If a profitable crop is followed by a flood of marriages and thus a rise in the marriage rate and birth rate for the relevant period, the analyst typically looks for no other important factors than the general correlation between prosperity and fertility. If there is a severe shortage of marriageable men after a war, and therewith an obvious change in the bargaining position of men, the analyst typically does not look for other important social changes that might have accentuated that change, or perhaps dampened it somewhat. As a consequence, the sometimes difficult problem of measuring these effects is ignored.

Trend Charting and Analysis

The causal interpretation of a particular event is closely linked with the charting of trends, because often the trend itself (divorce rates, age at marriage, male authority) *is* the special event to be analyzed. On the other hand, perhaps most research work is simply aimed at ascertaining the descriptive facts, with little effort at "explaining" the changes over time.

Trend mapping is also linked with the formulation of "timeless" equations (to be discussed next), because the trends may disprove or confirm such correlations. In turn, the decision as to *which* variables should be charted is based implicitly or explicitly on whether such data would be theoretically useful in such timeless relations.

As the historian knows, often more painfully than the sociologist, to ascertain trends is frequently difficult and tedious, and especially so in the area of the family. Indeed, for reasons we shall note in a moment, only in the past generation has this descriptive work gone forward steadily, perhaps because for the first time a more fruitful sociological framework has begun to suggest *which* data are most useful to unearth from the past.

Earlier, it was suggested that far from neglecting the topic of change, the sociology of the family has been preoccupied with it, and theoretical progress has perhaps been hampered by an overly strong commitment to one approach. In anthropology, this framework was evolutionistic; in sociology, it was first evolutionistic and then became a simplistic attempt to organize all trend data by reference to some version of "industrialization."

Karl Marx established this pattern firmly. In a section of *Capital* on the employment of women and children, he takes up a theme that has been central in family change analysis throughout the modern period: the impact of industrialization on the family, including such topics as the neglect of children, the lack of time to engage in family activities, the failure of women to sew or cook, the decline of domestic skills, the disintegration of family unity, and the increasing participation of married women in the labor force.[20] Marx drew his basic trend data from a mass of field reports on changing conditions in the factory areas of England. Many such reports were drawn up by British government commissions. For the most part, the changes were gross enough to be observed rather easily, and Marx did not aim at a *measure* of disintegration.

Social analysts have developed several sets of terms to describe this great trend, though few have tried to measure it. The cultural change from *Gemeinschaft* to *Gesellschaft* (Ferdinand Tönnies), status to contract (Sir Henry Maine), rural to urban, primary to secondary relationships (Charles Horton Cooley), immigrant to native-born, Negro to white, tribal systems to nations, with textbook statements of alterations in family patterns that accompany that secular trend, has been almost the sole major theme in discussions of family changes over the past century. The *substantive* trends noted have included the rise of the U.S. divorce rate since the Civil War, the decline of the birth rate since the early nineteenth century, the diminution of patriarchal authority since the colonial period and the concomitant decrease in familism, and the increase in the freedom of children (especially in courtship and mate selection).

Among such "trends," only the first two (divorce rates and birth rates) ever called forth any serious effort at measurement, or even proof. Although such descriptions (sometimes accompanied by anecdotal or diary materials) may well be correct if not very precise, they arouse some skepticism because they sound like complaints. While doubtless the charges of the older generation against the younger are sometimes valid—surely, children *are* less civil than children once were—and possibly this "trend" has been under way for two or three hundred years, it does seem odd that a change so gross as to be obvious to each generation should have continued in one direction for so long without some effective effort to stop it. In recent years, of course, the "discovery" of strong kin networks in urban areas has suggested that the family has declined much less than scholars once believed.[21]

Measurement Problems. Several measurement problems have made the simple charting of family changes difficult. A few of the major difficulties can be loosely labeled as follows:

1. Ideals in contrast to behavior
2. Class, sex, and generational perspectives
3. Absence of data on the process of building up larger kinship units
4. Periods of low literacy

Each of these technical problems overlaps somewhat with the others, but each does have some distinctive traits.

(1). The first of these includes several classical problems in data gathering which are intensified when trends over time are measured. Since the family sociologist lays special emphasis on the importance of values and attitudes, it is necessary to distinguish ideals from real behaviors. Ideals do not fully determine real behavior, but neither does behavior express ideals fully. For the past, this problem is made somewhat more difficult by the fact that we cannot easily obtain a set of survey data in which people have expressed their attitudes, and often we cannot reconstruct their actual behavior either. This problem is, however, related to a second distinction, which is of much greater importance for the past than for the present: the distinction between *real* ideals and *ideal* ideals, or public versus private ideals. The public exhortations to virtue that come down to us in manuals, handbooks, catechisms, or even in letters from father to son are not an adequate substitute for genuine attitudinal or value data that might have been available when men were speaking privately with one another at that time.

This difficulty may be illustrated by the effort to recapture family attitudes and behavior in early nineteenth-century America. One such study has recently shown that if one uses the reports by foreign observers from that period, for a wide range of family behavior the patterns seem to be similar to those of the present: freedom of the young from domination of their elders, relatively free courtship, etc.[22]

However, one might argue on the other hand that such a study really shows that the *standards* by which Europeans observed American family behavior have changed over time, and *in the same direction* as American family behavior. Consequently, what struck the European observer in the early nineteenth century as being very different from the European family pattern still strikes the European observer as different, though both values *and* behavior have changed. Or, one might argue on the other hand that such a study really shows that the "distinctive" American family pattern must have emerged earlier still in the history of the United States. If we could obtain an adequate sampling of both behavior and values at that time, we could far more easily make clear measurement of the changes since then.

(2). Class differences are especially important in measurements over time, because so high a percentage of past populations were made up of people without histories. A high percentage were illiterate, and in any event not important enough to figure in written records, or in the conversations of people who did write diaries, letters, and books. Analyses of "the Chinese family" until fairly recently described only the family ideals of the gentry and to a lesser extent their behavior, while omitting almost totally the family patterns of lower social strata. This omission has been equally true of research into Western family patterns.

That this omission is of great significance may be inferred from the various class differences which have been ascertained from modern research, but which have come to be thought of as relatively timeless, or at least applicable to a wide variety of populations over time: the lower strata probably had in the past a relatively high rate of marital disruption, a smaller and less active kin network, a weaker authority pattern of elders over children and husbands over wives, a lower rate of communication between husband and wife, etc. However, it is nearly impossible to ascertain whether there has been a *trend* in such variables over time, or even whether such formulations of class differentials are historically valid, since we cannot easily obtain such data for strata below the top level.

In survey terms, this problem is essentially one of obtaining an adequate *sample*. Our historical samples are primarily composed of the literate groups, with a heavy overweighting of the upper strata. For more recent periods, of course, we may begin to obtain better data on the lower social strata as each successive census of the past is open to public study. Thus, for example, Thernstrom has been able to probe ingeniously into the occupational and economic mobility of lower social strata in Newburyport in the mid-nineteenth century, by using census records.[23] Later in this discussion, we shall take note of additional work in Europe which is also opening up new records that will yield more adequate samples.

One example of the empirical consequence of this ommission may be seen by considering one type of individual datum noted above, age at marriage. Although the trend in age at marriage in the Western world has been generally toward a lower age over the past half-century we know in fact that this age has varied greatly in the past, and in any event depends upon particular kinds of socioeconomic structures. For example, where the young couple is not expected to be independent, the age may be fairly low (e.g., the Brahmins of India, and the nobles of France and England). Even for the more recent time period in the United States, it is very possible that the age at marriage among the *lower* social strata has changed very little, but that it has dropped far more in the middle social strata, and has thus become socially more conspicuous. Whether there has been a time trend would be very difficult to measure.

In a somewhat similar fashion, people have recently become very concerned with Negro illegitimacy rates, in which there has certainly been a short-term rise. However, we have no adequate figures for any period prior to 1938, and it is fairly obvious that if we expanded our time sample to include the past century, the secular trend would be downward, not upward.[24]

Of much more importance than the inability to count how many Negro members of the lower class had illegitimate children over the past century is the absence of their own observations. We know something about the public family values, and to some extent the private values, of *men* who were literate, and who were members of the middle or higher social classes. Few *women* have left their observations about how the family system operated (more in England and the United States than in other countries); almost no Negroes; and perhaps no children at all. It is not only difficult now to reconstruct a trend in their family role definitions as they saw them; we also lack their versions of the family role definitions accepted by their presumed betters.[25]

(3). A perhaps insuperable problem in trend charting is the lack of information about the processes by which large kin networks, kindreds, lineages, and so on were once built. Data on this general topic are available for periods of urbanization, secularization, or industrialization. As a consequence, the family change literature contains numerous propositions that relate such secular processes (or their traits, such as a market economy, a money system, etc.) with the breakdown of corporate kin structures, most large kin networks, or the domination of social structure by kinship variables. The long-term trend in the Western world since perhaps the High Middle Ages might be so described, and of course the modern world is witnessing such a trend generally.[26]

However, no matter where we place the point in history when Western (or any other) kinship structures began to decline in importance, they must at some time have been built up. We are witnesses to a large-scale destruction of corporate kin groups in societies over the world, but in some epoch they were constructed. Though we can assert a goodly number of correlations that seem to describe the disintegration process, we can make few propositions of any power or precision that describe the periods in which kin systems of some complexity were evolving. We have no data from which to make intelligent guesses. Those periods also included a decline (or low level) of literacy, the destruction of records, a lessened motivation to write books or collect data, and a dissolution of the political units that might have found useful the maintenance of archives. With reference to primitive societies, again their kinship patterns were constructed before any records were made, in periods of illiteracy.

(4). The significance of literacy for the problem of measurement has been evident throughout this discussion, but a final point deserves attention. When literacy is low, not only do fewer people record their private or public thoughts, and create fewer documents from which the trend analyst might chart ongoing changes, but all documents are socially less important in such a period, and thus less likely to survive. As an example, Stone remarks that it is not until the Elizabethan period that his close and detailed analysis of the British aristocracy became possible.[27] Not only do far more documents begin to appear, but far more are preserved (e.g., special rooms are constructed for documents). Censuses are uncommon, but the chances of a census, with its wider coverage of family-related data, increase with the expansion of literacy.

Although these problems exist for contemporary measurement, they can be solved by adequate research designs. For the charting of trends, however, they often cannot be solved, since *family* data are among the most evanescent of all facts. Political succession can be ascertained easily; the succession of family patterns cannot be. Indeed, one might hypothesize that in these historical periods of inadequate family records, family behavior was changing *rapidly,* but it would be difficult to disprove such an assertion.

The modern expansion in data collection has led many to suppose that for the mapping of family trends one need only write to the appropriate governmental agency. But though the United States has the distinction of having been the first nation to inaugurate a regular census (in 1790), our trend charting for the family is poor. With the exception of the birth rate (laboriously and ingeniously calculated from census data) and divorce rates (based on inadequate coverage until the 1930's), there is hardly a single family variable for which we can now draw a reliable time curve. Not one history of the American family can be taken seriously, though a few good monographs on specific time periods have been produced. *We are, in fact, deficient in the most basic data on which any important analyses of family change in the United States must be founded.*

"Timeless" Propositions in Family Change

Although this discussion concentrates on the analysis of family change, it must not be forgotten that only a small part of the research in *any* scientific field is devoted to change, and in every major field this subarea is the least developed, partly because of measurement problems. This fact about the development of science should be faced before going on to examine the place of timeless correlations in the study of family change.

Sidereal mechanics attained a high degree of elegance in Newton's time, but cosmogonical speculations remained the hobby of imaginative amateurs and a tiny minority of astronomers and physicists until well into the twentieth century. Chemists can hardly be said to have such a subfield at all, although they have contributed to the understanding of the phases of the solar system by their research in high-temperature chemical processes.

In the biological fields, perhaps only evolution (paleobotany, paleozoology, etc.) and ecology inquire into time trends. The two are theoretically closely linked, and in this type of inquiry they draw on roughly the same body of principles. These principles can best be tested by observing *contemporary* biological phenomena. Because of the difficulty of measuring which forces caused changes in the *past,* however—e.g., a clear fossil sequence from eohippus to the modern horse can be charted, but not which heel-nipping factors pushed it in that direction—this theory has not developed beyond a rudimentary form.[28]

Biological processes, like the processes that other great fields study, are assumed to occur in a *time dimension.* Nevertheless, these three advanced bodies of knowledge are made up mainly of timeless formulations, not propositions about *time trends.* The sociologist might well ponder the developmental gap between the first formulations of valid timeless correlation in a field and the development of a testable theory of change, in order to curb perhaps in some degree his overweening ambition to create *now* a valid, general theory of family (or social) change.

Such timeless propositions essentially state a correlation between (usually) two variables, which is thought to hold under a wide variety of conditions (or, hopefully, universally). Newton's gravitational formula (using three variables) is an example. Naturally, the illustrations used in the succeeding discussion will not be so esthetically satisfying as Newton's.

However, the family sociologist need not apologize if his formulations are somewhat less elegant, precise, or universally valid than those of even seventeenth-century physics. If the task were really so easy, doubtless many obscure physical scientists could achieve sudden great fame, now denied to them in their own field, simply by creating comparable propositions in this one.

Many critics would deny that sociology has achieved even one such proposition. Space does not permit a full explication of this issue. Viewed historically, such propositions have evolved in each science from simple correlations and observed regularities, as researchers have gradually seen which variables within a mass of disorderly phenomena seem always to be connected, to be functions of each other. Since each science continually re-examines skeptically its own findings, it is not possible invariably to assert that *now* a given sociological relationship fits the criteria of a "scientific law." In any event, we must consider the problem of measurement and theory by reference to the formulations that make up the body of knowledge we possess at present.

Such data are the core of any field and can be used to *correct* the grand "theories" of Type 1, the unifactorial hypotheses (e.g., climate has a low correlation with family patterns, and an even lower one with family *changes*). They are also the foundation for family change analyses in which general formulations are used to explain particular historical events. Any family change theory must ultimately be built from such formulations, since they describe the basic variables and processes of family patterns. This general relation is as true in sociology as it is in other fields.

This point is part of a more complex assertion that should be briefly stated here. Social change *data* can be studied in the service of several very different goals, the most notable of which are first, simply to understand and describe the *trends,* to find what is changing and how much; second, to develop a theory of family evolution, a set of presumably invariable *sequences;* and third, to *test* a supposedly timeless formulation.

My personal belief is that this last is the most profitable task of family change analysis in our generation. Thereby, the sociologist uses historical or trend data as he would data from other societies, i.e., to achieve a form of cross-cultural test. To study a hypothesis in very different time periods as well as in different societies subjects it to rigorous criteria. It is likely thereby to become more refined, precise, and valid.

Finally—a point to be looked at more closely in a moment—research in family *change* leads occasionally to a more general correlation, and a discovery that there has been less change than has generally been supposed.

Let us consider two brief examples of family change inquiry of this general type.

Social Class and Divorce Rate. As an outgrowth of my research on postdivorce adjustment, begun in 1946, I became aware that (contrary to the belief of most family sociologists) class position and divorce rate were *inversely correlated,* that is, that the lower the class, the higher the divorce rate. I presented this finding in 1948. In *After Divorce* I elaborated the datum considerably. Does it hold similarly for different class indicators, such as education, income, and occupation? Does it hold for caste as well as class? Does it hold for both Negroes and whites? Has it been observable *over time?* Finally, of course, if all these answers are affirmative, *why* does the relationship hold?[29]

That the relationship seemed to hold over time made the search for "causes" more imperative. Another set of factors increased the importance of that search. An extensive inquiry into possibly relevant data (marital adjustment by class, ecological distributions of divorce, juvenile delinquency, etc.) disclosed first, that published data in the past had often *contained* inverse correlations between some index of class and some index of "divorce proneness," but second, they were usually not discussed, often left unnoticed, and sometimes denied; and finally, no one had both announced the finding and given it the dignity of a formulation by attempting to show *why* it must be valid. Thus, a finding that had been relatively unnoticed previously became the focus of a longer inquiry which soon focused on the measurement of changes in divorce patterns over time.[30]

Let us list some of the data used to *measure* this relationship in the research discussed in *After Divorce.* As is clear, they can also be used for time trends:

1. Spatial distribution of divorcees among census tracts $\times$ income, density, and geographic mobility

2. Distribution of divorcees among enumeration districts $\times$ rent, income, home ownership, delinquency, and relief cases
3. Marital status $\times$ occupational level (data reported by high school children)
4. Remarried vs. married only once $\times$ occupational level
5. Marital instability (including separation and desertion) $\times$ class (composite index)
6. Negro vs. white percentage divorced, 1890–1950
7. Divorce proneness (whether a given population contains more divorcees than it forms of the general population) $\times$ specific occupation, 1887–1906
8. Divorce proneness $\times$ income
9. Negro vs. white proneness to divorce $\times$ education
10. Marital happiness $\times$ occupational level
11. Divorced vs. happily married $\times$ economic factors (long duration of employment, steadiness of work, savings)

Three comments on this early search for a general formulation are relevant to the broad problem of family change measurement. First, though it contains several observations over *time* (overlapping periods from 1887–1950) and *trend* descriptions, these are used primarily as a *test* of the basic datum. Different sets of time data were used to ascertain whether in fact the correlation seemed to exist, and just how strong the relationship seemed to be when different indexes were used. In addition, the analysis attempted to apply a Lazarsfeldian accounting scheme to the problem of measuring changing divorce proneness over generations.[31]

Second, various measurements themselves were approximations, or tentative gropings for an adequate measurement. Thus, for example, it was not possible (nor is it now) to obtain adequate data on proneness to divorce by occupation, by using actual divorces as recorded within each state. These records were far too incomplete even in the 1930's for such a test. Similarly, it appeared likely that though the percentage of Negroes reporting themselves as *divorced* in each census was higher than that of whites, such reports may have reflected merely the verbal customs of Negroes rather than the actuality of resorting to a divorce court. On the other hand, the census answers might well have reflected actual marriage *instability*.

Third, and again closely related to the problem of measurement, this analysis attempted a restatement of "economic factors" in *sociological* terms, rather than assuming the relationship was a simple economic one. In the 1930's and to some extent in the 1940's, many family analysts were skeptical of both economic and sexual factors as causes of marital adjustment. In this, their intuition was correct, but it sometimes led them to discount their own findings in which a gross correlation was visible between certain economic factors and proneness to divorce or marital unhappiness. Unfortunately, public records contain far more economic data (income, saving, home ownership, occupation) that can be used in such correlations than sociological data. Thus it is often necessary to develop a composite index which supposedly reflects *sociological* variables, or simply to accept the correlation with economic factors at its face value.

In groping toward a solution, then, the analysis moved generally toward the variable of marital instability rather than divorce, and toward the *role definitions* and social networks of different social strata. Thus, the analysis began with a relatively simple relationship, but moved toward an explanation in more general terms. This included such propositions as the following:

1. Because the distribution of income is more skewed than the wish to have the goods money can buy, the feeling of economic strain is higher toward the lower social strata.
2. Economic strain can be displaced (in the psychological sense) onto marital relations.
3. There is less censure and less catastrophe when the lower-class husband withdraws economic support from his wife, because there is more flexibility in income allocation (that is, more of it is devoted to consumer goods, less of it is committed to long-term investments), and the income difference between husband and wife is less.
4. Both the livelihood and the way of life of the couple toward the upper strata are more dependent on and involved in a supporting social network; and the cost of support given to the wife after divorce cannot be as easily evaded.
5. Among the lower social strata there is less emotional involvement and more open aggression between husband and wife, and less communication.
6. There is a higher percentage of working wives, but a lesser willingness of husband to share the household chores toward the lower strata.

In sum, if we view the family as a small social system, the strains arising from class-linked social factors are greater toward the lower classes. If this is true, then we should expect a higher rate of divorce, or at least a higher rate of marital disruption of some kind, among Negroes than among whites, and among lower occupational levels than higher occupational levels. We should expect this to hold true in rural populations as well, where we would then predict that migratory laborers or farm laborers exhibit a higher rate of marital instability than farm owners.

However, it is equally evident that within the Western world, this *cannot* be historically correct if we limit our measurement to legal divorces. Until fairly recently, it was only the upper strata who could obtain divorces at all, since these required either negotiations at the higher levels of Papal courts, or acts of provincial or national legislatures. Indeed, it is possible that this historical fact is the source of the general belief, until recently, that the divorce rate was *higher* toward the upper classes. Whatever their rate of marital instability, the poor could not divorce. On the other hand, in societies in which the divorce decision was largely a family matter, or in which access to some type of tribunal was fairly easy at all class levels, we would expect that reported divorces could be used as a fair approximation to the rate of marital instability. That is, which kind of observation can be used as an index of marital disruption depends in part on how easily such a disruption can appear in official records.

In the preceding paragraphs we have noted several inferences that can be drawn from the general formulations noted above. This is one characteristic of a fruitful generalization. Let us now specify further ones that focus on family change.

1. Within the Western world, where nations are in various degrees of technical development, we should find that at an early stage of development, when older legal patterns gave the right of divorce only to the somewhat higher social strata, marital disruption ought to correlate positively with class. As nations move into a more modern social political system, in which the masses acquire full citizenship rights and easier access to the courts, this relationship should gradually change.

2. In some nations at a modest level of development we ought to find that the proneness to divorce is not correlated well with class. Later, we should be able to show (as in most industrialized nations of the West) an *inverse* correlation between divorce proneness or marital instability and class.

3. On the other hand, in nations in which the administrative pro-

cedure for divorce was not the monopoly of the higher social strata, that inverse relationship ought to be found at almost any period.

4. Finally, however, in the most technologically developed nations, as certain kinds of class-induced strain differentials diminish, the class differentials in divorce proneness should also diminish. For example, we should find that over time the correlation between education as a class index and divorce proneness ought to diminish; and the marital disruption differential between Negroes and whites should also decline.[32]

This general test was attempted in a cross-cultural comparison, over time, of divorce in a fairly large number of Western and non-Western nations.[33] It is not relevant here to repeat these data, though by and large they support the inferences from this general formulation. The instance is cited, however, as an illustration of this use of family *change* data, i.e., to test the validity of a general, "timeless" formulation. If such a formulation does hold over time, then we can later use it in any steps toward the development of a full-scale family change theory.

Family Structure. A second example of utilizing time measurements to look for general formulations can be presented somewhat more briefly. As noted earlier, family sociologists have been much concerned with changes in U.S. family patterns, and many have described what I have labeled the "Classical Family of Western Nostalgia." According to this assumption, the typical early American household was a swarming, harmonious, extended one, made up of several generations and ruled by a patriarch. In a more or less cautious form, this assumption has been widespread, though doubtless here and there a skeptic could be found. Ogburn, for example, utilized census data to show that indeed the size of the American family had dropped since the early nineteenth century, but suggested that perhaps the family never had been very large in size.[34]

To test this general notion within a time perspective, Marion J. Levy and I approached this problem in the late 1950's with somewhat different modes of "measurement." Levy used hypothetical vital statistics data, and the computer made the "observations." Different sets of birth and death rates were fed into the computer, which thus carried a given population cohort through several generations of hypothetical birth and death experiences. If the large extended family described in the standard literature is to contain, say, three generations in one household, including some in-marrying spouses and their children, some people must live long enough to become grandmothers and some members of a set of brothers and sisters must live long enough to acquire spouses and children of their own. Computer calculations show that under most reasonable assumptions about birth rates in any society, a high percentage of such extended households is not statistically possible. Consequently, it must be concluded that in most time periods this type of family has not been common, even when it was an ideal.[35]

My own test was the simple one of using census and survey measurements of household size over the past fifty to one hundred years (in a few cases still farther back in time) in China, Japan, India, Arabic Islam, Sub-Saharan Africa, and several Western countries. Even allowing for observational and reporting errors as well as variations in definition, it is clear that only a small percentage of the households in any nation seem to have been large enough to contain even three generations in line (e.g., one set of grandparents, a son and his wife, and their children) plus unmarried sons or daughters of the grandparents.[36] The actual data over time, then, support the computer calculations from hypothetical data.

Nevertheless, such a set of measurements yields only a simple descriptive statement, not a general proposition, i.e., a correlation of wide empirical application, containing interesting theoretical implications; or a set of variables that predict such a correlation. All that we have been able to assert is that over rather great periods of time, a single variable (size of household) will vary within a small range. Here, then, a time study reveals relatively little change.

Leaving aside the rather interesting implications of this datum, let us consider the variables that might determine it. One possible set is the biological variables suggested by Levy, birth and death rates.[37] Sociological analysis would focus instead on these factors:

1. A social system can be maintained only if strong outside pressures and strong internal strains can be controlled, whatever the size of household.
2. The larger household has larger organizational *requirements* than does the smaller household. Among these are the following:
   a. Effective leadership by the male head of the household, which we can suppose is as uncommon as effective leadership generally.

    b. Similarly effective leadership by older females. This includes
not only "expressive leadership," but also instrumental
leadership of the internal organization of the household.

    c. Adequate resources, so as to offer better alternatives to ma-
turing young people than they could obtain by rejecting the
authority of their elders and looking elsewhere for opportunities.

This set of comments is the application of social system or organizational analysis to the problem of maintaining larger or smaller
households. For such general notions, there is a wide body of confirming data based on much research.

In addition, however, such a formulation permits several fruitful
inferences, which can in turn be tested by family change data and
by existing surveys from different societies. Some of these are the
following:

1. We would expect to find that size of household varies by class,
   in rural or urban families, wherever the large family ideal is
   widespread.
2. If the allegiance to the extended household ideal declines over
   time (as has happened in the Western world, and is happening
   elsewhere), class differentials in size of household will also
   decrease.
3. Where this ideal is widely held, families that become successful over a generation or so will aggregate into larger households;
   families that fail will diminish in size, and their extended households will break up.
4. Toward the upper social strata, the kin network will be larger,
   and more exchanges will occur within it, than toward the lower
   social strata.
5. As an index of the control by which the larger household is
   maintained, we would predict that toward the upper social
   strata the elders will be better able to impose their decisions
   about the courtship and marriage choices of their children (e.g.,
   through choice of neighborhood, companions, schools, economic threats, etc.).
6. If over time the control system of the upper stratum families
   weakens (as in the contemporary United States), then large
   extended households would become less common than before,
   and a larger percentage of the younger generation would be

successful in choosing their own spouses against the wishes of their elders.

Note that all of these are relatively simple measures, and most can be made over at least the time period of one generation if not more. For these predictions, a growing body of confirming data can be found.

Thus, we have considered two types of "timeless" findings. One is an implicit causal relation, expressed as a correlation. The other is a simple descriptive assertion, which rests in turn upon a set of relations that are asserted to hold for a wide range of times and places. Such formulations can always be applied within a time dimension, in that they do predict what can be observed over many time periods. However, they do not create any difficulties that are *specific* to the problems of family change. Essentially, we are using the same data for other periods that we would hope to use within our own. When that is not possible, the technical problems are the same as those of any historical investigation.

We are asserting, then, that sociologists will devote the main thrust of their energies to such correlations, and that they are not likely to develop a full-scale theory of evolutionary sequences, or measures to test them, in the near future. Moreover, this is not to be viewed as a failure, since in all other sciences we can observe the same lengthy time gap between the creation of a valid body of timeless formulations and an adequate theory of change.

Finally, we have argued that such a body of correlations is the necessary foundation for family *change* analysis: with that base, we can better interpret particular historical events and time trends; we can utilize measurements of change to test such formulations; we can predict what we shall find in particular time periods; and with some error we can even provisionally fill in time gaps with such data when adequate measurements are not available.

TYPES OF UNITS TO BE OBSERVED

Throughout the discussion to this point, we have been asking what kinds of observations can be made to solve the different types of family change problems, or which kinds of problems call for which kinds of measurements. This abstract dialogue between theory and measurement can be continued a step further by asking what types of family *units* we wish to study over time. We can thereby better con-

front some of the difficulties of ascertaining family change relationships, and also note that though each problem demands somewhat different kinds of data, different possibilities of measurement also suggest
new problems to be solved.

Individual and Structural Units

A simple way of classifying the types of units to be studied can be
drawn from the work of Lazarsfeld and his associates.[38] These may
be briefly labeled *individual, relational,* and *global* units. Data of
each type may be summarized or aggregated, to yield still other kinds
of measures for each class. An individual measure might be a person's
attitude toward having more children; a relational measure might be
the romantic attachment between two individuals; a global measure
might be the control of a matrilineage over land.

As just noted, however, observations on a particular unit may be
aggregated to yield more complex indexes or measures. For example,
the answers from a sample of *individual* respondents about fertility
values can be summarized to create a percentage, or an average "index of approval" of having a large family. In addition, the distribution
of approval, or a measure of its dispersion or variation within the
sample, can be calculated. These and other measures are ultimately
based on the recorded comments of an individual. Indeed, it is even
possible to construct structural or relational measures from individual
answers. For example, as a measure of group cohesion we may ask
what is the ratio of in-group to out-group choices made by individuals
when they name their close friends; or we may record the frequency
with which individuals communicate with one another within a kin
network.

Thus, with reference to the type of unit under observation, we
have suggested three levels of complexity, each of which may yield
other measures for a group through ordinary statistical transformations
(means, percentages, ratios, measures of dispersion, etc.). Before
commenting further on these three types of units, let us also note
that a further type of "unit" might be included, though it seems to
be less a unit than a mode of analysis: *contextual measures,* or the
unit-within-a-unit. Such observations analyze the behavior of one unit
(individual, dyad, lineage, etc.) within a larger unit. The focus is on
the relations between the two. Thus, we may attempt to record the
different behavior of the nuclear family in a time period when the kin
network is strong and when the network has become looser. Or, is
postdivorce adjustment different in a community with a high divorce

rate; does this adjustment differ over time, as more communities exhibit a higher divorce rate? Is a sister-sister dyad different in a sibling group made up otherwise of brothers, compared with one that is divided evenly among brothers and sisters?

To return now to the second of the three main types of units to be studied, *relational* data would include, e.g., the patterns of behavior of dyads or triads in a family: father-son, mother-daughter, superordinate authority-superordinate expressive-subordinates, and grandfather-father-son. Each of these has traits of its own that are not simply individual characteristics: e.g., mutual support and cohesion, conflict, ease of communication, etc.

A still larger or *global* type of unit would be families and kinship systems, though for various reasons one might wish to separate those two entities, and obtain measurements on each separately. Such collectivities, like relations made up of two or more individuals, have qualities of their own that individuals do not have. One can speak of the cohesion of a lineage, or of a family, but neither can be derived from the other; and neither can be derived from the "cohesion" of an individual.

A kinship system as a whole has the property of exchanging and circulating men and women, but individuals do not have that property. Thus, most systems require individuals to marry outside their own lineage, and often any two lineages do not make equal exchanges with one another. On the other hand, over generations the circulating system must yield an even exchange, or one or more lineages would die out.[39] In short, global units may have qualities in their own right.

Again, since at each level of unit-type the object under observation *is* a unit (family, individual, kin network, etc.) it is possible to aggregate or summarize the data on a sample of such units, and thus create additional indexes or measures.

An observational problem in family change analysis, as in sociology generally, is that most of our data are *individual,* but our most significant formulations are *structural,* i.e., relational or global. We ask individuals whether they visit their relatives, or exchange help with them, but from such data we aim at building up evidence about kin networks. We read individual diaries or travelers' reports, but we wish to describe a courtship or kinship system of a past generation. We question the individual, "Who makes the big decisions in your family?" but really seek through successive surveys over time to ascertain the *power structure* of samples of families over time. Individual data, often presented as aggregates and sometimes used as indices of system or global structural traits, have been perhaps the most common measures in family change.

Difficulties of Structural Measurement

In our earlier discussion we outlined the main problems of obtaining trends in such individual measures, and need not repeat them here. Let us instead comment further on the difficulties of structural or relational measures, where all those problems are compounded. It would be very difficult, for example, to sketch an analysis based on firm historical data, of the changing pattern of custody in the nineteenth century, when the possession of the child was gradually given to the wife rather than to the husband. *Kindreds* have been reported from isolated areas in the United States (e.g., the Hatfields and the McCoys) and they have played a role in ballad and fiction, but it would be a tedious if not impossible task to present an adequate analysis of the history of kindreds in this (or any other Western) country. As suggested in our earlier comments on trends, mainly of individual data, populations with low literacy, far removed from the upper social strata and of little political significance, have left us few records.

Gradually, we may hope to have some measurements over time of such simple relationships as grandfather-grandchild, or uncle-nephew, or sibling-sibling dyads, but even those relational data are more difficult to obtain than demographic observations on individuals, such as fertility or age at marriage.[40]

The technical problems in such an expansion in the unit of observation are well known to survey research. The procedures for obtaining a representative national sample in the United States, with the aim of measuring attitudes and values about certain aspects of family behavior, have been fairly well worked out. The costs can be calculated in advance, and are relatively modest by present-day standards. If however, the researcher wishes to obtain *sociometric data,* or to obtain "a snow ball sample" by which he starts with a given sample and obtains information on all the people in *their* social networks, or wishes instead to ask each individual about his exchanges with the many individuals in his kin network, the costs mount astronomically. These are costs in both money, time, and refusals. Moreover, the refusals are much more catastrophic, since substitutions cannot logically be made. The effort is to obtain relations with individuals in a network, and therefore other persons are not adequate substitutes. A system of substitute sampling by random numbers would not serve the purpose.

All this is intensified in time analysis, since with each link in the network, the measurement to be made is highly contingent upon the existence of records that may not have been made at all in the past.

Thus, for example, Rossi's recent ingenious analysis of the effect of kin relations on naming of children could be carried out on the basis of survey data, but would not be possible for any sample in the past, and perhaps not even for an upper-class sample, since we could not easily trace out the personal histories of each individual in the network to ascertain which members were more liked or disliked, exchanged more or less with the given family, or served as substitutes for an absent kinsman.[41]

Such gaps in the records make the establishment of simple time trends very difficult, and of course render somewhat suspect many of our "timeless" formulations noted above, since we cannot easily test them in prior generations. The absence of such a test is especially important for structural reasons, since to test them by reference to a sample of ethnographic observations on primitive societies is not identical with a test by reference to historical civilizations: sometimes the relevant relation or unit does not exist in both. Finally of course, such gaps make still more difficult the goal of ascertaining or testing for *patterned* sequences, or evolutionary developments.

Family Life Cycle Analysis

One further type of "unit" needs to be stressed, for its qualities emerge only over a period of years: the *life* or *developmental cycle* of the family. Any given domestic group goes through several phases before it breaks up from fission and the death of its older members.[42]

Sociologists of the family have not agreed on the most fruitful set of phases to be used in analyzing this unit theoretically, but laymen think naturally of a married couple, then parenthood, which is divided into the preschool, school, and young adulthood stages of the children. These young adults found their own households, and transform their parents into grandparents. Under contemporary mortality conditions a typical wife or husband is likely to live two decades or more after their children marry.

Diachronic analyses, viewing families as they pass through these phases, are rare, though social scientists have long recognized that such studies might illuminate not only the internal processes of the family but especially its exchanges with other segments of the society. Since, however, all these patterns change, it is useful to obtain developmental cycle data *over time*. That is, we should not only record the life cycle within a given generation, the distribution of the family developmental patterns of that generation, but the changes in the life cycle pattern itself over *successive generations*. Very likely, young adulthood was defined differently, and its place in the successive phases of the family entailed different role obligations, in colonial days than, say, at the turn of this century.

Families at the same stages of the developmental cycle engage in different kinds of exchanges with other segments of the society, over successive generations. How fission occurs and possibly how strong the family boundaries are, may vary from one generation to another.

Such data must be recorded periodically, and by an ongoing research organization, since the fruitfulness of life cycle data within one generation, or over successive generations, cannot easily outweigh the individual researcher's awareness that he will likely be dead before any substantial body of data has been analyzed. On the other hand, *panel* data ought to be collected on many other family traits (noted in this chapter) besides the developmental phases themselves. In addition, individual family data can be fed into a repository for life cycle measurements. Properly integrated, therefore, the task of collecting data on this "time unit" should not add exorbitantly to the total cost of recording all other family measures over time.

THE USES OF HISTORICAL DATA

The analysis of family change must rely upon historical data, but since all data are by definition historical, we cannot infer that sociologists should leave the task to historians. To some degree, the past generation has witnessed a rough division of labor between historians who look to the past, and sociologists, who have concentrated far more on the contemporary period. In addition, a division of labor based on theoretical aims has roughly differentiated the two disciplines. Sociologists have typically set themselves apart as aiming at generalizations of some kind, hopefully formulations of correlations that could be predicted over a wide variety of societies. They have, in short, used historical data to test these generalizations, rather than seeking historical data because of literary or political interest. They have been much less interested in the description of an epoch than in selecting particular data from that epoch to demonstrate some general idea.

However, this division was never fully accepted by either discipline, and the resurgence among sociologists of an interest in social change has occurred simultaneously with an increasing interest among historians in testing for general conclusions. This gives some hope for the future. However, historians have neglected the family more than other major social institutions. No doubt they have neglected it in part because they agreed that the major causal variables in history were to be found in political and economic factors, but the lack of adequate observations has also handicapped their work.

For example, if the historian wishes to deal with family life in ancient Rome, he is able to give us certain details about the wedding itself, because certain of the documents and descriptions of ceremonies have been preserved. If he concentrates, say, on the second century A.D., he is able in addition to offer us a considerable number of anecdotes and stories. However, he *must* focus on such bits of gossip, because they are most of what data he has. It is very difficult for him to give us a systematic statement about the family life of even the upper strata.[43]

The stories which illustrate the position of woman at that time would, for example, yield almost diametrically opposed inferences. If one collects stories about only the loose and bawdy women, Roman family life among the upper strata appears very different than if one selects by contrast the family patterns of the virtuous and noble women, but "balance" does not solve the problem. What we need to know for a given epoch are *systematic* data, that is, similar observations on a representative sample of people. Unfortunately, what is journalistically interesting may not be the most sociologically significant, and certainly does not often give an adequate picture of the family patterns at a given time.

Note, too, that the rare historian who has given much attention to the family does not often attempt an analysis over time. Rather, he concentrates on a *particular* epoch, the period in which he feels most expert. The historian who is expert in still another epoch may ask and answer very different questions, so that from even the comparison of two such works we do not obtain adequate time trends.[44]

Stone's work, mentioned earlier, is altogether different, in part because he begins at the point of an archival revolution, and attempts systematically to answer the kinds of questions a family sociologist would wish to know.[45] On the other hand, no comparable work at all has been done for any historical period of the United States. It can be supposed that more such work will appear in the future, as historians are increasingly challenged to answer the kinds of questions that sociologists raise, and as sociologists see the uses of historical data.

However, we cannot expect that any substantial percentage of sociologists will engage in genuine historical work in order to make adequate time measurement. The training of the modern sociologist focuses heavily upon contemporary data, which are both challenging and potentially available. The tedious kind of archival work, growing out of a scholarly tradition, is not likely to become a main career line of the typical young sociologist of the next generation. And for any important time comparison extending more than a decade or so in the past, archival inquiry is necessary.

As a consequence, sociologists will have to rely on historians in the future as in the past for the larger part of the data that they need to test a proposition. In Europe, where the two traditions have not been so separated as in the United States, some increased collaboration may take place. One especially fruitful development in the art of obtaining measurements on the past, and thus establishing time trends, has begun in France and England. This may be called the "reconstitution of past communities." Because in both England and France many types of church registries have been preserved, and some populations have been relatively nonmobile, in some regions it becomes possible to "take a census," or perhaps make vital statistics observations on people dead for hundreds of years.

In this process, the social scientists have essentially attempted to fill out "census schedules," as though they were trying to record contemporary information on each individual, or family, although the events happened hundreds of years ago. In some instances, they have been able to make rather complex cross-tabulations, after developing elaborate genealogies or in some cases reconstitutions of fairly large segments of a village population over several generations.[46] That is, by summarizing and analyzing individual or family data, they are able to describe at least some kinship patterns at one or more time points, so as to test both timeless correlations and hypotheses about trends.

Of course, such procedures cannot recapture most interpersonal relations, but can uncover family behavior that generated official records, e.g., age at marriage, whether pregnant at the time of marriage (by comparing this date with the date of a child's birth), numbers and sex of children, alliances between families, or whether families at a given class level were successful in enduring over many generations. Although each such investigation is tedious and complex, and covers usually only a small geographic region, it does give us a much greater body of information on a total population than has been achieved in the past.

We cannot carry out such a "census of the past" in the United States, since similar records either do not exist, or cover only one religious segment of the population, and in any event do not reach so far back in time. It is to be hoped that United States historians will continue to attempt to ascertain family changes of the past, even with less adequate data.

However, historians can contribute still more to the understanding of family change, by attempting the measurement of family alterations in the past as they relate to other areas of social action. Among these might be included the relations between family connections and jobs, such as Aronson has done with the higher political jobs in the Adams, Monroe, and Jackson administrations.[47] It is to be supposed that family networks played a large role in the economic transactions of the nineteenth century, but these have not been specified in detail, and we have no real trend measurements for such changes as may have occurred.

The frontier thesis has received a harsh drubbing from historians, but the question of class turnover during the economic expansion of the past century has not been fully answered. It is especially important for the understanding of social and family change in this period to know how successful were not only the leading families in maintaining their positions, but how important were family relations in both upward and downward mobility at levels *below* the top. During this period, inheritance laws changed in the United States, and presumably these affected or were affected by the existing kin networks. In turn, inheritance affected social mobility. Thus, all these factors are intertwined with family changes, and historians could help us to understand both the specific changes that took place, and the larger linkages with other areas of the society over time.

As yet, we have not been able to specify how industrialism—that ragbag of complex variables—has affected the family over the past century. Specifically, both have changed in ways that seem relatively clear, but perhaps only because we have not adequately investigated them, and we do not in any event know through which variables industrialization has had such effects on the family. We have not been able as yet to deny the possibility that changes in the family, or pre-existing traits of family systems in Western nations not only preceded industrialization, but also had a strong impact on its genesis and development.

As noted earlier, sociologists concerned with family change have been much enamored of the general notion that industrialization has had a great impact on the family system of the United States, but in fact there has been no adequate historical measurement of the specific family relations that have presumably changed. More precisely, as noted earlier, analysts have the general impression (confirmed by common observation but by no precise measurement) that within each generation the power of the elders has declined, as has that of parents generally over their children, and husbands over wives. Young children have acquired much greater freedom than before, in every area of family interaction. However, this has been a very long trend, moving presumably always in the same direction. Is there any possibility of measuring how fast that change has gone, and whether indeed it has been closely related to industrialization?

Similar questions can be raised about urbanism, a ragbag of variables nearly as large as that of industrialization. Many analysts have asserted that with the move from the country to the city, families became less neighborly and less kin-oriented. The kin network began to break down, and the ability to depend upon kin in time of crisis also declined. Whether this has been a long-term trend, or whether this type of report merely states what took place in the first generation of migration to the city, we do not know. On the other hand, we do know that at the present time, in every city in which this has been studied, large kin networks are very common.[48] Can historians ascertain whether there has been a real decline; whether there was a temporary decline during periods of rapid urbanization; or whether there has been no decline at all?

FAMILY CHANGE ANALYSIS
FOR THE FUTURE

While historians and sociologists are recapturing past trends, the entire society is creating *new* trends. History has been made, but it is also in the making. If we are to analyze family changes in the future more adequately than we have as yet done, we had better begin now to record the data that will be relevant then.[49] Such a conscious plan can be outlined only if we can decide which data we wish to record, and that in turn depends on which kinds of questions we want to answer.

The Theoretical and Pragmatic Utility of Family Data

The recording of time series is the complex outcome of many accidental variables, such as how difficult a given fact is to observe, measure, or record; which segments of the population want such data, and possibly whether specialized experts gradually come to have a vested interest in maintaining such a series. Such factors will doubtless determine the outcome of future data collection as well, but it may be possible to shape that outcome in part by making a clear choice among the possible kinds of information. Perhaps we can suggest variables that would be important for scientific questions, but which would at the same time be of some use for social accounting purposes.

Any time series represents only a small sampling of the information that could have been recorded, and is thus implicitly an answer to the question: Which data are important, which can best be used to cope with the nation's problems? All record-keeping is an implicit assertion that it would be costly to do without this information, and that additional facts would cost more than they would be worth. At the present time in the history of the United States, both social scientists and political leaders are increasingly coming to understand that a much wider range of information is needed for *practical* purposes, simply because the sociopolitical structure has become (or is thought to be) much more complex and is guided at so many points by conscious decisions that need to be based upon adequate information. As any organization becomes more complex, and multiform in its output, far more kinds of information are needed, and a much more adequate set of mechanisms is required to furnish an ongoing set of controls. People want to control more aspects of their society than before.

One of the indications of this change is the demand by economists that in calculating how much the nation as a whole "produced" in a given year, it is necessary also to make some estimates about the *costs* of producing that amount—for example, in stream, air, and noise pollution, in ragged nerves from highway congestion, in destroyed ghetto lives, in the destruction of wildlife through pesticides, etc.[50]

In the past, such pragmatic decisions about the recording of family change data have served theoretical goals only in part and by accident, and as a consequence researchers have frequently complained that the wrong time series, or incomplete data, are being recorded. They have tried to persuade government agencies to improve their practices. Unfortunately, they cannot wait for time series to be gathered; the theoretical question needs an answer *now,* but the time series were not recorded in the past. Moreover, each such question requires specific data, but these may not be useful for other researchers. The urgency of a theoretical question changes rapidly, but obviously the maintenance or creation of trend data cannot be so swiftly adjusted to such needs. Consequently, there will always be a substantial gap between the scientific needs of a field, and the practical exigencies of gathering time data.

On the other hand, as a field develops in rigor and precision, its needs correspond more closely to the practical needs of a society. The kinds of problems it wishes to solve may not be immediately practical, but they soon become so if the theoretical questions are adequately answered. In that case, the answer has a wide range of applications, and soon the fit between that answer and the urgencies of the day become apparent. Consequently, in looking for family change data that need to be reported for the immediate future, we may well utilize as our main guide the criterion of theoretical importance, while looking to see to what extent such information might be of some practical utility.

Political caution may also suggest that theoretical concerns might play a substantial role in suggesting the family trends to be reported for the future, since this is an especially sensitive area. States have always been most reluctant to interfere in the private domain of family life, although they have always promulgated various laws and norms for family life. Even at the present time, which represents an extreme in the state's willingness to intrude into family behavior, only a nearly catastrophic family situation is likely to evoke formal governmental intervention. It may therefore be more useful to ascertain how our family system operates while suggesting possible social accounting measures, rather than attempting to set up family standards by which states might wish to measure the performance of individual families or family behavior in the entire society.

We can, then, attempt to suggest some of the important variables that now seem to justify charting—for the past where possible, but certainly for the future—for reasons of theoretical significance, but note that the data can also be applied to the goals of social bookkeeping.

Wisely chosen, such data would be useful in uncovering problems in family behavior, or the *lack* of a major problem (e.g., more precise data on illegitimacy would locate more accurately where the problem is significant, and might prove that the general problem is not great). Such records would also permit a rough judgment as to how well the nation is coping with its family problems (e.g., fertility behavior and intentions within subsegments of the population would tell us how far our population growth is outstripping our resources).

Such data can also be used with caution for crude *predictions* of the immediate future. Of course, simple extrapolations from a present trend are often unwise in the absence of good theory. If we do not know why the curve is shaped as it is, mechanical extension may lead to errors. The age at marriage has been dropping, but it would be thoughtless to predict the age at marriage in 1985 by simply extrapolating the secular trend of the past generation.

On the other hand, in the absence of good analytic formulations, the best estimate is to assume that things will generally be tomorrow as they are today. The administrator cannot usually wait for adequate data. Within such limits, then, trend information can be useful for at least rough predictions.

Finally, if the variables are well chosen, they can also serve for testing or specifying more precisely whatever analytic variables we may suspect are powerful in the shaping of the family behavior, or the behavior in other institutional areas that may be related to the family. If, for example, trend data are gathered on the power structure within United States families, various hypotheses about the kinds of resources, actions, and interactions that generate power in the family can be checked.

One special theoretical problem makes the task of selection both important and difficult. As noted earlier, family sociology, and social science generally, has not developed an elaborate body of theory about social change, and for some decades has relied upon a crude formulation expressed by the terms *Gemeinschaft-Gesellschaft,* tribal-industrial, or folk-urban. As a consequence, though we can make some good guesses about the *general* pattern of development in, say, Mexico, we are without theoretical guides if we wish to predict the course of an already highly industrialized nation. We can draw curves *up to* high industrialization, but our theory does not permit us to predict what kind of society the United States itself is becoming. The fact that thousands of scholars in the United States are now trying to make just such charts should not obscure the fact that they are working entirely by intuition and by simple extrapolation from known curves, rather than any body of theory.

This failure is of special importance, since we can much more wisely choose which family variables to begin recording, if we have a clearer notion of what sort of society will emerge a generation or more from now. Which aspects of the social structure will be highly relevant? Which issue will be most significant? Much more specifically, what are some of the family patterns that are likely to emerge in the future? If we had a clearer answer to these questions, we should know much better which kinds of data would be practically and theoretically most useful for the social scientist of the future.

To predict the social structural problems with which the next generation will try to cope, and thus to suggest which data will be most significant, is to assume the mantle of prophet. But with the entrance of so many prophets on the stage at this time, one more can hardly be a burden.

As can be seen, these problems can be solved only in small part by the physical sciences. Most of the task will have to be given to the social sciences. After taking note of them, we shall venture to suggest which *family change* data might be of special theoretical and pragmatic utility within such a society.

One of the most important problems that will be faced is the increasing demand of lower social strata in the United States for political expression, and the contemporary and increasing loss of credence given to the dominant social strata. This problem is a modern version of a fundamental problem to be encountered in every society, the often conflicting demands of social order and those of justice. In the United States, of course, this problem is exacerbated by the difficulties of ethnic integration, and the long history of injustice to various ethnic groups, which themselves are becoming much more conscious in their demands, while dominant groups are becoming much more aware, in turn, that they have failed in their own civic duties. The increasing demand for social opportunities of all types is one aspect of this larger problem, but it extends to most areas of social participation and interpersonal relations.

A problem that is partly to be solved by the physical sciences, but whose solution has been retarded fundamentally by social variables is that of pollution—the pollution of air by both noise and foul chemicals; the destruction of natural life in the water, air, and forests; and the eradication of natural beauty. This pollution has been exacerbated by overpopulation, a problem in its own right. It is intensified in turn by the congestion of people in motion, on the highways and in the air. However, for the first time in the history of this country, a substantial change of opinion with respect to the esthetic and economic desirability of solving such problems is on the increase.

In addition, and again transforming these problems into nearly impending catastrophe, is the sociopolitical problem of attempting to cope with such tasks on a nationwide basis, while at the same time preserving a satisfying degree of freedom. The technical facilities for invading the privacy of individuals have increased, and constitute a continuing temptation and therefore a problem for the populace, but these only accentuate the growing power in the hands of governmental officials for controlling and shaping the lives of its own citizens. If some of these problems can be solved on the purely physical level, but the nation becomes regimented, then the basic values of the society will have been subverted.

Finally, the nation has had to face the problem openly, and must cope with it more strenuously in the future, that though some other nations have become richer during the past two decades, the United States is outstripping all of them at a rapid pace. The present pattern of international philanthropy is at best a sop to guilty feelings, and in turn creates some domestic resentment. It would hardly seem an adequate solution simply to give up economic growth (even if calculated by reference to collective achievements, and not merely the production of more automobiles), but gifts to poorer countries are no more than a step beyond that simplistic solution.

A society that confronts and tries to cope with such problems, rather than the spoliation of its natural resources, the exploration of its unknown hinterland, or the construction of cleverer and more complex machines, will also have a different family system. It will wish to have more adequate data on the functioning of its family system than it has had in the past. Let us now consider some of the data that we believe might well be included in a program of continuing time measurements, toward the end of a better comprehension of both how the family system works, and the extent to which it succeeds in performing many of the tasks for which it now has the responsibility.

Some Future Data Needs

Time and Money Budgets. We might well begin by recording periodic data on time and money *budgets* of families, both within successive samples of families, within each decade; and within time panels of families so as to obtain better data on life cycles. We could thereby exploit the insight of LePlay, which he himself did not adequately pursue, that such budgets express the value preferences and the social pressures on individuals and families.[51] From this point of view, these allocations are not to be considered "economic" except in the largest meaning of that term. How families invest their time and money, their energies and plans, will tell us far more about how individual families and a family system function, than mere public opinion surveys of value preferences. We could then better understand why some families are unwilling to invest in their children's talent, or to pay for psychological or physical therapy that might enable them to exploit the opportunities that come their way. We would also cast more light on another family change pattern, the operation of kin networks in an industrialized society. By developing life cycle budget patterns, we could understand far better the changes and exchanges of roles within a household over time, and individuals' increasing or decreasing participation in other areas of social behavior.

Variations in Family Patterns. Out of such data, we could in addition ascertain far better the *variations* of family patterns within the United States. Family change data should be periodically collected on these variant forms. The process of Americanization in past generations suggested to many analysts that assimilation could proceed rapidly. After all, thousands of children were transformed from Italians or Armenians or Norwegians into Americans within a generation. However, we now know that such ethnic and class differences survive many generations, though within any given generation a large segment assumes the family patterns of the dominant middle class.

We have become increasingly aware, in addition, that fundamental problems may exist among some segments of the population, notably lower-class Negroes and whites, and it would be highly useful to social planners, as well as to theorists, to obtain time data on the changing behavior of such families. In addition, of course, we could better understand how such family patterns, of so wide a variation, can interact effectively with other areas of the social structure. Consequently it would be useful to obtain time data on such family variations, whether ethnic or class in character.

Sexual Behavior. Although the "sexual revolution" has been heralded for decades, and more sober analysts have presented data to show that the gradual changes seem hardly revolutionary, we cannot deny that the place of sex in family and social life is changing. It would be difficult to predict the role that sex will play in the future, since it is so much under debate at present. Some essayists suggest that the new philosophy of sex plays down sexual differentiation, e.g., the similar appearance of male and female hippies. Others suggest that an industrialized society puts heavy emphasis upon sex differences, and especially on the glamour role of the female. Without question, sexual encounters have become commonplace, and most romantics would infer that they have much less emotional depth as a consequence. One might prophesy a future in which the dating and transient love relationships of the adolescent subculture become a much more widespread pattern at all age levels.

Only few would prophesy that we shall become more puritanical in the future. Whatever form our sexual behavior will take in the future, without question there will be a wider variation from one circle, clique, or segment of the population to another, and it seems unlikely that sex will play a small role in the marital relations of the future. Consequently, it would seem wise to begin taking periodic observations and soundings as to the place of sex in our society.

Changes in the Employment of Women. Although the rise of the employment of women has in Western nations been somewhat overstated, without question the qualitative changes have been profound. It is a commonplace to note that women have worked in all societies, and have done menial, tedious, hard labor. Indeed, men have typically managed to take over the challenging and exciting tasks for themselves, and though they have not rid themselves in any society of hard monotonous work, at worst they have shared it with the women. The qualitative change in the employment of women can be seen not only in the figure of "percentage of women in the labor market," or "percentage of the industrial labor force made up of women" (though in most western nations this figure has altered little in fifty years), but also in the entrance of women at almost all levels of responsibility, intellectual challenge, and power. The percentage is small, but it is growing.

We have only begun to measure the possible impact of this change on family relations. Preliminary studies suggest that the destructive impact on children is far less than had been supposed, but without question such participation increases the resources women have at their command, their ability to function independently of their husbands, the possibility of paying for child care, their self-conceptions, and the meaning of having children.[52] By contrast, we have few data on the role adjustments of *men* to this changed pattern in the United States.

Our concern, then, is not merely to ascertain how many women work at which kinds of jobs, but precisely how this type of participation in another institutional area affects family relations of all kinds. Since it is predictable that the social evaluation of women's employment will be changing, it must be predicted that the impact on the family will also change over time. At present, time budget data suggest that women do not spend any less time in household tasks now than they did half a century ago, since "labor saving devices" merely increase household production of various kinds and permit higher standards of cleanliness and performance, while men in turn object to taking women's tasks.[53] This process is not, of course, confined to the United States. However, since all these relations are changing, it would be useful to obtain periodic data on the impact of women's employment on family relations, for thereby we would understand how the family unit itself operates, and could also adopt more effective programs for coping with whatever problems that employment may create.

Functioning of Kin Networks. By now it has become a commonplace that kin networks are widespread in the most industrialized nation in the world, although it is equally evident that industrialization undermines large-scale kinship structures. However, the rediscovery of kin networks must be viewed as a theoretical problem, and not merely a set of descriptive facts. It is useful to know, for example, that in Western countries very likely a majority of old people live within a short distance of at least one of their children, and a majority may have seen a child within the past day, but we have not at all understood how such kin networks operate, or what their importance is for the functioning of the society as a whole.[54]

As noted earlier, social analysts had widely assumed in the early twentieth century that kin networks as well as ordinary neighboring had declined substantially with urbanization and with industrialization. In fact, we have no such data available, and thus cannot construct a trend for any of this period. Considerable data suggest that kin networks are larger, engage in more exchange, and control their children more effectively, toward the upper social strata, and these are in turn the more successful families within an industrialized society. This suggests the possible effectiveness of kin networks within a society whose role relationships are often defined as achievement-based, affectively neutral, universalistic, and self-oriented. Litwak has suggested a number of problems in an industrialized society for which the usual bureaucratic solutions are not adequate, and for which family participation may serve the goals better.[55] On the other hand, the precise definitions of who is to be in the kin network, and what are to be the role obligations of each person, have not been ascertained and indeed it seems likely that variant role definitions would be obtained if an adequate study were made.

Here again, it is clear that periodic readings on the *structure* of such networks, which tasks they assume, and who discharges them, would enhance considerably our understanding of how the family functions in modern society, and at the same time would be useful in social planning. These measurements ought to include the intensity of the emotional relations among the people in the network, as well as the labor and commodity exchanges among them. It would also be useful to obtain information on the extent to which such networks press toward various patterns of nepotism, and thus interact closely with the recruitment and mobility processes within industrialized societies. Coupled with such observations on nepotism would be data on the changing inheritance patterns within such networks, again contributing to our understanding of the linkages between economic and family processes.

Socialization Practices. At the present time, hundreds of studies are carried out each year on socialization. Most of these are planned and executed by psychologists, although often the variables are not limited to psychological factors. It has become apparent that periodic measurements of socialization practices in the United States would be of utility in social planning, especially among segments of the population that labor under the most disadvantages in the present opportunity system, but such readings would also help us better to understand both the inputs and the productivity of family processes. We refer not alone to the "effectiveness" of socialization, in the narrow sense of how well adults succeed in imposing their values and behavioral patterns on the next generation. Much more important might be the measurement of socialization practices as they bear on the production of neurosis and psychosis. Whatever psychodynamic theory we espouse, it seems clear that parent-child relations over time do create the particular personality structure that characterizes each individual, and that many persons are in effect crippled for life by these early experiences. It is unlikely that state intervention in such socialization processes will increase by much over the next few decades, but it would be of great theoretical importance to make such observations of socialization practices, with the end in view of achieving far greater precision in our prediction of neurosis and psychosis, of coping with those problems as they emerge, and of changing the educational system.

Crude theorizing has also suggested that the structural relations within the family and the particular socialization experiences of the child will affect greatly the child's need for achievement, and his ability to master the outside environment.[56] These theoretical formulations are suggestive but inadequate, and further measurement of this process is needed. Again, as an element in social planning, it would be useful to know how adequately the family is functioning to produce individuals who can utilize their talents in the problems they must face as adults.

It is not as yet clear that these socialization experiences affect greatly the degree of political participation of the next adult generation, or the particular form it will take. On the other hand, some formulations have offered specific hypotheses about the possibility that one of the outputs of the family is a political individual.[57] It might be wise to make at least some periodic measurements of this phenomenon, especially if our earlier suggestion is correct that we face special political problems relating to commitment to the political system, the willingness to grant freedom of participation and political expression to other groups, and the need for coping anew with the problem of order and justice.

Small-groups theory has continued to offer many hypotheses about the importance of resources in interpersonal relations, and a much older tradition has argued that wives and children have increased their freedom and participation in family decisions. This trend, if it is indeed a trend, is linked to the autonomy of the individual, the employment of women and the relative income of husband and wife, and the dependence of children (because of a lengthening period of education) on the family itself.

These changes are linked in turn with changes in socialization patterns as well as with changes in the time, energy, and money budgets of family. It would consequently be of both theoretical and practical importance to make periodic measurements of the individual resources of members of the family, their exchanges, and their role bargains, in short, to ascertain the power structure and processes within successive samples of families over the next few decades.[58] Here, too, added understanding of the interpersonal relations and changing role definitions of husband, wives, and children might be obtained from panels as well, since we know that these patterns alter within the life cycle of each family.

Social Costs of the Family System. A final body of time measurements would also aid our understanding of the linkages between family behavior and social behavior in other areas of the society. Characteristically family analysts have assumed that the stability of families and family systems is good, that family processes are to be viewed as desirable (except of course for those that are viewed as improper). It might be well now to undertake some better measurement of the *costs* of family life, to which thoughtful essayists have referred for generations.

It may be that some type of ideal "traditional" family in which everyone accepted his special role and discharged his obligations willingly might be a unit that would make everyone happier. In the contemporary United States, however, we have no such choice, if indeed any society ever did. A family *system* maintains itself with considerable stability, but individual families within it do not. The kin network helps its own members, but in so doing it may contribute substantially to the undermining or destruction of the aspirations held by other families. The very success of families of higher social strata in protecting their own inept from open competition may help erode political stability as well as credence in the social values of the society. The nepotism that may be applauded within the family circle may reduce not only physical production within a factory but may also prevent a more talented person from obtaining a position in which his talents could contribute substantially to the society.

In short, we ought also to examine the *costs* of our family system. More simply put, in examining the many linkages between familial and other processes that we have pointed out in this chapter, we ought not to lose sight of the fact that many of them create substantial costs. Families do in fact socialize their children, but they often produce criminals, psychopaths, neurotics, and psychotics. The family system that requires husband and wife to assume the obligations imposed upon them by the society, toward one another as well as toward their children, may also reduce their effectiveness as individuals, citizens, or even as producers. Some part of our program of time measurements, then, must look at the junctures at which the investment in family life may well yield little return, when balanced against the total costs, just as is true for other producing units of the society.

Many of the data that are suggested here as candidates for time measurements have been recorded for particular samples here and there, in isolated bits of research. Indeed, it is from such suggestive formulations that we have inferred their pragmatic and theoretical utility in the future, in a society that will be much changed from the present one. On the other hand, the importance of such data is great enough to argue for a continuing set of such observations, rather than relying upon the happenstance of an individual researcher's interest in a particular problem. All these time data would contribute, it is true, to a better analytic understanding of just how our family systems operate, both internally and in their linkages with other areas of social life, but the data from them could also be used to find out more adequately just how effectively the family serves the tasks that it has traditionally accepted.

NOTES

Work on this chapter was facilitated by NIMH Grant No. 11436-01. I am also indebted to Walter L. Goldfrank for his help.

1. Becker, Carl L., *The Heavenly City of the Eighteenth-Century Philosophers*, Yale University Press, New Haven, 1932, p. 118.
2. Morgan's first major work was *League of the Ho-De-No-Sau-Nee or Iroquois* (1851), reprinted by the Human Relations Area Files, New Haven, 1954, 2 vols.
3. *Ancient Society*, Cambridge University Press, Cambridge, 1964, 1st ed., 1877, pp. 325–328, 441–442.
4. Spencer, Herbert, *First Principles*, H. L. Fowler, New York, 1906 ed., pp. 640–641, 650–651.
5. Briffault, Robert, *The Mothers*, Macmillan, New York, 1927; Tylor, Edward B., *Primitive Culture*, J. Murray, London, 3 vols., 1871; see also Westermarck, Edward B., *The History of Human Marriage*, 2nd ed., Macmillan, London and New York, 1894.
6. Tylor had first suggested this measurement solution in a lecture given at the Royal Institution in 1869 and then in an article, "On the Survival of Savage Thought in Modern Civilization," *Proceedings of the Royal Institution*, which I have not been able to consult. The notion is also found in *Primitive Culture*, and elaborately treated in his article, "On a Method of Investigating the Development of Institutions: Applied to the Laws of Marriage and Descent," *Journal of the Royal Anthropological Institute*, 1888, pp. 245–272. See also Marett, R. R., *Psychology and Folklore*, Methuen, London, 1920, pp. 74ff.
7. See *Das Weltbild der Prmitiven*, E. Reinhodt, Minchers, 1924.
8. The Marxists were also the strongest admirers of Morgan, long after Americans had abandoned his ideas as unsatisfactory. See Engels, Friederich, *The Origin of the Family, Private Property and the State*, C. H. Kerr and Company, Chicago, 1902; Kautsky, Karl, *The Class Struggle*, C. H. Kerr and Company, Chicago, 1910; Kovalevsky, Maxim, *Tableau des Origines et de l'evolution de la famille et de la proprieté*, Samson & Wallin, Stockholm, 1890.
9. In an attempt to locate variables that might be correlated with societal complexity through the use of scalogram analysis, Robert F. Winch and Lynton C. Freeman found that neither religious nor family variables would "fit" into such a scale. See "Societal Complexity: An Empirical Test of a Typology of Societies," *American Journal of Sociology*, vol. 62, March, 1957, pp. 461–466.

10. See the careful discussion of the possible types of transitions in Murdock, G. P., *Social Structure,* Macmillan, New York, 1949, pp. 190ff.

11. Driver, H. E., and W. Massey, "Comparative Studies of North American Indians," *Transactions of the American Philosophical Society,* vol. 47, 1957, pp. 167–456. See also the evolutionary sequences worked out by Murdock, *op. cit.,* chap. 8; as well as Blalock, H. M., "Correlational Analysis and Causal Inferences," *American Anthropologist,* vol. 62, 1960, pp. 624–632; and Marsh, Robert M., *Comparative Sociology,* Harcourt, Brace & World, New York, 1967, chaps. 2, 3.

12. See the clear discussion of these issues in Marsh, Robert, *Comparative Sociology, op. cit.,* pp. 57ff., as well as his chap. 1 on evolutionary theory generally.

13. See the discussion of this method in Knut Bergslund and Hans Vogt, "On the Validity of Glottochronology," *Current Anthropology,* vol. 3, 1962, pp. 115–153; and Hymes, D. H., "Lexicostatistics so Far," *Current Anthropology,* vol. 1, 1960, pp. 3–44.

14. Levy, Marion J., "Contrasting Factors in the Modernization of China and Japan," in Kuznets, Simon S., Wilbert E. Moore, and Joseph K. Spengler, editors, *Economic Growth: Brazil, India, Japan,* Duke University Press, Durham, N.C., 1955, pp. 496–536.

15. Davis, Kingsley, *Human Society,* Macmillan, New York, 1949, pp. 598–600.

16. For further complexities, see the discussion in Marsh, Robert M., *Comparative Sociology, op. cit.,* pp. 198ff.

17. *Ibid.,* p. 428; see also Davis, Kingsley, "The Sociology of Parent-Youth Conflict," *American Sociological Review,* vol. 5, August, 1940, pp. 523–535.

18. See the discussion of this point in Goode, William J., *World Revolution and Family Patterns,* The Free Press, New York, 1963, pp. 42–43; and Connell, K. H., *The Population of Ireland, 1750–1845,* Clarendon Press, Oxford, 1950, pp. 49–60.

19. See Goode, William J., "Illegitimacy in the Caribbean Social Structure," *American Sociological Review,* vol. 25, February, 1960, pp. 21–30.

20. See especially pp. 429ff. in *Capital,* Modern Library Edition, New York, 1936.

21. For a review of this "discovery," see Sussman, Marvin B., and Lee Burchinal, "Kin Family Network: Unheralded Structure in Current Conceptualization of Family Functioning," *Marriage and Family Living,* vol. 24, 1962, pp. 231–240.

22. See Furstenberg, Frank F., Jr., "Industrialization and the American Family: A Look Backward," *American Sociological Review,* vol. 31, June, 1966, pp. 326–337.

23. Thernstrom, Stephan, *Poverty and Progress: Social Mobility in a Nineteenth-Century City,* Harvard University Press, Cambridge, 1964.

24. On this measurement problem, see Goode, William J., "A Policy Paper for Illegitimacy," in Zald, Meyer N., editor, *Organizing for Community Welfare,* Quadrangle, Chicago, 1967, pp. 274ff.

25. That their opinions were not recorded, but are now, is, however, a rough measure of a "trend," i.e., their increasing power and literacy. There is now a market for their observations.

26. See Goode, William J., *World Revolution and Family Patterns, op. cit.,* for a detailed theoretical analysis of this set of great trends.

27. Stone, Lawrence, *The Crisis of the Aristocracy: 1558–1641,* Clarendon Press, Oxford, 1965, pp. 2, 274ff.

28. For a recent attack on this problem, see Martin, P. S., and H. E. Wright, editors, *Pleistocene Extinctions: The Search for a Cause,* Yale University Press, New Haven, 1968.

29. See Goode, William J., "Problems in Postdivorce Adjustment," *American*

Sociological Review, vol. 14, June, 1949, pp. 294–401. See also chaps. 4 and 5 in *After Divorce,* The Free Press, Glencoe, 1956. The monograph has been reissued as *Women in Divorce,* The Free Press, New York, 1964.

This elaboration may be found in chaps. 4 and 5 in *After Divorce,* The Free Press, Glencoe, 1956. The monograph has been reissued as *Women in Divorce,* The Free Press, New York, 1964.

30. That others shared my belief can be documented from the literature but I also tested this by reporting the finding orally to colleagues, who invariably responded with a "double take," i.e., they nodded in assent at hearing an affirmation of accepted knowledge, but then expressed surprise when they realized the relationship was *negative.*
31. Goode, William J., *After Divorce, op. cit.,* pp. 64–66.
32. For this last point, see Goode, William, *Women in Divorce, op. cit.,* p. 51.
33. "Marital Satisfaction and Instability: A Cross-Cultural Class Analysis of Divorce Rates," *International Social Science Journal,* vol. 14, no. 3, 1962, pp. 507–526.
34. Ogburn, William F., *Technology and the Changing Family,* Houghton Mifflin, Boston, 1955, pp. 99–100.
35. See Levy, Marion J., "Aspects of the Analysis of Family Structure," as well as "The Range of Variation in Actual Family Size: A Critique of Marion J. Levy, Jr.'s Argument," by Lloyd A. Fallers, in *Aspects of the Analysis of Family Structure,* Ansley J. Coale, *et al.,* editors, Princeton University Press, Princeton, N.J., 1965.
36. Goode, William, *World Revolution and Family Patterns, op. cit.,* pp. 5ff., 129ff., 188ff., 239ff., 296ff., 356ff.
37. Though both can be given sociological and specifically family meanings, Levy uses them with no such redefinition, and within his approach a sociological redefinition is not necessary.
38. See, for example, Lazarsfeld, Paul F., and Herbert Menzel, "On the Relations between Individual and Collective Properties," in Etzioni, Amitai, editor, *Complex Organizations,* Holt, Rinehart, and Winston, New York, 1961, pp. 422–440; and Barton, Allen H., "Methods of Research on Organizations," Bureau of Applied Social Research, New York, 1966, prepared for the *International Encyclopedia of the Social Sciences.* Mimeographed.
39. Claude Lévi-Strauss has analyzed certain of these patterns extensively, in his *Les Structures Élémentaires de la Parenté,* Presses Universitaires de France, Paris, 1949; see also the critique of this work by George C. Homans and David M. Schneider, *Marriage, Authority, and Final Causes: A Study of Unilateral Cross-Cousin Marriage,* The Free Press, Glencoe, Ill., 1955; and Rodney Needham's counterattack, *Structure and Sentiment,* University of Chicago Press, Chicago, 1962.
40. As a refreshing contrast to the general lack of such observations, however, see Aronson, Sidney H., *Status and Kinship in the Higher Civil Service,* Harvard University Press, Cambridge, 1964, in which the author compares the importance of kin network relations in obtaining government jobs in the Adams, Monroe, and Jackson administrations.
41. Rossi, Alice S., "Naming Children in Middle Class Families," *American Sociological Review,* vol. 30, August, 1965, pp. 499–513.
42. Glick, Paul C., *American Families,* a volume in the Census Monograph Series, Wiley, New York, 1957.
43. As an example, see Carcopino, Jerome, *Daily Life in Ancient Rome,* E. O. Lorimer, translator, Yale University Press, New Haven, 1940, chap. 4; or even the magisterial work of Mark Bloch, *Feudal Society,* L. A. Manyon, translator, 2 vols., University of Chicago Press, Chicago, 1961.
44. For example, M. I. Finley, in his *The World of Odysseus,* basically tries to

utilize the Homeric epic in a content analysis, in order to reconstruct family life and social patterns generally in that period. The archeological materials give us something of the background, and he tries to read between and through Homer's descriptions of family relations. Nevertheless, this is not a *time analysis*. For an example of how historians neglect the family, see Cantor, Norman F., *Medieval History,* Macmillan, New York, 1963, in which there is no discussion of the place of the family in that society.

45. Stone, Lawrence, *The Crisis of Aristocracy: 1588–1641, op. cit.*
46. Fleury, M., and L. Henry, *Des Registres Paroissiaux a L'Histoire De La Population: Manuel de depouillement et d'exploitation de l'Etat Civil Ancien,* Presses Universitaires de France, Paris, 1956. See also the related uses of detailed demographic work in measuring family trends in Glass, D. V., and C. D. Eversley, editors, *Population in History,* Aldine Publishing Co., Chicago, 1965; and Wrigley, E. A., editor, *An Introduction to English Historical Demography,* Basic Books, New York, 1966.
47. Aronson, Sidney, *Status and Kinship in the Higher Civil Service, op. cit.*
48. Goode, William J., *World Revolution and Family Patterns, op. cit.,* pp. 70–76.
49. See the interesting suggestion of this kind made by Paul S. Lazarsfeld, "The Obligation of the 1950 Pollster to the 1984 Historian," *Public Opinion Quarterly,* vol. 14, 1950, pp. 618–638.
50. See, for example, the essays in Bauer, Raymond A., editor, *Social Indicators,* Massachusetts Institute of Technology, Cambridge, 1966; as well as the series of volumes now appearing on the trends of events in the United States that are predicted in the next forty years, prepared by the American Academy of Arts and Sciences, *Working Papers of the Commission on the Year 2000,* Hudson Institute, Croton-on-Hudson, N.Y., 1967.
51. For an exposition of these inadequate beginnings, see Goldfrank, Walter L., "The Sociology of Frederic LePlay," Columbia University, unpublished ms., 1965.
52. Nye, F. Ivan, and Lois W. Hoffman, *The Employed Mother in America,* Rand McNally, Chicago, 1963.
53. For recent time budget studies, see Guilbert, Madelaine, Nicole Lowit, and Joseph Crevsen, "Problèmes de méthode pour une enqûete de budgets-temps. Les cumuls d'occupations," *Revue Française de Sociologie,* vol. VI, 1965, pp. 325–335; "Enquête comparative de budgets-temps," *ibid.,* vol. VI, 1965, pp. 487–512; "Les budget-temps et l'étude des horaìres de la vie quotidienne," *ibid.,* vol. VII, 1967, pp. 169–183.
54. On these points, see Goode, William, *World Revolution and Family Patterns, op. cit.,* pp. 70–76; Sussman, Marvin B., and Lee Burchinal, "Kin Family Network," *op. cit.;* Stehouwer, Jan, "Relations between Generations and the Three Generational Household in Denmark," in Shanas, Ethel, and Gordon F. Streib, editors, *Social Structure and the Family: Generational Relationships,* Prentice-Hall, Englewood Cliffs, N.J., 1965, p. 147.
55. Litwak, Eugene, "Technological Innovation and Ideal Forms of Family Structure in an Industrial Society," paper read at the Ninth International Seminar on Family Research, Tokyo, 1965.
56. See McClelland, David C., *et al., Talent and Society,* Van Nostrand, Princeton, N.J., 1958.
57. See Hyman, Herbert, *Political Socialization,* The Free Press, Glencoe, Ill., 1959.
58. See the suggestive formulations of Blood, Robert O., and Donald M. Wolfe, *Husbands and Wives,* Free Press, New York, 1960, chap. 2.

8. TRENDS AND ANTI-TRENDS IN RELIGIOUS CHANGE

N. J. Demerath III

ONE OF THE fundamental ingredients of any meaningful religion may be a confidence that it has undergone and is still undergoing change. Few would doubt that American religion has changed since the nineteenth century, but few would agree on the patterns, and certainly sociologists have provided little basis for unanimity. Ask any question and our response is likely to be a contemplative silence, a scholarly scowl, and finally a long list of methodological conundrums leading to that ultimate conclusion: "It all depends."

But, of course, changes in American religion have hardly been ignored. Historians, both theological and academic, have frequently chronicled the passing religious times, and some of this chapter will rely on such accounts. And yet there are also considerable differences between the sociological and historical approaches to change. For one thing, the historian is often more specific in his interest and is able to chart the development of ideas and institutions without feeling obliged to place them in an overarching context that will permit causal interpretation. Traditionally, the historian has been more concerned with change for its own sake and less concerned with theory concerning change; the sociologist is inclined to reverse the priorities and sometimes analyzes change solely for its theoretical import. Then too, there are fundamental differences in data. Classical historiography has been more concerned with the march of prominent events and prominent ideas; the sociologist has been more concerned with the less prominent characteristics of smaller events and more commonplace ideas, those that are rarely recorded in books and records and are less accessible through standard historiographic techniques. In the simplest terms, the historian is trained to deal with "soft" data, while the sociologist hankers after "hard" statistics. This may seem to glorify the sociologist at the expense of the historian, but as this chapter will indicate, hard data on social change—particularly religious change—are generally either

349

in scarce supply, unreliable, or unilluminating. In short, the monographic historian asks limited questions of a limited phenomenon for which sound answers are more readily available. The sociologist asks grandiose questions of universal phenomena and sets severely restrictive criteria for his answers.

The traditional differences between history and sociology may no longer pertain, since the new generation of historians tends to be more social scientific and the new wave of sociologists more historical. But before this happy convergence is consummated, a defense of the traditional sociological orientation may be in order. Surely there remains room for analyses of change that are organized theoretically rather than chronologically. Surely it is also worthwhile to hold out for the hardest data possible in the hope of ultimately increasing the reliability of our judgments. Finally, as long as one holds fast to the rigorous criteria of both good theory and good methodology, there is ample justification for tackling big topics as well as small. The results may unify some currently disparate knowledge, expose the gamut of our past inadequacies as scholars, and provide a challenge for the future.

These are the goals of this chapter. On the one hand, it will raise a host of issues concerning major processes and trends alleged to be afoot in twentieth-century American religion. On the other hand, its guesses will be tempered by a search for numerical evidence wherever it is available. Unhappily, the evidence will be no match for the speculation. But if the chapter were confined to reliable evidence alone, it might even now be ending instead of just beginning.

The chapter includes four major sections. First, we shall look at the intriguing issues and doubtful data surrounding the putative religious revival in America. What has happened to church membership, Sunday School registration, church finances, religious publications, and church attendance over time? A quick reading of the available statistics seems to indicate a substantial growth, if not revival, of "religiosity," but further reflection reveals two qualifications. First, the statistics themselves are thoroughly suspicious. Second, even if one could demonstrate that, say, church membership had increased, the questions remain: what sort of membership and membership in what sort of religious organizations? The balance of the section deals with these more elusive but perhaps more important issues.

The second section has to do with religious belief. Has there been a death of God in the minds of the laity? What evidence is there of general secularization in the relation between the church and the individual? Once again there is a paucity of solid data. There are few reliable measures of current beliefs, let alone the beliefs of the past. While we know that the Altizers of today were preceded by the Nietzsches of yesteryear, we have little knowledge of changes in belief in the general population.

But, of course, religion is more than belief, and the chapter's third section will deal with changes in its organizational aspect. Has the church become more differentiated and more bureaucratized, and with what causes and consequences? Here good data should be more abundant than they actually are. Surely something can be gleaned from denominational budgets and the changing staff sizes of denominational headquarters and local parishes. But these data are not standardized either across time or across denominations, and they are difficult to rely upon. While somewhat better evidence is available concerning changes in the clerical functionaries of religious organizations, this too is spotty and shall often be confined to case studies of several particular denominations that are not necessarily representative. Throughout this section, issues such as changing church goals and patterns of influence will be implicated. But often the discussion will use illustrative materials as flimsy support for flights of speculative fancy.

The fourth section deals with ecumenism, which many herald as a sign of the contemporary times. Certainly ecumenism is a twentieth-century phenomenon. But formal mergers are not easily institutionalized; they are sometimes more symbolic nationally than meaningful locally; and they may create as many problems as they solve. Moreover, ecumenical tendencies must be evaluated with respect to more than actual unions and reunions. For example, what is the current state of relations between white and Negro Protestants; what is happening to the Protestant-Catholic differences that have occupied us since Max Weber; and what are the trends in anti-Semitism and the relations between Christians and Jews as revealed in, say, interfaith marriage?

Several cautions are advised throughout, in addition to the methodological snares already noted. First, although this chapter may seem long, it is clearly too short to do justice to the topic. Many footnotes are substantive and strategic; indeed, some matters only alluded to in footnotes deserve whole sections of their own. A second caution concerns a variety in American religion that is both intoxicating and bewildering. Even the most substantiated conclusion concerning one part of it cannot be safely generalized to other parts. After all, how does one leap from Reform Judaism to the Negro churches, or from the Two-Seed-in-the-Spirit Predestinarian Baptists to The American Humanist Association? The chapter will go to some pains to take account of such differences. Still, it will generally cleave close to mainstream Protestantism simply because its data are somewhat less scarce.

A final admonition is both more abstract and more important. The title of this chapter is in many ways misleading in emphasizing "religion." For the most part, the emphasis will lie instead with churches and religious organizations, and any sociologist hesitates to equate religion at large with its institutional manifestations. Indeed, it is quite possible to define religion so that it encompasses all of man's "ultimate concerns" and "superordinate values." From this view, a chapter on religious trends would necessarily deal with nothing less than the entire American value system. This is plainly not my intention, and it is worth noting a corollary. Statements about the waxing and waning of the church in American life by no means justify extrapolations to either the "American character" or the degree of "progress versus decay" in the society's general morality. As we shall see, it is quite possible to view the church as both a positive and a negative force in American society. Any ultimate evaluation depends upon perspectives beyond the province of this investigation.

DISCERNING AND DISPUTING TRENDS IN FORMAL RELIGIOUS PARTICIPATION

Writing in 1887, Daniel Dorchester arrived at the following conclusion after reviewing a mass of church statistics for the nineteenth century as a whole:

> All persons familiar with the history of Christianity will agree that the above exhibit of religious progress cannot be paralleled in the history of God's kingdom in any land or any age. It is all the more remarkable because only about ninety years ago it was a common boast of infidels that "Christianity would not survive two generations" in this country. Instead of that, Christianity, since then, has achieved her grandest triumph. How often has the progress of Christianity in the apostolic age been cited as a marvel of growth which the church of our times should emulate. Such persons forget that the growth of the churches of the United States in this century has far transcended that of the first centuries. (Between 1800 and 1886 the number of adherents of evangelical Christianity in our country has seen an increase of 41,287,226, or more than in the whole world at the close of the first nine centuries of the Christian era.) "Not unto us, O Lord, not unto us, but unto they name give glory, for thy mercy, and for thy truth's sake."[1]

Such celebrations of growth and progress are still common today. Nor are data lacking to feed the euphoria. Consider, for example, Table

TABLE 1. CHURCH MEMBERSHIP AS A PERCENTAGE OF
THE POPULATION, 1800–1965

Year	Percentage
1800	7
1850	16
1860	23
1870	18
1880	20
1890	22
1900	36
1910	43
1920	43
1930	47
1940	49
1950	57
1955	61
1960	63.6
1965	64.3

SOURCE: *Yearbook of American Churches,* 1967, Department of Publication Services, National Council of the Church of Christ in the U.S.A., New York, 1967, p. 218. However, the figure for 1800 is my own calculation, based upon data from Dorchester, Daniel, *Christianity in the United States from the First Settlement Down to the Present Time,* Phillips and Hunt, New York, 1888.

1, comparing the proportion of church members in the population between 1800 and 1965. The figure was roughly 7 per cent at the dawn of the nineteenth century, but it spurted to 23 per cent by 1860, to 43 per cent between 1890 and 1910, and enjoyed its last upsurge between 1940 and 1965 when it rose from 49 per cent to 64.3 per cent.[2] Although we shall consider several other accepted indicators of religious growth, this one is certainly the cornerstone of the argument. Hence, this is a good place to begin some methodological lint-picking that may ultimately unravel the cloth itself.

Even in Dorchester's day, such statistics had their detractors. Henry K. Carroll recorded a number of deficiencies in his volume, *The Religious Forces of the United States Enumerated, Classified, and Described on the Basis of the Government Census of 1890.*[3] In particular, Carroll recognized the problems inherent in relying on the churches to gather and report their own figures to the Census Bureau instead of simply including religion in the standard census schedule so that data might be collected directly from individuals. This policy of church reporting has been constant throughout the period with which we are concerned.[4] While a postcript to this section will present the case for a U.S. Census enumeration of individual religion, let us pause now to consider some of the consequences of *not* having such enumerations in the past.

Perhaps the most crucial source of error in church-reported figures arises because churches have varied definitions of "membership," varied not only among themselves but also over time. Thus, many Protestant denominations have included only adults over the age of thirteen in their membership counts—owing partly to the Protestants' sect-like emphasis on knowledgeable conversion as opposed to infant baptism. On the other hand, the Catholics and, in some cases the Lutherans and Episcopalians as well, have included baptized infants in their totals; and the Jews have frequently included all Jewish residents in the ecological area served by a temple or synagogue. Of course, such differences have been acknowledged by many church and census statisticians. Carroll, for example, attempted a noble but necessarily crude standardization for the 1890 figures. But Carroll was among the first to do so, and few subsequent church statisticians have followed his lead. Thus, the data prior to 1890 are especially suspect, and suspicion is also justified for the twentieth-century figures reported since.

Unsystematic variation in membership definitions *over time* is even more strategic. Looking again at Table 1, note the considerable growth that occurred between 1890 and 1910. S. M. Lipset's thorough and circumspect appraisal of the figures indicates that the growth is more illusory than real, since many churches changed their definition of membership to admit children to the tallies during these years.[5] Indeed, Lipset relies on a later work of Henry Carroll's to establish the point. Carroll has noted that many Protestant churches relaxed their membership criteria, perhaps to compete with the totals released by the Roman Catholic, Greek Orthodox, and Jewish organizations, all of which benefited statistically not only from the enormous influx of immigrants in the period but also from more embracing membership standards so that maximum numbers were counted. Even so, according to Lipset, the Protestants were probably grossly underestimated by 1910. This may still be the case, although it is equally serious from the standpoint of larger trends to note that many Protestant groups have been continually "catching up" throughout the interim by expanding their membership criteria. For example, Truman Douglass points out that in 1916 only 1 per cent of Episcopalian church members were under thirteen, but this had increased to 26 per cent by 1926.[6] Such alterations may account for a good bit of what has passed for "growth" in this century.

This possibility is given succor by Michael Argyle's recomputations of church membership proportions only for those *over thirteen* years old.[7] Table 2 provides Argyle's figures, ranging from 1906 to 1950.

TABLE 2. PERCENTAGE OF THE U.S. POPULATION AGED THIRTEEN AND OVER WHO ARE CHURCH MEMBERS, 1906–1950

Year	Percentage
1906	55
1916	55
1926	52.7
1930	53.4
1935	52.1
1940	50.7
1950	63.7

SOURCE: Argyle, Michael, *Religious Behavior,* The Free Press, Glencoe, 1959, p. 28.

Contrary to Table 1, these data indicate a *drop* in church membership between 1906 and 1940, though an increase after 1940. Argyle argues that the heralded religious revival is almost exclusively a post-1940 phenomenon. But even this may be risky, since still other errors remain to be taken into account.

One of these errors involves the uneven and haphazard addition of *new* churches to the total membership rolls. Recall that the figures depend upon self-reporting by the churches themselves. Not all churches or denominations make reports, and some have begun reporting only recently. This is a major reason why Winthrop Hudson answered negatively to the question posed in his 1955 article, "Are the Churches Really Booming?"[8] Hudson provides an example for the years 1952–1954, one that I have taken from Lipset's own citation:

> . . . when the Christ Unity Church was listed for the first time in the 1952 *Yearbook* [the *Yearbook of American Churches* is published by the Research Division of the National Council of Churches and is the most frequently cited source of national church statistics] with 682,172 members, it alone accounted for more than one-third of the 1,842,515 gain reported that year. The following year, the American Carpatho-Russian Orthodox Greek Catholic Church and the Ukrainian Orthodox Church, each with 75,000 members, were listed for the first time. The year after that, five bodies listed for the first time contributed 195,804 to the total increase in church membership.[9]

Here is one more error that can be easily imagined to have operated throughout the 165 years covered in Table 1. Indeed, it is only reasonable to suppose that the error has been a constant feature of the time lapse, as first the U.S. Census Bureau and then the federal and National Council of Churches grew more respected as successive keepers of the national religious records. One can even argue that the figures reflect less concerning numerical growth than they do concerning the rising spirit of ecumenism and the increasing importance of numbers themselves in the bureaucratizing world of American religious organization. Of course, the tabulators themselves are constrained. On the one hand, they have every reason to encourage delinquent churches to report for the first time to make their future tallies more accurate. On the other hand, the more successful they are in prompting first-time cooperation, the less reliable will be their trend reports, barring the sort of systematic corrections that are so difficult and so conspicuously absent.

Still another uncontrolled factor that tends artificially to inflate growth estimates is *mobility*. While it is by no means clear that vertical mobility in the class system has markedly increased over time, it is accepted that geographical mobility has accelerated throughout the country. As people move from town to town, they move from church to church. Because the churches are somewhat less vigilant in purging their rolls than they are in augmenting them, there are increasing instances in which the same person may be counted twice or more within the same year by different parishes and even different denominations. Unhappily, there are no available data with which to gauge the extent of the distortion, much less correct it.[10]

Finally, a last error may seem to be random, but has probably also led to inflated illusions of growth. There has always been a tendency for many churches to round their counts, most at the nearest hundred, some at the nearest thousand, and a few at the nearest hundred thousand. Of 251 religious bodies for which data are available in the 1967 *Yearbook,* the inclusive membership figures for 42 churches are rounded to the nearest thousand; of these, four are rounded to the nearest hundred thousand, and one is rounded to the nearest half-million. Such symmetry strains credibility. Thus, Winthrop Hudson has expressed doubt that the membership of the Church of Christ actually increased from 1,500,000 to 1,600,000 as reported between 1955 and 1956. As Hudson and others have noted, it is a fair assumption that rounding generally errs on the side of overestimating growth, since numbers have become an area of religious competition, and budgets, staffs, and general prestige depend upon them. Indeed, it should come as no surprise that the largest single Protestant group—

the Southern Baptist—has aroused considerable suspicion among statisticians guarding the floodgates against figures that may be more
boastful than accurate. For example, T. Lynn Smith dryly points out
the discrepancy between the figures listed in 1937 by the Handbook of
the Southern Baptist Convention and the figures listed for the Southern
Baptists in the more accurate 1936 Census of Religious Bodies to explain why the membership appeared to have dropped between 1926
and 1936.

> . . . the 1937 Handbook of the Southern Baptist Convention reports a
> total of . . . 4,482,315 members. If these figures are compared with the
> . . . 2,700,155 given by the 1936 Census of Religious Bodies, the ex-
> planation of why the membership of the denomination appeared to have
> fallen [in 1936] from 3,524,378 in 1926 [in the Southern Baptist Hand-
> book] would seem to be fairly apparent.[11]

The issue is not honesty but misplaced zeal. No one disputes the numerical strength of the largest groups, but questions remain as to the
exactitude of the figures listed.

Trends in Denominational Membership

This, however, takes us into a different and perhaps more important
range of issues concerning church membership. In addition to looking
at trends in *aggregate* membership rates, it is also possible to compare
the membership trends of various religious bodies and denominations
since the turn of the century. It is true that these comparisons are vulnerable to the aforementioned errors of the membership data they
rely upon. Still, they may be crudely suggestive. For a start, Table 3
presents the relative proportions of Protestant and Catholic church
members in the population since 1926, a period that postdates the

TABLE 3.   PROTESTANT AND CATHOLIC CHURCH
MEMBERS AS PERCENTAGES OF THE POPULATION,
1926–1965

Year	Protestants	Catholics
	(percentages)	
1926	27.0	16.0
1940	28.7	16.1
1950	33.8	18.9
1955	35.5	20.3
1960	35.4	23.3
1965	35.6	23.8

SOURCE: *Yearbook of American Churches,* 1967, p. 219.

greatest surge of Catholic immigration. Both Catholics and Protestants gained in the period, especially in the years between 1940 and 1955, and, if anything, the Protestants had a slight edge in growth. But there is another way to look at the data. The one instance in which the U.S. Census Bureau did conduct an individual enumeration of religion on a special subsample in 1957 employed only one question asking those over age fourteen their religious "preference." The results were Protestant (66.2 per cent), Catholic (25.7 per cent), Jewish (3.2 per cent), "other" (1.3 per cent), and no religion (2.7 per cent).[12] Now there is certainly a difference between formal church membership as reported in Table 3 and nominal religious identification as indicated in the 1957 Census figures. Indeed, while the Protestants have had a slightly higher growth of membership per se, the Catholics seem to be more efficient in converting nominal identification into membership. Only a little more than one-half the nominal Protestants are church members (and this may be inflated because of the inflations in the membership data themselves); it is more like 90 per cent of the Catholics, although we have already seen that Catholics count the baptized infant as well as the adult and hence have more embracing membership criteria in general.

But comparisons between Catholics and Protestants as such are not very illuminating because of wide internal variance. More detailed analysis of differential changes in church membership comes from Richard C. Wolf, who compared rates for various denominations between 1905 and 1955.[13] Table 4 summarizes his findings, in which the

TABLE 4.   COMPARATIVE GROWTH AND GROWTH RATES FOR ELEVEN MAJOR RELIGIOUS GROUPS, 1905–1955

Denomination	1905	1955	Percentage growth
Eastern Orthodox	129,606	2,396,906	1754.7
Churches of Christ	159,649	1,700,000	964.8
Latter-Day Saints	256,647	1,372,640	430.9
Lutheran	2,112,494	7,286,589	244.4
Baptist	5,662,234	19,165,780	238.4
Protestant Episcopal	886,942	2,759,944	210.9
Roman Catholic	12,079,142	33,574,017	177.9
Presbyterian	1,830,555	3,858,709	110.7
Methodist	5,749,838	11,775,731	104.8
Disciples of Christ	982,701	1,897,736	93.1
Congregational	845,301	1,342,045	58.7

Source: Wolf, Richard C., "1900–1950 Survey: Religious Trends in the United States," *Christianity Today*, April 27, 1959, p. 4.

Eastern Orthodox Church had the highest percentage of growth at 1754.7 per cent, while the Congregationalists had the lowest rate at 58.7 per cent. Wolf speculates on the variables which best distinguish between denominations (or more accurately "denominational families") that have high versus low rates of growth. He concludes that a simple distinction between "conservative" and "liberal" with respect to doctrine, worship style, and church organization accounts for most of the variance. Thus, it is the conservative groups who grew the most in the first half of the twentieth century, while the liberal groups grew the least. Wolf buttresses his conclusion with two further sets of comparisons. First, he compares conservative and liberal subdenominations within several of the denominational families and finds, for example, that liberal Presbyterians, Baptists, and Lutherans have lower rates of growth than their more conservative kin. Second, he looks at a number of smaller groups between 1905 and 1955 and finds that the Mennonites (207.7 per cent), the Brethren (154.6 per cent), and the Adventists (237.3 per cent) all have higher growth percentages than the Unitarians (43.9 per cent), the Universalists (9.4 per cent), and the Quakers (7.1 per cent)—again corroborating his thesis. He acknowledges one major exception, however, in the Roman Catholics, who combine conservatism with a relatively low growth rate. Wolf accounts for this by asserting that Catholicism's authoritarian style is at odds with American democratic ideals.

Certainly Wolf's interpretation is consistent with Winthrop Hudson's finding that the twelve largest denominational affiliates of the liberal National Council of Churches actually declined relative to the population increase between 1940 and 1954,[14] a finding that questions even the limited interpretation of a general religious revival in the post-1940 period. While a revival may have occurred, it appears to be restricted to the conservative rather than the liberal and to the smaller rather than the larger groups among the Protestants.

And yet Wolf's central thesis concerning the differences between conservative and liberal denominations has had its detractors as well. Glen Trimble has argued that the interpretation of the 1905 to 1955 period is oversimplified,[15] since the distinction between conservative and liberal is drawn along dimensions that few would accept without very serious reservations, and since a welter of other factors must also be seen in relation to church growth, such as ethnicity, patterns of merger, changing regional distributions of denominational strength, and the general migration from rural to urban areas. Trimble also provides similar data for the years 1955 to 1965 in an effort to bring the trend analysis up to date. The results indicate that Wolf's findings for the century's first fifty years do not apply accurately to the last decade. Table 5 presents logarithmic computations of *annual growth rates* in

TABLE 5. COMPARISON OF ANNUAL GROWTH RATES FOR ELEVEN DENOMINATIONS WITHIN THE PERIODS 1905–1955 AND 1955–1965

| Denomination | Annual growth rates for | |
	1905–1955	1955–1965
	(percentages)	
Eastern Orthodox	6.0	2.9
Churches of Christ	4.8	3.9
Latter-Day Saints	3.4	3.6
Lutheran	2.5	2.3
Baptist	2.5	2.4
Protestant Episcopal	2.3	2.2
Roman Catholic	2.1	3.4
Presbyterian	1.5	1.4
Methodist	1.4	1.2
Disciples of Christ	1.3	0.1
Congregational	0.9	4.4

SOURCE: Recomputed from data in Trimble, Glenn, unpublished paper, Research Division, National Council of Churches, February, 1967.

the two periods, computations which show a leveling off of the earlier differences. Indeed, seven of the eleven denominations show at least a slight decline in annual growth between the two periods. The largest increase occurs among the Congregationalists, and may be largely accountable through their merger with the Evangelical and Reformed Church in 1957. Although the Evangelical and Reformed total membership was only 4.4 per cent of the Congregationalists at the time of the merger, some Evangelical and Reformed members may have been encouraged by the merger to identify themselves as full-fledged Congregationalists instead of simply members of the joint United Church of Christ.

Before leaving the murky area of membership statistics, it is important to emphasize Trimble's point that factors other than "religious enthusiasm" may account for any actual increase in church membership over time. Later we shall see that mergers have been increasingly characteristic of the twentieth century. Certainly they are factors in the growth of particular denominations during particular periods, as evidenced by the Congregational example. But they may also produce more general inflations. Sometimes they serve to bring formerly non-reporting groups into the countable fold, and they may also result in more vigilant counting. Beyond this, however, one wonders to what extent the natural demographic changes in American life might have produced membership growth, even with "religiosity" held constant. We have already mentioned the possible bias inherent in the increase of geographical mobility with its consequences for multiple-counting. Quite apart from bias, the rural-urban migration may have had consequences for either increasing or decreasing the rate of membership growth, although the direction is difficult to determine. A more readily interpretable phenomenon is the suburban shift within the urban areas themselves.

For example, E. Digby Baltzell's discourse on *Philadelphia Gentlemen*[16] indicates that between 1860 and 1900 a number of fashionable Quakers left the fold to become even more fashionable Episcopalians. But he also demonstrates that, at least among Episcopalians, membership in the old, urban churches declined between 1900 and 1940, while membership in the new, suburban churches increased enormously during the same period. That the increase in the suburban churches was more than five times as great as the decline in the urban churches suggests that others were picked up in the outreach. While many of these were from other denominations, some of them may have been those who preceded the church to the suburbs and were only led to take out membership once they had a neighborhood parish. In any event, it is clear that the move from the inner-city to the suburbs is a general phenomenon of the times. J. Milton Yinger summarizes some statistics of Truman Douglass as follows:

> In Cleveland between 1920 and 1950, five of the largest Protestant denominations declined by 13%. Fifty-three churches left the heart of Detroit in a fifteen-year period. Between 1930 and 1955, while the population of the country was increasing by 19%, and its own membership by 41%, the number of churches related to one of the largest Protestant denominations declined, in 16 major cities, by 20%.[17]

Elsewhere, Douglass accounts for this partly in terms of a Protestant ministry that is largely small-town in its own roots, so that even by 1955 only 36 per cent came from cities of more than 25,000.[18] Although this is more relevant to a later section on qualitative changes in the church and the clergy, Douglass is plainly concerned about the implicit tendency of the church to skirt problems where they are greatest. He is among the clerical avant-garde that seeks to promote a move back to the inner-city with a self-consciously and sociologically re-vitalized ministry.

So far we have been considering data on church membership almost exclusively. The data have certainly been pivotal in assessments of American religious change, partly because of their abundance, but also because of the tendency to overlook their many inadequacies. Surely one would be hard pressed to offer any precise interpretation of the reality behind the statistical facade. While most churches do indeed have more members now than ever before, the most crucial, yet most elusive, issue concerns church membership in proportion to the popula-tion, since the country as a whole has more "members" than ever be-fore. It is clear that the seeming growth in proportional church mem-bership may be more spurious than real; this is even possible for the more circumspect thesis of a revival only after 1940. Lipset's conclu-sion that there is no substantial evidence of *any* real change since the middle of the nineteenth century may be apt. But it is also possible that proportional membership has actually *declined* over the past century or so. This is an interpretation which I have never seen advanced, but one which I would be willing to hazard as no more difficult to defend than any of the others.

Still, it is fortunate that church membership hardly exhausts the available measures of religiosity, since evidence suggests that it taps only one dimension of adherence, inadequately at that, and wholly neglects other issues.[19] Indeed, it is plausible to argue that propor-tional church membership may have declined over the years, while other, and possibly more important, aspects of American religion have increased. Let us now turn to some alternative indicators of change in individual religious behavior.

Other Indicators of Change

Many of the alternatives are quite similar to membership itself in that they are church-reported statistics and subject to some of the same errors. For example, Table 6 presents the proportion of the total popu-lation registered in Sunday schools between 1906 and 1960. Like Argyle's figures for adult church members, Sunday school enrollment surges only after 1940, though it seems to level off after 1955. But much of the increase here is related to the proportional increase of youth generally in the population. Moreover, insofar as any rise in Sunday school registration is genuine, it may not be due to any in-crease in religious proclivity. The further one moves from the tradi-tional aspects of religion, the more questionable the interpretations be-

TABLE 6. SUNDAY SCHOOL ENROLLMENT AS PERCENTAGE
OF THE POPULATION, 1906–1960

Year	Percentage
1906	17.2
1916	19.6
1926	17.9
1936	14.4
1945	17.6
1950	18.0
1956	22.9
1960	22.0

SOURCE: *Yearbook of American Churches,* 1962, p. 255.

come. Thus, it may well be that Sunday schools began to serve subtly and not so subtly different functions after 1940. To what extent does the trend represent religious expression for the children or the parents; to what extent does it reflect greater babysitting service to facilitate adult church attendance or other parental activities that are frustrated by the presence of children?

But it is not only Sunday school registration that has increased; the same is true of church-related or parochial day schools.[20] In 1937, the Protestants had 2,000 church-related day schools with 110,000 students; by 1959, the count was substantially higher and seemingly more precise with 4,794 schools and 358,739 students. Still, it is instructive to note that in 1959 the Catholics had some 11,710 schools with 4,090,200 students. Clearly religious education is on the upswing in absolute terms. The wave of recent referenda and court decisions allowing state funds for parochial school transportation and the like should cause the figures to mount at an accelerating rate in future years. Again, however, one must be wary of imputing religious causes to formally religious phenomena and assuming that figures on church-related schools reflect renewed interest in the church itself. It may be related to increasing affluence, increasingly overcrowded urban public schools, and other such factors. After all, enrollment in nonpublic schools has increased generally from 9.4 per cent to 15 per cent of the total school enrollment between 1940 and 1962, and at least a part of this comes from increasing enrollment in nonreligious private schools.

Another general aspect of religious growth for which there are available data concerns church finances. In fact, this is one of the few areas for which government figures are available, especially figures on church construction and per capita personal consumption expenditures. One of the most celebrated trends in defense of a religious revival is the

364   INDICATORS OF SOCIAL CHANGE

TABLE 7.   ESTIMATES OF THE ANNUAL VALUE OF NEW
CONSTRUCTION OF RELIGIOUS BUILDINGS, 1925–1965

Year	Value
1925	$ 165,000,000
1930	135,000,000
1935	28,000,000
1940	59,000,000
1945	26,000,000
1950	409,000,000
1955	736,000,000
1960	1,016,000,000
1965	985,000,000

SOURCE: "Construction Volume and Costs," U.S. Department of Commerce,
as reprinted in *Yearbook of American Churches,* 1967, p. 225.

changing yearly value of new church construction.[21] Table 7 presents
these data, but note its obvious disadvantages. It is uncorrected for
either the changing value of the dollar or the general tightness of money
in a fluctuating economy, though the damper effect of the depression is
obvious, as is the effect of post-World War II prosperity. While the
statistics seem to support the thesis of a postwar religious revival, note
that we find something here that was also evident earlier: the middle-
1960's seem to be a tapering-off period. Of course, crude data can
make a mockery of such close interpretations of short-term trends.
Nevertheless, the data so far and the support still to come make the
thesis plausible.

Consider, for example, the findings in Table 8 on U.S. personal consumption expenditures between 1929 and 1965. These data are probably more reliable since they reflect a proportion of the money available and require no correction for the value of the dollar. At the same
time, note that the census category on which they are based is labeled
"religious and welfare expenditures," and the relation between religion and welfare has been frequently uncertain and sometimes stormy.
Despite such peculiarities, the figures parallel the pattern in Table 7
for new church construction. Once again there is a depression sag and
a post-World War II boom; in addition, there is also a decline for the
middle 1960's. And yet the findings on personal consumption expenditures do depart from the church construction data in that they show
no real evidence of increase between the 1920's and the current day.
Lipset makes a good deal of the finding that per capita religious contributions were actually higher during the depression (1933) than they
have been at any time since.[22] Of course, one must recall the problems

TABLE 8.   ANNUAL CONTRIBUTIONS TO "RELIGION AND
WELFARE" AS PERCENTAGE OF PER CAPITA INCOME
EXPENDITURES, 1929–1965

Year	Percentage
1929	1.3
1933	1.5
1935	1.1
1937	1.0
1938	1.1
1943	.7
1945	.8
1949	1.0
1952	1.1
1955	1.3
1960	1.5
1965	1.3

SOURCE: *Statistical Abstract of the United States, 1966,* U.S. Department of Commerce, Bureau of the Census, Washington, 1966, and "Survey of Current Business," Department of Commerce, Office of Business Economics.

with data collected on religion and welfare together, and note that the trend may be different if one counts per capita donations for church members alone. Still, one church economist who has looked at recent church member donations relative to the national GNP finds the trend sobering. Oliver Fix examined changes in donations between 1956 and 1966 for 23 denominations which have suitable data available. He concludes: "Significantly, only one denomination, The Christian Church, has remained consistently ahead of national growth and inflation. . . . Many denominations have maintained an average giving which keeps pace with GNP but a number have recently fallen far behind. . . . Such a trend can only indicate impending financial disaster."[23] Later we shall see that Fix's pessimism may be unwarranted in the light of a current level of religious business assets in the U.S. that is almost double the combined assets of the nation's five largest corporations. Once again there are widely divergent views, even on church finances.

But let us leave the world of big business and turn to the more academic climes of publishing. Here too we have access to data collected by nonreligious agencies, since data on the religious press and its trends can be obtained directly from general publishing figures. In 1948, Alfred McClung Lee analyzed some of these figures and concluded:

. . . rather than reaching three-fourths of America's reading public as it did a century ago, the church press's impact—in terms of copies published—is now probably somewhere near one-tenth that of the secular daily press. This is in terms of mere number of copies and does not take into consideration differences in size of issues and in psychological impact. Church newspapers and magazines alone, in similar terms, probably circulate not more than one-third of the church press's total, possibly one-thirtieth that of the secular daily press, in the course of a given month or year. This decreased proportion of printed impact is one reason church spokesmen try to penetrate more effectively the great mass audiences of the secular press and radio, motion pictures, and public schools. But they are hobbled in the press, the radio, and the motion pictures by many of the ideological and technical problems that curtail the effectiveness of the religious press, and American tradition and law fortunately supply something of a brake on church proselytizing in the public schools.[24]

Lee's analysis leaves a number of strings untied, as he himself would admit. One could hardly expect the religious press to compete with the rise of the secular daily press. Perhaps a fairer analysis would ask how books on religion compete over time with books on other topics. Samuel Klausner relies on data from *Publisher's Weekly* for just such an analysis and summarizes his findings this way:

> Between 1918 and 1957 the total number of books published in the United States increased by slightly more than half. Population rose by two-thirds during this time, so this would not indicate increased reading. Certain groups of the population may, however, read more today while others read less. . . . The number of books in medicine and hygiene rose by about 63 per cent and those in science by about 89 per cent during this same period. This corresponds with the general population rise. . . . The number of religious books rose by only about 22 per cent, while the books and articles in psychology nearly doubled through the last three decades.[25]

An earlier analysis by Hornell Hart examined the percentage of religious articles in a sample of popular journals and notes that it fell regularly from 2 per cent in the 1905–1909 period to 0.7 per cent by 1940. Hart previously sorted these articles according to whether they were favorable or unfavorable to religion and found a steady decline in the percentage proreligious, from 77 per cent in 1905 to 58 per cent in 1920 and to 40 per cent in 1931.[26] Unfortunately, Hart's data do not extend into the period in which Argyle and others consider the religious revival to have occurred. While one work does cover the entire period from 1875 to 1955 in a content analysis of the changing *tone* of inspirational literature in America, I shall defer consideration to a later section on trends in belief patterns. Here we are still concerned with the presumably more straightforward issues concerning changes in formal participation alone.

I have saved one obvious datum for last—the changing rate of church attendance, evidence that bows only to the membership data in its prominence in defense of a religious revival. Unfortunately, national figures on attendance are only available as far back as 1939, when the Gallup Poll (The American Institute of Public Opinion) began including it as a regular item in their schedules. Still, since 1939, there have been frequent soundings, as indicated in Table 9. Thus, 41 per

TABLE 9. PERCENTAGE OF ADULTS REPORTING CHURCH ATTENDANCE DURING WEEK PRECEDING INTERVIEW, 1939–1965

Year	Percentage
1939	41
1940	37
1942	36
1947	45
1950	39
1954	46
1955	49
1956	46
1957	47
1958	49
1959	47
1960	47
1961	47
1962	46
1963	46
1964	45
1965	44

SOURCE: American Institute of Public Opinion as reprinted in *Yearbook of American Churches*, 1967, p. 220.

cent of a sample of American adults claimed to have attended church during the week preceding the interview in 1939. After a series of erratic fluctuations, the rate climbed as high as 49 per cent by 1958, after which it began to taper off to 44 per cent by 1965. Once again there is at least meager evidence of a religious surge after World War II and in the 1950's. Also once again, we find a more recent decline.

Certainly these data on church attendance are more reliable than many of the foregoing measures of religious change. Even so, there are doubts as well. Michael Argyle compared the results of similar polls in England (where the rate of church attendance is much lower, hovering at roughly 15 per cent since World War II) with actual countings at representative British church services.[27] He found that the polls tend to overestimate actual attendance by as much as 20 per cent. And if this is so in a country where church attendance is relatively rare, the error may be much greater in the United States where attendance is more common, hence, more normative. Here the tendency to add a bit to improve one's image should be greater.

It can be argued, of course, that this sort of bias should be constant over time so that poll figures on *relative* changes will be approximately reliable even though absolute estimates of church attendance at any single moment are too crude to be credible. Perhaps, but the argument has a rebuttal. There may be a self-fulfilling prophecy crescendoing as the phrase "religious revival" is trumpeted from steeple to steeple. The tendency to conform artificially to this newly religious image in a poll response may be a factor in documenting the image itself. But then, one must be cautious of poll data over time for other reasons. Where the differences at issue average roughly 5 per cent and are nowhere greater than 12 per cent, sampling variability from year to year may be a factor. Note, too, that poll series are rarely standardized with respect to the time of year at which the interviews are conducted. It is possible that some are "high" because they fall closer to the Christmas and Easter season, while others are "low" because they were taken during the "off-season" moments in the Christian calendar. Argyle himself dismisses the trends in American church attendance as statistically unreliable.

But even if the trends were statistically unassailable, there would remain questions of their import. I have elsewhere argued that church attendance, like church membership, measures only one facet of religiosity and one that is decidedly "middle-class" in style.[28] According to some recent but unpublished data, ministers are also somewhat cynical in evaluating attendance per se. Thus, of a sample of more than 8,000 clergymen from six Protestant denominations, two-thirds agreed with the statement: "Many loyal church-goers are using religion as an escape from their responsibilities in the world."[29] Alas, church attendance illustrates a problem that is recurrent throughout this chapter: those phenomena on which we have any trend data at all are often the most superficial phenomena on which to base meaningful generalizations.

As promised, this first section on trends in religious participation has raised more questions than answers. The issue of the putative religious revival remains inconclusive with no prospect of ultimate settlement. The chance for collecting reliable data on the past has vanished. But surely this need not be the case for the future. And if there is any single recommendation that emerges from this review, it is that *the Census should include questions concerning religion in its regular enumerations.* Indeed this recommendation is so urgent and so passionately debated that it deserves a postscript of its own.

The Case for Census Questions on Religion

A brief history of religious enumeration policies may serve as prologue. Since its inception in 1790, the decennial U.S. Census has never asked individuals their religion or political beliefs. However, beginning in 1850, the Census Bureau did begin to collect data on churches, data reported to federal marshals in the various judicial districts by local church officials. This policy continued with various alterations in the particular information collected until 1890. At that point, it was decided to dissociate these tabulations from the regular decennial census and to collect them instead in the sixth year of each decade. Thus, data were gathered for 1906, 1916, 1926, and 1936. Congress failed to make the necessary appropriations for 1946, perhaps because of the war. Apparently a precedent was established, because appropriations have been generally lacking in subsequent years as well. However, independent Congressional appropriations are not necessary for the Census Bureau to add another item to its various and more frequent Current Population Surveys. And in 1957, after a Milwaukee pretest in 1956, the Census did include a single question on religion asked of individuals in 35,000 households in 330 sample areas. As noted earlier, the question elicited only general religious preference, an item not to be confused with actual church membership, church attendance, or religious belief. So far only one report on the data has been released. However, as a result of the 1966 Public Information Availability Act, the Census Bureau made available additional materials on request.

In a comprehensive review of this policy and the prospects for changing it as of 1959, Dorothy Good lists (and partially rebuts) five major objections to adding a question on general religious preference to the regular census schedule.[30] First, it is argued that such questions would violate the principle of separation of church and state. Opponents on this ground cite the First Amendment and its clause that "Congress shall make no law respecting an establishment of religion, or prohibiting the free exercise thereof . . ." Good points out that the clause has never been mentioned in Census legislation nor has it been interpreted for its applicability by the judicial system. In fact, T. Lynn Smith notes that "The Permanent Census Act in 1902—the legislation that established our Bureau of Census—(actually) specified that the data about the religious bodies should be gathered every 10 years . . ."[31]

It is difficult to see how a census question on religion is equivalent to making a "law respecting an establishment of religion, or prohibiting (its) free exercise." A census item is likely to do far less in indicating respect for "an establishment of religion" than a great many other current governmental practices, ranging from the church's tax-exempt status to parochial school aid, from the existence of army chaplains and religious edifices on federal property to the acknowledgement of religious factors in such policy areas as birth control aid. Indeed, one wonders whether the inclusion of an item on religion would not indicate less respect for "an establishment of religion" than *excluding* such an item because of the anticipated objection of the religious establishment itself. But a good deal of the opposition is based on the spectre of the European system, wherein census data on religion are linked with the state's role in helping the church collect its taxes. Surely laws are sufficiently clear in prohibiting this. Moreover, do the presently collected data on race, income, and occupation indicate a violation of the neutrality of the state on these issues? In fact, the NAACP and the Urban League are now solidly behind the policy of collecting data on race, despite their earlier opposition.

A second major objection to a census question on religion also seeks to guard against abuses of systems in other countries. Some have opposed recording an individual's religion on the grounds that it might become the basis of the kind of national files and national policies that characterized the Nazis. But again strict laws prohibit such usages or disclosures. Moreover, Donald Bogue points out that no dictator would want to rely on out-of-date census returns; he would do what Hitler in fact did in commissioning a new and irregular enumeration for his own purposes.[32] Finally, Bogue also suggests that insofar as such dangers are involved, they already reside with data presently available for most persons in other places. While military, educational, and church records are too dispersed for scientific aggregation, they all contain religious information which an interested despot would have little trouble collecting for particular individuals.

Third, it is argued that such questions would be violations of privacy, especially since respondents are required by law to answer census questions. Of course, this argument applies to the census' current items, including income and age, both of which give social scientific interviewers far more difficulty than religion. The experience of many survey researchers is that income in particular is likely to prompt more problems than inquiries concerning the most perverse and intimate sexual behavior, much less religious affiliation. Good reports that when the Census Bureau itself asked a subsample of respondents their reactions to the 1957 religious item, less than 3 per cent expressed mild resentment, and less than 1 per cent expressed strong resentment.

But a fourth criticism is in behalf of those particular religious groups who resist any sort of enumeration on principle. Some of these are small sects, but they also include the sizable Christian Science body. Of course, it is difficult to counsel a policy that will run roughshod over the stated principles of a religious group. It might be possible to make exceptions in these cases. It might even be possible to make an exception for the religious item as a whole in order to make it voluntary for all. Judging from past experience, more than 95 per cent will answer it anyway, but this may be reduced if it is *singled out* as voluntary, and one quakes at the consequences of making other "special" items voluntary as well. The problem is a real one and not to be dismissed. However, it applies to only a fraction and is not unresolvable.

Finally, Good lists a fifth objection that is of a different character altogether. Some critics argue that a single question on general religious preference is worse than no information at all, since its ambiguity will almost surely lead to misinterpretation. Certainly any sociologist of religion familiar with survey techniques could quickly supplement the one question with fifteen others that are also "crucial." Nor is there any doubt that this one question—like any other—is vulnerable to misinterpretation. Still, one question is better than none, and all things considered, this one may be preferable because it should be fairly reliable in eliciting the very broad answer that is sought. As it is, various other phenomena may now be misinterpreted, since Census data are crucial to a host of important analyses and religion is left "loosely flapping about," in the words of T. Lynn Smith. Finally, there is always the appeal to international conformity. As of Good's estimate in 1959, religious preference was included in the census schedules of ten countries in the Americas, twelve in Europe, sixteen in Africa, and two in Oceania. The numbers have probably increased considerably in the interim.

In one sense, of course, the debate concerning religion and the census is an important bellwether of religion and politics in American society. Quite apart from the theoretical objections and their possible rebuttals, it would be instructive to look at the alignments of various interest groups on the matter. It should come as no surprise that proposals for adding religion to the enumeration schedule have been supported by the American Sociological Association, the Population Association of America, the Association of Statisticians of Religious Bodies, the American Statistical Association, and other scholarly groups. Perhaps more surprising is the support from the National Council of Churches of Christ in the U.S.A., the Catholic Press Association, and the Catholic hierarchy of the United States. The opposition is more narrowly confined. As of 1959, it included the American Civil Liberties Union, the American Jewish Congress, the Anti-Defamation League of B'nai B'rith, the Union of American Hebrew Congregations, and the Jewish Statistical Bureau, together with an assortment of individual Protestants, Catholics, and Jews.

But note that the alignment may have changed since 1959. Opposition is now more informal than formal. It is interesting to quote a news release from the Bureau of the Census, announcing that the 1970 census will *not* contain a question on religion (I have italicized two points in particular):

> The Bureau has been considering a number of requests from individuals and organizations which proposed that a question on religion be added to the nationwide census which is to be taken beginning in April, 1970. The decision not to add this question is based on the fact that *a substantial number of persons again expressed an extremely strong belief that asking such a question in the Decennial Population Census, in which replies are mandatory, would infringe upon the traditional separation of church and state. . . .* The issues again were widely discussed at a series of public meetings held in all parts of the country and were also reviewed in recent hearings before the Post Office and Civil Service Committee of the House of Representatives. *Since there appears to be no basic change in the nature of the arguments pro and con, there seems to be no reason to delay the decision.*

One wonders how big is a "substantial number of persons" and whether a Bureau of a democratic government hasn't already violated the separation of church and state by emulating the Quakers in requiring full consensus before making a positive decision. One also wonders what sort of change could be expected in the "arguments pro and con." A change in favor of the proponents might be the vastly increased experience of survey researchers with religious items and their unanimous conclusion that questions on religious preference pose little difficulty. But surely one does not expect the arguments to change so much as the evaluation of them. Since this evaluation has been altered by a great many groups, and since the general climate is generally hospitable to the proposal, the question is now how long can the Bureau of the Census hold out? There is serious consideration of a plan that would involve taking the census every five years, instead of every ten, beginning in 1975. To cite an earlier comment of Donald Bogue's: "It is to be hoped that the Bureau of the Census will give a high priority to this item in (1975), as penance for the policy forced on it for (1970)."[33]

But as important as census data on religion would be, they should not be regarded as a panacea for the difficulties of deciphering U.S. religious trends. It is obviously crucial to know what proportions of the population are religiously identified and participate in the churches, but it is just as important to examine changes in the quality of the identification and participation. The next section begins this exploration by examining the more subtle and subjective issue of religious belief. The following sections will examine changes in the organizational fabric of religion and trends in ecumenism.

YESTERDAY'S VILLAGE ATHEIST, TODAY'S THEOLOGIAN, TOMORROW'S PARISHIONER: TRENDS IN RELIGIOUS BELIEF?

One of the most peculiar aspects of the current American religious scene is not that God is proclaimed dead but rather that the obituaries are being written by churchmen. As an example, consider the following excerpts from a parody of *The New York Times* style in necrology, a satire that appeared in the twenty-fifth anniversary issue of the Methodist student magazine, *Motive,* in February, 1966.[34] The piece is both an important datum concerning belief and a fascinating document in the little-attended realm of religious humor:

Atlanta, Ga., Nov. 9—God, creator of the universe, principal deity of the world's Jews, ultimate reality of Christians, and most eminent of all divinities, died late yesterday during major surgery undertaken to correct a massive diminishing influence. His exact age is not known, but close friends estimate that it greatly exceeded that of all other extant beings.

The cause of death could not be immediately determined, but the deity's surgeon, Thomas J. J. Altizer, 38, of Emory University in Atlanta, indicated possible cardiac insufficiency. . . .

In Johnson City, Texas, President Johnson was described by aides as "profoundly upset." He at once directed that all flags should be at half-staff until after the funeral. The First Lady and the two Presidential daughters, Luci and Lynda, were understood to have wept openly. Both houses of Congress met in Washington at noon today and promptly adjourned after passing a joint resolution expressing "grief and great respect for the departed spiritual leader." Senator Wayne Morse, Democrat of Oregon, objected on the grounds that the resolution violated the principle of separation of church and state, but he was overruled by Vice President Hubert Humphrey, who remarked that "this is not a time for partisan politics."

. . . Reaction from the world's great and from the man in the street was uniformly incredulous. "At least he's out of his misery," commented one housewife in an Elmira, N.Y. supermarket. "I can't believe it," said the Right Rev. Horace W. B. Donegan, Protestant Episcopal Bishop of New York. In Paris, President de Gaulle in a 30-second appearance on national television, proclaimed "God is dead! Long live the republic! Long live France!" News of the death was included in a one-sentence statement, without comment, on the 3rd page of Izvestia, official organ of the Soviet Government. The passing of God has not been disclosed to the 800 million Chinese who live behind the bamboo curtain.

Public reaction in this country was perhaps summed up by an elderly retired streetcar conductor in Passaic, N.J., who said: "I never met him, of course. Never even saw him. But from what I heard I guess he was a real nice fellow. Tops." From Independence, Mo., former President Harry S. Truman, who received the news in his Kansas City barbershop, said: "I'm always sorry to hear somebody is dead. It's a damn shame." In Gettysburg, Pa., former President Dwight D. Eisenhower released through a military aid the following statement: "Mrs. Eisenhower joins me in heartfelt sympathy to the family and many friends of the late God. He was, I always felt, a force for moral good in the universe. Those of us who were privileged to know him admired the probity of his character, the breadth of his compassion, the depth of his intellect. Generous almost to a fault, his many acts of kindness to America will never be forgotten. It is a very great loss indeed. He will be missed."

. . . Dr. Altizer, God's surgeon, in an exclusive interview with the Times, stated this morning that the death was "not unexpected." "He had been ailing for some time," Dr. Altizer said, "and lived much longer than most of us thought possible." He noted that the death of God, had, in fact, been prematurely announced in the last century by the famed German surgeon, Nietzsche. Nietzsche, who was insane the last 10 years of his life, may have confused "certain symptoms of morbidity in the aged patient with actual death, a mistake any busy surgeon will occasionally make." Dr. Altizer suggested, "God was an excellent patient, compliant, cheerful, alert. Every comfort modern science could provide was made available to him. He did not suffer—he just, as it were, slipped out of our grasp."

There is, of course, the possibility of overstatement here. At the same time, the satire's cutting edge is not necessarily inconsistent with any of the trends that have been alleged for church membership and participation. It makes obvious sense in conjunction with a thesis that membership and participation have actually declined. It can even be plausibly linked to interpretations of churchly revival. Indeed, this last is so plausible that it deserves special attention.

One of the most ardent advocates of a "contemporary upswing in religion" in the United States is Will Herberg,[35] who cites many of the membership and attendance trends discussed in the last section. But note that Herberg is more widely known for another thesis advanced in the same book; namely, that American religion has gradually become the religion of democracy and the "American Way of Life." It no longer matters what a man's religion is, so long as he has one, and belief is less important than affiliation. Consider one of Herberg's concluding statements, a statement that is tinged with the despair of an older theologian:

> Americans fill the houses of worship, but their conceptions, standards, and values, their institutions and loyalties, bear a strangely ambiguous relation to the teachings that the churches presumably stand for. The goals and values of life are apparently established autonomously, and religion is brought in to provide an enthusiastic mobilization. . . . Of the very same Americans who so overwhelmingly affirm their belief in God and their membership in historic churches, a majority also affirm, without any sense of incongruousness, that their religion has little to do with their politics or business affairs. . . . But this way of looking at things is precisely the way of secularism, for what is secularism but the practice of the absence of God in the affairs of life?[36]

One could quibble with Herberg's conception of secularism and view it instead as "the practice of the absence of God in the affairs of the [*church*]." But the two conceptions are compatible, and Herberg is not alone in seeing secularism in both senses as a corollary of the putative revival in church participation. Earlier I noted Michael Argyle's thesis that there had been such a revival, if only since the 1940's in America. The phenomenon itself may be empirically dubious, but Argyle's explanation of it is interesting nonetheless:

> It may be suggested tentatively that the decline of religion down to 1940 was due to slow changes in society and personality away from the authoritarianism of Catholic-type bodies, and from the guilt-feelings of traditional Protestantism. Since the war, the churches have become both more secular and more liberal, hence more appealing to the prosperous middle class.[37]

Once again secularism is seen as complementary rather than antithetical to a revival in church participation. Indeed, Argyle is suggesting that secularization is a *precondition* for revival because religious groups had to abandon some of their traditional theological formulations to attract parishioners to an emancipated and modern institution.

This thesis is both provocative and theoretically appealing. Even if there has been no revival, one can argue that secularization was necessary to allow religion to maintain as many participating adherents as it has. But the problem again is one of documentation. What evidence is there of secularization? What kinds of data are available concerning a drop in the level of religious orthodoxy? Note first that the two ques-

tions are not identical. One can certainly imagine a process of secularization that leaves traditional belief intact and at a high level of acceptance. For example, one can continue to believe in an intellectual sense
but with reduced saliency and relevance to the everyday rounds of life.
Moreover, the church has developed a number of "secular" programs
to recruit parishioners—programs such as recreation leagues, nursery
schools, group therapy, religious night clubs, and such proselytizing
techniques as spot radio commercials and church services on commuter
trains—but it is quite possible that such organizational changes are not
reflected in changes in the actual religious beliefs of individuals. Such
beliefs are the focus of this section. Let us begin by more closely examining the new theologians themselves.

It should be clear at the outset that the theological proclamation of
the "Death of God" is neither universal among theologians nor to be
equated with a rejection of traditional religion itself. Many theologians,
even some of the current radicals, quake at the announcement; they
disagree with its logic and they disparage its bravado. For example, the
former Bishop James Pike, for all of his alleged heresy, has taken public issue with the "Death of God" argument in that lively barrel of religious ferment, *Playboy* magazine.[38] Harvey Cox's widely read book,
The Secular City, explores the matter with some misgivings.[39] And
clearly the phrase, "Death of God," means different things to different
people using it, as is evident in the various exchanges among, for example, Thomas J. J. Altizer, William Hamilton, Gabriel Vahanian, and
Paul M. Van Buren.

But insofar as the phrase resonates at all among theologians, what
does it mean? Certainly the phrase is more spectacular than its import.
The movement proclaims only the death of a particular conception of
God, one that is abstract, other-worldly, and psychologically "out-
there" rather than within the believer himself. Moreover, the interpretation places renewed emphasis on Jesus in order to place renewed emphasis on the ethical as opposed to the metaphysical. The new theology
seeks rationale and motivation for involvement in the problems of the
world—racial, political, military, economic—and it finds the older conception of God wanting in this respect. God is dead not only because
people no longer find the traditional image salient, but also because that
image is largely irrelevant to man's existential plight.

This is not the place for a thorough exegesis of this literature, nor
am I equipped to undertake it. There are, however, two points that are
well within the ken of the sociologist of religion: the extent to which
the "new" theologians are in fact new, and, more important, the de-

gree to which the theologian represents the mass of religious sentiment.

Unhappily, I am aware of no statistical data on the dispositions of theologians over time.[40] But certainly there is ample historical support for the argument that theologians have been engaged in a steady retreat since the Reformation, a retreat that involves a succession of moves to slightly more liberal ground that is temporarily more defensible. Thus, Martin Marty's analysis of nineteenth-century American theological developments indicates that orthodoxy won a series of battles, while losing the war.[41] Still, it seems reasonable to suppose that there is a newness about the current breed of theological mavericks, a novelty not so much in what is said but in the stridency of the saying and the extent to which it has achieved a hearing. At the same time, the reaction of those listening remains moot. While the theologians think of themselves as responding to the loss of faith of men everywhere, one wonders about the source of their data. And if the loss is a consequence rather than a cause of their message, one wonders what sort of evidence would be necessary to show it. There has always been a slip between the theological cup and the parishioners' lips, and some have argued that contemporary theologians, especially those in academic settings, are more estranged and differentiated from the religious mainstream than any of their predecessors.[42] Many parishioners are no doubt yawning in the midst of such seeming excitement. Others are surprised to find their own beliefs so bowdlerized and misrepresented. Still others may be shocked to find that theologians are willing to admit doubts that they themselves have guiltily suppressed; somehow the professional "men of God" are supposed to hold the banner high, however tattered and windblown it may be.

Assessments of Religious Belief

The difficulty is to find a valid and reliable measure of general religious belief today, much less yesterday. Americans have long been reputed the most religious nation in the West on the strength of consistent polling evidence that somewhere between 95 per cent and 98 per cent "believe in God." But more detailed research has cast doubt on the inferences to be drawn from these data. As only one example, in a recent study of religious belief among undergraduates[43]—an admittedly poor sample for anything—a colleague and I asked first whether the respondent believed in God (yes or no) and found that 86 per cent of our students did. Later, in the same questionnaire, however, we asked the respondents to choose from among five statements the one which best approximated their own particular conception of

God. Some 45 per cent of the sample and almost a third of the original "believers" opted for statements that were basically agnostic. This suggests, however tentatively, that much of the alleged orthodoxy in the United States may be a methodological artifact of standard interview questions which are too general to uncover more specific doubts. Moreover, there is also the distinct possibility that religious doubts continue to be normatively stigmatizing. No matter how pervasive in one's private thoughts, they are not easily confessed publicly, for atheism ranks second only to communism as a target of public scorn.[44] And since these normative pressures may be greater in a Gallup-type personal interview than in an anonymous and faceless questionnaire, this may add to an inflated orthodoxy reflected in poll results. To test the effects of such biases, my colleague and I manipulated bias itself in our questionnaire study of undergraduates. It came as no surprise to find that, when biases are combined to give maximally orthodox and dissident versions of belief questions, the responses vary widely. But the interesting point is not that respondents can be manipulated, but rather their reactions to the manipulation itself. None protested, and when we later asked them to assess the extent to which their questionnaire answers reflected their "real" beliefs and attitudes, the dissident bias emerged as somewhat preferable to the orthodox. Thus, it may be that accurate assessments of religious belief require the researcher to counterbalance natural normative constraints with biases of his own so as to give legitimacy to unorthodoxy.

But even without such gimmicks, religious doubt is apparent on the part of contemporary church members. Table 10, for example, presents denominational data on belief in God from a national random sample of Christian church members. This study, by Charles Y. Glock and Rodney Stark,[45] uncovers similar patterns for other belief items as well, ranging from the divinity of Jesus to life beyond death and the credibility of the Bible. Although doubt is the rule rather than the exception only among the Unitarians, and a little bit of doubt need not signify a deity's death, some questioning is obviously apparent here. And recalling that these data apply only to church members, it is tempting to speculate on doubt among the unchurched, though one should be careful about assuming that disbelief or doubt will rise precipitously among nonmembers. As we noted earlier, church membership leaves a good deal to be desired as a general measure of religiosity. For example, a number of low-status persons belong to sects with no formal membership categories but believe devoutly nevertheless.[46]

Still another temptation is to assume that the amount of doubt that

TABLE 10. DENOMINATION DATA ON BELIEF IN GOD
(NATIONAL SAMPLE)

Denomination[a]	Percentage agreeing with statement: "I know God really exists and I have no doubts about it."
Unitarian (9)	22
Congregational (44)[b]	63
United Presbyterian (75)	67
Protestant Episcopal (56)	72
Methodist (217)	78
Presbyterian Church USA (40)	70
Disciples of Christ (42)[c]	73
American Lutheran bodies (146)[d]	70
Total moderate Protestants (628)	72
Lutheran, Missouri Synod (45)	70
Evangelical and Reformed (28)[b]	71
American Baptist (91)	82
Southern Baptist (187)	93
Other Baptist bodies (90)	86
Sects (128)[e]	90
Total conservative Protestants (569)	86
Total Protestants (1,197)	79
Catholics (507)	85

[a] Figures in parentheses show total number of respondents.

[b] The Congregational and the Evangelical and Reformed denominations merged several years ago to form a single body under the name of the United Church of Christ. However, because of the extreme contrasts in religious outlook between members of the two original bodies we have presented them here separately under their old names.

[c] Officially the Christian Church.

[d] Included here are the Lutheran Church in America and the American Lutheran Church. There were no important differences between members of these two bodies.

[e] Included in the category of sects were: Assemblies of God, Church of Christ, Church of God, Four Square Gospel, Free Methodist, Mennonite, Nazarene, Pentecostal, Salvation Army, Seventh Day Adventist, Campbellite, Jehovah's Witnesses, Christian Missionary Alliance, Mission Covenant, and various tiny holiness bodies. Excluded were such groups as Christian Science, Unity, Divine Science, Theosophy, Spiritualists, and other such bodies which most properly should be classified as cults for our analysis, but since only eleven persons in the sample claimed affiliation with bodies of this type, such a general category seemed futile. Also excluded were persons who claimed affiliation with the various Eastern Orthodox churches, and one member of each of the major Asian faiths.

SOURCE: Glock, Charles Y., and Rodney Stark, *Christian Beliefs and Anti-Semitism,* Harper and Row, New York, 1966, p. 190.

exists in Glock and Stark's contemporary data is unparalleled in the past. Perhaps so, but this is even more difficult to substantiate empirically. Moreover, there is a good deal of qualitative testimony indicating that the nineteenth century was not the period of feverish orthodoxy that is often imagined. Lipset notes at length that foreign observers, even in the early 1800's, wondered at the simultaneous importance of religious affiliation and the relative unimportance of dogma and doctrine. Thus, Lipset quotes the reflections of an Italian Jesuit, Giovanni Grassi, after his stay in the country between 1812 and 1817:

> Those who describe themselves as members of one or another of the sects do not thereby profess an abiding adherence to the doctrines of the founders of the sect. . . . Thus the Anglicans of today no longer take much account of their thirty-nine articles, nor the Lutherans of Calvin or of Knox. . . .
> Among the peculiarities of America, not the most extreme is that of finding persons who live together for several years without knowing each other's religion. And many, when asked, do not answer, "I believe," but simply, "I was brought up in such a persuasion."[47]

Or consider the following from De Tocqueville which, as Lipset notes, has much in common with Herberg's diagnosis more than a hundred years later:

> Each sect adores the Deity in its own peculiar manner, but all sects preach the same moral law in the name of God. . . . Society has no future life to hope for or to fear; and provided the citizens profess a religion, the peculiar tenets of that religion are of little importance to its interests.[48]

In a slightly different spirit, some eighty years later H. L. Mencken made some observations on the religious climate among the brethren of Dayton, Tennessee, during the famous "monkey" trial of the evolutionist Scopes in 1926. Here one would expect orthodoxy to be coursing through every local vein, but Mencken brings his cynicism to bear as follows:

> Even in Dayton, I found, though the mob was up to do execution upon Scopes, that there was a strong smell of antinomianism. The nine churches of the village were all half empty on Sunday, and weeds choked their yards. Only two or three of the resident pastors managed to sustain themselves by their ghostly science; the rest had to take orders for mail-order pantaloons or work in the adjacent strawberry fields; one, I heard, was a barber. On the courthouse green a score of sweating theologians debated the darker passages of the Holy Writ day and night, but I soon found that they were all volunteers, and that the local faithful, while interested in their exegesis as an intellectual exercise, did not

permit it to impede the indigenous debaucheries. Exactly twelve minutes after I reached the village, I was taken in tow by a Christian man and introduced to the favorite tipple of the Cumberland range. : . . They were all hot for Genesis, but their faces were far too florid to belong to teetotalers, and when a pretty girl came tripping down the main street which was very often, they reached for the places where their neckties should have been with all the amorous enterprise of movie actors. It seemed somehow strange. . . . Dayton was having a roaring time. It was better than the circus. But the note of devotion was simply not there.[49]

Mencken highlights an irony that pervades this section. On the one hand, Americans prosecute public doubters of faith; on the other hand, their own beliefs are often either privately doubted or characterized by low saliency and a lack of urgency. Both sides of the irony can be amply illustrated for the current scene as well as for the past.

Qualitative evidence for measuring belief over time is provocative but highly selective and unreliable. Quantitative data are both rare and clumsy in picking up the subtler facets of the issue. How does one measure a belief's saliency or urgency as opposed to its content? And how can content itself be measured apart from very general questions or questions that measure doubt as opposed to substance? Keeping this limitation in mind, as well as the standard problems of sampling and the like, let us critically inspect the few quantitative clues available. Most of these clues are for limited time periods and limited groups. While most support a decline in orthodox belief, none is unassailable.

For example, James H. Leuba compared the beliefs of samples of well-known scientists in 1914 and 1933. He found a sizable decline in orthodoxy in the interim, although the report is out of print, and the precise statistics are not available to me.[50] Scientists are no doubt important, but they are also atypical. Moreover, the period in question precedes the later years in which both the religious revival and the rise of the new theology are alleged to have occurred. More extensive time data on more representative groups are needed.

Given the captive respondents of the academic social scientist, it should be no surprise to learn that at least crude data are available over time for college students. For example, Argyle cites the work of Dudycha at "an American college" comparing belief in 1930 and 1949. Again, the statistics are unavailable to me, but Argyle cites the study as indicating a "slight decline in belief—particularly on the ideas of forgiveness of sin, Salvation by faith, and final judgment."[51] More quantitative, though perhaps no more reliable evidence, can be put together for student beliefs in God in 1913, 1952, and 1965. Leuba also analyzed belief in God among students at nine "high-ranked" colleges in 1913 and found that 87 per cent of the men and 93 per cent of the women "believed." In 1952, a team of Cornell sociologists studied male students at eleven colleges and found that some 24 per cent were either atheists or agnostics, hence only 76 per cent were "believers."[52] I can supply data on students at the University of Wisconsin for 1965, but they come in two forms and it is difficult to tell which is most comparable with the unavailable Leuba data. I have already indicated that some 86 per cent of one sample answer "yes" to the simple question: "Do you believe in God?" On the other hand, if it is more appropriate to ask the student to pick one of several statements about God, 60 per cent or less would be classified as believers.[53] Clearly it is difficult to justify any firm conclusions from these data. Not only are the questions dissimilar but so are the samples. While the comparisons would seem to suggest a decline in student belief in God, the suggestion is far from a command, and the data are presented more to illustrate foibles than to document a fact.

Turning to adults, there is some meager evidence available concerning religious belief from public opinion polls with national samples. I have already mentioned that the amount of variance in the percentage claiming to believe in God is very low, since the figure vacillates between 95 per cent and 98 per cent. But there is more variance concerning another facet of belief: life after death. The Gallup polls have asked the question several times in the past; the percentage believing in an afterlife was 64 per cent in 1936, 76 per cent in 1944, and 74 per cent in 1961.[54] One explanation advanced for the jump between 1936 and 1944 was World War II and the consequent drama of military death. But the 1961 evidence seems to uphold the high previous figure; is there anything to discredit the pattern? Possibly. It is interesting to note that the 1961 poll was taken in December, perilously close to the Christmas season. Even the data in 1944 might be somewhat suspect on the basis of their November date—although the commercial extension of Christmas into the early fall may be a more recent phenomenon. In any event, the low figure in 1936 may be partially accountable through the May date of the poll cited.

A radically different sort of evidence on changing religious beliefs stems from a content analysis of 46 best-sellers of inspirational religious literature between 1875 and 1955. Needless to say, one must be cautious in hazarding extrapolations from these books to the American religious scene generally. Still, a few possible implications are worth noting. The authors, Louis Schneider and Sanford Dornbusch, indicate

that the notion of an afterlife has never been prominent in the literature, and that there is a steady tendency to maximize adjustment in this
life rather than escape to a life beyond. Since World War II, there has
been increasing emphasis on the importance of institutional religion in
facilitating such adjustment. Schneider and Dornbusch comment on the
trend as follows:

> We therefore have the paradoxical situation that institutional religion
> gets to be favored in principle (dogma being a component thereof also
> recently regarded in more friendly fashion), while the "old-time reli-
> gion," the "faith," which might underpin and make a support of ritual,
> dogma, and the like other than *formally* "pro-religious," shows no sign
> of reinforcement in our literature. If the literature supports the notion
> of a religious revival, it does so in most equivocal fashion.[55]

Here is yet another hint of a revival in formal religious adherence that
is accompanied by an eclipse of traditional religious fervor. Dogma is
stressed insofar as it is tied to religious institutions, but there is an increasingly important difference between a respected dogma and an
urgently compelling faith. Indeed, Schneider and Dornbusch raise a
crucial question in this regard: Is it possible for religion to make its
latent functions manifest and continue to fulfill them without the old-
time trappings? Their answer is pessimistic and is couched in terms of
a "self-defeating prophecy." Thus, the very act of declaring one's functions baldly and in nonreligious terms may strip away the religious
mystique that is so necessary to fulfill the functions.

But let us return again to the search for numbers. Perhaps the best
empirical data available on trends in religious belief pertains neither to
national samples of adults nor even to parishioners. Instead, it involves
the changing beliefs of ministers. It is clearly perilous to generalize from
ministers to almost anyone else. At the same time, if we are concerned
with the climate of religious belief within the churches themselves,
ministerial evidence should be crucial. At least these data afford a
check on the extent to which the new theologians have affected and reflected the beliefs of their less erudite colleagues.

The data in question have been assembled for this chapter from two
studies. In 1929, George Herbert Betts published a little-known work,
The Beliefs of 700 Ministers,[56] in which he asked some 56 belief questions of 500 ministers and 200 seminary students representing seven denominations in the Chicago area. Betts' own argument revolved about
his finding that the seminary students were more "liberal" in belief than
their elders, from which Betts concluded that liberalism was the wave of
the future. Of course, the conclusion may well be spurious since youth

tends to mellow in its aging, and one can imagine that every generation of ministers was more liberal in its seminary salad days. Nevertheless, the data on the 500 ministers are useful for our purposes, since nine of Betts' items are close enough to items in a more recent study of ministers to warrant comparison. In 1965 Jeffrey K. Hadden asked a sample of more than 8,000 ministers, also from six denominations, a battery of questions concerning not only their religious beliefs but a host of other issues as well.[57]

Before we begin with the nine comparisons, a few caveats are in order. First, it will be obvious that the questions under comparison are slightly different in their 1929 and 1965 versions. While it is always difficult to estimate the impact of semantic variance, caution is certainly indicated, and at points the admonition will be underlined. A second reason for suspicion concerns the form of the responses. Whereas Betts apparently asked ministers only whether they believed, disbelieved, or were uncertain concerning a given statement, Hadden used a now-conventional six-point scale, ranging from strongly agree to moderately agree, slightly agree, slightly disagree, moderately disagree, and strongly disagree. In order to provide comparable categories, I have collapsed Hadden's six-point scale into three groups: agree (strongly or moderate agree); uncertain (slightly agree and slightly disagree); and disagree (moderately disagree and strongly disagree). An obvious third difficulty with the data concerns the samples. Not only was Betts dealing with a Chicago sample exclusively while Hadden's was nationwide, but the denominational categories are different in the two studies. For example, Betts talks of Lutherans and Baptists categorically without specifying *which* Lutherans and *which* Baptists in denominations where the question is far from idle. Hadden is much more careful, sorting out subcategories wherever appropriate. For this reason, I have decided against comparing the pooled results from both samples and have restricted the analysis to separate data for three common denominations which have been relatively cohesive and constant over time: the Episcopalian, the Methodist, and the Presbyterian.

The lengthy Table 11 contains the data in nine tiers, representing the nine items that were comparable in the two ministerial surveys for 1929 and 1965. Note that on seven of the nine comparative items, the ministers of today do indeed seem more liberal than the ministers of yesterday. The only two exceptions concern the "devil" (or the "demonic") and a literal interpretation of the Bible, but surely the 1965 items are more liberal themselves in both cases. Thus, it makes a difference whether one is asked to agree that "the Devil exists as an actual being" or, in a more sophisticated form, "I believe in the demonic as a per-

TABLE 11. SOME COMPARISONS OF THE BELIEFS OF
EPISCOPALIAN, METHODIST, AND PRESBYTERIAN
MINISTERS IN 1929 AND IN 1965

Statement and response	Episcopalians	Methodists	Presbyterians
	(percentages)		
A. (1929) "God exists"			
believe	100	100	100
uncertain	0	0	0
disbelieve	0	0	0
(1965) "I find it increasingly diffi-cult to believe in a God."			
disagree	90.6	90.0	91.0
uncertain	6.7	6.7	6.0
agree	3.9	3.2	3.0
(1965) "I would expect a think-ing Christian to have doubts about the existence of God."			
disagree	17.9	32.0	21.4
uncertain	15.6	21.1	20.0
agree	66.6	46.4	58.6
B. (1929) "The Devil exists as an actual being."			
believe	47.0	41.0	44.0
uncertain	21.0	12.0	17.0
disbelieve	32.0	47.0	39.0
(1965) "I believe in the demonic as a personal power in the world."			
agree	63.3	38.0	52.9
uncertain	23.9	26.7	26.1
disagree	13.0	35.3	21.2
C. (1929) "The Bible is wholly free from legend or myth."			
believe	11.0	13.0	18.0
uncertain	0.0	7.0	9.0
disbelieve	89.0	80.0	73.0
(1965) "I believe in a literal or nearly literal interpretation of the Bible."			
agree	11.1	17.9	19.5
uncertain	9.3	12.2	11.8
disagree	79.6	69.5	78.7
D. (1929) "Hell exists as an actual place or location."			
believe	27.0	41.0	44.0
uncertain	19.0	13.0	17.0
disbelieve	54.0	46.0	39.0
(1965) "Hell does not refer to a special location after death but to the experience of self-estrangement, guilt, and meaningless in this life.			
disagree	22.1	24.2	28.6
uncertain	18.3	17.8	17.2
agree	59.7	57.5	54.2

TABLE 11 (*cont.*)

Statement and response	Episcopalians	Methodists	Presbyterians
		(*percentages*)	
E. (1929) "There is a continuance of life after death."			
believe	100.0	94.0	98.0
uncertain	0.0	3.0	2.0
disbelieve	0.0	3.0	0.0
(1965) "I expect to live after death."			
agree	98.3	87.9	86.9
uncertain	8.9	9.0	10.6
disagree	1.9	3.1	2.5
F. (1929) "Jesus was born of a virgin without a human father."			
believe	75.0	54.0	69.0
uncertain	14.0	13.0	13.0
disbelieve	11.0	33.0	18.0
(1965) "I believe that the virgin birth of Jesus was a biological miracle."			
agree	55.9	40.4	50.5
uncertain	22.3	22.7	25.0
disagree	21.8	36.5	24.6
G. (1929) "After Jesus was dead and buried, he actually rose from the dead, leaving the tomb empty."			
believe	100.0	74.0	86.0
uncertain	0.0	7.0	4.0
disbelieve	0.0	19.0	10.0
(1965) "I accept Jesus' physical resurrection as an objective historical fact in the same sense that Lincoln's physical death was a historical fact."			
agree	70.4	49.2	64.9
uncertain	10.7	15.6	12.4
disagree	19.0	34.7	22.7
H. (1929) "(I believe) in a visible, bodily, second coming of Jesus to establish a reign on earth."			
believe	54.0	20.0	36.0
uncertain	14.0	9.0	16.0
disbelieve	32.0	71.0	48.0
(1965) "As described in Revelations, Christ and his Saints will historically rule the earth during the millennium."			
agree	14.7	17.9	16.7
uncertain	30.1	29.7	34.6
disagree	55.3	51.9	48.8

TABLE 11 (*cont.*)

Statement and response	Episcopalians	Methodists	Presbyterians
	(*percentages*)		
I. (1929) "The creation of the world occurred in the manner and time recorded in Genesis."			
believe	11.0	24.0	35.0
uncertain	4.0	9.0	7.0
disbelieve	85.0	67.0	58.0
(1965) "The Biblical account of creation provides us with the clearest evidence that Darwin's theory of evolution is wrong."			
agree	2.1	12.2	8.2
uncertain	3.3	13.8	12.5
disagree	94.4	73.9	79.3

SOURCE: Betts, George Herbert, *The Beliefs of 700 Ministers*, The Abingdon Press, Nashville, 1929, pp. 26–30; and Hadden, Jeffrey K., unpublished 1965 data on some 8,000 ministers.

sonal power . . ."; it makes a more obvious difference whether one is asked to judge the Bible "wholly free from legend or myth" or "I believe in a literal *or nearly literal* interpretation of the Bible" (italics added). Indeed, in the light of these differences, it may be remarkable that the increment of orthodox agreement in the 1965 sample is no greater than it is, especially with regard to the Bible.

But there are other problems of comparability as well. Consider, for example, the first tier dealing with belief in God, where I have actually used two items from Hadden's recent study to compare with Betts' more straightforward question. The first of Hadden's items asks whether the current ministers find it increasingly difficult to believe in God, and the answer seems to be a resounding "no," indicating a level of firm belief that is only slightly less than the orthodoxy unanimity manifest in 1929. But Hadden's second item concerning God suggests an alternative interpretation of the first. Perhaps many ministers do not find it increasingly difficult to believe in God because they have had substantial difficulties all along. Thus, the proportion expecting a "thinking Christian to have doubts about the existence of God" ranges from 46.4 per cent among the Methodists to 66.6 per cent among the Episcopalians. A different sort of problem is posed by the questions concerning Hell. Betts is characteristically unambiguous, but Hadden's item is vulnerable to the difficulties in interpreting any item that involves assessment of more than one sentiment. Thus, does disagreement with the item indicate that the respondent accepts Hell as "a special location after death" or does it mean simply that he does not accept the psychoexistential alternative of "the experience of self-estrangement, guilt, and meaninglessness in life"?

Despite such problems, the data do seem to lend credence to a liberalization of doctrine among ministers and to the notion that the new theologians may represent something more than scholarly rebellion and the natural aberration of the philosopher. Betts may have been right, after all, in suggesting that the greater liberalism of the seminary students of 1929 presaged greater liberalism for ensuing generations of ministers. The data are also suggestive in their tenuous evidence that the Methodist ministers may be somewhat more liberal than either the Episcopalian or the Presbyterian. This is at least the case for three items on which there were substantial denominational differences concerning the devil, the resurrection, and the virgin birth. And note that on these items, as with most of the others, the denominational patterning of any wide differences was very similar in 1965 to 1929. This suggests first that the comparisons deserve at least a modicum of confidence. It also suggests—if this confidence is deserved—that the three denominational ministries have not changed at radically different rates over time. This augurs well for ever-cautious extrapolation to other Protestant groups, and perhaps to Catholics as well. Although I know of no specific data on the changing beliefs of Catholic priests over time, there is clearly ferment arising from the yeast in Vatican II.[58]

Of course, one cannot overemphasize the perils in generalizing trends in the beliefs of clergymen to trends in the belief of parishioners or the population at large, largely because we are not even sure of the direction in which differences might run. On the one hand, one could argue based on common sense that clergymen should naturally be more orthodox and traditional in their beliefs than nonclergymen, and that any changes that have occurred among clergymen themselves might underestimate changes among the less institutionally constrained laity. But the opposite is also plausible. Theological change and revolution often reach the clergy long before others. Indeed, the position of many clergymen within the church may be increasingly tense these days because their beliefs are far more liberal than their parishioners suspect. Since it is also possible that the beliefs of parishioners are less orthodox and less salient than their clergymen suspect, this may produce further tension through mutual misperception based upon stereotypes of "what ought to be" rather than empirical knowledge of "what is."

Unfortunately, there are no data for national samples of nonclergymen that allow reliable analysis of the changing content of belief. And yet there is another dimension to belief for which crude data are available, the dimension pertaining to the urgency and influence of religion in everyday life. In a recent news release, George Gallup presented the trend since 1957 in response to the question: "At the present time, do you think religion as a whole is increasing its influence on American life, or losing its influence?" Gallup cites the results in Table 12 as

TABLE 12. CHANGES IN RELIGIOUS INFLUENCE, ACCORD-
ING TO NATIONAL SAMPLES OF ADULTS, 1957–1968

	1957	1962	1965	1967	1968
	(percentages)				
Increasing	69	45	33	23	18
Losing	14	31	45	57	67
No difference	10	17	13	14	8
No opinion	7	7	9	6	7

SOURCE: American Institute of Public Opinion press release, April 11, 1967; *The New York Times,* May 25, 1968.

"one of the most dramatic shifts in surveys of American life." Looking only at the percentage who say that religion is *losing* influence, it rises from 14 per cent in 1957 to 31 per cent by 1962, 45 per cent by 1965, and to fully 67 per cent by 1968. Insofar as one can regard this as a projective test of sorts, it seems to indicate that the saliency of religion is indeed declining. Certainly many churchmen have interpreted the pattern this way. And perhaps no single poll result has produced as much discussion and consternation among those who keep their ears attuned to such findings.

And yet the question of interpretation looms large. First, the Gallup data are based on national samples of adults rather than church members or believers, and it is risky to conclude that this trend reflects a loss of saliency for the latter—though it probably does. Second, one wonders about such specifics as the date of the poll interviews in the respective years, since we have already seen that this may be a factor in Gallup's evidence concerning church attendance and belief in an afterlife. Third, one also wonders what the results might have been prior to 1957. Table 12 seems to indicate that an extrapolation would produce virtually nobody arguing for a loss of religious influence in earlier years. But there are data available which indicate quite the contrary.

Hadley Cantril's massive compilation of polls on *Public Opinion: 1935–1946*[59] presents two earlier soundings on the matter. In January, 1937, fully 49.9 per cent of a national sample studied by Elmo Roper for *Fortune* magazine indicated that religion was losing influence. In February, 1939, 34 per cent of a Gallup sample indicated that "influence of religion in this community has decreased during the last few years." Note that these two studies—especially the first—were done in the afterglow of the Christmas season and still present high estimates of loss of influence (unless the findings are accountable by a lingering resentment over Christmas gifts). The pattern seems to indicate that, while the proportion perceiving a loss of influence is higher today than it was then, it is not a unilinear trend. Instead once again we see a peak of religion in the 1940's and 1950's[60] and thereafter a decline that seems to restore some of the characteristics of the 1930's and perhaps earlier.

How then to summarize all these data on belief? The best single answer is, of course, "cautiously." One must be wary of pouncing on specifics at the risk of speciousness. Insofar as the foregoing has dealt with details, it was primarily to point out methodological problems that inhere in such analyses. Thus, there is evidence of a liberalization, if not a loss, of faith. And yet it is difficult to tell whether this represents a long-term trend or a reversion to an earlier state after a recrudescense of traditionalism. It is also difficult to tell how characteristic this is of the nation as a whole. Certainly there remain substantial pockets of orthodoxy, even fundamentalism, that are lost in national figures. Moreover, it may very well be that liberalization reflects changes within individuals less than changes in the society at large. The dramatic increases in urbanization and education, as well as the much less dramatic increase in vertical mobility, should all have the effect of reducing the traditional content and saliency of beliefs simply because there are more people in social categories that have always scored relatively low in such matters.

However, several rays of methodological hope brighten the future. In the mid-1960's sophisticated interest in religious belief on the part of social scientists has flowered. Glock and Stark and Hadden are but a few who have sought to elicit the various dimensions of belief, and who have begun to produce solid evidence for meaningful population segments. While some of these data await further analysis, they do offer a substantial benchmark for comparison with studies of the future. An author undertaking the present task in the year 2000 should not be nearly so disadvantaged in the area of beliefs as he will be with respect to formal church membership and church participation.

CHANGES IN CHURCH ORGANIZATION: DIFFERENTIATION AND BUREAUCRATIZATION

Every institution is beset with a tension between the dictates of its ideology and the restraints of its organizational form. But few institutions have been more consistently agonized than the church. The historian Robert Moats Miller puts the matter this way in his analysis of *American Protestantism and Social Issues, 1919–1939:*

> After all, to survive religion must be institutionalized, and as institutions the churches are as subject to the pressures and mores of society as any other agencies. And just because the treasure of religion is perpetuated in earthen vessels, compromise and corruption is (sic) inevitable. This is the tragedy of religion: institutionalized it becomes corrupt, without the churches it dies.[61]

Or consider the remarks of theological sociologist Robert Lee:

> The dilemma is simply this; on the one hand, if the church is to take seriously its obligation as a missionary and witnessing movement, it must maintain some semblance of continuity, stability, and persistence; it must develop appropriate organizational and institutional forms. Yet, on the other hand, the very institutional embodiments necessary for the survival of the church may threaten, obscure, distort, or deflect from the purposes for which the institution was originally founded.[62]

Lee sums up the problem by citing an aphorism: " 'After the doxology, comes the theology, then the sociology.' " And indeed it is precisely at this point that the sociologist should come into his own as a student of religion. Although 80 per cent of Hadden's sample of Protestant ministers agree that "it is impossible for the sociologist to fully comprehend the meaning and significance of religion unless he is himself a member of the faith," the judgments of Lee, Miller, and others offer hope that even the noninvolved sociologist can fathom the church as an organization, if not religion as a personal experience. Nor are the two unrelated. The organizational nature of the church provides context and boundaries for individual experiences within it. Just as it was important to explore religious belief to understand the quality of church membership and participation, it is important to be aware of church structure as the arena in which both belief and participation are played out.

Continuity and Change in Organizational Problems

Certainly sociologists of religion have directed increasing attention to religion's organizational aspect since World War II. And studies of Protestant, Catholic, and Jewish groups indicate a surprising ecumenism with respect to shared organizational problems.[63] But what about the *changing* nature of religious organization? Organizational problems are not new, and it would be improper to suggest that earlier students of religion were wholly oblivious to them. There are several landmark studies from the 1930's that do not deserve their current neglect.[64] Moreover, there was a still earlier period at the turn of the century when sociologists, especially Europeans, regarded organizational issues as central to an understanding of religion. The works of Max Weber, Ernst Troeltsch, and, to a lesser extent, Émile Durkheim remain profoundly relevant. Indeed, Weber's analysis of religion is virtually prophetic in its analysis of the problems accompanying the development of the contemporary parish.[65]

But Weber and Troeltsch[66] are best known for advancing a general perspective on church organization that has dominated the field since. This is the celebrated distinction between the ideal-types of "sect" and "church," a distinction based on a conception of the sect as an organizationally uncorrupted and perfervid ideological movement in contrast to the church, which is more compromising, more bureaucratized, more professionalized, and more heterogeneous. Further, there is a crucial dynamic link between the sect and the church in that the sect is often spawned out of rebellion against a church but then gradually takes on churchlike attributes of its own over time.

This perspective can be applied to American religious trends in two quite different ways, yielding two quite different conclusions. First, it can be argued that the cyclical drama of church-sect relations is as old as religion itself and is likely to persist throughout its life course. From this perspective, no religious group is immune to organizational problems and dynamics, and every age has experienced the disorders. Thus, one finds organizational tensions within sixth-century Catholicism no less than among twentieth-century Baptists. The succession of organizational forms as represented in the Protestant Reformation can be seen in the later developments of Reform and Conservative Judaism, not to mention more recent changes in Christianity itself. It can be argued that the most important attribute distinguishing religious organizational problems in one era versus another is the attention accorded them. Perhaps much of the emphasis on current organizational dilem-

mas of the church simply reflects the increased currency of the sociological perspective itself.

But there is another way of interpreting the church-sect implications. Thus, twentieth-century American religion has been unusual in
witnessing the maturation into churches of an unusual number of sects
born several centuries earlier. The Baptists, Congregationalists, Methodists, and Presbyterians all have deep roots in the past but are only
now reaching churchly adulthood. Indeed, it can be argued that the
whole process of moving from sect to church has been accelerated by
the conditions of American life. Many younger and indigenous American groups are catching up with the development of their older brethren. The Disciples of Christ, the Church of God, and many of the
Pentecostalist groups are but a few who are now wincing from growing
pains and *rites du passage*.

Undoubtedly both these general interpretations have merit. On one
hand, it would be folly to argue that the contemporary church faces
unique organizational problems of religion. On the other hand, it is
difficult to deny that many of these problems have been steadily
exacerbated throughout this century. Both positions are "reasonable,"
but how does one go beyond reason to proof? Once again we are confronted by a methodological diet that reduces already skimpy evidence
to skeletal proportions.

Here as before, many of the problems stem from religious diversity.
Whatever the separation of church and state has meant to others in
this country, its resulting variety has been a sty in the generalizing eye
of the sociologist. Religious groups differ not only in style and substance but also in their data collection. In part, this is a matter of degree, since some denominations simply collect more data than others.
But more troublesome problems arise because different groups often
use different categories to sort what is fundamentally the same information. For example, a study of organizational trends in American religion might well include analyses of changes in church budgets. But
each church uses a somewhat different budgetary classification, and the
few common categories are too general to be illuminating. Much the
same can be said of trends in staffing. One *should* be able to rely on
formal organization charts to inspect changing role conceptions, responsibilities, and relationships, but the staff data are equally capricious
across religious groups.

Because of these difficulties in aggregation, much of what follows
will rely upon case studies of single denominations. Generalization is,

of course, especially vulnerable to religious diversity. Moreover, many of these studies are qualitative with very little "hard data." Churches not only differ from each other in collecting data, but also each single church is likely to change its techniques of data collection and classification over time. A few suggestive bits and pieces have survived, but they are rare indeed.

For all these reasons, then, this section will take an approach that is quite different from its predecessors. Instead of using available data and methodological considerations to puncture pre-existing balloons, I shall inflate some balloons of my own, seeking support in the form of illustrative examples. By now the reader should be accustomed to viewing any assertion about American religion, including what follows, with suspicion. The principal justification is not to dictate "the truth" but rather to offer a framework that can be utilized by future scholars attempting similar assessment, hopefully with more and better evidence at their disposal.

Earlier we saw how the implications of classic church-sect theory can lead to two quite different though mutually plausible interpretations of American religious change, or the lack of it. My own view is closer to the second than to the first. While organizational *problems* have always characterized religion, this century has witnessed an uncommon number of organizational *changes,* partly as new responses to old problems recently exacerbated. Indeed, I am convinced that more change has occurred in the organizational facet of religion during the twentieth century than in either individual participation or individual belief.

But what are the factors generating change? Certainly one is size itself. Regardless of whether religion has grown *proportionately* in American society, it has certainly grown in absolute numbers. Riding the crest of the national population growth, virtually every major religious group in this country has at least tripled in membership since the turn of the century.[67] After a point, quantitative changes in numbers become qualitative changes in scale, especially when the numerical increase is accompanied by other changes as well. For example, most churches not only have much larger memberships, but their members are also more widely dispersed around the country. Problems of communication and coordination require new solutions, if they are solvable at all. Still other factors are associated with historical changes in polity for many groups. For example, the rise of the Social Gospel Movement within American Protestantism ultimately had the effect of sharpening the churches' confrontation with secular society and social problems. This in turn required a quite different structural apparatus with new specialists and new authority relations. These changes have had further ramifications, of which some are acknowledged and purposeful, while others are covert or unintended. Certainly the consequences extend to the type of ministerial candidates recruited, the nature of church polity, and the changing institutional saliency of traditional mandates and doctrine. Some tensions are relieved, but many others are created. Without pressing the point, as the church structure seeks greater efficiency, the traditional religious aspect loses prominence—a point that is implicit in the quotes from Miller and Lee which began this section.

But perhaps the most important source of change resides less within the churches themselves and more in the society at large. Granted that most religious groups have come to confront that society more pragmatically, they are increasingly forced to do so on society's own terms. For example, if one seeks to alter the policies of an increasingly bureaucratized government (whether with respect to civil rights, poverty, foreign policy, or education), one must fight bureaucratic fire with bureaucratic fire. Or if the churches are anxious to increase their memberships further, they must compete with alternative organizations and activities for potential members, and the competition is often on the changing terms dictated by the secular competitors themselves. Thus, we get a proliferation of recreation leagues, nursery schools, religio-psychiatric clinics, businessmen's luncheon groups, and even organized political activity represented by the alignment of some religious groups with the left and others with the right. These are the consequences as churches grow impatient for society to come to them and as they begin to grope outward on their own.

So much for a very brief summary. One could go on at length, growing steadily more romantic. But surely this whole approach is severely limited by a lack of data, and perhaps a concept or two can serve as poor substitutes. What kind of sociological rubrics are appropriate for these putative changes? How can we gain at least analytic closure?

The Growth of Differentiation

One key concept here is that of *differentiation*. As a result of increasing size, increasing dispersion, and increasing tasks and specialties, the typical denomination has played host to a series of cleavages in what is idealized as a seamless web. This differentiation takes a number of different forms. There are, of course, the expected regional, political, and doctrinal splits. But more to the organizational point, one finds increasing gaps between the three levels of the laity, the local parish clergy, and the national headquarters. The levels are increasingly separate in tasks and understandings. Moreover, the tension between them mounts as each becomes aware of how the others differ.

One example of differentiation between the national headquarters staff and the church as a whole is provided by M. Moran Weston in his analysis of the *Social Policy of the Episcopal Church in the Twentieth Century*. Weston provides a detailed analysis of the "failure of communication" between the church's national agencies and its local levels. Nor is the failure entirely unintentional:

> As a matter of fact, the prevailing policy of the National Council in 1952 was that there should not be general mailings to all of the clergy or to any other church-wide group except under very, very special circumstances, which must be jointly agreed upon by the executive officer of the department or division sponsoring the publication and the officials of the Department of Promotion.[68]

But Weston's general summary of his study is more helpful in exploring further aspects of differentiation:

> . . . prior to 1920 there existed no national machinery for coordinating and prosecuting the social politics enacted by the General Convention of the Church. After 1920, the National Council, as the chief executive agency of the General Convention, and the departments established under it, made possible a coordination and integration of programs in a way that led to greater efficiency and effectiveness. However, the failure to provide adequately in the way of funds, staff, and other resources left the Department entrusted with the Church's national social work program without the necessary tools with which to do the job. Further, the long years of the depression interrupted the growth of the Department and the development of its program for approximately ten years. Only since World War II has there been an upward turn in the program of the National Council generally, and of the Department of Social Relations, in particular. It would be fair to state, however, that, even at the present time, there does not exist enough in the way of leadership, machinery, or financial resources to implement existing social policy effectively on a church-wide basis. The channels for communicating policy and program from General Convention, National Council, and national department to the various diocesan departments, parishes, and missions are by no means adequate. Also, these same channels cannot be relied on to transmit effectively and fully the thinking of the parishes and missions and diocesan leadership to the national department, Council, and Convention. In those dioceses where there is paid social relations staff, communication is more efficient. There still remains in the Episcopal Church a strong current of distrust of central agencies and an emphasis on diocesan and parish autonomy. This sentiment, as much as any other factor, may account for the slow growth in the work of the

National Council, generally, and of the social service department in particular. The fear of bureaucracy is especially acute in matters dealing with controversial social issues, developments, and relationships.[69]

Clearly differentiation is no simple phenomenon, nor can it be evaluated in a single phrase, leaping over tall issues. On the one hand, it allows the national headquarters more autonomy, more thrust, and more coordination at the top. On the other hand, it poses problems concerning the allocation of resources, communication, mobilization, and resentment from below. Later I shall explore several of Weston's points independently. Meanwhile, there is a further aspect of differentiation itself that deserves consideration.

So far I have stressed the increase in *vertical* differentiation between levels as increasingly common, but there has also been an increase in *horizontal* differentiation within levels; e.g., between various departments within a denomination's national headquarters, between various types of clergymen within the same denomination, and even between different categories of parishioners within the same congregation. Clearly the phenomenon of specialization is at issue here, and there can be little doubt that the church has gone the way of most institutions in hosting its increase. Of course, specialization and physical differentiation are not *necessarily* related, since it is possible to imagine specialists working side-by-side in fully cooperative arrangements. But such cooperation generally depends upon a calculated organizational framework that is rarely present in the church. Recent developments in religious organizations have tended to be catch as catch can; they have often developed without explicit design and sometimes in covert and emergent opposition to stated principles. Moreover, because some specialists are seen as illegitimate or boat-rocking in their expertise, they are sometimes granted autonomy on the theory, "out of sight, out of mind."

One consequence of such differentiated specialization is a loss of control over the specialists themselves. And indeed many churches are now undergoing an especially heavy siege from specialists who are increasingly critical and increasingly radical in their suggestions for change. A particularly striking instance is the case of the campus ministry, as recently analyzed by Phillip E. Hammond and Robert E. Mitchell.[70] The authors point out that the campus ministry has come to function as a kind of "escape-valve" for radicals among the clergy who might be an embarrassment in a suburban pulpit. But they also suggest that this "segmentation of radicalism" is not wholly effective; specifically, they hypothesize a number of mechanisms through which the exiled radicals may ultimately effect even radical changes in the parent churches themselves. Of course, the campus minister is only one of a number of clerical types that could be described as radical. Indeed, the proliferation of this "new breed" has become a common subject for popular analysis. For a good example, Harvey Cox has made a recent career out of writing on the fermentation among church functionaries.[71] Cox may certainly draw upon himself as an illustration of his thesis, but there are many others as well, including the "death of God" theologians, clerics in civil rights work, those who are in full-time poverty programs in urban ghettoes, and at least one who presides over emancipated soul-searching in a night-club setting. It is difficult to judge the change represented by such types, though their own rhetoric certainly points to changes in the future.

The Growth of Bureaucratization

But this should not suggest that twentieth-century religion has become a "happening" in all respects or that the future of church organization lies with the blithe spirit. Processes of differentiation should not be confused with anarchy. Actually there is still another process long underway that suggests quite the opposite; the process of *bureaucratization*. I mentioned earlier the difficulties of standardizing quantitative data to yield empirical measures of organizational change. Trends in budgets, role allocation, agency growth and development are all difficult to measure not only across denominations but also within any given denomination because of changing categories over time. A sound empirical analysis of such dynamics would require more intensive effort than I could muster in the context of an explicitly extensive review of American religious change. And yet, just as I had convinced myself of the hopeless difficulties involved, Gibson Winter published a rebuttal that is a classic in the rare genre of empirical treatments of American religious organization.[72] Focusing especially on the Disciples of Christ, Methodists, Roman Catholics, and Judaism, Winter documents increasing bureaucratization within each beyond a glimmer of a doubt. Relying largely on his own innovative data collection from denominational yearbooks, Winter does in fact analyze budgetary trends in terms of administrative cost ratios, allocations to specific national agencies, and the changing source and distribution of member contributions. He also examines the rise of national staffs as well as such things as the ratio of "primary bureaucratic functionaries" to urban and rural Catholic dioceses from 1900–1960. While the empirical treatment is especially thorough for the Catholic case, Winter demonstrates convincingly that bureaucratization and organizational growth are trans-denominational phenomena in twentieth-century American religion.

All of Winter's twenty-two tables are relevant here; however, I shall offer only an enthusiastic citation and move on to some further evidence of bureaucratization. Earlier I cited Weston's analysis of the national agencies of the Episcopalian church in connection with the process of differentiation. But Weston's points are germane to bureaucratization as well. Nor should increasing bureaucratization be surprising in an Episcopalian church whose polity has always been strongly hierarchic, with the "Catholic" principle of "apostolic succession" reinforcing a nationally centralized structure of authority. However, other denominations have opposite principles of organization; for example, the Baptists have a revered tradition of "local autonomy," in which every parish determines its own fate on its own terms. If an increasingly centralized national bureaucracy can develop among the Baptists as well, it may suggest that bureaucratization is less a passing fancy than an organizational necessity in American religion.

Paul Harrison's analysis of the Baptist case[73] is a classic not only among sociologists of religion but among students of organizations generally. Harrison documents a process by which the goals of the Baptist national agencies and councils began to demand increasing attention if they were to be served adequately. This involved the recruitment of organizational specialists who, in turn, exercised their professional competence to gain necessary organizational control. Harrison talks of the development of "rational-pragmatic authority" and a bureaucratic structure that emerges not because it is democratically ordained but rather because it is the most efficient way of meeting responsibilities. In fact, the most peculiar aspect of this bureaucracy is that it arises covertly and without consent—the only conditions under which it could arise at all among the Baptists. And precisely because the process is unacknowledged, it is largely uncontrolled. Ironically, then, the Baptists' tendency to turn their back on bureaucracy meant that they were ultimately saddled with a bureaucracy that is doubly entrenched. Harrison concludes his analysis with a further irony concerning the relations between national headquarters, the American Baptist Convention, and the local churches:

> ... the original function of the Convention—to serve the churches and help them achieve their common goals—has been drastically altered. The preservation of the Convention's organization and program has now become an ultimate purpose of the denomination. In a sense the role of the churches has been displaced by the role of the Convention. It is now

the purpose of the congregations to increase and preserve the life of the national organization. The organizational imperatives of the Convention are now so stringent that the ministers are the local servants of the Convention and the executives are the national servants.[74]

Note the crucial phrase, "organizational imperatives." It suggests that the church may be more responsive to its structure than its doctrine, and that this structure makes relentless demands that may have little to do with the doctrine itself. Throughout Harrison's analysis, one is reminded of the precarious quality of the church's traditional goals. Certainly, there is nothing new about this precariousness, but there may be at least two reasons why it has increased. First, many of the traditional goals, such as providing "salvation," are other-worldly in nature; hence they are not sufficiently concrete or immediate to allow an increasingly bureaucratized church to mobilize, coordinate, and evaluate its efforts efficiently. A second reason derives from the assumption that society as a whole has undergone substantial secularization so that other-worldly objectives are now deviant in the light of more prominent this-worldly concerns. If the church is to be an effective instrument in the larger world, it must relate to the goals of that world, requiring an abandonment of some of its more distinctively "sacred" objectives.

Now one consequence of precarious goals may be goal-lessness itself. Certainly many denominations and local congregations flounder for lack of specific direction. Informal ministerial testimony indicates that increasing numbers of clergymen are beginning to have doubts about their own roles and missions; later we shall show that ministers are increasingly oriented to nonparish specialties. But goal-lessness in its strict sense may be tantamount to organizational death, which is rare. Instead, another process is more common, that of "goal displacement" or the process by which means become ends in themselves. Here are two illustrations from the Baptists:

> When Baptist leaders think of the work of missions, education, publications, or ministerial benefits, *they must think in terms of the agencies which carry on these activities and of the organizational procedures which have been established. There is no possible way of organizing to achieve a goal and at the same time avoid the demands of organizational imperatives.* The Baptists in local churches, when they consider the missionary enterprise, must necessarily accept the interpretation given them by the professional workers. It is not a false interpretation, but neither is it derived from first-hand experience. *The executives tend to interpret the mission work in terms of impressive budgets, numbers of missionaries, quantitative analysis of annual conversions, the world*

situation as viewed by a secretary in New York, public relations, and personnel problems and organizational difficulties.[75] [italics added]

But not only is there a tendency to reduce activities to their most instrumental denominators; it is also common for the most instrumental departments to command increasing power:

> Promotional activity is a requisite of any large-scale organizational activity, whether it is voluntary or inclusive, religious or secular. American Protestantism's general acceptance of the methods of mass communication is in the first instance motivated by the need to support an ambitious organizational and missionary program. The institutionalized work of all the large religious groups in America is characterized by rationalized social structures with special staffs of executives, sub-executives, office secretaries, file clerks, business managers, editors, bookkeepers, file workers, missionaries, etc. Among all these workers, the promotional men enjoy a unique position. They can make the claim that they husband all the activities and provide the essential income for the work of the organizations. In many cases their position is supreme, for nothing must stand in the way of promotion.[76]

There are, of course, many further examples of goal displacement within religious organizations. Earlier I mentioned the competition over membership recruitment as an instance in which the means to an end has become partially an end in itself. Perhaps a more demonstrable example concerns church finances.

Churches, like most organizations, depend upon money to fulfill their functions. Church bureaucracies, like most bureaucracies, tend to measure their success in monetary terms as one of the few quantitative indicators available.[77] Certainly it is true that the corporate wealth of American religion has reached colossal proportions in this century, partly because of wise investments, and partly because of a tax-exempt status that is so unusual that the churches are not even obligated to report their earnings, with the consequence that precise estimates of wealth are precluded. Of course, it is not easy to decide when money is a means and when it has become an end in its own right. But if a sociologist's judgment is suspect, perhaps the judgment of religious officials is more convincing. Recently a number of church officials and church bodies have indicated concern. Thus, the former Bishop James Pike has at times called for an abolishment of the church's tax-exempt status on the grounds that ". . . church wealth has become a menace."[78] He elaborates the point both in terms of the internal corruption of churchly ideals and in terms of the potential danger that lies in posing a threat to secular bodies through combined religious real estate assets that are more than twice the aggregate assets of the nation's five largest corporations: "Let the churches render unto Caesar what is Caesar's— before he comes to take it with a sword." Nor is Pike alone in this position. He cites the support of Eugene Carson Blake, the current General Secretary of the World Council of Churches, as well as that of the National Council of Christians and Jews, the Baptist Joint Committee on Public Affairs, and other groups. In the same spirit are the very recent remarks by John Dillenberger, Dean of the San Francisco Graduate Theological Union, who indicates that five out of every six church buildings in the country could be razed, and the church mission would not suffer. Indeed, if the properties were sold, the mission could be furthered by putting the monies to more laudable ends.[79]

So far this discussion of bureaucratization has been largely restricted to the national staffs and agencies of religious organizations. But it may also apply to the local level as well. Earlier I mentioned the sheer increase in size as a factor in any organizational changes that have occurred. Just as whole denominations have grown spectacularly, so have the average number of members per local church. Table 13 presents

TABLE 13.   AVERAGE NUMBER OF MEMBERS PER CHURCH:
ALL RELIGIOUS BODIES, 1926–1965

Year	Number
1926	235
1936	262
1940	265
1945	249
1950	304
1960	359
1961	363
1965	382

SOURCE: *Yearbook of American Churches,* 1967, p. 218.

figures of the National Council of Churches that indicate almost a 60 per cent increase in average parish membership between 1926 and 1965. Although these figures may be as suspect as the more general membership statistics, they do suggest the possibility of increasing administrative complexity. While bureaucracy may not be an accurate term for the result, there is no doubt that local church structures have begun to approximate organizational mazes. For example, Martin E. Marty's analysis of *The New Shape of American Religion*[80] cites a number of recent pamphlets and books on "how to organize your church." He quotes one that recommends some 22 official positions and 23 committees, all to be filled by parishioners quite apart from the paid staff.

Now such a list is not necessarily representative of all suggestions, let alone typical of all churches. Nor does it necessarily reflect change, though this should be testable by a content analysis of such programmatic suggestions over time, or, more preferably, by a survey of actual church structures as a beginning for longitudinal data extending into the future. Meanwhile, Marty's own verdict of change may be granted some credibility, especially since he is himself a parish minister of considerable experience. Indeed, Marty finds the future so foreboding that he too is anxious to explore alternatives. For example, he dubs the current system one of "multitudinism" in which the church is subverted by its massive size; he opts instead for a "remnant" model in which membership is restricted to the very few who "really care."

Marty is presumably not alone in his disenchantment with current trends. And here is one instance in which there is empirical confirmation of a trend. According to Douglass and Brunner,[81] the average Protestant minister spent 11.4 per cent of his time on *administrative duties* in the early 1930's. In contrast, recent analyses of the roles of the minister indicate that he now spends some 40 per cent of his time on administration, a responsibility for which he continues to receive poor seminary training and little reinforcement from his parishioners, who give administration the lowest priority on their list of what a minister should be doing, a judgment in which the minister himself concurs.[82] Clearly the minister receives administrative help from lay workers. At the same time, the effort of filling and coordinating such positions is substantial in itself. And from the standpoint of many parishioners, the positions may be filled according to criteria of secular expertise rather than religious dedication or a devotion to common churchly ideals. Thus, the members of the important finance committee are likely to be relatively high-status businessmen, whereas many of the most personally committed parishioners are low-status women who may have quite different notions about church programs and expenditures. This raises still another organizational problem for the minister to contend with—that of integrating a church that has grown more heterogeneous as it has grown larger.

Changes in the Clerical Profession

In view of the impact that all the changes hypothesized in this section should have on the clergy, it is appropriate to examine the few other bits of clerical trend data available for possible support. Of course, some of the trends have no necessary bearing on organizational structure. For example, a study of *The Education of American Ministers* by Mark A. May and Frank K. Shuttleworth in 1934 presented a good deal of information on changes in the proportion of university graduates who entered the ministry between 1640 and 1907;[83] the percentage stood at 65.5 per cent for the years between 1642–1660, and it thereafter decreased to 44.1 per cent (1721–1740), 16.7 per cent (1811–1880), and to 3.1 per cent for the years 1901–1907. Although I know of no more recent data to bring the series crudely up to date, there is little reason to suspect an upsurge. Still, it is true that ministerial training has had a curvilinear association with educational quality. In the very early days of the seventeenth and eighteenth centuries, a very high proportion of ministers came from such elite colleges as Harvard, simply because (1) these colleges were explicitly devoted to training for the pulpit; (2) they were among the very few colleges that existed in general; and (3) the ministry was a peculiarly prestigeful and even remunerative occupation in this pre-industrial era.

During the nineteenth century, however, Richard Hofstadter's distinction between a "living and a learned" religion[84] took force, and increasing numbers of ministers came from Bible Institutes rather than universities. It has been only in the twentieth century that we see the new marriage between seminary education and the university as increasing numbers of seminaries move into the academic orbit as satellites, recruiting from the secular liberal arts programs. It is apparent, however, that the problems of ministerial education are far from solved. Like every other facet of the American educational system, the seminaries face a drop-out problem that may be accelerating rather than coming to a halt. And even when the seminarian does not drop out during the course of his studies, it is increasingly doubtful that he will enter the ministry after graduation. May and Shuttleworth indicate the long-term trend as follows: 92.5 per cent of seminary graduates in the period 1870–1879 had actually entered the ministry itself five years after their graduation; the percentage drops to 92.2 per cent for 1880–1889; to 86.6 per cent for 1910–1919; and to 77 per cent for 1920.[85] Again there are no recent data to complete the series. However, crude evidence for the United Presbyterians suggests that the number of their seminary graduates who were not subsequently ordained has increased considerably between 1953 and 1965.[86] Of course, this sort of trend may be difficult to evaluate unless one knows what sort of people are opting out. Unfortunately, there is no study of the matter over time, though research by H. G. Duncan on 111 ex-ministers in 1932 indicated that it was the best-trained that withdrew and the mediocre who stayed.[87]

The year 1932 is a bell that stimulates a natural economic salivation. It is quite possible that the low salary level of ministers, not only during the depression but afterwards, has been a factor in the attrition. David Moberg indicates that between 1929 and 1949 the average incomes of "employees of religious organizations" dropped from $200 to $750 below the national average.[88] But while it is clear that clergymen have low salaries, it remains unclear how low. The term "employees" includes too many people. Moreover, such figures are often capricious since they do not indicate whether customary fringe benefits (housing, living allowance, ceremonial fees, etc.) are included. In any event, since the Social Security Act of 1950, many clergymen's salaries have been raised to a statutory minimum—perhaps a sad commentary in itself.

Of course, there is a constant lament over the shortage of clergymen. Moberg indicates, for example, that between 1945 and 1955, Catholic Church membership increased by 36 per cent but the number of priests by only 22 per cent. During the same period, the Protestant Churches reported an annual need for 10,000 new ministers, while only 6,500 were graduating annually from seminaries. To take a specific example, some 2,500 Southern Baptist churches were without any minister, and another 9,000 had only part-time ministerial help. Note, however, that such estimates call for important qualifications. Statistics of dire need are often used as recruiting devices by every sort of organization from the churches to the schools. They are sometimes more fancy than fact. For example, how many of the vacant 2,500 Southern Baptist pulpits are in churches that could support even a part-time minister? The countryside is dotted with skeletal churches that have lost dramatic membership weight on involuntary diets of urbanization and regional mobility. This is especially the case for rural areas and the South, and hence may be particularly apt for the Southern Baptists.

For quite a different perspective on the supply of ministers, it is worth noting a recent internal memorandum of the United Presbyterian Church in the U.S.A.[89] This report is remarkable in its awareness of methodological errors and its reluctance to leap to facile conclusions. It indicates that popular estimates of the Presbyterian growth rate are inflated just as conventional estimates of the ministerial supply are understated. In fact, the report concludes that if one adds ministers who have switched from other denominations to the supply of new

Presbyterian ordinations, the net gain between 1959 and 1965 is 1,022 —a figure "which is considerably more than the actual need of 639 based on net gain in membership. . . ." Indeed, the report goes on to cite a factor that is frequently neglected in such trend analyses. It points out that if pastors are to move from one pastorate to another in line with church policy, between 700 and 800 vacancies in churches willing and able to make the call are required. This leads to a close analysis of the churches formally listed as vacant. Of 1,518 churches without pastors in 1965, a total of 863 had less than 100 members, leaving only 655 crudely estimated to be in any position to support a professional clergyman. Comparing 655 with the 700 to 800 needed vacancies produces the startling conclusion that there is now a surfeit of ministers, at least among Presbyterians, who are now beginning to press for quality rather than quantity. Perhaps this surfeit applies to other denominations as well.

In all these trends and countertrends, there is very little other than the important data on administrative time to confirm the earlier assertions concerning differentiation and bureaucratization in the church as a whole. It is true that the clerical career seems to have dropped in favor among college graduates, which may reflect changes in the churches doing the recruiting. It is also true that ministers have been increasingly well educated since the 1930's, which may lead to more sophisticated organizational techniques and structures. Finally, the Presbyterian data note the number of ministers who have switched denominations. Moberg indicates that this is an increasing tendency,[90] and it is possible to infer from it an increasing professionalization as career considerations take precedence over denominational ties and doctrinal allegiances. But all these deductions are tenuous at best. What is sorely needed is an analysis of the changing allocation of the clergy. Rather than debate their quantitative waxing and waning, it would be far more important to determine what they are doing now, as opposed to what they did earlier.

For a preliminary step, let us again consider data from the Presbyterians. If one compares categories of ministerial employment between 1945 and 1965, there is both stability and change. Stability is best represented by the proportion of ministers who were classified as "pastors"; this largest of all groups included 45.2 per cent in 1945 and 47.06 per cent in 1965. Change is partially exemplified by the proportions who are classified as "executives." In 1945, this accounted for only 0.4 per cent of the Presbyterian clergy; but by 1965, the figure had risen to 3.5 per cent. If the increase seems insignificant at first glance, it is more impressive with a second look. Translated into absolute terms, the increase is from some 38 executives in 1945 to some 449 in 1965. Put another way, the number of executives in 1965 was almost twelve times the number in 1945, during a period when the Presbyterian membership increased by no more than one-half. This seems to substantiate claims of increasing bureaucratization, at least at the level of formal executive positions in one major denomination.[91]

Another change in the Presbyterian ministry also seems to corroborate claims of bureaucratization, this time at the level of the local parish. In 1951, the Presbyterians began collecting data for a new category of ministerial employment, that of "assistant and associate pastor." In that year, 3.0 per cent or 278 ordained ministers fell into the cluster, but by 1965 the figures had reached 9.5 per cent or 1,218. Of course, it is still possible that the number of churches served by assistant and associate pastors actually declined in the period if the absolute number of churches vastly increased. But the data indicate the contrary; at least between 1955 and 1965, the number of Presbyterian churches decreased from 9,226 to 9,060.

One additional implication of these data involves possible changes in the age structure of the ministry. As more subordinate positions are available for in-service training, it may well be that more younger clergymen are either cause or consequence. Here is one point at which national figures are available. E. Wilbur Bock has recently analyzed trends for white and Negro clergymen since 1930,[92] and Table 14 presents Bock's tabulations on the changing age distributions of both groups, as drawn from U.S. Census data. As one might expect, the pattern for Negroes is considerably different from that of the whites. Whereas the Negro clergy get proportionately older over time (perhaps an important commentary on Negro churches generally), white clergymen get proportionately younger. Thus, the percentage of Negro ministers over sixty-five rises from 9.8 per cent in 1930 to fully 18.1 per cent by 1960, but the percentage of white ministers in this age group falls from 10.8 per cent to 7.7 per cent. And among whites the most obvious trend can be seen in the under-thirty-five category which included 20.7 per cent in 1930 but 30.8 per cent in 1960, a leap from roughly one-fifth to almost one third.

For several reasons, this is an appropriate end point for the present section. First, it can be seen as a qualification of any prior suggestions that such organizational changes as differentiation and bureaucratiza-

TABLE 14. PERCENTAGES OF THE EMPLOYED CLERGY, BY AGE AND COLOR, UNITED STATES, 1930–1960

Color and year	Number	Total	Less than 35	35–44	45–54	55–64	65 and over
				(percentages)			
White							
1930	120,181	100.0	20.7	24.8	24.0	19.7	10.8
1940	116,800	100.0	25.7	24.7	22.0	17.4	10.2
1950	139,020	100.0	27.2	27.1	20.3	16.2	9.2
1960	181,312	100.0	30.8	25.8	21.8	13.9	7.7
Nonwhite							
1930[a]	24,540	100.0	10.2	26.4	34.2	19.4	9.8
1940	17,920	100.0	10.8	23.3	34.0	21.3	10.6
1950	18,360	100.0	8.2	19.0	30.0	25.2	17.6
1960	13,980	100.0	11.1	15.8	29.1	25.9	18.1

[a] The figures for 1930 are for Negroes only; those for the other years are for all nonwhites.

SOURCE: Bock, E. Wilbur, "The Decline of the Negro Clergy: Changes in Formal Religious Leadership in the Twentieth Century," paper presented at the annual meeting of the Southern Sociological Society, New Orleans, April, 1966, p. 11.

Derived from: U.S. Bureau of the Census, *Fifteenth Census of the United States, 1930,* vol. V, *Population—General Reports on Occupation,* Government Printing Office, Washington, 1933, chap. 4, Table 7, pp. 154–155, Table 8, pp. 174–175, and Table 9, pp. 192–193; U.S. Bureau of the Census, *Sixteenth Census of the United States: 1940, Population, The Labor Force, Special Report on Occupational Characteristics,* Government Printing Office, Washington, 1943, Table 1, pp. 11 and 17; U.S. Bureau of the Census, *U.S. Census of Population: 1950,* vol. IV, *Special Reports,* part 1, chap. B, *"Occupational Characteristics,"* Government Printing Office, Washington, 1956, Table 6, p. 69, and Table 7, p. 81; U.S. Bureau of the Census, *U.S. Census of Population: 1960, Subject Reports, Occupational Characteristics,* Final Report PC (2)–7A, Government Printing Office, Washington, 1963, Table 6, p. 71, and Table 7, p. 91.

tion have sapped the church's vitality. It may very well be that younger ministers are more vigorous, more restless, and more innovative. If so, this trend promises a continuation of change itself. But a second reason for ending here concerns a different sort of qualification. The importance of the unhappy distinction between Negroes and whites reminds us of something that has been seriously neglected throughout this chapter; namely, the difficulty of generalizing from mainstream Protestantism to a host of other groups. This is a common consequence of inadequate data and the wholesale use of concepts in their stead. The area of organizational change is particularly ripe for more detailed research in the future.

THE ECUMENICAL TIDE AND ITS BACKWASH

Two words stand out in any semantic analysis of recent church literature: "dialogue" and "ecumenism." Nor is the talk idle. Communication, cooperation, and actual denominational mergers have indeed increased during this century, particularly among Protestants. This is one trend for which substantial historical documentation is available. Let us consider some of it before seeking explanation, qualification, and elaboration.

Throughout the eighteenth and nineteenth centuries, American religion was known for rampant denominationalism. H. Richard Niebuhr's classic, *The Social Sources of Denominationalism*[93] documents the vigorous variegation that resulted from the influences of class, race, nationalism, and sectionalism. But Niebuhr's book was published in 1929, and by then a tendency toward convergence was underway. In 1960, Robert Lee wrote a sequel to Niebuhr's book entitled *The Social Sources of Church Unity,* in which he summarized the switch from the centrifugal to the centripetal in this way:

> The important point to ponder . . . is that organic mergers are now a fact, whereas previously they were non-existent. Between 1870—when the Old School and the New School Presbyterians reunited—and 1905, not a single instance of church union is recorded in the United States.
>
> Since 1905, no less than eleven organic mergers within the same denominational family and four unions across denominational lines have been consummated. These unions have reduced the number of major Protestant groups from thirty-four to fifteen. Moreover, various merger discussions now pending include at least thirty parties.[94]

Note that Lee restricts his count to "major" groups; in a footnote, he indicates that "excluded from this counting are countless consolations (sic) of smaller groups and synods. Also excluded are mergers like the Pillar Fire with the Fire Baptized Holiness Church. Indeed, since 1911, fourteen Pentecostal groups have merged into five bodies with a combined membership of 556,000." But note too that Lee's count is now eight years old. For example, his category of "trans-denominational" mergers does not include the 1961 merger of the Unitarians and the Universalists; nor, of course, the union in 1968 of the Methodists and the Evangelical United Brethren. Finally, as of 1960, Lee could make no mention of the current discussions underway concerning a dramatic merger of Methodists, Episcopalians, Presbyterians, the United Church of Christ, and other groups. Although formal merger is hardly around the corner for this "Consultation on Church Union," the discussions are noteworthy in themselves.

Ecumenical Forms

It is important to distinguish various forms of ecumenism. Lee mentions two that may be termed *union* and *reunion*. Union refers to the marriage of denominations that have no prior history of togetherness, such as the various mergers culminating in the final binding of the Congregational and Evangelical and Reformed Churches into the United Church of Christ in 1957. In reunion, denominations that were once together, then divorced, find mutual happiness anew. For example, the 1906 merger between the Presbyterian Church USA and the Cumberland Presbyterians; the 1911 consolidation of the Northern Baptist Convention and the Free Baptist Churches into the American Baptist Convention; and the 1939 convergence of the Methodist Episcopal Church with the Methodist Episcopal Church, South, and the Methodist Protestant Church.

At least three other ecumenical forms involve no actual merger at all. One is what Lee and others have termed the "conciliar movement." Its most important case is generally considered the start of twentieth-century ecumenism generally—the formation of the Federal Council of Churches in 1908 as the organizational wedge of the heralded Social Gospel Movement. Conceived in large part "to secure a larger combined influence for the churches of Christ in all matters affecting the moral and social condition of the people, as to promote the application of the law of Christ in every relation of human life,"[95] the Federal Council was a consolidated agency for social action, and as such it thrived insofar as success can be measured in budgetary terms. Lee notes that its budget was $9,000 in 1909, but $649,644 in 1948. By then, however, the Federal Council was only one of a number of national, trans-Protestant agencies concerning such matters as stewardship, foreign missions, the ministry, etc. In 1950, the Federal Council joined with many of these various groups to form the National Council of Churches, an organizational behemoth whose annual budget now pushes $30,000,000 and whose constituency includes more than thirty denominations with another thirty or so holding the status of "associate" or "affiliate."

Still, the National Council hardly exhausts the conciliar movement, despite its dominance. On one hand, it is strongly related to the World Council of Churches, founded in 1948. On the other hand, it has increasingly close ties with the formally autonomous state and local councils of churches. The growth of the local community councils from 1917 to 1956 is presented in Table 15. Like many of the foregoing trend statistics, these suggest that 1940 was a crucial take-off point

TABLE 15.   GROWTH OF LOCAL COUNCILS OF CHURCHES,
1917–1966

Year	City councils with paid staff	City councils volunteer staff
1917	c. 31	no data
1919	c. 40	no data
1921	c. 60	no data
1930	c. 50	no data
1941	98	87
1943	116	230
1945	147	354
1947	257	420
1956	281	657
1966	205	609

SOURCE: Lee, Robert, *Social Sources of Church Unity,* Abingdon Press, Nashville, 1960, p. 133.

and that the 1960's produced a dip. Certainly one thing is clear, however; the surge of ecumenism in this century is not a revival but a wholly new phenomenon. As one of the prime movers put it in 1958, "The whole course of what we call the ecumenical movement has taken place within fifty years. My generation has seen it all."[96]

Nor has the conciliar movement been confined to the major, liberal Protestant groups. In 1941, partly in self-defense, Carl McIntire rallied several fundamentalist groups into the American Council of Christian Churches (ACC). According to William G. McLoughlin's excellent analysis,[97] the ACC claimed to represent one and a half million parishioners and some fifteen denominations by 1965. But it was not only competing with the liberals. In 1942, the National Association of Evangelicals (NAE) was formed as a neo-fundamentalist group, eschewing the militant posture of the ACC. Also by 1965, the NAE claimed a total strength of some thirty-four denominations and 1,654,278 members, however credible these figures may be. Clearly both these groups are statistically insignificant when contrasted to the National Council. However, they too have international and local affiliates, and they may even command greater support than their statistics indicate since fundamentalism has been traditionally suspicious of the overarching organizations that ecumenism entails.

Needless to say, the conciliar movement has also extended to Catholics and Jews as well. Certainly the Vatican Council is not to be dismissed on the international scene,[98] and its ecumenical implications for the United States may be considerable as well. Within Judaism, observers have commented on the increasing communication and cooperation between the Reform, Conservative, and Orthodox wings. Groups ranging from the American Jewish Congress, the B'nai B'rith Anti-Defamation League, and the Synagogue Council of America give at least symbolic manifestation to the spirit. Finally, the National Conference of Christians and Jews marks a small step toward interfaith convergence, though later we shall examine anti-Semitism more specifically.

So far then we have considered three forms of ecumenism in unions, reunions, and the emergence of transdenominational councils. Two other forms deserve at least brief mention. One is the emergence of the *community church,* an institution that had much of its impetus as a result of ministerial and financial shortages during World War II. Actually, there are a number of subtypes here, including the "old circuit" plan, in which a single minister serves multiple churches, the "federated church," in which several churches from different denominations pool their resources for purposes of worship services, etc., and the "nondenominational community church," hosting members from a variety of faiths but with formal ties to none. Summary statistics on the development of the various forms of community churches are elusive, though Lee cites David Piper's early estimate that the number had grown from a "handful" in 1917 to 1,296 in 1927.[99] Some forms have increased more than others—apparently nondenominational churches have declined somewhat since the 1920's, according to *their* council, the "Council of Community Churches"—but the general trend seems to be steadily increasing. Indeed, some have gone so far as to speculate that the current development of the community church may produce a distinctive denomination in its own right. After all, its development so far parallels the nineteenth-century beginnings of the Disciples of Christ, founded as it was on the basis of a frontier ecumenism.

Finally, even in communities where there is no formal community church or even a local council of churches, there is an apparently increasing *comity process.* Although the term itself is losing favor, it refers to an arrangement whereby local churches establish and sometimes police rules for recruitment, public ministerial appearances at holiday ceremonials, interfaith visitation, etc. The emphasis is on mutual planning to avoid "overlapping and overlooking." This often involves vigorous community surveys to determine denominational distributions and to arrive at precisely calculated ratios of churches to church members that should hold for given areas. It may even involve explicit antipoaching laws to protect one church against raids from another, or to protect lackluster clergymen from the threat of a dazzling personality in a competing pulpit. For the most part, comity arrangements are restricted to Protestant churches, and even more to the major liberal and moderate denominations as fundamentalist churches and sects generally opt out. There are, of course, exceptions; but some of these are questionable in their ecumenical import. For example, W. Seward Salisbury reports the case of Oswego, New York, in the early 1950's in which the threat of a growing Catholicism drew virtually all the Protestant groups together, along with the Jewish synagogue, in an alliance of self-defense.[100]

A thorough explanation of the rise in ecumenism is clearly impossible here. A range of factors are important, including the slow healing of Civil War wounds and the splits over slavery, the rise of geographical mobility and the decline of sectionalism generally, urbanization, the acculturation of ethnic groups and churches, increased denominational mobility among both parishioners and ministers, the correlates of perceived increases in vertical mobility, the changing quality of church participation, the decline in saliency and particularistic content of religious beliefs, the increase in differentiation itself allowing ecumenically inclined leaders further autonomy for their ventures, and the rise of bureaucratic goals and policies that require cooperation for maximum achievement. Of course, some of these factors can be seen as consequences as well as causes.

But one of the challenges throughout this analysis has been to chip away the veneer of change to examine its qualifications, problems, and prospects more realistically. Certainly one should be on guard against the assumption that formal ecumenism has permeated all levels and all aspects of American religion. There is continuing opposition even within denominations that have already merged with seeming success. For example, the union between the Congregational-Christian and the Evangelical and Reformed bodies is still plagued by local law suits, not to mention local parishes that refuse to adopt the new title of "United Church of Christ" and earlier banded together in variously titled councils of opposition. In general, one can chart opposition to ecumenism simply by noting those for whom the foregoing conditions do not apply. Opposition is more likely among unreconstructed Southerners, those whose regional and ethnic identities remain strong, those who are localites rather than mobile cosmopolitans, those who are anxious about their status rather than flush with the satisfaction of mobility, and those who continue to cling to traditional doctrine and, more importantly, traditional church organizational forms. It is not surprising to find fundamentalist groups suspicious of merger; nor to discover opposition in denominations with long-standing principles of local autonomy, and hence long-standing opposition to the requisite of centralization. But in addition to enmity, there is apathy as well. Many mergers simply fail to crystallize at the local level. The spirit of ecumenism tends to prevail more at the top than at the bottom, i.e., more among national leaders than local clergymen, and more among interdenominational officials than among the denominational leaders themselves. It is worth recalling the title of an earlier exploration of the matter: Edmund de S. Brunner's *The Larger Parish: A Movement or an Enthusiasm.*[101]

Enthusiasm notwithstanding, there is little evidence that ecumenism is a panacea. Some students of religion have taken positions which suggest that the demise of denominationalism itself may be "dysfunctional" if religion is to meet the variegated needs of a still variegated population.[102] And while it is true that ecumenism is a new response to old problems, it has sometimes exacerbated these older problems and created new ones in the bargain. Certainly this is the case if increasing differentiation and bureaucratization are perceived as problems, and if one clings to grass-roots control as a model of proper church polity. For example, James Gustafson has analyzed the administrative agonies and readjustments that were entailed in the United Church of Christ merger.[103] There one finds increasingly centralized control for two former denominations with hallowed traditions of relative decentralization. Moreover, the centralized administration is often inefficient and a source of conflict. There are frequent instances of "double-staffing." There is a tendency to alternate the denominational backgrounds of high-ranking national leaders with little regard for relative competence. Financial problems and conflicts stem from the quite different fiscal histories and policies of the denominations. As a result, more than one UCC official has indicated that the merger produced an organization that was larger rather than better, more cumbersome rather than more streamlined. Indeed, the pathologies of formal mergers have so disenchanted many church officials that they have transferred their enthusiasm to lower levels of cooperation over specific programs; e.g., the increasing numbers of interdenominational efforts and parishes within the troublesome "inner cities" of the nation. Cooperation at this level is far easier than any formal merger. It may even be more important.

But so far this discussion has centered on ecumenism almost exclusively among white Protestant groups. Surely the term is meant to embrace more. Even within Protestantism, one wonders about ecumenical efforts to integrate white and Negro churches. Within American Christianity, it is worth asking about the current status of Protestant-Catholic differences. Finally, what about the relations between Christians generally and other faiths; more specifically, to what extent is the spirit of cooperative enterprise, interdominational tolerance, and religious homogeneity manifest in changing patterns of anti-Semitism? Of course, all three topics deserve (and have had) lengthy treatments of their own, and all three pose vexing methodological problems. The following attempts only to highlight the issues with no illusions of definitiveness.

Race and Religion

There is an abiding paradox in the relationship between whites and Negroes in American religion. On the one hand, white religious leaders of various faiths have been in the forefront of the civil rights movement, and several major denominational bodies have explicitly demanded integration of the local parishes themselves. On the other hand, the cliché that "Sunday morning within the churches is the most segregated time in America" is still true. In part this discrepancy is methodological, since the first half of the paradox is revealed in the soft data of public statements, council declarations, and individual acts of clerical valor, while the second half can be gleaned from the few pieces of hard data available concerning trends in church membership, etc.

But there is another resolution to the paradox as well, one that turns on the level of church hierarchy involved.[104] It is certainly true that spokesmen of most national religious agencies have been consistently integrationist in their statements and formal policies. Not only have they joined in the liberal consensus crying for an end to segregation, but they have taken more concrete steps as well. Indeed, the National Council of Churches has recently discontinued its annual message on race relations on the grounds that the area has been infused with pious talk at the expense of hard-nosed action. It has begun to give more attention to such concrete projects as the Delta Ministry with its militant civil rights work in Mississippi, and exchange programs in which Negro and white clergymen would switch pulpits for a month or so during the year. The Consultation on Church Union has included several Negro denominations in its exploratory discussions toward the merger of six of the country's largest denominations. Both the Presbyterians and the Methodists have recently elected Negroes to top national offices. These changes are taking place at the *top* of the white Protestant structure. But once one penetrates to less exalted levels of church organization where any lasting ecumenism must be put into effect, the results are considerably less encouraging.

Consider that there are now an estimated 1.6 million Negroes in predominantly white religious groups in this country. Not only is this less than 1 per cent of the total 123.3 million church members, but it is also less than 10 per cent of Negro church members alone. Moreover, some of the "integration" is itself more token than genuine. For example, the Methodists claim almost 375,000 black members; but this figure includes some 225,000 members of the all-Negro "Central Jurisdiction," an organizational enclave set apart to facilitate the merger between northern and southern Methodists in 1939, an enclave that has only recently shown signs of giving way. Such arrangements are not atypical among major Protestant denominations. David M. Reimers points out similar arrangements in the recent past for Presbyterians and the former Congregationalist-Christians.[105] Reimers indicates that Negroes have not only been frequently neglected in ecumenical moves, but they have also been common obstacles, as among the Southern Presbyterians contemplating reunion with the Northern wing.

One would expect few church-collected statistics on this issue, since the statistics can be so embarrassing. But probably the most thorough investigation of a single denomination's racial exclusiveness was conducted from within: Herman H. Long's *Fellowship for Whom? A Study of Racial Inclusiveness in Congregational Christian Churches.*[106] After studying over 1,000 parishes in large metropolitan areas in 1958, Long concluded that only 26.6 per cent included members of a "minority group" (not necessarily Negro). Roughly 70 per cent of these urban parishes reported they had never confronted a situation of possible minority group membership. But at least in the midwest, over half the lay respondents could point to exceptions in the announced policy of open hospitality across racial and minority group lines. Many qualitative comments from lay members suggested that ministers were often far more willing to pursue integration in the wider community than in their own parishes. And yet it would be a mistake to leap to the conclusion that ministers are solely or even primarily responsible for the dragging of churchly heels.

A recent study of Episcopalians by Glock, Ringer, and Babbie notes that the percentage who feel that "people of different races should have their own parish churches" is 10 per cent among Episcopalian Bishops, 9 per cent among Episcopalian priests, and fully 27 per cent among Episcopalian parishioners.[107] And Yoshio Fukuyama has recently surveyed the parishioners of the merged United Church of Christ in similar detail.[108] Thus, the percentage who would admit Negroes to "my church as members" declines from 78 per cent among those under thirty years old, to 77 per cent for those between thirty and forty-four, 70 per cent for the age group between forty-five and fifty-nine, and to 55 per cent for those sixty and over. Roughly 50 per cent of Fuku-yama's white parishioners agreed that "Negroes are happier in Negro churches and Negro schools." (This is contrasted to only 8 per cent of the Negro parishioners in his sample.) Like countless other studies, this one finds a consistent correlation[109] between anti-Negro sentiment and the orthodoxy of religious beliefs. It is probably true that these attitudinal studies of parishioners indicate greater hypothetical receptivity to Negro church members now than in the past. On the other hand, there is still a substantial pocket of opposition, and even a minority is apparently sufficient to exclude.

Suffice it to say then that the verbal invitations to black-white ecumenism from the top have not generally been accompanied by gracious hospitality at the bottom. The overwhelming majority of Negro church members continue to be members of Negro churches (predominantly Baptist with a large minority of Methodists). While it is true that the three separate Negro Methodist groups are now working towards a merger in 1972 and there is interdenominational cooperation among the Negro churches[110] as represented by the larger Fraternal Council of Churches, this must seem empty ecumenism indeed when compared to integration with white Protestants. Not surprisingly perhaps, it is the Roman Catholic Church whose Negro membership has increased most rapidly in the past quarter of a century. This increase is in no small measure due to the Catholic organizational structure, which allows its officials far more authority than the Protestants in outweighing the predilections of parishioners.

Protestant-Catholic Relations

But what about the relations between Protestants and Catholics themselves? The alternating current of Protestant-Catholic differences has been a major source of religious energy in this country since the nineteenth century. The alternating judgments concerning their persistence and attrition have been equally important in energizing scholarly debate. Certainly the issues are too complicated to be resolved in any brief summary. In particular, there seem to be at least three issues involved at three quite different levels. First, what is the past, present, and future state of Protestant-Catholic differences with respect to economic, educational, and family matters? These hoary differences trace back to

Weber's analysis linking the Protestant Reformation and the rise of capitalism.[111] Second, what are the trends in actual cooperation and dissociation among Protestant and Catholic laymen? Third, what is happening to the institutional relationships between Protestant and Catholic church organizations?

Perhaps the most provocative sociological prognosis for Protestant-Catholic tensions in the U.S. is found in Gerhard Lenski's book *The Religious Factor*. Lenski notes that the number of Catholics in the country has been increasing disproportionately to both Protestants and the population at large. He then cautiously predicts an increasing "compartmentalization" of the Protestant and Catholic camps with a result somewhat similar to the highly polarized religious structures of Holland and Lebanon. But Lenski's argument is not simply that Protestants and Catholics will retreat to neutral corners and bombard each other with contemptuous glances. He also argues that, if Catholicism continues to grow in relative strength, the following eventualities may occur as a result of Catholic influence:

1. Rising rates of church attendance in American Society;
2. Strengthening of socio-religious group communalism;
3. Strengthening of both nuclear and extended family systems;
4. Increase in intellectual heteronomy and decline in the importance attached to intellectual independence;
5. Increasing support for welfare state policies;
6. Increasing support for the Democratic Party;
7. Shifting focus of interest from work group to kin group;
8. Slowing rate of material progress, and perhaps also of scientific advance;
9. Rising birth rates;
10. Narrowing latitude for exercise of the right of free speech;
11. Increasing restraints on Sunday business and divorce, and possibly birth control;
12. Declining restraints on gambling and drinking.[112]

This is a list of possibilities to be reckoned with morally, politically, and perhaps most important, methodologically. Lenski's logic involves an extrapolation from the traditional position of the Catholic Church to its parishioners and then to the country as a whole. But this is risky, as Lenski himself might admit with the opportunity of hindsight over the events that have occurred in Catholicism since his book was published in 1961. There are, to be sure, continued points of friction between the Catholic Church and other religious groups, especially evident in the church-state arena with issues such as state aid to parochial schools, Bible reading in the schools, birth control, divorce, and abortion. On the other hand, Catholic officialdom is undergoing changes on some of these issues. But even if the winds of change should dissipate within the Catholic church structure, there is evidence that Catholics are changing anyway as individuals. Moreover, the changes involved seem to point in increasingly Protestant (or at least "secular") directions, suggesting a lay ecumenism of attitudes and behavior, quite apart from any formal union, or more properly, "reunion." And yet methodological vagaries appear here as well.

Consider the realm of fertility and birth control itself. If one had asked about trends in Catholic-Protestant fertility differentials a decade ago, many social scientists would have described a convergence since the 1940's. But a number of changes in the mid-1950's compelled revision of such trend analyses. Perhaps partly because of increased affluence encouraging more children for lower-status couples and partly because of earlier marriages and longer childbearing periods, Catholic fertility took a turn upwards relative to Protestants. Because the increase was more pronounced among practicing than nonpracticing Catholics, it suggests an intrinsically religious effect. Indeed, Freedman, Goldberg, and Slesinger note that the increase in birth *expectations* for the general population between 1955 and 1962 "was produced entirely by the Catholic population and in particular by the regular church-going Catholics."[113] Table 16 presents the 1962 differentials between Catholics and non-Catholics for both births and expected children in the white population. Note that it is important to control for race, since otherwise the high fertility of the dominantly Protestant Negroes would produce an artificial closure with the Catholics. Note too that the religious differences persist despite controls for education, income, wife working, and farm background. While one might also control for ethnicity (e.g., Irish Catholics have higher birth rates than Italian Catholics) and for Protestant denomination (Baptists tend to have especially high rates, even among whites alone), there was a virtual consensus among demographers as late as 1965 that the Protestant-Catholic fertility differential was real and possibly even increasing.

But more recent evidence suggests yet another reversal and perhaps the beginning of a long-term narrowing of the gap. In 1965, Charles Westoff and Norman Ryder collected a third set of data in the Growth of American Families series, data that were explicitly comparative with the earlier studies of 1960 and 1955.[114] Certainly the most remarkable aspect of the Westoff and Ryder study concerns changing patterns of

TABLE 16. MEAN NUMBER OF LIVE AND EXPECTED BIRTHS BY SELECTED SOCIAL AND ECONOMIC CHARACTERISTICS FOR CATHOLICS AND NON-CATHOLICS FOR THE WHITE POPULATION, 1962

Selected characteristics	Catholics			Non-Catholics		
	Live births	Expected births	(N)	Live births	Expected births	(N)
Husband's education						
under 12 years	3.0	3.8	115	2.6	3.1	284
12 years	2.6	4.0	69	2.0	2.8	193
over 12 years	2.7	4.0	140	2.0	2.8	427
Wife's education						
under 12 years	3.2	3.8	96	2.6	3.1	270
12 years	2.7	3.8	134	2.0	2.8	325
over 12 years	2.5	4.1	91	2.0	2.8	308
Family income						
under $6,000	2.8	4.0	142	2.1	2.9	358
$6,000 and over	2.8	3.9	176	2.3	2.9	535
Years wife worked since marriage						
0	3.2	4.4	96	2.3	3.2	237
1–4	2.7	4.0	165	2.2	3.0	447
5+	2.6	3.0	45	2.0	2.4	192
Couple's farm background						
some	2.9	4.2	109	2.2	2.9	550
none	2.7	3.8	215	2.2	2.9	362
Total	*2.8*	*3.9*	*324*	*2.2*	*2.9*	*912*

SOURCE: Freedman, Ronald, David Goldberg, and Doris Slesinger, "Current Fertility Expectations of Married Couples in the United States," *Population Index,* vol. 29, October, 1963, p. 384.

contraception, and the changes are especially marked among Catholics themselves. Table 17, for example, presents data for the three years on the percentage of Catholics who report conformity to the position of the Church on birth control, i.e., the percentage who use rhythm alone. Not only does the conformity drop off steadily, but this decrease occurs among both frequent and infrequent church attenders. Although space precludes it, further data from the Westoff and Ryder research might also be included to show, for example, that the changes in contraceptive practices have been particularly marked among younger Catholics and those with greater education. Clearly a cohort view of the phenomenon is instructive. One might very well expect a fertility convergence as older cohorts are replaced by younger. This convergence did not show up in the 1962 data on expected and actual

TABLE 17. PERCENTAGE OF CATHOLIC WOMEN CONFORM-
ING TO CATHOLIC DOCTRINE ON CONTRACEPTION BY
FREQUENCY OF CHURCH ATTENDANCE:
1955, 1960, AND 1965

Year and frequency[a] of church attendance	All Catholic Women	
	Number of women	Total conformed
Total		
1955	787	70
1960	668	62
1965	843	47
Regular		
1955	533	78
1960	525	69
1965	607	56
Less frequent		
1955	254	53
1960	143	35
1965	236	26

[a] "Regular" means "regularly" in the 1955 and "once a week" in the 1960 survey to questions on the frequency of attendance at religious services. In the 1965 survey the category means "once a week or more" to a question on attendance at Mass. Percentages for 1955 and 1960 adapted from Whelpton, Pascal, et al., *Fertility and Family Planning in the United States,* Princeton University Press, Princeton, N.J., 1966, p. 285.

SOURCE: Westoff, Charles F., and Norman B. Ryder, "United States: Methods of Fertility Control, 1955, 1960 and 1965," *Studies in Family Planning,* vol. 17, February, 1967, p. 5.

birth rates partly because the contraceptive revolution was only just beginning,[115] and partly because the younger cohorts were relatively small and still working on their first and second children while the crucial variance only begins to emerge with the third. Extrapolation is risky in demography or any other area; still, today more than ever before, the cards seem stacked for a growing convergence of Catholic-Protestant fertility patterns.

These findings for fertility and birth control carry two important implications for Lenski's argument. First, they suggest that the crucial condition behind the argument—that Catholics should continue to increase disproportionately—may be less and less the case. Second, they suggest that other Protestant-Catholic differences are declining as well. For example, the decreasing contraceptive gap may be partially a function of a decreasing status gap. Recently Glenn and Hyland have published data which support the inference.[116] Comparing a 1943 survey conducted by the National Opinion Research Center and four 1963

TABLE 18. PERCENTAGE DISTRIBUTION OF WHITE
RESPONDENTS BY ECONOMIC LEVEL TO A 1943 NORC
SURVEY AND TO FOUR RECENT GALLUP POLLS, BY
RELIGIOUS PREFERENCE

	1943 NORC SURVEY[a]			
Economic level[b]	Protestants	Catholics	Jews	Total
	(percentages)			
Upper	26.3	21.6	50.0	25.9
Middle	51.4	48.1	41.2	50.2
Lower	22.3	30.2	8.8	23.9
	100.0	100.0	100.0	100.0
Number of respondents	1,638	485	67	2,190

	FOUR RECENT GALLUP POLLS (DECEMBER, 1963, TO MARCH, 1965)			
Economic level[b]	Protestants	Catholics	Jews	Total
	(percentages)			
Upper	35.9	41.0	58.0	37.8
Middle	41.5	43.3	26.7	41.5
Lower	22.7	15.6	15.3	20.7
	100.0	100.0	100.0	100.0
Number of respondents	8,660	2,884	435	12,209

[a] The original 1943 NORC data give religious identification for church members only. The nonmembers had lower average status than the members; they were allocated between the Protestants and Catholics on the basis of information on church membership from a 1945 Gallup poll. Jewish members and nonmembers do not differ appreciably in economic status; therefore the 1943 Jewish data presented here are for members only.

[b] The respondents to the 1943 NORC Survey were divided into four economic levels largely on the basis of rent, or, if they were homeowners, estimated rental value of home. Here the two upper levels are combined into one. The Gallup respondents were divided into economic levels on the basis of income data. The upper level starts at $7,000 and the lower level is below $3,000.

SOURCE: Glenn, Norval D., and Ruth Hyland, "Religious Preference and Worldly Success: Some Evidence From National Surveys," *American Sociological Review,* vol. 32, February, 1967, p. 75.

Gallup Polls, they find that, if anything, the status comparisons between the two religious groups have reversed. Table 18 presents the findings, but again there are necessary qualifications somewhat similar to those entered above. Catholics *should* rank higher in status because they are more concentrated in urban, metropolitan areas with greater opportunity. Therefore, they may be religiously disadvantaged in that they do not rank even higher. And yet one must not conclude too quickly that Catholicism is itself a status depressant. Certainly the Catholics have been catching up; moreover, any real obstacles may relate more to ethnicity, low parental status, and consequently disadvantaged educational careers.

This, of course, moves us into the methodological hornets' nest of Catholic-Protestant differences in economic and educational aspirations and achievements. Here the legacy of Max Weber is both imposing and ironic. It is imposing because sociologists have continued to seek out in the twentieth century the kinds of religious differences that Weber advanced for the sixteenth and seventeenth centuries. But it is also ironic because Weber was careful to qualify his assertions concerning early religious differences and even went out of his way to indicate that these differences would give way before the pervasive force of the capitalist ethic itself.[117] In short, many recent sociologists have been looking for a needle that Weber himself had removed from the haystack. As Glenn and Hyland put it after their very careful review of old and new data on the topic:

> This study shows that the effects of any Protestantism and Catholicism on income, occupation, and education explains at best only a small fraction of the variance. Our analysis provides no conclusive answer to the question that has commanded so much sociological attention in recent years, but it suggests that arriving at a more nearly conclusive answer is not very important.[118]

This is not the place for a thorough review of the literature on Protestant-Catholic differences. Suffice it to say that Glenn and Hyland's analysis of status differences is paralleled by findings on other issues elsewhere. For example, Leonard Broom and Norval Glenn explored a host of attitudes on matters as diverse as international politics, premarital sex, general happiness, and approval of women wearing Bermuda shorts on the streets.[119] They find that there are few differences between Catholics and Protestants that are not either small or totally lacking after controls for region of the country and community size; presumably still other controls such as ethnicity, parental status, etc. would reduce the remaining differences even further. Indeed, it was the failure to provide a control for ethnicity that damaged the credibility of Lenski's earlier findings on the differences between Protestants and Catholics in Detroit. Many observers have pointed out that Detroit Catholics are primarily Polish in background, and that Poles generally have tended to lag behind other Catholic immigrant groups in acculturation and status mobility. The point, however, is not that Lenski was wrong while his critics are right. Rather it is increasingly difficult to make an unassailable case for major differences between Catholics and Protestants in the general population. According to methodological justice, one is guilty until proven innocent; and proof of any intrinsically religious difference is increasingly hard to come by.

One reason for this may concern convergent Protestant-Catholic socialization patterns for the young. A number of recent studies have focused on differences among Protestant and Catholic youth, and especially on differences attributable to public versus parochial education. Thus, Bressler and Westoff find no significant differences in the economic values and achievements of Catholic youth who attended parochial versus public elementary schools, high schools, and colleges.[120] Andrew Greeley finds no evidence of intellectual impoverishment among Catholic college seniors, even seniors in parochial colleges, when compared to Protestant seniors in an NORC sample of 40,000.[121] And Greeley and Rossi extend the thesis in studying Catholic adults who have been exposed to different types of schooling.[122] These findings may help to explain why many other studies find that any differences that continue to occur between Catholics and Protestants are smaller for young adults than old. While it is possible to argue that young adults will ultimately be socialized into the patterns of the old, it is perhaps more likely that the youth of today bodes well for the ecumenism of tomorrow.

And yet so far I have presented very little evidence of any actual ecumenism in the sense of greater contact and cooperation between Catholics and Protestants. Let us now consider one measure that may be revealing. J. Milton Yinger argues that interfaith marriage "can well be considered the most sensitive index of the extent of separation across religious lines."[123] He also provides a sophisticated summary of its trends over time. For example, Ruby Jo Kennedy's work in New Haven[124] indicates that the rate of interfaith marriages among Catholics increased from 5 per cent in 1870 to 16 per cent in 1940, and then to 30 per cent by 1950. These local data jibe well with John Thomas's conclusions from the 1950 national *Catholic Directory:* 30 per cent of all marriages involving a Catholic also involved a member of a non-Catholic faith—predominantly Protestant.[125] And using the data collected in the 1957 special Census study of religion, Paul Glick finds that the Catholic rate of mixed marriage was slightly more than one-fourth of the interfaith marriages that would be expected if religion were not a factor and marriage depended solely on population distribution.[126] Yinger argues that such figures probably underestimate the actual amount of intermarriage. Thus, they fail to count those marriages in which there is a change in religion on the part of one or both spouses after marriage so that homogeneity appears as the tabular result. For example, Lenski's Detroit study indicated that 32 per cent of Catholic marriages were originally interfaith, but only 15 per cent of the couples were religiously mixed at the time of the actual interview.[127] Yinger also points out that the Protestant intermarriage rate is low for whites because the figures include Negroes, who are vastly underrepresented in non-Protestant groups and have such low rates of *interracial* marriage.

But lest we overestimate the trend and its import, let us consider some qualifications as well. For example, how stable are interreligious marriages as measured by divorce rates? Clark Vincent cites three recent studies conducted in Maryland, Michigan, and Washington with combined cases of more than 24,000 marriages.[128] The rate of divorce was 5 per cent for all-Catholic marriages, 8 per cent for all-Protestant marriages, but 15 per cent for mixed Catholic-Protestant marriages. Even here, however, there are problems of interpretation. A substantially greater proportion of all-Catholic marriages end in annulment rather than divorce. One would surely expect divorce to underestimate instability and dissatisfaction in all-Catholic marriages, because of the strictures and stigma against divorce within the Church. And it may be that a substantial proportion of the religiously homogeneous marriages were heterogeneous until courtship resulted in conversion.

A more important caution concerning the trend in marriage also applies to most of the other analyses of Protestant-Catholic differences cited. That is, the data are based on broad religious preferences and do not typically take gradations of religious involvement into account. It may be that the rise in mixed marriages and the decline of Protestant-Catholic educational, economic, and fertility differences are all accounted for by a decline in religious commitment in the population at large; if true, these statistics may say little about trends within the churches themselves. Although a decline in particularistic commitment may augur well for increasing informal ecumenism at the level of lay attitudes and behavior, ecumenism is much more problematic at the level of the churches as organizations. Of course, one obstacle here has been the international authority of Catholicism and the consequent difficulty of contriving a distinctively American reunion. And yet there is some sign that this authority is beginning to give way in a process of decentralization. Paradoxically, one of the major products of the council of unity at Vatican II was a trend toward a more Protestant differentiation in which national churches obtained greater autonomy and in which local Bishops and priests gained independence not only from Rome and the Papacy but from each other. Though any formal Protestant-Catholic merger is no doubt very distant, it is becoming imaginable. In fact, American Protestantism and Catholicism may attain general solidarity before either sees an end to their internal hostilities, between the Irish, Italians, and the Poles among the Catholics, and between Negroes and whites among the Protestants.

The Prevalence of Anti-Semitism

Finally, let us consider the trends and prospects for ecumenism beyond the Christian community and specifically with the Jews. There is no doubt that Judaism deserves far more attention than it has received so far in this report. Its distinctiveness defies thorough treatment in a discussion heavily oriented to Protestantism as a more reliable indicator of Amercian religion generally. Ironically, part of the Jews' distinctiveness smacks of the Weberian version of Protestantism itself. Many of the foregoing studies of religious differences note that Jews are not only more different from Protestants and Catholics than either are from each other, but also that Jews are the statistical embodiment of an emphasis on educational -and scientific rationality, economic aspiration and achievement, and rational family planning. Of course, none of this necessarily implies specifically "secular" religious effects of Judaism itself. Indeed, many observers have pointed to the increase of secular Judaism in this century, reflecting changes in status, ethnicity, and educational patterns. Unhappily, most research on the Jews makes no differentiation within the category. Thus, we are left without knowledge of the particular attributes of Orthodox, Conservative, Reform, and areligious Jews.

But this section is explicitly devoted to ecumenism. While no formal mergers compel attention, there are two sorts of data available on informal patterns of solidarity and cleavage: first, trends in intermarriage; second, trends in anti-Semitism. It is indisputable that Jews have considerably lower rates of interfaith marriage than either Catholics or Protestants. According to the 1957 special census of religion, only 7.2 per cent of Jews were married to non-Jews (4.2 per cent to Protestants; 3.0 per cent to Catholics) as compared to 8.6 per cent of Protestants and 21.6 per cent of Catholics.[129] While the Jewish and the Protestant rates seem similar, note that Protestants *should* have a very low rate of intermarriage because of their population dominance, but by the same logic, Jews *should* have a very high rate of intermarriage because of their underrepresentation. Put more precisely, if religion played no role at all in mate selection, only 4 per cent of Jewish marriages would be *intra*-faith, in contrast to the 92.8 per cent that is revealed in the census figures.

Despite the national endogamy of Jews, there is a great deal of variation in smaller studies of specific localities. For example, Kennedy's work in New Haven indicates that Jewish intermarriages increased from 0 per cent in 1870 to 6 per cent in 1940, although there was a subsequent drop-off to 4 per cent by 1950. While the last figure is reasonably close to a 7 per cent figure reported for New Orleans Jews in 1953 by Goldman and Chenkin,[130] both figures seem low relative to those cited for other areas. Rosenthal reports percentages for various years between 1953 and 1959 that range from 11.5 per cent in Washington to 17.2 per cent in San Francisco and 31 per cent in Iowa.[131] And Heiss finds an intermarriage rate of 18.4 per cent for Manhattan in 1954.[132] But note that there are problems of comparability. The earlier estimates for the U.S. at large, New Haven, and New Orleans are undoubtedly low, since they count only marriages in which the partners have retained their separate religious affiliations while ignoring those in which there has been a conversion after the marriage itself. By contrast, the studies by Heiss and Rosenthal look at either the spouses' religious background or their faith at marriage.

It is difficult to assess *changing* intermarriage rates for Jews. There are no national data over time, and the local data are subject to enormous variation, partly through methodological discrepancies and partly because intermarriage rates tend to be higher in those areas where small Jewish subcommunities are less able to sustain endogamy. While there has no doubt been a slight rise over time, intermarriage is still rare among Jews. This parallels the findings of various other studies on the rate of Jewish participation with gentiles generally in this country, studies well summarized by Milton Gordon.[133] To borrow the title from Rosenthal's article, Jewish life in America may well represent "acculturation without assimilation." As Gordon, Glazer, and Moynihan,[134] and others have indicated, we have consistently tended to overestimate the effects of the "melting pot."

It is no doubt true that many Jews choose not to assimilate, but this by no means exhausts the explanation. Anti-Semitism has long been a virulent factor in American society and religion; it is a force that must be reckoned with in any assessment of ecumenism itself. Recently, Charles Herbert Stember conducted a thorough analysis of our changing patterns of anti-Semitism for the American Jewish Committee.

After sifting through a mass of public opinion polls and other evidence, he concludes rather hopefully:

> Anti-Jewish prejudice obviously is not yet a thing of the past, any more than anti-Jewish discrimination is, but both are unmistakably in a state of decline. As we have seen, hostile attitudes toward Jews are finding less widespread support in the 1960's than at any other time since the systematic study of public attitudes began. Actual discriminatory practices also have lessened to a marked degree during that period, so that we probably are safe in asserting that prejudice and discrimination to-day are not prevalent enough to reinforce or perpetuate each other significantly, as they formerly did. In both feeling and behavior toward Jews, our society has undergone a profound change within the span of one generation.[135]

Most of Stember's data refer to the attitudes and hypothetical practices of national samples of non-Jews, but he also offers several specific comparisons over time for Protestants and Catholics. Table 19 presents comparisons on nine issues for time periods that range from 1939–1962 to 1946–1962. Both religious groups show a decline in attitudinal anti-Semitism on every item, though Catholics seem to have undergone a greater decrease and seem to be less prejudiced as of 1962. Of course, there are also methodological problems here. The link between attitudes and behavior is always problematic. More important, one must be wary of overgeneralizing to either Protestants or Catholics, since differences of status, ethnicity, levels of involvement, and subaffiliation are factors in both groups. Finally, there are problems of comparability over time as well, since the 1962 data are based on nominal religious preference, while the early polls use actual church membership as the religious criterion. Stember is aware of this, but he defends the comparisons on the grounds that "we have no evidence that the church members of the early polls differed in any significant way from the church adherents represented in the 1962 study, as far as attitudes towards Jews were concerned." Actually there are several plausible sources of suspicion. For one thing, because formal church membership is directly related to social class, and because anti-Semitism is inversely related to social class, a comparison of church members at one time with token identifiers at a later time may underestimate the decline in prejudice. One could also argue that church members tend more often to be "believers" than do nominal affiliators; and there are a host of findings that indicate direct relationships between orthodox beliefs and authoritarianism generally. By this logic, the tables may over-

TABLE 19.   PROTESTANTS' AND CATHOLICS' RESPONSES
TO ITEMS REFLECTING ANTI-SEMITISM, 1939–1962[a]

Belief items	Year	Per cent Protestants	Catholics
Think Jewish businessmen less			
honest than others	1939	52	53
	1962	22	15
Think Jews tend to be more			
radical than others	1939	32	42
	1962	26	22
Would tend to vote for anti-Semitic			
Congressional candidate	1940	15	18
	1962	4	5
Think Jews generally have			
objectionable qualities	1940	66	61
	1962	25	23
Think Jews have too much power in			
the United States	1940	51	54
	1962	21	20
Would mind a Jewish neighbor	1940	27	26
	1962	3	1
Would mind a Jewish employee	1940	39	32
	1962	7	4
Think Jews are a threat to America	1946	14	15
	1962	3	5
Think of Jews as a race	1946	36	42
	1962	31	32
Number of cases		1,860–2,315	557–781

[a] Other religions and "no religion" excluded.

SOURCE: Stember, Charles, et al., Jews in the Mind of America, Basic Books, New York, 1966, p. 228.

estimate the decline of prejudice within the churches by comparing a high starting point with an artificially low end point.

To understand the dynamics of anti-Semitism within the churches themselves, we need more detailed causal studies of contemporary church members and their prejudices. Fortunately, one is available in the recent book by Glock and Stark, Christian Beliefs and Anti-Semitism.[136] The authors were frankly unprepared for the magnitude of anti-Semitism uncovered. But they posit a causal chain as follows: orthodoxy in Christian beliefs often leads to religious particularism (the tendency to see one's own beliefs as the *only* truth); particularism, in turn, leads to *hostility* against those who reject the view; this hostility is especially great toward a group whose identity is largely sustained on the basis of such rejection. Thus, the Jews provoke special enmity not only by their participation in the Crucifixion but also by their continued refusal to seek atonement through conversion. Table 20 offers

TABLE 20.   ORTHODOXY, PARTICULARISM, AND JEWISH GUILT AMONG A SAMPLE OF CHURCH MEMBERS IN THE SAN FRANCISCO BAY AREA

(PER CENT WHO AGREED: "THE JEWS CAN NEVER BE FORGIVEN FOR WHAT THEY DID TO JESUS UNTIL THEY ACCEPT HIM AS THE TRUE SAVIOR.")

Rank on Particularism Index	Orthodoxy Index		
	High	Medium	Low
Protestants			
High			
per cent	77	42	29
number	(360)	(183)	(52)
Medium			
per cent	63	20	8
number	(219)	(403)	(235)
Low			
per cent	13	5	1
number	(24)	(131)	(280)
Catholics			
High			
per cent	33	10	a
number	(105)	(30)	(9)
Medium			
per cent	13	6	0
number	(135)	(66)	(25)
Low			
per cent	5	0	0
number	(19)	(17)	(29)

ᵃ Too few cases for stable percentage.

SOURCE: Glock, Charles Y., and Rodney Stark, *Christian Beliefs and Anti-Semitism,* Harper & Row, New York, 1966, p. 66.

empirical support. Indexes of orthodoxy and particularism are related to agreement with the statement, "The Jews can never be forgiven for what they did to Jesus until they accept Him as the True Savior." The percentage differences are plainly remarkable in all directions. While the relationships even so may be inadequate to support the *causal* interpretation given them, it appears that Christianity, at least at the level of individual doctrinal interpretations, is hardly innocent of anti-Semitism. Clearly some substantial degree of prejudice continues, despite the best efforts of many church members and officials to combat it.

But there is also variation among Christian groups. Glock and Stark show denominational differences on an over-all index of anti-Semitism, reproduced here in Table 21. Our earlier concerns about generalizing to all Protestants seem well-founded. Thus, "high" anti-Semitism characterizes as few as 7 per cent among the Congregationalists and 9 per cent among the Methodists; but as many as 23 per cent for the Missouri Synod Lutherans, 24 per cent for Southern Baptists, and 26 per cent for members of fundamentalist sects. Note too that Table 21 supports both Stember's data and the findings in Table 20 in that Catholics have slightly lower rates of anti-Semitism than either Protestants generally or than eight of the ten specific Protestant denominations. Still, Glock and Stark estimated that more than five million American Catholics manifest an anti-Semitism buttressed by their views of church doctrine. A report to this effect was widely circulated in various languages during the deliberations at Vatican II and was probably helpful in producing the major change in Catholicism's doctrinal position with respect to the Jews.

In summary, this section has probed various aspects of American ecumenism, one of the most celebrated features of twentieth-century American religion. It is clear that ecumenism has been a mounting force, especially among the Protestants. But it is also clear that ecumenism neglects old problems and creates new ones. Hopefully future research will involve not only bigger and better tabulations of mergers and instances of cooperation but also closer examination of the differences between quantitative facade and the qualitative reality.

SUMMARY AND QUALIFICATIONS

Recently an Arizona prospector left an estate of $200,000 to go to the most promising scientific research proving the existence of the soul, preferably by photographing its release from the body at death. Some ninety-two proposals were entered at the opening court session, and I am myself led to wonder if such research might not be more feasible than any attempt to provide a definitive analysis of American religious change. But this report operated under two more specific mandates. On the one hand, it sought to pry beneath a number of commonly accepted axioms to indicate methodological problems of interpretation

TABLE 21. DENOMINATIONAL AFFILIATION AND CHRISTIAN ANTI-SEMITISM AMONG A SAMPLE OF SAN FRANCISCO BAY AREA CHURCH MEMBERS

Index of Anti-Semitic Beliefs[a]	Congregationalists	Methodists	Episcopalians	Disciples of Christ	Presbyterians	American Lutherans	American Baptists	Missouri Lutherans	Southern Baptists	Sects	Total Protestant	Catholic
						(percentages)						
High	7	9	12	21	18	19	12	23	24	26	15	11
Medium high	14	14	19	15	18	17	19	16	22	27	18	18
High and medium high	(21)	(23)	(31)	(36)	(36)	(36)	(31)	(39)	(46)	(53)	(33)	(29)
Medium	53	51	45	46	46	40	56	45	49	39	47	45
None	26	26	24	18	18	24	13	16	5	8	20	26
Total	100	100	100	100	100	100	100	100	100	100	100	100
Number	(115)	(297)	(305)	(33)	(353)	(140)	(104)	(81)	(55)	(159)	(1,645)	(409)

[a] Index includes only persons who responded to all six items.

SOURCE: Glock, Charles Y., and Rodney Stark, *Christian Beliefs and Anti-Semitism*, Harper & Row, New York, 1966, p. 129.

432

and inadequate data. On the other hand, it tried to offer new data and new formulations to highlight aspects of change hitherto neglected. In the first function, it was frequently critical of past efforts; in the latter respect, it is itself intended as a foil for future scholars.

I have defined the subject matter of religious change broadly on the assumption that religion is a multifaceted institution that requires multifaceted understanding. At times the report sacrifices depth for breadth, and the pursuit of breadth has had another consequence as well. This is very likely the most extensive sociological analysis of religious change in recent years, but for that very reason it may be the least conclusive. After examining phenomena as diverse as membership growth, religious beliefs, organizational differentiation, bureaucratization, and the various formal and informal aspects of ecumenism, the results may seem an empirical hodgepodge related by the most tenuous theory. Surely discretion militates against any quick summary or overarching interpretation.

For example, consider the thesis of increasing religiosity. It is true that many statistics seem to indicate an extraordinary surge of formal religious participation in the last century. But it is also true that these same statistics are methodologically vulnerable, especially in the case of church-collected membership data. It is more than merely possible that there has been a proportional *decline* in participation, once these biases are taken into account. At the very least, one must restrict growth to certain time periods, noting that if the churches seemed to flourish between the mid-1940's and mid-1950's, they seem to have undergone a decline since the early 1960's.

But just as important as such quantitative matters are the qualitative changes that accompany them. There is some evidence that religious belief is losing in both orthodoxy and saliency, though one must be careful even here. Whatever the "death of God" means to theologians, it is hardly universally acknowledged among the citizenry at large. Indeed, the phrase may signify more concerning changes in the organizational contexts of professional churchmen than changes in the laity itself. The current stridency among many clergymen and religious officials is both cause and consequence of important organizational processes underway throughout American religion. The twin tendencies toward differentiation and bureaucratization are not only important within denominations, but they are also implicated in the relations between denominations. Ecumenism is perhaps the most distinctive aspect of twentieth-century American religion, but even so conspicuous gaps remain at both the institutional and interpersonal levels.

Throughout we have seen the danger of allowing facile judgments to masquerade as detailed investigations; at times I have lapsed into speculation to sustain an argument where evidence is lacking. But it cannot be overemphasized that the enthusiasm for generalization often represents a misplaced zeal that would be better spent in rectifying the persistent problems of inadequate data and spurious interpretation. Methodologists may be theoretically meek, but for that reason alone, they may inherit the earth.

Finally, there is the nagging but always legitimate question, "So what?" Even if one could discern unequivocal trends toward the increasing or decreasing well-being of religion, any inference to the well-being of society itself would be precarious. Indeed, the changing nature of American religion may be less important to society now than it was a century ago. I am myself persuaded that society as a whole is undergoing an institutional differentiation under which traditional religion is increasingly autonomous but decreasingly relevant. No longer is religion inextricably woven into a close-knit institutional fabric so that it must act and react in conjunction with economic, educational, political, and other agencies. Religion seems to have developed a niche of its own. On the one hand, this means that it has more freedom; on the other hand, it may involve less import.[137] Thus, churchmen can speak out more readily and more radically precisely because their judgments are less urgent and less listened to in centers of authority; even the church's veto power over societal affairs is now crumbling both by choice and by circumstance.

And yet this line of argument can obviously be carried too far. Variables such as autonomy, urgency, and influence are extremely difficult to measure at the level of a total society.[138] Moreover, to say that religion is losing influence is not to say that it has lost it altogether. Clearly religion is still a force to be reckoned with. But we can reckon with it better if we apply the same standards for evidence and interpretation that we apply to other institutions. Insofar as *this* is a trend among students of religion it bodes well for the future. Not only will it aid us in understanding religious change itself, but it is possible that what is learned for religion will be increasingly applicable to other institutions as well.

NOTES

1. Dorchester, Daniel, *Christianity in the United States From the First Settlement Down to the Present Time*. Phillips and Hunt, New York, 1888, p. 742.

2. Later I shall comment on the increasing importance of the religious "numbers game" in interdenominational competition. Here it is interesting to note the use of decimals for the last two entries in Table 1. It is possible, of course, that such exact figures are only recently available. But this is surely specious precision, and one must wonder whether the decimals are not used to suggest more of an increase than would be indicated by the rounded figures.

3. Carroll, Henry K., *The Religious Forces of the United States Enumerated, Classified, and Described on the Basis of the Government Census of 1890.* The Christian Literature Co., New York, 1893.

4. Actually earlier nineteenth-century church membership figures were computed as a ratio of religious preference figures. See Baird, Rev. Robert, *Religion in America.* Harper and Brothers, New York, 1856. For minor variations in subsequent policy concerning membership counts, see p. 368 of this chapter.

5. Lipset, S. M., *The First New Nation.* Basic Books, New York, 1963, pp. 147–148. Lipset's chapter on religion in this volume is an elaboration of his earlier argument, "Religion in America: What Religious Revival?" *Columbia University Forum,* vol. 2, Winter, 1959. In both instances, Lipset argues that there is no good evidence of any substantial change in the rate or tone of religious practice. This is, of course, in response to the substantial literature arguing the case for a religious revival, especially Herberg, Will, *Protestant, Catholic, Jew,* Doubleday, Garden City, 1955, pp. 59–84. For a position that mediates between Lipset and Herberg, see Glock, Charles Y., "The Religious Revival in America?" in Zahn, Jane C., editor, *Religion and the Face of America,* University Extension, University of California, 1959, Berkeley, pp. 25–42. Glock delineates four (later five) dimensions of religiosity and argues that revival may have occurred in one while decline may characterize another. Thus, *behavioral* participation may have increased, while *doctrinal* orthodoxy may have decreased.

6. Douglass, Truman B., "Ecological Changes and the Church," *The Annals of the American Academy of Political and Social Science,* vol. 332, November, 1960, pp. 80–88. Note that this problem would not be so severe if all denominations had made the shift at once, or even if all denominations had proclaimed their shifts when they occurred. As it is, the source of error is left dangling and difficult to control for in precise terms. And yet it would be improper to imply that the collectors of church statistics have been unaware of this and other problems to follow. See, for example, Landis, Benson Y., "Confessions of a Church Statistician," *National Council Outlook,* vol. 7, February, 1957.

7. Argyle, Michael, *Religious Behavior.* The Free Press, Glencoe, 1959, esp. pp. 28–38.

8. Hudson, Winthrop S., "Are Churches Really Booming?" *The Christian Century,* vol. 72, 1955, pp. 1494–1496. For the Catholic case, see Mulvaney, B. G., "Catholic Population Revealed in Catholic Baptisms," *American Ecclesiastical Review,* vol. 133, 1955, pp. 183–193.

9. Lipset, S. M., *First New Nation, op. cit.,* p. 145.

10. In addition to the shift from parish to parish within the same denomination, mobility has probably also been a factor in shifts from one denomination to another. In a good discussion of this point, David O. Moberg points out that the "typical Protestant Church grows more by transfer of members than by evangelism (transforming people into church members for the first time)." See Moberg, David O., *The Church as a Social Institution.* Prentice-Hall, Inc., Englewood-Cliffs, N.J., 1962, pp. 253–254. And, in a similar vein, Clark E. Vincent notes that interfaith marriage is an increasing inflationary factor in membership rolls, since converted spouses

are often carried on the rolls of both the original and the new denomination. See Vincent, Clark E., "Interfaith Marriages," in Raab, Earl, editor, *Religious Conflict in America,* Doubleday Anchor Books, Garden City, 1964, p. 51.

11. Smith, T. Lynn, *Population Analysis.* McGraw-Hill, New York, 1948, p. 178.

12. "Religion Reported by the Civilian Population of the United States, March, 1957," *Current Population Reports,* U.S. Bureau of Census, Series P-20, No. 79, Washington, February 2, 1958.

13. Wolf, Richard C., "1900–1950 Survey: Religious Trends in the United States," *Christianity Today,* April 27, 1959, pp. 3–5.

14. Hudson, Winthrop S., *op. cit.*

15. Trimble, Glen, unpublished manuscript, Research Division, National Council of Churches, February, 1967.

16. Baltzell, E. Digby, *Philadelphia Gentlemen.* The Free Press, New York, 1958, pp. 246–261.

17. Yinger, J. Milton, *Sociology Looks at Religion.* Macmillan, New York, 1963, p. 28.

18. Douglass, Truman B., *op. cit.,* p. 86.

19. For a critique of church membership as a measure of religiosity, see Demerath, N. J. III, *Social Class in American Protestantism.* Rand McNally, Chicago, 1965, pp. 8–10; and Goode, Erich, "Some Critical Observations on the Church-Sect Dimension," *Journal for the Scientific Study of Religion,* Spring, 1967, together with my rejoinder in the same issue, "In a Sow's Ear."

20. *Yearbook of American Churches for 1967,* National Council of Churches of Christ in the U.S.A., p. 224.

21. For a thorough if somewhat dated analysis of changing patterns of church finances and church construction, see the work by C. Luther Fry, particularly his *The U.S. Looks at Its Churches,* Institute of Social and Religious Research, New York, 1930, and his chapter on "Changes in Religious Organizations," in *Recent Social Trends,* McGraw-Hill, New York, 1933, pp. 1009–1060. Of course, it is highly questionable whether church finances are reliable as a measure of religious worth. Indeed, as we shall see later, a number of churchmen have begun to argue that the two are negatively instead of positively related. Both the state of church finances and the scholarly use of them may involve a certain opportunism.

22. Lipset, S. M., "Religion in America: What Religious Revival?" *op. cit.* One might ask how the value of church construction can increase, while per capita donations do not. The answers are several. First, the greater absolute numbers of church members means more money despite a drop in average individual donations. Second, the churches are well-known for their sound financial investments, and many are still living handsomely off of funds collected earlier. Third, I have already noted that part of the seeming increase in the value of construction lies in inflation itself, a factor that is not so crucial to per capita donation figures.

23. Fix, Oliver W., "Is Giving Predictable?" Paper delivered at the annual meeting of the Section on Stewardship and Benevolence, National Council of Churches, December, 1966, p. 25. Actually it is interesting to compare Fix's dire warnings of the dangers of too little money with the equally dire warnings of others, such as James Pike, Eugene Carson Blake, and John Dillenberger, on the dangers of too much money. The difference between the two positions is largely reflective of different organizational roles. That such roles should be so different within the church structure is an important observation.

24. Lee, Alfred McClung, "The Press and Public Relations of Religious Bodies," *The Annals of the American Academy of Political and Social Science,* vol. 256, March, 1948, p. 121.

25. Klausner, Samuel Z., *Psychiatry and Religion,* Free Press, New York, 1964, p. 21.

26. Hart, Hornell, "Changing Social Attitudes and Interests," chap. 8 in *Recent Social Trends, op. cit.,* and "Religion," *American Journal of Sociology,* vol. 47, 1941, pp. 888–897.

27. Argyle, Michael, *op. cit.,* pp. 6–7.

28. Demerath, N. J. III, *Social Class in American Protestantism, op. cit.,* pp. 10–14ff.

29. I am indebted to Jeffrey K. Hadden for permission to use this finding and other data to be seen later. Hadden's study of the beliefs and attitudes of the Protestant ministry on a host of issues bids fair to become a landmark. Certainly his forthcoming book with Raymond Rymph on the ministry and the civil rights movement will be an important empirical addition to the all-too qualitative literature on the church and social change. Meanwhile, see his article, "A Protestant Paradox—Divided They Merge," *Trans-action,* vol. 4, July/August, 1967, pp. 63–69.

30. Good, Dorothy, "Questions on Religion in the United States Census," *Population Index,* vol. 25, January, 1959, pp. 3–16. For another excellent statement of this position, in addition to a general methodological critique of religious data, see Peterson, William, "Religious Statistics in the United States," *Journal of the Scientific Study of Religion,* vol. I, Spring, 1962, pp. 165–178.

31. Smith, T. Lynn, *op. cit.,* pp. 175–176.

32. Bogue, Donald, *The Population of the United States.* The Free Press, Glencoe, 1959, p. 688.

33. *Ibid.,* p. 709. Bogue originally was referring to the years 1970 and 1960 respectively, hence the parentheses in the quotation.

34. Towne, Anthony, *Motive,* February, 1966.

35. Herberg, Will, *op. cit.*

36. *Ibid.,* p. 270. For a very recent and extremely provocative statement of a similar position, see Bellah, Robert N., "Civil Religion in America," *Daedalus,* vol. 97, Winter, 1967, pp. 1–21.

37. Argyle, Michael, *op. cit.,* p. 34.

38. See the exchange between Pike and Hamilton in the January, 1967, *Playboy,* concerning Hamilton's statement of his own position in the preceding issue. Of course, "playboy religion" is a phenomenon worth studying in its own right. The number of ministers who write letters to the editor in praise of positions taken and articles printed may evidence change in the pulpit itself. On the other hand, a cynic might also speculate that some of these ministers are suffering in conventional pulpits and hope to use the letter to prompt a quick exit. Many have observed that as other institutions perform what were once religious functions, religious institutions reciprocate by meeting secular needs.

39. Cox, Harvey, *The Secular City.* Macmillan, New York, 1965, pp. 241–269.

40. And yet there is one recent approximation of such work, an empirical analysis of the changing social backgrounds of Catholic saints from the first to the twentieth centuries. See George, Katherine and Charles H., "Roman Catholic Sainthood and Social Status," *Journal of Religion,* vol. 5, 1953–55, pp. 33–35, revised for inclusion in Bendix, Reinhard and S. M. Lipset, editors, *Class, Status and Power,* 2nd edition, The Free Press, New York, 1966, pp. 394–401.

41. Marty, Martin E., *The Infidel: Freethought and American Religion.*

Meridian Books, New York, 1961. In fact, Marty uses the military analogue of Omar Bradley in noting that religion continued to fight "the wrong war at the wrong place, at the wrong time and with the wrong enemy" (p. 197).

42. See Cox, Harvey, *op. cit.*, pp. 246–248.

43. Demerath, N. J. III, and Richard M. Levinson, "Baiting the Dissident Hook: Some Effects of Bias in Measuring Religious Belief," unpublished paper, Department of Sociology, University of Wisconsin, 1968.

44. See Stouffer, Samuel A., *Communism, Conformity and Civil Liberties,* Doubleday, Garden City, 1955, for survey indications that 84 per cent of the public would ban the nonreligious from teaching posts at the college level, and 60 per cent favor removing all books "against religion" from their libraries. (Results cited in Rosenberg, Bernard, Israel Gerver, and F. William Howton, *Mass Society in Crisis,* Macmillan, New York, 1964, p. 528).

45. Glock, Charles Y., and Rodney Stark, *Christian Beliefs and Anti-Semitism.* Harper and Row, New York, 1966. For a more elaborate analysis of the beliefs of a sample of church members in the San Francisco Bay area, see Glock and Stark, *Religion and Society in Tension,* Rand McNally, Chicago, 1965, pp. 86–122.

46. For an excellent brief analysis of the changing theology of the Protestant sects, see McLoughlin, William G., "Is There a Third Force in Christendom?" *Daedalus,* vol. 96, Winter, 1967, pp. 43–68.

47. Lipset, S. M., *First New Nation, op. cit.,* p. 153.

48. *Ibid.,* p. 158.

49. Mencken, H. L., "The Hills of Zion," in Cooke, Alistair, editor, *The Vintage Mencken,* Vintage Books, New York, 1955, pp. 154, 161.

50. Leuba, James H., "Religious Beliefs of American Scientists," *Harper's Magazine,* vol. 169, 1934, as cited in Argyle, Michael, *op. cit.,* p. 31.

51. *Ibid.*

52. Jacob, Philip E., *Changing Values in College.* Harper and Brothers, New York, 1957, p. 108. Actually the Cornell study is only one of many that Jacob examined before concluding that the college has little effect at all in changing values. For a good methodological critique of this literature, see Barton, Allen H., *Studying the Effects of College Education,* The Hazen Foundation, New Haven, 1959.

53. These data refer to the study by myself and Levinson cited in footnote 43. Another colleague, Kenneth G. Lutterman, and I are now working on a larger study of student values and campus religious groups that includes not only the University of Wisconsin but four other strategically different midwestern campuses as well. Unfortunately, we have only begun to analyze the Wisconsin data at this point, and the evidence concerning belief in God raises even greater problems of comparability when compared to the Leuba and Cornell studies. Still, it is worth noting that of a sample of 1,288 undergraduates at the University of Wisconsin in 1965, only 34 per cent opted for the most traditional and literal statement concerning God: "I have faith in God as a person who is concerned about me and all mankind and to whom I am accountable." Interestingly enough, the variance in agreement for the members of particular campus religious groups ranges from 97 per cent of the Southern Baptists, to 81 per cent of the Catholics, 49 per cent of the Episcopalians, 26 per cent of the United Church of Christ, 14 per cent of Hillel, and 0 per cent of the Unitarians, to cite but a few. For a preliminary analysis of these and other data and their implications, see Demerath and Lutterman, "The Student Parishioner: Radical Rhetoric and Traditional Reality," paper delivered at the annual meeting of the American Sociological Association, San Francisco, 1967.

54. For the 1936 and 1944 results, see Cantril, Hadley, *Public Opinion, 1935–1946,* Princeton University Press, Princeton, 1951, p. 310. For the 1961 finding, see Rosten, Leo, editor, *Religions in America,* rev. edition, Simon and Schuster, New York, 1963, p. 320.

55. Schneider, Louis, and Sanford M. Dornbusch, *Popular Religion: Inspirational Books in America,* University of Chicago Press, Chicago, 1958, p. 56. For a somewhat similar analysis of trends in hymn content between 1836 and 1935, see Crawford, B. F., *Religious Trends in a Century of Hymns,* Carnegie Press, New York, 1938. Crawford finds that the theme of fear is replaced by love and gratitude, and that textual emphasis on traditional dogma declined, while there was increasing reference to the humanity of Jesus. Insofar as this parallels much of the change represented by the "new theology," it suggests that this theology may have been gathering momentum for some time and within full earshot of the parishioners themselves.

56. Betts, George Herbert, *The Beliefs of 700 Ministers,* The Abingdon Press, Nashville, 1929, esp. pp. 26–30.

57. See footnote 29 for the Hadden citation, and let me repeat here my appreciation for his generosity in allowing me to use his results in this way.

58. One very recent instance of this ferment is a survey of Catholic priests in New York, Connecticut, and New Jersey concerning the tradition of clerical celibacy. Although a response rate of 36.5 per cent is ominously low, 47.1 per cent of the 2,905 respondents favored a policy of optional celibacy, and the percentage increased to a clear majority among the younger priests specifically (*New York Times,* June 8, 1967, p. 41). Of course, it is possible that priests have felt this way since the year 1150 when celibacy was established. It may be that the only new thing here is the survey itself. Still, this seems unlikely conjecture. The priesthood does indeed seem to be changing, and not the least of this change concerns matters of traditional doctrine.

59. Cantril, Hadley, *op. cit.,* p. 742.

60. For somewhat similar poll data that seem to corroborate this increase during the 1940's and 1950's, see Elmo Roper and Associates, *The Public Pulse,* December 21, 1957, as cited in Rosten, Leo, *op. cit.,* p. 319. Roper asked his national samples of adults the following question, "Which one of these groups do you feel is doing the MOST good for the country at the present time?" The groups included religious leaders, government leaders, business leaders, etc. In 1942, religious leaders got 18 per cent of the "vote," but this increased to 34 per cent by 1948, and to 46 per cent by 1957. One might infer from the Gallup poll that the percentages should begin to drop off drastically *after* 1957. On the other hand, it is also possible that the two questions are radically different and unrelated, despite their seeming similarity. Thus, Gallup may have elicited responses concerning personal religious saliency, while Roper's data were more overtly political on a wider societal scale. Or Gallup's reference to influence might have triggered responses in terms of the actual situation whereas Roper's reference to "good" may have elicited responses in a more philosophical context.

61. Miller, Robert Moats, *American Protestantism and Social Issues, 1919–1939,* University of North Carolina Press, Chapel Hill, 1958, p. 347.

62. Lee, Robert, "The Organizational Dilemma in American Protestantism," in Cleveland, Harlan, and Harold D. Lasswell, editors, *Ethics and Bigness,* Harper and Row, New York, 1962, pp. 187–188.

63. For the Protestant classic, see Harrison, Paul M., *Authority and Power in the Free Church Tradition: A Social Case Study of the American Baptist Convention,* Princeton University Press, Princeton, 1959; for Judaism,

see Sklare, Marshall, *Conservative Judaism,* The Free Press, Glencoe, 1955; and for the Catholics, see Fichter, Joseph H., S. J., *Southern Parish: Dynamics of a City Church,* University of Chicago Press, Chicago, 1952.

64. See the several important works of H. Paul Douglass and Edmund de S. Brunner; for example, *The Protestant Church as a Social Institution,* Institute of Social and Religious Research, New York, 1935.

65. Weber, Max, *The Sociology of Religion.* Translated by Ephraim Fiscoff, Beacon Press, Boston, 1963, chap. V.

66. For the latter's contributions, see Troeltsch, Ernst, *The Social Teachings of the Christian Churches,* Macmillan, New York, 1932, esp. vol. I, pp. 331–382. Actually Troeltsch relied upon the distinction more than Weber, who used other conceptual frameworks for his most incisive theoretical studies of the church. And even Troeltsch himself offered a third category of religiosity, that of "mysticism" which, contrary to its connotations, was seen as an emancipated, liberal, and noninstitutional form of adherence for which Troeltsch envisaged an ascendancy in the twentieth century. The church-sect distinction is by now a battle-scarred veteran of the analytic wars under increasing attack (see the symposium with Goode, Demerath, and Eister in the *Journal for the Scientific Study of Religion, op. cit.*). However, it shows no sign of losing its position in the front-line trenches.

67. In 1890, there were 20.5 million church members in the nation's twenty largest religious groups; in 1960, these same twenty groups claimed a total of 114 million members. See Winter, Gibson, "Religious Organizations," in Warner, W. Lloyd, editor, *The Emergent American Society,* vol. I, Yale University Press, New Haven, 1967, p. 408.

68. Weston, M. Moran, *Social Policy of the Episcopal Church in the Twentieth Century,* The Seabury Press, New York, 1964, p. 394. For a more empirical study of current political differentiation within the Episcopalian Church, see Glock, Charles Y., and Benjamin B. Ringer, "Church Policy and the Attitudes of Ministers and Parishioners on Social Issues," *American Sociological Review,* vol. 21, April, 1956, pp. 148–156.

69. Weston, M. Moran, *op. cit.,* p. 403.

70. Hammond, Phillip E., and Robert E. Mitchell, "Segmentation of Radicalism—The Case of the Protestant Campus Minister," *American Journal of Sociology,* vol. 71, September, 1965, pp. 133–143. For a longer discussion of the problems of professionalization within the campus ministry, see Hammond, Phillip E., *The Campus Clergyman,* Basic Books, New York, 1966.

71. See, for example, Cox, Harvey G., "The 'New Breed' in American Churches: Sources of Social Activism in American Religion," *Daedalus,* vol. 96, Winter, 1967, pp. 135–150. But note that even if activism has increased among churchmen generally, influence is another matter. Indeed, as I shall argue gingerly in the chapter's brief concluding section, it is possible to see the church gaining autonomy but losing influence as society itself undergoes differentiation.

72. Winter, Gibson, *op. cit.*

73. Harrison, Paul, *op. cit.*

74. *Ibid.,* p. 206.

75. *Ibid.,* p. 137.

76. *Ibid.,* p. 179.

77. In this connection, it is worth noting that religious bureaucracies now commonly hire managerial consultants whose expertise is generally directed toward business firms. For example, Winter notes a still confidential study of the National Council of Churches conducted by the firm of Booz, Allen, and Hamilton; Harrison notes that the American Baptist Convention called in the American Institute of Management. Both are noteworthy

for their indications of secularization and bureaucratization. The latter study showed, however, that at least the Baptist bureaucratic machinery is hardly well-oiled. In fact, the AIM declared it to be "appallingly archaic."

78. Pike, Bishop James, "Tax Organized Religion," *Playboy*, vol. 14, April, 1967, pp. 94, 100, 144, 147–148.

79. As reported in the *Wisconsin State Journal*, May 6, 1967, p. 10.

80. Marty, Martin E., *The New Shape of American Religion*, Harper and Row, New York, 1958, p. 155–157. For further work in a similar vein, see Berger, Peter L., *The Noise of Solemn Assemblies*, Doubleday, Garden City, 1961.

81. Douglass and Brunner, *op. cit.*, p. 119, as cited in Moberg, David, *op. cit.*, p. 497.

82. See, for example, Blizzard, Samuel, "The Protestant Parish Minister's Integrating Roles," *Religious Education*, vol. 53, July-August, 1958, pp. 374–380; Glock, Charles Y., and Philip Roos, "Parishioners' Views of How Ministers Spend Their Time," *Review of Religious Research*, vol. 2, Spring, 1961, pp. 170–175. And for a bit of first-rate sociology masquerading as satire, see Smith, Charles Merrill, *How to Become a Bishop Without Being Religious*, Doubleday, Garden City, 1965.

83. May, Mark A., and Frank K. Shuttleworth, *The Education of American Ministers*, vol. IV, Institute of Social and Religious Research, New York, 1934. For a more recent examination of trends and prospects in ministerial training, see Niebuhr, H. Richard, Daniel Day Williams, and James M. Gustafson, *The Advancement of Theological Education*, Harper and Row, New York, 1957.

84. Hofstadter, Richard, *Anti-Intellectualism in American Life*, Random House, New York, 1965.

85. May and Shuttleworth, *op. cit.*

86. Henderson, William H., "Some Factors to Consider in Regard to Candidates," mimeographed research report, Division of Vocation, Board of Christian Education, The United Presbyterian Church, 1967. In this connection, it is worth noting some forthcoming recommendations from Paul M. Harrison, whose current study of clerical education reveals a great deal of disenchantment among seminarians themselves. Harrison urges that seminaries also make provision for training students in other, nonreligious roles so that their subsequent career choices are more flexible.

87. Duncan, H. G., "Reactions of Ex-Ministers Toward the Ministry," *Journal of Religion*, vol. 12, January, 1932, pp. 100–115, as cited in Moberg, David, *op. cit.*, p. 486.

88. Moberg, David, *op. cit.*, pp. 505–506.

89. Henderson, William H., *op. cit.*

90. Moberg, David, *op. cit.*, pp. 254–255.

91. Note, however, that Gibson Winter corroborates the trend among his denominations. For example, among the Disciples of Christ, the number of national staff members increased from 10 to 68 from 1892 to 1940 and from 68 to 162 by 1962. The trend is even more spectacular among the Catholics. "Chancel functionaries" in urban areas increased from 100 to 341 between 1900 and 1940, and from 341 to 575 by 1960. "Agency functionaries" in urban areas increased from 0 to 480 between 1900 and 1940, and from 480 to 1,540 by 1960. These urban trends are closely paralleled by trends for rural districts as well. See Winter, *op. cit.*, pp. 417, 450.

92. Bock, E. Wilbur, "The Decline of the Negro Clergy: Changes in Formal Religious Leadership in the Twentieth Century," paper presented at the annual meeting of the Southern Sociological Society, New Orleans, April, 1966. See also Bock, "The Female Clergy: A Case of Professional Mar-

ginality," *American Journal of Sociology,* vol. 72, March, 1967, pp. 531–539.

93. Niebuhr, H. Richard, *The Social Sources of Denominationalism,* Henry Holt and Co., New York, 1929.
94. Lee, Robert, *The Social Sources of Church Unity,* Abingdon Press, Nashville, 1960, p. 100.
95. *Ibid.,* p. 78. Throughout I have alluded to the Social Gospel Movement. For several historical works that deal with this major ideological development in American Protestantism, see May, Henry F., *Protestant Churches and Industrial America,* Harper and Brothers, New York, 1949; Meyer, Donald B., *The Protestant Search for Political Realism, 1919–1941,* University of California Press, Berkeley, 1960, and Miller, *op. cit.* Note, however, that the Social Gospel Movement had neither the exclusive backing nor the spectacular successes that are sometimes claimed for it. It was a minority movement within Protestantism, and one that many have characterized as naive and with goals that were more evangelical than realistic.
96. Lee, Robert, *The Social Sources of Church Unity, op. cit.,* p. 78.
97. McLoughlin, William G., *op. cit.*
98. One of the most spectacular evidences of the new ecumenism among the Catholics is the newly created secretariat for atheism. But in some respects it may be easier to join hands with atheists than with other "religious" groups. Matters of doctrine have not been as crucial in blocking ecumenism as matters of organizational polity, and the atheists have little polity to contend with.
99. Lee, Robert, *The Social Sources of Church Unity, op. cit.,* p. 146.
100. Salisbury, W. Seward, "The Structure of Religious Action in a Small City," paper delivered to the annual meeting of the American Sociological Society, Atlantic City, 1952.
101. Brunner, Edmund de S., *The Larger Parish: A Movement or an Enthusiasm,* Institute of Social and Religious Research, New York, 1934. And for an indication that mergers occur despite doctrinal differences rather than because of doctrinal rapprochements, see Hadden, Jeffrey, "A Protestant Paradox," *op. cit.*
102. See, for example, Parsons, Talcott, *Structure and Process in Modern Societies,* The Free Press, Glencoe, 1960, chap. X; Lipset, S. M., *The First New Nation, op. cit.,* pp. 159–169. Indeed, it is interesting to note the discrepancy between such "sociological" views of denominationalism and other, more "theoretical" perspectives. For example, Niebuhr, H. Richard, *op. cit.* viewed denominationalism as a pathological fragmentation of religious unity.
103. See Ehrenstrom, Nils, and Walter C. Muelder, editors, *Institutionalism and Church Unity: A Symposium,* Association Press, New York, 1963, pp. 332–346.
104. This, of course, recalls the earlier discussion of the importance of differentiation and bureaucratization within the church for the development of controversial programs of social change. A number of studies have indicated that church policies are apt to be more strident and more innovative the more the policy-makers are removed from the influence of local parishioners. See, for example, Pope, Liston, *op. cit.,* Glock and Ringer, *op. cit.,* and, more specifically on race relations, Campbell, Ernest Q., and Thomas F. Pettigrew, *Christians in Racial Crisis: A Study of Little Rock's Ministers,* Public Affairs Press, Washington, 1959. On the other hand, one must be cautious not to overestimate the influence of such stridency at the top. This chapter's brief conclusion will indicate that here societal differentiation had a damper effect.

105. Reimers, David M., *White Protestantism and the Negro,* Oxford University Press, New York, 1965, pp. 134–157.

106. Long, Herman H., *Fellowship For Whom? A Study of Racial Inclusiveness in Congregational-Christian Churches,* Department of Race Relations, Board of Home Missions, United Church of Christ, New York, 1958.

107. Glock, Charles Y., Benjamin B. Ringer, and Earl R. Babbie, *To Comfort and To Challenge,* University of California Press, Berkeley, 1967, p. 155.

108. Fukuyama, Yoshio, *The Parishioners: A Sociological Interpretation,* The Research Department, Board for Homeland Ministries, United Church of Christ, New York, 1966, p. 21ff.

109. It is true, of course, that correlation should not be interpreted as causation. And yet later, we shall offer one recent argument for interpreting the correlation between orthodoxy and anti-Semitism as causal. Some of the logic that applies there may also apply here, but then so might many of the methodological qualifications.

110. Recently a good deal has been made of the importance of the Negro churches in the wider civil rights movement. Certainly many Negro civil rights leaders are ministers; it is also possible to trace the roots of "freedom songs" into hymnals of the past. But one must be careful about overgeneralizing the point. Negro churches are also vulnerable to the conservatism of parishioners, and there has always been an other-worldly aspect to Negro religion that runs counter to any tendency towards this-worldly activism. For a recent empirical study that indicates a negative relationship between religiosity and civil rights militancy for a national sample of Negroes, see Marx, Gary T., "Religion: Opiate or Inspiration of Civil Rights Militancy Among Negroes?" *American Sociological Review,* vol. 32, February, 1967, pp. 64–72.

111. Weber, Max, *The Protestant Ethic and the Spirit of Capitalism.* Charles Scribners Sons, New York, 1928.

112. Lenski, Gerhard, *The Religious Factor,* Doubleday, Garden City, 1961, p. 325.

113. Freedman, Ronald, David Goldberg, and Doris Slesinger, "Current Fertility Expectations of Married Couples in the United States," *Population Index,* vol. 29, October, 1963, p. 379.

114. Westoff, Charles F., and Norman B. Ryder, "United States: Methods of Fertility Control, 1955, 1960 and 1965," *Studies in Family Planning,* vol. 17, February, 1967.

115. Of course, there is a profound distinction between a couple's ability and willingness to use contraceptives and its desired family size. It is possible that even though Catholics are more contraceptively-inclined, they will be no less desirous of large families. And yet this does not seem likely. Technological change often produces changes in behavior and norms. While we may now be in the midst of the familiar "cultural lag," one might expect the lag to be short-lived in the light of other changes currently affecting not only the Catholic Church but also the position of the Catholic laity in society at large.

116. Glenn, Norval D., and Ruth Hyland, "Religious Preference and Worldly Success: Some Evidence From National Surveys," *American Sociological Review,* vol. 32, February, 1967.

117. Weber, Max, *op. cit.,* pp. 181–182.

118. Glenn, Norval D., and Ruth Hyland, *op. cit.,* p. 85.

119. Broom, Leonard, and Norval D. Glenn, "Religious Differences in Reported Attitudes and Behavior," *Sociological Analysis,* vol. 27, Winter, 1966, pp. 187–209. For a review of other studies and a treatment of reputed Protestant-Catholic differences as a problem in the sociology of

knowledge, see Greeley, Andrew M., "The Protestant Ethic: Time for a Moratorium," *Sociological Analysis*, vol. 25, Spring, 1964, pp. 20–33.

But one must be wary of overzealousness on behalf of the null hypothesis. Lenski is not alone in his position to the contrary. Consider also the findings in the voting literature. Alford notes that, with class held constant, the difference between Protestant and Catholics in their support of the Democratic presidential candidate dropped almost by half between 1944 and 1956, but that the difference was larger than ever before in 1960. Clearly 1960 was a prime year for religion and politics, and a careful analysis of the Kennedy election by Campbell, Miller, and Stokes indicates that Kennedy gained 4 per cent from the Catholics but lost 6 per cent from the Protestants, so that the religious factor produced a net loss of some 2 per cent in the aggregate—considerably less, however, than was the case for Al Smith in 1928. But once again caution is in order here. While there is little doubt that religion was itself an issue in 1960, one must be generally careful about imputing religious causes to seeming religious differences. Although Alford did control for social class, he might have found an even greater decline in religious differences between 1944 and 1956 had he been able to control for ethnicity, community size, and a host of other factors. See Alford, Robert R., *Party and Society*, Rand McNally, Chicago, 1963, pp. 241–249; and Campbell, A., W. E. Miller, and D. E. Stokes, "Stability and Change in 1960: A Reinstating Election," *American Political Science Review*, vol. 55, June 1961, pp. 269–280.

120. Bressler, Marvin, and Charles F. Westoff, "Catholic Education, Economic Values, and Achievement," *American Journal of Sociology*, vol. 69, November, 1963, pp. 225–233.
121. Greeley, Andrew M., *Religion and Career*, Sheed and Ward, New York, 1963.
122. Greeley, Andrew M., and Peter H. Rossi, *The Education of Catholic Americans*, Aldine Publishing Co., Chicago, 1966.
123. Yinger, J. Milton, *op. cit.*, p. 81.
124. Kennedy, Ruby Jo, "Single or Triple Melting Pot? Intermarriage Trends in New Haven, 1870–1950," *American Journal of Sociology*, vol. 58, July, 1952, pp. 56–59.
125. Thomas, John L., "The Factor of Religion in the Selection of Marriage Mates," *American Sociological Review*, vol. 16, August, 1951, pp. 487–491.
126. Glick, Paul C., "Intermarriage and Fertility Patterns among Persons in Major Religious Groups," *Eugenics Quarterly*, vol. 7, March, 1960, pp. 31–38.
127. Lenski, *op. cit.*, p. 49, as cited in Yinger, *op. cit.*, pp. 83–84.
128. Vincent, Clark, *op. cit.*, pp. 56–57. Actually the rate of divorce is higher where the mixed marriage involves a Catholic husband (21 per cent) rather than a Catholic wife (7 per cent). But the divorce rate is highest among those with no formal religious affiliation (18 per cent), though the latter finding needs more careful scrutiny before being used to support the bromide that "the family that prays together stays together."
129. Yinger, *op. cit.*, p. 83.
130. Goldman, Benjamin B., and Alvin Chenkin, "The Jewish Population of New Orleans, 1953," Council of Jewish Federation and Welfare Funds, 1954, cited in Ben B. Seligman, "Some Aspects of Jewish Demography," in Marshall Sklare, editor, *The Jews: Social Patterns of an American Group*, The Free Press, Glencoe, 1958.
131. Rosenthal, Erich, "Acculturation Without Assimilation? The Jewish Community in Chicago, Illinois," *American Journal of Sociology*, vol. 66, November, 1960, pp. 275–288.

132. Heiss, Jerold, "Premarital Characteristics of the Religiously Intermarried in an Urban Area," *American Sociological Review,* vol. 25, February, 1960, pp. 47–55.

133. Gordon, Milton M., *Assimilation in American Life,* Oxford University Press, New York, 1964, pp. 173–195.

134. Glazer, Nathan, and Daniel Patrick Moynihan, *Beyond the Melting Pot,* The M.I.T. Press, Cambridge, 1963. See also the two-volume series on the Jews in "Lakeville," a midwestern suburb. Sklare, Marshall, and Joseph Greenblum, *Jewish Identity on the Suburban Frontier: A Study of Group Survival in the Open Society,* vol. I; and Ringer, Benjamin B., *The Edge of Friendliness: A Study of Jewish-Gentile Relations,* vol. II, Basic Books, New York, 1967.

135. Stember, Charles Herbert, *et al., Jews in the Mind of America,* Basic Books, New York, 1966, p. 128.

136. Glock and Stark, *Christian Beliefs and Anti-Semitism, op. cit.* But for a three-person critique of the methodology here, see Williams, Robin, Andrew Greeley, and Daniel J. Levinson in the "Review Symposium" for the December, 1967, *American Sociological Review.* All three agree that Glock and Stark, perhaps in the interest of their research client, the Anti-Defamation League of B'nai B'rith, tend to exaggerate the amount of anti-Semitism within the churches and tend to overstate the case for religion as a causal, rather than merely correlated, factor.

137. This sort of trend is implicit in a number of historic-sociological works. It can be seen as the real thrust of the Protestant Reformation itself in breaking the spell of Catholic dominance over secular affairs and ultimately producing a religious relativism that allowed men to regard the churches themselves as less monolithic and hence less influential. This is an interpretation that rescues part of Weber's thesis in *The Protestant Ethic and the Spirit of Capitalism* without swallowing it all. It is an interpretation that can be applied not only to whole societies but also to the changing nature of community structures within any given society. For a more elaborate statement of this position, see Demerath, N.J. III, and Phillip E. Hammond, *Religion in Social Context: Tradition and Transition,* Random House, New York, 1968, esp. chaps. 3 and 6.

138. See, for example, the vagaries in interpreting the public opinion data concerning religious influence and the relative contributions of religious and other leaders, cited earlier, and footnote 60. It is true that some evidence in support of this thesis is available from the community power literature: for example, Dahl, Robert, *Who Governs?* Yale University Press, New Haven, 1961; and Lynd, Robert and Helen, *Middletown* and *Middletown in Transition,* Harcourt, Brace and Co., New York, 1929 and 1937, note an eclipse in religious influence over time. But then this literature is also difficult to evaluate, and any thorough exegesis would require far more space than is available here.

IV. DISTRIBUTIVE FEATURES

9. CONSUMPTION: A REPORT ON CONTEMPORARY ISSUES

Milton Moss

IN A VERY broad sense all that is required to upgrade the economic well-being of everyone in American society is an expanding economy supplemented by selective policies to overcome economic hardship. Living standards could be improved for all households if growing incomes were provided. For the poor, increases in income and earning capacity would mean more nutritious and varied foods, improved health care, upgraded housing, and better education for their children. Even for families well above a poverty line, much of the growth in incomes could be expected to be used to upgrade these basic necessities.

The proportion of income used to acquire personal possessions, and to enjoy travel and recreation, has been shown to rise with generally rising incomes, while for increases into the uppermost levels of income the shares going for accumulation of investments of many types expands even more. Finally, a growing economy provides the resources for increased provision of a wide variety of public goods and services.

This familiar and very broad description of consumption in a growing economy and in an egalitarian-oriented society should be kept in mind as a fundamental background to this chapter. In the forefront, however, is a sharper focus on certain issues in American society which seem at this juncture to require resolution.

What are these issues and what quantitative measures are useful in appraising social change in these areas?

In this chapter we focus on three broad issues:

First, the American economy has reached general levels of prosperity that are unparalleled in time and among the countries of the world. The expectation that marked growth in the physical and cultural resources available to consumers will continue, barring widespread war and destruction, appears at this juncture to be unquestioned.

Not only is increased consumption considered a prime goal of total economic effort—but many, if not most, features of the American pattern of consumption are believed by many observers to constitute the goal of other industrialized countries and, more distantly, the goal of developing countries. At the same time economic growth has, at least in this country, put a new focus on economic disadvantage. Poverty, absolute or relative, seen as pockets in the midst of widespread and rapidly growing prosperity may be a different phenomenon from poverty which was more widely experienced during periods of economic instability and general depression. The first issue, then, is assessing the severity of economic disadvantage, and the extent to which it is changing.

Second, choice has always been an important issue for households. Choice of vocation, location of job, size of family, selection of goods of desirable quality and price, choice of profitable investments—all these have in some sense always been important in relatively advanced societies. Two developments have heightened, on the one hand, and diminished or altered, on the other hand, this problem of choice.

1. The problem of personal choice has been complicated by the increase in the share of expenditures or time requiring specialized knowledge and discretion, particularly in connection with the growth over a long period in tangible possessions, in financial investments, in the use of credit, in the decrease in working time, in the lengthening of the life span, and in the rapidity with which occupations may become obsolete during one's working lifetime.

2. At the same time there has been a decline in the range of individual discretion, resulting largely from the increase in the size of government activity. The proportion of personal income subject to individual discretion has diminished somewhat because of increases in taxes and increases in the size of consumption collectively provided, and the area of public choice has widened.

To illustrate the general problem posed by these two developments, this chapter will provide statistical measurements of only a limited number of the changes which they reflect. Specifically:

1. The general nature of growth in income, consumption, and assets with adult maturation;
2. The general growth in consumer investment, mostly tangible;
3. The changing role of the government sector as it affects consumption and the choices these imply.

The third and last issue for this study we discuss only briefly, although it has dominated discussion of consumer behavior at least since the time of Keynes. This concerns the study of consumer behavior as it affects the economy—essentially studying those facets of consumer demand that are particularly relevant for production. Our intention is not to tackle this subject in any sense of completeness but to focus on one feature, namely, that changes in the timing of consumer investment decisions, particularly for durable goods, such as an automobile, accentuate fluctuations in the economy. The task here is to improve our understanding of this process so that we may better anticipate such oscillations in consumer behavior and hopefully moderate their effects.

These three issues (the term "issue" indicates that they are unsolved problems rather than clear-cut goals) cover a very broad spectrum, and will require many measurements for appraising the extent to which the issues are moving toward resolution.

We define, for the moment, consumption in a very broad sense, to include all that persons and families purchase or acquire, in order to maintain their existence, to increase their earning power (or economic aspirations), and to obtain cultural and recreational opportunities. In a strict sense, *consumption* can be defined as immediate satisfaction, *income* as the financing of consumption and investment, and *investment* as contributing to future income and consumption. We believe, however, that immediate satisfactions are an abstraction and cannot be easily disentwined from income and investment.

For this reason the chapter deals with the processes of income, consumption, and investment, rather than consumption per se. Moreover, the chapter emphasizes the need to see these processes over a life span of personal and familial maturation. This involves evaluating for different groups of young and old the interplay of streams of earnings, of changing patterns of consumption together with investments which in varying degrees are fulfilled or thwarted.

The chapter only very partially provides the details of quantitative measurement required for a continued appraisal of social change in this area. While data on income and consumption and to a lesser extent investment are abundant, we have not attempted to present them all. Moreover, in one area, which this inquiry insists deserves great emphasis—namely, the study of the life span of the household—the data are rather meager.

As a final introductory comment, while consideration must be given to the role of publicly provided goods and services as well as other public activities directly affecting consumption, this broad area is not separately emphasized (however fundamental it may be in another context) but is brought in at various junctures to indicate its relevance to the three issues delineated earlier.

GROWTH IN THE TOTAL ECONOMY

For everyone's real income and consumption to grow, the total economy (and hopefully its productivity) must rise faster than the increase in population. Whatever measurements are employed to gauge improvements in consumption levels, a *starting* point should show basic aggregates of total economic performance, then proceed to more critical dissection, and possibly to come back again to broad aggregates if we are fortunate enough in finding new ones.

Our aim at this point is to indicate in simple terms, the growth in the total economy as measured by Gross National Product (GNP) and how that has been translated into a growing volume of goods and services, in total and per capita. This growth is summarized in the two panels in Figure 1. (Data on which the figure is based are given in Reference Table A at the end of the chapter.)

The unmistakable upward trends—in production, productivity, and in the flow of goods and services to consumers—are shown in this figure. Since the beginning of this century, as the left panel indicates, Gross National Product, in dollars of constant purchasing power had grown over the two-thirds of a century eightfold, or an increase of about 3.2 per cent per year compounded.[1] This growth has been accomplished with lessened effort. As the bottom panel of the figure shows, product per man-hour has more than quadrupled over the period, rising at a rate of 2.3 per cent per year.

The total volume of goods and services purchased by persons and families (also in constant prices), shown in the right panel of the figure, has paralleled the increase in GNP, while in per capita terms, the growth has been from about $630 to $2,306, a rise of 3.7 times or about 2 per cent per year. Note that this rise is almost parallel but not quite as marked as the rate of growth in productivity mentioned earlier.

Shown in the bottom panel is the percentage in total GNP that the economy provided for personal consumption. Personal consumption expenditures now constitute 63 per cent of GNP. The share was as low as 56 per cent in World War I, and 46 per cent in World War II. It was as high as 83 per cent in the depth of the Depression. But a straight line through the fluctuations would show up as a horizontal level of approximately 63 per cent. As is well known, these are the purchases in the market, but also include estimates of the rental value of owner-occupied housing, of food made and consumed on farms, and of services provided by financial intermediaries for which no express charge is made. Excluded are illegal transactions (e.g., a large fraction of the "food and beverage" consumption component during Prohibition) and production within the household, including cooking, baking, sewing, home repair, parent tutoring, home entertainment—each of which could be purchased in the market, but is not traditionally part of measured GNP.

The significance of these broad measures for a study of social change is that they portray the necessary conditions for well-being. As a set of necessary conditions, their meaning is clear—they show that the economic base, by growing and by continuing to devote a large (but secularly constant) share to personal consumption, provides the resource base for meeting the objectives of health of body, economic security and growth, and cultural and recreational opportunities.

These measures have another meaning in the *welfare* sense. That is, in order for any person or group to receive some improvement without requiring some sacrifice from others, the total economy must grow. But this too is only a necessary condition. To determine whether in fact the fruits of economic growth are distributed in a manner "adequately" to meet the three aforementioned objectives for all persons and families, an examination of persons and families, of goods and services, must be made in many dimensions.

MEASURES OF THE INEQUITIES OF ECONOMIC GROWTH

One broad question to ask is whether, simply in the course of economic growth, there can be a significant reduction in the number of poor people—even granting that the rewards of economic growth are inequitably distributed. An interesting attempt to measure this effect was made by L. E. Galloway.[2] By relating the percentage of families in poverty, as defined by the well-known Social Security standard, to the growth in total incomes he projected a decline in the incidence of poverty from around one-fifth of all families in the mid-1960's to 4 per cent by 1980.

This need not imply that policies to promote total economic growth suffice to resolve the issue of economic disadvantage. First, the process

FIGURE 1. GROSS PRODUCT, PRODUCTIVITY, AND CONSUMPTION, 1900–1965

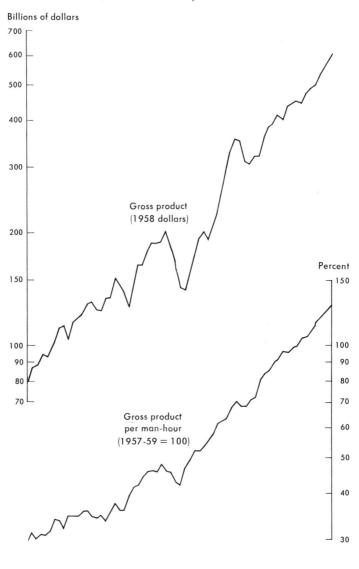

Billions of dollars

Gross product
(1958 dollars)

Percent

Gross product
per man-hour
(1957-59 = 100)

1900   '10   '20   '30   '40   '50   '60

FIGURE 1. GROSS PRODUCT, PRODUCTIVITY, AND CONSUMPTION, 1900–1965 (*cont.*)

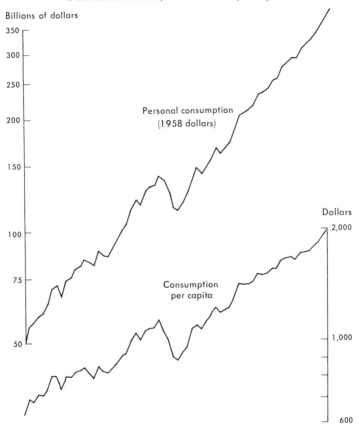

NOTE: This chart is plotted on a ratio scale.
SOURCES: See notes to Reference Table A, pp. 518–519.

455

may be regarded as much too slow. Second, some of the features of economic disadvantage (not necessarily taken into account in a fixed standard measure of poverty) may not be eradicated by economic growth.

Economic growth generally provides growing income for nearly everyone, if the growth is at least as fast as the growth in the number of people available for jobs. In fact, it particularly helps the poor in the sense that a failure of the economy to grow, as in a recession, generally affects the unskilled, uneducated worker more than others. A strongly rising economy benefits the poor more than one rising less strongly.

Our purpose in this section is to discuss various measures of poverty—or, more broadly, economic disadvantage. The intent is not, of course, to range over the entire field of poverty research so much as to show the bearing of some of these measures on an improved evaluation of consumption goals. We deal with measures of the number in a disadvantaged position and measures of the "nature of that disadvantage."

The Incidence of Poverty

Our main interest at this point is merely to show first, that in terms of a fixed standard, say, a given income for a family of a given size, in constant purchasing power there has been a decline in the incidence of poverty. Second, in terms of the simplest of relative standards which relates the lowest incomes to the middle incomes, there has not been such a decline.

As Table 1 shows, using the fixed standard, the number and percentage of persons in families and unrelated individuals in poverty declined significantly between 1959 and 1966. In terms of constant purchasing power, persons having the equivalent income of $3,130 or less for a nonfarm family of four members declined to 15 per cent of all persons—a drop of seven percentage points in the seven-year span shown. A much bigger decline in poverty has taken place for white persons than for nonwhites. These findings are quite familiar by now and are mentioned only as background for our presentation of the general problem.

Increasing attention has been given over the years to the concept of relative deprivation.[3] This is a difficult concept—because the reference point, or group, cannot always be clearly specified. Nevertheless, it is worth serious consideration because all standards are relative in time and place and some measures along this line should be examined.

TABLE 1. INCIDENCE OF POVERTY BY COLOR, 1959–1966

Year	Number of persons			Number in poverty			Percentage in poverty		
	Total	White	Non-white	Total	White	Non-white	Total	White	Non-white
	(in millions)								
1959	176.5	156.9	19.6	38.9	28.2	10.7	22.1	18.0	54.6
1961	181.4	160.4	20.9	38.1	26.5	11.6	21.0	16.5	55.4
1963	187.2	165.2	22.0	35.3	24.1	11.2	18.9	14.6	50.9
1965	191.5	168.9	22.7	31.9	21.4	10.5	16.7	12.7	46.4
1966	193.4	170.2	23.2	29.7	20.1	9.6	15.4	11.8	41.4

SOURCE: Condensation of Table H in "Income in 1966 of Families and Persons in the United States," *Current Population Reports*, Series P-60, no. 53, U.S. Bureau of the Census, December, 1967. The definition of poverty in this table is that now officially current, and was developed by Mollie Orshansky, taking as its base the Level 1 definition scaled roughly to an income of $3,000 for a family of four.

Note that figures in this table refer to persons rather than households. In 1966 there were 10.3 million nonfarm households, and 0.6 million farm households in poverty according to the Social Security Administration definition, or 17.6 and 20.8 per cent, respectively, of the total number of households. These percentages were down from 22.5 and 40.9 in 1959. See *Economic Report of the President*, February, 1968, p. 143.

TABLE 2. PERCENTAGE OF U.S. FAMILIES
CLASSIFIED AS POOR BY RELATIVE AND
ABSOLUTE STANDARDS, 1947–1960

Year	Median income (1959 dollars)	Percentage of families with income		
		Less than one-half the median[a]	Less than $3,000 (1959 prices)	Less than $2,000 (1959 prices)
1947	3,957	19.0	33.9	19.1
1948	3,868	19.4	34.7	19.8
1949	3,807	20.1	35.9	21.3
1950	4,036	20.0	33.0	19.8
1951	4,164	19.0	30.9	17.9
1952	4,277	19.0	29.3	17.8
1953	4,627	19.9	27.1	16.8
1954	4,530	20.7	28.7	18.1
1955	4,817	19.9	25.9	16.0
1956	5,129	19.5	23.6	14.2
1957	5,148	20.0	23.5	14.2
1958	5,143	19.9	23.8	14.1
1959	5,417	19.9	22.7	13.4
1960	5,547	20.2	22.1	13.2

[a] Estimated by interpolation.

SOURCE: Fuchs, Victor R., "Toward A Theory of Poverty," in Task Force on Economic Growth and Opportunity, *The Concept of Poverty*, Chamber of Commerce of the United States, Washington, 1965; reprinted in Miller, S. M., M. Rein, P. Roby, and B. M. Cross, "Poverty, Inequality, and Conflict," *The Annals of the American Academy of Political and Social Science*, September, 1967.

We start by showing data in Table 2 representing a broad measure of relative disadvantage presented by Victor Fuchs. The important point stressed here is that relative to some fraction (say half) of income in the middle position of U.S. families, the proportion of families with incomes less than that fraction has remained constant.

An alternative view of the same phenomenon is shown in Table 3. This measure has the advantage of avoiding Fuchs' need to resort to interpolation, and is brought forward to 1964. Also the data are based on current dollars rather than 1959 dollars. Constant dollar data are redundant for purposes of this measure inasmuch as deflation of all incomes by the same price index leaves unaffected the ratio of median to bottom fifth income.

As shown in this table, the top limit of income received by the families in the lowest fifth of the income distribution remained at close to

TABLE 3. INCOMES OF THE LOWEST FIFTH
COMPARED WITH THE
MEDIAN INCOME OF FAMILIES
IN THE UNITED STATES, 1947–1964

Year	Lowest fifth	Median	Ratio to median
	(current dollars)		
1947	1,580	3,031	.52
1948	1,656	3,187	.52
1949	1,540	3,107	.50
1950	1,665	3,319	.50
1951	1,959	3,709	.53
1952	2,052	3,890	.53
1953	2,132	4,233	.50
1954	2,018	4,173	.48
1955	2,228	4,421	.50
1956	2,451	4,783	.51
1957	2,491	4,971	.50
1958	2,564	5,087	.50
1959	2,713	5,417	.50
1960	2,798	5,620	.50
1961	2,829	5,737	.49
1962	3,018	5,956	.51
1963	3,150	6,249	.50
1964	3,279	6,569	.50

SOURCES: The income figures for the lowest fifth represent the upper limit of that group. Data are calculated from "Consumer Income," *Current Population Reports*, Series P-60, no. 53, Table G; and Henson, Mary F., "Trends in the Income of Families and Persons in the United States, 1947–1964," Technical Report No. 17, U.S. Bureau of the Census, Washington, 1967.

one-half the median income of all families throughout the post-World War II period.

The measure of relative disadvantage, ceteris paribus, can be sharpened further by controlling for the differences that are due to age, as shown in Table 4 for the years 1964, 1957 and 1947. This table provides essentially the same income data as in Table 3 for the relevant age groups.

For most groups income in the lowest quintile of the given age group is approximately half of the average income for the same group. In the oldest group the ratio is much lower, however, indicating that the relative deprivation in the oldest ages tends to be greatest. This is also consistent with the finding that inequality in income size distributions tends to be greatest for the aged. Between 1947 and 1964 there appears to have been some improvement for this group though the "deprivation ratio" has apparently remained quite low. Moreover, other measurements are needed before one can determine any significant change in the economic status of the aged. We note parenthetically that our interest at this point is in focusing on the lowest end of the income distribution rather than in the degree of general inequality or dispersion of all incomes. For this reason we have not used the more familiar measures of inequality (for example, the Gini ratio) which, like the standard deviation or coefficient of variation, are really measures of general dispersion—not measures of poverty.

Based on these relative measures the lowest income recipients have neither lost nor gained ground in the growth of the economy.[4] Based on an absolute standard such recipients have gained ground. The different trends shown by the absolute and relative standards are consistent in the sense that with a growing economy, if no change occurs in group-to-group disadvantage then, by the process of income growth, all groups (advantaged and disadvantaged) must have grown in relation to some fixed income standard.

It is difficult to deny that with a general rise in real income there is also some upgrading in standards, suggesting that a relative standard may be preferable to a fixed one particularly if economic growth is rapid. The nature and extent of the upgrading among different groups —the poor, the middle-income, and the rich—are not known. Some evidence on upgrading in some average sense, however, is suggested, if not demonstrated, in the work of the U.S. Bureau of Labor Statistics (BLS) in their special budget studies. The most recent, dealing with the City Worker's Family Budget, illustrates the upgrading process.[5] In this study an attempt was made to compare changes for renter families in the cost of a standard budget resulting from price changes and from consumption standards per se. According to this study the total cost of a moderate standard of living for the four-person family averaged about $4,200 in 1951, and $8,700 for all renter families covered. These increases in the level of total budget costs reflect increases in federal, state, and local income taxes and Social Security taxes as well as the rise in prices and in the upgraded standard of living. In an effort to separate these component sources of change in cost, BLS found that in the fifteen-year span from 1951 to 1966 the increase in total cost was attributable to a 40 per cent increase in price and a 50 per cent increase in the standard. This increase in the standard compares with a rise of 78 per cent in disposable personal income, after correction for price change.

While the procedure used by BLS to obtain a changed standard

TABLE 4. RELATION BETWEEN LOWEST AND MEAN INCOMES OF U.S. NONFARM FAMILIES, BY AGE, 1964, 1957, AND 1947

Age group	1964 Lowest quintile	1964 Mean	1964 Ratio	1957 Lowest quintile	1957 Mean	1957 Ratio	1947 Lowest quintile	1947 Mean	1947 Ratio
Total	*3,279*	*7,438*	*.44*	*2,491*	*5,483*	*.45*	*1,580*	*3,566*	*.44*
14–24	2,675	4,975	.54	2,250	4,041	.56	1,361	2,425	.56
25–34	3,973	6,987	.57	3,357	5,399	.62	1,815	3,254	.56
35–44	4,512	8,323	.54	3,479	6,187	.56	1,926	3,857	.50
45–54	4,402	8,760	.50	2,930	6,306	.47	1,908	4,099	.47
55–64	3,248	7,866	.41	2,265	5,510	.41	1,541	3,795	.41
65 and over	1,831	5,269	.35	1,198	3,564	.34	689	2,848	.24

NOTE: The use of the median would have been preferable to eliminate correlation between the two income positions which is present in use of mean. However, as shown in the total column the results seem to differ only slightly compared with the preceding table in which the median was used. For age group data, only the mean figure was available in the published source.

SOURCE: Henson, Mary F., "Trends in the Income of Families and Persons in the United States, 1947–64," Technical Report No. 17, U.S. Bureau of the Census, Washington, 1967, Table D, p. 33, and Table 25, pp. 182–187.

461

budget is no precise demonstration of the upgrading process for a moderate position in the income scale, it does strongly suggest that the process of general income growth is accompanied by an upgrading and that it by no means exceeds the rate of general economic growth. It might be noted parenthetically that the new standard budget is some 16 or 20 per cent below the average level of living for families of the type represented in the budget (a family of four persons: an employed husband, age thirty-eight; a wife not employed outside the home; and two children, a girl eight and a boy thirteen).

Consumption Patterns and Assets of the Poor

Measures of levels of living among the poor more direct than those provided by income data are evident from information on consumption patterns; yet even these represent only broad averages and do not reveal the full range of presence or absence of acute economic hardship. Data mainly from the 1960–1961 Consumer Expenditures Survey,[6] but also from other sources, reveal the following main conclusions of consumption patterns of families at low or the lowest income levels.

1. For such families, income understates consumption by wide margins. This is clearly shown in Table 5 where expenditures for current consumption are shown to be appreciably in excess of money receipts by percentages ranging as high as 71 per cent for a single-person family in the lowest consumption class. The large percentages by which current consumption exceeds income imply the use of assets

TABLE 5. CURRENT CONSUMPTION AS A PERCENTAGE OF MONEY INCOME, BY SIZE OF FAMILY, 1960–1961

	Percentage of after-tax income and other money receipts					
	Number of persons in family					
Type of family	1	2	3	4	5	6 or more
In "low-consumption" classes						
Current expenditures	105	105	107	113	105	99
Expenditures plus value received without expense	114	110	113	119	109	103
Under "low-consumption" classes						
Current expenditures	151	118	123	125	125	109
Expenditures plus value received without expense	171	133	137	134	135	116

SOURCE: Lamale, Helen H., "Levels of Living Among the Poor," Report No. 238–12, U.S. Bureau of Labor Statistics, Washington, August, 1965, p. 6.

or credit, the receipt of public or private assistance, gifts from persons outside the family, and insurance benefits—all of which are seen in the survey to be important resources for families at low income levels.

2. In the low-consumption classes, the percentage of total consumption spent for food varied from 27 per cent for three-person families to 31 per cent for families of six persons or more. It was as high as 34 per cent for very large families in the lowest consumption levels in the survey. These high percentages compare with an average of 24 per cent for all nonfarm families. While persons in the lowest income classes on the average spent amounts for food which were within the range of expense that the U.S. Department of Agriculture specifies as providing nutritional adequacy, the chances are that the diets in fact could be well below the standards necessary for nutritional health. The knowledge of nutrient adequacy of foods and skill in food preparation or the motivation for proper application of such skills as may be known are believed to be generally lacking among those in the lowest income levels—at least to a greater extent than those with higher incomes.

3. In 1960 about one-third of all U.S. families with incomes below the poverty line lived in housing that was dilapidated or lacked plumbing (that is, hot and cold running water or private toilet or bathing facilities inside the structure). This total is made up of some 2 million American families who live in completely dilapidated housing, that is, dwelling units with structural defects that endanger the health and safety of the inhabitants, and close to 4 million families who live in units that lack basic plumbing facilities. Data collected in the 1950 and 1960 censuses suggest a reduction in the number of occupied substandard units from 15.3 to 9.0 million units. The data shown in Table 6 indicate further improvement since 1960. The improvement in the quality of occupied housing in nonmetropolitan areas has been much more marked than in metropolitan areas. Part of this relative improvement reflects the continued migration to urban areas of poor farm families, many of whom have abandoned substandard units.

4. Prices paid by families at the lower end of the income scale averaged lower than families in the middle range of income. For example, 6 per cent of the low-consumption families bought refrigerators at an average cost of $176 compared with an average of $266 for the 8 per cent of families in the $6,000 to $7,500 class who bought refrigerators. For washing machines, the comparable figures were 7 per cent at $140 and 9 per cent at $197. For vacuum cleaners, 4 per cent at $68 compared with 9 per cent at $85. Lower average prices are of

TABLE 6. OCCUPIED HOUSING UNITS, BY QUALITY
AND AREA, 1960 AND 1966

Quality by area[a]	1960	1966
	(thousands)	
Standard units	44,418	52,138
Substandard units	8,469	5,754
Metropolitan areas	3,231	2,470
Nonmetropolitan areas	5,238	3,284
Dilapidated	2,353	1,995
Metropolitan areas	1,052	n.a.
Nonmetropolitan areas	1,301	n.a.
Nondilapidated, lacking plumbing	6,116	3,759
Metropolitan areas	2,179	n.a.
Nonmetropolitan areas	3,937	n.a.

[a] Based on 1960 definitions of quality and metropolitan areas.

SOURCE: Department of Commerce and Department of Housing and Urban Development, as given in the *Economic Report of the President,* February, 1968, p. 150.

course to be expected. There is no evidence, though, from survey figures whether the quality of goods purchased is or is not disproportionately lower for the poor. To the extent, however, that those with low and unstable incomes include a greater proportion of families with less familiarity with retail practices and facilities (because of lack of education or other reasons) vulnerability to the possibility of overcharge may be great.[7]

Since assets might constitute an important source of consumption expenditures for those with "inadequate" incomes, some appraisal of the importance of these assets among low-income families should be noted. This brief discussion relies on information gathered in a survey of wealth conducted for the Federal Reserve Board by the Census Bureau.[8] According to this source, most of those classified as poor on basis of income levels had little or no reserves of wealth (as of the end of 1962) but there were some with fairly sizable holdings in the form of equity in a home and/or liquid and investment assets. Were these amounts sufficiently large to alter our present notions of the number in poverty?

The survey found that four in ten units in the low-income level group were homeowners, and the mean wealth holdings amounted to $6,200 for families and $5,800 for one-person units. Older persons or heads of families (say, sixty-five or older) had larger amounts of wealth on the average than the younger. All in all, however, even if account were taken of these assets, and an estimate made of their income yield for purposes of consumption, the survey concluded that perhaps one in seven of the families, and one in four of the one-person units classified as poor on the basis of current income would not be so classified on the basis of their wealth to supplement their income. The survey based this estimate on an allowance of 4 per cent yield on equity from home ownership *plus* liquidation of financial assets both sufficient to just overcome the gap between the poverty level and current income less indebtedness as of 1962. The data are shown in Table 7.

The survey concludes, and this writer agrees, that "As a predictable program for raising consumption levels of units with incomes be-

TABLE 7. ASSETS IN RELATION TO INCOME DEFICIENCY
FOR UNITS WITH INCOME BELOW POVERTY LEVEL 1,
DECEMBER 31, 1962

Income deficiency and compensation	All units	Unrelated individuals	Families of 2 or more
	(*percentages*)		
Units with income below Level 1[a]	100	100	100
Deficiency compensated			
By allowance for home equity[b]	6	7	6
By allowance for home *plus* liquid and investment assets[c]			
Sufficient[d] for:			
5 years or more	13	19	9
3 years but less than 5	2	2	1
2 years but less than 3	3	4	1
1 year but less than 2	3	5	2
Deficiency not compensated			
Some liquid and investment assets[c]	13	14	12
No liquid and investment assets[c]	61	49	70

[a] Level 1 is the economy level as defined by the Society Security Administration.

[b] Allowance estimated at 4 per cent of equity.

[c] After deduction of personal noninstalment debt and instalment debt incurred for purposes other than purchases of durable goods and home repair and modernization.

[d] Liquid and investment assets sufficient to meet gap between poverty income Level 1 and 1962 money income plus allowance for a 4 per cent return on home equity.

NOTE: Details may not add to totals because of rounding.

SOURCE: Projector, D. S., and G. S. Weiss, "Survey of Financial Characteristics of Consumers," Federal Reserve Board, August, 1966.

low poverty criteria, use of accumulated savings has limits." Obviously, the amount of wealth in the hands of the poor appears inadequate to raise their living conditions for any appreciable period of time. Furthermore, most of the wealth held by those classified as poor in terms of current income is owned by the elderly. The many special situations for the elderly occasioned by differing life expectancies, individual uncertainties, and special emergencies would very likely make such a program quite difficult to administer.

At a later point we discuss patterns of asset holdings in more detail. See, for example, the discussion of Table 17, which shows the severely disadvantaged position of Negroes with respect to accumulation of assets.

Actual and Expected Earning Power

The foregoing measures pertained largely to *inequality* in income, consumption, or assets. In large degree, it is supposed that these measures of inequality imply deficiency or hardship or injustice of some sort. But of what sort? In point of fact, apart from data on housing, and possibly an *implication* of some nutritional deficiency or lack of variety in diet, there is nothing in the foregoing figures which *prima facie* implies hardship or injustice. To pursue this matter further we seek other measures which may be more pertinent to family aspirations.

First, we deal with the matter of earning power or of actual or prospective growth in income over the life span. We conjecture that growth in real income as the adult earner and the family matures is one of the most important indicators of dynamic strength in an economy and of the relative well-being of a family. We *assume* that the goal of growth in family income is widespread and that the failure to achieve or expect this growth (for social or personal reasons) is a source of acute dissatisfaction, particularly when the general economy is expanding rapidly.

It is clear that there are at least two components of this income growth with family or personal maturation. One reflects growth in the economy—if the economy grows, the income of each family or potential earner should rise with this growth. The other reflects increase in income with maturation. As a person grows older (short of retirement) one would expect his income to rise with his added experience. As with all indicators, one might object to any stringent interpretation —in this instance, the need at times to qualify the function of the age-income relationship. How much of the rise in income with age results from rules governing seniority per se and how much from increased productivity with job training and added responsibilities is a further challenge to analysis.

The study of earning power over the life span involves essentially an examination of various data on income by age. Following in part the work done by Herman Miller,[9] in examination of the relationship between income and age, we attempt to separate the effect of (1) the difference in income due to age in any given year, and (2) the cohort difference due to both age and the general rise in incomes. Table 8 uses cross-sectional age differences as a measure of the first effect, and cohort differences as a measure of the second effect. Since the second effect includes both the effect of aging *and* the effect of a general rise in incomes associated with economic growth, the difference between the two is an estimate of the effect of economic growth.

In this table data are shown by moving or successive decades starting with the 1947 to 1957 span and all the way to the one for 1954 to 1964. This represents additional time series data not presented by Miller. He used only the 1949–1959 decade but in considerably more detail as discussed at a further point in this analysis.

Median family income, as a result of age, per se, rises more sharply in the earliest stage of life shown in the table and for each cross-section except for 1949. Income rises up to the forty-five to fifty-four age range and then declines. The rise in income associated with economic growth (the difference between the data based on cross-section and on cohorts) is also quite a bit higher for the younger than for the older groups.

The families with youngest family heads showed increases (due to general economic growth) in almost every decade that exceeded the general growth in the economy as measured by GNP or disposable income in constant prices. The oldest benefited the least from economic growth. While there seems to be general stability in the age-income relationships over the years shown in the table, some discontinuity is evident, which may be more indicative of the approximate accuracy of the data than of any significant change in actual incomes. See, for example, the very small percentage changes due to age in 1951 and 1952 for the group forty-five to fifty-four compared with thirty-five to forty-four.

We discuss the income-age relationship further using more detailed data for only the 1949–1959 decade for male earners developed by Miller. Miller divided the increase in income over the 1949–1959 period into the two components described above—age and the general rise in income due to economic growth. As shown in Table 9, in

TABLE 8. PERCENTAGE CHANGES IN MEDIAN FAMILY INCOME DUE TO AGE AND ECONOMIC GROWTH, BY DECADES, 1947–1964

Decade	GNP	Disposable income	25-34 to 35-44			35-44 to 45-54			45-54 to 55-64			55-64 to 65 and over		
			Age	Age plus growth	Difference	Age	Age plus growth	Difference	Age	Age plus growth	Difference	Age	Age plus growth	Difference
1947–1957	46.0	44.9	12.3	50.6	38.3	4.8	34.8	30.0	− 7.3	9.9	+17.2	−42.8	−37.4	+ 5.4
1948–1958	38.2	38.7	9.4	51.1	41.7	4.8	38.8	34.0	−10.0	18.3	+28.3	−41.2	−31.5	+ 9.7
1949–1959	46.8	44.3	4.2	57.8	53.6	4.4	51.3	46.9	− 9.5	27.9	+37.4	−40.0	−26.3	+13.7
1950–1960	37.3	36.3	6.8	55.0	48.2	2.5	46.6	44.1	− 9.1	22.9	+32.0	−43.0	−29.5	+13.5
1951–1961	29.7	37.2	6.3	48.0	41.7	−0.2	43.3	43.5	−10.1	24.7	+34.8	−46.2	−27.8	+18.4
1952–1962	34.1	39.5	7.3	48.2	40.9	0.4	43.2	42.8	−12.7	25.6	+38.3	−40.1	−25.9	+14.2
1953–1963	33.5	38.5	5.9	41.6	35.7	5.3	40.1	34.8	−15.1	16.3	+31.4	−46.1	−29.2	+16.9
1954–1964	42.8	46.6	9.8	52.6	42.8	3.3	43.4	40.1	−15.9	19.9	+35.8	−43.4	−28.1	+15.3

NOTE: Family median income changes are calculated from data in Henson, Mary F., "Trends in the Income of Families and Persons in the United States, 1947–1964," Technical Report No. 17, Table 3, U.S. Bureau of the Census, Washington, 1967. Data are in constant prices for 1964. "Age" refers to cross-section data in the initial year of the decade and "age plus growth" to cohort data over the decade. "Difference" represents the estimated change in income due to economic growth. See Table 9 for fuller description. The "family median income" data refer to income before taxes and are therefore only broadly comparable with the aggregate measure of disposable income, which is after taxes. The aggregate figures on GNP and disposable income in the first two columns are provided for very broad comparisons between these aggregate measures of economic growth and those estimated for family median income shown under each age group and labeled "difference." GNP and disposable income are also in constant prices but pertain to 1958.

TABLE 9. CHANGE IN U.S. MALE INCOMES DUE TO AGE AND ECONOMIC GROWTH, BY COLOR AND EDUCATION, 1949–1959

Years of school completed and color	Age 25–34 and 35–44			Age 35–44 and 45–54			Age 45–54 and 55–64		
	Age[a]	Age plus growth[b]	Difference[c]	Age[a]	Age plus growth[b]	Difference[c]	Age[a]	Age plus growth[b]	Difference[c]
All classes									
Total	24	75	51	3	40	37	-13	22	35
Elementary, 8 yrs.	19	53	34	7	33	26	-7	18	25
High school, 4 yrs.	24	63	39	17	38	21	-3	18	21
College, 4 yrs. or more	76	127	51	15	35	20	-6	12	18
White									
Total	25	76	51	3	39	36	-15	21	36
Elementary	19	54	35	7	33	26	-8	18	26
High school	24	64	40	17	38	21	-3	19	22
College	76	128	52	15	35	20	-6	12	18
Nonwhite									
Total	6	63	57	-4	39	43	-16	24	40
Elementary	9	52	43	3	37	34	-8	24	32
High school	11	59	48	—	36	36	-10	26	36
College	40	103	63	6	56	50	-16	37	53

[a] Change based on ratio of income between age groups in 1949; e.g., group 35–44 had a 24 per cent higher income than the 25–34-year-olds in 1949.

[b] Change based on ratio for given age group as it grew older from 1949 to 1959; e.g., the 25–34-year-olds increased their income 75 per cent as they grew older from 1949 to 1959, and as the economy grew.

[c] The difference between the first two columns represents the change due to economic growth.

SOURCE: Based on data from Miller, Herman P., *Income Distribution in the United States*, A 1960 Census Monograph, U.S. Bureau of the Census, Washington, 1966, Table VI-2.

469

1949 males between the ages of thirty-five to forty-four had a mean income 24 per cent higher than those in the group twenty-five to thirty-four. The table also shows that the group thirty-five to forty-four years of age in 1959 had a mean income 75 per cent higher than this age group had when in 1949 they were ten years younger. Over the ten-year span they increased their income, both because of the increase due to added experience with age and also because of the general growth in income of the economy. The difference, 51 per cent, may be said to be the increase resulting from economic growth. For the 1949–1959 decade it was about twice the increase due to age alone. This is equivalent to about 4.2 per cent per year compounded. The rise in total U.S. personal income (before taxes but corrected for price changes as is the census measure) over this period as estimated by the Department of Commerce was 43 per cent or at a rate of 3.7 per cent per year.

Further examination of the table shows that for each education level the young men benefited more from economic growth than the older men. For example, in the case of college graduates, the increase from 1949 to 1959 due to economic growth was 51 per cent for the group that was twenty-five to thirty-four in 1949, while the increase in incomes as a result of economic growth for the graduates who were thirty-five to forty-four in 1949 was 20 per cent by 1959. In the next age grouping shown in the table the increase due to economic growth was 18 per cent.

A higher increase due to economic growth for the young is evident for other education levels for both white and nonwhite. The familiar finding that education provides larger percentage increases in income with age for whites than for nonwhites is illustrated in this table. Thus a white college graduate in 1949 could expect on the average to increase his income by 76 per cent in about ten years in the process of maturing from age twenty-five to thirty-four to age thirty-five to forty-four. His nonwhite counterpart, based on these findings, could expect a 40 per cent rise, partly because of much less opportunity and partly because of generally poorer quality of education. The rise in later age groups while diminishing for both white and nonwhite, diminishes far less for white.

The increases due to economic growth, however, seem to tell a somewhat different story. Thus a young nonwhite college graduate in 1959 showed a rise of 63 per cent on the average due to economic growth from 1949 to 1959 compared to a 52 per cent rise for his white counterpart. The larger percentage rise for nonwhites due to economic growth is evident in all of the age groups shown in the table.

It is also noteworthy that in the older two age spans shown, economic growth has benefited the well-educated nonwhite *in relation to the less-educated nonwhite* to a much greater extent than was true of this relationship for whites. Thus the table shows that in the thirty-five to forty-four to forty-five to fifty-four age span incomes of non-white college graduates grew 50 per cent from 1949 to 1959 as a result of economic growth. For high school graduates it was 40 per cent. In the case of whites for this and the next age group, there was no appreciable difference in income gain due to economic growth between high school and college graduates. In fact, the figures suggest a slightly higher rise for the high school graduates.

Note that some of those who were college graduates in 1959 may not have been in that educational status in 1949—so that there is some error in the measurement of the extent to which economic growth confers benefits on those with high educational status. A panel study—holding both the age cohorts constant and recording the shift in education status—would be needed to record the full effect of education on differences in growth of income.

Analysis by region yields results which are less clear, probably reflecting the difficulties of too much aggregation, though still suggestive of the relation between high income and growth with age. We compare the combined North and West with the South, keeping in mind that incomes of men in the North and West averaged about a third higher than in the South for whites and for the nonwhites about 2.7 times higher, according to the census statistics for 1959.

As shown in Tables 10 and 11, college graduates in the North and West in 1949 evidenced more growth in income with age than in the South. But for nonwhites the difference was less pronounced, although the drop-off in income in later years in the South for nonwhites was greater than for nonwhites in the North and West.

The general stability of the tendency for marked growth of income with age for all groups, with especially marked differences in the rate of growth for nonwhite and white, men and women, highly and lowly educated, has been evident in the averages over the ten-year spans shown in the several tables above.

The differential growth in income with maturation is of interest in comparing men and women. It seems clear from the evidence in Table 12 giving data over a period of some twenty-five years that while in-

TABLE 10. CHANGE IN U.S. MALE INCOMES DUE TO AGE AND
ECONOMIC GROWTH BY COLOR, EDUCATION, AND REGION
(NORTH AND WEST), 1949–1959

Years of school completed and color	Age 25–34 and 35–44			Age 35–44 and 45–54			Age 45–54 and 55–64		
	Age[a]	Age plus growth[b]	Difference[c]	Age[a]	Age plus growth[b]	Difference[c]	Age[a]	Age plus growth[b]	Difference[c]
All classes									
Total	25	74	49	3	39	36	-14	21	36
Elementary, 8 years	18	52	34	6	33	27	-8	19	27
High school, 4 yrs.	23	64	41	17	39	22	-3	19	22
College, 4 yrs. or more	55	134	55	15	36	21	-6	13	19
White									
Total	26	76	50	3	40	37	-15	22	37
Elementary	18	53	35	6	33	27	-8	19	27
High school	24	65	41	17	40	23	-3	19	22
College	79	135	56	15	36	21	-6	13	19
Nonwhite									
Total	8	59	51	-3	37	40	-9	25	34
Elementary	8	48	40	1	36	35	-4	24	28
High school	10	61	51	1	41	40	-11	27	38
College	48	110	62	-1	64	65	-9	45	54

Source and notes: See Table 9.

472

TABLE 11. CHANGE IN U.S. MALE INCOMES DUE TO AGE AND ECONOMIC GROWTH BY COLOR, EDUCATION AND REGION (SOUTH), 1949–1959

Years of school completed and color	Age 25–34 and 35–44			Age 35–44 and 45–54			Age 45–54 and 55–64		
	Age[a]	Age plus growth[b]	Difference[c]	Age[a]	Age plus growth[b]	Difference[c]	Age[a]	Age plus growth[b]	Difference[c]
All classes									
Total	18	73	58	2	39	37	−14	22	36
Elementary, 8 yrs.	17	53	36	7	33	26	−7	18	25
High school, 4 yrs.	28	58	30	16	32	16	−4	16	20
College, 4 yrs. or more	63	107	44	16	55	39	−6	9	15
White									
Total	21	74	53	3	38	35	−15	21	36
Elementary	17	54	37	5	32	27	−7	18	25
High school	28	59	31	16	32	16	−5	16	21
College	65	108	43	15	55	40	−6	8	14
Nonwhite									
Total	4	50	46	−5	30	35	−20	12	32
Elementary	7	45	38	1	32	31	−17	16	33
High school	14	47	33	−8	25	33	−10	17	27
College	29	83	54	14	49	35	−19	23	42

SOURCE and notes: See Table 9.

TABLE 12. MEDIAN INCOME OF PERSONS BY AGE
AND SEX, SELECTED YEARS, 1941–1966

Sex and year	Age group					
	20–24	25–34	35–44	45–54	55–64	65 and over
Men						
1941	699	1,095	1,321	1,297	796	446
1951	1,855	3,004	3,219	2,887	2,315	823
1961	2,095	4,388	5,085	4,580	3,787	1,420
1965	3,191	6,007	6,714	6,363	5,250	2,116
1966	3,330	6,507	7,305	6,918	5,750	2,162
Women						
1941	267	278	259	291	224	240
1951	1,072	1,185	1,110	913	756	421
1961	1,130	1,309	1,494	1,515	1,034	734
1965	2,187	2,257	2,484	2,560	2,019	984
1966	2,126	2,350	2,590	2,758	2,214	1,085

SOURCES:
> 1941 data—Brady, Dorothy, "Age and the Income Distribution," Department of Health, Education and Welfare, Social Security Administration, Research Report No. 8, Washington, 1965.
> 1951, 1961—Henson, Mary F., "Trends in the Income of Families and Persons, 1947–64," Technical Paper No. 17, U.S. Bureau of the Census, Washington, 1967.
> 1965—*Current Population Reports,* Series P-60, no. 51, January, 1967, U.S. Bureau of the Census.
> 1966—*Current Population Reports,* Series P-60, no. 53, December, 1967, U. S. Bureau of the Census.

come levels are obviously higher for men than for women and the growth in income over the life span is also more pronounced, what is of particular interest is that in the earliest year shown there is no growth pattern by age for women. Even as late as 1951 the average income growth pattern shows a tapering off quite early in life. But by 1961 the shape of the growth curve (though at a lower level) is much more like those of men.

Note that for the comparisons in this table it was not necessary to correct for price changes since from one year to the next, the relation between incomes of young and older persons may change only very slightly as a result of differences in the prices of things each requires for living. It is therefore pertinent merely to examine the changing pattern from year to year in the difference in income between the younger and older persons.

A final measure discussed in this section on income and age is one which might be considered as an expectational measure. It is not expectational in the sense that it is a measure of what people *would say* or think they expect—but râther of what people might expect on the basis of past experience of persons in their broad groupings by color and education. This is the measure of lifetime earnings shown in Figure 2. (Data are given in Reference Tables B and C at the end of the chapter.)

In 1959, young white males could expect their earnings to rise to a peak about twice that of a nonwhite. For equivalent educational levels (nominally equivalent, i.e., without regard to quality differences) white college graduates could look forward to an even higher relative difference in income growth than a nonwhite. Equally important, according to our conjecture on the significance of growth with maturation, is the fact that income for a white person continues to rise for a number of years after the earlier peak is reached for a nonwhite. The longer period of income growth with age is even more marked for white college graduates compared with their nonwhite counterparts. Clearly, however, both white and nonwhite college graduates could look forward to substantially more growth in income than their corresponding group average.

The data in Figure 2 are intended to illustrate only broadly the different patterns of expectation of income growth. They are by no means precise for several reasons. First, of course, a cross-section for 1959 may not fully reflect changes over time. Second, no adjustment is made in these figures (although data are available in the original source) for differences resulting from economic growth. This factor has been discussed earlier. Third, no adjustment was made for the difference between whites and nonwhites in their evaluation of the future. It seems reasonable to suppose at least at this writing that nonwhites discount the future at a higher rate (in other words, value it less) than whites. A higher discount rate for nonwhites than for whites, in order to show the present value of expected earnings, would widen the relative differences between whites and nonwhites shown in Figure 2.

By way of summary, the examination of data on income in relation to age has shown that this growth with age is far less evident for the disadvantaged than for others. More specifically it has shown:

1. The growth in income with age is much more marked for men than for women, though the growth pattern for women has shown considerable improvement.
2. It is far more marked for whites than nonwhites for each level of education completed. This was particularly evident in the

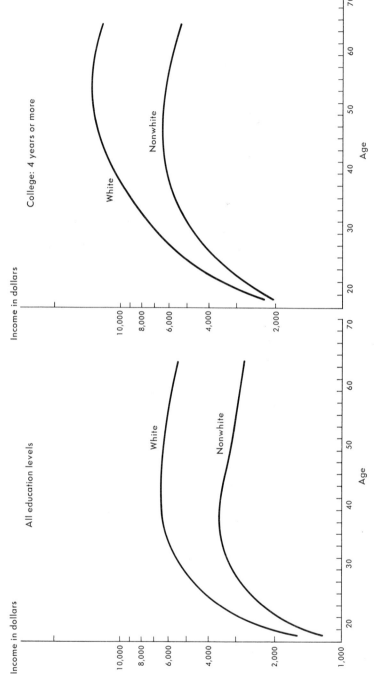

FIGURE 2. EXPECTED LIFETIME EARNINGS FOR MALES IN 1959

NOTE: This chart is plotted on a ratio scale.

SOURCES: Based on data from Miller, H. P., and R. A. Hornseth, "Present Value of Estimated Lifetime Earnings," U.S. Bureau of the Census Technical Paper No. 16, Washington, 1967. See this source for description of estimates. Basic data for this chart are in Reference Tables B and C, pp. 520–521.

measure of earning power as indicated in the figure on lifetime earnings.

3. College graduates have a much more pronounced growth in income with age than those with less schooling, but the difference between white and nonwhite is greater at this level than at lower education levels.

It is suggested that the nature of growth in income with maturation be explored much more fully as an added dimension to comparisons of levels of living over time and among different regions and countries. This should be done not only to sharpen the study of economic disadvantage, at any one time, but more broadly to include a study of the changing pattern of differences in economic expectation among all significant groupings, including key groups within a middle range of income.

In this connection some emphasis should be put on the fact that our data are quite inadequate to the task of dealing with significant groupings within the middle range of income. In particular the blue-collar (sometimes referred to clumsily as "nonsupervisory personnel"), the low-income white-collar, and possibly the small proprietor are in a special situation today. These groups have had to bear much of the problem of adjustments resulting from special advantages that have been conferred upon the poor through improved housing, job training, and lowering the barriers to job entry. The problems of adjustments within neighborhoods, in the schools, and on the job have doubtless been more severe for these groups in the lower-middle range of incomes than for those at much higher levels, and might explain some of the antagonisms expressed by these groups toward policies designed to help the most disadvantaged classes.

This note on where our data frontier seems to stop should be seen as a call to enrich research on the distribution of social benefits and costs. Socioeconomic groupings other than size groupings of income are needed. The white-nonwhite classification discussed earlier is a significant step in this direction, but it is clear that other social groupings of data are needed.

While information on income by occupation is surely helpful in this connection, the need is greater and requires not only a measure of economic benefit (such as income and assets) and by significant socioeconomic groupings—but also of cost—including taxes and perhaps less measurable—the major problems of adjustment to social change, such as those faced by people in the low-middle range of income, and others.

CHOICE AND CONSUMER BEHAVIOR

Is consumption absolute? Obviously not. Certainly no economic goal should be expected to provide the answer to all things. But beyond a fruitless metaphysical probe on the meaning of consumer satisfaction, it is useful to ask how one evaluates the goal of ever-increasing levels of material well-being. Does this goal lead to longer life, greater opportunities for fulfilling individual abilities and expectations, lessened crime and disease, and in general to enhanced benefits to individuals and society? This search for a gain in terms that include but go beyond the measuring rod of income and wealth is one of the essential tasks of appraising social change and is especially challenging in the area of consumption. We will briefly examine some aspects of this issue in the latter part of this section. We raise this question now in order to emphasize one main, perhaps obvious, point: The importance of the continued increase in economic well-being cannot be appraised simply by charting its growing volume.

It is true, of course, that an increasing volume of production and consumption of goods and services necessarily implies that society, through individual and collective choice, has been willing to pay for this growing volume of goods and services. The fact that production and consumption has been growing implies a growing "willingness" to pay the requisite prices.

However, the issue of appraising changing consumption levels goes deeper. Consider the following:

1. Consumption per se, by apparent preference, diminishes and investment rises in relation to total personal income as one goes up the income scale, suggesting a diminishing marginal utility to purchases of goods and services. This is true at least in comparing different families at a given point in time. Over time the problem is more complicated and will be discussed further in this section. That there is diminishing preference for food and certain other basics as income increases over time as well as among families is well established—and can even be numbered as one of the very few laws of economics.

2. Consumption goods may conceivably increase their "productivity" in the sense of satisfaction per unit of consumption. To the extent, therefore, that some consumer goods are inputs to satisfaction, the smaller the input for the given level of satisfaction, the higher the "productivity" of consumer goods and the lower will be the requirement per unit of satisfaction. Thus, for example, a person who can

make do with less expense for housing plus transportation would be better off than if he has more expense, assuming equal satisfaction.

3. The person, family, or community that has greater public facilities for general use as supplements rather than as substitutes for what may be financed out of personal income is better off than one with lesser facilities. By this we mean, clearly, that comparing two persons in different communities, enjoying the same personal income and personal consumption, the one with greater public facilities is better off than the one with the lesser. To what extent, however, the person enjoying added public facilities is better off than a person in another community with the same total value of consumption but in which the same facilities (say, education) must be paid for privately—is a particularly challenging question.

4. A person with more information about consumption and investment is potentially better off than his counterpart with less information but with the same amount of time to choose. The more knowledgable person may obtain the same bundle of goods for lower prices, or out of a given income obtain a larger bundle, or make a better choice, because enhanced knowledge permits him to find the lower prices or the better quality goods or the investments with the higher rates of return.

5. Finally, the person whose choices can be made with little danger of personal harm or risk of loss of income—under conditions in which either markets are functioning efficiently or public protection is provided—is better off than the person without such protective conditions.

We suggest that all of the above may be subsumed under the general issue of choice. That is, at almost any level of income, and certainly as income levels rise higher and higher—*choices* become the main issue of personal, family, and social improvement. These choices involve the allocation of income and time among various goods and services, the choices among investments, and between consumption and investment. Finally, for society as a whole choices must be made as to how much of total effort and resources should go to private and how much to public goods and services.

To deal with this broad problem we propose to consider four aspects:

1. The life cycle over which choices must be made;
2. The growing importance of investment in all forms;
3. The growing importance of consumption that is collectively provided and used;

4. The significance of time as a fundamental element of cost in consumption.

The Life Cycle

Levels of living encompass all the economic costs and rewards that span a lifetime. An adequate study of living conditions must take into account the process by which resources are used to enable persons and households to take care of their bodily needs and tastes, to plan their future in the way of major expenses for a growing career, a home and its furnishings, or for a car, for major medical expenses, and for major educational expenses for themselves and their children. It comprises the need to meet the stream of expenses that come in small amounts day by day and for those that come in large chunks—the ones that require large outlays, special financing, and particular judgments based on one's aspirations or status.

As the family or single adult matures, changes in consumption and investment unavoidably occur. The young consumer seeks a different volume and composition of goods and services from the old, and he devotes a different portion of his time and income to investment in the form of training or financial or tangible asset formation.

The process of maturation, as far as consumer behavior is concerned, is a threefold one involving (1) changing growth in income both as maturation proceeds and the total economy grows, (2) differing tastes as people grow older and their incomes change, and (3) asset formation.

Since these processes involve decisions concerning trade-offs between present and future, between consumption and investment (i.e., between immediate satisfactions and increasing future earning or consuming capability) they are at the very core of the issue of choice.

Income. In an earlier section we conjectured that different patterns of growth in income with age were basic to the measurement of relative well-being or deprivation. The different patterns of *actual* growth in income over the life cycle, and the implications of these existing or past patterns of expectations, clearly make for a considerable difference in ability to plan for the future and to meet changing needs.

In this section, we do not stress the differences, though they are especially marked by color, occupation, and sex. What we do place emphasis on at this point is the showing that by and large for a broad mass of the people in our society income does grow markedly with age, and that this pattern is probably highly predictable in a statistical sense (rather than for any one individual). The curves of lifetime earnings in Figure 2 and the suggestion emerging from Table 8 that the tapering off in growth in incomes in later stages of life may be diminishing underscore the stability of this relationship. Also, as was shown in Table 12, while the growth in income with age for women has been a relatively recent phenomenon, it is apparently now well established.

As was pointed out earlier, the rise in income with age is associated both with maturation or rising individual productivity as well as with a generally rising and more productive economy. One force presumably reinforces the other. In particular, if the growth in economy is more stable—less cyclical fluctuation—the predictability of the increase in income with age is reinforced.

The increased stability of growth in the economy is illustrated in Figure 1 which shows that the growth in total income during the period after World War II is the most stable in the entire period since the beginning of the century. The upward trend in income in the chart shows up as nearly a straight line (plotted on a ratio scale), suggesting that in the past two decades the predictability of growth in income over the life span has probably been strengthened.

In the sections which follow on consumption and asset formation we illustrate the simple and obvious fact that the allocation of income varies considerably over the life cycle. The broad aggregate data show this rather imprecisely but adequately enough to emphasize that the study of family maturation in terms of income growth and use needs much more attention. But following this path is likely to be necessary if depth in the measurement of consumer choice is to be achieved.

Consumption. The changing character of expenditures by age is illustrated in Table 13, based on the Labor Department's Survey of Consumer Expenditures. The percentage shares of major expenditures for house furnishings and equipment and for autos predominate in the earliest adult family stages, education expenses nearer the middle and later stages, and food and medical care in the latest phases. The percentage share for shelter is highest at the earliest and latest stages.

Because income and age are positively correlated up to approximately a middle range of income and then negatively correlated, expenditure and age are cross-classified with income in Tables 14 and 15, the first on house furnishings, the second on auto purchase.

For all age groups, the percentage spent for house furnishings and equipment declines with age. It starts at around 6 to 7 per cent of total expenditures at age twenty-five and declines to under 4 per cent in the

TABLE 13. PERCENTAGE DISTRIBUTION OF PERSONAL CONSUMPTION EXPENDITURES, BY AGE OF HEAD, 1960–1961

Age group	Total	Food	Shelter	House Furnishings and Equip.	Clothing	Medical care	Education	Auto	All other
Total	100.0	24.5	13.0	5.3	10.3	6.7	1.0	13.7	25.5
Under 25	100.0	21.6	15.1	6.6	9.2	5.9	1.0	18.3	22.3
25–34	100.0	23.6	14.3	6.0	9.8	6.0	0.7	14.7	24.9
35–44	100.0	25.0	12.3	5.5	11.4	5.8	1.1	13.7	25.2
45–54	100.0	24.2	11.8	4.9	11.4	6.2	1.8	14.1	25.6
55–64	100.0	24.8	12.6	4.8	9.6	7.8	0.8	13.3	26.3
65–74	100.0	25.5	14.6	4.3	7.5	9.7	0.3	10.7	27.4
75 and over	100.0	27.4	16.1	3.6	6.1	12.1	0.2	7.6	26.9

SOURCE: "Consumer Expenditures and Income," Report No. 237–93, U.S. Bureau of Labor Statistics, June, 1966, Table 3A. Includes all urban and rural families and single consumers in the U.S.

TABLE 14. PERCENTAGE DISTRIBUTION OF HOUSE FURNISHINGS AND EQUIPMENT, BY INCOME AND AGE OF HEAD, 1960–1961

Income	Total	Age						
		Under 25	25–34	35–44	45–54	55–64	65–74	75 and over
Total	5.3	6.6	6.0	5.5	4.9	4.8	4.3	3.6
Under $ 1,000	3.8	3.7	8.2	2.8	3.6	3.9	4.1	2.9
1,000– 1,900	4.0	5.1	4.8	5.9	5.0	3.8	3.6	3.2
2,000– 2,900	4.4	4.4	4.8	4.6	5.0	4.1	4.1	3.6
3,000– 3,900	4.9	5.9	5.2	4.9	5.0	4.7	4.1	4.9
4,000– 4,900	5.1	5.6	5.5	5.0	4.8	4.8	4.9	3.2
5,000– 5,900	5.5	8.3	6.4	4.9	4.8	4.8	4.6	2.5
6,000– 7,400	5.5	8.4	6.2	5.4	4.9	5.3	5.0	4.2
7,500– 9,900	5.5	6.5	6.2	5.7	5.1	4.7	4.3	4.3
10,000–14,900	5.5	1.9	6.8	5.7	5.3	5.1	3.8	3.9
15,000 and over	5.4	7.9	9.5	7.2	4.2	5.2	4.5	3.7

SOURCE: See Table 13; "Consumer Expenditures and Income," Table 1A and Supplement 2, Tables 14a–14g.

TABLE 15. PERCENTAGE DISTRIBUTION OF AUTOMOBILE PURCHASE, BY INCOME AND AGE OF HEAD, 1960–1961

Income	Total	Age						
		Under 25	25–34	35–44	45–54	55–64	65–74	75 and over
Total	13.7	18.2	14.7	13.7	14.1	13.3	10.7	7.6
Under $ 1,000	5.3	5.8	6.9	11.9	6.5	5.8	3.2	2.0
1,000– 1,900	6.3	9.5	8.6	6.1	8.6	7.9	5.6	3.2
2,000– 2,900	9.4	12.2	10.9	11.8	8.4	9.0	8.3	6.9
3,000– 3,900	12.8	17.7	14.9	12.5	12.2	11.1	10.9	8.6
4,000– 4,900	15.0	22.1	15.2	13.2	14.9	14.9	13.3	10.9
5,000– 5,900	14.8	19.3	15.6	13.6	15.2	14.1	12.8	12.8
6,000– 7,400	14.6	17.2	15.2	13.7	15.0	14.7	14.1	5.4
7,500– 9,900	15.1	21.0	14.4	15.0	15.0	15.7	15.6	12.8
10,000–14,900	14.6	25.3	15.3	14.0	15.2	14.6	12.3	15.1
15,000 and over	11.2	7.3	7.9	11.5	11.8	10.3	9.5	19.8

SOURCE: See Table 13; "Consumer Expenditures and Income," Table 1A and Supplement 2, Tables 14a–14g.

484

late ages. The lowest income groups show the same general pattern, but it is somewhat more erratic, either peaking at a somewhat later age or having more than one peak. For example, for incomes under $3,000 or $4,000, peaks in the percentage share show up after thirty-five years of age. As incomes rise, the tendency for the high peak to show up in the earlier age groups (under thirty-four) is most marked and the decline in the share in later stages of life more pronounced. The exceptionally low percentage shown for the group with $10,000 to $14,900 in income and under twenty-five is very likely a result of large sampling error.

A straightforward reading of Table 15 shows that the share of expenditures for autos declines with age more clearly for the lower income than for the higher income groups. This contrast in the decline with age between high and low income groups is less evident for house furnishings than for autos.

One should consider in tables of this sort an adjustment that takes into account that income rises in nearly all cases with age. Keeping income constant, as these tables purport to do, doesn't truly reflect the life cycle effect. A proper adjustment would need to be based on a longitudinal study of families. But a very rough notion can be obtained. If one lets income and age rise by, say, roughly going along a diagonal, rather than horizontal, path in the tables there is a clearer decline in the percentage spent for autos and house furnishings, as age and income increase together.

These tables are largely illustrative of what is essentially an obvious point, namely, that the timing of major expenditures varies over the life span. These and other major outlays may be more predictable if examined more closely than can be done here. To what extent these outlays could be made more rational in terms of their amount, their timing, use of income, of credit, and assets is a challenge in future study of consumption.

Personal Wealth. One of the most comprehensive sources of information on personal wealth holdings by type of wealth and wealth holder is the Survey of Financial Characteristics of Consumers conducted for the Federal Reserve Board in the spring of 1963. Questions on assets and debt were asked in great detail as of December, 1962, and related to income and various other characteristics. The sample was specially designed to include a large number of relatively wealthy consumers and to still be representative of all units in the United States.

The unprecedented detail obtained on wealth and the various checks made on reliability for this survey give it a special place in an extremely difficult area of economic observation. At the same time, it should be recognized that data of this kind are especially subject to error—broadly speaking, subject to understatement. It is believed, however, that the distributions tend to provide a reasonably reliable profile of wealth holdings, even though the broad aggregates derivable from the survey tend to be below national totals obtained from financial institutions.

Our purpose in using these data is to stress the relation of wealth and its composition to the life cycle, using age of the head of the consumer unit as the life cycle variable.

The relationship of amount of wealth with age is shown in Table 16. The data are cross-classified with income. As the table shows, in all but two income classes, the amount of wealth rises systematically with age to a peak in the oldest age group. In the relatively high income classes the relationship is somewhat less systematic. For example, in the income ranging between $25,000 to $50,000, the youngest age group shown has the largest amount of wealth. This is caused by exceptionally large holdings of miscellaneous assets, mostly personal trusts, which is probably a random occurrence, to be expected when the numbers in the cells become rather small as a result of the three-way tabulation of income, age, and wealth. Sampling error is probably also responsible for the decline in wealth at age sixty-five and over for the $100,000 and over income group.

The rise in wealth with age would probably be even more substantial and the decline for the poorest of the oldest age group somewhat reduced if instead of a cross-section analysis as shown in this table, a cohort or longitudinal analysis for a significant time span were shown instead. Unfortunately, such data are not available in this survey.

An interesting attempt at a cohort analysis was undertaken by Lansing and Sonquist using data from the Surveys of Consumer Finances in 1953 and 1962 of the Survey Research Center at the University of Michigan.[10] Samples of heads of spending units born within ± five years of 1890, 1900, 1910, 1920, and 1929 formed the cohorts whose change in wealth from 1953 to 1962 was examined in this study.

The familiar pattern of wealth increasing in level with age is shown in Table 17 for the year 1962 for both whites and Negroes. Increases in wealth from 1953 to 1962 were generally more marked for the young than for the old and somewhat higher for the ones with more schooling. Whites had far more wealth than Negroes. Note, for ex-

TABLE 16. COMPOSITION OF WEALTH, MEAN AMOUNT BY INCOME AND AGE, DECEMBER 31, 1962

1962 income	All units	Age Under 35	35–54	55–64	65 and over
All units	20,982	6,304	19,305	32,527	30,838
0– 2,999	7,609	1,802	4,500	11,127	9,702
3,000– 4,999	10,025	1,158	7,176	16,781	22,474
5,000– 7,499	13,207	5,005	12,534	20,677	37,767
7,500– 9,999	19,131	5,904	15,190	39,917	58,545
10,000–14,999	28,021	10,807	24,626	36,565	89,148
15,000–24,999	62,966	22,734	47,112	83,009	169,315
25,000–49,999	291,317	1,396,328	190,297	262,028	432,882
50,000–99,999	653,223	647,323	743,609	549,204	688,613
100,000 and over	1,698,021	n.a.	2,120,093	3,006,155	1,193,042

NOTE: Wealth is defined in this survey to be the value (generally market value as of the end of 1962) of assets minus the debts secured by these assets. Assets covered in the survey included two tangibles: homes and autos, financial assets including the value of equities in family-owned farms, businesses, or professions, liquid assets (checking and savings accounts and U.S. savings bonds), investment assets (mainly marketable securities, investment in real estate, and mortages), and a miscellaneous group consisting largely of assets held in trust.

SOURCE: Projector, D. S., and G. S. Weiss, "Survey of Financial Characteristics of Consumers," Federal Reserve Board, 1966, based on data from Table A8, pp. 110–111.

487

TABLE 17. MEAN NET WORTH OF SPENDING UNITS BY AGE AND COLOR OF HEAD OF UNIT AND EDUCATION OF WHITE

WHITE

Cohort	Grammar School		High School		College	
	Level in 1962	Percentage increase 1953–1962	Level in 1962	Percentage increase 1953–1962	Level in 1962	Percentage increase 1953–1962
1929	2,700	3.8	7,900	139.4	14,200	173.1
1920	7,500	44.2	15,400	94.9	23,800	91.9
1910	14,100	67.9	21,200	43.2	35,800	59.8
1900	14,000	12.0	23,700	9.2	33,200	-1.5
1890	11,400	-16.2	19,800	-18.2	61,200	35.4

NEGRO—ALL EDUCATION LEVELS

Cohort	Level in 1962	Percentage increase 1953–1962
1929	1,900	216.7
1920	3,500	105.9
1910	3,800	22.6
1900	4,100	2.5
1890	3,400	-30.6

SOURCE: Lansing, J. B., and J. Sonquist, "A Cohort Analysis of Changes in the Distribution of Wealth," Conference on Research in Income and Wealth, March, 1967.

488

ample, that the average amount of wealth for each Negro cohort at all education levels was only a small fraction of the wealth held by whites who had only a grammar school education. The percentage increase from 1953 to 1962, however, for the youngest Negro cohort (those born in 1929) was larger than for any white group.

Lansing and Sonquist caution against precise use of the data, particularly the very small rise for the young white persons with only a grammar school education and the very large rise in the oldest of the white college graduates (probably due to sampling error possibly arising from an exceptional captial gain in stocks).

Returning to the Federal Reserve Survey, Table 18 provides information on types of assets in relation to age. Ownership of tangible assets (a house or car) or a private business is relatively important in the earlier stages of life. In the later stages liquid assets and particularly investment assets (e.g., marketable securities) increase in importance.

TABLE 18. PERCENTAGE DISTRIBUTION OF FORMS OF WEALTH BY AGE GROUP

| Form of wealth | All units | Age of head | | | | |
		Under 35	35–44	45–54	55–64	65 and over
Total	100	100	100	100	100	100
Own home	27	26	31	33	25	22
Automobile	3	7	5	4	2	1
Business	18	12	23	23	20	12
Liquid assets	13	9	10	11	13	16
Investment assets	33	13	22	26	38	47
Miscellaneous assets	5	32	9	3	2	1

Source: See Table 16.

Following the Federal Reserve Board survey, which was taken in the spring of 1963 and which emphasized the amount of net worth at the end of 1962, the same group was reinterviewed a year later to emphasize the flow of savings during 1963. The two interviews together provide a basis for measuring changes in family finances. A study based on this second survey was made available to me prior to publication by the Federal Reserve Board.[11]

A highly useful series of distributions for 1946, 1948, 1949, 1950, 1960–1961, and 1963 shown in Table 19 was put together in this study showing the relation between age and income and saving (see footnotes to this and earlier tables for definition of saving).

The column in the table entitled "income mean ratio" is the ratio of mean income of the given age group to the mean income for all groups. Thus, according to the 1963 Survey of Changes in Family Finances (the last bank of figures in the lower right corner of Table 19) the mean income for the youngest units was 71 per cent of the general mean. This ratio reaches a peak, about a fourth higher than the general mean, in the forty-five to fifty-four age group. The life cycle patterns of income and saving are broadly similar from one survey to the next.

The saving mean ratio reached higher peaks than income in the older but not the oldest age groups in all surveys. Saving in relation to income is shown to be an increasing function of age for all surveys except that for 1963. The exception in the 1963 survey results from a high saving-income ratio in the twenty-five to thirty-four age group. The 1963 survey, however, was believed to have understated debt (and hence overstated saving) presumably in the youngest age. If this understatement is allowed for, a significant part of the departure of the 1963 data from the tendency of saving to increase with age is reduced.

The Projector study attempts to examine the results of the 1963 survey in the light of several theories which determine saving. Most theories deal with *total* saving in relation to income not its differing composition in relation to income.

One of the most important theories for our purpose examined in the Projector study is the Modigliani and Ando theory of the life cycle. According to this theory, "the purpose of saving is to enable the household to redistribute the resources it gets (and expects to get) over its life cycle in order to secure the most desirable pattern of consumption over life."[12]

Without attempting to define what this "most desirable pattern" might mean, the relevant question is whether the optimum sought by consumers is over the general span of life or in any current period in relation to current income.

The significant variables of importance in this hypothesis are: current income, income to be expected over the remaining life span (expressed in terms of a present value of future earnings—as we have shown earlier in Figure 2) and the current worth of saving (assets minus debt).

Younger consumers would be expected on the basis of this hypothesis to spend in a given year a smaller fraction of their *current net worth* than older consumers because the use of a given amount of resources is supposed to extend over a longer period for the young than for the old.

With regard to the use of *current income,* this hypothesis says that as current income varies (generally upward with age aside from short-run changes), the fraction of the change in income spent for consumption depends upon the total anticipated resources over the life span. A given rise in current income, according to this view, will produce a larger increase in expected total future resources for the young than for the old. As a consequence, younger people will spend a larger fraction of a given increase in current income—and this fraction will decline with age until the oldest working age group (fifty-five to sixty-four). Beyond this age the fraction increases. The Projector survey found its data "to be in accord with a modified life cycle theory," although various complications of data, definitions of savings, and assumptions about bequests, make a precise test difficult.

What is important for our purpose is not so much the question of whether some optimum consumption-saving pattern *in fact* is *planned* over a life span as that major changes in economic and social requirements over the life span necessitate understanding of the pattern of growth of economic resources. If the level of well-being is to be appraised in this context, it is well to know to what extent consumption and saving is or has been guided by foolish or wise hopes and by the presence or absence of regrets—vain or otherwise.

The significance of the age-income, consumption-and-asset relationships has not been fully explicated in this writing. The data presented are largely illustrative of the pervasive importance of the age factor and the implication that research be oriented more to an understanding of the decision process over the life span.

Growth in Assets and Debt

The expansion in holdings of wealth in financial and physical form constitutes one of the major trends in recent history of U.S. households. Accompanying this expansion has been a continuation of the upward trend in consumer debt—particularly long-term mortgage debt and also shorter-term instalment and noninstalment credit.

The changing amounts outstanding and composition of financial assets and liabilities are shown in Table 20 based on data published by the Federal Reserve Board. In the twenty-year period shown, total financial assets grew fourfold to an estimated figure of $1,438.8 billion by the end of 1965, while debt grew tenfold to a level of $342.5 bil-

TABLE 19. RELATION AMONG SAVING, INCOME, AND AGE OF CONSUMER UNIT, SELECTED YEARS, 1946–1963

Age of head	1946 Income mean ratio	1946 Saving mean ratio	1946 Mean saving as percentage of mean income	1948 Income mean ratio	1948 Saving mean ratio	1948 Mean saving as percentage of mean income	1949 Income mean ratio	1949 Saving mean ratio	1949 Mean saving as percentage of mean income
18–24	57	−15	−3	65	−27	−3	64	−36	−3
25–34	95	57	6	98	56	4	97	40	2
35–44	118	136	12	119	149	8	118	113	5
45–54	{116	{149	{13	122	197	11	121	179	8
55–64				103	122	8	109	225	11
65 and over	57	55	10	61	13	1	64	36	3

Age of head	1950 Income mean ratio	1950 Saving mean ratio	1950 Mean saving as percentage of mean income	1960–61 Saving A Income mean ratio	1960–61 Saving A Saving mean ratio	1960–61 Saving A Mean saving as percentage of mean income
18–24	67	22	3	76	14	2
25–34	104	67	5	103	94	8
35–44	119	143	9	122	126	9
45–54	118	158	10	120	143	11
55–64	103	141	11	96	114	11
65 and over	54	2	a	60	41	6

	1960–61 Saving C			1963		
18–24	76	−61	−3	71	37	5
25–34	103	80	3	105	145	13
35–44	122	116	3	122	118	9
45–54	120	152	5	124	180	14
55–64	96	145	5	95	74	8
65 and over	60	50	3	57	−8	−1

a Less than ½ of 1 per cent.

SOURCES: Projector, D., "Survey of Changes in Family Finances," Federal Reserve Board, in press.

Data for 1946, 1948–1950 are from Surveys of Consumer Finances. Data for 1946 are published in Fisher, Janet A., "Income, Spending, and Saving Patterns of Consumer Units in Different Age Groups," *Studies in Income and Wealth*, vol. XV, National Bureau of Economic Research, New York, 1952, p. 92. Data on saving and its distribution by age group for 1948–1950 are from "1951 Survey of Consumer Finances, Part IV, Distribution of Consumer Saving in 1950," *Federal Reserve Bulletin*, September, 1951, Tables 7 and 16. Data on mean income are shown in "1951 Survey of Consumer Finances, Part III, Distribution of Consumer Income in 1950," *Federal Reserve Bulletin*, August, 1951, Table 1. The distribution of income by age group is from unpublished data. Saving excludes purchases of consumer durable goods and includes life insurance premiums. Income is before tax.

Data for 1960–1961 are from the Survey of Consumer Expenditures. The figures shown in the table are derived from the following publications of U.S. Bureau of Labor Statistics: "Consumer Expenditures and Income, Total United States, Urban and Rural, 1960–61," BLS Report No. 237–93 (USDA Report CES-15), February 1965, Table 3A, p. 13. Saving A is the sum of the Survey of Consumer Expenditures items "net change in assets and liabilities" and "personal insurance." Saving C is the Survey of Consumer Expenditures item "net change in assets and liabilities." Income is money income after taxes.

Data for 1963 are from the Survey of Changes in Family Finances. Saving is the Survey of Changes in Family Finances concept of saving less net purchases of automobiles and less payments to retirement plans. Income is disposable income.

TABLE 20. FINANCIAL ASSETS AND LIABILITIES OF U.S. HOUSEHOLDS (YEAR-END AMOUNTS OUTSTANDING), 1945–1965

Assets and liabilities	1945	1950	1955	1960	1965	Percentage increases 1945–55	1955–65
	(billions of dollars)						
Total Assets	355.4	431.5	683.7	931.0	1,438.8	92.4	110.4
Checking accounts and currency	54.1	55.8	63.7	65.9	86.7	17.7	36.1
Savings accounts	50.0	67.1	105.5	165.3	279.5	111.0	164.9
Life insurance reserves	39.5	55.0	69.3	85.2	105.9	75.4	52.8
Pension reserves	9.9	23.8	49.6	89.4	150.8	401.0	104.0
U.S. government securities	65.1	66.7	66.8	69.8	77.6	2.6	16.2
State and local obligations	7.2	9.6	18.6	28.7	38.4	158.3	106.5
Corporate and foreign bonds	7.6	3.9	4.8	6.7	4.6	-33.8	-4.2
Corporate stock	110.6	133.3	284.9	394.3	666.3	157.6	133.9
Mortgages	5.4	7.7	9.3	11.8	10.3	72.2	10.8
Other	5.9	8.6	11.3	13.9	18.7	91.5	65.5
Total Liabilities	31.0	72.3	139.9	221.9	342.5	351.3	144.8
Mortgage debt	14.5	39.7	84.9	142.2	217.6	485.5	156.3
Short-term debt	5.7	21.5	38.8	56.0	87.9	580.7	126.5
Other	10.8	11.1	16.2	23.7	37.0	50.0	128.4

SOURCES: Derived from "Flow of Funds Accounts, 1945–1967," Federal Reserve Board, 1968, Table 8, p. 160. The household sector in the Flow of Funds accounts include—in addition to persons as members of households—personal trusts and nonprofit organizations serving individuals, such as foundations, private schools and hospitals, labor unions, churches, and charitable organizations. While no separate data on a continuing basis are available, the importance of personal trusts and nonprofit organizations in the early 1960's is estimated at about $60 billion in bank-administered personal trusts and roughly $25 to $30 billion in nonprofit organizations, or slightly under 1 per cent of the total household sector holdings ($1,100 billion in the early 1960's).

For slightly different levels than shown in the table, resulting mainly from a different definition of the household sector, see Goldsmith, R. W., R. E. Lipsey, and M. Mendelson, *Studies in the National Balance Sheet of the United States*, vol. II, National Bureau of Economic Research, New York, 1963. The trends in that source are in the main almost identical to the Federal Reserve for the period covered by both sources (1945–1958).

lion. The rate of increase in assets has apparently accelerated in the past ten years compared with the preceding decade, while the expansion rate for debt has declined though still remaining quite rapid.

The largest single financial asset category in all the years shown is corporate stock amounting at market value in 1965 to $666.3 billion. The rapid increase in stock holdings of 158 per cent in the first decade has abated only slightly in the second partly reflecting differential increases in stock market prices, which were more rapid in the first decade after World War II (mainly between 1950 and 1955) than in the second.

The growth in the various asset categories was particularly marked for pension and life insurance reserves and checking and savings accounts. Corporate bonds were the only holdings to decline in the twenty-year span, partly reflecting the marked increase in preference for corporate stock and the general inflation of prices. Since 1965 (the last year shown in the table), however, bond holdings have increased because of the sizable upswing in interest rates.

The expansion in financial assets of households described above has been accompanied by a considerable increase in ownership of wealth in tangible form. Data on the amount of tangible wealth (houses, autos, house furnishings, and other personal property in physical form) is much less reliable or even quantifiable than for financial assets largely because active markets and prices for tangible property (though widespread for houses and autos) are much less pervasive and specific than for financial assets.

In recent years the current gross outlays for purchase of houses, autos, and personal or household equipment has constituted about 10 per cent of the Gross National Product. It is estimated that in 1965 persons and families in the United States had in their possession a total value outstanding of property in the form of houses, equipment, furnishings, and automobiles amounting to around $700 billion in current market prices. (This includes about $70 billion in autos, approximately $120 billion in major household or other durables, roughly $450 billion in nonfarm owner-occupied housing plus land, and some $60 billion in miscellaneous physical holdings in business properties and other possessions.) [13]

Of course, these figures do not imply that if all of these goods were sold at once, so much cash would accrue to the owners. Nor do these values equal the amount of equity in those goods since debt on owner-occupied housing ($204 billion) and on autos and durables ($46 billion) totaled $250 billion or about 35 per cent of the asset value of tangible property. What the values do signify in a general way is that there exists an accumulation of capital or durable goods which at current market prices will provide the services to meet current goals of shelter, recreation, transportation, and other intangible goals over an extended period of time. Such considerations are important in the aggregate in time of war or depression when output and buying of such goods are curtailed. Anticipation of war shortages has led to "panic" buying of durables, for example, at the outbreak of the Korean war.

The dollar figures on trends for all households taken together surely imply that, on the whole, the increase in wealth has been very substantial indeed. But the wins, losses, and draws among various households over the years cannot easily be revealed. For a determination of such differences, as in many other evaluations of household behavior, a longitudinal study would be important to identify over a significant period of time, the shifts in fortunes of individual households.

In the absence of such in-depth studies some notion of the distribution of total wealth would be helpful. An approximate measure of how wealth in financial and tangible form is distributed among consumers is available from the Federal Reserve–Census Survey of Financial Characteristics. As indicated in Table 21, and as might well have been expected, investment assets (mortgages, real estate, corporate stock and other marketable securities) are much less equally distributed than ownership of a home, liquid assets (savings accounts, U.S. savings bonds, and checking accounts) or automobiles. For example, the 1 per cent of the consumer units whose total wealth holdings are $200,000 and over account for some 55 per cent of the total value of investment assets.

If we were to array consumer units by current income and by wealth (not shown in this table) we would find that wealth holdings are much more unequal than current income. We would also find that ownership of a home and of liquid assets are more nearly distributed like income than investment assets, particularly marketable securities.

Studies of the change in the concentration of wealth suggest that large holdings are becoming only slightly more widespread.[14] It will be recalled (see discussion of Table 17) that the accumulation of assets for Negroes has been very meager indeed, even compared with whites who have had only a grammar school education.

Holdings of major consumer durables are, of course, very widespread in the United States, and in terms of mass consumption, are probably the most apparent hallmark of our economy. This often-heralded accomplishment of U.S. industry is clearly seen in Table 22.

The distribution of households with one or more of the items of

TABLE 21. DISTRIBUTION OF WEALTH
BY SIZE OF WEALTH
(PERCENTAGE OF EQUITY IN SPECIFIED ASSETS),
DECEMBER 31, 1962

Size of wealth in dollars	Distribution of consumer units	Distribution of wealth by form			
		Own home	Auto- mobile	Liquid assets	Invest- ment assets
All units[a]	100	100	100	100	100
Negative	2	b	−1	b	b
Zero	8	b	b	b	b
1–999	15	b	5	1	b
1,000–4,999	19	4	13	5	b
5,000–9,999	16	12	15	7	1
10,000–24,999	23	36	30	23	7
25,000–49,999	11	24	19	25	11
50,000–99,999	4	11	10	17	15
100,000–199,999	1	5	4	8	11
200,000–499,999 } 500,000 and over }	1	4 4	3 2	7 6	22 32

[a] Figures are rounded and may not always total 100.
[b] Less than ½ of 1 per cent.
SOURCE: Based on Projector, D. S., and G. S. Weiss, "Survey of Financial Characteristics of Consumers," Federal Reserve Board, 1966, Tables A-16 and A-36.

equipment shown is very widespread among all income groups, particularly for standard items such as autos, refrigerators, television sets, and washing machines. Of course, these distributions say nothing of the value or condition of these items. In value terms, the distributions would be far less equal.

In connection with these widespread holdings of durables, the rising trend of costs associated with their maintenance is noteworthy. As Table 23 shows, these costs are estimated to have grown from $4.1 billion in 1929 to $37.5 billion in 1965 or a ninefold increase. This compares with a growth of sevenfold in the amounts spent on purchase of durable goods (not shown in the table). Maintenance costs were 5 per cent of total consumer outlays in 1929 and by 1965 had grown to 9 per cent.

Not all household operations services as defined by the Department of Commerce are included in the estimate for maintaining personal and household durable goods, e.g., domestic service, water, telephone, or most important, home repairs. At the same time much of the above includes services associated with rental housing, that is, electricity and

TABLE 22. PERCENTAGE OF HOUSEHOLD OWNERSHIP OF MAJOR DURABLES BY INCOME GROUP, JANUARY, 1967

Total money income before taxes	One or more autos	Washing machine	Refrig-erator	Tele-vision set	Air con-ditioner	Dryer	Radio and phonograph equipment	Dish-washer
All households	78.6	71.8	84.6	93.2	20.5	30.1	35.3	11.6
Under $1,000	24.5	46.9	75.4	68.9	4.3	2.8	6.3	0.6
$1,000–$1,999	39.4	51.4	73.4	80.0	6.8	4.2	8.1	0.7
$2,000–$2,999	56.9	58.7	80.4	90.6	10.5	9.0	13.6	1.4
$3,000–$3,999	71.6	61.5	79.2	93.2	12.9	13.2	19.2	2.2
$4,000–$4,999	76.8	66.3	80.0	93.4	14.7	20.7	27.3	4.4
$5,000–$5,999	87.6	70.3	83.4	96.7	18.9	25.9	32.0	5.4
$6,000–$7,499	90.9	78.3	87.2	96.7	21.6	34.7	39.0	7.0
$7,500–$9,999	94.4	81.3	89.0	98.4	28.5	47.0	48.2	13.3
$10,000–$14,999	96.1	85.9	92.0	98.4	33.7	56.6	58.7	27.4
$15,000 and over	97.1	84.8	90.7	98.6	44.9	64.0	72.2	50.9

SOURCE: Based on U.S. Bureau of the Census, "Consumer Buying Indicators," *Current Population Reports*, Series P-65, No. 18, August 11, 1967, Tables 1 and 4.

TABLE 23. COST OF MAINTAINING PERSONAL AND HOUSEHOLD POSSESSIONS, 1929 AND 1965

Personal consumption	1929	1965
	(billions of dollars)	
Total	77.2	431.5
Costs of maintaining and using tangible wealth	4.1	37.5
Electricity	0.6	6.6
Gas	0.5	4.0
Auto repair	0.8	6.2
Auto insurance less claims paid	0.1	2.5
Tolls, road, bridge, etc.	a	0.4
Auto gasoline and oil	1.8	15.1
Appliance and TV repairs, fire insurance, and other miscellaneous expenses	0.3	2.7
Percentage of total consumption	5	9

a Less than $50 million.

SOURCE: Derived from U.S. Department of Commerce, "The National Income and Product Accounts of the United States, 1929–1965," Table 2.5, pp. 44–49.

gas. Also, the figures for gasoline and oil include that paid for rental autos. All expenditures, however, are for personal use and do not include commercial or business use. Consumer interest, which is presently not included in national income, should be counted as a service cost, in this writer's view. The present amount of interest, as estimated from personal income tax returns, is approximately $15 billion. This would raise total costs associated with maintaining durable goods to about $53 billion, or about 12 per cent of total current consumption, inclusive of such interest.[15]

The discussion of costs of maintaining personally owned durable goods is necessarily fragmentary. The major gap in this discussion is that of social costs (or "externalities," as they are sometimes called). The most serious of the social costs pertain to the auto, including the inconveniences of highway construction and maintenance, air pollution, and traffic snarls, accidents and deaths. No attempt at such calculations is made in this study.

Growth in the Public Sector

The rise in the importance of government as it affects personal incomes, consumption, and the general welfare is perhaps the most marked shift in the composition of major income flows during the century. This is evident in the increase in payments to government via taxes and contributions for social insurance on the one hand, and the rise in payments by government to individuals on the other hand. Contributions for taxes and insurance which totaled $2.7 billion in 1929 by 1965 had grown to $79 billion or nearly 30 times the earlier level. This meant that such contributions or payments to government had risen from about 3 per cent of personal incomes to 14 per cent. Nothing like such a major shift in the disposition of personal income has occurred over the years and most of it occurred since World War II (Table 24).

TABLE 24.   DISPOSITION OF PERSONAL INCOME, 1929–1965

Disposition	1929	1939	1950	1960	1965
	(billions of dollars)				
Personal income	85.9	72.8	227.6	401.0	535.1
Payments to government	2.7	3.0	23.6	60.2	79.2
Taxes	2.6	2.4	20.7	50.9	66.0
Social insurance	.1	.6	2.9	9.3	13.2
Disposable income	83.3	70.3	206.9	350.0	469.1
Outlays	79.1	67.7	193.9	333.0	443.4
Consumption	77.2	66.8	191.0	325.2	431.5
Transfers	1.8	.9	2.9	7.8	11.9
interest	1.5	.7	2.4	7.3	11.3
to foreigners	.3	.2	.5	.5	.6
Personal saving	4.2	2.6	13.1	17.0	25.7

SOURCE: Based on U.S. Department of Commerce, "The National Income and Product Accounts of the United States, 1929–1965," Table 2.1. In adding to personal income in this table, keep in mind that by accounting convention payments for social insurance are considered in the national accounts as a deduction from personal income even though taxes are included. Figures may not add because of rounding.

A counterpart of this shift (as far as personal income and consumption is concerned) is seen in the analysis of the source of personal income (Table 25). Transfers of cash to persons show the largest percentage rise by far of all major sources of income. These transfers of cash from government to persons increased to $37 billion by 1965— as of early 1968 they were around $53 billion or nearly sixty times the 1929 level. They have grown from about 1 per cent of all sources of income in 1929 to 7 per cent in 1965. They represent mostly pension and other payments from federal, state, and local governments to older people, and constitute approximately 30 per cent of the total sources of income of the aged.

As obligations to government have greatly increased, the discre-

TABLE 25. SOURCES OF PERSONAL INCOME, 1929–1965

Source	1929	1939	1950	1960	1965
	(billions of dollars)				
Personal income	85.9	72.8	227.6	401.0	535.1
Earnings	66.1	58.3	188.0	329.0	432.6
Wages	50.4	45.9	146.7	270.8	358.4
Other	.6	.6	3.8	12.0	18.5
Proprietor's	15.1	11.8	37.5	46.2	55.7
Property	18.4	12.0	27.4	52.6	75.9
Rent	5.4	2.7	9.4	15.8	18.3
Dividends	5.8	3.8	8.8	13.4	19.2
Interest	7.2	5.5	9.2	23.4	38.4
Transfer payments	1.5	3.0	15.1	28.5	39.7
From business	.6	.5	.8	1.9	2.6
From government	.9	2.5	14.3	26.6	37.1
Less personal contributions for social insurance	.1	.6	2.9	9.3	13.2

SOURCE: See Table 24, "National Income and Product Accounts," Tables 2.1 and 3.9. Figures may not add because of rounding.

tionary power over total personal income has lessened over the years. By contrast, within disposable income, the share devoted to personal consumption and savings has shown relatively little change at 94 per cent for personal outlays and 6 per cent for savings in both 1929 and 1965.

Resulting from the broad shifts in government activity as reflected in the changing sources and disposition of income is some redistribution of income and consumption that presumably is different from what it would have been if these major shifts had not occurred. The information needed, however, in order to determine the magnitude of such redistribution effects among households—taking into account both the differing taxes they pay and the varying benefits they receive —is woefully inadequate. Until such an analysis of redistribution effects is made, the broad aggregates will remain without essential appraisal.[16]

The essential difficulty with appraising these broad trends is that it is not possible with existing data (except by broad assumption) to know who gets what from public expenditures. Nor do we know the real distribution of tax burdens. It is well known, of course, that the income tax as actually paid is much less progressive than the schedule of nominal tax rates. For example, as Pechman points out, if incomes were taxed according to nominal rates without any exemptions, deductions, or other special allowances, then effective tax rates for each income group would begin at 14 per cent and rise to almost 70 per cent in the very highest brackets. But in consequence of all the various allowances, the average tax rate for any income group as a whole never rises above 30 per cent and actually begins to *decline* slightly for income groups above $200,000.[17]

Apart from personal income taxes, the burden of all taxes is not fully known. Thus the extent to which business taxes are either passed on directly to consumers in higher prices or indirectly through lower wages, or not passed on at all by lower profits is a subtle and inconclusive area of economic analysis.

In place of a microanalysis to determine who pays for and who benefits from public expenditures, some notion of the nature of public expenditures is of help, so that the reader, if he is so inclined, may supply his own assumptions. We have grouped public expenditures in Table 26 by functional categories to suggest the broad intent or goals of public expenditures. It is not possible from these figures to measure how government expenditures in fact redistribute the national income among the various groups of households. The table does indicate, however, that over the recent decade, a considerable expansion has occurred in expenditures affecting "human capital" (education and health) and the sociophysical environment. The enormity of defense and space expenditures in the total requires no amplification.

While the rearrangement of federal budget figures in Table 26 may be more helpful than the official tabulations in examining and making more explicit the goals of public expenditures, they are still much too broad for any serious evaluation. Even figures for a metropolitan area may be too broad. Thus, the serious overcrowding and pressure on public facilities in particular sections of central cities (such as Anacostia in Washington, D.C.) may be obscured in the figures for a metropolitan area as a whole. However desirable, a substantial increase in public housing for particular *people* may put an added strain on already overstrained school and recreational facilities, as well as other community facilities, if the additions take place in particular *areas* of the city. In a particularly revealing column in *The Washington Post* (June 19, 1968), William Raspberry says: "The question is not one of the need for housing but of the necessity of locating new units in Anacostia." In the figures for a metropolitan area as a whole, an increase in moneys spent for public housing may look salutary as a socioeconomic indicator; but the essential imbalance of population in relationship to such figures would need to be examined much more closely.

The need for closer examination of federal aid is particularly true for increases in expenditures for health. There is little question that these expenditures have risen greatly. There is also little question that medical services have become increasingly available to the poor and the elderly. But not all details of such services may necessarily be wanted by patients, and, moreover, there has been an enormous increase in the cost of medical care partly resulting from increased federal assistance.

Therefore, in any study of public or private consumption, including the study of the balances within such expenditures as between different public goals and of the balances between public and private consumption goals, newer, more micro (more down-to-earth) analyses are needed.

The figures in Table 26 represent money costs, obviously. The study of the extent to which these costs have served the ends sought is a subject of great ferment today in and out of government. Such studies are still largely exploratory, but it is hoped that their methodology and results will have important implications in coming years for the evaluation of the impact of government policy on social change.

Time and Choice

There has been a considerable increase in interest in analysis of how time is spent. This interest by sociologists, economists, and others has ranged from considerations of changing hours of work, time spent on journeying to work, the extent and nature of leisure, or the analysis of the content of time divided between the direct or indirect pursuit of earnings, and other pursuits.

The problem is both simple and subtle. It is simple because there are clearly accepted units of time which make it possible to determine that various people in different times and places have allocated so many hours a day or year to working, sleeping, eating, and various other activities or inactivities. The subtlety intrudes as soon as one attempts to evaluate how time is spent in terms of irksomeness, leisure, "free time," unobligated time, etc. Needless to say, partly because of the unavoidable ambiguities in the definition of leisure or "free time" the results have been somewhat ambiguous. De Grazia, for example, has shown with some effectiveness that notwithstanding a considerable reduction in average hours of work as reported in official statistics, the amount of so-called "free time" has not appreciably increased because of (1) expansion in the number of women in the labor force; (2) considerable increase in part-time work by persons who cus-

TABLE 26. GOVERNMENT EXPENDITURES BY FUNCTION, 1956 AND 1966

	1956			1966		
Type of expenditure	Total	Federal	State and local	Total	Federal	State and local
	(millions of dollars)					
Total	*107,433*	*71,866*	*35,567*	*224,605*	*142,855*	*81,750*
Human resource development	*18,192*	*2,373*	*15,819*	*47,659*	*7,062*	*40,597*
Education	14,129	1,176	12,953	37,648	3,562	34,086
Health	4,063	1,197	2,866	10,011	3,500	6,511
Welfare benefits	*19,945*	*15,904*	*4,041*	*49,237*	*40,554*	*8,683*
Public assistance and relief	4,911	1,539	3,372	11,118	3,904	7,214
Unemployment	1,470	1,470	—	1,836	1,836	—
Old age and retirement	6,427	6,427	—	22,578	22,578	—
Disability and pension allowances	2,760	2,731	29	4,027	4,015	12
Other	4,377	3,737	640	9,678	8,221	1,457
Recreation and culture	*563*	*50*	*513*	*1,440*	*208*	*1,232*
Housing, environment and utilities	*11,224*	*3,023*	*8,201*	*25,346*	*10,162*	*15,184*
Housing	17	—6	23	1,146	712	434
Urban renewal	17 }	22 }	23	1,146 }	520 }	434
Public housing		—28 }			192 }	
Physical environment	9,442	2,325	7,117	20,748	8,023	12,725
Highways	7,381	827	6,554	15,894	4,249	11,645
Water	450	394	56	787	664	123
Air	266	188	78	1,014	921	93
Conservation and development of resources	1,345	916	429	3,053	2,189	864

Utilities	1,765	704	1,061	3,452	1,427	2,025
Transit	38	—	38	268	—	268
Electricity	−47	—	−47	−218	—	−218
Water and gas	145	—	145	212	—	212
Postal services	644	644	—	1,100	1,100	—
Sanitation	1,094	—	1,094	1,965	—	1,965
Other	−109	60	−169	125	327	−202
Regulation and safety	*3,174*	*69*	*3,105*	*7,035*	*157*	*6,878*
Police	1,409	—	1,409	3,015	—	3,015
Fire	773	—	773	1,457	—	1,457
Correction	498	30	468	1,174	66	1,108
Regulation of commerce and finance	494	39	455	1,389	91	1,298
National defense	*41,290*	*41,113*	*177*	*62,695*	*62,303*	*392*
Space	—	—	—	*5,947*	*5,947*	—
General government and foreign affairs	*13,045*	*9,334*	*3,711*	*25,246*	*16,462*	*8,784*
General government	10,898	7,187	3,711	22,385	13,601	8,784
International affairs and finance	2,147	2,147	—	2,861	2,861	—

SOURCES: These figures have been regrouped from data on government expenditures by function as presented in the National Economic Accounts of the Office of Business Economics, Department of Commerce. Data for 1966 are from their *Survey of Current Business* for July, 1967, Table 3.10, p. 29; and for 1956 from their publication "The National Income and Product Accounts of the United States, 1929–1965," Table 3.10, p. 63. A number of the items in the table are on a net basis in which receipts for services rendered are deducted from government outlays. The most important of these is the line for postal services, indicating that government outlays exceed postal receipts. The few negative figures in the table indicate in these instances that receipts exceeded outlays.

The large figure for "Other" in the category of "welfare benefits" includes subsidies and supports for the agricultural sector of the economy, which, as is well known, do not in large part go to needy farmers but to the very large farm enterprises.

tomarily do not work full time; (3) increase in moonlighting; (4) probable increase in time spent journeying to work; and (5) increase in work around the home.[18]

Our interest in time in this report is mainly concerned with how it relates to the broad subject of choice. While it is undoubtedly true that the range of choice among goods and services and investments has markedly increased in recent decades, knowledge of all the varying costs of these alternatives is itself a costly and difficult process.

One fundamental element of cost, largely neglected in the study of household behavior, is that of time. Largely in consequence of work undertaken by such economists as Jacob Mincer and Gary Becker, there has been provided a sharpened focus on the analysis of time in terms of cost.[19]

According to this approach, commodities and income are given an extended concept, by including the cost of time. The concept of commodities is broadened by including the money price (usually market price) and the time required to acquire and consume the commodity. The concept of income is broadened by distinguishing between earnings for which working time is important and other sources of income for which such time is of much less importance. It is recognized in this approach that work-time may occasionally be a form of "consumption" to the extent that the job in itself is a source of satisfaction and pleasure.

One advantage of this approach is that it provides some perspective on the concept of consumption, which we essentially avoided defining at the outset of this study. We can conceive, according to the Becker approach, of two activities, each constituting an abstract limiting condition: "pure" work which contributes only to earnings and nothing to satisfaction (or consumption) per se, and "pure" consumption which contributes nothing to earnings only to satisfaction (presumably "leisure"). In between are the intermediate "commodities" or activities, which contribute (directly and indirectly) *both* to earnings and consumption, e.g., food, sleep, durable goods, education, an enjoyable job, even a vacation—in fact, the range of most commodities.

More important, this approach gives promise to providing a sharpened analysis of the choices among consumption goods and as between consumption and work. Two variables central to this approach are: (1) market prices of goods and services, and (2) earnings rates, which not only measure the earnings-time required to pay the money prices, but put a cost on the value of time for persons with differing wage rates. These two variables considered *jointly* (i.e., relative to one another) provide a basis for determining *changes* in choices that have occurred over long periods, and *differences* in a given period among households with differing earnings.

For example, one of the most significant trends in the U.S. economy in the first half of this century has been the decline in the hours worked in given types of jobs, and the rise in wage rates. According to this approach, a rise in wage rates per se would have induced a rise in hours worked. In fact, however, the opposite occurred, because relative market prices of time-intensive "recreation" goods (e.g., television sets and vacations) fell even more than the rise in wage rates.

The decline in hours has leveled off in recent decades, consistent with the fact that the decline in market prices of "recreation" goods relative to the rise in wages had been more rapid in the earlier than in the latter half of this century.

This approach also seeks to tie together the increased labor force participation of women with the increase in purchase of labor-saving appliances and other consumption trends that save housework time (such as quick dinners in and out of the home). The rise in earnings rates for women has increased the value of their working time, which taken together with the relative decline in market prices of household durables and quick preparation foods has induced, according to this approach, an increase in entry of women into the labor force and increased purchases of appliances.

Apart from trends over time, the theory attempts to explain why people in relatively high earnings brackets tend to have a higher purchase rate of goods whose market price is high but time cost is low, such as plane transportation. Other examples are summer camps for children and night-clubbing (which also takes time but not working time).

While various approaches to the study of time imply the need for more information on the allocation of time, the incisiveness of this particular approach requires more than merely "time budgets." It requires that such information also be coupled with data on earnings, as well as other sources of income, in order to separate the effect on consumption from income that takes time and income that does not. In addition, these time budgets must be interrelated with the traditional type of consumption budget in order to rank goods by their relative "time intensities" involved in their use or acquisition. This poses a difficult but challenging task for our information system.

In concluding this section, we would like, with some diffidence, to ask for a somewhat broadened approach. In the Becker analysis consideration is given largely to the two limiting conditions of "pure" work and "pure" consumption as applied to a *current* picture of consumption and work. We would add the concept of investment (including tangible, financial, and "intangible" such as education). This implies that time must be considered not only in a very current sense, but over the time horizon which can include major phases of the life span. Indeed, in other highly significant studies, Becker gives a central place to such considerations[20] and it is hoped they might be integrated more in the study of the allocation of time. This broadened view of time to include study of households over their life cycle, or of choices that have implications for the family's *future* as well as current earnings and consumption, will pose an even more severe strain on our information system.

ANTICIPATING EFFECTS OF CONSUMER BEHAVIOR ON THE ECONOMY

The focus in the main body of the chapter was on questions of (1) adequacy of income and consumption, and (2) on the complexity of household choices. Both are concerned essentially with consumer welfare either under conditions of deprivation or affluence. In this section we discuss another type of question. Instead of seeking to determine how well society takes care of its citizens and how well they take care of themselves, we ask what impact does household behavior have upon society?

Consumer preferences and behavior, no matter how conditioned, have long-run and short-run effects on the economy. This is a large subject indeed, and we focus on only one aspect: that associated with short-run effects. Even this is a large subject and discussion of this, too, we must limit considerably as will be noted as we proceed.

Figure 3 provides some perspective on the problem. (Data on which the figure is based are found in Reference Table D at the end of the chapter.) As shown in the right-hand panel of the figure, there has been a *secular* stability of savings as a percentage of disposable income. Except for certain sharp short-run changes, this percentage has moved within a narrow range above and below 6 per cent. This secular stability has persisted notwithstanding a substantial increase in personal taxes, rising from less than 3 per cent nearly forty years ago to about 13 per cent at the present time. (See left panel of the figure.)

Our focus for the moment, however, is on the short-run changes in the savings rate. The very large swings have been associated with the

Depression in the 1930's and World War II. During the 1930's the very severe drop in income was accompanied by a pronounced fall in the rate of savings to negative levels, as spending in the effort to maintain living standards exceeded current incomes, and people either spent part of their assets or borrowed, or both. An almost similar, but much shorter-lived, drop in the rate of savings occurred in the 1938 recession. During World War II, the rate of savings rose to unprecedented levels as output and buying of many goods, particularly consumer durable goods, was sharply curtailed. In the period since World War II, changes in rate of savings reflected less cataclysmic forces, and were more in line with present notions of consumer behavior. In 1950 and again in 1954–1955, for example, the rate of savings dipped as credit and cash buying of autos and other durables greatly accelerated.

Following these increases in buying of durables (and associated decreases in the rate of savings), in 1951 and again by 1958 the savings rate rose as buying of these goods was sharply reduced. The increase in the saving rate in 1967 accompanied, among other things, a contracted rate of buying of autos.

Because changes in the savings rate in recent years have been associated with swings in purchase of durables, much research on consumer behavior has focused on understanding and, if possible, anticipating such swings. The efforts of households to distribute their expenditures over time—and to alter their timing—deciding when and when not to make a major purchase—i.e., before, after, or during a particular month or year, is a central feature of these swings. These alterations in timing, which produce fluctuations in consumption, is one of the prime causes of fluctuations in total GNP. They take the form of postponing or advancing the timing of a major purchase. If consumers in general have postponed such purchases, there is a cyclical drop; if accelerated, a cyclical rise.

Recently research has been undertaken in the area of understanding and anticipating such shifts in major purchase decisions—in particular, the survey work on consumer buying anticipations. Many factors underlie such alterations in timing which may be related to actual or expected changes in personal finances or to the condition of particular durable goods. Indeed, a myriad of reasons may propel persons toward or set up barriers to major purchase decisions. Notwithstanding the complexity of motivation possibly causing these fluctuations, the interesting fact is that general tendencies are observable for a broad profile of persons and households to curtail at one time or increase at other times the purchase of a major durable good. Such general

FIGURE 3.   INCOME, TAXES, AND SAVINGS, 1929–1967

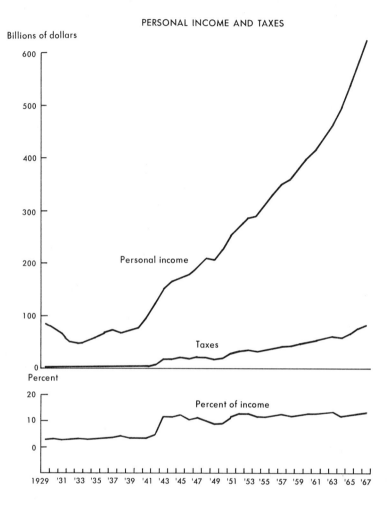

tendencies have been evident during the postwar periods of major swings in the savings rate throughout the country, in all broad income groupings, and including those with increases as well as decreases in income.

While research on such behavior is a long way from explaining the sharp short-run changes (though more successful in explaining secular growth in consumer durable goods with secular growth in income), considerable effort and some significant progress has been made in an

FIGURE 3.   INCOME, TAXES, AND SAVINGS, 1929–1967 (*cont.*)

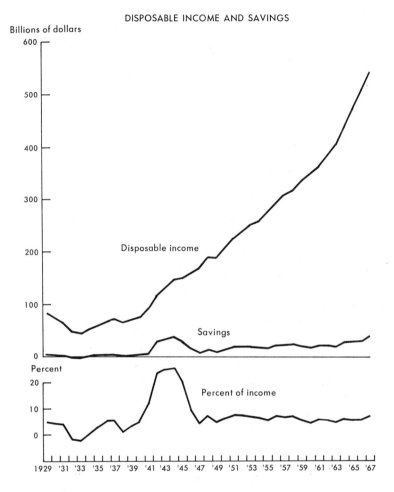

NOTE: This chart is plotted on an arithmetic scale.
SOURCES: See notes to Reference Table D, pp. 522–523.

effort to measure buying anticipations. The purpose of such measurement is to see whether forces are observable through household interviews that might foreshadow important changes in the rate of buying.

Among the most notable approaches in this field include that pioneered by George Katona, presently carried forward at the Survey Research Center at the University of Michigan, and the work at the Bureau of the Census under the consultative guidance of F. Thomas Juster.

Katona's work centers on the study of attitudes, including such attitudes as personal financial well-being (e.g., whether persons consider or expect themselves to be better off financially than a year ago); expectations about changes in general; business conditions; market conditions for household goods (is this a good time to buy?); and buying intentions (e.g., intend to buy a house or car, etc., within the next twelve months).

The underlying theory that justifies this kind of study is the alleged rise in the discretionary "power" of U.S. consumers.[21] It has resulted from (1) expansion in incomes to levels well above subsistence standards for a broad mass of the population; (2) widespread increase in asset holdings, which came about largely during World War II but continued in the ensuing period; (3) extensive use of instalment credit; (4) widespread expenditures for durable goods; and (5) increase in economic intelligence, or awareness by a sizable part of the population of changes in business conditions which can contribute to a "social contagion" when signs of change in business occur, and result in widespread increases or decreases in consumption. The first four points are well grounded in fact; the fifth point is in large part assumed.

Katona and his associates, particularly Eva Mueller, constructed a time series (largely quarterly and dating back to 1953) of an aggregate index based on answers to such attitudinal type questions. When optimistic expectations about personal finances or general business or particular market conditions rose, the index would be expected to foreshadow a rise in purchases and vice versa. This index was dramatically successful in preceding the 1954–1955 boom and 1957–1958 recession in buying of consumer durables. Yet when analysis was made of particular households, those with optimistic attitudes were not necessarily the buyers during the booms, nor were the pessimists predominant among the nonbuyers during the recessions. A surprisingly large literature developed concerning this seeming paradox,[22] but we cannot examine it here.

The main advantage of the attitude data, apparently, is that they may catch changes in consumer sentiment that affect the purchase probabilities of a broader group than the relatively few who (as indicated by their stated intentions) are very near to purchase but who for random reasons may not be able to fulfill their intentions. Even if few persons are able to perform an act in a given time it may be possible to detect influences among the many (through their attitudes) which propel only the few.

The work of Juster initially focused on measurement of buying intentions, per se. Data for such measurements were based on changes in the proportion of households which expressed positive intentions to purchase an auto or household durable within the next three, six, or twelve months. The difficulties with this approach stemmed from the fact that the actual buying of durables (as observed in successive surveys) was accounted for largely by nonintenders. As a consequence, and contrary to Katona's attitude index, the intentions data per se tended to be doubtful predictors of aggregate changes in buying of durables. At the same time, and again contrary to the attitude index, analysis of individual households showed that if a person was an "intender," there was a very high probability he would buy an auto or other durable in the period ahead. Unfortunately, mainly because intenders were such a small fraction of all respondents, the more important proposition—namely, if a person bought was there a high probability that he had been an "intender" in earlier survey?—was not true.

In recent years, largely in order to sharpen the measurement of consumer anticipations, a new approach has been instituted at the Census Bureau under Juster's leadership. Following earlier pilot surveys, the Census Bureau in September, 1967, began quarterly publication of a report on Consumer Buying Indicators.[23] The main change in this approach, aside from ancillary questions on income and income changes and on the list of durable goods, is the shift from measuring an expressed intention to buy, to measuring the subjective probabilities of purchase of each household. A respondent is asked to select his chances of purchasing given items, within given time periods, from an answer sheet scaled from 0 to 100. The mean probability for a group of households is the average value reported by these households. The survey in its present form is still essentially exploratory. A principal advantage observed from results of pilot surveys has been that the probability scale provides a much wider spread of responses than did the intender-type surveys. That is to say, in the intender-type surveys the responses were distributed dichotomously: divided sharply between the tiny fraction who were intenders, and a large amorphous remainder who either didn't have an intention or said definitely they didn't intend to buy. In the new approach the frequency distribution of responses according to their probability of making a major purchase is much more spread out.[24]

Work is going forward in improving this experimental survey dealing with different time horizons, different items of major expenditures, and including different financing arrangements.[25] As data accumulates and successive surveys are matched, it should be possible to provide substantial tests of the relation between changes in mean purchase probabilities and changes in aggregate purchases. It may also be possible to press further and actually observe the act of postponing or accelerating the timing of purchase decisions by observing shifts of *given* individuals in their purchase probabilities from high to low or vice versa.

KNOWLEDGE AND THE CONSUMER: CONCLUDING REMARKS

The choices households must make over the life span have become increasingly complex as alternatives need to be selected among careers, houses, durables, colleges, personal finance and insurance arrangements, and capital market possibilities. Trends in consumer behavior toward increased activities of an investment nature, including both the accumulation of tangible and financial assets and the increased expenditures of time and money (public and private) for higher education and job training, have all contributed to the complexity of consumer choice. They have correspondingly heightened the need for specialized information. How can this knowledge best be provided?

The sources of information and regulation to enlighten and protect the consumer, in order to minimize the risks to his health, safety, and to his income include: business advertising, consumer organizations, federal, state, and local governments, and the consumer himself. It is much beyond the scope of this chapter to undertake an analysis of the efficacy of each of these sources and a determination of where increased efforts are needed.

It is probably too costly and highly impractical, however, to expect the individual consumer to have the knowledge necessary or the "individual laboratory" available, in the words of George Stigler, to search out the best among alternative choices of major expenditures of time and money during each of the major phases of investment and consumption over the life span, as well as in the purchases vital to day-to-day living.

It is probably safe to say that as the trends toward complexity of choice continue the roles of private and public organizations will become more challenging: for business, to increase the potential functions of advertising (in terms of consumer knowledge) beyond merely identifying the major sellers in each market; for government, to provide a growing role of consumer protection in health, safety, and personal finance; and for other organizations, including testing organizations and cooperatives, to enable consumers to pay for the services they require but cannot provide individually.

The present ferment in this area of consumer information and protection within government and business, owing largely to the strong prodding of private citizens, presents an augury of dynamic change in a complex and significant area of human behavior.

Thus knowledge needed *by* the consumer whether provided individually and/or collectively is likely to present an increasing challenge for policy and research. What of knowledge *about* the consumer?

We have stressed the need for understanding the life span and the changing requirements faced over that span.

We have stressed that consumer investment decisions, for example, the purchase of tangible assets, may have destabilizing effects on the economy and that anticipation of changes in such decisions has become an important area of research on consumer behavior.

We are aware that these aspects of consumption require much more information, particularly of a longitudinal sort, than is now available and will probably entail a significant change in approach to consumer surveys.

But we wish to end with a caveat and a challenge. A caveat because we feel that inordinate and perhaps unnecessary demands for information will be demanded of households in the years ahead. There is a tendency to want to know everything, from everyone, from cradle to grave. We believe this is not only costly in the usual sense of resources needed to collect the data, but much more important in the burden on respondents, in the waste of information proliferation, and in the danger of abuse.

Our challenge then is to all in this profession to seek the pertinent, the significant; to find ways through pilot surveys and multivariate analysis—to determine through trial and analysis what factors are important for information gathering, and how small our samples can be kept. That we need more information from households is unquestioned, that the demands for information should not go on without limit is the challenge.

NOTES

1. The measure of "actual" GNP used here could be sharpened to show "potential GNP," or the output that would be possible given fuller utilization of manpower and capital capacity. This would not only show performance

in relation to the past but in relation to our fullest potential. (See estimates of potential GNP in the 1968 *President's Report of the Council of Economic Advisers*, p. 61.) It would be useful also to show the changes in prices and in the degree of unemployment but these facets, while important to a study of living conditions, are not necessarily the specific subject of this chapter.

2. Galloway, L. E., "The Foundations of the 'War on Poverty,'" *American Economic Review*, March, 1965. See also further discussions by H. Aaron and L. E. Galloway in the *American Economic Review*, December, 1967, p. 1243 *et seq*.

3. See, for example, Miller, S. M., M. Rein, P. Roby, and B. M. Gross, "Poverty, Inequality, and Conflict," *The Annals of the American Academy of Political and Social Science*, September, 1967, for a recent discussion.

4. For attempts to measure incidence of poverty based on estimated standard budgets, see Ornati, Oscar, "The Poverty Band and the Count of the Poor," in *Inequality and Poverty*, E. Budd, ed., W. W. Norton Co., New York, 1967. Based on contemporary standards, a decline since the Depression is evident in number below a minimum subsistence level but no change since 1941. See material on upgrading of standards in later discussion in this chapter.

5. "City Worker's Family Budget for A Moderate Living Standard," 1966, Bulletin No. 1570–1, U.S. Bureau of Labor Statistics, Washington.

6. Lamale, Helen H., "Levels of Living Among the Poor," Report No. 238–12, U.S. Bureau of Labor Statistics, Washington, August, 1965.

7. See, for example, Caplovitz, D., *The Poor Pay More*, Free Press of Glencoe, New York, 1963. For a finding of relatively little discrimination, see "Comparison of Prices Paid for Selected Foods in Chain Stores in High and Low Income Areas of Six Cities," U.S. Department of Agriculture, Washington, June, 1968.

8. See Projector, D. S., and G. S. Weiss, "Survey of Financial Characteristics of Consumers," Federal Reserve Board, August, 1966.

9. Miller, H., *Income Distribution in the United States*, A 1960 Census Monograph, U.S. Bureau of the Census, Washington, 1966, chap. 6.

10. Lansing, J. B., and J. Sonquist, "A Cohort Analysis of Changes in the Distribution of Wealth," Conference on Research in Income and Wealth, March, 1967, to be published by the National Bureau of Economic Research.

11. Projector, D., "Survey of Changes in Family Finances—1963," to be published by the Federal Reserve Board.

12. Modigliani, F., and A. Ando, "Tests of the Life Cycle Hypothesis of Savings," *Bulletin of the Oxford University Institute of Statistics*, 1957, p. 105.

13. The estimates are quite rough representing: for housing and land, and miscellaneous holdings, extrapolations from 1958 and 1962 from Goldsmith, R. W., R. E. Lipsey, and M. Mendelson, *Studies in the National Balance Sheet of the United States*, vol. II, National Bureau of Economic Research, New York, 1963, Table III-1; and Juster, F. T., *Household Capital Formation and Financing, 1897–1962*, National Bureau of Economic Research, New York, 1966, Table B-1; for autos owned by households, estimates are derived and extrapolated from data provided in Friedman, C. S., "The Stock of Automobiles in the United States," *Survey of Current Business*, October, 1965, Table 5 (market value data); and Friedman, C. S., "Auto Ownership by Households in Mid-1964," *Survey of Current Business*, October, 1966; for major household durables, estimates are by the author in cooperation with the Office of Business Economics, and based on the depreciated value of accumulated purchases of furniture, appliances, televisions, radios, and minor durables.

14. See Lampman, R. J., *The Share of Top Wealth-Holders in National Wealth,* National Bureau of Economic Research, New York, 1962, which studied trends from 1922 to 1956. See pp. 197 *et seq.* Data published by the Internal Revenue Service indicate that top wealth holders (holders of gross estates of $60,000 or more) increased from about 2 per cent of the adult population in 1953 to just less than 4 percent in 1962. See "Personal Wealth, Estimated from Estate Tax Returns," *Statistics of Income—1962,* Internal Revenue Service, Washington, May, 1967, p. 57.

15. A full accounting of the services received in relation to the costs paid for durables is a difficult matter. The costs shown above are very broadly estimated and probably on the whole are on the low side. For a very interesting effort to calculate the services less costs (or net income) obtained from durables, see Juster, F. T., "Household Capital Formation and Financing 1897–1962," Appendix B, National Bureau of Economic Research, New York, 1966. The estimate of consumer interest is from "Preliminary Report, Statistics of Income—1966, Individual Income Tax Returns," Publication No. 198 (1–68), U.S. Treasury Department, Washington, 1968.

16. For recent attempts at such evaluation, largely by assumption, see: "Tax Burdens and Benefits of Government Expenditures By Income Class, 1961 and 1965," Tax Foundation, New York, 1965; Gillespie, W. Irwin, "Effect of Public Expenditures on the Distribution of Income" in Robert A. Musgrave, ed., *Essays in Fiscal Federalism,* The Brookings Institution, Washington, 1965; Bishop, George A., "Income Redistribution in the Framework of the National Income Accounts," *National Tax Journal,* December, 1966, pp. 378–390.

17. Pechman, J., *Federal Tax Policy,* The Brookings Institution, Washington, 1966, p. 65 and chart 4–2, p. 66, based on analysis of 1962 tax returns.

18. De Grazia, Sebastian, *Of Time, Work and Leisure,* Twentieth Century Fund, New York, 1962.

19. Mincer, J., "Market Prices, Opportunity Costs, and Income Effects" in *Measurement in Economics,* Stanford University Press, Stanford, 1963; and Becker, G., "A Theory of the Allocation of Time," *The Economic Journal,* September, 1965. The latter article undertakes to tie together theoretically and to some extent empirically the work along this line.

20. Becker, G., *Human Capital,* National Bureau of Economic Research, New York, 1964; and *Human Capital and the Personal Distribution of Income,* University of Michigan Press, Ann Arbor, 1967.

21. Katona, G., *The Powerful Consumer,* McGraw-Hill, New York, 1960.

22. For a recent defense of this work, see Katona, G., "Anticipations Statistics and Consumer Behavior," *The American Statistician,* April, 1967.

23. Series P-65 of *Current Population Reports.*

24. See Juster, F. Thomas, "Consumer Buying Intentions and Purchase Probability: An Experiment in Survey Design," *Journal of the American Statistical Association,* September, 1966.

25. For interesting recommendations on future work in this and related areas (particularly in emphasizing the need for more longitudinal studies), see Ferber, Robert, "Anticipations Statistics and Consumer Behavior," *The American Statistician,* October, 1966. For an overview of the vast literature on the subject of consumer behavior, also by Ferber, see "Research on Household Behavior," *Surveys of Economic Theory,* vol. III, American Economic Association and Royal Economic Society

REFERENCE TABLE A. GROSS PRODUCT, PRODUCTIVITY,
AND CONSUMPTION, 1900–1965

Year	(1) Gross Product (1958 $ billions)	(2) Personal consumption (1958 $ billions)	(3) Consumption per dollar of Gross Product	(4) Consumption per capita	(5) Gross Product per man-hour
1900	79.8	48.3	.61	$ 634	29.2
1901	89.0	54.2	.61	698	31.1
1902	89.9	54.7	.61	689	30.0
1903	94.3	57.9	.61	717	30.7
1904	93.1	58.7	.63	714	30.6
1905	100.0	62.0	.62	740	31.4
1906	111.6	68.9	.62	806	33.8
1907	113.4	70.2	.62	806	33.7
1908	104.0	65.8	.63	740	32.0
1909	116.8	73.0	.63	806	34.4
1910	120.1	74.3	.62	804	34.4
1911	123.2	77.9	.63	829	34.6
1912	130.2	79.9	.61	838	35.4
1913	131.4	82.6	.63	848	35.5
1914	125.6	81.6	.65	822	34.3
1915	124.5	80.1	.64	797	34.2
1916	134.3	87.4	.65	857	34.7
1917	135.2	85.5	.63	827	33.6
1918	151.8	85.1	.56	823	35.5
1919	146.4	88.8	.61	850	36.9
1920	140.0	93.2	.67	875	35.7
1921	127.8	99.2	.78	914	35.8
1922	148.0	102.8	.69	933	39.3
1923	165.9	112.1	.68	1,002	41.2
1924	165.5	120.5	.73	1,055	41.9
1925	179.4	116.9	.65	1,009	43.9
1926	190.0	126.5	.67	1,076	45.1
1927	189.8	129.4	.68	1,087	45.3
1928	190.9	132.3	.69	1,097	45.2
1929	203.6	139.6	.69	1,145	47.3
1930	183.5	130.4	.71	1,059	45.1
1931	169.3	126.1	.74	1,016	45.0
1932	144.2	114.8	.80	919	42.4
1933	141.5	112.8	.80	897	41.7
1934	154.3	118.1	.77	934	46.2
1935	169.5	125.5	.74	985	48.4
1936	193.0	138.4	.72	1,080	51.4
1937	203.2	143.1	.70	1,110	51.5
1938	192.9	140.2	.73	1,079	52.7
1939	209.4	148.2	.71	1,131	54.8

REFERENCE TABLE A (*cont.*)

Year	(1) Gross Product (1958 $ billions)	(2) Personal consumption (1958 $ billions)	(3) Consumption per dollar of Gross Product	(4) Consumption per capita	(5) Gross Product per man-hour
1940	227.2	155.7	.69	$1,178	57.4
1941	263.7	165.4	.63	1,240	60.9
1942	297.8	161.4	.54	1,197	61.5
1943	337.1	165.8	.49	1,213	63.0
1944	361.3	171.4	.47	1,238	67.2
1945	355.2	183.0	.52	1,308	70.0
1946	312.6	203.5	.65	1,439	67.7
1947	309.9	206.3	.67	1,431	67.9
1948	323.7	210.8	.65	1,438	70.2
1949	324.1	216.5	.67	1,451	71.9
1950	355.3	230.5	.65	1,520	78.5
1951	383.4	232.8	.61	1,509	82.1
1952	395.1	239.4	.61	1,525	84.5
1953	412.8	250.8	.61	1,572	88.4
1954	407.0	255.7	.63	1,575	90.8
1955	438.0	274.2	.63	1,659	94.7
1956	446.1	281.4	.63	1,673	94.6
1957	452.5	288.2	.64	1,683	97.2
1958	447.8	290.1	.65	1,666	99.4
1959	475.9	307.3	.65	1,735	103.4
1960	487.7	316.1	.65	1,749	104.6
1961	497.2	322.5	.65	1,755	107.4
1962	529.8	338.4	.64	1,813	113.0
1963	551.0	353.3	.64	1,865	116.7
1964	580.0	373.8	.64	1,946	120.7
1965	614.4	396.2	.64	2,036	124.2

SOURCES:

Col. (1) and (2)—Years from 1909 to the present are from the Office of Business Economics. 1900–1908 are based on data from Kendrick, John W., *Productivity Trends in the United States,* National Bureau of Economic Research, New York, applying the 1909 ratio to OBE data to earlier data.

Col. 3—The calculated ratio of Personal Consumption (Col. 2) to Gross Product (Col. 1).

Col. 4—Personal consumption divided by the total population of the United States, based on data from the *Current Population Reports,* Bureau of the Census.

Col. 5—This series from 1909 on represents labor productivity for the total private economy derived by the Bureau of Labor Statistics. 1900–1908 are based on data from Kendrick for the total private domestic economy, applying the 1909 ratio to BLS data to earlier data.

REFERENCE TABLE B.   EXPECTED LIFETIME EARNINGS
FOR MALES IN 1959, ALL EDUCATION LEVELS

Age	White	Nonwhite
	(thousands of dollars)	
18 years	1,570	1,208
20 years	2,434	1,674
22 years	3,215	2,088
24 years	3,914	2,452
26 years	4,530	2,765
28 years	5,065	3,027
30 years	5,516	3,237
32 years	5,866	3,383
34 years	6,125	3,473
36 years	6,314	3,520
38 years	6,454	3,539
40 years	6,564	3,541
42 years	6,620	3,506
44 years	6,621	3,436
46 years	6,585	3,349
48 years	6,530	3,262
50 years	6,472	3,193
52 years	6,404	3,133
54 years	6,319	3,076
56 years	6,216	3,020
58 years	6,095	2,967
60 years	5,956	2,916
62 years	5,800	2,867
64 years	5,626	2,820

SOURCE: U.S. Bureau of the Census, *Present Value of Estimated Lifetime Earnings, Technical Paper No. 16*. Table 1, Page 7. U.S. Government Printing Office, Washington, D.C., 1967.

REFERENCE TABLE C.   EXPECTED LIFETIME EARNINGS
FOR MALES IN 1959, 4 YEARS OF COLLEGE

Age	White	Nonwhite
	(thousands of dollars)	
18 years	2,236	2,048
20 years	3,124	2,585
22 years	3,998	3,095
24 years	4,857	3,577
26 years	5,702	4,031
28 years	6,532	4,458
30 years	7,349	4,858
32 years	8,173	5,248
34 years	8,993	5,619
36 years	9,784	5,951
38 years	10,522	6,223
40 years	11,186	6,416
42 years	11,815	6,521
44 years	12,402	6,556
46 years	12,915	6,542
48 years	13,321	6,500
50 years	13,589	6,450
52 years	13,734	6,381
54 years	13,769	6,287
56 years	13,694	6,166
58 years	13,510	6,018
60 years	13,216	5,845
62 years	12,812	5,645
64 years	12,298	5,418

SOURCE: U.S. Bureau of the Census, *Present Value of Estimated Lifetime Earnings, Technical Paper No. 16.* Table 1, Page 10. U.S. Government Printing Office, Washington D.C., 1967.

REFERENCE TABLE D.   INCOME, TAXES, AND SAVINGS, 1929–1967

Year	Personal Income and Taxes			Disposable Income and Savings		
	Personal income	Taxes	Percentage of income	Disposable income	Savings	Percentage of income
	(billions of dollars)			(billions of dollars)		
1929	85.9	2.6	3.0	83.3	4.2	5.0
1930	77.0	2.5	3.2	74.5	3.4	4.6
1931	65.9	1.9	2.9	64.0	2.6	4.1
1932	50.2	1.5	3.0	48.7	−.6	−1.2
1933	47.0	1.5	3.2	45.5	−.9	−2.0
1934	54.0	1.6	3.0	52.4	.4	.7
1935	60.4	1.9	3.1	58.5	2.1	3.6
1936	68.6	2.3	3.4	66.3	3.6	5.4
1937	74.1	2.9	3.9	71.2	3.8	5.3
1938	68.3	2.9	4.2	65.5	.7	1.1
1939	72.8	2.4	3.3	70.3	2.6	3.7
1940	78.3	2.6	3.3	75.7	3.8	5.1
1941	96.0	3.3	3.4	92.7	11.0	11.9
1942	122.9	6.0	4.9	116.9	27.6	23.6
1943	151.3	17.8	11.8	133.5	33.4	25.0
1944	165.3	18.9	11.4	146.3	37.3	25.5
1945	171.1	20.9	12.2	150.2	29.6	19.7
1946	178.7	18.7	10.5	160.0	15.2	9.5
1947	191.3	21.4	11.2	169.8	7.3	4.3
1948	210.2	21.1	10.0	189.1	13.4	7.1
1949	207.2	18.6	9.0	188.6	9.4	5.0
1950	227.6	20.7	9.1	206.9	13.1	6.3
1951	255.6	29.0	11.3	226.6	17.3	7.6
1952	272.5	34.1	12.5	238.3	18.1	7.6
1953	288.2	35.6	12.4	252.6	18.3	7.2
1954	290.1	32.7	11.3	257.4	16.4	6.4
1955	310.9	35.5	11.4	275.3	15.8	5.7
1956	333.0	39.8	12.0	293.2	20.6	7.0
1957	351.1	42.6	12.1	308.5	20.7	6.7
1958	361.2	42.3	11.7	318.8	22.3	7.0
1959	383.5	46.2	12.0	337.3	19.1	5.6

REFERENCE TABLE D (*cont.*)

Year	Personal Income and Taxes			Disposable Income and Savings		
	Personal income	Taxes	Percentage of income	Disposable income	Savings	Percentage of income
1960	401.0	50.9	12.7	350.0	17.0	4.9
1961	416.8	52.4	12.6	364.4	21.2	5.8
1962	442.6	57.4	13.0	385.3	21.6	5.6
1963	465.5	60.9	13.1	404.6	19.9	4.9
1964	497.5	59.4	11.9	438.1	26.2	6.0
1965	537.8	65.6	12.2	472.2	27.2	5.8
1966	584.0	75.2	12.9	508.8	29.8	5.9
1967	626.3	81.7	13.0	544.6	38.7	7.1

SOURCE: "The National Income and Product Accounts of the United States, 1929–1965" and recent issues of the *Survey of Current Business,* U.S. Department of Commerce.

NOTE: Definitions, which may be obtained in more detail from official national income sources (principally "National Income 1954 Edition" and "The National Income and Product Accounts of the United States: Revised Estimates 1929–64," *Survey of Current Business,* August 1965) are briefly as follows:

1. Personal income includes all types of money income (from earnings and property); and certain types of "imputed income" or income in kind including rental income of home owners, wages in kind, and imputed interest paid by banks on checking accounts; and transfer payments.
2. Taxes include mainly personal income and property taxes.
3. Disposable income represents personal income less taxes, and savings represents a statistical residual after deduction of consumption expenditures from disposable income. While savings are *calculated* in the national accounts as a residual it is by no means clear that savings are in fact regarded as a residual by many classes of consumers.

10. THE DEFINITION AND MEASUREMENT OF LEISURE

Philip H. Ennis

O F ALL THE great categories of life, leisure is surely one of the most untidy. As individual experience or as behavior of large numbers of people, it is more diverse, more resistant to secure definition and measurement than most other aspects of social life. The variety of everyday words relating to leisure—recreation, relaxation, idleness, fun, play, games, entertainment, and diversion—underscores the complexity of the subject.

Expressive behavior is also a puzzling category. Its familiar forms —art, entertainment, and sports—are almost too multifarious for continuous monitoring; but insofar as they are manifested in leisure they become one more general type to be described as well as data and definition allow. Yet the connection between leisure and expressive behavior is not quite that simple. Practically *all* patterned behavior shows an expressive component. Voting in a presidential election, putting on a gray flannel suit for work, setting the dinner table with the "good" silver are all expressive acts to some degree. On the other side, much leisure has an instrumental element, the craft and do-it-yourself hobbies being the most obvious examples. Moreover, in everyday language expressive behavior implies participation in "culture," which is regarded as an important value. It is considered even better if the culture is "high" rather than "low," and if the person is active rather than passive. Thus, while some part of expressive behavior eludes the net of leisure, that part which is caught will be treated here as but one kind of leisure.

A discussion of the formidable definitional problems involved in these areas comprises the first part of this chapter. The second part will examine the problems of measuring leisure, dealing especially with sources of data and the difficulties of integrating different types of material and matching them to the definitions. The third section discusses the distribution of leisure across the social landscape; the fourth section considers the organization and structure of leisure. The final part explores the difficult problem of the quality of leisure; for it is, after all, an evaluation of the quality of life that lies behind most inquiries into leisure.

PROBLEMS OF DEFINITION

The three central problems in defining leisure are first, to find sensible boundaries between leisure and other great categories of life; second, to develop flexible and sensitive ways of deciding if something is or is not leisure; and third, to reconcile the differences among the several aspects of leisure. That is, leisure involves *activities,* carried out through *time,* involving direct or indirect expenditures of *money* on the part of some numbers of *people*. Thus, any social accounting of leisure has to involve one or more of these four things—time, dollars, activities, and numbers of people. Various students of leisure, concentrating on one or the other of these aspects, develop different operative conceptions of leisure as a result of the particular data they use. The conventions of collecting and organizing time, dollar, or activity data are different; some components of leisure are thereby ignored or distorted. These have to be reconciled or at least confronted.[1] Yet no matter how fully they are described these aspects do not constitute a definition of leisure. What then is leisure?

Leisure is socially patterned behavior, guided by the peculiar norm that it be subjectively "free." A typical expression of this fundamental prescription for leisure was reported in one of the Depression studies sponsored by the National Recovery Administration. It was said that "Leisure time by definition is free time. Any sense of obligation to do anything other than what one's tastes and interests invite is a denial of the very essence of leisure."[2] This popular view recounts the normative prescription of leisure, but it leaves us with two difficult questions—one is the perennial difficulty of translating subjective states into objective measures; the other is specifying what things are chosen by whom to occupy this "free" time. Lundberg, Komarovsky, and McInerny's *Leisure,* a classic study, formulated and resolved the issues in this type of definitional statement.

> Leisure is popularly defined as the time we are free from the more obvious and formal duties which a paid job or other obligatory occupations impose upon us. It is in this sense that we have used the term. Tentatively and for practical purposes, we shall accept this definition because it is relatively objective. In so doing, we shall not overlook the

important subjective differences which distinguish mere idleness, rest, or loafing, from relaxation, recreation, or a certain mental release or exaltation. In this more limited sense, leisure is primarily an attitude, a state of mind, a process of pleasureable adjustment to one's situation. Leisure in this subjective sense will always depend upon personality, temperament, education, and the activities that have preceded. An activity which is recreation to one person is onerous labor to another. The same activity may be either labor or relaxation to the same person at different times. But by the same reasoning it would be impossible to define work objectively on the basis of overt activity for it is frequently largely interwoven with recreational elements. Yet for many purposes we find such classifications of activity useful.[3]

Implicit in this optimistic expectation that leisure can be so readily objectively determined is the assumption that individual differences in the definition of leisure are really slight, that there is a dominant consensus on what is and what isn't leisure. To some extent this is obviously the case. For most people the ten-minute coffee break is so sharply *bounded off from the constraints of work* that its meaning is unmistakable.

The shape of the ground makes the figure. Even what is done during the coffee break is greatly influenced by the physical and social surroundings; the use of the free time is strongly determined by the surrounding situation. At the other extreme, retirement is as equally well bounded off from the constraints of work. Its meaning with respect to work is also unmistakable. Yet what is done in the "golden years" is much more problematical and undefined.

But what about the *daily* leisure hours, the *weekend,* and the *vacation?* These sectors of leisure are even more open and normatively varied. In addition to the different kinds of *measuring perspectives* for leisure (i.e., time, dollars, activity), there are also different "envelopes" of leisure, that is, constraining boundary points at each end of the leisure experience.

Structural Setting

What makes the whole picture complex is the structural setting of leisure as a mode of experience.[4] It is institutionally interstitial, a patterned gap in the social anatomy. To oversimplify somewhat, work is institutionalized into corporations, businesses, professional-client and buyer-seller relations; the family fairly well encompasses sexual relations, procreation, and the early socialization of the young. Authority and its administration are organized into political parties and the agencies of government; religious needs and sentiment, especially those related to the ceremonies of birth, marriage, and death, are located within the church. Of course, there is "leakage" of these functions into other institutions and a multiplicity of functions for each institutional grouping; nevertheless, there is a dominant locus for these needs and activities. Leisure, on the other hand, is not contained in any single institutional area but can be expressed in any of them. It can fit into any of them; to a limited extent it can also create its own institutions.

A second structural feature of leisure arises from the content of its "master norm," i.e., leisure as free time. Thus, it can fulfill a variety of functions for the individual. At various times a person can find in his leisure either tension release, creative expression, self-improvement, social integration, symbolic status defense or enhancement, and other gratifications, some of which are less consciously apprehended than others. Other modes of experience, such as work, family relations, and religion are also multifunctional, but leisure differs from them in an interesting and strategic way. There is no hierarchical valuation among the possible uses of one's free time that has community (or national) consensus, since there is no agreed-upon or clear-cut conception of their relative importance to the individual or to society as a whole.

The functions of work, on the other hand, are stamped with a fairly clear order of precedence, the maximization of economic return being the leading and almost unchallenged value. Religion and family life also are fairly unambiguous in their ranking of important values. But the multiplicity of possible leisure goals and especially their lack of consensual ordering gives a kind of unpriced cafeteria-selection quality to leisure and thus strengthens its shifting and problematical character.

A third feature of leisure is that the operation of its norm of being "free" invites specific normative control from other sources, notably from the specific social contexts in which a given leisure activity is placed or from the general values which permeate the culture as a whole. Before we examine these norms in more detail, it is important to identify the consequences of these structural defining properties of leisure.

From the institutional side, since leisure is contained within no single institutional context, it is competed for by all. This competition is not only for leisure dollars and hours but even more importantly for the public's value commitment. Churches and symphony orchestras, voluntary organizations and the television industry all want financial support or participation or attendance, to be sure; but even more they want their public to accept them fully and to become regular devotees.

Each institutional structure seeks to convert the casual dabbler, the occasional participant, into a full-fledged member. These vested leisure interests, as we might call them, have learned that the indeterminacy of leisure is bad for their business. The casual moviegoer or churchgoer, the occasional bowler or book reader is a greater risk than the avid fan, since he can be more easily wooed away by the ubiquitous competition. In these attempts to enclose leisure, organization has proved to be a major weapon. It is easier to sell one man twelve books than it is to sell twelve men one book, as the publishing industry has discovered. Thus industry, religious institutions, civic groups, art galleries, and symphony orchestras, not to mention commercial leisure interests ranging from bowling alley operators to the Mickey Mouse club popular in the 1950's, have elaborated endless ingenious organizational devices to contain the volatile leisure habits of the American public.

Were these tendencies unchecked, all leisure would eventually be encapsulated into vast sealed compartments with little crossing over from one context to another. The counterpressures which scatter leisure among a variety of activities stem in part from a person's roots in different institutions (he might want to spend all his free time with the boys in the company's bowling team, but the demands of his wife force participation in other leisure contexts—the family and the community). Moreover, the sheer force of satiation and desire for variety, when coupled with the fact that some leisure interests are almost incapable of being contained within the same organizational structure, also place limits on the organizational drift. The measurement of the extent of organization or dispersion of various leisure activities is thus an important part in the assessment of American leisure. The problems of measurement will be discussed later.

Normative Setting

We return now to the question of what leisure is subjectively, as defined by the norms that the culture offers beyond the imperative that it should be free. While it is necessary at some point to be quite concrete and say that leisure is skiing and going to movies and loafing, it is even more vital to give a normative definition of what the leisure experience is. Not only will the activities change over time, but their cultural meaning will also change; and if the range of normatively dictated meanings are not identified, then the endlessly changing catalogue of activities will be uninterpretable in broader terms. Yet it also is difficult to specify the full range of norms that define leisure for the same reasons that applied to its structural position. All institutions want to extend their influence and control. From the world of work, still perhaps our major institutional anchoring point, there are two sets of powerful norms which seek to define leisure.

One set is to be inferred from the negative or residual definition of leisure given Arthur Stinchcombe in a recent sociology textbook.

> There is a fundamental difference between activities that are systematically planned to achieve some purpose and those that are spontaneous. Generally we call systematically planned, purposeful activities "work," and spontaneous activities "leisure" or "play." Some people have more fun studying than dancing; professors are recruited from this group. But we still call studying "work," and dancing "play" because unlike studying, dancing is not systematically planned to achieve some purpose. As de Man, a Belgian pioneer of survey research on workers, asserted:
>
>> . . . all work is felt to be coercive. Even the worker who is free in the social sense, the peasant or the handicraftsman, feels this compulsion, were it not only because while he is at work, his activities are dominated and determined by the aim of his work, by the idea of a willed or necessary creation. . . . Work inevitably signifies subordination of the worker to remoter aims, felt to be necessary, and therefore involving a renunciation of the freedoms and enjoyment of the present for the sake of a future advantage.
>
> Sociologists often call work "instrumental activity" and play "expressive activity."[5]

Three normative definitions of leisure are involved here. The first is the now familiar contraposition of coercive work to leisure as everything else spontaneous or "free." Clearly, this distinction obscures the coercive elements in the family, religion, the civil community, and the other major institutions we all participate in. While we may not have really come all the way down the secular road to anomie, there is no question that the pervasive polarization of work vs. leisure is a powerful indicator of the erosion of community, church, and family power. Direction by these previously central anchorings has clearly shifted from consensually supported imperatives to personally chosen options. Their inclusion in the category of leisure is only recognition of this fact.

The second norm is that leisure should be "fun," that leisure hours and activities are those in which the search for personal pleasure is pre-eminent. The third norm, apparently added as an afterthought, is that leisure should be expressive rather than instrumental. Since Stinchcombe is so abrupt here, it is not possible to tell how much he intends the polarity of expressive-instrumental simply to coincide with that of consumption-production or to reach beyond in the directions discussed earlier. Whichever is meant, American culture as a whole stresses both meanings as important in leisure. We have, then, leisure implicitly defined by the norms directing people toward freedom (spontaneity), pleasure, and expressiveness. Work at the other extreme is coercive, serious, and instrumental. This distinction is in normative terms. The irrepressible currents of horseplay, gossip, and sociability at work, on the one hand, and the diligence and effortfulness of some leisure, on the other hand, modulate the polarity of the two extremes.

The ethos of work, paradoxically, attempts to invade and stamp leisure with its own values of achievement and purposeful activity and give leisure a contradictory set of norms. The following injunction from a book entitled *The Leisure Wasters* is typical of the evangelical tone of such preachments:

> There is a ready-made purpose allied with one's vocational life. It is to get the job done, to receive an income, to spend a certain number of hours in a place of business. Leisure has no such built-in purposes. Then it is up to the individual to give it a purpose, or to spend it without purpose. . . . It's time to unpack purpose and get it into operation again. Leisure time should be filled with a sense of purpose if we are to have any sense of *living* at all.[6]

The tension between the values of work and those of leisure pointed up in this quotation lead to a discussion of the quality of leisure; but we postpone this for later consideration.

Guidelines

Having located leisure in an unsettled structural and normative situation, we return to the two major initial questions: How is leisure to be distinguished from the other major categories of living and how is any given item to be assigned? As to the first question, the tripartite division of work, nurturance-maintenance, and leisure is the broadest categorization that has a viable tradition of usage in the social sciences. It is an approach that maximizes inquiry into the central question of how the restless, shifting quality of leisure is differentially channeled into various institutional contexts and differentially defined by the values of those contexts. By implication this view acknowledges the still dominant coercive power of work and the *relatively* weak coercion that comes from family, religious, civic, and political settings.

The second question is not so easily answered. Just as hard cases make bad law, difficult research decisions can make weak generalizations. The decisions as to what is leisure, what is work, and what is maintenance-nurturance are indeed difficult for those gray areas at the boundaries.

Three guidelines which can help make these decisions more consistent constitute what can be called a *modular strategy*. First, the life cycle of the individual or the family should be taken into account. Thus, for example, schooling has the coercive power for the young that work has for adults; educational activities should therefore be treated differently for different age groups.

Second, the natural distinctions of leisure "envelopes" should be maintained where feasible. The weekday, the weekend, the vacation, and retirement are each constrained by different forces and activities and have different meanings.

Third, the time, activities, or dollars devoted to leisure should be recorded and reported in as microscopic a form as is practical; first, so that the mosaic of leisure can be mapped in its complexity, and second and more important, so that the components can be put together for different purposes. Social policy planning for leisure is likely to be aimed at specific types of leisure for particular groups of people. The factual basis of that planning, therefore, should have the flexibility necessary to isolate the relevant data without contamination.

While these three guides help delimit the field there remains the alternate question of how to classify an activity. Ten minutes of setting-up exercises in the morning is clearly to be counted in the maintenance-nurturance entry of a time budget. Participation in a health club, whose activities involve considerable opportunity for expressive behavior, is a mixed case, though the maintenance-nurturance elements appear to outweigh the leisure aspects. But what of nudist camps? While they make appeals to health concerns they appear predominantly to serve a social and ideological expressive function within the context of leisure. Or, to focus on a different issue, where do sex and courting belong?

The answer has to come from either an intuited or an empirically determined *consensus*. For the latter, periodic surveys on leisure are clearly necessary to clarify and refine the intuitions that will have to suffice until there is a stronger empirical basis for decision.

PROBLEMS OF MEASUREMENT

The heart of the issue is to assign numbers to the time, the dollars, and the activities that are designated leisure in such a way that they are relevant to the definition we have developed and are coherent with each other. This does not mean that the statistical indicators have to match perfectly; one of the major purposes of this section in fact is to discuss the failure of various leisure indicators to do just that. First, however, two other problems: one has to do with the criteria that these numbers should satisfy before they can be considered useful indicators of the nation's leisure and the other has to do with the different kinds of units by which leisure can be measured. The various criteria governing social indicators have been discussed extensively;[7] those which raise special problems for leisure are reviewed here briefly.

Criteria for Leisure Indicators

The first criterion is that if national policy is to be guided, or at least tracked by, factual accounting of national life then a truly national set of indicators is necessary. Insofar as statistical series are gathered or controlled by leisure industries, especially by trade associations or specialized publishers connected to some leisure activity, their coverage is likely to be uneven and incomplete to an unknown degree. *Historical Statistics of the United States,* for example, contains a table showing the numbers of bowling teams from 1896 through 1957. The source of the data is *Bowling Magazine,* a publication of the American Bowling Congress (ABC). Beneath the surface authority of this appealing set of data, however, lies the turbulent history of American bowling. The ABC, organized in 1895, extended its reach over existent bowling slowly and sporadically. In 1906–1907 Eastern bowlers seceded and formed their own organizations, yet there is no indication in the table whether the departing teams were or were not included. In 1920–1921 a large number of teams from New York City were reunited with the parent organization; again there is no way of knowing whether these teams were counted for the first time. Moreover, in 1915–1916 membership in the ABC was limited to "male white sex."[8] How many teams of women and nonwhites were there then; and when the clause was removed, did the number of teams jump to include them?

These particular figures obviously should be regarded with considerable skepticism, and there is every reason to suspect that most other leisure associations have had a similar history of partial coverage as they evolve from scattered beginnings into more complete saturation over their fields. The resulting bias is likely to show more rapid initial growth than actually exists.

A second criterion is standardization. The natural and almost inescapable tendency of each state and large city, each leisure industry and each research enterprise is to define its categories and measuring instruments according to its own needs and traditions. This is difficult to overcome, requiring something like the steady, disinterested, and virtuoso skills that have been used by the American Standard Association in achieving standardization in vast areas of American industry. Similar skills, in addition to federal support, would have to be applied, but applied flexibly to avoid the inherent difficulty in standardization, that is, a frozen rigidity wherein the categories of a statistical series can over time let reality slip beneath the measures. Consumer expenditures for "sports equipment," for example, have been recorded in U.S. government series from 1909 to the present.[9] As valuable as it is to have something that captures this important type of leisure expenditure, the meaning of this category is far from clear given the changes in the types and technology of sports over the past sixty years.

Thus a third and somewhat contradictory criterion is specificity of categories. Whether the measures are time, dollars, or activities, they should be kept to the smallest, most homogeneous scale possible within the bounds of reasonable length of the entire list. For instance, the category of "radio and television receivers, phonographs, parts and records" (though detachable from musical instruments to which it is generally joined) in the series of consumer expenditures cited above is still less than useless if we wanted to analyze the interrelations and the functional equivalence among these three different kinds of leisure expenditure as they changed, grew, and declined from 1909 forward.

Finally, there is the criterion of meaningfulness. An indicator has to tell us something unambiguously about some aspect of leisure. It is too much to ask that the subjective meaning and quality of life expressed in the leisure indicator be immediately interpretable. However, there should be some precision as to what unit, which people, and how many of them are doing what under known social conditions.

A few examples illustrate the point. Marion Clawson, in discussing outdoor recreation, states:

> Data on visits are frequently described as though they relate to visitors, thus leading the uninitiated into erroneous conclusions. There were 55 million visits to the national park system in 1956, for instance; this figure surely represents far fewer than 55 million people, but we do not know if it represents 30 million persons or 20 million, or some smaller or larger number.[10]

Here is a more serious failure to relate numbers meaningfully to definitions:

> A survey of 21 museums alone showed an aggregate attendance of 19,370,000 in 1958. Within two years this had climbed to 21,360,000—

a gain of more than ten per cent. Across the country museums are making room for unaccustomed crowds.[11]

The implication here, relentlessly pursued by the author, is that we are in the midst of a "culture explosion." We are not told though, which 21 cities these were, whether their population growth was more or less than 10 per cent, whether these figures represent people coming in by themselves or as part of organized groups, or how many *people* not *visits* these figures represent, or whether they represent adults or children.

Finally the apparently phenomenal growth from 1929 to 1963 of total expenditures for "Admissions to Legitimate Theater and Opera and Entertainments of Nonprofit Institutions (Except Athletics)," to use the 1954 Survey of Current Business classification, is radically brought back to a meaningful level through the corrections of inflation, population growth, and allocation of disposable income in Figure 1.

Equally important for meaningful indicators is having statistical series as wide-ranging in their content as the extended definition we have proposed for leisure. Adult education and the myriad forms of community participation, for example, are two obvious items that are all too often omitted in either time or dollar statistical series on leisure. A related problem is the present inability to disentangle the leisure from the work components in such activities as travel, eating, and reading. Considerable experimentation in data collection techniques is necessary in order to clarify these ambiguities.

In short, the sources and nature of statistical series on leisure have to be carefully filtered through at least these four screens before they can be considered as useful for establishing national yardsticks on leisure.

Units of Leisure Output

Now let us consider the units by which leisure can be measured. On the output side there are two different ways of quantifying the element of time, two different ways of assessing the leisure dollars expended, and several ways of counting the variety of leisure activities along with the number of people engaged in them.

Time Measures. Of the two types of temporal accounting of leisure, one is the attempt to specify the *total amount of leisure available* to the country, to answer the question: How much leisure time do we have and how is it changing? Just as a major definition of leisure was a negative one, that is, the "leftovers" from work, this approach has the

FIGURE 1. INDEXES OF EXPENDITURES ON ADMISSIONS, 1929–1963

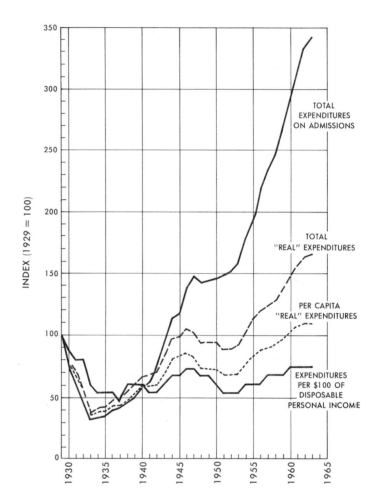

To permit comparisons among statistics as heterogeneous as total expenditures and per capita expenditures, the data are all expressed in terms of the corresponding 1929 figure, which is taken as 100. For example, the total expenditure on admissions in 1939, $64 million, is approximately 50 per cent of the 1929 figure, so that the 1939 index number is 50, and that is the admissions figure plotted for 1939 in the graph. All of the lines start off from exactly the same level (100) because the 1929 figure is, by definition, always equal to 100 per cent of itself.

SOURCE: Baumol, William J., and William G. Bowen, *Performing Arts: The Economic Dilemma,* Twentieth Century Fund, New York, 1966, p. 46.

same strategy of answering the questions by counting the residual hours, often removing those which are not leisure. A particularly sophisticated example of this kind of aggregate analysis was used by Clawson and Knetsch. They show in Table 1, for the years 1900, 1950, and 2000, the total number of hours available to the total U.S. population. The basic trichotomy of work (and its equivalents for students and housewives—school and housekeeping), maintenance-nurturance, and leisure is clearly visible. From the turn of the century our total leisure hours have increased by 25 per cent from 1900 to 1950.[12]

As one would expect, the separate entries for weekday, weekend, vacation, and "retired" leisure show different rates of change, with the weekend showing the largest rate of increase. Yet how are their data to be interpreted? The authors themselves indicate two difficulties, one of which is really not a problem. They worry that their data cannot show how different classes of people have different amounts and types of leisure, but aggregate data simply are not designed to tell what groups have more or less leisure of different kinds. The other difficulty is more serious. The authors indicate considerable disagreement as to whether their estimates are correct, some critics claiming there is more leisure available, others less.

Sebastian De Grazia's work[13] is cited, for example, as suggesting that there is considerably less leisure now than Clawson and Knetsch claim. Since the two sets of data are both in aggregate form and gathered for roughly comparable time periods, a direct comparison seems possible. But the two sets of data simply don't match. The Clawson aggregate data are based on a yearly basis for the entire population. The De Grazia data are a complex and fastidious reconstruction of the *changes in the weekly hours* of leisure from one time period (1850) to another (1950). This factor alone makes comparisons difficult, since the Clawson data deal with *annual totals*. Direct translation is impossible for other reasons. The De Grazia material treat vacations, which are almost always taken in a lump sum of time, in terms of fraction of hours per week; it considers only the adult male full-time worker; and it does not give an estimation of the total maintenance time during the week. It is a genuine puzzle why the two sets of data do not match. It could not be the surprisingly large percentage of time for sleep (about 40 per cent) in the Clawson data compared to the more expected 33 per cent for sleep in De Grazia's calculations, because this goes the wrong way. That is, the Clawson data would show even more leisure, for if hours devoted to sleep were counted, the problem then would be a matter of calculation and definition. De Grazia does not automatically

TABLE 1. NATIONAL TIME BUDGET AND TIME DIVISION OF LEISURE, 1900, 1950, AND 2000

Use of time	1900			1950			2000		
	Billion hours	Per cent of total time	Per cent of leisure time	Billion hours	Per cent of total time	Per cent of leisure time	Billion hours	Per cent of total time	Per cent of leisure time
1. Total time for entire population	667	100		1,329	100		2,907	100	
2. Sleep	265	40		514	39		1,131	39	
3. Work	86	13		132	10		206	7	
4. School	11	2		32	2		90	3	
5. Housekeeping	61	9		68	5		93	3	
6. Preschool population, non-sleeping hours	30	4		56	4		110	4	
7. Personal care	37	6		74	6		164	6	
8. *Total* (items 2–7)	*490*	*73*		*876*	*66*		*1,794*	*62*	
9. Remaining hours, largely leisure	177	27	100	453	34	100	1,113	38	100
10. Daily leisure hours	72		41	189		42	375		34
11. Weekend leisure hours	50		28	179		39	483		44
12. Vacation	17		10	35		8	182		16
13. Retired	6		3	24		5	56		5
14. Other, including unaccounted	32		18	26		6	16		1

SOURCE: Clawson, Marion, and J. L. Knetsch, *Economies of Outdoor Recreation*, The Johns Hopkins Press, Baltimore, 1966, p. 22; adapted from Holman, Mary A., "A National Time-Budget for the Year 2000," *Sociology and Social Research*, vol. 46, no. 1, October, 1961.

538

count the reduction of work time as a gain in leisure. De Grazia recognized, in short, the coercive power of other institutions to drain away the "free time" won by less work. The conclusion, however, is that not until there is agreement as to these definitional issues will there be the possibility of gaining an estimate of our aggregate leisure time.

The second way leisure time can be measured is through *time budgets of individuals*. This relatively expensive data collection method can yield intensive and specific information as to how much leisure time a person has, how he uses it, how it fits into the rest of his life, and most important, how different kinds of people have different leisure patterns. For reasons that are not at all clear this style of data collection has not flourished in the United States. As Nelson Foote recounts its history, only two major sociological monographs and three large-scale social-bookkeeping studies (the last being in 1950), have kept this research tradition alive.[14]

In Europe, however, time budget analysis has been more securely rooted, and appears at present to be thriving by virtue of UNESCO sponsorship of a multination project directed by Alexander Szalai.[15] Such a coordinated approach, recently discussed by Robinson,[16] is essential if time budgets are to become a reliable social yardstick, because this microsocial technique has to standardize a very large number of procedures and agree upon so many important points of variation.

The methodological issues discussed by Foote point to fundamental questions of how people define and name the moments and activities of their everyday lives and how they give temporal and social boundaries to them. If the *social scientist* specifies the categories of leisure and work in advance, he sacrifices the immediacy and reality of the experience in favor of reliability of observation over large samples. If, on the other hand, the *respondent* records in his own terms the flow of activity (or nonactivity) over time, then the costs of such "validity" are sampling bias (how many people can keep diaries), and noncommensurability of categories. The time budget technique, in sum, is so much at the mercy of definitional predilections as to the meaning of activities and their measurement that it is probably best suited at this point as a basic research tool rather than as an instrument for the social monitoring of leisure behavior.

A widely used modification of the time budget is the use of diaries or surveys focused to measure the use of time for specific purposes. Travel to and from work, visits to public recreational areas, and television viewing are common examples. Widespread agreement as to the definition of these activities, their relatively sharp delimitation from the totality of everyday life plus their immediate social utility are factors that account for the extensive use of such survey and diary studies. Yet the very concentration on a single activity without the context of the rest of the day can distort its extent and meaning.[17]

What can we conclude about the systematic measurement of the "time envelope" for leisure? As social indicators neither the macrosocial aggregate measure of available leisure time nor the microsocial time budgets have enough definitional consensus or methodological clarity at this time to qualify them as immediately serviceable indicators. They both have most promise when they retreat from the extremes of either attempting to measure the total leisure hours in the country or the minute-by-minute recounting of what a given day is like toward a middle level of familiar activity categories and temporal units. When they do this there are impressive regularities and findings that are plausible and inviting for further research.

Money Measures. We turn now to the economic side of leisure. As with the temporal dimension, there are two comparable kinds of measures. One is an aggregate of all consumer expenditures for leisure and the other is the dollar budget study of persons or households. The latter are expensive and require considerable efforts to mount; thus they have been done on a national scale only infrequently.[18]

The longest and most stable statistical series of aggregate leisure expenditure data comes from the Survey of Current Business.[19] It has used approximately the same data collection methods and categories since 1929. In *America's Needs and Resources, A New Survey,* Dewhurst extended the series back to 1909 with the aid of a variety of sources. Thus we have a continuous accounting of leisure expenditures for the entire United States for about sixty years, but it should be emphasized that this accounting reflects the viewpoint and definitional practices of the *producers* of leisure, not those of the *consumer.* The dollar amounts expended for leisure, however, are positive quantities, not residuals as was the case with the aggregate estimates of leisure time.

The first question which arises, then, is how well the categories organizing these quantities fit into the rubric of the threefold division of work, maintenance-nurturance, and leisure. Superficially they appear to fit quite well. Of the twelve major expenditure categories in the 1966 version of the Survey of Current Business Consumer Expenditure reports, five are readily identified with maintenance-nurturance, one with work, three fall into our definition of leisure, and three are mixed.

The maintenance-nurturance categories are clothing, personal care, housing, housing operation, and medical expenses. The categories which can be included in the definition of leisure are recreation, education, and welfare. The one category clearly related to work includes a variety of items ranging from working equipment, union dues, and so forth.[20] The mixed ones—food, domestic and foreign transportation— comprise, unfortunately, about 45 per cent of the total in recent years. The largest component of the mixed group is food purchases. From one point of view, this item is clearly maintenance-nurturance; from another, that of time, *eating* has a strong leisure component. In fact, eating is included in the aggregate leisure time assessments, since everything that is not work is included in leisure. There is no easy way to resolve this paradox. Even if the dollar and the time conceptions of food consumption could be harmonized, there remains the difficulty of segregating the portion that should be allocated to work, to maintenance, and to leisure. The contrast of home expenditures for food vs. restaurant expenditures is only a partial solution, since the functions of both are mixed.

The same problems apply to transportation. Some travel dollars (and time) should clearly be included in leisure; some involve the journey to work and should therefore be considered as maintenance. Yet the organization of the data precludes the differentiation. Moreover, the expenditures for hotel and motels, an obvious part of the cost of travel, are buried with expenditures for costs of "clubs, schools and institutions" in "Other Housing" which is in the Housing category, ordinarily considered as maintenance-nurturance. The situation in these mixed-expenditure categories, is, to say the least, unsatisfactory. No clear and reliable distinctions as to their leisure share can be made; and therefore, until clear and refined definitions are agreed upon, we are blocked in making aggregate estimates.

A close examination of the subcategories under recreation reveals the same unhappy result, one that has worsened over the years. The categories used in the Survey of Current Business prior to 1947, whatever their deficiencies, were radically compressed and reorganized in 1954. Probably the sheer growth in size and diversity of leisure enterprises strained the resources of the voluntary and trade associations upon whom the government relies and those governmental agencies themselves. Therefore, the commendable aims of completeness and modular disaggregation became too expensive to support. The response of the Survey in any case has been to reduce the specificity of the categories. Table 2 compares the organization of the earliest and the present recreational categories.

TABLE 2.   RECREATION CATEGORIES FROM THE
NATIONAL INCOME SUPPLEMENT
TO THE SURVEY OF CURRENT BUSINESS, 1947, 1954

1954	*Recreation*	*1947*
1. Books and maps		5a. Informal recreation Books and maps
2. Magazines, newspapers, and sheet music		5b. Magazines, newspapers, and sheet music
3. Nondurable toys and sports supplies		5d. Nondurable toys and sports supplies
4. Wheel goods, durable toys, sports equipment, boats, and pleasure aircraft		5e. Wheel goods, durable toys, and sports equipment 5f. Boats and pleasure aircraft
5. Radios and television receivers, records and musical instruments		5h. Radios, phonographs, parts and records 5i. Pianos and other musical instruments
6. Radio and television repairs		5j. Radio repairs
7. Flowers, seeds, and potted plants		6. Flowers, seeds and potted plants
8. Admissions to specified spectator amusements 8a. Motion picture theatres 8b. Legitimate theatre and opera and entertainments of nonprofit institutions (except athletics) 8c. Spectator sports (footnote specifies this as including the 1947 categories and neither specifies nor implies others)		1. Admissions to specified spectator amusements 1a. Motion picture theatres 1b. Legitimate theatres and opera 1c. Entertainments of nonprofit organizations (except athletics) [Spectator Sports] 1d. Professional baseball 1e. Professional football 1f. Professional hockey 1g. Horse and dog race tracks 1h. College football 1i. Other amateur sports 1j. Ticket brokers, markup on admissions 1k. Purchase of programs
9. Clubs and fraternal organizations, except insurance (footnote specifies this as including the 1947 categories and neither specifies nor implies others)		8. Clubs. 8a. Athletic and social dues and fees 8b. Social fraternities dues and fees 8c. Fraternal, patriotic, and women's organizations 8d. Luncheon clubs

TABLE 2 (*cont.*)

1954	Recreation	1947
10. Commercial participant amusements (footnote specifies this as including the 1947 categories and neither specifies nor implies others)	4.	Specified commercial participant amusements
	4a.	Billiard parlors and bowling alleys
	4b.	Dancing, riding, shooting, skating, and swimming places
	4c.	Amusement devices and parks
	4d.	Daily fee golf courses, greens fees
	4e.	Golf instructions; club rental, and caddy fees
	4f.	Sightseeing buses and guides
	4g.	Private flying operations
11. Pari-mutuel net receipts	2.	Pari-mutuel net receipts
12. Other (footnote specifies this as including the 1947 categories and neither specifies nor implies others)	Other	
	5k.	Photo developing and printing
	5l.	Photographic studios
	5m.	Collectors' net acquisition of stamps and coins
	5n.	Hunting dog purchase and training, and sport guide service
	5o.	Veterinary service and purchase of pets
	7.	Camping fees
	3.	Nonvending coin machines receipts minus payoff
	9.	Commercial amusements
[Not visible in 1954]	5c.	Book rental and repair
	5g.	Boat and bicycle rental, storage and repairs

SOURCE: I am grateful to Don Parker of Wesleyan University for this reconstruction.

Two general observations about the reorganization of these categories: First, in spite of extensive reshuffling, the categories are basically identical. Whether this is a deliberate policy to maintain historical continuity or simply administrative somnolence or concerted resistance by the nation's retail establishment to extensive record-keeping (which appears the most likely possibility), the result is a failure to capture the changing leisure scene. None of the new types of leisure expenditure is included. Second, the glacial packing of specific activities into larger categories—commercial participant amusements, clubs, and "other" in particular—precludes microscopic analyses of leisure trends. We are, in addition, frozen into an acceptance of these larger predetermined groupings without the opportunity of rearranging the specific items into different configurations and combinations.

A closer look at the resulting groupings reveals that hardly any is satisfactory. "Books and maps," for example. Perhaps it is unnecessary to carp at a mixture of books with maps if the latter constitutes as small a proportion of the whole as common sense would suggest. But how small is it; and how many of the dollars spent on maps are spent by *individuals* in the pursuit of leisure rather than museums, libraries, etc.? Previous data show that 22 per cent of all books sold in 1960 were educational (purchased largely by schools) and 20 per cent were juvenile books.[21] The ordinary meaning of "book buying" is certainly inflated by these figures. At the other extreme is the almost certain understatement of commercial participant leisure. Any random scanning of the weekend newspapers from Byron, Illinois, home of one of the country's busiest drag strips, to New York City will reveal more varieties of participant entertainment than appears in the Survey's list. A similar understatement is to be found in the admissions to spectator amusements.

A different kind of difficulty results from the splitting of expenditures for *equipment* (only partially contained in the "Wheel goods, durable toys, sports equipment, boats and pleasure aircraft" category), from the *fees and attendant expenses* involved in the use of that equipment. Thus it is impossible from these figures to secure an accurate picture of the relative position of such rapidly expanding activities as camping, boating, skiing, or golfing. Then the survey combines some items that make little sense together and separates others that should be combined. Why, for example, should sheet music be included with magazines and newspapers? Shouldn't reading be regarded differently from music-making; and if music-making is a useful category, why should the expenses for musical instruments be included in the expenditures for radio and television receivers and records? (The advantages of separating these last three items from each other was noted above.)

Another puzzle: while gardening is a widespread activity, why should it be traced only by the money spent on flowers, seeds, and potted plants? Such a combination, in fact, mixes the florists' products with the home-grown variety. More important is the absence of a separate accounting for the very large expenditures for garden and lawn equipment, which, judging from the periodicals on the subject, loom large, and another for perhaps from 10 to 20 per cent of the leisure gardeners who hire people to work in or to design their gardens.[22] The equipment expenses are buried in the sports equipment category and the hired personnel expenses do not appear to be caught anywhere. Why should gardening be singled out, in short, if only to be badly reported? Again, why should pari-mutuel receipts be separated from the item of nonvending machine receipts, if the latter are, as appears, largely from gambling devices? The two items should be kept together even though it is obvious that the amounts spent on gambling are far greater. No one has as yet documented the estimates ranging from 3 to 20 illegal dollars bet for every legally reported gambling dollar—another instance of underreporting leisure expenditure.

Finally, there is the problem of "Other." The general difficulties with the revision of the series is underscored by the way that eight specific activities previously reported in various parts of the schedule were clumped and homogenized into the residual "Other" category. This is an unfortunate loss, since in 1965 "Other" constituted about 7.5 per cent of all leisure spending and ranked sixth among the twelve types of leisure activity. In 1929 these items amounted to only 5 per cent and together ranked eighth indicating an expanding role for this kind of leisure, which though heterogenous points to an active, high-skill type of activity.

These criticisms may appear quarrelsome and unresponsive to the exigencies imposed on the compilers of the series. While internal reformulation of the categories along the lines suggested above is still an imperative—at least a cessation of aggregation is called for—perhaps we have been imposing an unsuitable purpose on the series. It may be that the aggregate expenditures approach is best suited for gross comparisons of leisure with other kinds of consumer spending rather than as a tool of internal comparison among different types of leisure activity. In any case the obvious question as to how much money is spent for leisure as a whole and how that amount varies with restricted or broadened definitions of leisure we postpone for a comparison with family budget data.

An analogous question is how the aggregate measures of leisure dollars compares to the aggregate measures of leisure time. This is really only meaningful as a time series confrontation, seeing, that is, the changes in the relative share of the consumer budget allotted to

FIGURE 2.　PERCENTAGE OF CONSUMER EXPENDITURES
FOR RECREATION AND LENGTH OF AVERAGE
WORK WEEK, 1909–1965

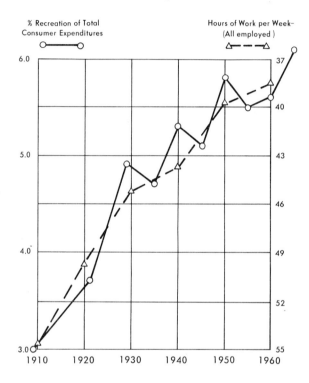

SOURCE: Derived from De Grazia, Sebastian, *Of Time, Work and Leisure,*
Twentieth Century Fund, New York, 1962, Table 1; and Dewhurst, J. Frederic,
et al., America's Needs and Resources; A New Survey, Twentieth Century Fund,
New York, 1955, Table 4.4.

leisure matched to the change in the available leisure time. The latter
is measurable most clearly by using the hours of work as the indicator
and assuming that the hours of maintenance-nurturance have either
not changed radically from the turn of the century until the present
or that some of that maintenance is now at the borderline with leisure,
as well might be the case with gardening and home upkeep. Thus
Figure 2 shows the percentage of consumer dollars going into "recreation"—a minimum definition—along with the decline in the average
length of the work week from 1909 to 1965.

The relationship is clear and regular; as the hours of work decline, there is a parallel increase in the relative outlay for recreation. The interpretation of this pattern is far from clear, however, and it raises more questions than can be answered within the scope of this chapter. The first question is to determine how much of the time gained from work goes into leisure and how much into maintenance-nurturance. The second question is the differentially changing price levels of leisure activities and their relation to the general increase in income over the years. Third, has the cost of leisure, differential pricing aside, increased due to more complex and extensive equipment and technology and the use of more expensive human and natural resources? Fourth, how do the different types of recreation differentially contribute to the over-all growth of leisure spending—which items have grown rapidly, which have declined? These are the kinds of questions the aggregate approach invites, and while there is considerable room for disagreement over the theoretical definition and its empirical indicators, there is nothing like a multiple regression to give some answers.

Fisk's monograph, *Leisure Spending-Behavior* is a particularly useful beginning in this respect, demonstrating quite nicely the influences of differential inflation and income elasticities on recreational spending. The conclusions in brief appear that in recent decades "the amount of money spent on recreation goes up when the relative price of recreation goes down" and that variations in leisure expenditures are closely tied to changes in income.[23]

How does the aggregate dollar picture compare to the family budget method in its categories and its dollar estimates? With respect to the first, the important comparisons are in the *range and detail* of specific leisure expenditure categories. Of the previously cited major family budget studies in recent years the two Bureau of Labor Statistics Surveys of 1950 and 1960 elaborate a set of categories essentially similar in scope and detail to that of the Survey of Current Business' aggregate list. Yet the Life-Politz survey strongly suggests that far more detailed specific information can be gathered and separately tabulated than we might expect from the two BLS studies.[24] This may be accounted for by the larger scope of the latter enterprises, or their desire to conform to the categories of the Survey of Current Business, as well as the Life-Politz interest in serving specific commercial clients. But why couldn't the aggregate method be more detailed? The reasons, beyond those of cost, must lie in the nature of the leisure spending. Some kinds of activity may elude tracing through aggregate market indicators by being too diffuse—entertaining at home, gardening, or even vacations and outings, for example.

It is an open question whether one method of documenting the full range of leisure spending is better than another. A case can be made that either of the two is superior in identifying the obscure and infrequent kinds of leisure spending and that only experimentation and careful cost estimates can provide the answer. It is possible at present, though, to compare them on their absolute and relative dollar estimates of leisure spending. One such comparison was made by Lester D. Taylor who matched the 1960 BLS Survey of Consumer Expenditures with the National Income and Product Accounts (aggregate data) for that year.[25] He reports that when weighted to the total U.S. households the individual budget method is nearly $20 billion lower than the aggregate one. The single largest discrepancy is a $6 billion gap attributable to alcoholic beverages; that is, the percentage of alcohol to total consumer expenditures in the Survey of Consumer Expenditures (household budgets) is only 42 per cent of the comparable aggregate percentage. Taylor concludes that a "Puritan" effect is responsible. Whatever the social value that distorts the reporting of alcoholic beverage consumption, the quality of the statistical data is so good that there can be little doubt that the individual reporting is at fault. The important fact is that there are discrepancies in the two series, discrepancies in estimating how large or small a share a given type of leisure occupies in the total leisure budget. Table 3 shows the ratio of individual to aggregate proportions of total expenditures in each leisure category.

Total recreation, for example, was estimated by the aggregate method to be $18,901,000 or 6.71 per cent of the aggregate total consumer expenditures. The individual estimate of leisure spending was $16,082,000 or 6.15 per cent of total individual consumption. The ratio of the two percentages is 85.1 (6.15/6.71) indicating that the individual method *understates* the level of recreational spending compared to the aggregate approach. (A ratio of 100 indicates the two methods are identical in estimating an item.)

While the grouping of the items in the larger clusters appears almost idiosyncratic, it does have an attractive logic; e.g., participation activities are conjoined to equipment costs. Even if wrong, it illustrates the case for maximum flexibility through disaggregation.

The two methods are closest in estimating spectator admissions (99.9) and radio, television, records, phonographs, and musical instruments (90.2) and newspapers and magazines (84.4). Is this because these items are the most routinized both in production and in their place in family life and therefore most readily accountable? This

TABLE 3.   REPORTED RATIO OF INDIVIDUAL
TO AGGREGATE EXPENDITURES FOR VARIOUS
LEISURE ACTIVITIES

Activity	Ratio of individual to aggregate expenditures
Total recreation	*85.1*
Books	60.4
Newspapers and magazines	84.4
Toys and play equipment, participant sports, other transportation, club dues and memberships	65.7
Television, radio, phonograph, etc. includes maintenance, musical instruments	90.2
Spectator admissions, recreation out of home city	99.9
Other recreation, hobbies, pets (purchase and care)	161.5

SOURCE: Taylor, Lester D., "Combining the 1960–61 BLS Survey of Consumer Expenditures and OBE Time Series Data in Projecting Personal Consumption Expenditures," unpublished manuscript, 1967, Table 1.

conclusion gains some support in that the aggregate method understates most radically the level of spending for hobbies, pets, and the ubiquitous "Other." This may mean, either alternatively or in addition, that these fragmentary and scattered activities are so fine-grained they slip beneath the screen of aggregate accounting.

Plausibility, that great enemy of social science, shows itself at this point in the significant aggregate *overestimation* (compared to the individual data) of participant sports, sport equipment, toys, etc. (65.7). Why wouldn't these diverse and multifarious activities yield the same result as did hobbies and the like? Again, only close and systematic scouting can provide the answers.

Leisure dollars can be monitored in another way, one that is more fragmentary and more displaced from *total leisure spending* of either families or the total economy. This way is the special study of some particular activity, e.g., boating, outdoor recreation, television, or book reading. While such surveys gain in depth they are generally unattached to the larger loom of the individual's or the society's total leisure patterns.

Activity Measures. Dollars and hours track leisure at a distance. To get a closer look we want to know how many people are doing what kinds of things. Here is a typical popular conception:

"It has been estimated that more than twice as many people now go to art museums as ball games."[26] This kind of statement quantitatively relates leisure activities to some fairly clear though implicit social value—"high culture is better than a passive spectator sport." Leaving aside such a judgment, for the moment we turn instead to the question of how the diversity of activities and numbers of people engaging in them can be measured. One way is to study the *individual,* asking him about his interest and activities. Another is to trace the leisure *activities* themselves through their more or less organized forms. Studies focusing on the individual are devoted to one type of leisure activity[27] or they sweep across all of leisure asking their respondents what activities they engage in, how often, and sometimes how much money they spend on each. Generally such surveys often contain additional questions about the respondents' attitudes and experiences with respect to work, leisure, self, community, family, and so on. The analyses then typically describe the relative rates of various activities and the differences in the people who engage in them.[28]

Essentially the same kind of information can be gathered by investigating the organized forms of a given leisure activity, for these "organizations" often conduct surveys of their actual and potential users. One difficulty with such surveys is the diversity of their methodology and their general lack of sophistication. The reasons are familiar —scanty financing, inadequate professional expertise, over-restricted objectives. Even so, these surveys form a fascinating if fragmentary mosaic portraying the spread and growth of leisure's multifarious activities.[29]

For example, how much would we know about that common but mysterious expressive act, the purchase of flowers, without the aid of the survey reported by the U.S. Department of Agriculture?[30] This anonymous study (why can't we know its director and its methodological description?) tells us two interesting facts. One is that from 1930 to 1964 the sales of flowers by telegraphic wire increased from two to nine million orders, an increase quite accurately predicted by changes in disposable personal income, employment levels, confectionery sales, and the sales of household appliances. The other is the distribution of customers' uses of flower purchases; in 1964 46 per cent of florists' total sales were for funerals, 19 per cent were for hospitals, 9 per cent for weddings, 4 per cent for conventions and business openings, 5 per cent for church use, and only 10 per cent for home use (the remaining 7 per cent was for "other" uses).[31]

It is no surprise that the basic ceremonies of birth, marriage, and death are the important occasions of flower sales, but how much more we would know about the whole range of expressive behavior in these situations and in everyday life if there were large-scale, broad-ranged studies instead of these slivers of information unanchored to any context. Such consolidated or at least centrally coordinated studies might bring about standardization of such basic categories as "member," or "user," not to speak of more agreement on softer terms such as "heavy" or "regular" users. These difficulties are seen quite visibly in the National Ski Census, a useful but flawed attempt to describe the universe of skiers.[32] The strength of leisure organizations lies, it appears, in their ability to collect and organize the harder facts such as the *number of licenses or permits* if there are any involved, as in the case of hunting and fishing, or in the *numbers of units sold* as in boating (what about the growing secondhand market for boats?) or the *numbers of members* enrolled in formal organizations as in bowling. These too could become more rigorous and standardized with the assistance and guidance of an agency devoted to such systematic collection of data.

Measurement of Leisure Resources

Since the measurement of leisure resources or inputs is a task more for economists than for sociologists, it will be sketched lightly and only in general terms here. The resources for leisure are diverse in type and the documentation of their worth varies in availability and reliability. Following the suggestion of Clawson, these inputs can be divided into natural resources and man-made ones, cross-classified into those which are publicly or privately owned.[33]

The key measures that would appear necessary to assess the supply trends in leisure are the space (land area) involved, the capital invested, and the manpower utilized. It does not seem an overstatement to say that there is little possibility at this time of bringing together the information required for a full-dress economic analysis of leisure in the same way that other industries are studied, partly because it is difficult to decide how much of a given area or resource is used for leisure purposes. How much of the national highway investment, for example, should be considered recreation, or how should wildlife preserves, open lands, rivers and other water areas be allocated for leisure purposes? Or how much of the publishing industry should be considered as educational and how much as recreation? In fact, every definitional problem of this sort on the output side has its counterpart on the input side.

Our inability to estimate the supply of leisure is also due to a lack of knowledge of land use, capital investment, and manpower utilization.

These gaps are largely in the private sector, for in the field of outdoor recreation the Outdoor Recreation Resources Review Commission has done outstanding work in mapping the federal, state, and local resources.[34] And some states, New York for example, have contributed more detailed inventories.[35] Still, however, the contribution of the private sector to the supply of outdoor recreation facilities is hardly known. Aside from the potential use of the data from the Census of Manufactures the only other known study analyzing a part of the leisure scene in depth is Baumol and Bowen's work on the performing arts.[36] Even in this intensive study the authors concentrated mainly on visible professional performing arts organizations; the large but relatively unknown amateur and semiprofessional resources had to be ignored.

While there have been impressive reviews of public policy problems in the performing arts[37] and public television,[38] there has been little concentrated research designed to collect and organize the basic economic facts of the leisure industries. Some of the data are actually available for those agencies which regularly gather the routine statistics of their operations, the public libraries of the nation being a case in point. For over a decade there has been published a fairly good national series reporting operating expenditures, capital investment, and manpower figures for most of the public libraries in the country.[39]

Art, historical, and other museums have not been as systematically monitored. The professional and trade associations of leisure industries vary in their ability and willingness to gather their basic statistical facts of life. Perhaps only a centralized and well-funded agency could persuade or induce standardization of such activity.

Finally, a particularly ignored area has been the resources *producing* leisure skills, both amateur and professional. How many "leisure" teachers are there? Where do they teach, how are they trained, how much are they paid? A careful survey of the manpower involved in teaching leisure skills—from schools of baton, karate, or French cooking to the employees in the public schools teaching music, art, and sports—is an important facet of the entire picture, not only for the economic point of view but for the understanding of the institutional structure of leisure and its underlying values.

PROBLEMS OF DISTRIBUTION

Leisure time and dollars are unequally expended by various social groupings; leisure activities as well as leisure resources are clustered differentially in the nation. A full accounting of leisure trends requires the mapping of these uneven distributions, not only because of our society's concern with equality of opportunity but also because of our need to understand more fully the social processes that generate class, ethnic, regional, and age-linked differences in leisure.

Socioeconomic Differences

What is the range of these distributional differences and how can they best be traced? First, and most obvious, are the differences in individual leisure patterns among the various occupational, income, educational, ethnic, and age groupings in the nation. The data for showing them comes by and large from individual level studies of dollar expenditures, time budgets, and activity inventories. The second difference is the unequal distribution of leisure resources in the nation. The basic data here are necessarily diverse, ranging from descriptions of local, state, and federal parks and recreation areas to aggregate community (again local to national) expenditures for leisure institutions. Also to be considered are the more scattered information sources about private leisure complexes, e.g., the ski resorts in New England, the theater industry in New York, the tourist establishments in Florida, and so forth.

A third kind of unequal distribution stands halfway between the first two. It is the clustering of specific types of people with known leisure patterns into particular communities or regions, either temporarily or for longer time periods. The retirement communities, summer or winter resorts, and bedroom suburbs are typical of the range.

Time Measures. Two kinds of material on individual differences in leisure time are at hand. One is the set of periodic special reports from the Bureau of Labor Statistics, which surveys hours of work for different types of workers. Table 4, for example, shows for different occupational groups the average weekly numbers of hours worked, and the proportions working less than thirty-five hours, thirty-five to forty hours, and more than forty-one hours per week. There are some impressive differences in these figures. The overworked executive emerges here as a strong, albeit statistical, reality as does the farmer and the underemployed domestic worker. More important than the differences *between* occupational strata, however, is the range of variation *within* them. The question raised is how different are the styles of life among the salesmen working less than thirty-five hours (30 per cent of the total) from that of the 36 per cent of the salesmen working more than forty-one hours per week? Even these figures are too crude.

TABLE 4.　HOURS AT WORK AND OCCUPATIONAL
GROUP, 1965

Type of occupation	Percentage distribution of weekly hours at work				Average hours weekly
	Less than 35 hours	35–40 hours	41 or more hours	Total	
Professional, technical, and kindred workers	16	49	35	100	41.4
Managers, officials, and proprietors, except farm	8	32	60	100	49.4
Clerical and kindred workers	20	64	16	100	37.4
Sales workers	30	34	36	100	37.8
Craftsmen, foremen, and kindred workers	11	52	37	100	42.3
Operative and kindred workers	14	53	33	100	41.2
Domestics	66	19	15	100	24.1
Service workers, except private household	29	41	30	100	37.8
Laborers	31	46	23	100	35.5
Farmers and farm workers	23	13	64	100	52.1
Farm laborers and foremen	42	17	41	100	39.4

SOURCE: Bureau of Labor Statistics, *Labor Force and Employment in 1965,* Special Labor Force Report No. 69, Washington, 1966, Table D-6, p. A-31.

Occupations should be even more specifically identified, since there is some evidence that leisure patterns vary quite sharply for different occupational groups; and within each occupation the hours worked by men and women should be differentiated.[40]

For a closer look at the time spent on various activities, we must turn to time budget analysis. The studies reported by Robinson[41] for example, contrast the time spent in a variety of activities by male "executives and professionals," "white-collar workers" and "labor" and for employed women (white-collar vs. labor) and housewives. Table 5 shows a contrast of the Lundberg 1934 study of leisure with Robinson's current work (1965–1966). There are too many internal comparisons and too many questions raised in this table for full discussion here—comparisons of total leisure or specific activities in the two time periods between men at different occupational levels, women in different occupations and between men and women. Does, for example, the Depression of 1934 as opposed to near-full employment of 1965 account for more sleeping, less work, and more leisure for men and white-collar working women (work hours excepted) in the earlier

TABLE 5. COMPARISON OF BUDGET AVERAGE FOR VARIOUS GROUPS IN 1934 LUNDBERG STUDY WITH SIMILAR GROUPS OF THE 1965-1966 STUDY (IN PARENTHESES)

Activity	Men			Employed women		Housewives	Overall
	Executives and professionals	White-collar	Labor	White-collar	Labor		
Nonleisure (Hours per day)							
Sleep	8.2 (7.7)	8.3 (7.6)	9.0 (7.4)	8.2 (7.6)	8.3 (7.4)	8.6 (7.5)	8.4 (7.5)
Work for pay	6.2 (6.8)	6.4 (7.2)	5.9 (7.5)	5.9 (5.4)	6.7 (3.9)	0.1 (0.2)	4.5 (4.5)
Care of self	0.7 (0.9)	0.7 (1.0)	0.8 (1.3)	1.0 (1.3)	1.0 (1.3)	1.0 (1.3)	0.9 (1.2)
Transportation	1.2 (1.6)	0.8 (1.5)	0.9 (1.3)	1.1 (1.3)	1.0 (1.3)	0.8 (1.0)	1.0 (1.3)
Household and children	0.9 (0.7)	0.5 (0.6)	0.6 (0.3)	1.2 (2.9)	1.4 (2.9)	4.2 (6.2)	1.9 (2.8)
Total	17.2(17.7)	16.7(18.1)	17.2(17.8)	17.4(18.5)	18.4(16.8)	14.7(16.2)	16.7(17.3)
Shopping	— (0.4)	— (0.3)	— (0.2)	— (0.5)	— (0.7)	— (0.7)	— (0.5)
Leisure (Minutes per day)							
Eating	106 (78)	114 (73)	101 (76)	116 (59)	109 (52)	106 (79)	108 (71)
Visiting	79 (68)	81 (74)	94 (39)	94 (74)	74 (132)	151 (138)	103 (95)
Reading	74 (50)	61 (36)	95 (24)	43 (29)	38 (23)	84 (40)	68 (35)
Entertainment	15 (11)	45 (13)	35 (13)	48 (14)	29 (16)	44 (10)	37 (12)
Sports	40 (10)	34 (12)	35 (5)	19 (5)	20 (0)	16 (2)	47 (10)
Radio	22 (5)	34 (4)	32 (10)	18 (5)	45 (7)	29 (2)	30 (5)
Motoring	15 (2)	20 (2)	12 (1)	25 (4)	13 (1)	10 (3)	15 (2)
Clubs	10 (5)	8 (8)	0 (5)	3 (7)	0 (5)	61 (12)	20 (8)
Television	— (80)	— (75)	— (159)	— (58)	— (102)	— (75)	— (89)
Miscellaneous	40 (51)	35 (51)	5 (24)	33 (61)	8 (64)	50 (65)	32 (54)
Total leisure minutes	401 (360)	438 (348)	409 (366)	399 (306)	336 (402)	551 (426)	470 (381)
Total leisure hours	6.7 (6.0)	7.3 (5.8)	6.8 (6.1)	6.6 (5.1)	5.6 (6.7)	9.2 (7.1)	7.6 (6.3)
Total	23.9(24.1)	24.0(24.2)	24.0(24.1)	24.0(24.1)	24.0(24.2)	23.9(24.0)	24.3(24.1)

SOURCES: 1934 data from Lundberg, F., M. Komarovsky, and E. McInerny, Leisure: A Suburban Study, Columbia University Press, New York, 1934; 1965–1966 data from Robinson, John R., "Social Change as Measured by Time Budgets," paper presented at American Sociological Association meetings, San Francisco, 1967.

period? But where did the hour and a half to two and a half hours of television watching really come from and how do we explain the decline of time spent *reading* (almost cut in half) in the face of a known increase in expenditure for reading across these years?

An even more frustrating question is how this table, which indicates only slight differences in total leisure time among different occupations, is to be reconciled with Table 4, which showed executives working a far longer week than people in white-collar or blue-collar jobs. Is the combination of professional with executive categories in Table 5 responsible for this discrepancy or is it the inclusion of women in Table 4 but their segregation in Table 5, or is there no discrepancy at all? That is, is it possible that the higher-level occupations work longer hours but have the same amount of leisure because they spend less time (but maybe more money) on maintenance-nurturance? The working man might, for example, spend his *free* Saturday morning washing his car, but still not report this as leisure while the executive works Saturday morning and pays for an "instant" car wash on the way home. The problem is clearly to examine the various temporal patterns of leisure and work for specific occupational groups and for different income and educational levels.

Money Measures. Money for leisure as a whole and for specific kinds of leisure is unequally distributed. The single most comprehensive source of data is the Bureau of Labor Statistics' Survey of Consumer Expenditures. These are vast and relatively unexplored compilations showing for different income educational and occupational levels and for different family sizes and types living in varying kinds of communities the distribution of expenditures for leisure categories discussed above. From these data we can see, for instance, the extent of income and educational influence on leisure expenditures. Figure 3 shows the total recreational expenditures in 1960–1961 for ten income classes at four educational levels.

There is a discernible increase in the percentage of people's income (money after taxes) allocated for recreation as both income and educational levels rise. How significant are these differences—that is, how elastic are leisure expenditures and how does the spending for the different leisure subcategories shift as the total amount increases or decreases? The last question raises the following methodological problem: not all the families in the sample reported expenditures for all the items. For example, in 1960–1961 only 7 per cent of the lowest income group (less than $1,000 per year) reported spending anything

FIGURE 3. RECREATIONAL EXPENDITURES BY INCOME
CLASS AND EDUCATIONAL LEVEL, 1960–1961

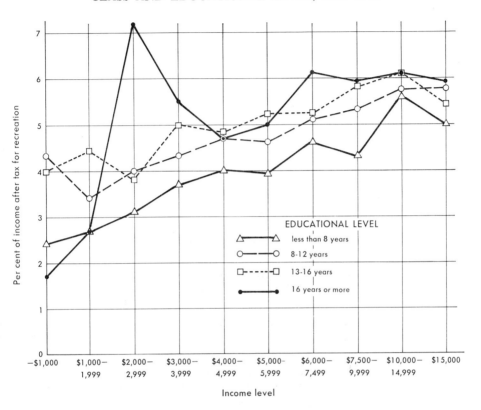

SOURCE: Bureau of Labor Statistics, Survey of Consumer Expenditures, 1960–1961.

for *books* in contrast to 74 per cent of the highest ($15,000 or more). The range of those reporting purchases of *newspapers* was much narrower—53 per cent of the lowest income group to 99 per cent of the highest. The question that has to be resolved, and resolved separately for each type of activity, is whether spending nothing can be considered as a "zero" dollar purchase. In other words, should book buyers be considered *qualitatively* different from nonbook buyers or should *everyone* be considered as part of the audience for books? This question is complex and will be discussed subsequently with problems of the structuring of leisure. Without resolving the issue it is still possible to demonstrate the uneven participation in different types of

TABLE 6.   ALLOCATION OF LEISURE EXPENDITURES
BY INCOME, 1950

	Income	
Type of leisure spending	From $3,000–$6,000	More than $6,000
	(percentages)	
Purchase of radio, TV, etc.	40	30
Admissions (movies, sports events, etc.)	17	18
Other (hobbies, sports equipment, etc.)	28	39
Reading (magazines, books, newspapers)	15	13
Total	100	100

SOURCE: Adapted from Wharton School, Study of Consumer Expenditures, Vol. IX, Table 1, p. 3, as cited in Ennis, P. H., "Leisure in the Suburbs," in William Dobriner, ed., *The Suburban Community*, G. P. Putnam's Sons, 1958, pp. 255–260. Occupational level and type of residence community have been held constant.

leisure activities as a function of income or education. For example, Table 6 shows the shift away from spending on radio, television, and records and toward "other" leisure (that is, presumably, made up of more active and individualized activities) as income rises.

While the data are crude compared to fine-grained demographic characteristics in the BLS material, the table suggests the kind of differences in leisure spending among various age groups and family types. These differences are restricted, though, to the narrow range of leisure categories included in the Consumer Survey schedule. For more detailed specific analysis of the distribution of leisure, we must turn to the single-purpose, one-time-only surveys. The gain in specificity and intensiveness of information is, however, traded for a loss in continuity.

These studies tell us, for example, that participation in voluntary organizations is very high at the upper end of the socioeconomic ladder and falls off quite sharply at lower levels.[42] An important difficulty with these researches is the restricted definition of voluntary associational participation. Membership in formal organizations is taken as the criterion of participation in most of these studies; if this restriction is relaxed to include the more amorphous kinds of associational behavior among people of lower socioeconomic status, then it is less likely that such sharp differences in participation rates will be observed. Other studies show clear, strong social class differences in leisure pursuits, ranging from adult education[43] to attendance at the performing arts.[44] Still others show for extended lists of activities differential participation by socioeconomic status.[45]

Activity Measures. All these data contribute to the by now familiar "brow level" categorizations of leisure activities, and there can be no quarrel with the general picture. Yet the brow-ranking of ten or twenty leisure activities on the basis of what social class pursues them "most frequently" distorts the fact that for almost any given activity the participant or audience mix is far broader than indicated. Leisure activities are rarely the exclusive property of a single social stratum. The participation of lower strata may be quite large in total numbers even though small in percentage terms. This can be shown dramatically for, say, television viewing. An audience for the so-called "cultural ghetto," that is, serious programing, contains proportionately more college-educated people than those with high school or less education. However, since the total number of the less well-educated is so much greater than those who went to college, the audience for serious programing has a rather high loading of low-educated individuals.[46] Furthermore, the boundaries sealing off the activities of one level from those of others are not impermeable. Activities once regarded as the province of higher-status people are increasingly enjoyed by lower strata. Conversely, the known participation of higher-status people in middlebrow or lowbrow activities is well documented.[47] While it is all but inescapable to associate specific activities with positions in the stratification system, the familiar "brow" categories are threadbare and ill-fitting. Differentiations by age, type of community, and region appear to be increasingly important determinants of leisure for one thing; the continued vigor of ethnic styles cutting across income levels for another, the diffusion and scatter of many activities across a widening range of social classes for a third, all point to a more heterogeneous and complex picture than in previous years.

Before the policy implications of this complex distribution of leisure can be understood an important methodological issue must be clarified: Some inequal distributions of leisure may result from individual choices among ubiquitous alternatives—almost all people have access to television, the choice of whether or not to watch is up to the individual (or family). Preferences for and participation in other activities are related to the availability of external resources— a ski slope, a museum, a bowling alley, a book store. What we do with our leisure depends in good measure on what choices are available. Most studies of leisure have ignored the matching of activity to availability of resources either because of an assumption (warranted or not) that the differential appearance of facilities is irrelevant or because the categories of activity explored are defined so broadly that they are unaffected by the presence or absence of particular facilities. Such studies may indeed be valuable, but it should be clear that the more intensive, specific, and detailed a leisure inquiry is the more imperative it is to include an equally detailed inventory of the available leisure resources. Thus Steiner's study of television viewing carefully traced the viewers' "diet" and the screen's "menu." Johnstone's study of adult education did the same thing in a partial way by assessing a sample of individuals' adult education activities and at the same time measuring the educational facilities in their communities.

Mapping Leisure Resources

Finally, let us turn to the problems of mapping the distribution of leisure resources. The ORRRC materials cited above are major sources of information for outdoor recreation, and an agency for future collection and organization of leisure data. The careful methods of Baumol and Bowen are a model for data handling in the performing arts.

The distributional inequities of outdoor recreational areas are strangely parallel but opposite to those of the performing arts. As Clawson and Knetsch observe, ". . . over two-thirds of all the public non-urban recreation areas were under 40 acres in size, but altogether these small areas contain less than 1 per cent of the total recreation acreage in the country. In contrast slightly over 1 per cent of the areas were greater than 100,000 acres, but together these total 88 per cent of the total area."[48] Most of these large tracts obviously are in the West where population density is the lowest. With a few notable exceptions, most of the nation's cultural resources (museums, theaters, music) are comparably concentrated in the East.

There are basically two problems in measuring the distribution of leisure resources. One is the difficult administrative task of amassing the relevant data about the location of "outlets" from all the diverse leisure activities—bowling alleys, movie houses, libraries, television stations, and so forth. This is not an easy assignment. It requires considerable energy and patience to track down and develop rapport with these national and regional organizations and associations through which the local resources can be located. Standardized categories have to be developed and the various associations have to be persuaded to organize their record-keeping accordingly.

The second problem is both practical and theoretical. What are the sensible and relevant spatial boundaries for defining a community's (or an individual's) leisure resources? How are the different practices of record-keeping by leisure associations and public bodies going to be coordinated? Some leisure data are reported on a state level, others by county, others on a local basis.

The theoretical problem is how to assign spatial boundaries that are "natural" to some population unit, taking into account the divergent distances that people will ordinarily travel for various leisure activities. Can the presence or absence of a leisure resource (supply) be decided upon independently of its use (demand)? Suppose a town in California has a lake a hundred miles away, a distance regarded by the population as a "normal" drive for a weekend. Is that lake equivalent to one twenty miles from an Ohio town which is a "normal" drive for its weekenders? If such a dependence on the users' habits places an intolerable burden on record-keeping and research facilities, then what spatial unit is to be selected? City and suburb are so interconnected in both work and leisure that they should be treated as a unit. The difficulty here is largely administrative, because record-keeping of leisure organizations rarely matches the proper geographical units.

ORGANIZATIONAL PATTERNS

How the average American spends his free time is, naturally, the main interest of the nation's pulse-taker. Total concentration on the individual, however, obscures a pervasive fact about leisure. Because of its peculiar location in the institutional structure there is a relentless pressure toward the organization of individual leisure activities into larger units.

> *Item:* The *Middletown* (Conn.) *Press* announced on February 15, 1968, that Peter Spano had formed the Connecticut Ocelot Club with a charter membership of 14. Mr. Spano indicated that local veterinarians don't know how to treat exotic cats. The Connecticut Ocelot Club is, according to its founder, one of 800 such ocelot organizations in the United States.
> *Item:* The Chicago *Daily News* reported in a four-part series (June 27–30, 1967) the activities of organized spouse-swapping groups in many of Chicago's suburban and middle-class city neighborhoods. Estimates range from 1,500 to 2,500 couples involved in weekly symposia, meetings, and swinging parties. The story reported: "Their most important rule . . . is that husband and wife are in it as a team." One man explained—"You get active in something new . . . so you drop things you used to be active in . . . I started out being active in churchwork I was head of a youth group. From there I went to the Masons and I dropped the churchwork. I used to be out three or four nights a week for lodge work . . . and then I started going into politics in the

new town that we moved into. So I stopped being active in the Masons. Then we got into this and about the same time, I got into a higher job, so I didn't have time for nothing else. I dropped it all."

Item: Gale Research's Encyclopedia of Associations (4th edition, 1964) described 87 national horticultural organizations with 17,177 state and local affiliates and a membership of 566,821 persons. It also lists 28 national philatelic associations, comprising 980 state and local groups with a total membership of 245,369. (The American Kennel Club Registrations in 1966 totaled 804,400 for 112 different breeds of dog, each with its own organization.) Also listed are 583 fraternal and ethnic national associations made up of 80,503 state and local units whose total membership is slightly over 28 million persons. In the American Contract Bridge League there are listed about 5,000 subunits whose members total 125,000. There are no listed national poker associations.

Item: The New York Times on February 2, 1968, reported that the long feud between the American Amateur Union (AAU) and the National Collegiate Athletic Association (NCAA) reached a momentary stopping point when the Sports Arbitration Board appointed by Vice President Humphrey concluded its deliberations, announcing "that the AAU is not entitled to be the sole governing body for domestic purposes," giving the NCAA's self-created federation (USTFF) the right to conduct open meets. The federation must apply for AAU sanction and the AAU must grant it. The warfare between the two bodies dates back several decades, erupting periodically. The last fitful peace treaty was imposed by General Douglas McArthur in 1963.

Item: The New York Times on December 17, 1967, reported that the introduction of the five-day work week in the Soviet Union has produced unanticipated problems: "The sale of vodka has increased sharply (a 25 per cent increase in Moscow) the reading of books has declined and people are wasting more time than ever on their days off standing in long lines at food stores, barber shops and bath houses." The inadequacies of Russian consumer services are seen as responsible. A Soviet official was quoted as saying, "Before changing work schedules of service and cultural facilities, an agreement must be reached on just what is rest. Rest is not just sitting around idle or going to visit friends. One of every 50 workers must be kept on the job to insure that people can do what they want during their free time."

These examples illustrate some of the organizational tendencies and problems in leisure. At the lowest level, to elaborate for a moment on the Russian five-day work week, there is the problem of the temporal envelope of leisure. Beneath the surface of ordinary observation there is a deep structuring of many social institutions which sustain a given mix of leisure intervals—the coffee break, the holiday, the weekend, the vacation. Sudden or even slow changes in familiar arrangements dislocate those invisible structures. The extension in the United States of paid vacations, experiments in the six-hour work day, three-day weekends, and the increased work-force participation of women all invite the closest scrutiny. What is clearly needed is a twofold research and data collection operation. One part should be a careful measurement of the changes in the temporal patterning of leisure sequences, and the second and closely connected part should be an intensive study of the consequences of changes in these patterns.[49]

Next, as the ocelot and spouse-swapping incidents illustrate, is the difficult problem of identifying the ceaseless and microscopic coagulation (and dissolution) of individual leisure interests into various forms of organized activity. These processes are resistant to study by ordinary social science research techniques, yet their consequences for the individual and the community may be great. The central task here, it seems, is basic research into the social processes which move individual preferences seen in the large as statistical aggregates through the stages of audiences or quasi-groups into the more or less self-conscious organized leisure organizations.

A step beyond this is the extension of special or community groups into larger, ultimately national associations. The stunning facts on the extensiveness of national leisure organizations calls attention to another basic organizational dimension of leisure. For every committed, nationally affiliated gardener, dog lover, or bridge player there is a large but unknown number of participants giving less time and effort. But how many? Each activity is likely to have a distinctive percentage of active fans to moderate or peripheral participants. This is the phenomenon of "concentration of use," readily illustrated in the contrast between newspaper and book reading. Most newspaper readers tend to read one newspaper a day so that, say, 80 per cent of the newspaper readers account for about 80 per cent of the newspapers read. Book reading is different; many people read few books, a few people read many books, so that about 20 per cent of the book readers account for 80 per cent of all the books read.

Leisure activities vary in the concentration or dispersion of their participants' engagement. Insofar as the activity requires or involves some professional expertise, especially situations involving the performance before an audience, then the shape of the concentration-of-use curve is critical. The reason is that both audiences and performers have to be educated to the standard of the medium. While no one knows how many peripheral audience members or fans, amateurs or semiprofessional actors, writers, tennis players, or whatever, are necessary to sustain the total system, the professionals need the amateurs and the amateurs need the professionals. In terms of maintaining a cultural system over time, writers need readers from whom will come the next generation of writers.

The concentration-of-use configuration for a given activity is important in another sense. It can provide the basis of deciding how to draw the boundary of who is in and who is out of the activity for those statistical accounting purposes discussed in the previous section. The shape of the concentration-of-use curve for picnicking is probably much like that for newspaper reading—almost everyone goes on a picnic now and then. The concentration-of-use curve for sky diving, on the other hand, would probably show that 1 per cent of the population accounts for 90 per cent of the sky dives. This relationship does not imply that there is a simple relationship between total numbers of participants and the shape of the concentration-of-use curve, however. This is an empirical question and requires the collection of individual-level data on participation rates in a variety of activities. One final word on this point. Why do some leisure activities resist organization beyond a certain point and others pyramid into a vast national structure—bridge vs. poker, for example—and what is the relation between degree of organization and concentration of use?

Now to the implications of the final item—the clash between the AAU and the NCAA. As leisure organizations mobilize large numbers of people around one or more activities, the prizes become significant and the struggles approximate those of the political arena. These are in fact political struggles between social forces with immediate *interests* in the pragmatic sense and *ideologies* in the sense of a set of values being expounded and defended. The contestants vary considerably: here the ideals of the amateur athlete clash with the imperatives of modern organized athletics. Each of these sets of values expresses the beliefs of different institutional forces, not all readily identifiable.

There is another kind of contest that goes on in many cities in which various interests vie for domination of the "cultural" life of the community. Often active in these battles are the commercial booking agencies who dispatch specialists in community organization to help "the ladies" create community concert umbrella organizations, which, of course, hire their company's performers. The recent acceleration in the growth of local and state arts councils (some 63 art centers are listed by the Associated Councils of the Arts in January, 1967) is but another example of the organizational drive in leisure.

It is important to examine and re-examine periodically which institutional forces are gaining or losing in the various leisure fields. How fares, for instance, organized religion's entry into nonchurch leisure, as seen for example in their attempts to move into the "coffee house" field or into outdoor recreation?[50] Or to what extent have federal governmental influences been extended in the field of boating though the U.S. Power Squadron, in the amateur radio field through civil defense, or other governmental arrangements with the 100,000 member American Radio Relay Association and in the amateur aviation field through the Civil Air Patrol?

A vast and complex political struggle has been waged over open lands in wilderness areas and over park and recreational areas closer to population centers. The participants have changed and have formed shifting alliances over the years. These controversies date back to the planning of most American cities, in fact, and thus offer a rich historical source of data for research into the course of such battles.

Closer to the individual is his immediate and extended family. To what extent is leisure retreating back into the confines of the family or to what is it cutting those ties under the influence of age- and sex-segregated leisure patterns?

The difficulties in measuring the organizational dimension in leisure are great. It is necessary to give more quantitative yet sensitive expression to the observations made on the question by the Lynds about the other "Middletown" back in 1925.

> In the main . . . leisure activities are carried on by people in groups rather than singly. . . . many of the earlier informal ties are being displaced by more rigid lines of union and demarcation. (p. 272)
>
> This trend toward greater organization appearing in so many leisure pursuits culminates in the proliferating system of clubs which touches the life of the city in all its major activities. (p. 285)
>
> With greater organization has come increasing standardization of leisure time pursuits. . . . (p. 309)
>
> Finally, the greater organization of leisure is not altogether a substitute for the informal contacts of a generation ago; opportunities to touch elbows with people are multiplied in the mobile and organized group life of today, but these contacts appear to be more casual and to leave the individual somewhat more isolated from the close friends of earlier days. In view of the tightening of social and economic lines in the growing city, it is not surprising that the type of leisure today tends in the main to erect barriers to keep others out. (p. 312)[51]

THE QUALITY OF LEISURE

This last question is the most difficult. All the refinements and complexities of measuring leisure discussed above do not provide answers to the questions: How well do we live as individuals; how human

and civilized is our society? Even if we could render an exact judgment as to the quality of our leisure it would still not be enough, because the whole life—work, maintenance, and leisure—in all its social
settings have to be added, first for each individual and then summed
for the total population. Yet all attempts to find such a calculus of
happiness have failed. We are left with the view that the quality of
society's leisure rests on a subjective judgment as to how well our
values are being realized in a general way. Beyond that is the philosophical debate about whether or not the values are any good, or
rather, which values comes first and which should be defended at all.
This is not the place for that debate. Instead several different attempts
to assess leisure's quality in quantitative terms are discussed.

The first is the question of standards. Many organized leisure interests respond to the intangible nature of leisure by establishing minimal conditions under which their particular activity can be carried
out. Such standards or guidelines, for example, a limit to the number
of visitors allowed per acre on certain kinds of open land, or rules
defining the size and diversity of the book collection for a branch library, illustrate rational attempts to realize the values shared by the
managers and presumably the users of an activity.

Long experience and consensus among experts are the only tools
available at present for establishing standards. While the health, safety,
and conservation standards underlying leisure guidelines probably rest
on firmer ground and set some limits on them, the process of standard-
setting is little understood. Agencies vary widely, for example, in defining the park acreage required per 1,000 population.[52] How much
are such decisions determined simply by the geography and the population density, how much by political negotiations among interested
parties, and how much by studies of users' needs and substitution ratios? If it is useful to understand the social (and technical) processes
involved in establishing standards for leisure activities, it is imperative
that they be paralleled with studies of users' perceived satisfactions
so that some sort, no matter how crude, of cost-benefit analysis can
be made, relating standards to outcome. This can be done, from the
user's point of view, by having them estimate the relative desirability
of the activity under different conditions (i.e., different levels of the
standardized items), by having them assign dollar values to the activity or alternative uses of their time and money at given levels of conditions.

A second approach to leisure's quality is to evaluate the extent that a
person, a community, or a whole society has the structural opportunity

to carry into behavior leisure's main norm, "to do what you want to do." While this prescription clearly invites an examination of the individual's skills, motivations, and interests, we postpone that to examine the external conditions guaranteeing the exercise of the norm. In terms of the institutional setting of leisure described above, this means that the person or group requires both a *multiplicity* of institutional connections and the *flexibility* of moving among them, that is, there are limits on the extent to which any single institutional context (family, work, etc.) is able to constrain the person's behavior. Such a view is a defense of pluralistic society, an ideological bias frankly confessed. Other kinds of social structures might very well provide an equivalent to leisure guided by different normative directives, but if individual free choice of activity is the dominant prescription, then the conditions of multiplicity and flexibility of institutional engagement seem critical.

The useful research to fill in this viewpoint should consist of two parts. The first should specify for some population the patterns of their work, family, and other institutional attachments. The second should identify their leisure habits, and evaluate the cultural level of that leisure. This latter point is critical and involves an explicit or implicit subjective judgment as to leisure's quality. Only two studies fulfilling these requirements come to mind, Steiner's television study and Wilensky's analysis of the leisure habits of men in a specific group of occupations. Wilensky's study is especially noteworthy because both the degree of his respondents' institutional connectedness and their cultural level are carefully documented. Panels of judges evaluated the "brow" level of reading, television fare, and other leisure activities with high reliability. Sophisticated statistical analysis then confronted the institutional data and the leisure data. While the main substantive results are admittedly ambiguous, they point to several quite different styles of life. There is a low-competence leisure person who compulsively absorbs large doses of low-level television, engages in much aimless leisure and—this is critical—"has weak attachments to secondary associations and fluid friendships and . . . a short work week."[53] A second type identified as the "Happy Good Citizen-Consumer" is strongly attached to multiple institutions in his community and has "no leisure malaise." Another important conclusion of Wilensky's work is the blending and blurring of brow levels and the relative noncorrelation of leisure quality levels with ordinary demographic variables. Much in this study needs elaboration and qualification. It should also be noted that there is no attempt to give baseline estimates of the relative prevalence of these types in the total population, nor is there any assessment of the availability of leisure resources. Nevertheless, this study is clearly an important research model that calls for continued elaboration and extension.

The third empirical attempt at quantifying the quality of our life are the National Opinion Research Center studies of "happiness."[54] Here again the survey method was used on a large sample of individuals in several different communities. In addition to the familiar background information, and some items on family, work, and other social relations, the critical part of the interview schedule probed into the respondents' positive and negative feelings toward his life. The picture that emerges is one of substantial satisfaction by a large majority of people, even though many people experience "negative affect." A full report of these studies is still in preparation; at present there appears enough solid evidence to say that reported satisfaction with life is a meaningful concept for the measurement of the quality of leisure.

The final example is the remarkable tour de force of Bernard Berelson, "In the Presence of Culture,"[55] wherein he turns his unremitting search for the facts on the question: "How much time do American adults voluntarily spend in the presence of culture in an average month and in what ways?" Culture is then given the following criterion—"any time—book, film, concert, television program, play, etc.—would presumably have to be given serious attention as part of a liberal education in a good college." Berelson then scans every conceivable source of information, surveys, published records, educated estimates for all possible media. "The answer is 447,021,000 hours, or an average of about 4 hours a month per American adult or about 4½ percent of his leisure time (figured at an average of three hours a day)." The study then differentiates this involvement by educational levels and by types of cultural fare.

What can be concluded about this effort? Its faults are obvious. There is no baseline against which to measure the result; is this a little or a lot of culture? There is no assessment of how much culture was *offered* during that month. The definition of culture is arbitrary and difficult to implement. Notwithstanding these problems, however, Berelson's method has the attractiveness of a large clean sweep. When modified to meet the difficulties mentioned above, the "head count" approach might provide a periodic census of cultural participation. When associated with institutional and educational information such a monitoring could be of considerable analytic value in addition to its cultural thermometer function.

In summary, while there is nothing like the immediacy of a perceptive intelligence describing the quality of a community's style of life in discursive terms there is also nothing more persuasive than a solid empirical estimate of that same style. Can these two modes of understanding be conjoined? This is the challenge that has to be met if a continuing evaluation of the nation's leisure is to be a vital one.

There is, finally, no easy way to assess the balance of forces in the ceaseless struggle among major institutions, including commercial enterprises, to enfold leisure, to define its meaning, and to validate its dominion in the name of the nation's highest values. The competition for leisure commitment often produces viewpoints that overburden leisure with more emotional or social freight than it should bear. We need to assess how much leisure as a whole is invaded by such postures as that of the American Bowling Congress.

> Bowling is life. It is comedy, tragedy and drama . . . Only the right sport, the right organization and the right people could do these things: PROVIDE the greatest weapon against juvenile delinquency . . . TEACH the lessons of democracy and sportsmanship through upwards of 20,000 business and factory leagues where the bosses and employees play together . . . BAND 35,000 church teams into leagues for the benefit of these churches . . . And finally . . . bowling was best described as the great battleground for individualism against regimentation "Anyone who wants to put over a foreign 'ism' will have to lick the ABC first."[56]

NOTES

I am indebted to my colleagues Hubert J. O'Gorman and Stanley Lebergott for critical readings of parts of this chapter, and to Ken Krich for assistance in collecting the materials. I am responsible for errors of fact or interpretation.

1. Contrast, for example, the definition and categories developed for a study of leisure expenditures in Fisk, George, *Leisure Spending-Behavior,* University of Pennsylvania Press, Philadelphia, 1963, p. 7, with the categories in a study of time budgets in Robinson, John P., "Social Change as Measured by Time Budgets," paper presented at American Sociological Association meetings, San Francisco, 1967.
2. National Recovery Administration, *Report of the New York Committee on the Use of Leisure Time,* 1930, p. 15.
3. Lundberg, F., M. Komarovsky, and E. McInerny, *Leisure: A Suburban Study,* Columbia University Press, New York, 1934, pp. 2, 3.
4. The following discussion of the structure of leisure is a modification of views stated in Ennis, Philip H., "Leisure in the Suburbs" in William Dobriner, ed., *The Suburban Community,* G. P. Putnam's Sons, New York, 1958, pp. 248–270.
5. Stinchcombe, Arthur, "Formal Organizations" in N. Smelser, ed., *Sociology,* John Wiley, New York, 1967, p. 154.

6. O'Connor, Connie, *The Leisure Wasters,* A. S. Barnes Co., Cranbury, N.J., 1966, p. 158.
7. See, for example, Bauer, Raymond, ed., *Social Indicators,* MIT Press, Cambridge, 1966.
8. *Bowling Magazine,* September, 1955, pp. 13–24.
9. Dewhurst, J. Frederic, *et al., America's Needs and Resources: A New Survey,* Twentieth Century Fund, New York, 1955, p. 366, Table 161. From 1929 to the present, at least, U.S. government series provide the information. From 1909 to 1929 Dewhurst uses privately collected sources as approximations.
10. Clawson, Marion, *Statistics on Outdoor Recreation,* Resources for the Future, Washington, 1958, p. 14.
11. Toffler, Alvin, *The Culture Consumers,* Penguin Books, Baltimore, 1965, p. 25.
12. Clawson, Marion, and J. L. Knetsch, *Economics of Outdoor Recreation,* The Johns Hopkins Press, Baltimore, 1966, p. 22.
13. De Grazia, Sebastian, *Of Time, Work and Leisure,* Twentieth Century Fund, New York, 1962.
14. Foote, Nelson, "Methods for Study of Meaning in Use of Time," in *Aging and Leisure,* Robert Kleemeier, ed., Oxford University Press, New York, 1961, pp. 155–157.
15. Szalai, Alexander, "Trends in Comparative Time Budget Research," *American Behavioral Scientist,* May, 1966, pp. 3–8.
16. Robinson, John P., "Social Change as Measured by Time-Budgets," *op. cit.*
17. An example is the discrepancy between the amount of radio listening as recorded from the time budget studies of Robinson and Converse and specialized studies directed toward radio listening. The latter, not surprisingly showed higher rates of listening. The studies are reported in Robinson, *op. cit.,* p. 26.
18. The three most important of these studies in recent years are the 1950 *Study of Consumer Expenditures, Incomes and Savings,* 28 vols., University of Pennsylvania, Philadelphia, 1957, 1958; the 1960 repetition of the 1950 study; and *Life Study of Consumer Expenditures* (conducted for *Life* by Alfred Politz Research), Simon and Schuster, New York, 1958.
19. U.S. Department of Commerce, *National Income Supplement* to the Survey of Current Business, Washington, 1929–
20. The *National Income Supplement* to the Survey of Current Business, 1929–1946, Table 30, has a slightly different organization of these major categories and will be discussed further below.
21. From Ennis, P. H., "The Library Consumer" in *The Public Library and the City,* Ralph Conant, ed., MIT Press, Cambridge, 1965, p. 22. These are numbers of books, it should be noted, not dollar sales, but there is enough of a relationship between the two—children's books being somewhat less expensive than other types—to get a general picture.
22. See Meyersohn, Rolf, and Robin Jackson, "Gardening in Suburbia," in William Dobriner, ed., *The Suburban Community, op. cit.,* pp. 271–286.
23. George Fisk in his *Leisure Spending-Behavior, op. cit.,* chap. 2, reaches essentially the same conclusion as shown in Figure 2 with respect to leisure expenditures, though he shows a less steady growth due to his use of refinements in per capita figures, constant dollars, and a different definition of leisure.
24. See *Life Study of Consumer Expenditures, op. cit.* The questionnaires of the BLS studies apparently do have great detail in their consumption categories, but they are not presented to the public in the fine-grained manner in which

they are collected. The reasons are complex and beyond the present scope to explore.

25. Taylor, Lester D., "Combining the 1960–61 BLS Survey of Consumer Expenditures and OBE Time Series Data in Projecting Personal Consumption Expenditures," unpublished manuscript, 1967.
26. *Newsweek*, April 1, 1968, p. 54.
27. Abbott Ferriss notes that individual recreation surveys differ according to the methods of their data collection. Samples of individuals can be drawn from (1) people passing a transportation point, something like the traditional arrival and departure study; (2) persons found at a particular recreation facility, a park, wilderness site, etc.; and (3) individuals or families in their homes. These different sampling procedures with their differing bases have to be chosen in accordance with the purpose of the inquiry. See Abbott L. Ferriss, "Application of Recreation Surveys," *Public Opinion Quarterly*, vol. 27, Fall, 1963, pp. 443–445.
28. Three important studies on a national scale are: Johnstone, John, and Ramon J. Rivera, *Volunteers for Learning*, Aldine Publishing Co., Chicago, 1965, a national study estimating the rates and types of participation in adult education; the *National Recreation Survey*, a report prepared by Abbott Ferriss for the Outdoor Recreation Resources Review Commission, 1962, reporting on the participation of different kinds of people in a variety of outdoor recreational activities; and Steiner, Gary A., *The People Look at Television*, Alfred A. Knopf, New York, 1963, an intensive study of the television viewing habits and attitudes of the American public.
29. Two sources reporting some of these studies are *Outdoor Recreation Research, a Reference Catalog*, Washington, 1966, published by the U.S. Department of Interior, Bureau of Outdoor Recreation, in cooperation with the Science Information Exchange of the Smithsonian Institution; and *Tourism and Recreation, A State of the Art Study*, Office of Regional Development Planning, U.S. Department of Commerce, Economic Development Administration, Washington, n.d.
30. *A Graphic View of the Retail Florest Industry*, U.S. Department of Agriculture, Economic Research Service, Marketing Research Report No. 788, Washington, 1967, p. 18.
31. *Ibid.*, p. 14.
32. See *Tourism and Recreation, op. cit.*, pp. 154–157.
33. Clawson, Marion, "Statistical Data Available for Economic Research on Certain Types of Recreation," *American Statistical Association Journal*, March, 1959, pp. 281–309.
34. *Outdoor Recreation For America*, Final Report to the President and to the Congress by the Outdoor Recreation Resources Review Commission, 1962. This is the summary report for 27 specific research efforts in the field of outdoor recreation.
35. *Statewide Comprehensive Outdoor Recreation Manual* prepared by Robert E. Young, N.Y. Conservation Department and Vollmer Ostrower Associates, 1966.
36. Baumol, William J., and William G. Bowen, *Performing Arts: The Economic Dilemma*, Twentieth Century Fund, New York, 1966.
37. *The Performing Arts: Problems & Prospects*, Rockefeller Panel Report on the Future of the Theatre, Dance and Music in America, McGraw-Hill, New York, 1965.
38. *Public Television, A Program for Actors*, Report of the Carnegie Commission on Educational Television, Bantam Books, New York, 1967.
39. U.S. Office of Education, Library Services Branch, *Library Statistics:*

Statistics of Public Library Systems Serving Populations of 100,000 or more (37,000–49,999 and 50,000–99,999), 1952–60.

40. See, for example, the occupational community of the printer in Coleman, J. S., S. M. Lipset, and M. A. Trow, *Union Democracy,* Free Press, Glencoe, Ill., 1956.

41. Robinson, John R., "Social Change as Measured by Time Budgets," *op. cit.*

42. Wright, Charles, and Herbert H. Hyman, "Voluntary Association Memberships of American Adults," *American Sociology Review,* vol. 23, 1958, pp. 284–294.

43. Johnstone and Rivera, *Volunteers for Learning, op. cit.*

44. Baumol and Bowen, *Performing Arts: The Economic Dilemma, op. cit.*

45. For example, White, R. C., "Social Class Differences in the Uses of Leisure," and Clarke, Alfred C., "Leisure and Occupational Prestige," in Eric Larabee and Rolf Meyersohn, eds., *Mass Leisure,* Free Press, Glencoe, Ill., 1958.

46. Steiner, Gary, *op. cit.,* chap. 6.

47. *Ibid.,* and Wilensky, Harold L., "Mass Society and Mass Culture: Interdependence or Independence?" *American Sociological Review,* vol. 29, no. 2, 1964, pp. 173–197.

48. Clawson and Knetsch, *Economics of Outdoor Recreation, op. cit.,* p. 183.

49. See Swados, Harvey, "Less Work—Less Leisure," in *Mass Leisure, op. cit.,* pp. 353–363.

50. See Perry, Rev. John D., Jr., *Report of the Coffee House Study Project,* National Council of Churches and National Coffee Association, New York, 1965; and *Report of the Task Force on Leisure,* A Christian Ministry in National Parks, division of National Council of Churches, Rev. Warren W. Ost, Director, New York, 1965.

51. Lynd, Robert S., and Helen Merrell Lynd, *Middletown,* Harvest Books, Harcourt, Brace & World, New York, 1956.

52. Clawson and Knetsch, *Economics of Outdoor Recreation, op. cit.,* pp. 146–150.

53. Wilensky, Harold L., "Mass Society and Mass Culture," *op. cit.,* p. 183.

54. Bradburn, Norman, and David Caplovitz, *Reports on Happiness,* Aldine Publishing Co., Chicago, 1964.

55. Berelson, Bernard, "In the Presence of Culture," *Public Opinion Quarterly,* Spring, 1964, pp. 1–12.

56. *Bowling Magazine,* September, 1955, pp. 13, 14, 24.

11. PROBLEMS IN THE MEASUREMENT OF HEALTH STATUS

Iwao M. Moriyama

THE AVERAGE life expectancy at birth in the United States increased from 47.3 years in 1900 to 70.2 years in 1964. The remarkable increase in longevity is frequently presented as evidence of health progress made by the general population in the United States.

What these figures conceal is that the increase in expectation of life has not been uniform over the age scale. For example, in the period 1900 to 1964 the increase in the expectation of life of white males at age sixty-five is only 1.5 years, whereas at age one it is 13.8 years. Actually, a large part of the increase in life expectancy at birth resulted from the reduction in the death rate during the first year of life. It is therefore relevant to examine the course of the infant mortality rate. This statistical measure is of special interest because it has long been regarded as the most sensitive index of the level of living and of sanitary conditions.

INFANT MORTALITY

For years the infant mortality rate declined at a rapid pace in the United States[1] (Figure 1). During the period 1933–1949, the total infant mortality rate decreased about 4.3 per cent each year. However, beginning about 1950, the rate of decrease dropped to 1.1 per cent per annum.

The mortality experience of white infants follows the same pattern as that for all infants. For the nonwhites, the deceleration in the downward trend is even more marked. During the period 1933–1949, the mortality rate for nonwhite infants decreased 4.6 per cent per annum. Between 1950 and 1964 the decline slowed down to 0.6 per cent per year. The gap between the rate for white and nonwhite infants has widened during the past decade.

Because of the change in mortality trend in the United States, the

FIGURE 1. INFANT MORTALITY RATES, BY COLOR: UNITED STATES, 1933–1965

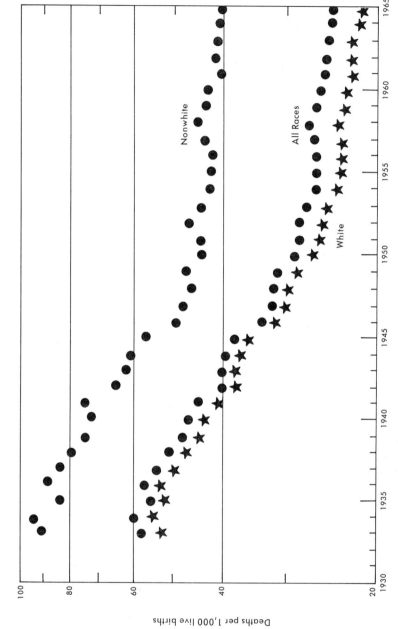

SOURCE: National Center for Health Statistics

present situation in this country is less favorable relative to other countries than was the case twenty-five to thirty years ago. Although there are indications of a similar change in trend in other countries such as Australia, England and Wales, New Zealand, Norway, and Sweden, these changes are not nearly as great as those experienced in the United States. On the other hand, the rates for many countries of low mortality continue to decline. As a consequence, the infant mortality rate for the United States ranks relatively high in international comparisons. Also, the gap between the rate for the United States and those of other countries is widening.

The infant mortality rate in the United States is currently significantly higher than the rates for the various Scandinavian countries, the Netherlands, Switzerland, England and Wales, Australia, New Zealand, Japan, France, and a number of other countries. The difference between the infant mortality rate for the United States and the rates of other countries cannot be readily accounted for on the basis of differences in definitions, methods of data collection, and possible incompleteness of registration.[2]

Do these findings mean that the socioeconomic status of the U.S. population is declining, or that sanitary conditions in the United States are deteriorating? Are conditions in other countries improving, whereas they are now static in the United States? Or are these changes merely the results of a statistical artifact?

Because significant changes have taken place over the years in the United States in the distribution of live births by age of mother, birth order, birth weight, and other factors related to the increased risk of infant death, it is possible for total infant mortality to be affected by the change in the proportion of births by these characteristics even if the force of mortality remained unchanged. Adjustment of rates for the changing distribution of live births by birth order and age of mother does not make it apparent that these factors account for the change in the infant mortality trend. Neither the changing number of annual births nor the slight increase in the proportion of low birth-weight infants explains the phenomenon. There is little evidence to suggest that the leveling off of the infant mortality trend in the United States is not real.

Perhaps the most significant finding is the changing relationship between the deaths occurring in the neonatal (under twenty-eight days of age) period and those in the postneonatal (twenty-eight days to one year) period. During the past thirty-five years or so, the neonatal mortality rate has changed very slowly, whereas the postneonatal mortality rate has declined rapidly. Most of the past decline in the infant mortality rate has been due to reductions in deaths from the exogenous factors (principally pneumonia and diarrhea and enteritis), and relatively little headway has been made in the prevention of deaths from factors relating to the birth process such as birth injuries, postnatal asphyxia, congenital malformations, and prematurity.

The leveling off of the infant mortality rate appears to be a consequence of two factors, the first being the deceleration in the rate of decline in the death rate for pneumonia. The second retarding effect is the relatively unyielding course of mortality among the neonates.

The infant mortality rate does not reflect the rising level of living during the postwar era. As for the future, further declines in the infant mortality rate in the United States are possible, but they are likely to be modest ones in the absence of important breakthroughs in the prevention of deaths in the neonatal period. Therefore, it appears that the infant mortality rate is no longer a particularly useful indicator of the level of living and sanitary condition for a country like the United States.

TOTAL MORTALITY

For a very similar reason, mortality data for the other ages are no longer adequate as measures of "health" of the population. Here again it has been shown[3] that the past declines in the death rate at the various ages are due primarily to reductions in the death rates for the infectious diseases. With the successive introduction of pneumonia serum and the antimicrobials starting in the late 1930's, there was an acceleration in the rate of mortality decline. However, by 1950 the mortality from the diseases of infectious origin had reached a level where death rates for the infectious diseases no longer contributed in a major way to the over-all mortality rate.

The long-term decline in mortality from the infectious diseases resulted in a major realignment of the principal causes of death. As in the case of the causes of infant mortality, there has been a significant shift in the numerically important causes of death. The prominent causes are now malignant neoplasms and cardiovascular-renal diseases at all ages, congenital malformations through the childhood years, accidents and other violence from childhood through middle age, cirrhosis of the liver in middle age, and diabetes mellitus from middle age into old age.

New problems are also emerging. The dramatic upward trend of the chronic bronchopulmonary disease mortality from middle age onward seems particularly significant. None of the trends for these causes of death exhibits the same rate of decline as the trend for the infective diseases. In fact, many of the trends are rising by different degrees. The combined effect of these various trends is to slow down the rate of decline of the total death rate (see Figure 2).

Further reductions in total mortality in the United States are possible, but any substantial decreases must come from the lowering of the death rates for the chronic noninfective diseases and for accidents and other violence. On the basis of a life table analysis of mortality data for 1949–1951, Woodhall and Jablon[4] concluded that large increases in longevity will result, not as a consequence of the solution of any single disease process, but as the result of a general breakthrough on the whole front of aging. The elimination of certain causes of death such as the infective and parasitic diseases, malignant neoplasms, diabetes, and accidents would result only in small increases in the average life expectancy. The largest increment would come from the elimination of cardiovascular diseases as a cause of death. The cardiovascular disease problem was noted as an exception to the generalization about future changes in life expectancy.

The nature of the past changes in mortality and the present behavior of the death rates have made moot the value of statistics of deaths from all causes as a measure of health in countries like the United States. Fuchs[5] defends the usefulness of mortality statistics and suggests that the lack of change in the death rate might be an indication that "the increase in health services has not resulted in improved health levels and the scientific advances of recent years have not had much effect on health. An alternative explanation is that changes in environmental factors in these years have had, on balance, a negative effect on health, thus offsetting the favorable effects of increases in services and medical knowledge. The latter explanation seems to be a real possibility."

This is an interesting possibility, but no evidence has been found to indicate that environmental changes caused a retardation in the decline of the death rate. Also, there is little to suggest that the increase in health services over the years has resulted in improvements in the level of health. On the other hand, the accelerated decline in the death rate resulting from the reduction of mortality from diseases of infectious origin does suggest that medical advances were responsible for the prevention of deaths from the infective diseases. Even here, it must be admitted this is a *post hoc, ergo propter hoc* reasoning.

Because various biological, environmental, demographic, and socioeconomic factors can influence the course of mortality, it is not possible

FIGURE 2. CRUDE DEATH RATES: UNITED STATES, 1900–1965

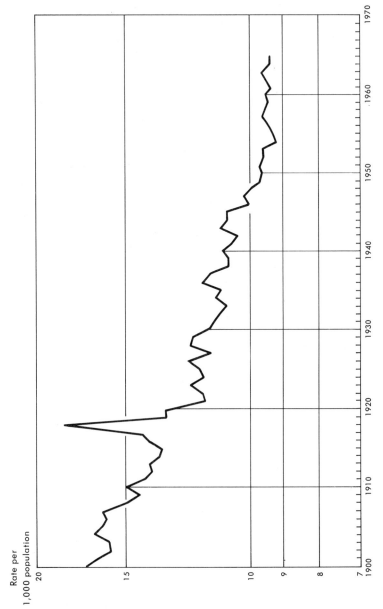

SOURCE: National Center for Health Statistics

578

to isolate the specific effects of any one factor nor is it possible to state categorically whether or not there has been any improvement in the level of health. This, of course, does not mean that mortality rates for specific diseases are not useful for the assessment of certain health problems. Mortality studies have done much to elucidate health problems and etiological factors relating to disease.

By far the most frequent use of mortality statistics has been in the study of trends and differentials in mortality. For example, from a study of mortality rates, Merrill,[6] Dorn,[7] Moriyama,[8] and others have called attention to the chronic obstructive lung diseases as an emerging public health problem. The rising mortality trend of cancer of the respiratory system suggested lung cancer as a special problem, and subsequent studies of mortality experience of smokers and nonsmokers by Doll and Hill,[9] Dorn,[10] Hammond and Horn,[11] and others have implicated cigarette smoking.

Frequent use has been made of mortality data for epidemiological studies. These studies of descriptive epidemiology have been, and still are, of value in suggesting hypotheses to be tested. There are also numerous examples[12] of epidemiological studies utilizing death certificates as the starting or end points. These retrospective and prospective studies have dealt mainly with leukemia and other malignant neoplasms, cardiovascular diseases, and with maternal and perinatal events.

The great virtue of mortality data is the availability of a long and generally comparable series of statistics. There is no other body of routine statistics that provide diagnostic data for the country as a whole as well as for the smaller civil subdivisions.

Mortality data are available for many countries. For this reason, it has been recommended[13] that the life expectancy at birth, the infant mortality rate, the crude death rate, and the proportionate mortality rate for ages fifty years and over be used as indicators of level of living for international comparisons.

The disadvantage of mortality data is that in countries where the need for statistical information is greatest, the data are nonexistent or of poor quality. An inherent weakness of mortality statistics is that diseases or conditions of high lethality are well represented, whereas nonfatal conditions do not have the same probability of appearing in the statistics. For example, almost all primary lung cancer deaths appear in the primary mortality tabulations, while conditions like arthritis, a frequent cause of disability, are not often found as causes of death. Also, one would not expect mortality data to provide measures which would indicate satisfactorily the levels of, say, dental health or mental health. For example, it is not possible to deduce from mortality statistics that the 111 million adults in the United States had a total of 2.25 billion decayed, missing, and filled teeth[14] or that approximately 22 million persons,[15] or 13 per cent of the population in 1957–1958 were edentulous (have lost all their permanent teeth). Although dental diseases are rarely causes of death, they are resultants of nutritional problems in the general population, infections of the teeth and oral tissues, and inadequate oral hygiene and dental care.

Although mortality data were originally developed as a measure of health, the relationship between mortality and morbidity has not been clear. Recently, Moriyama and Chiang[16] developed a model for estimation of prevalence and incidence of chronic diseases from mortality data using cardiovascular-renal diseases as an example. This model, based on the theory of competing risks, requires information on the number of deaths among the cases of chronic diseases. This statistic is not now generally available, but it may be possible to estimate this parameter from data on multiple causes of death when they become available, possibly starting with data year 1968 in the United States.

Lerner and Anderson[17] refer to the death rate as the best indicator of health levels at an earlier stage in development of sanitation, public health practice, and medical knowledge. At the turn of the century the American Public Health Association and the American Medical Association jointly memorialized the Congress of the United States and proposed the annual collection of mortality statistics to provide measures of health conditions for the U.S. population. The results were the establishment of the Permanent Census Office in 1902 and the annual federal collection of mortality statistics.

At the turn of the century, tuberculosis, influenza and pneumonia, and diarrhea and enteritis were numerically the most important causes of death. As mortality from the infective diseases declined, the chronic noninfective diseases increased in relative frequency as causes of death. This change gave rise to problems in the classification and interpretation of cause-of-death statistics. The procedure for selecting the cause of death to be tabulated became more and more inadequate with the increase in chronic disease mortality because of the difficulty in determining and coding the underlying cause of death. There was growing dissatisfaction with mortality statistics and a consequent demand for morbidity data. In 1956, the U.S. Congress authorized the annual collection of statistics on illness and disability in the general population.

With regard to the measurement problem, Lerner and Anderson state that "health levels are now most adequately measured when mortality rates are supplemented by morbidity rates and even by other measures of social well-being." They hasten to add that statistics of morbidity are only now becoming available and that their use poses numerous problems.

NATIONAL ILLNESS STATISTICS

Until the establishment of the National Health Survey in 1956, the only available national illness data related to the notifiable diseases. These are the communicable disease statistics collected for public health surveillance purposes.

The National Health Survey[18] is a three-pronged coverage of illness in the general population. The Health Interview Survey is a continuing nationwide sampling and interviewing of households; the Health Examination Survey consists of physical examinations and testing of samples of individuals in a series of separate surveys; and the Health Records Survey is a series of sample surveys in which the sources of information are establishments which provide medical, dental, nursing, and other types of health-related care to the general population.

Health Interview Survey

The Health Interview Survey became operational in 1957. At the present time, members of about 42,000 households are interviewed each year covering about 134,000 individuals. The survey covers the civilian noninstitutional population and provides data on the incidence of illness and accidental injuries; the prevalence of diseases and impairments; the extent of disability; the volume and kinds of medical, dental, and hospital care received; and other health-related topics.

In the Health Interview Survey,[19] morbidity is defined as a departure from a state of physical or mental well-being, resulting from disease or injury, *of which the affected individual is aware.* For the purpose of the survey, the concept of morbid condition is "further limited by specifying that it includes only conditions as a result of which the person has taken one or more of various actions. Such actions might be the restricting of usual activities, bed disability, work loss, the seeking of medical advice, or the taking of medicine."

The following are a few of the findings[20] from the Health Interview Survey:

> During the period July 1964–June 1965 an estimated incidence of 400.9 million acute illnesses and injuries requiring either medical attention or restriction of daily activity occurred among the civilian non-

institutional population of the United States. This estimate represents an average of about 212.7 conditions per 100 persons per year which represents a slight increase over the incidence rate of 208.5 per 100 persons per year.

Acute illness and injury caused each person in the population an average of 8.3 days of restricted activity during the year, including about 3.5 days spent in bed. Acute conditions were responsible for an estimated 4.6 days lost from school per school-age child (6–16 years) and 3.4 days lost from work per currently employed person.

An estimated 87.3 million persons, or 46.3 per cent of the population, exclusive of the Armed Forces and inmates of institutions, reported one or more chronic diseases or impairments. The comparable percentage for the 12-month period ending June 1964 was 45.2.

An estimated 24.2 million discharges from short-stay hospitals involving one or more nights of hospital stay, or 12.9 discharges per 100 persons, occurred during the reference period ending between July 1964 and June 1965.

Data are also available on activity limitation resulting from various diseases and conditions. Generally speaking, diagnostic data obtained in population surveys through interviews are not particularly specific nor precise. Aside from response errors present in surveys of this type, many do not know the specific nature of their afflictions. In many cases, the respondent provides information concerning other members of the household. There is evidence to indicate that the information supplied by proxy respondents for other adults in the household is not as complete or accurate as that which those adults can supply for themselves. The inadequacy of diagnostic information secured by the interview method has been fairly thoroughly documented.[21, 22, 23, 24]

Health Examination Survey

Undiagnosed or unrecognized disease is also a problem. There is no way of obtaining information on undiagnosed and/or nonmanifest disease without appropriate laboratory and direct physical examinations of a sample of the population. The Health Examination Survey[25] is designed to provide statistics on prevalence of specific diseases in certain segments of the population using standardized diagnostic criteria, and to secure distributions of the general population with respect to certain physical and physiological measurements.

In the first cycle of examination, the group selected for study was the adult population eighteen to seventy-nine years, inclusive. This cycle focused attention on certain cardiovascular diseases, arthritis and rheumatism, and diabetes. According to the results of the first cycle,[26] of the 111.1 million adults, eighteen to seventy-nine years, in the

United States in 1960–1962, some 14.6 million had definite heart disease and about 13 million had suspected heart disease. This represents a prevalence rate of about 13.2 per 100 population with definite heart disease and 11.7 with suspected heart disease. These estimates do not include the prevalence of heart disease in the approximately 1.4 million inmates of institutions not covered by the Health Examination Survey. Nor do they include the prevalence in the population eighty years and over, which numbered about 2.5 million in 1960.

The Health Examination Survey[27] indicated that about 2 million people in the United States have diabetes and are aware of it. In addition, there are probably about twice as many unknown as there are known diabetics, depending upon the interpretation of the results of glucose tolerance tests. Other interesting findings from the first cycle of the Health Examination Survey are prevalence data on arthritis and rheumatism, and dental diseases and defects; visual acuity and hearing levels; and the results of physiological measurements such as blood glucose, blood pressure, and serum cholesterol levels in the general population.

The second cycle dealt with children between the ages of six and eleven years, inclusive. Special emphasis was given to problems of growth and development. A physical examination was given as well as a selected battery of psychometric tests. A dental examination was also made, as were tests of respiratory function and exercise tolerance. Data from this cycle are now being processed.

The third cycle of the Health Examination Survey now underway is concerned with the population ages twelve to seventeen, inclusive. A physical examination is given with special reference to the stage of pubertal development, abnormalities, illnesses, and injuries which may affect growth and development. Psychological tests are also given to measure performance in various situations as related to growth in thinking, socialization, and motor coordination. Other tests include visual and aural acuity, respiratory function, electrocardiogram, exercise tolerance, and grip strength. Height and weight and other body measurements are also taken.

An important gap in national illness data relates to the mental diseases. The staff of the Health Examination Statistics Division has been conducting a series of seminars on the problem of devising a simple method of measuring the prevalence of mental disorders. This is an exceedingly complex area of measurement. Most of the data now available are based on statistics of utilization of psychiatric facilities. For example, Kramer[28] reported that the year-end resident patient population of state and county mental hospitals increased at an average rate of 2.1 per cent per year between 1946 and 1955. From that year, the population decreased at about 1 per cent per year to the level of 504,604 patients at the end of 1963. This reduction in the population occurred at the same time that the admissions were increasing at an average rate of 7.4 per cent per year.

According to the Group for the Advancement of Psychiatry,[29] estimations of the frequency of mental disorders involve problems of changes in incidence, duration, and prognosis of mental diseases. The problem of measurement becomes even more complicated because "(1) social attitudes toward illness change and may affect the number of patients who seek help; (2) available psychiatric resources increase or diminish—contributing to an increase or decrease in the number of reported cases; (3) changes in diagnostic skills, fashions and nomenclature also increase or decrease the total number of reported cases in any specific diagnostic category."

It remains to be seen if a battery of tests can be devised and incorporated into the Health Examination Survey procedures to measure the magnitude of the mental illness problem. It also remains to be seen if suitable methodology can be devised for the measurement of certain physical diseases such as cancer and stroke.

Health Records Survey

The Health Examination Survey has certain limitations imposed by the type of diagnostic equipment possible for mobile units and by the fact that repeated examinations are not feasible. Therefore, the National Health Survey takes the third approach through the Health Records Survey. The purpose of this survey is to produce statistics on the characteristics of health services received by the U.S. population and the characteristics of those receiving the services.

An important component of the Health Records Survey is the Hospital Discharge Survey. This is a continuing survey of short-stay hospitals to obtain statistics on the use of hospitals, on services provided in hospitals, and on characteristics of the patients. Another component of the Health Records Survey is the survey of resident institutions. This is the population not covered by the Health Interview Survey. Data will be obtained for inmates of resident institutions, both medical and nonmedical. This includes long-stay hospitals, penal institutions, orphanages, nursing homes, homes for the aged, and other facilities providing domiciliary care.

With the various data collection mechanisms provided by the National Health Survey, the measurement of the health of the population apparently would be a simple matter of adding the various pieces from the different surveys. However, the various components of the National Health Survey are not yet unified in terms of definitions, classification, population, and time coverage, so the different pieces cannot be articulated in a satisfactory manner. Perhaps more important is the lack of a conceptual definition of health capable of being translated into suitable operational definitions.

DEFINITION OF HEALTH AND DISEASE

The discussion up to this point has been concerned mainly with illness from disease, disability, and mortality. In turn, the terms "disease," "disability," and "mortality" have been used interchangeably to mean the obverse of "health." Also the term "health" has not been specifically defined and has been used in a general and loose sense.

From the dawn of civilization, man has been concerned with the question of health and disease. Galdston[30] refers to the Hippocratic treatise on Airs, Waters and Places, and suggests that Hippocrates was more concerned with the epidemiology of health than with the epidemiology of disease. Thus, Galdston believes that the epidemiology of health antedated that of disease. However, at present, much more is known about the epidemiology of disease than about the epidemiology of health.

Siegerist[31] has the following to say about health:

> Like the Romans and John Locke, we think of health as a physical and mental condition. "Mens sana in corpore sano" remains our slogan. But we may go one step further and consider it in a social sense also. A healthy individual is a man who is well balanced bodily and mentally, and well adjusted to his physical and social environment. He is in full control of his physical and mental facilities, can adapt to environmental changes, so long as they do not exceed normal limits; and contributes to the welfare of society according to his ability. Health is, therefore, not simply the absence of disease: it is something positive, a joyful attitude toward life, and a cheerful acceptance of the responsibilities that life puts on the individual.

Siegerist's idea is perhaps more succinctly expressed by the Constitution of the World Health Organization,[32] which defines health as "a state of complete physical, mental and social well being and not merely the absence of disease and infirmity." It is easy to agree with the desirability of attaining the state of positive health, but it will be much more difficult to find agreement as to what is meant by "complete physical, mental and social well being" or even as to the meaning of "absence of disease and infirmity." May[33] criticizes the WHO definition because no criterion is given "by which to decide where the disease state begins and ends. They suggest that 'norms' or 'health,' or 'disease and infirmity' are clear-cut notions, since they define one of the terms by opposing it to the other."

The WHO definition of health may serve the Organization admirably as an ideal or a slogan, but not as a goal to be achieved. Without satisfactory operational definitions of the various terms, it would not be possible to determine if and when a state of health has been achieved by any population.

There seems to be a general recognition of the existence of some kind of continuum between "health" or "well-being" at one extreme and death at the other extreme. However, there are various views as to the gradations that may exist between "perfect health" and "death." For example, Dorn's[34] rough representation of the health spectrum includes the various stages of disease leading to death. His continuum starts with perfect health and passes through conditions predisposing to disease, e.g., obesity, latent or incipient disease, early apparent disease, far advanced disease, and then to death.

In this scale, latent or incipient diseases are usually unrecognized by the person affected. As a rule, these conditions can be discovered only by special tests. Dorn lists as examples the earliest detectable stages of tuberculosis, diabetes, and cancer. Opinions may differ as to the stage at which these conditions should be diagnosed as the clinical disease of which they are the precursors.

The disease may or may not manifest itself for a period of time, but signs and symptoms begin to appear as the disease develops. The existence of a disease state may or may not be recognized by the individual affected, but for practical purposes only those diseases that have been identified should be counted. This will depend on the physicians' diagnoses.

In any disease, the person affected passes from health to disease, and either to death or freedom from disease. In chronic diseases, the change from absence of disease to manifest disease is frequently insidious and imperceptible. In addition, the state of ill-health may persist for years with alternating periods of exacerbation and remission, or with steady progression through various stages of disease until death intervenes.

In moving along the continuum, at what point is it decided that a state of health no longer exists? Is the presence of a predisposing factor or condition such as slight overweight a deviation from health? Or is it necessary to move further down the scale to latent and incipient disease? If so, all nonmanifest diseases must be discovered through some kind of mass screening process. Although "manifest disease" is unquestionably a departure from health even in the early stages, the term is difficult to define. One operational definition might be that a manifest disease is what a clinician diagnoses. This, of course, would depend upon a number of factors, among them the diagnostic criteria used. This factor alone could make a large difference in the frequency count of disease. For example, it has been mentioned that the Health Examination Survey used a standardized technique in examining adults for heart disease. According to certain criteria, 14.6 million adults were considered to have definite heart disease. By another set of criteria, the frequency count could be almost doubled by including what have been termed the suspected heart disease cases.

Woolsey and Nisselson[35] refer to Dorn's spectrum of health as the continuum of pathological change. The other model is a scale of feeling, or lack of feeling, of well-being, which they termed the continuum of sickness. For this continuum, Merrell and Reed[36] visualized "a graded scale of health from positive through zero to negative health. On such a scale people would be classified from those who are in top-notch condition with abundant energy, through the people who are well, to fairly well, down to the people who are feeling rather poorly, and finally to the definitely ill. The word health rather than illness is chosen deliberately to emphasize the positive side of this scale, for in the past we have focused our attention thoroughly on the disease side."

Merrell and Reed give as an example of a meaningful classification with regard to health the classification used by Collins and Downes in the Eastern Health District of Baltimore. This scheme included the following rubrics: chronically ill, ill enough to require hospitalization, ill enough to be confined to bed at home, ill enough to require attendance of a physician, ill enough to prevent engaging in usual occupation, and no reported illness. Merrell and Reed felt that the greatest weakness of this classification was that it does not break down the title "no reported illness" into different degrees of positive health.

In commenting on the pathological and sickness scales, Woolsey and Nisselson point out that a large number of cases of chronic diseases would be counted identically in these two methods. However, the two methods do not necessarily agree on the point where the existence of a disease will be first noted because the feeling of sickness is not always correlated with the extent of pathological change. Woolsey and Nisselson also observe that the stepping up of the intensity of clinical examination is capable of producing more cases of chronic diseases than would be identified by increasing the intensity of interviews in a survey.

In the continua of pathological change and of sickness, measurement is confined to the identification of disease or disability. Some feel that this is a negative approach, and that the public health and medical profession should focus on health and wellness. Dunn[37] and others postulate varying degrees of positive health or different levels of wellness. The concept of positive health goes far beyond the mere absence of disease or disability. It is concerned with the functional efficiency of mind and body and social adjustment, and it is related to ability of individuals to realize their full potentials for valued achievement.

Reed[38] feels that the problem of positive health calls for research in physiological fields and that a real solution will come when we have better knowledge of the development of the human being as a functioning organism. Reed further states, "Rather than a seeming separation of pediatrics from geriatrics, we need knowledge as to the growth and development of physiological processes as we proceed from infancy to old age. This knowledge may give us some yardsticks for an evaluation of 'positive health' and may help us to lay down objectives in this field." Reed suggests the desirability of placing emphasis in the direction of positive health, but he also recognizes the lack of axes of classification that are necessary if it is proposed to carry through the notion of positive health.

The psychologists have been struggling with the concept of health and disease in their field. Smith[39] says, "The signs are increasingly clear that 'mental health' and its complement, 'mental illness' are terms that embarrass psychologists. . . . Unable to define or conceptualize them to our satisfaction, we use the terms in spite of ourselves, since they label the goals, however nebulous, of many of our service activities and the auspices of much of our research support. . . . And from as many quarters we encounter the call for a more positive view of mental health than is involved in the mere absence of manifest mental disorder. . . . The discussion goes on in articles, conferences, and symposia, with little evidence of consensus in the offing."

With respect to program activities in the field of public health, a pragmatic view is taken of the problems of health and disease by a work party of the American Public Health Association. In its report on "A Broadened Spectrum of Health and Morbidity,"[40] the following four levels of public health concern and effort are outlined: (1) mortality; (2) serious morbidity; (3) minor morbidity; and (4) positive health.

The group regarded the conservation of life as the first essential of public health. Therefore, the reduction of mortality is listed as the first problem of concern to public health activities. As a public health program moves progressively from level (1) to level (4), it adds new concerns and efforts which do not displace the previous ones.

The work party saw the United States in 1960 as ready for level (3) work. With regard to positive health, they said, "Society's standards and expectations for all men must be such that public health, together with other social efforts, would naturally be concerned with helping all persons toward attaining a full sense of physical vigor and mental well-being and maintaining a constructive and wholesome relationship with others in a safe and pleasant environment that promotes longevity and happiness."

POSSIBLE INDICATORS OF HEALTH

The Study Group on the Measurement of Levels of Health[41] of the World Health Organization classified health indicators into three groups as follows: (1) Those associated with the health status of persons and populations in a given area (vital statistics, nutrition, etc.); (2) those related to physical environmental conditions having a more or less direct bearing on the health status of the area under review; and (3) those concerned with health services and activities directed to the improvement of health conditions (availability and use of hospitals, physicians, and other health personnel).

Backett[42] would add to this list biochemical and other indicators of "healthiness" such as the proportion of persons of various ages and different sexes with "normal" hemoglobin, "normal" blood cholesterol, and with "normal" urinalysis and the proportion of persons without, for example, ova in stools, palpable spleens, bacteria in the urine, and evidence of malnutrition; more specialized indexes, for example, verbal or other tests of mental functions (standardized intelligence test scores and scores on various tests of personality adjustment); and verbal or other tests of vulnerability to disease (various types of screening such as genetic screening, screening for special occupational risks or for other kinds of risks such as smoking, patterns of behavior, diet, poverty, etc.).

Backett suggests the possibility of crude measures of the health of the population from information on the nature of the environment. Environmental hazards such as radioactivity, air pollution, insecticides, or other obvious features such as heat, cold, humidity, and absence of rainfall may provide useful indicators. Other measures of the physical environment may be clean water or adequate sewage disposal. Backett points to needed measures of the "healthiness" of the social environment such as tolerance of mental defects, illness, or sexual and other deviance, and to still another kind of indicator of the health of communities by the measurement of the extent to which health needs are met. This is a new concept where one aspect of the health of a community is determined by early case finding and bringing the cases of different diseases under effective treatment.

Sanders'[43] method of measuring community health levels is based on the assumption that improved health care would increase survival and thus increase the known prevalence of disease in a community. A modified life table is proposed for measuring the adequacy of health services. In this analysis, the probability of survival is to be based on functional effectiveness, that is, ability to carry on daily living activities. The comparative health levels of different communities would then be measured in terms of productive man-years. According to Sanders' hypothesis, the community which shows a higher number of productive man-years per 100,000 conceptions will be considered to have more adequate health care even though it experienced higher age-specific morbidity rates for the various chronic diseases.

Sullivan[44] has extended Sanders' notion of probability of survival based on functional effectiveness and computed what may be termed the expectancy of disability-free life. According to these computations,[45] a person born in 1965 may look forward to about sixty-five years of life free of disability out of a total future lifetime of about seventy years. In terms of bed disability, the expected future lifetime free of bed disability is about sixty-eight years. The corresponding figures at age sixty-five years are: expectation of life, fifteen years; expected future lifetime free of disability, eleven years; and expected future lifetime free of bed disability, about fourteen years.

Disability-free years of life is a hypothetical measure subject to the same kind of assumptions implicit in the conventional life table. Because the major component of the measure is the expectation of life at specified ages, there may be some question as to the sensitivity of the measure. Also, both the expectation of life and the duration of disability may vary independently. Therefore, it would be necessary to analyze the two parts separately in the assessment of the disability problem.

Sanders proposes other measures of community health levels such as an index of preventive health services (laboratory determination of immunity levels); a measure of quality of medical care; the construction of life tables for mortality from various diseases; and a measure of early diagnoses of diseases.

Chiang[46] has developed a mathematical model of an index of health. This index is based on the probability distribution of the frequency and duration of illness, and the time lost due to deaths. Chiang asks the question, "What is the average fraction of the year in which an individual is healthy?" This fraction, or the mean duration of health, is used as an index of health of a population.

Woolsey[47] suggested the use of a disability measure as an indicator of the state of public health. More specifically, he used the distribution of the population according to chronic limitation of activity and chronic limitation of mobility. Woolsey points out that the greatest advantage of the scales that he suggested is that they are comparatively simple to apply in interview-type population sample surveys. On the other hand, the greatest methodological disadvantage is that the scales divide the population into groups that are widely different in size.

From the examples of proposed health indicators given here, it is apparent that various approaches can be, and have been, applied to the problem of measurement of the level of health of a population. Some deal directly with the population affected, while others are concerned with environmental factors or services which are presumed to have an impact on the population. Some are specific in that they relate to the effect of a particular factor, while others are more general in terms of the stimulus as well as response.

It is also apparent that the different indicators will give different results. Even the same indicator can produce widely different results by varying, say, certain definitions. An example was noted in determining the prevalence of heart disease in the Health Examination Survey, which may differ by almost as much as a factor of 2 depending on the criteria used in defining heart disease.

The question of which indicator to use would depend on the purpose to be served. Operational definitions also need to be developed, which would be necessarily arbitrary in nature.

PROBLEMS IN DEVELOPING AN INDEX OF HEALTH

Linder[48] expressed a need for an over-all index such as the Gross National Product used in the measurement of economic progress which brings together a number of disparate factors into a single index of the state of national economy. He suggests the possibility of developing a GNP-like health index, the "gross national health deficit (GNHD)" that "could blend together in one number the days of healthful living lost each year by the chronically and acutely ill, the days of life lost through death that comes too soon and all the impairment suffered for lack of medical treatment and advice." In a less optimistic tone, Linder goes on to say "Even if it were logically possible to construct a GNHD, it might not meet all needs because it would still stress, as conventional health statistics do, the negative aspects of health." One could probably generalize further and say that any measure which has involved in it one or more arbitrary elements will not meet all the needs for a health index. However, what seems to be important here is not that an index be suitable for all purposes, but that it be useful for at least one stated purpose which is considered worthwhile.

Sullivan[49] reviewed the various methods of measuring levels of health and proposed a measure of impact of illness upon the population. The suggested index of health status involves morbidity in terms of disability. Those disabled for a particular day are to be classified as follows: (1) persons confined to resident institutions because of ill health; (2) persons not in resident institutions with serious continuing limitation of mobility; (3) persons not classified above with serious continuing activity limitations; and (4) persons not classified above who restricted their usual activities for the day in question. Because the various categories are mutually exclusive and the reference period is one day, the number of persons in each category is additive; and it is possible to obtain a measure of all persons disabled on a single day. This would provide a single measure of the impact of morbidity in the living population for that day. In practice, it would be desirable for the index to cover a longer period of time, possibly a year. For this purpose, the estimated number of days in each disability category will be summed to obtain the total number of days of disability during the year. Essentially, this is the morbidity component of Linder's GNHD.

An important advantage of this proposal is that a good part of the data, at least for the civilian noninstitutional population, are already available from the Health Interview Survey. Data on chronic activity limitation are collected annually, but information on chronic mobility limitation is obtained only periodically. Sullivan discusses these and other problems involved in the derivation of estimates of disability days. He also considers the problems affecting the reliability and validity of measures of morbidity based upon disability criteria.

Regardless of how it is derived, an index of health should have certain desirable properties, such as:

1. It should be meaningful and understandable.
2. It should be sensitive to variations in the phenomenon being measured.
3. The assumptions underlying the index should be theoretically justifiable and intuitively reasonable.
4. It should consist of clearly defined component parts.
5. Each component part should make an independent contribution to variations in the phenomenon being measured.
6. The index should be derivable from data that are available or quite feasible to obtain.

If availability of data is a requirement, the index would by necessity have to deal with the disease and disability part of the spectrum rather than the obverse, health or positive health. Further, the additive property of the component parts would severely limit the choice of indicators. Very few, if any, of the measures of the environment, for example, have a common denominator so that conversion into a single unit is not practicable. On the other hand, measures of disease and disability do seem to have several elements in common. For example, the common factor in incidence or prevalence of disease is the case of the disease. Thus, one can obtain a total count of diseases and disability. However, such totals would not be particularly useful without taking into account the impact of the various diseases in some meaningful term yet to be specified. This leads to questions such as how one equates a case of coryza with a case of primary lung cancer, or a case of congenital anomaly with a case of senile psychosis.

Disability data have as a common factor the duration of disability, which in itself is a rough measure of the severity of the condition. Here, a different set of questions arise. For example, how does one equate absence from school with absence from work, or days of limitation of usual activities with days in bed?

There are other problems in obtaining reliable and valid measures of behavioral evidence of morbidity. Sullivan points out:

> . . . while a period of restricted activity is a more objective event than a report of "feeling ill" it also has a subjective aspect which must be recognized. The decision to reduce his usual activities reflects the individual's attitude toward illness and self-care, the expectations or demands of his family, his employer and his associates, his knowledge or beliefs about the symptoms present, and other social and cultural

factors. . . . Disability occurs in a social setting and, like other social phenomena, cannot be measured in isolation from the setting. It has social consequences regardless of the nonmedical factors which may influence its occurrence. A condition which disables a salaried worker may not disable a person paid on a daily basis—this makes the disability no less real for the salaried worker and his employer. Disability measures reflect the impact of morbid conditions as they influence the social participation of members of the population. In this respect they measure an aspect of morbidity important in any evaluation of the health status of a population.[50]

The measurement of duration of disability in the living population might be accomplished through some mechanism such as the Health Interview Survey as suggested by Sullivan. The population that die during the study period presents something of a problem. Because one-half year, on the average, is lost by each decedent, Chiang took this figure as the time lost by each death. Some would like to go further and include the future lifetime of those who failed to live out their life expectancy. Such a figure may be fairly substantial. For example, the future years lost by the U.S. population in 1963 by failure to survive their life expectancy is about 34 million. This figure overshadows the estimated 12 million person-years of disability (based on restricted activity criterion) suffered by the civilian noninstitutional population of the United States during a period of a year. Thus, it may be seen that loading the future lifetime lost due to premature deaths into a single calendar year of disability experience gives undue weight to this factor.

The index of health, however it is derived, will presumably be a single measure of the impact of morbidity and mortality. However, such an index will be a nonspecific measure of the effects of disability, that is, it will not be possible to identify the specific factors that affect the index. In this sense, the index is much like the death rate. Many things including the age, sex, and color composition of the population would have an effect on the index.

Ideally, one would like to have built into the index certain components which give an indication of the factors influencing the duration of disability. It is not likely that this will be possible in the foreseeable future. It will usually require an epidemiological investigation of considerable complexity to determine the specific reasons for the improvement or deterioration in health indexes of this type.

If the index is to be limited to the measurement of nonspecific effects, it would be essential to have as one of the axes of classification the demographic characteristics of the population. Because the problems of mortality and morbidity differ so much, the mortality component of the index should be differentiated from the morbidity component. If it were possible to obtain reasonably precise diagnostic information for the living population, it would be useful to have diagnostic categories as another axis of classification. Other cross sections should be taken for the purpose of delineating as specifically as possible the various problem areas. In this regard, morbidity surveys have a decided advantage over the registration method because it is possible to collect simultaneously new data for the population at risk and for those who are disabled. For example, the collection of income data for the survey population makes possible the computation of rates by income, whereas in mortality data it is necessary to collect mortality data on income and income data on the living population before rates can be computed. On the other hand, the sample size in morbidity surveys necessarily limits the kinds of data that can be collected. For example, it is not economically feasible to collect morbidity data for minor civil subdivisions in a national survey. Yet data for small geographic areas are useful in pinpointing or localizing problem areas. Thus, one can foresee the index of health being analyzed in various ways, each designed to narrow the problem area to possibly disease categories in identifiable segments of the population and/or to specific geographic areas.

Serious consideration of an index of health is just beginning. More work on a conceptual basis is needed. Because of the dynamic nature of health and disease, it is not likely that an index of health, no matter how health is defined or how the index is constructed, will satisfy all users from the standpoint of definition or of needs. Not all the data that might be needed to compute the index would be immediately available. However, it is important to make a start. The development and use of a health index based on a blend of morbidity and mortality data will represent an important forward step in the measurement of health progress in the United States.

SUMMARY

The substantial reductions in mortality rates in the past sixty years or so as measured by life expectancy at birth and by death rates suggest a remarkable improvement in the health of the general population. However, analyses of death rates indicate that the significant declines in the death rates have occurred primarily in the younger ages, especially among the infants. Great progress has been made in the prevention of deaths from the infective diseases. On the other hand, little, if any, gains have been made in the reduction of mortality from the chronic diseases. For many chronic diseases, increases in mortality have been recorded. As a consequence, there has been a change in the rate of decline of the mortality trend in the United States. Further declines in the death rate are possible, but the gains in the future are likely to be modest until important breakthroughs are made in the prevention of the major chronic diseases.

In retrospect, it seems apparent that mortality rates have not been a particularly good index of health except insofar as the infective diseases are concerned. However, mortality data have been helpful in identifying the emergence of certain public health problems, and in the conduct of epidemiological studies.

A major problem in the development of a health index is the lack of a satisfactory conceptual definition of health capable of being translated into operational terms. The various definitions imply that "health" and "disease" are clear-cut notions, but none of the definitions, including that of the World Health Organization, is satisfactory for measurement purposes because none gives any criteria to determine ·where the state of health or disease begins and ends.

The existence of some kind of a health spectrum with optimum health at one end and death at the other extreme is generally recognized. In between there may be a continuum of disease or pathological change. Or it may be a scale of feeling of well-being, a continuum of sickness. Still another scale may relate to behavioral reactions to illness.

Some feel that the concern with disease or disability is a negative approach to the study of the problem of health. Positive health or levels of wellness should be the order of the day! Conceptually, there is much to be said for focusing on positive health. However, it will be some time before it will be possible to define and differentiate between the various degrees of wellness. Even if it were possible to measure positive health, variations in morbidity and mortality would still be major considerations under present conditions. Any effort to improve the general health of the population at this time would have to deal with problems of disease and disability.

Various kinds of health indicators have been suggested. These range from physiological measurements to those of pathological change, and from the physical hazards of the environment to measures of the social environment. Numerous approaches can be made to the problem of measurement of what might be termed the level of health of the population. Each of these approaches would measure something different, and not many of the suggested indicators can be integrated into a single index.

An index of health utilizing disability data has been proposed. This index will provide a single measure of morbidity, and will have socio-economic meaning in terms of time lost by disability. For analytical purposes, it would be essential to express the index in terms of the demographic characteristics of the population to delineate as specifically as possible the contributions to the index made by the various segments of the population. Also, it would be useful to show causes of disability if reasonably precise diagnostic information can be obtained on the living population. Finally, some consideration might be given to the development of adjustment factors to take into account the effect of changes or differences in situations such as in health insurance coverage which may affect the behavior of the population in regard to curtailment of activities, or seeking of medical care. These adjustment factors will be useful in trend analyses or in assessing differences in the disability experience of different segments of the population.

Further clarification is needed on the uses to be made of the index. More study should be devoted to conceptual problems, especially those relating to the definition of health. Meaningful operational definitions will have to be developed. It will also be useful to make an empirical approach using available data. A study of variations in the numerical values should provide helpful leads for the eventual development of an index of health progress in the United States.

NOTES

1. Moriyama, I. M., "Recent Change in Infant Mortality Trend," *Public Health Reports,* vol. 75, May, 1960, pp. 391–405.
2. Shapiro, S., and I. M. Moriyama, "International Trends in Infant Mortality and Their Implications for the United States," *American Journal of Public Health,* vol. 53, May, 1963, pp. 747–760.
3. Moriyama, I. M., "The Change in Mortality Trend in the United States," National Center for Health Statistics, Series 3, No. 1, U.S. Dept. Health, Education and Welfare, Public Health Service, Washington, 1964.
4. Woodhall, B., and S. Jablon, "Prospects for Further Increase in Average Longevity," *Geriatrics,* vol. 12, October, 1957, pp. 586–591.
5. Fuchs, V. R., "The Contribution of Health Services to the American Economy," *Milbank Memorial Fund Quarterly,* vol. 44, no. 4, pt. 2, October, 1966, pp. 65–103.
6. Merrill, M. H., "Public Health Responsibilities and Program Responsibilities in Chronic Respiratory Diseases," *Supplement American Journal of Public Health,* vol. 53, March, 1963, pp. 25–33.

7. Dorn, H. F., "The Increasing Mortality from Chronic Respiratory Disease," in *Proceedings of the Social Statistics Section.* American Statistical Assn., Washington, 1961, pp. 148–152.

8. Moriyama, I. M., "Chronic Respiratory Disease Mortality in the United States," *Public Health Reports,* vol. 78, September, 1963, pp. 743–748.

9. Doll, R., and B. A. Hill, "Lung Cancer and Other Causes of Death in Relation to Smoking," *British Medical Journal,* vol. 2, 1956, p. 1071.

10. Dorn, H. F., "Tobacco Consumption and Mortality from Cancer and Other Diseases," *Public Health Reports,* vol. 74, July, 1959, pp. 581–593.

11. Hammond, E. C., and D. Horn, "Smoking and Death Rates—A Report on Forty-four Months of Follow Up of 187,783 Men," *Journal American Medical Association,* vol. 166, 1958, p. 1159.

12. Moriyama, I. M., "Uses of Vital Records for Epidemiological Research," *Journal of Chronic Diseases,* vol. 17, 1964, pp. 889–897.

13. "Measurement of Levels of Health," Technical Reports Series No. 137, World Health Organization, Geneva, 1957.

14. National Center for Health Statistics, "Selected Dental Findings in Adults by Age, Race and Sex; United States 1960–1962," Publication No. 1000, Series 11, No. 7, Public Health Service, Washington, November, 1965.

15. U.S. National Health Survey, "Loss of Teeth, United States, July 1957–June 1958," Series B–22, National Center for Health Statistics, Public Health Service, Washington, 1960.

16. Moriyama, I. M., and C. L. Chiang, "A Model for Estimation of Prevalence and Incidence of Cardiovascular-Renal Diseases from Mortality Data," presented at the Epidemiology and Statistics Session, Annual Meeting of the American Public Health Association, October 31, 1966.

17. Lerner, M., and O. W. Anderson, *Health Progress in the United States, 1900–1960,* University of Chicago Press, Chicago, 1963.

18. National Center for Health Statistics, "Origin, Program and Operation of the U.S. National Health Survey," Publication No. 1000, Series 1, No. 1, Public Health Service, Washington, reprinted April, 1965.

19. National Center for Health Statistics, "Health Survey Procedures: Concepts, Questionnaire Development and Definitions in the Health Interview Survey," Publication No. 1000, Series 1, No. 2, Public Health Service, Washington, May, 1964.

20. National Center for Health Statistics, "Current Estimates from the Health Interview Survey," Publication No. 1000, Series 10, No. 25, Public Health Service, Washington, November, 1965.

21. Trussel, R. E., J. Elinson, and M. L. Levin, "Comparisons of Various Methods of Estimating the Prevalence of Chronic Disease in a Community—The Hunterdon County Study," *American Journal of Public Health,* vol. 46, February, 1956, pp. 173–182.

22. Commission on Chronic Illness, *Chronic Illness in the United States,* vol. IV, *Chronic Illness in a Large City: The Baltimore Study,* Harvard University Press, Cambridge, 1957.

23. U.S. National Health Survey, "Health Interview Responses Compared with Medical Records," Public Health Service Publication No. 584–05. Public Health Service, Washington, 1961.

24. Sanders, B. S., "Have Morbidity Surveys Been Oversold?" *American Journal of Public Health,* vol. 52, October, 1962, pp. 1648–1659.

25. National Center for Health Statistics, "Plan and Initial Program of the Health Examination Survey," Publication No. 1000, Series 1, No. 4, Public Health Service, Washington, July, 1965.

26. National Center for Health Statistics, "Heart Disease in Adults, United States 1960–1962," Publication No. 1000, Series 11, No. 6, Public Health Service, Washington, September, 1964.

27. National Center for Health Statistics, "Blood Glucose Levels in Adults, United States, 1960–1962," Publication No. 1000, Series 11, No. 18, Public Health Service, Washington, September, 1966.

28. Kramer, M., "Some Implications of Trends in the Usage of Psychiatric Facilities for Community Mental Health Programs and Related Research," Publication No. 1434, Public Health Service, Washington, 1966, p. 77.

29. Group for Advancement of Psychiatry, "Problems of Estimating Changes in Frequency of Mental Disorders," Report No. 50, New York, August, 1961, pp. 469–517.

30. Galdston, Iago, editor, *The Epidemiology of Health,* Health Education Council, New York, 1953, p. 2.

31. Siegerist, H. E., *Medicine and Human Welfare,* Yale University Press, New Haven, 1941, p. 100.

32. World Health Organization, "Constitution of the World Health Organization, Annex I," in *The First Ten Years of the World Health Organization,* WHO, Geneva, 1958.

33. May, J. M., *The Ecology of Human Disease,* MD Publishers, Inc., New York, 1958, p. 321.

34. Dorn, H. F., "Some Applications of Biometry in the Collection and Evaluation of Medical Data," *Journal of Chronic Diseases,* vol. 1, no. 6, June, 1955, pp. 638–664.

35. Woolsey, T. D., and H. Nisselson, "Some Problems in the Statistical Measurement of Chronic Diseases," papers contributed as a memorial to Samuel Weiss, sponsored by the Washington Statistical Society in collaboration with the American Statistical Association, 1956, pp. 75–87.

36. Merrell, M., and L. J. Reed, *The Epidemiology of Health, Social Medicine, Its Derivations and Objectives,* The Commonwealth Fund, New York, 1949, pp. 105–110.

37. Dunn, H. L., "Points of Attack for Raising the Levels of Wellness," *Journal of the National Medical Association,* vol. 49, no. 4, July, 1957, pp. 225–235.

38. Reed, L. J., "Principles Applying to the Collection of Information on Health as Related to Socio-environmental Factors," in *Backgrounds of Social Medicine.* Milbank Memorial Fund, New York, 1949, pp. 24–32.

39. Smith, M. B., "Mental Health Reconsidered: A Special Case of the Problem of Values in Psychology," *American Psychologists,* 1961, pp. 299–306.

40. "Report of the Chairman of the Technical Development Board to the Governing Council, 1959–1960," *American Journal of Public Health,* vol. 51, February, 1961, pp. 287–294.

41. "Measurement of Levels of Health," *op. cit.*

42. Backett, E. M., "The Measurement of Health and Disease in a Population," Euro-250/5, mimeographed paper prepared for the European Conference on Morbidity Statistics, February 6, 1963.

43. Sanders, B. S., "Measuring Community Health Levels," *American Journal of Public Health,* vol. 54, no. 7, July, 1964, pp. 1063–1070.

44. Personal communication.

45. Computed by applying person years of disability (or bed disability) to L_x values of the life table to derive disability (or bed disability) free years of life. These modified L_x values are then summed up in the conventional manner and expectation figures derived.

46. Chiang, C. L., "An Index of Health, Mathematical Models," Public Health Publication No. 1000, Series 2, No. 5, National Center for Health Statistics, Public Health Service, Washington, May, 1965.

47. Woolsey, T. D., "Classification of Population in Terms of Disability." World Population Congress, Belgrade, Yugoslavia (in press).

48. Linder, F. E., "The Health of the American People," *Scientific American,* vol. 214, no. 6, June, 1966, pp. 21–29.

49. Sullivan, D. F., "Conceptual Problems in Developing an Index of Health," Public Health Service Publication No. 1000, Series 2, No. 17, National Center for Health Statistics, Public Health Service, Washington, May, 1966, p. 18.

50. *Ibid.*

12. TRENDS IN OUTPUT AND DISTRIBUTION OF SCHOOLING

Beverly Duncan

THE AMOUNT of knowledge that an individual can command is not limited by the amount of knowledge held by other individuals, except insofar as their aggregate holdings are the sum of what is known. The primary mechanism for transmitting knowledge from one individual to another, however, is schooling. The amount of schooling that one individual receives can be increased only by reducing the share of another individual or by increasing the aggregate amount of schooling provided by the society. Although to an extent the amount of schooling provided can be increased, a limit does exist. A society in which all are full-time workers in the education industry, either as students or teachers, is not viable.

How the available schooling is distributed among members of the society is a point of more than academic interest. If an opportunity for training is made available to some members, it must be denied others. The outcome of these decisions affects not only the life chances of the individual, but also the resilience of the society. Whether the decisions are made consciously or not, whether they are made centrally or not is irrelevant to their implications.

The aim of this chapter is a narrow one: to identify a few basic data sets that bear on twentieth-century trends in the output and distribution of schooling in America. Nearly all the sets brought under scrutiny have been generated by the United States Bureau of the Census, deservedly called the "fact finder of the nation." The selection of data sets is in part, of course, a matter of personal predilection. On the other hand, the Bureau has pioneered in the control of data quality and the use of the sample survey as a supplement to complete enumeration.

In the course of identifying these basic data sets, certain issues are raised about their analytical utility. The most fundamental issue revolves around the demographer's concept of the cohort.[1] Put quite simply, the value of information collected in different surveys is enhanced when it is compiled for a cohort, that is, a group of people who have in common the timing of an event defining their membership, such as birth in a given year or period of adjacent years. Moreover, schooling measured in years of school attendance or grades completed is cumulative and irreversible for the cohort as for the individual.

At least as early as 1910, census statisticians were cognizant of the potential utility of cohort analysis. In the General Report and Analysis of the census taken in that year, they noted that: "Each age group represents in its illiteracy the extent to which educational advantages were lacking or inaccessible during its childhood. If the illiteracy of each age group is designated as that of persons born in a given period of time, a much clearer view is obtained of the gradual improvement of educational conditions."[2] They also observed that within each cohort or group of persons defined by period of birth, the illiteracy rate recorded in the 1910 census was lower than the illiteracy rate recorded in the 1900 census which, in turn, was lower than the rate recorded in the 1890 census. They correctly identified the possible bases of change in the rate as a differential in mortality favoring literates and mastery of reading and writing skills by illiterates during the intercensal periods. Unfortunately, census statisticians have not pursued this lead as to the most effective format for presenting statistics on schooling.

No exhaustive review of the substance of discernible trends in education is attempted here.[3] In reviewing the record on the output of schooling since 1900, three trends become clear, however: first, a threefold increase in the number of school years distributed among Americans annually; second, a one-third increase in the per capita output of school years; and third, an increase of some five-and-a-half years in the mean duration of schooling. Also to be observed are a growing equality in the distribution of education among members of successively younger birth cohorts and a diffusion of near-universal school attendance from age eleven toward both younger and older ages. Series on the schooling of subpopulations point to: an increasingly favorable position of males vis-à-vis females; a static influence of social background; and a lessening handicap associated with being a Negro.

OUTPUT AND DURATION OF SCHOOLING

In the year 1900, some 13 million school years were distributed among Americans. Thirty years later, the annual output of school years totaled nearly 28 million. By 1960, the annual output had reached about 44 million school years. That the increase in the annual ouput of schooling over the past six decades has been on the order of threefold is a certainty.

Any closer estimate of the increase in the output of school years over the sixty-year span or of the change occurring in particular time segments of that span must be qualified. The available series on output is correct as to approximate magnitude, but the figures are not fully comparable from one year to another. The statistics have been generated by the Bureau of the Census either as part of the decennial-census operation or through sample surveys which have been carried out annually since 1945. Survey month, the attendance-period referent, constraints on the ages of the enrolled, and the definition of a school have not been constant, however; and each affects the count of school years produced (Table 1).

Some evaluation of the statistics that make up the record on aggregate schooling and its distribution among Americans is in order. A detailed account of the demonstrable deficiencies and the disturbing uncertainties that inhere in these data offers tedious reading. Since these are the data on which most substantive materials presented here rest, it seems expedient to outline their limitations at the outset nevertheless.

Data Evaluation

For expository convenience, the problems that arise from the choice of survey month and attendance-period referent are considered together. Similarly, the influences of constraints on the ages of the enrolled and the definition of a school are treated together. Finally, the series of observations which underlie the substantive materials presented here is compared with an alternative enrollment series.

Survey Date and Attendance Period. Because neither school entry nor school leaving occurs evenly over the course of a year, the survey month and the length of the period preceding the survey date to which the attendance query refers have pronounced effects on the size of the enrolled population. The evidence now at hand on gross and net turnover in the enrolled population in the course of a year is meager, but the volume appears sufficiently large to merit systematic investigation. Four pieces of evidence can be introduced.

(1). The data reported by the Bureau of the Census that bear most directly on the magnitude of fluctuations in enrollment from one academic term to another are twenty years old. A question on enroll-

TABLE 1. PERSONS ENROLLED IN SCHOOL, BY AGE, FOR THE CONTERMINOUS UNITED STATES AS RECORDED IN DECENNIAL CENSUSES, 1900–1960, AND FOR THE UNITED STATES AS RECORDED IN A SAMPLE SURVEY OF THE CIVILIAN NONINSTITUTIONAL POPULATION, 1962 AND 1964

Year	Survey month	Attendance period[a] in months	Age span[b]	School type[c]		Enrolled, by age (thousands)		
					All	Under 5	5 to 20	21 or more
1900	June	12	Total	Any	13,367	41	13,161	150
1910	April	7	Total	Any	18,010	49	17,647	313
1920	January	4	Total	Any	21,763	45	21,374	345
1930	April	7	5+	Any	27,884	—	26,850	1,035
1940	April	1	5–24	Graded	26,759	—	26,293	466
1950	April	2	5–29	Graded	29,884	—	27,997	1,887
1960	April	2	5–34	Graded	43,538	—	41,444	2,094
1962	October	1	5–34	Graded	48,704	—	46,704[d]	2,000[d]
1964	October	1	3–34	Graded[e]	52,458	798[e]	49,456[d]	2,204[d]

[a] Period preceding survey date during which attendance at some time results in classification of individual as enrolled.

[b] Ages of individuals included in the enrolled population.

[c] Types of school for which attendance results in classification of individual as enrolled.

[d] Includes half the enrolled persons ages 20 and 21.

[e] Includes 439,000 persons attending nursery schools.

SOURCES: Decennial Censuses, June, 1900, through April, 1960; *Current Population Reports,* Series P-20, no. 126, September, 1963, and no. 148, February, 1966.

ment status was included in sample surveys conducted in October, 1946, April, 1947, and October, 1947. The attendance-period referent was the "current term or school year" in the October surveys and "since March 1" in the April survey. Sampling variability is sufficiently large to account for most changes recorded, but the increase in enrolled persons aged eighteen to twenty-four between the first and second terms of the 1946–1947 school year probably is not a chance fluctuation.[4]

(2). More recently the Bureau has compared enrollment counts estimated from the October, 1959, Current Population Survey with those based on the April, 1960, census. The difference amounts to no more than 1 per cent below the college level, but the census count at the college level was 12 per cent below the survey estimate. The apparent decrease in college-level enrollment is consistent with the substantial attrition between the first and second terms of the 1959–1960 school year reported by colleges.[5]

(3). An indication of the size of one component of gross turnover in the enrolled population recently became available through a 1965 resurvey of noninstitutional males who in 1963 had been between the ages of sixteen and twenty-one and were not attending school. Resurveyed were the 90 per cent of the original group who were civilians at the time of the 1965 survey. Some 13 per cent had re-entered school at some time since 1963; 8 per cent were attending school at the 1965 resurvey date.[6]

(4). Another component of gross turnover has been measured by following the schooling of a group of 1952 male college entrants over a ten-year period. Some 28 per cent had left college for a year or more, but returned and graduated within ten years of the date of first entry.[7]

Age Span and School Type. In 1940 constraints on the permissible ages of the enrolled were most severe and the definition of schooling which could lead to inclusion in the enrolled population was most restrictive. There has been subsequent relaxation of the constraints and broadening of the definition, but the inclusiveness of censuses taken early in this century has not been regained.

Justification for prejudgment of the age span within which the enrolled population will fall is not clear. Nonetheless, the Bureau of the Census has made such judgments, sometimes at the point of questionnaire design, other times at the point of tabulation specification. The pattern which seems to have guided the Bureau in this regard is more explicit in "a general picture of the structure of education in the

United States" which appeared in issues of the "Digest of Educational Statistics" prepared by the United States Office of Education. Among its features are an equation of grade one with age six and advances of one grade accompanied by increases of a year in age. Data generated by the Bureau of the Census cast doubt on the utility of any such representation of the educational structure as a guide for survey-operation procedures, however (Table 2).

TABLE 2. PERCENTAGES OF PERSONS ENROLLED IN SELECTED GRADES WHO ARE YOUNGER OR OLDER THAN THE AGES USUALLY ASSOCIATED WITH THE GRADE, APRIL, 1960

Grade	Usual age[a]	Younger	Older		
			All	1–3 yrs.	4 yrs. or more[b]
1	6–7	5.8[c]	5.2	4.3	0.9
5	10–11	3.7	11.8	10.5	1.3
11	16–17	6.5	10.9	7.8	3.1
15	20–21	8.0	35.0	16.5	18.5
17+	22–24[d]	3.6	62.7	41.1[e]	21.6

[a] As suggested in publications issued by the U.S. Office of Education; see text.

[b] Underestimated because enrolled persons aged 35 or more excluded from basic tabulation.

[c] Underestimated because enrolled persons age 4 or less excluded from basic tabulation.

[d] Instead of 22–25 because grade distribution of enrolled 25-year-olds unknown.

[e] Persons aged 25 to 29.

SOURCE: *U.S. Census of Population: 1960,* vol. I, part 1, Table 168.

The effect of change in the permissible ages of the enrolled cannot be measured systematically between successive observations because other procedural changes were occurring simultaneously. It can be established, however, that had twenty-four been set as the upper age limit of the enrolled in 1950 as in 1940, the count of enrolled persons aged twenty-one or more would have numbered 1.1 million rather than 1.9 million in 1950. No other procedural changes were introduced between these censuses which would influence significantly the enrollment count.

Attendance at any type of school resulted in the classification of the respondent as enrolled in the censuses taken early in this century. More recently, only regular schooling, "that which advances a person toward an elementary or high school diploma, or a college, university, or professional school degree," could result in classification of the respondent as enrolled. The starting point of regular schooling has been lowered, however, from the first grade through the kindergarten to the nursery school in the past twenty years.

A possible resolution, and one which would facilitate comparison between surveys with their inevitable procedural changes, is a return to the inclusiveness of the early censuses. The school attendance of each respondent would be ascertained, irrespective of age. The enrolled respondent then would be queried with respect to the type of school. Under such procedures, the independent as well as joint effects of change in the age span and school type on the count of the enrolled could be determined with reasonable precision.

An Alternative Enrollment Series. A word of explanation may be in order about why the results of population surveys conducted by the Bureau of the Census rather than the compilations of school records made available through the Office of Education are relied on here for time series on schooling. First, the user of enrollment statistics is seldom interested only in aggregate schooling or a count of the enrolled. To investigate the distribution of schooling among socially significant groups in the population requires a linkage of enrollment status with other personal characteristics on an individual basis. Second, the statistical capability of the Bureau of the Census has been and is unmatched by the Office of Education. Whatever the potential merits of individuals and schools, respectively, may be as a source of statistics on schooling, the population-survey data have been collected under more carefully controlled procedures than the school-survey data.

Although less is known about the quality of enrollment data gathered by the Office of Education than about the quality of the enrollment data collected by the Bureau of the Census, a comparison of the two series may be informative (Table 3). The census count consistently has been lower than the school-record count, presumably because an enrolled individual can be counted only once in the census operation but can be enrolled in more than one school in a given year. The counts have tended to converge over time, however, save in 1940 when the census count of the enrolled is known to have been usually restrictive because of procedural decisions.

The comparison of alternative series is reassuring on one point, specifically, the slackening of growth in the output of school years during the 1930's. The census count of the enrolled in the year 1940 was smaller than the count a decade earlier, but the apparent decrease

TABLE 3. OUTPUT OF SCHOOLING IN THE CONTERMINOUS
UNITED STATES IN DECENNIAL CENSUS YEARS, 1900–1960

Item	1900	1910	1920	1930	1940	1950	1960
Enrolled, in millions							
(a) Decennial census	13.4	18.0	21.8	27.9	26.8	29.9	43.5
(b) School records	17.0	19.8	23.9	29.4	29.5	31.1	44.8
Ratio (a) to (b)	.78	.91	.91	.95	.90	.96	.97
Mean days, annual							
(a) School year	144	157	162	173	175	178	178
(b) Attended per pupil	99	113	121	143	152	158	160
Ratio (b) to (a)	.69	.72	.75	.83	.87	.89	.90
Per capita output							
School years							
Decennial census	.18	.20	.21	.23	.20	.20	.24
School records	.22	.21	.23	.24	.22	.21	.25
School days							
Decennial census	26	32	34	40	35	36	43
School records	32	33	37	41	38	37	44
School-days attended							
Decennial census	18	23	25	33	30	32	38
School records	22	24	28	34	33	33	40

SOURCES: Table 1 and U.S. Bureau of the Census, *Historical Statistics of the
United States* and *Continuation to 1962* thereof, Washington, 1960 and 1965,
Series A-20, H-223, H-230, H-231, and H-321.

could be an artifact of procedural change. The school-records counts
reveal no corresponding decrease, but the increase between 1930 and
1940 is notably less than the increase registered over any other ten-
year span.

Per Capita Output and Duration of Schooling

An informative, though somewhat unconventional, measure of the
American performance in the educational sphere is the per capita
output of school years. Although the number of school years provided Americans annually increased threefold between 1900 and
1960, the per capita output of school years in 1960 was no more than
a third greater than the per capita output in 1900.

In a sense, the school-year measure underestimates the growth of
schooling since the turn of the century. That the mean number of days
in the school year has increased is well known. Moreover, it is true,
though perhaps less well known, that the mean days of school attended
per pupil has risen even more rapidly than the number of days in the
school year. When the per capita output measure is school-days attended rather than school years, growth in the per capita output of
schooling between 1900 and 1960 is estimated as twofold.

Irregularities in the decennial changes in per capita output can be observed, however. Indeed, the changes appear so irregular that there is no basis for inferring a long-run trend toward a higher per capita output of schooling. The several alternative series—school years based on either census or school-records counts or years translated into days or days attended—indicate a peak per capita output in 1930, lesser output in 1940 and 1950, and a new peak in 1960. (The several series are shown in Table 3.)

For the past two decades, an annual output series can be constructed from results of the sample surveys conducted by the Bureau of the Census. Procedural changes have occurred, most frequently in the early years of the survey operation; but the series offers a reasonable approximation to a "true" record of the annual output of regular schooling since 1945 (Table 4). Year-to-year gains in the per capita output are recorded with the sole exception of the 1949–1950 and

TABLE 4.   ANNUAL OUTPUT OF SCHOOLING IN THE
UNITED STATES, 1945–1966

Year	Enrolled, millions	Per capita output	
		School years	Days attended
1945	25.5	.182	27.2
1946	27.2	.192	28.9
1947	28.7	.199	30.4
1948	29.5	.201	31.2
1949	30.3	.203	31.8
1950	30.3	.200	31.6
1951	30.9	.200	31.4
1952	32.5	.207	32.3
1953	34.4	.216	34.0
1954	36.1	.222	35.3
1955	37.4	.226	35.9
1956	39.4	.234	37.1
1957	41.2	.240	37.9
1958	42.9	.246	38.7
1959	44.4	.251	39.9
1960	46.3	.256	41.0
1961	47.7	.260	41.9
1962	48.7	.261	42.4
1963	50.4	.266	43.3
1964	51.7	.269	43.9
1965	53.8	.276	n.a.
1966	55.1	.280	n.a.

Sources: U.S. Bureau of the Census, *Historical Statistics of the United States* and *Continuation to 1962* thereof, Washington, 1960 and 1965, Series A-22 and H-231; and *Statistical Abstract of the United States: 1960*, 1966, Tables 2 and 164; *Current Population Reports*, Series P-20 for enrolled ages 5 and over.

1950–1951 period. A cumulative increase of a tenth of a school year or some seventeen days of school attendance is recorded over the twenty-year span.

It could be argued that the per capita output of schooling is only an awkward way of indexing the age structure of the American population and the conventions about the ages at which Americans attend school. To some extent this is true, but over time the ages of "usual" attendance have become both younger and older. To assume that changes in the per capita output of schooling reflect nothing more than changes in the relative numbers of the population falling within some fixed span of ages is too simplistic.

Most of the output of schooling during this century has been distributed among the nation's youth. Given their relative numbers, a specified mean duration of schooling implies an approximate per capita output; or a given per capita output implies an approximate mean duration of schooling. The per capita output now stands at about .28 school years, and recent projections of the enrolled and total populations through 1985 imply a per capita output of school years as great as .29.[8] Although the current per capita output level probably is higher than any that has prevailed in the past, it appears sufficient only to maintain the trend toward a longer mean duration of schooling for each successive birth cohort of Americans.

To illustrate how the age structure of the population intervenes between the per capita output and mean duration measures, an arbitrary assumption about who receives schooling is made. All six-year-olds attend school, and as many individuals of each older age attend school as is possible given the aggregate schooling available for distribution. The age composition of the population is assumed to remain fixed for a more or less indefinite period. A given per capita output of schooling then can be equated with a mean duration of schooling.

The aggregate schooling or enrollment count and the size and age composition of the population as reported in a census are taken as given. With these items of information, the per capita output can be calculated; with the addition of the simplifying assumptions noted above, a mean duration of schooling for the birth cohort aged six on the census date also can be calculated. The irregular changes in per capita output observed between censuses taken in this century are found to be consistent with steady gains in the mean duration of schooling when allowance is made for shifts in the age composition of the American population (Table 5).

Measures of the mean duration of schooling derived in this fashion

TABLE 5. PER CAPITA OUTPUT OF SCHOOL YEARS AS REPORTED IN DECENNIAL CENSUS, IMPLIED MEAN DURATION OF SCHOOLING FOR SIX-YEAR-OLDS ON THE CENSUS DATE, AND GRADES COMPLETED AS REPORTED BY AMERICANS WHO WERE SIX-YEAR-OLDS IN THE GIVEN YEAR, FOR THE SOUTH AND NON-SOUTH, 1900–1960

Year cohort age six or census year	United States Per capita output	United States Implied mean duration	United States Grades completed By 1965	United States Grades completed Ultimate	South Per capita output	South Implied mean duration	South Grades completed by 1960	Non-South Per capita output	Non-South Implied mean duration	Non-South Grades completed by 1960
1891–1895	—	—	7.5	7.5	—	—	6.5	—	—	8.6
1896–1900	—	—	7.9	7.9	—	—	—	—	—	—
1900	.175	7.9	—	—	.159	6.1	—	.183	8.9	—
1901–1905	—	—	8.5	8.5	—	—	7.4	—	—	9.4
1906–1910	—	—	9.0	9.0	—	—	—	—	—	—
1910	.196	9.7	—	—	.202	8.4	—	.193	10.4	—
1911–1915	—	—	9.6	9.6	—	—	8.3	—	—	10.4
1916–1920	—	—	10.0	10.0	—	—	—	—	—	—
1920	.206	10.1	—	—	.222	9.7	—	.199	10.6	—
1921–1925	—	—	10.5	10.5	—	—	9.4	—	—	11.4
1926–1930	—	—	10.9	10.9	—	—	—	—	—	—
1930	.227	11.5	—	—	.235	10.4	—	.224	12.1	—
1931–1935	—	—	11.1	11.2	—	—	9.9	—	—	11.7
1936–1940	—	—	11.6	11.7	—	—	10.4	—	—	12.0
1940	.203	11.7	—	—	.212	10.5	—	.199	12.2	—
1941–1945	—	—	11.8	12.1	—	—	10.5[a]	—	—	12.0[a]
1946–1950	—	—	11.9	12.6	—	—	n.a.	—	—	n.a.
1950	.199	12.9	—	—	.212	11.9	—	.193	13.4	—
1951–1952	—	—	11.1	12.9	—	—	n.a.	—	—	n.a.
1953–1956	—	—	8.8	12.9	—	—	n.a.	—	—	n.a.
1960	.244	13.5	—	—	.247	12.6	—	.242	14.1	—

[a] Cohort age 6 in 1941–1943.

NOTE: Ultimate number of grades completed estimated on the assumption that schooling continues with the current schedule of age-specific attendance rates.

SOURCES: Enrolled population and size and age composition of the total population from reports of the decennial census taken in the given year; grades completed by age and place of birth from *U.S. Census of Population: 1960*, Subject Report PC(2)–5B, Table 3, and *Current Population Reports*, Series P–20, no. 158, December, 1966, current schedule of age-specific attendance rates from *Current Population Reports*, Series P–20, no. 162, March, 1967.

are not proposed as estimators of educational attainment or grades completed. It is, nonetheless, of some interest to compare trends in the implied mean duration of schooling with trends in the mean number of grades completed, as inferred from the reports of Americans about their birth year and educational attainment. The series resemble one another rather closely. The similarity can be taken to mean that reports made recently by survey respondents about their educational attainment are, at least, compatible with enrollment counts made at past dates.

Similar calculations and comparisons carried out separately for the Southern and non-Southern populations reveal that the "effort" of Southerners to provide schooling has been somewhat greater than that of other Americans, although the performance of the South would be judged deficient on the basis of outcome. The per capita output of school years in the Southern states has exceeded the per capita output in the rest of the nation throughout most of this century. Nonetheless, Southern youth have received nearly two years less schooling than their age-mates in the North and West. The intervening factor is, of course, the relatively large number of children in the Southern population.

"Goals" for Per Capita Output

Looking ahead, it becomes clear that "goals" with respect to educational attainment cannot be set realistically without taking into account the full range of activities that must be performed to maintain a viable society and the age composition of the population which must perform these activities. Sixteen years of schooling seems a modest goal for children entering the school system around 1985. In fact, it is implied by projection of the trend toward a rising mean duration of schooling for successive birth cohorts. The Bureau of the Census recently has published alternative projections of the age composition and size of the American population in 1985.[9] To provide an average of sixteen years schooling for the young in a population with the 1985 age composition would require a per capita output of no less than .26 school years and perhaps as much as .31 school years.

Complementary goals might well be an extension of "preschool" training to younger age groups and an expansion of training for adult members of the population. The training of children between the ages of two and five would call for a per capita output on the order of .08 to .10 school years. Training for a tenth of the adults would require a per capita output on the order of .06 school years. The per capita output of all types of formal schooling then takes on values between .40 and .46 school years.

To meet these goals, perhaps half the members of the population would be engaged solely in education: some 46 per cent as students and 4 per cent as full-time workers in the education industry. In the absence of change in economic and family organization, the upper limit on the practicable size of the education sector is approximated. The full-time work force for industries other than education must be allocated a quarter of the members of the population. Infants and persons engaged in their care may account for a tenth. Unaccounted for is something on the order of 15 per cent of the population, including the permanently and temporarily disabled and the institutionalized.

Trends in enrollment and attainment typically are assessed and projected independently not only of one another, but also of probable or desirable changes in competing sectors of organized activity. The risk of officially promulgated, but inherently contradictory, "goals" increases as government attempts to influence performance in more sectors of activity. The practicable aggregate output of schooling remains a limiting factor on educational goals; although, to be sure, alternative goals are consistent with a given output.

THE DISTRIBUTION OF SCHOOLING

The aggregate schooling provided can be distributed among individuals in such a way that each receives the same amount of schooling as his age-mates, or all schooling can be directed to some small minority within the population. Several years ago, analysts of education statistics noted that "schooling is one of the most equally distributed 'goods' in American society." Moreover, the distribution of schooling among individuals appeared to be becoming more even over time.[10]

Readings on the distribution of schooling among members of birth cohorts who had reached their majority only a few years before the observation date were somewhat inconclusive, however. By no means all members of these cohorts had completed their schooling. Because the timing of schooling within the life cycle need not be constant from one cohort to another, it was difficult to forcast the shape that their educational distribution ultimately would take.

Statistics that bear on the equality with which schooling is distributed and the timing of schooling within the life cycle are now more voluminous. The relevant data sets are arrays by number of grades completed and age-specific rates of school attendance, each compiled for cohorts identified by year of birth. Before offering substantive comment on trends in the equality and timing of schooling, it is appropriate to review some characteristics of the basic data, however.

Characteristics of the Data

The Arrays. Measures of the equality of distribution must be derived from arrays of individuals by the number of grades of regular schooling completed. Neither completion of nursery-school or kindergarten programs nor completion of training programs in the trades or business practice offered by "special" schools is reflected in the distributions. The extent to which coverage of these types of schooling would modify the measures of equality, or changes therein over time, remains unknown. There do exist, however, some indications of the frequency with which individuals obtain such training.

Among children who entered the regular school system before World War II, perhaps no more than a fifth and probably no more than a fourth began their schooling in kindergarten. This order of magnitude is suggested both by the school-attendance rate for five-year-olds as reported in decennial censuses and by the ratio of kindergarten enrollment reported by schools to the number of five-year-olds in the national population. Since World War II, perhaps as many as half the children have entered the school system through a kindergarten. By the mid-1960's, 9 per cent of the four-year-olds, 60 per cent of the five-year-olds, and 4 per cent of the six-year-olds were enrolled in a kindergarten. Moreover, 5 per cent of the three-year-olds and 7 per cent of the four-year-olds were attending a nursery school that included "instruction as an important and integral phase of its program of child care."[11]

Results of a recent survey suggest that perhaps a tenth of the nation's adults have received training in "special" schools other than nursery schools and kindergartens. In 1960, a nationwide sample of heads of spending units were surveyed with respect to their schooling. Eleven per cent of the heads in the age range eighteen to fifty-four reported that they had completed exactly twelve grades in the regular school system and had, in addition, some training outside that system.[12] Spending-unit heads are perhaps more likely to have received such training than other adults. When allowance is made for the possibility of combining "special" training with formal schooling of fewer or more than twelve grades, however, an estimate of 10 per cent for the adult population as a whole seems conservative.

A second set of issues concerns the form of the array. Its detail, that is, whether the distribution is by single grade or by grouped grade levels, varies from one tabulation to another. A constant feature is, however, the open-ended terminal interval. When information on grades completed began to be collected by the Bureau of the Census in 1940, no more than 3 per cent of the members of any birth cohort had completed as many as seventeen grades. The open-ended interval of "college, five years or more," may then have been appropriate for tabulation purposes. As many as 6 per cent of more recent birth cohorts are completing seventeen grades, however. The distribution of this highly educated group by number of grades completed is not known, yet some assumption about their attainment must be made in order to estimate the total number of grades completed by a cohort and the equality with which the grades have been distributed among cohort members.

There are available counts of the number of higher degrees conferred each year since 1870, but these fail to yield a satisfactory estimate of the mean grades completed by cohort members who have completed at least seventeen grades. A first, and the less serious, problem is coverage. Completion of the seventeenth grade need not result in the receipt of a master's (or equivalent) degree. The more serious problem is posed by the fact that recipients of the doctorate in a given year include individuals who have received the master's degree no more than one year or as many as twenty years earlier and are still more heterogeneous with respect to birth cohort. The ratio of doctorates to master's degrees is found to be highly sensitive to the assumed time lag between degrees (Table 6). Moreover, an assumption that the "true" lag has remained constant over time appears untenable. Discernible in the basic series on degrees conferred, for example, is the impact of World War II: the dearth of doctorates awarded in the war years; the "making up" in the immediate postwar period. Implied, of course, is change in spacing between the master's degree and the doctorate.

Quite arbitrarily, the problem has been resolved by assigning a mean of eighteen as the number of grades completed by the group "college, five years or more" in cohorts reaching the age of six before World War II and a mean of nineteen as the number of grades completed by members of this group in more recent cohorts. The relative numbers now receiving postgraduate education are sufficient, however, to justify the routine collection and reporting of more detailed information on the attainment of the nation's most highly educated group.

TABLE 6. GRADUATE DEGREES CONFERRED BY
AMERICAN INSTITUTIONS OF HIGHER EDUCATION,
1912–1962

Year (ratio base)	Degrees conferred[a]		Ratio, doctor's to master's, with lag (yrs.)		
	Master's	Doctor's	4	6	8
	(thousands)				
1912	3.0	0.5	.22	.18	.20
1914	3.3	0.6	.17	.19	.26
1916	3.9	0.7	.16	.21	.28
1918	2.9	0.6	.29	.38	.49
1920	4.3	0.6	.26	.33	.34
1922	6.0	0.8	.24	.24	.38
1924	8.2	1.1	.18	.28	.32
1926	9.7	1.4	.24	.27	.29
1928	12.4	1.4	.21	.23	.22
1930	15.0	2.3	.19	.19	.20
1932	19.4	2.7	.14	.15	.17
1934	18.3	2.8	.16	.18	.19
1936	18.3	2.8	.18	.19	.13
1938	21.6	2.9	.16	.11	.09
1940	26.7	3.3	.09	.07	.15
1942	24.6	3.5	.08	.16	.27
1944	13.4	2.3	.30	.49	.57
1946	19.2	2.0	.35	.40	.47
1948	42.4	4.0	.18	.21	.21
1950	58.2	6.6	.15	.15	.15
1952	63.5	7.7	.14	.14	.15
1952[b]	63.6	7.7	.14	.14	.15
1954[b]	56.8	9.0	.16	.17	.20
1956[b]	59.3	8.9	.17	.20	.24
1958[b]	65.6	8.9	.18	.22	—
1960[b]	74.5	9.8	.19	—	—
1962[b]	84.9	11.6	—	—	—

[a] Master's includes second professional degrees; doctor's includes equivalent degrees.
[b] Includes Alaska and Hawaii.

SOURCES: U.S. Bureau of the Census, *Historical Statistics of the United States* and *Continuation to 1962* thereof, Washington, 1960 and 1965, Series H-333 and H-336; and *Statistical Abstract of the United States, 1966,* Washington, 1966, Table 194.

The Rates. Schedules of age-specific rates of school attendance as of the survey date are commonly reported. Such a schedule does not represent the relative frequency with which individuals of any given age on the survey date have attended school in the past. Neither does it represent a forecast of the relative frequency with which individuals of any given age on the survey date will attend school in the future.

In fact, because age-specific rates of school enrollment have been increasing over time, the schedule of rates as of a given date consistently overstates the rates of attendance at young ages relative to the rates of attendance at older ages by comparison with a schedule of rates representing the actual experience of a birth cohort (or the group of individuals of any given age on the survey date). The point can be illustrated readily with reference to selected rates drawn from recent decennial censuses. Shown below are attendance rates at the ages of six and sixteen as reported in the censuses of 1940, 1950, and 1960.

Census	Rate at age	
	6	16
1940	68	—
1950	76	81
1960	—	86

These same rates are displayed below in a format which facilitates cohort analysis.

Cohort age six in	Rate at age	
	6	16
1940	68	81
1950	76	86

Schedules of attendance rates reported in the decennial censuses can be spliced in such a way that they approximate a "true" cohort schedule. Available in successive censuses are the rates of attendance by single year of age. Assume that the cohort aged six on the census date attends school at the rates reported in that census between the ages of five and nine; that between the ages of ten and fourteen, cohort members attend school at rates which represent an average of the rates reported in the census taken when they were six and the census taken ten years later, when they were sixteen; and that between the ages of fifteen and nineteen, the cohort attends school at the rates reported in the census taken when they were sixteen. The hypothetical cohort schedule constructed in this way can be faulted, but a better alternative is not obvious.

Through its recurring sample-survey operation, the Bureau of the Census has the capability of generating true schedules of school-attendance rates for cohorts born during the past three decades. This involves nothing more than the tabulation of data collected through the annual October survey of school attendance by either enrollment status and single year of age or enrollment status and single year of birth. Six-year-olds covered in the first survey, that of October, 1945, had been born between October, 1938, and September, 1939, for example. As seven-year-olds, this cohort appeared in the survey conducted in October, 1946. The cohort appeared in the survey conducted in October, 1956, as seventeen-year-olds; and in the October, 1966, survey as twenty-seven-year-olds.

Should the argument be invoked that sample size is too small to calculate annual attendance rates by single year of age or birth, two counterarguments can be set forth. First, a rate has been published for a single year of age group on occasion. Second, a proper pooling of data from successive surveys would yield an enrollment schedule by a single year of age for a multiple birth-year cohort. Such problems as retabulation may pose do not seem sufficiently severe obstacles. Until the Bureau of the Census undertakes to arrange data from the recurring surveys of attendance in such a way that repeated observations on a cohort can be effected, the timing of schooling must be inferred from the hypothetical cohort schedules constructed from decennial census data.

Equality of Distribution

Among individuals who reached the age of six shortly before World War I, the most-educated fifth received some 30 per cent of the schooling; the share of the least-educated fifth was about 10 per cent. The share of the most-educated fifth fell by about three percentage points for the six-year-olds of the late 1930's, and a corresponding increase was recorded in the share of the least-educated fifth. The six-year-olds of the 1940's have not yet completed their schooling, but projected distributions by grades completed imply no lessening in the equality of distribution (Table 7).

The relative equality with which education is distributed can be highlighted by contrasting the education distribution with the income distribution.[13] The top fifth of the spending units received just over half the aggregate family personal income in the early 1930's and about 45 per cent of the income in the years since World War II. The share of the bottom fifth has amounted to no more than 5 per cent. The corresponding measures on the education distribution are a little less than three-tenths for the top fifth and a little more than a tenth for the bottom fifth.

TABLE 7. PERCENTAGE OF AGGREGATE SCHOOLING RECEIVED BY THE MOST-EDUCATED AND LEAST-EDUCATED MEMBERS OF COHORTS AGE SIX BETWEEN 1906 AND 1950

Year cohort age six	Most educated			Least educated			Gini coefficient
	10%	20%	30%	30%	20%	10%	
1906–1910	17.7	31.6	44.8	16.4	8.7	2.6	.23
1911–1915	17.1	30.6	43.1	17.5	9.5	3.1	.21
1916–1920	16.3	29.2	41.2	18.2	10.2	3.9	.19
1921–1925	15.7	28.3	39.7	18.6	10.9	3.8	.18
1926–1930	15.5	27.9	38.9	19.1	11.2	4.2	.16
1931–1935	15.2	28.0	38.9	19.7	11.5	4.4	.16
1936–1940	14.7	27.3	38.4	20.9	12.4	4.7	.14
1941–1945	15	28	39	21	13	5	.15
1946–1950	15	27	39	22	14	6	.13

SOURCES: *U.S. Census of Population: 1960* for cohorts 1906–1910 through 1931–1935; *Current Population Reports*, Series P-20, no. 158, December, 1966, for cohort 1936–1940, and Series P-25, no. 305, April, 1965, for cohorts 1941–1945 and 1946–1950.

It could be argued that the equality with which education is distributed is overstated because the unit is a grade completed. The cost of providing a year's schooling increases with the grade level. Hence, were a dollar value attached to each grade completed, the equality with which education was distributed would diminish. Appropriate dollar values per grade are open to question. Simply assume that per-grade costs are in the ratio of 3 at the elementary level, 5 at the high-school level, 8 in the thirteenth and fourteenth grades, 12 in the fifteenth and sixteenth grades, and 17 thereafter. The top fifth of the six-year-olds of 1926–1930 received 36 per cent of the schooling, and the bottom fifth received 9 per cent. It seems likely that the equality of the education distribution will remain greater than the equality of the income distribution under any reasonable translation of grade units into dollar-cost units.

Although the equality with which schooling is distributed has increased over time in both the Southern states and the states to their north and west, education in grade units has been distributed with less equality in the South at any given time. There is, however, some evidence of convergence between the Southern and non-Southern systems in this regard (Table 8). Minor qualification on the conclusion is necessary because the distributions which underlie the measures of equality pertain to persons born in or residing in the South. That they received their schooling within the region is not a certainty.

Barriers in School Progression. The increasing equality with which the distributive process operates in the regular school system implies change in the shape of the distribution by grades completed. At each grade level, the formal schooling of some individuals comes to an end; others continue to progress through the graded system. The continuation ratios between successive grades over all levels of the system underlie the distribution by grades completed, of course.

Among children who entered the school system in the early part of this century, continuation ratios between successively higher grades in the elementary system fell gradually from 98 to 89 per hundred. Only two-thirds of the children who completed the eighth grade effected the transition into the secondary system successfully, however. Of those who succeeded in the transition or completed the ninth grade, 86 per cent went on to complete the tenth grade. The transition thus constituted a major barrier or stringent screening point within the school system.

With the passing of time, the point at which a major barrier within

TABLE 8. PERCENTAGE OF AGGREGATE SCHOOLING RECEIVED BY THE MOST-EDUCATED AND LEAST-EDUCATED MEMBERS OF COHORTS AGE SIX BETWEEN 1906 AND 1935 BY REGION OF RESIDENCE IN 1960 AND BY REGION OF BIRTH

Year cohort age six	South						Non-South					
	Most educated			Least educated			Most educated			Least educated		
	10%	20%	30%	30%	20%	10%	10%	20%	30%	30%	20%	10%
	(by region of residence)											
1906–1910	19.4	34.4	48.2	13.1	6.3	1.6	17.2	30.7	43.6	18.4	10.2	3.5
1911–1915	18.4	32.9	46.6	13.9	7.2	2.1	16.3	29.4	41.4	19.4	11.4	4.2
1916–1920	17.9	31.8	44.9	14.7	7.7	2.2	15.8	28.4	40.0	19.7	11.9	4.6
1921–1925	17.0	30.4	43.0	15.6	8.3	2.7	15.3	27.5	38.6	20.1	12.3	5.0
1926–1930	16.5	29.7	41.7	16.3	8.8	2.9	14.9	27.1	37.8	20.8	12.5	5.3
1931–1935	16.2	29.3	41.0	17.0	9.3	3.2	14.8	27.5	38.2	20.8	12.4	5.1
	(by region of birth)											
1901–1910	19.1	34.4	47.1	14.4	6.7	2.5	16.2	29.6	41.8	19.6	11.5	5.0
1911–1920	17.6	31.7	44.9	16.1	8.9	2.9	15.6	28.5	39.9	20.2	12.6	5.3
1921–1930	16.4	29.7	42.1	16.8	9.8	3.1	14.8	27.0	37.7	21.9	13.1	5.8
1931–1935	15.9	29.0	40.8	17.8	10.1	3.9	14.5	26.8	37.8	22.2	13.7	5.8

SOURCES: *U.S. Census of Population: 1960*, vol. I, part 1, Table 173, and Subject Report PC(2)–5B, Table 3.

the system is encountered has been deferred. Among children entering the school system around 1940, continuation ratios between successively higher grades in the elementary and secondary systems fell gradually from 99 to 90 per hundred. The rate of high-school graduation for this recent cohort, some 70 per cent, matches the elementary-completion rate for the cohort entering school three decades earlier.

It is now not until the point of transition from the secondary system into the institutions of higher education that the first major barrier to progression is encountered. For older cohorts, this point had constituted a second barrier. The continuation ratio between the twelfth and thirteenth grades also may be of interest because only at this point in the school system did the ratio become lower over time. Some 48 per cent of the relatively few high-school graduates in the cohort aged six in 1906–1910 completed at least one year of college as compared with 36 per cent of the more numerous high-school graduates in the cohorts aged six in 1921–1925 and 1926–1930. Although a final judgment is premature, the ratio may be found to have increased for members of more recent cohorts when their schooling is completed (Table 9).

Although members of the cohorts who entered school around 1940 were by 1960 beyond the "usual" age of college entry, a sizable number reported that they still were attending secondary school. Sizable numbers in more recent cohorts who had passed the "usual" age of high-school entry reported that they still were attending elementary school. The effect of such enrollment on the ultimate continuation ratios between higher levels of schooling is not clear. It remains to be seen whether late-completers will continue to progress through the system at the same rate as their age-mates who completed the grade at a younger age.

When continuation ratios for the Southern and non-Southern populations are examined, it becomes clear that convergence in the equality with which schooling is distributed has come about through a narrowing of the regional difference in selectivity below the secondary level. Children in the Southern system have been less likely to continue between successive grades through the elementary system than have their age-mates in the North and West. Continuation ratios between higher grades have been similar for Southerners and non-Southerners throughout the observation period, in contrast.

Regional Disparity. The stringent screening at the lower levels characteristic of the South results in a distinctive array by grades com-

TABLE 9. CONTINUATION RATIOS BETWEEN SPECIFIED GRADE LEVELS, PER HUNDRED PERSONS COMPLETING LOWER LEVEL, FOR AMERICANS ATTAINING THE AGE OF SIX BETWEEN 1906 AND 1948

Year cohort age six	Grade levels													
	0–1	1–3	3–5	5–7	7–8	8–9	9–10	10–11	11–12	12–13	13–14	14–15	15–16	16–17
1906–1910	98	98	94	89	89	65	86	82	87	48	80	69	81	41
1911–1915	98	98	95	91	91	72	87	83	87	46	80	71	81	43
1916–1920	99	99	96	93	92	77	88	85	88	40	79	71	82	44
1921–1925	99	99	97	94	94	83	90	87	88	36	79	72	83	42
1926–1930	99	99	98	95	95	87	92	88	89	36	79	73	84	41
1931–1935	99	99	98	96	96	89	91	88	89[a]	38	81	76	83	38[a]
1936–1940	99	99	98	97	96	91	92	89	90[b]	38	80[a]	76[a]	80[b]	35[b]
1941	99	99	99	97	97	92	92	89	90[b]	37[a]	77[a]	73[a]	75[b]	29[c]
1942	99	99	99	97	97	93	92	89	90[b]	37[b]	76[b]	72[b]	72[c]	—
1943	99	100	99	97	97	93	92	90	90[c]	37[b]	75[c]	70[c]	—	—
1944	99	100	99	98	97	94	93	90	89[c]	37[c]	72[c]	—	—	—
1945	99	100	99	98	97	94	92[a]	89[a]	88[c]	38[c]	—	—	—	—
1946	99	99	99	98	97	94	93[a]	89[b]	84[c]	—	—	—	—	—
1947	100	99	99	98	97[a]	94[a]	92[c]	86[c]	—	—	—	—	—	—
1948	99	99	99	98	97[b]	94[c]	88[c]	—	—	—	—	—	—	—

[a] 0.50 to 0.99 per cent of cohort enrolled in higher grade in 1960.
[b] 1.00 to 1.49 per cent of cohort enrolled in higher grade in 1960.
[c] 1.50 per cent or more of cohort enrolled in higher grade in 1960.

SOURCE: *U.S. Census of Population: 1960*, vol. I, part 1, Tables 168 and 173.

pleted. Its most noteworthy feature is described by the phrase "the too-empty middle of the southern educational pyramid."[14] Moreover, this distributive feature of the Southern school system has supra-regional significance. Here the educational characteristics and sizes of the interregional migration streams become relevant.

Just under a fourth of the Southern-born residing in the nation in 1960 were living in the North or West, and about 6 per cent of the persons born in the North or West were living in the South. About one of every seven adults residing in the South in 1960 had been born outside the region, and about one of every six young adults and one of every four adults residing in the North and West had been born else-where. The interregional flows are, then, of substantial size relative to the size of either the originating or receiving population.

The stream moving north and west from the South includes dis-proportionate numbers of Southerners who have completed at least elementary school. In fact, it is precisely at grade eight that the relative number of out-migrants reaches its maximum. The stream moving into the South compensates only the loss of college-trained Southerners, however. The migration flows serve to accentuate the "too-empty middle" of the Southern distribution.

From the North and West, disproportionate numbers of college-trained natives move into the South; but their loss is roughly compen-sated by the in-movement of college-trained Southerners. Although the out-migration rates from the South peak at the "too-empty middle" of the Southern distribution, the relative number of Southern in-mi-grants in the North and West attains a maximum among functional illiterates, a stratum particularly ill-equipped to adjust to new circum-stances (Table 10).

By one definition, "the first educational task, North or South, is to pull the bottom up toward the middle, to bring these men and women and their children into the orbit of the national culture and econ-omy."[15] The problems posed by this task are rather different in the respective regions, however.

For the North and West, the so-called bottom is weighted heavily with in-migrants from the South. Attempts to discourage the in-migra-tion of the undereducated or to encourage adult in-migrants to ac-quire elementary training may not meet much success, but they appear possible lines of action for pulling the bottom up toward the middle.

At first thought, the Southern problem may seem to revolve wholly around the equality with which schooling is distributed. The least-educated three-tenths received only 18 per cent of the schooling

TABLE 10. INTERREGIONAL MIGRANTS PER 100 PERSONS REMAINING IN THEIR REGION OF BIRTH IN 1960, BY GRADES COMPLETED, FOR COHORTS ATTAINING THE AGE OF SIX BETWEEN 1901 AND 1936

Region and year cohort age six	All	Grades completed									
		0	1–4	5–7	8	9–11	12	13–15	16	17+
South											
1901–1910											
Out-migrants	27	17	22	25	37	28	29	26	24	28
In-migrants	13	1	2	6	16	17	28	29	34	41
1911–1920											
Out-migrants	29	15	20	25	41	32	30	30	24	29
In-migrants	12	1	1	3	10	12	21	27	32	43
1921–1930											
Out-migrants	32	16	19	26	44	37	33	38	28	37
In-migrants	14	1	1	2	8	11	22	33	35	47
1931–1936											
Out-migrants	31	16	20	25	44	37	30	31	26	35
In-migrants	13	3	2	3	7	10	17	24	30	42
Non-South											
1901–1910											
Out-migrants	6	5	5	4	4	6	8	9	11	12
In-migrants	12	62	51	18	10	10	8	9	8	8
1911–1920											
Out-migrants	5	4	5	3	3	5	6	8	11	11
In-migrants	13	48	76	26	13	12	9	9	8	8
1921–1930											
Out-migrants	6	3	6	4	3	4	6	10	12	12
In-migrants	14	37	91	43	18	15	9	11	9	10
1931–1936											
Out-migrants	6	4	6	5	3	5	5	8	10	11
In-migrants	14	24	83	47	22	17	9	11	9	9

SOURCE: *U.S. Census of Population: 1960*, Subject Report PC(2)–5B, Table 3.

available to natives of the South who reached the age of six in 1931–1936, resulting in an average of 6.0 grades completed. The corresponding figures for the non-South are 22 per cent of the schooling and an average of 8.6 grades completed. Had the least-educated three-tenths of the Southerners received 22 per cent of the available schooling, however, their average schooling still would have been only 7.5 grades. The mean number of grades completed was fewer for all Southerners than for their age-mates in the North and West. An attempt to trace the Southern "problem" back still further would lead to the earlier observation that the mean duration of schooling is lower in the South despite the higher per capita output of schooling.

The measures of the educational distribution necessarily reflect the experience of persons whose schooling was essentially complete at the time of the most recent census, the youngest of whom now are nearly forty years old. There is, however, no basis for thinking that the outlines of the regional disparity have changed. At the time of the 1960 census, literal high-school dropouts were no more numerous among teen-agers in the Southern population than in the rest of the national population; but the proportion of out-of-school youth with no more than elementary training was substantially higher in the South. Moreover, among the youth still attending school, relatively many Southerners had completed no more than seven grades and represented potential increments to the out-of-school group with only elementary training (Table 11).

The Timing of Schooling

The chances that an individual will be attending school depend more upon his age than upon any other personal characteristic, save perhaps the presence of severe mental or physical impairment. Throughout this century, the age-specific enrollment curve for Americans has taken the form of an inverted-U with its apex at age eleven. Among the very young and the very old, the school-attendance rate has been and is effectively zero. At more central ages, increases in attendance have been recorded. Because the increases over time in attendance rates form a U when plotted in relation to age, the enrollment curves for successively younger cohorts become less peaked. Near-universal attendance has diffused from age eleven toward both younger and older ages during the past six decades.

Because attendance has diffused toward both younger and older ages over time, intercohort differences in per capita school years attended widen with advances in age. Contrast, for example, the co-

TABLE 11. DISTRIBUTION PER 1,000 YOUTH BY ENROLLMENT STATUS AND GRADES COMPLETED, FOR COHORTS AGE SIX BETWEEN 1948 AND 1951 BY REGION OF RESIDENCE IN 1960

Year cohort age six and region	Not enrolled, by grades completed					Enrolled, by grades completed				
	12+	9–11	8	5–7	0–4	0–4	5–7	8	9–11	12+
1948–1949										
South	21	100	45	55	16	13	56	69	618	7
Non-South	31	90	25	13	7	9	19	40	754	13
1950–1951										
South	1	19	18	29	15	29	341	327	220	0
Non-South	1	18	14	8	6	10	231	403	307	0

SOURCE: *U.S. Census of Population: 1960*, Subject Report PC(2)–5A, Table 12.

hort of males who entered the school system around 1950 with the cohort who had entered around 1910. The mean number of school years attended by the more recent cohort exceeded the mean for the earlier cohort by 0.6 years at age eight; by 1.3 years at age sixteen; and by 2.6 years at age twenty. In fact, members of the more recent cohort had received as much schooling by the time they were sixteen as the members of the earlier cohort had received by the time they were twenty (Table 12).

More generally, the intercohort comparisons raise the issue of the timing of schooling within the life cycle. Many different schedules of age-specific attendance rates imply the same mean duration of schooling for the cohort as its members reach adulthood. From another perspective, identical age-specific attendance rates over a part of the age range do not ensure the same ultimate mean duration of schooling. Not only are these observations true in some formal sense; differences in the timing of schooling among cohorts of Americans are pronounced enough to render difficult any inference about the magnitude of the ultimate differential in schooling.

Differentials by Color. Assume, for example, the task of gauging the progress of nonwhite boys who reached the age of six in 1950 with respect to formal schooling. Plausible norms of comparison might be the progress of their white age-mates, of white boys born a decade earlier, and nonwhite boys in that earlier birth cohort (Table 13). Annual reports issued as the nonwhite boys progressed would almost certainly appear to contradict one another.

1. Reports on attendance at ages five and six and at ages eighteen and nineteen will point out that the nonwhite boys are attending in relatively greater numbers than had the white boys ten years their senior, but reports on attendance at ages seven through seventeen will assert that they are attending in relatively lesser numbers than had the white boys ten years their senior.

2. The report issued when the nonwhite boys are six will note that the gap with their white age-mates is less than the gain recorded over the earlier nonwhite cohort, but the report issued when they are fifteen will note that the gap with white age-mates is greater than the gain over the earlier nonwhite cohort.

3. When the nonwhite boys reach the age of seventeen, the point will be made that they have attended school a half year less than their white age-mates and a half year more than the nonwhite boys ten years their senior; but when they reach the age of

TABLE 12. AGE-SPECIFIC RATES OF SCHOOL ATTENDANCE AND PER CAPITA SCHOOL YEARS ATTENDED BY AGE, FOR COHORTS OF AMERICAN MALES AGE SIX IN GIVEN YEAR

Age	Attendance rate per 1,000					Per capita school years attended				
	1910	1920	1930	1940	1950	1910	1920	1930	1940	1950
5	167	180	195	175	339	—	—	—	—	—
6	517	544	655	682	764	0.2	0.2	0.2	0.2	0.3
7	747	799	890	922	942	0.7	0.7	0.9	0.9	1.1
8	825	874	940	947	956	1.4	1.5	1.7	1.8	2.0
9	861	896	954	955	960	2.3	2.4	2.7	2.7	3.0
10	910	947	962	958	968	3.1	3.3	3.6	3.7	4.0
11	924	956	966	960	969	4.0	4.2	4.6	4.6	4.9
12	911	950	961	954	965	5.0	5.2	5.6	5.6	5.9
13	906	947	955	952	963	5.9	6.1	6.5	6.6	6.9
14	846	907	926	934	950	6.8	7.1	7.5	7.5	7.8
15	771	848	873	915	931	7.6	8.0	8.4	8.4	8.8
16	533	658	757	806	865	8.4	8.8	9.3	9.4	9.7
17	357	471	605	679	763	8.9	9.5	10.0	10.2	10.6
18	228	311	381	424	548	9.3	10.0	10.6	10.8	11.3
19	154	208	232	278	375	9.5	10.3	11.0	11.3	11.9
20	—	—	—	—	—	9.7	10.5	11.3	11.5	12.3

SOURCE: Duncan, Beverly, *Family Factors and School Dropout*, Final Report on Cooperative Research Project No. 2258, U.S. Office of Education, The University of Michigan, Ann Arbor, 1965, Table 6–1.

629

TABLE 13. AGE-SPECIFIC RATES OF SCHOOL ATTENDANCE FOR COHORTS OF AMERICAN MALES AGED SIX IN 1950 AND 1940, BY COLOR

| | Male | | | | Nonwhite, 1950, less | | |
| | White | | Nonwhite | | White | | Nonwhite |
Age	1950	1940	1950	1940	1950	1940	1940
	(attendance rate per 1,000)						
5	351	184	248	117	−103	64	131
6	772	696	702	588	− 70	6	114
7	947	931	907	854	− 40	−24	53
8	959	953	935	903	− 24	−18	32
9	963	959	945	922	− 18	−14	23
10	970	960	953	932	− 17	− 7	21
11	972	962	953	936	− 19	− 9	17
12	968	958	949	928	− 19	− 9	21
13	966	956	941	914	− 25	−15	27
14	954	941	916	880	− 38	−25	36
15	938	923	884	857	− 54	−39	27
16	874	818	800	722	− 74	−18	78
17	775	696	671	550	−104	−25	121
18	556	437	485	324	− 71	48	161
19	384	287	309	201	− 75	22	108
	(per capita school years attended)						
6	0.4	0.2	0.2	0.1	− 0.2	0.0	0.1
7	1.1	0.9	1.0	0.7	− 0.1	0.1	0.3
8	2.1	1.8	1.9	1.6	− 0.2	0.1	0.3
9	3.0	2.8	2.8	2.5	− 0.2	0.0	0.3
10	4.0	3.7	3.7	3.4	− 0.3	0.0	0.3
11	5.0	4.7	4.7	4.3	− 0.3	0.0	0.4
12	5.9	5.6	5.6	5.3	− 0.3	0.0	0.3
13	6.9	6.6	6.6	6.2	− 0.3	0.0	0.4
14	7.9	7.6	7.5	7.1	− 0.4	− 0.1	0.4
15	8.8	8.5	8.4	8.0	− 0.4	− 0.1	0.4
16	9.8	9.4	9.3	8.8	− 0.5	− 0.1	0.5
17	10.6	10.2	10.1	9.6	− 0.5	− 0.1	0.5
18	11.4	10.9	10.8	10.1	− 0.6	− 0.1	0.7
19	12.0	11.4	11.3	10.4	− 0.7	− 0.1	0.9
20	12.3	11.7	11.6	10.6	− 0.7	− 0.1	1.0

SOURCE: *Census of Population: 1950*, vol. II, part 1, Table 110.

twenty, the point will be made that they lag behind their white age-mates by less than a year, whereas a gain of a full year is registered over the nonwhites ten years their senior.

Any recurring theme will be limited mainly to the observation that nonwhite boys are attending in relatively lesser numbers than are their white age-mates, but in relatively greater numbers than had the nonwhite boys ten years their senior.

Differentials by Locality. There are, moreover, somewhat persistent differentials in timing among localities. Precise measurement of these differentials would require age-specific enrollment schedules for cohort members whose schooling occurred wholly within the locality. The closest approximation is a schedule for cohort members resident in the locality on a given observation date, a changing rather than fixed group of persons born in the same year. Nonetheless, the outlines of the distinctive regional patterns can be sketched. The Northern pattern, exemplified by Massachusetts, is distinguished by: a relatively young school-entry age; a relatively high rate of attendance in the ages of maximum attendance; and a relatively early age of school leaving. The key features of the Western pattern, exemplified by Utah, are: a relatively late school-entry age; a relatively high rate of attendance in the ages of maximum attendance; and a relatively late age of school leaving. The Southern pattern, exemplified by Texas, is distinguished by: a relatively late school-entry age; a relatively low rate of attendance in the ages of maximum attendance; and a relatively early school leaving age. Such differentials imply that the school-age migrant is likely to be defined as retarded or accelerated by the norm of the receiving locality (Table 14).

Differentials by Social Background. The timing of schooling probably varies among age-mates who differ with respect to social background. Such differentials are much more difficult to document, but at least three pieces of relevant evidence are available.

First, the age of school entry can be shown to be younger for children whose parents are well educated than for children whose parents have a lesser educational attainment. Among children whose father (or mother in the absence of the father) had not completed elementary school, 31 per cent of the five-year-olds and 51 per cent of the six-year-olds were attending school in 1960. The corresponding figures for children whose father was a high-school graduate were 73 and 88 per cent. A lesser differential in the same direction appears at ages seven through thirteen. If the attendance rates for the five-year-olds in each background stratum at successively higher ages were the same as those observed for children of the given age and in the same stratum in 1960, the mean duration of schooling by age fourteen would be 7.8 years if the father had not completed elementary school as compared with 8.3 years if the father was a high-school graduate.[16]

Second, among children who would have been fourteen years old at the opening of the 1959–1960 school year, the mean number of

TABLE 14. AGE-SPECIFIC RATES OF SCHOOL ATTENDANCE FOR URBAN RESIDENTS IN THE STATES OF MASSACHUSETTS, UTAH, AND TEXAS IN THE 1950'S AND 1940'S

Age	1950			1940			Mass., 1950's, less		Mass., 1940's, less	
	Mass.	Utah	Texas	Mass.	Utah	Texas	Utah	Texas	Utah	Texas
				(attendance rate per 1,000)						
5	508	327	155	334	186	49	181	353	148	285
6	885	804	550	865	737	481	81	335	128	384
7	948	972	921	968	967	902	-24	27	1	66
8	956	977	949	975	984	952	-21	7	-9	23
9	956	977	959	978	983	965	-21	-3	-5	13
10	968	981	968	969	980	963	-13	0	-11	6
11	969	982	970	971	979	966	-13	-1	-8	5
12	966	981	964	969	982	960	-15	2	-13	9
13	962	979	958	968	979	951	-17	4	-11	17
14	958	974	938	964	979	925	-16	20	-15	39
15	942	961	899	947	975	870	-19	43	-28	77
16	862	915	818	847	931	755	-53	44	-84	92
17	748	839	692	731	835	593	-91	56	-104	138
18	571	656	498	473	536	360	-85	73	-63	113
19	444	508	352	343	396	260	-64	92	-53	83
				(per capita school years attended)						
14	8.1	8.0	7.4	8.0	7.8	7.2	0.1	0.7	0.2	0.8
16	10.0	9.9	9.2	9.9	9.7	9.0	0.1	0.8	0.2	0.9
18	11.6	11.7	10.7	11.5	11.5	10.3	-0.1	0.9	0.0	1.2
20	12.6	12.8	11.6	12.3	12.4	11.0	-0.3	1.0	-0.1	1.3

SOURCE: *U.S. Census of Population: 1960*, Reports by States, vol I, Table 45; *U.S. Census of Population: 1950*, Reports by States, vol. II, Table 62; *U.S. Census of Population: 1940*, Reports by States, vol. IV, Table 15.

TABLE 15. SCHOOLING OF AMERICANS AGED 14 AT THE
OPENING OF THE 1959–1960 SCHOOL YEAR,
BY EDUCATION OF THEIR FAMILY HEADS

Grades completed by family head	Enrolled per 1,000	Mean grades completed	Percentage completing at least grade			
			5	7	8	9
7 or less	918	7.3	95.4	78.7	58.1	16.5
8	946	7.7	97.6	90.6	73.2	20.0
9 to 11	955	7.8	98.3	91.1	75.9	23.3
12	981	8.0	98.1	95.4	86.1	24.4
13 or more	982	8.1	99.6	98.4	90.6	28.6

SOURCE: Special tabulations from a computer tape file furnished under a joint project sponsored by the U.S. Bureau of the Census and the Population Council and containing selected 1960 census information from a .001 sample of the population of the United States.

grades completed was 7.3 if the father had not completed elementary school and 8.0 if he was a high-school graduate (Table 15). The order of magnitude of the differential is similar to that implied by the enrollment schedules at ages younger than fourteen recorded in the 1960 census and referred to earlier. The major factor producing the differential may be presumed to be a difference in the usual age of school entry, rather than a difference in enrollment rates at ages seven through thirteen or in the relative frequency with which a grade is repeated.

The third piece of evidence pertains to the timing of attendance after entering college. The college careers of a group of 1952 male entrants were traced over a ten-year period. Entrants whose parents were well educated were less likely to interrupt their schooling after college entry. They were also less likely to interrupt their schooling temporarily. Among the men who had completed college in the ten-year period, interruption had been as common among the men with well-educated parents as among the other entrants, however.[17] The relevant data are summarized below in the form of percentage distributions for males in each background stratum.

Closely spaced readings on the influence of social background on the

Interruption of schooling	Parents' education		
	High	Mid	Low
None	53.6	49.5	45.5
Temporary	29.0	25.1	23.8
Permanent	17.4	25.4	30.7

timing of schooling in the life cycle will not be easy to effect from the results of "general-purpose" surveys. Measurement may appear to require only that information be collected about each member of each household contacted, including indicators of schooling for the young and socioeconomic position for the household or its head. Two distinct sets of problems arise, however. First, social background can itself change as the child matures. Family heads obtain more schooling; main wage-earners change jobs; secondary family workers begin to augment the family income; or, for that matter, family units dissolve and reform. Second, upon leaving school or entering college, sizable numbers of children terminate residence in the family home. They do not, then, appear on the household roster; and their characteristics can no longer be linked to those of other family members. For example, about a third of the young males who are eighteen years old at the opening of the school year are not living in a family unit.[18]

If there is a serious interest in measuring the influence of social background on schooling as that schooling is occurring and not after the fact, large-scale special surveys must be fielded periodically. The design would call for a baseline survey of "preschool" children in which the composition and socioeconomic position of their families were ascertained. One of two strategies then must be followed. The children covered in the baseline survey can be traced forward. Information about their schooling and the composition and socioeconomic position of their families would be collected at each subsequent contact. Alternatively, subsequent surveys of the birth cohort in which the "preschool" children of the baseline survey hold membership could obtain some retrospective information as well as current information about schooling and family circumstances. Such retrospective information, if used judiciously, should permit a splicing between surveys, such that the series would approximate a set of repeated observations on the same group of children.

Intervention in the Distributive Process

How the school system should distribute education depends on the kind of society Americans envisage at the close of this century. If, for example, it is one in which individuals are valued not for the mechanical energy they can provide, but rather for their ability to manipulate symbols, then the functional illiterate can play no productive role. If it is a society in which the right to migrate is inviolable, then both the output of schooling and its distribution within each locality are truly national concerns. Whatever the vision of the society to come, it may not be amiss to question the implication of each policy proposal for the shape of the education distribution, under conditions of both a fixed and changing output of schooling.

An active role on the part of the federal government would represent something of a break with tradition. Education has been conceived as a state, if not local, responsibility. Insofar as federal action has occurred in the past, it typically has been directed to the most-educated segment of the population nearing adulthood.

For example, just over a hundred years ago Congress acted to, in effect, set up a permanent endowment for each state in support of a college. At the time that the "land-grant" colleges were endowed, the youngsters they would serve were, indeed, an educational elite. Fewer than half the children between the ages of five and twenty were attending school. A sixth of the teen-agers were illiterate.

Two decades ago, education allowances were made available to veterans of World War II. They had been a somewhat select group at the time of induction. A 1947 survey revealed that 78 per cent of the veterans aged twenty-five to twenty-nine as compared with 59 per cent of their nonveteran age-mates had completed some high-school training.[19] A resurvey of the cohort in 1952 revealed no change in the respective proportions with some high-school training. Neither was change in the continuation ratios between higher levels of schooling observed among the nonveterans. Among the veterans, however, continuation ratios had risen from 67 to 74 per hundred between grades nine and twelve; from 31 to 36 per hundred between grades twelve and thirteen; and from 33 to 51 per hundred between grades thirteen and sixteen.[20]

Programs such as "Head Start" and "Job Corps" may signal a new direction in federal activity in the educational sphere. Whether they will have a detectable influence on the education distribution remains to be seen, of course. It is not only that these programs are of very recent origin. Thus far, analysts of education statistics have met with little success in identifying a change in the distribution which can unambiguously be designated as an effect of a program as such. To be sure, substantial numbers of veterans resumed schooling with an education allowance; but a substantial number of these men whose schooling had been interrupted by military service would have resumed schooling in the absence of such an allowance.

DIFFERENTIAL SCHOOLING
AMONG SUBPOPULATIONS

What are commonly referred to as the inequalities in the American educational system frequently are inferred from more or less persistent differences in the mean years of formal schooling received by the young in diverse subpopulations. If it were possible to obtain an unambiguous measure of how educable a child is, the inequalities might be conceived as the differences among subpopulations with respect to the mean amount of schooling received by children with the same ability to learn. Inasmuch as this measurement problem remains unresolved, the gross differences must be taken to represent the inequality or, perhaps more accurately, inequity with which the system operates.

Compounded in a gross difference between groups are differences in their access to educational opportunity; in the extent to which they capitalize on available opportunities; in their exposure to out-of-school experiences which facilitate progress in the school system; and in the frequency and severity of impairments, of whatever origin, in the ability to learn. How much of an intergroup difference in educational attainment should be attributed to inequities in the operation of the school system depends on one's conception of the role of the school in American society. The provision of adequate school facilities within the effective commuting range of each child is one order of task. Compensation for intergroup differences in resources and motivation or health and housing is quite another order.

One other point should be made clear at the outset. The annual per capita amount of schooling received by a subpopulation does not alone determine the mean duration of schooling for its members; the age structure of the subpopulation intervenes. Since the 1930's, for example, the amount of schooling received by members of America's racial minorities appears to have exceeded the amount received by members of the so-called white majority on a per capita basis. The differential is unequivocal each year since the close of World War II (Table 16). Given the age compositions of the respective populations as of 1960, however, the per capita amount of schooling received by the minorities would have to be about .04 school years greater than the per capita amount received by the majority if the mean schooling received by the young in the two populations were to be equalized at about twelve years. The foregoing calculation is exceedingly rough, but it illustrates the point that equality in the mean duration of schooling between subpopulations is likely to entail inequality in the

TABLE 16. PER CAPITA SCHOOL YEARS RECEIVED BY
MEMBERS OF THE WHITE AND NONWHITE POPULATIONS,
1900–1964

Year	White	Nonwhite	Year	White	Nonwhite
1900	.183	.124	1953	.203	.223
1910	.199	.170	1954	.220	.240
1920	.207	.196	1955	.231	.252
1930	.224	.211	1956	.231	.258
1940	.201	.212	1957	.237	.268
			1958	.243	.273
1947	.179	.206	1959	.247	.280
1948	.195	.206	1960	.252	.286
1949	.198	.212	1961	.255	.293
1950	.198	.225	1962	.258	.286
1951	.200	.233	1963	.262	.295
1952	.208	.237	1964	.265	.300

SOURCE: 1900 through 1940 from reports of the decennial censuses; 1947 through 1964 from reports of the Current Population Survey conducted by the U.S. Bureau of the Census.

per capita amounts of schooling received by the respective subpopulations.

Trends in the differential schooling of several subpopulations are assessed below. The data are drawn exclusively from surveys conducted by the U.S. Bureau of the Census, and the measure of schooling is the number of grades completed. Most of the statistical series reported are terminated with the birth cohort which entered the school system shortly before World War II although the same items of information often are available for more recent birth cohorts. Readings based on the experience of a cohort which includes an appreciable number of members whose schooling still is in progress cannot be interpreted readily within a trend framework and, therefore, are not reported here.

Sex

As indexed by mean grades completed, the differential in schooling by sex has been modest in magnitude throughout this century; but the direction of the differential has reversed over time. The initial difference of 0.3 grades in favor of females decreased for successive cohorts reaching school age before the 1920's. A difference in favor of males, which then appeared, had increased to 0.4 grades for the cohort reaching school age in the late 1930's. The increasingly favorable position of males with respect to educational attainment also is revealed by a narrowing of the male deficit of elementary and secondary graduates and a widening of the male excess of college graduates (Table 17).

Continuation between successive grade levels in the elementary system and at the point of transition into the secondary system has remained relatively more frequent for females than for males, although the trend toward convergence in the respective continuation ratios is clear. Within the secondary level, the continuation ratios have typically, but by no means consistently, been higher for females than for males. Possibly a reversal in the direction of the sex differential with respect to continuation between these grade levels will be confirmed when the series can be extended forward in time. Continuation at the point of transition from the secondary system into the institutions of higher education and between successive levels in the colleges and universities has consistently been more frequent for males than for females, and the sex difference has tended to widen over time (Table 18).

Comparisons with respect to educational attainment between males and their female age-mates have a special property which will be absent in comparisons between most other subpopulations. The sex ratio at birth and in childhood is essentially invariant among families of high and low social status, urban and rural families, families with few and many children, minority-group and majority-group families. Differences in the composition of the male and female subpopulations with respect to such background characteristics or in their educational opportunities, at least in the sense of presence of school facilities, cannot be the source of the sex differential in schooling. This is not to say that the sex differential in schooling cannot vary among social-origin strata, of course.

A very few comparisons can be made between males and their female age-mates in the same social-origin stratum. The data for males derive from their reports in the March, 1962, Current Population Survey and its supplement, "Occupational Changes in a Generation." The data for females are based on the reports made by married men included in the survey about their wives.[21] Each survey respondent was asked the number of grades he had completed, the number of brothers and sisters he had had, and what kind of job had been held by the head of the family in which he was living at age sixteen. If the respondent was married, he was asked to report the same items of information for his wife.

The study design and the specification of tabulations now available result in some slippage in the comparisons between the schooling of

TABLE 17. MEASURES OF SCHOOLING RECEIVED FOR COHORTS AGE SIX BETWEEN 1906 AND 1945, BY SEX

Year cohort age six	Mean grades completed		Percentage completing					
			Grade 16		Grade 12		Grade 8	
	Males	Females	Males	Females	Males	Females	Males	Females
1906–1910	8.8	9.1	7.0	5.4	26.1	30.7	68.1	72.7
1911–1915	9.4	9.7	8.2	6.5	32.6	37.2	74.2	78.3
1916–1920	9.9	10.1	8.6	6.2	38.9	42.3	78.3	82.0
1921–1925	10.5	10.5	10.0	6.2	47.1	49.7	83.1	86.0
1926–1930	10.9	10.8	13.0	6.2	52.8	56.5	85.7	88.5
1931–1935	11.1	11.0	14.7	7.3	53.4	58.0	86.9	90.1
1936–1940[a]	11.8	11.4	18.5	9.3	66.5	64.8	90.0	92.6
1941–1945[a]	—[b]	—[b]	—[b]	—[b]	70.5	70.1	93.2	94.9

[a] Educational attainment for the two most recent cohorts probably is overstated relative to attainment for earlier cohorts because of differences in the source survey operations.
[b] Ultimate attainment cannot yet be evaluated.

SOURCE: *U.S. Census of Population: 1960*, vol. I, part 1, Table 173 for cohorts 1906–1935; *Current Population Reports*, Series P-20, No. 158, December, 1966, Table 4 for cohorts 1936–1945.

TABLE 18. CONTINUATION RATIO BETWEEN SUCCESSIVE GRADES PER 1,000 COMPLETING LOWER GRADE FOR COHORTS AGE SIX BETWEEN 1906 AND 1944, BY SEX

Year cohort age six, and sex	Grades													
	0–1	1–3	3–5	5–7	7–8	8–9	9–10	10–11	11–12	12–13	13–14	14–15	15–16	16–17
1906–1910														
Male	974	976	930	880	876	631	855	820	866	526	824	732	842	468
Female	977	983	944	893	897	672	866	827	877	452	774	646	776	349
1911–1915														
Male	982	981	947	905	898	708	868	828	862	490	823	738	844	492
Female	986	988	960	916	914	737	878	834	878	428	783	678	767	349
1916–1920														
Male	987	984	957	921	914	762	883	847	871	434	818	734	849	503
Female	990	990	970	931	926	782	886	845	882	360	769	682	772	345
1921–1925														
Male	990	987	966	940	936	825	901	867	880	410	822	734	856	486
Female	992	992	976	948	944	836	901	865	886	310	751	683	785	314
1926–1930														
Male	991	989	972	948	948	864	912	878	890	438	836	769	876	470
Female	993	993	980	957	956	882	918	882	894	291	729	669	778	288
1931–1935														
Male	992	991	976	954	950	875	902	872	892	475	845	792	865[a]	447[b]
Female	994	994	984	963	961	901	915	878	889[a]	306	754	701	775	251
1936–1940														
Male	992	992	981	962	960	901	918	896	903[b]	459[a]	825[a]	782[b]	819[c]	421[c]
Female	994	995	988	971	968	920	920	886	895[a]	307	756	715	760	213
1942														
Male	991	993	984	967	964	917	919	898	848[c]	426[b]	770[c]	733[c]	732[c]	308[c]
Female	995	996	991	977	975	935	925	891	899	321	749	711	714[a]	128[a]
1944														
Male	994	995	988	973	970	928	922	897[a]	886[c]	416[c]	722[c]	531[c]	168[c]	167[a]
Female	995	997	992	982	978	944	930	896	890[c]	334[a]	727[b]	571[c]	211[c]	76

[a] 0.50 to 0.99 per cent of cohort enrolled in higher grades in 1960.
[b] 1.00 to 1.49 per cent of cohort enrolled in higher grade in 1960.
[c] 1.50 or more per cent of cohort enrolled in higher grade in 1960.

males and the schooling of their female age-mates in the same social-origin stratum that can be reported here (Table 19). The match is close enough to make the comparisons substantively interesting, however. Equally important, the comparisons illustrate the feasibility of reconstructing past differentials in schooling from the retrospective reports of persons still living. The possibility that the school experience of the cohort will not be reflected faithfully in the retrospective reports of survivors increases as the cohort ages. Evaluations of data quality undertaken as part of the original study suggest that these data are adequate for the purpose to which they are put here, however.

The increasingly favorable position of males vis-à-vis females with respect to educational attainment is a noteworthy trend not only for the American population as a whole, but also for the subgroups examined here—persons reared in small families, in large families, in nonfarm families, and in farm families. The direction of the sex differential at the first observation, the cohort reaching school age between 1906 and 1920, was not constant over subgroups or origin strata, however. The mean grades completed by males with no more than three siblings or by males living in a family headed by a nonfarm worker was slightly greater than the mean attainment of their female age-mates in the same origin stratum. The disparity in attainment by sex has become greater for more recent cohorts. In contrast, males reared in large families or in farm families were completing substantially fewer grades than their female age-mates in the same origin stratum at the initial observation. The difference in attainment by sex for these groups has become less for the cohorts reaching school age in the 1920's and the 1930's.

In each stratum, a differential favoring females is detectable with respect to continuation through the elementary and secondary systems. At higher levels of education, the continuation ratios are higher for males than for females, however. Although the direction of these differentials is constant over origin strata, the magnitude is variable. The differential favoring females at the lower levels of schooling is less pronounced for cohort members from small or nonfarm families than for cohort members from large or farm families. The differential favoring males at the higher levels of schooling, on the other hand, is more pronounced for the cohort members from small or nonfarm families.

Two pieces of evidence can be offered to support the contention that past differentials can be inferred from retrospective reports of cohort survivors. The first is an estimate of mean school years at-

TABLE 19. MEASURES OF SCHOOLING RECEIVED FOR COHORTS AGE SIX BETWEEN 1906 AND 1940, BY SEX AND NUMBER OF SIBLINGS OR OCCUPATION OF FAMILY HEAD

Origin stratum, year cohort age six and sex	Mean grades completed	Percentage completing grade			Continuation ratio between grades per 1,000 completing lower grade					
		8	12	16	0–5	5–8	8–9	9–12	12–13	13–16
Three or fewer siblings										
1906–1920										
Male	11.1	87.1	53.1	14.8	955	912	838	727	507	551
Female[a]	11.0	89.2	55.8	10.0	965	925	829	754	445	404
1921–1930										
Male	12.0	91.5	68.0	20.8	973	941	913	814	501	610
Female[a]	11.8	95.8	71.4	10.0	989	969	915	814	336	417
1931–1940										
Male	12.6	94.8	74.3	24.7	984	963	950	826	520	639
Female	12.1	96.6	76.5	12.7	988	978	964	821	359	462
Four or more siblings										
1906–1920										
Male	8.9	70.6	27.8	5.5	882	801	661	595	376	532
Female[a]	9.5	78.6	35.4	4.2	948	829	709	635	297	398
1921–30										
Male	9.9	80.9	41.5	5.3	928	872	799	641	314	407
Female[a]	10.4	87.5	49.3	4.0	964	908	817	689	226	356
1931–1940										
Male	10.6	86.2	48.8	8.3	955	903	858	659	360	475
Female	10.8	91.5	54.1	4.7	981	933	862	686	234	373

Nonfarm family head										
1906–1920										
Male	10.9	86.1	48.8	13.4	966	891	816	695	494	556
Female[a]	10.7	89.4	51.1	8.1	979	913	798	717	371	430
1921–1930										
Male	11.7	91.3	64.0	16.9	972	939	906	773	454	580
Female[a]	11.5	94.4	66.5	8.5	986	957	914	770	309	413
1931–1940										
Male	12.3	95.1	70.0	21.6	985	966	939	783	503	613
Female	11.9	96.4	72.3	11.1	991	973	950	790	320	478
Farm family head										
1906–1920										
Male	8.3	65.8	22.9	3.5	852	773	591	589	321	469
Female[a]	9.4	74.2	34.9	4.9	920	806	693	680	413	342
1921–1930										
Male	9.5	75.8	37.0	5.3	905	837	737	663	325	441
Female[a]	10.2	86.0	48.7	3.7	961	895	773	732	240	318
1931–1940										
Male	10.1	81.0	45.4	6.1	933	868	814	689	309	432
Female	10.5	88.2	52.1	4.8	966	913	815	725	269	342

[a] Nonwhite females age six in 1921–1925 included in 1906–1920 cohort.

NOTE: Male cohorts include only natives of the United States; female cohorts include only women married to a male between the ages of 20 and 64 in 1962.

SOURCE: Special tabulations from March, 1962, Current Population Survey and supplement thereto, "Occupation Changes in a Generation," conducted by the U.S. Bureau of the Census.

tended by members of a cohort who entered school around 1930. Cumulating school-attendance rates by single year of age and sex as reported in the 1930 census through age thirteen and as reported in the 1940 census from ages fourteen through twenty-four for the non-farm population yields means of 12.2 school years attended for males and 11.8 school years attended for females. Cumulation of the corresponding school-attendance rates for the farm population yields means of 10.3 years for males and 10.6 years for females. The estimates compare quite satisfactorily with the measures of mean grades completed by the cohort reaching school age in the 1930's which were derived from the retrospective reports of survivors (reported in Table 19).

The second, and substantively more interesting, piece of evidence is the sex differential in attainment for sixteen-year-olds living in non-farm and farm families, respectively, at the time of the 1960 census (Table 20). By this age, 93.6 per cent of the nonfarm males had com-

TABLE 20. PERCENTAGE DISTRIBUTION BY ENROLLMENT STATUS AND GRADES COMPLETED, FOR PERSONS AGE 16 AT OPENING OF 1959–1960 SCHOOL YEAR BY SEX AND FAMILY HEAD'S OCCUPATION

Stratum of origin and sex	Not enrolled by grades completed					Enrolled by grades completed				
	0–6	7	8	9–10	11+	0–6	7	8	9–10	11+
Nonfarm family head										
Male	1.5	1.3	2.9	5.3	3.4	2.0	1.5	4.4	59.6	18.0
Female	1.1	0.9	2.0	5.2	3.2	1.5	1.5	2.6	60.0	22.0
Farm family head										
Male	5.5	7.6	5.5	6.2	2.1	5.5	4.1	4.8	47.6	11.0
Female	2.5	2.5	5.0	3.3	3.3	1.7	1.7	4.1	56.2	19.8

SOURCE: Special tabulations based on .001 sample of records from the 1960 Census of Population.

pleted the eighth grade and 3.5 per cent continued to attend elementary school. The corresponding proportions for nonfarm females were 95.0 and 3.0 per cent. The percentage of elementary graduates probably will be something less than one point higher for females than for males when all schooling is completed. The excess of female elementary graduates has been reported as 0.7, 3.1, and 3.3 percentage points for nonfarm-reared members of successively older cohorts. Of the male sixteen-year-olds living in farm families, 77.2 per cent had completed eighth grade and 9.6 per cent continued to attend elementary school. The corresponding proportions for females were 91.7 and 3.4. If the youngsters attending elementary school ultimately complete eighth grade, the percentage of elementary graduates will be 8.3 points higher for females than for males. The excess of female elementary graduates has been reported as 7.2, 10.2, and 8.4 percentage points for farm-reared members of successively older cohorts.

Family Size

Not only does the direction of the sex differential in schooling differ between cohort members who grew up in small families and their age-mates who grew up in large families; family size itself has a very substantial influence on the amount of schooling received for both males and females. The number of grades completed is related negatively to the number of siblings. The female with no more than one sibling completes an average of two grades more than the female with at least seven siblings (Table 21). The effect of family size on schooling is even more pronounced for males. The male with no more than one sibling completes an average of three grades more than the male with at least seven siblings (Table 22). Increases in mean schooling between members of the cohort reaching school age in 1906–1920 and the cohort reaching school age in 1931–1940 amounted to about a grade for females in each family-size stratum and a grade and a half for males in each stratum.

Although the sample of respondents who provided the information summarized here was large by usual standards, it is not sufficiently large to subclassify respondents into both detailed birth cohorts and detailed origin strata and, then, to measure the educational attainment of each subclass. In an earlier report on these data, it was assumed that the relation of the number of grades completed to the number of siblings could be described adequately with linear regression techniques. This assumption permitted a finer subclassification by birth cohort, although it ruled out the possibility of exploring potentially interesting details of the educational distribution of youth in a particular origin stratum. Results of the regression analyses suggested that the family-size effect had been essentially constant for some decades. The regression coefficient measuring the change in mean grades completed associated with an increase of one in the number of siblings fluctuated only between −.32 and −.42 for seven successive birth cohorts of native white males reaching the age of six between 1906–1910 and 1936–1940.[22]

TABLE 21. MEASURES OF SCHOOLING RECEIVED BY FEMALES AGE SIX BETWEEN 1906 AND 1940, BY NUMBER OF SIBLINGS

Year cohort age six and number of siblings[a]	Percentage distribution	Mean grades completed	Percentage completing grade			Continuation ratio between grades per 1,000 completing lower grade					
			8	12	16	0–5	5–8	8–9	9–12	12–13	13–16
1906–1920[a]											
0	5.5	11.4	86.4	59.2	13.2	979	883	871	786	592	—[b]
1	9.8	11.4	91.1	63.4	11.4	968	942	865	805	445	402
2	13.4	11.0	90.6	55.0	10.6	966	938	808	751	452	425
3	12.9	10.5	87.6	49.3	7.1	956	917	807	697	361	—[b]
4	11.1	10.2	86.1	42.1	5.0	975	883	749	652	329	—[b]
5 or 6	20.5	9.7	79.9	38.2	4.3	954	838	720	664	292	—[b]
7 or more	26.7	9.1	74.3	30.4	3.7	931	798	681	600	283	—[b]
1921–1930[a]											
0	7.3	11.9	96.3	74.5	11.1	986	977	929	832	371	—[b]
1	13.0	12.4	97.5	79.7	14.4	994	981	954	856	405	447
2	15.9	11.5	95.1	66.5	8.1	990	960	880	795	300	404
3	13.3	11.4	94.7	67.3	7.4	983	963	910	781	275	—[b]
4	12.1	10.9	92.1	59.2	5.3	986	933	843	764	247	—[b]
5 or 6	16.7	10.4	87.3	50.1	3.5	963	906	856	671	208	—[b]
7 or more	21.6	10.0	85.3	43.0	3.6	953	895	770	655	226	—[b]
1931–1940											
0	7.9	12.5	97.3	79.7	19.4	992	980	969	845	450	542
1	17.9	12.4	98.0	81.5	15.2	991	989	975	854	388	480
2	16.3	11.9	95.8	73.3	11.6	985	972	951	804	340	467
3	13.6	11.6	95.4	71.8	6.8	984	969	962	782	280	337
4	10.6	11.5	95.0	66.6	8.5	983	966	913	767	291	—[b]
5 or 6	15.0	11.1	93.2	57.1	6.0	988	944	884	693	296	—[b]
7 or more	18.7	10.1	88.2	44.8	1.5	974	906	813	624	122	—[b]

[a] Nonwhite females age six in 1921–1925 included in 1906–1920 cohort.
[b] Base fewer than 100 sample cases.

NOTE: Cohorts include only women married to a male between the ages of 20 and 64 in 1962.
SOURCE: Special tabulations from March, 1962, Current Population Survey and supplement thereto, "Occupation Changes in a Generation," conducted by the U.S. Bureau of the Census.

TABLE 22. MEASURES OF SCHOOLING RECEIVED BY NATIVE MALES AGE SIX BETWEEN 1906 AND 1940, BY NUMBER OF SIBLINGS

Year cohort age six and number of siblings	Percentage distribution	Mean grades completed	Percentage completing grade			Continuation ratio between grades per 1,000 completing lower grade					
			8	12	16	0–5	5–8	8–9	9–12	12–13	13–16
1906–1920											
0	5.0	11.7	89.6	60.7	18.3	979	916	903	750	528	—[a]
1	9.4	11.6	88.4	60.8	19.8	951	930	877	785	555	587
2	12.6	11.3	89.0	55.4	15.0	964	924	848	733	535	506
3	12.7	10.2	83.2	42.1	9.7	940	885	769	658	410	559
4	11.8	9.7	76.7	37.6	8.5	902	850	771	637	420	—[a]
5 or 6	19.7	9.3	75.2	30.8	5.8	908	828	695	588	360	522
7 or more	28.7	8.3	65.0	21.6	4.2	856	759	580	574	359	536
1921–1930											
0	6.2	12.5	91.6	75.4	25.2	966	948	917	898	582	574
1	12.6	12.7	94.3	74.9	27.2	987	955	945	841	557	653
2	14.3	12.1	94.8	67.4	20.0	989	959	891	799	472	629
3	15.1	11.1	86.1	59.8	14.4	948	908	907	765	434	555
4	11.7	10.8	89.1	51.1	8.2	957	931	856	670	397	404
5 or 6	17.0	10.1	83.9	44.6	5.5	936	895	815	652	303	410
7 or more	23.0	9.3	74.7	34.3	3.7	908	822	751	612	262	—[a]
1931–1940											
0	7.7	12.9	95.9	78.6	27.8	989	970	959	854	533	665
1	16.1	13.1	96.5	79.9	30.4	988	977	956	866	576	661
2	16.7	12.4	95.0	73.1	22.1	986	964	963	799	520	581
3	13.2	11.8	91.8	66.6	19.2	975	941	918	791	429	673
4	10.8	11.5	91.4	63.1	11.6	980	933	898	768	368	500
5 or 6	14.9	10.9	89.2	51.5	9.0	978	913	879	657	386	452
7 or more	20.6	9.9	81.4	39.3	6.2	926	878	818	590	328	478

[a] Base fewer than 100 sample cases.

SOURCE: Special tabulations from March, 1962, Current Population Survey and supplement thereto, "Occupation Changes in a Generation," conducted by the U.S. Bureau of the Census.

The influence of family size appears more pronounced with respect to some measures of schooling than with respect to others, and the several measures of schooling suggest different answers about the presence and direction of trend in the family-size effect. For example, the series on percentage completing elementary school suggests diminution in the family-size effect; but the series on percentage completing college suggests that the influence of family size became more pronounced over time (Tables 21 and 22). Such apparent inconsistencies follow from a rise in average grades completed and a constant association between number of grades completed and number of siblings. More significant is the fact that whichever indicator of progress through the school system is selected, there is an average tendency for an increase in siblings to coincide with a decrease in educational attainment.

Intuitively, it is clear that there is overlap between family size and other background factors which are presumed to influence progress through the schools. For example, youth with many siblings are more likely to grow up in a family whose head is poorly educated than are youth with few siblings; or youth with many siblings are relatively more likely to grow up in a rural area. Some, but by no means all, of the family-size effect arises from the association of family size with other background characteristics. When six other background characteristics have been "held constant" statistically, the difference in mean grades completed between males with no more than one sibling and their age-mates with at least seven siblings is found to be about two grades (Table 23). By way of comparison, the gross or observed difference reported earlier was about three grades.

The regression coefficients describing the relation of grades completed to siblings implied, on the average, a decrease of just over 0.3 grades with each additional sibling. The slope of a line fitted, on the criterion of least squares, to the adjusted means can serve as a counterpart to the regression coefficient. The slope takes on values in the range of $-.15$ to $-.23$ for seven successive birth cohorts of native white males reaching the age of six between 1906–1910 and 1936–1940. Each additional sibling, then, results in a decrease of about 0.2 grades net of the effects of the six other background characteristics.[23]

Education of Family Head

The male whose family head had attended college received about five years more schooling than his male age-mate who grew up in a

TABLE 23. MEAN GRADES COMPLETED BY NATIVE WHITE MALES AGE SIX BETWEEN 1906 AND 1940, BY NUMBER OF SIBLINGS, OBSERVED AND ADJUSTED FOR OTHER BACKGROUND CHARACTERISTICS

Year cohort age six and statistic	Number of siblings						
	0	1	2	3	4	5 or 6	7 or more
1906–1910							
Observed	—[b]	11.1	11.4	9.8	8.5	8.8	8.5
Adjusted[a]	—[b]	10.5	10.8	9.5	8.8	9.0	8.9
1911–1915							
Observed	—[b]	11.9	11.2	10.2	10.7	9.7	8.5
Adjusted	—[b]	11.1	10.6	10.0	10.5	9.9	9.2
1916–1920							
Observed	—[b]	12.3	11.8	11.1	10.2	9.9	9.1
Adjusted	—[b]	11.3	11.2	11.0	10.3	10.3	9.9
1921–1925							
Observed	12.6	12.4	12.1	11.6	11.0	10.3	9.7
Adjusted	12.4	11.7	11.6	11.2	11.3	10.6	10.3
1926–1930							
Observed	13.1	13.2	12.4	11.4	11.3	10.5	9.6
Adjusted	12.5	12.2	12.0	11.4	11.4	11.0	10.2
1931–1935							
Observed	13.0	13.0	12.4	12.0	11.7	10.9	10.2
Adjusted	12.3	12.5	12.0	12.0	11.8	11.3	11.0
1936–1940							
Observed	13.5	13.5	12.8	11.8	11.6	11.3	10.0
Adjusted	12.8	12.8	12.4	11.7	11.9	11.7	10.9

[a] Adjusted for differences in composition by family type, family head's education and occupation, ethnic status, type of school attended, and region and rural-urban status of community of residence as a youth through a multiple-classification analysis.

[b] Base fewer than 100 sample cases.

SOURCE: Special tabulations from March, 1962, Current Population Survey and supplement thereto, "Occupation Changes in a Generation," conducted by the U.S. Bureau of the Census.

family headed by a functional illiterate, irrespective of whether he was born in the first decade of this century or in the fourth decade. The influence of the family head's education on schooling appears more pronounced with respect to some measures of schooling than with respect to others, but an average tendency for an increase in the youth's schooling to coincide with an increase in the number of grades completed by the head of his family is unambiguous (Table 24).

A recurring feature in the pattern of continuation ratios perhaps should be singled out for comment. The number of grades completed by the head of the family apparently takes on special signifi-

TABLE 24. MEASURES OF SCHOOLING RECEIVED BY NATIVE MALES AGE SIX BETWEEN 1906 AND 1940, BY GRADES COMPLETED BY THE FAMILY HEAD

Year cohort age six and grades completed by head	Percentage distribution	Mean grades completed	Percentage completing grade			Continuation ratio between grades per 1,000 completing lower grade					
			8	12	16	0–5	5–8	8–9	9–12	12–13	13–16
1906–1920											
16 or more	3.8	13.8	96.2	81.2	40.0	988	975	951	888	803	613
13 to 15	3.4	12.5	96.1	65.2	25.6	997	964	907	748	—a	—a
12	10.4	12.1	94.5	69.2	17.4	986	958	900	814	493	511
9 to 11	7.2	10.9	88.7	49.3	11.5	972	913	836	664	489	—a
8	29.1	10.3	88.2	40.4	8.6	976	905	717	639	399	530
5 to 7	21.3	9.5	74.1	34.0	6.9	935	792	715	642	371	550
4 or fewer	25.0	7.8	57.7	20.2	4.1	787	732	630	555	354	—a
1921–1930											
16 or more	4.5	15.3	99.5	95.6	61.7	995	1000	1000	960	834	774
13 to 15	4.5	13.9	97.9	89.3	37.4	995	984	988	923	699	599
12	12.2	12.7	96.1	78.1	22.7	990	971	947	859	509	572
9 to 11	8.7	11.9	93.9	67.4	15.1	984	954	933	769	406	—a
8	27.5	11.0	92.2	54.9	8.6	970	951	838	710	341	462
5 to 7	22.1	10.5	83.3	47.6	8.9	951	876	846	676	359	521
4 or fewer	20.6	9.3	70.9	38.8	5.6	871	814	780	702	347	417
1931–1940											
16 or more	4.4	15.3	100.0	94.1	63.4	1000	1000	976	964	886	761
13 to 15	5.2	14.3	98.8	90.5	44.3	996	992	994	922	762	642
12	14.4	13.0	97.5	84.3	24.6	990	985	983	880	518	564
9 to 11	13.8	12.1	94.1	69.8	19.1	976	965	956	776	479	572
8	27.9	11.7	94.3	65.5	15.1	975	967	896	775	377	613
5 to 7	19.4	11.0	89.4	53.4	9.6	977	915	867	688	367	490
4 or fewer	14.9	9.8	78.2	37.4	6.2	937	834	822	581	349	—a

a Base fewer than 100 sample cases.

SOURCE: Special tabulations from March, 1962, Current Population Survey and supplement thereto, "Occupation Changes in a Generation," conducted by the U.S. Bureau of the Census.

cance as the minimum schooling required by or for the youth. The continuation ratio between any given pair of grades tends to decrease between successively lower origin strata defined by the family head's educational attainment. An unusually sharp drop in the ratio tends to occur between the stratum for which continuation implies attainment equal to that of the family head and the next lower stratum. For example, males from families whose heads terminated their schooling after the ninth grade are much more likely to continue between the eighth and ninth grades than are their male age-mates whose family heads left school upon completing the eighth grade. The proportion of males continuing from ninth through twelfth grade is substantially higher for the group whose family heads had completed twelfth grade than for the group whose family heads left the secondary system before completion.

The influence of family head's education on schooling also can be detected in the differential educational attainment of children of a given age. At the time of the 1960 census, for example, differentials by head's education with respect to progress in the school system were pronounced among youth who had been sixteen years old at the opening of the 1959–1960 school year. Fewer than 1 per cent of the males whose family head had attended college had left school with no more than an elementary education, in contrast to a fifth of their male age-mates whose family head had completed fewer than eight grades. In the group whose family head had attended college, 28 per cent were entering their senior year of high school or beginning college; only 6 per cent of the group whose family head had completed fewer than eight grades had progressed equally far through the school system. The rapidity with which females progress through the school system also varies directly with the educational attainment of the family head, although the differentials are somewhat less sharp than those observed for males (Table 25).

When allowance is made for the overlap between the family head's educational attainment and other background factors that influence a youth's schooling, the effect of family head's education is reduced, but by no means eliminated. The regression coefficients describing the relation of grades completed by the respondent to grades completed by his family head range from .39 to .42 over seven cohorts of native white males reaching age six between 1906–1910 and 1936–1940. After the mean number of grades completed by respondents in each origin stratum has been adjusted to "hold constant" six other background characteristics which influence schooling, sizable differences in

TABLE 25. PERCENTAGE DISTRIBUTION BY ENROLLMENT STATUS AND GRADES COMPLETED, FOR PERSONS AGE 16 AT OPENING OF 1959–1960 SCHOOL YEAR BY SEX AND GRADES COMPLETED BY THE FAMILY HEAD

Sex and grades completed by family head	Not enrolled, by grades completed					Enrolled, by grades completed				
	0–6	7	8	9–10	11+	0–6	7	8	9–10	11+
Male										
13 or more	0.0	0.0	0.5	0.5	2.0	1.0	0.5	2.0	65.3	28.2
12	0.0	0.7	1.3	3.7	3.3	1.0	0.0	1.3	67.3	21.3
9 to 11	1.8	1.8	2.9	7.5	3.6	0.7	1.1	4.6	57.1	18.9
8	1.2	1.2	4.9	4.0	2.8	2.8	0.8	8.5	59.1	14.6
7 or fewer	6.3	5.7	7.2	9.3	3.9	5.4	5.4	6.3	44.1	6.3
Female										
13 or more	0.6	0.6	0.6	1.7	1.1	1.1	0.6	1.1	67.4	25.3
12	1.1	0.0	0.7	3.4	3.4	1.1	0.7	3.4	59.7	26.5
9 to 11	0.0	0.0	1.6	5.0	3.8	1.9	1.3	1.3	60.9	24.3
8	1.1	0.4	2.8	6.4	4.9	0.7	1.1	2.8	59.0	20.8
7 or fewer	3.3	3.3	4.8	7.3	2.7	2.4	3.0	6.0	53.5	13.6

SOURCE: Special tabulations based on .001 sample of records from the 1960 Census of Population.

attainment by head's education remain. The slope of a line fitted, on the criterion of least squares, to the adjusted means takes on values in the range of .18 to .25 for the seven cohorts. The observed increase of 0.4 grades in respondent's educational attainment for each incremental grade completed by the family head is reduced, then, to an increase of about 0.2 grades when allowance has been made for the overlap in background characteristics. There is no evidence of trend in the extent to which the educational attainment of the family head influences the attainment of the respondent.

Other Background Indicators

The influences on schooling of not only number of siblings and education of the family head, but also the head's occupation, the presence of both parents in the family home, ethnic status, the type of school attended, and the region and rural-urban status of the community of residence have been examined for the several birth cohorts of adult native males. The substantive findings are not recapitulated here, inasmuch as they have been reported at some length elsewhere.[24] About a third of the variance in educational attainment for each cohort and for both whites and nonwhites can be attributed to the additive effects of the seven background indicators. Social background, as indexed by these seven characteristics, has become neither more nor less important as a determinant of the amount of schooling received.

Father's occupation and the region and rural-urban status of the community of residence, as well as family size and the education of the father, also have been found to influence the progression of children through the school system. Their effects on both enrollment status and the number of grades completed at a given age have been documented for teen-age boys with statistics from the 1960 census.[25] The direction in which these background characteristics influence educational attainment is the same for the teen-agers and for the older men. Whether the magnitudes of their effects will be the same when the teen-agers have completed all schooling remains unknown, of course.

Perhaps the most important question left unanswered by these analyses is how much of the effect of social background on schooling should be attributed to overlap between background and intelligence rather than to background as such. Even if the issue of possible contamination of measures of intelligence by background is set aside, evidence on the relation between measured intelligence and social background is scant. One recent set of estimates, based on a sifting of the available evidence about the relations among educational attainment, number of siblings, father's education, father's occupation, and measured intelligence, implies that the three background indicators and ability had substantial independent effects on the amount of schooling completed by white males who reached school age around 1940. About two-fifths of variance in attainment can be attributed to the additive effects of the three background characteristics and measured intelligence. Social background alone accounts for 15 per cent of the variance in grades completed; intelligence as measured early in life alone accounts for 16 per cent of the variance; and 11 per cent of the variance must be allocated to the joint effects of background and intelligence.[26]

Unfortunately, there is no prospect that better estimates of the relations among ultimate educational attainment, social background, and intelligence measured early in life will become available in this century, let alone that it will be possible to determine whether the importance of background relative to intelligence has been changing over time. One opportunity to establish a firm benchmark was lost within the past few years. As part of the Civil Rights Act of 1964, Congress instructed the Commissioner of Education to undertake a survey "concerning the lack of availability of equal educational opportunities for individuals by reason of race, color, religion, or national origin in public educational institutions." As part of the survey operation, about 76,000 first-graders were administered standard achievement tests within a month of the opening of the 1965–1966 school year. The ability measurements antecede regular schooling for these children, who can, moreover, be subclassified on the basis of kindergarten attendance. Indicators of social background, such as the type of family and the education of the family head, also were obtained for each student. The name of the student was not made a part of the basic record, however. As a consequence, any chance of resurveying these individuals to obtain estimates of the influence of their background and ability at the point of school entry on their subsequent progress through the schools has been eliminated.[27]

Color

The public interest in the differential in schooling that obtains between so-called white Americans and the racial minorities is attested by the section calling for a survey of educational opportunities in the Civil Rights Act of 1964. That a differential in favor of whites exists with respect to educational attainment is well-known, of course. As indexed by mean grades completed, the white-nonwhite differential in

TABLE 26. MEASURES OF SCHOOLING RECEIVED FOR
COHORTS AGE SIX BETWEEN 1906 AND 1945,
BY SEX AND COLOR

	Mean grades completed		Percentage completing							
			Grade 16		Grade 12		Grade 8	
Sex and year cohort age six	White	Non-white	White	Non-white	White	Non-white	White	Non-white
Male								
1906–1910	9.1	5.8	7.5	1.9	27.8	9.8	71.9	32.7
1911–1915	9.8	6.4	8.8	2.4	34.7	12.4	77.9	38.2
1916–1920	10.2	7.0	9.2	2.9	41.4	15.5	82.0	44.3
1921–1925	10.8	7.8	10.7	3.6	49.9	21.4	86.3	53.5
1926–1930	11.2	8.5	14.0	4.5	55.8	26.7	88.4	62.2
1931–1935	11.4	9.0	15.8	5.5	56.2	29.8	89.2	67.7
1936–1940[b]	12.0	10.2	19.4	10.9	69.3	43.8	91.8	75.9
1941–1945[b]	—[a]	—[a]	—[a]	—[a]	72.7	53.4	94.1	86.0
Female								
1906–1910	9.4	6.5	5.7	2.3	32.7	11.5	76.4	38.7
1911–1915	10.0	7.2	6.8	3.1	39.5	14.8	81.7	46.0
1916–1920	10.3	7.7	6.5	3.2	45.1	17.7	85.3	52.3
1921–1925	10.7	8.3	6.5	3.7	52.8	23.2	89.0	60.4
1926–1930	11.0	9.1	6.5	4.2	59.8	30.3	91.0	68.8
1931–1935	11.2	9.6	7.6	4.8	61.1	35.2	92.0	75.8
1936–1940[b]	11.5	10.4	9.6	7.3	68.1	41.8	93.3	87.4
1941–1945[b]	—[a]	—[a]	—[a]	—[a]	72.8	51.3	95.8	88.7

[a] Ultimate attainment cannot yet be evaluated.
[b] Educational attainment for the two most recent cohorts probably is overstated relative to attainment for earlier cohorts because of differences in the source survey operations.

SOURCE: *U.S. Census of Population: 1960*, vol. I, part 1, Table 173 for cohorts 1906–1935; *Current Population Reports*, Series P-20, no. 158, December, 1966, Table 4, for cohorts 1936–1945.

attainment has narrowed appreciably over the past six decades; but there remains a difference of just under two grades for males and just over a grade for females in the most recent cohort whose schooling can be assumed essentially complete (Table 26).

Another way of expressing the white-nonwhite difference in schooling is in terms of the difference in birth year between cohorts of whites and nonwhites, respectively, who have attained the same level of schooling. The most recent cohort of nonwhites for whom a reading on ultimate educational attainment is available reached the age of six in the late 1930's and had been born in the years 1930–1935. The mean number of grades completed by this cohort, 10.2 for males and 10.4 for females, matches the attainment of the cohort of whites who reached the age of six in the late 1910's and had been born in the years 1910–1915. The attainment of nonwhites, then, lagged behind the attainment of whites by twenty years.

One interesting feature of the white-nonwhite difference in schooling is not captured by the difference in mean grades completed. Schooling is distributed with less equality among nonwhites than among whites, that is, the variability in grades completed is greater within the non-white population than in the white population. The lag in the attainment of nonwhites relative to that of whites, expressed as the difference in birth year between cohorts with like attainment, is substantially less with respect to the college-graduation rate than with respect to the elementary-completion rate. For example, the college-graduation rate for the nonwhite cohort reaching the age of six in the late 1930's (11 per cent) matches the rate for white males who reached the age of six in the early 1920's. The elementary-completion rate for the late-1930's cohort of nonwhites (76 per cent) matches the rate for white males who reached the age of six in the early 1910's, however. Implied is a lag of fifteen years with respect to the college-graduation rate, in contrast to a lag of twenty-five years with respect to the elementary-completion rate.

It has not been at the point of college entry nor within the institutions of higher education that the nonwhite, by comparison with his white age-mate, has been handicapped most severely in his progress through the school system. The sharpest differences between the continuation ratios for nonwhites and whites, respectively, have occurred at lower grade levels (Tables 27 and 28). For the cohort whose members reached the age of six between 1906 and 1910, for example, the deficit in the continuation ratio for nonwhites widened between successive grade levels to a maximum of twenty percentage points be-

TABLE 27. CONTINUATION RATIO BETWEEN SUCCESSIVE GRADES PER 1,000 COMPLETING LOWER GRADE FOR COHORTS OF MALES AGE SIX BETWEEN 1906 AND 1944, BY COLOR

Year cohort age six, and color	Grades													
	0– 1	1– 3	3– 5	5– 7	7– 8	8– 9	9– 10	10– 11	11– 12	12– 13	13– 14	14– 15	15– 16	16– 17
1906–1910														
White	982	985	946	893	881	633	857	822	868	528	824	734	843	468
Nonwhite	900	883	746	690	784	595	804	783	817	451	804	672	807	468
1911–1915														
White	988	989	961	918	903	712	871	831	864	492	824	740	844	493
Nonwhite	930	907	786	722	799	642	806	775	810	435	800	671	839	488
1916–1920														
White	991	991	970	935	920	766	887	850	874	436	819	735	850	503
Nonwhite	947	921	821	756	819	686	815	779	804	395	801	694	841	484
1921–1925														
White	993	992	977	952	943	830	905	871	883	412	824	735	858	486
Nonwhite	962	940	863	805	851	750	836	792	805	372	793	691	826	510
1926–1930														
White	993	993	980	959	955	870	917	884	896	442	838	772	878	468
Nonwhite	973	959	899	846	876	792	850	799	800	369	798	704	819	504
1931–1935														
White	993	994	983	962	956	880	906	878	899[a]	480	847	795	868[b]	446[b]
Nonwhite	980	968	920	870	892	820	853	794	794[a]	398	801	724	800	475[a]
1936–1940														
White	993	994	986	969	964	906	923	904	912[b]	465[a]	828[b]	786[b]	822[c]	421[c]
Nonwhite	984	977	940	901	914	859	871	814	801[b]	372	762[a]	698[a]	742[a]	409[b]
1942														
White	993	995	989	974	969	921	924	906[a]	908[c]	436[b]	775[c]	739[c]	737[c]	—[d]
Nonwhite	982	978	950	911	926	879	871[a]	817	790[c]	307[a]	696[b]	619[b]	613[b]	—[d]
1944														
White	994	996	991	979	974	933	927	906[a]	897[c]	426[c]	728[c]	535[c]	166[c]	—[d]
Nonwhite	989	986	962	926	933	889	872[a]	808[a]	775[c]	286[b]	614[c]	436[c]	238[c]	—[d]

[a] 0.50 to 0.99 per cent of cohort enrolled in higher grade in 1960. [b] 1.00 to 1.49 per cent of cohort enrolled in higher grade in 1960. [c] 1.50 or more per cent of cohort enrolled in higher grade in 1960. [d] Not calculated.

SOURCE: *U.S. Census of Population: 1960*, vol. I, part 1, Tables 168, 172, and 173.

TABLE 28. CONTINUATION RATIO BETWEEN SUCCESSIVE GRADES PER 1,000 COMPLETING LOWER GRADE FOR COHORTS OF FEMALES AGE SIX BETWEEN 1906 AND 1944, BY COLOR

Year cohort age six, and color	Grades													
	0–1	1–3	3–5	5–7	7–8	8–9	9–10	10–11	11–12	12–13	13–14	14–15	15–16	16–17
1906–1910														
White	982	988	958	908	904	676	870	830	879	452	773	645	774	200
Nonwhite	937	927	806	705	784	604	788	765	817	438	824	679	826	353
1911–1915														
White	989	992	971	931	921	742	883	838	881	428	781	677	764	348
Nonwhite	958	947	848	746	802	658	796	762	806	432	825	710	838	380
1916–1920														
White	992	994	979	945	935	788	891	849	886	359	767	680	768	343
Nonwhite	969	959	878	782	820	698	801	764	791	374	815	712	844	386
1921–1925														
White	994	995	984	960	952	843	907	871	892	308	749	682	782	309
Nonwhite	977	968	907	828	850	752	824	780	797	340	796	710	838	383
1926–1930														
White	994	995	986	967	964	889	924	889	901	290	726	667	774	282
Nonwhite	983	978	935	869	881	809	848	802	801	308	772	695	831	366
1931–1935														
White	995	996	988	971	968	908	921	885	898[a]	305	753	700	773	246
Nonwhite	986	986	957	902	904	845	861	805	793[a]	317	766	708	798	308
1936–1940														
White	995	996	990	977	974	926	926	894	905[a]	306	756	715	758	210
Nonwhite	988	989	970	929	927	876	873	814	800[a]	312	765	712	786	248
1942														
White	996	997	993	982	979	940	930	899	910[a]	324	750	713	716[a]	—[d]
Nonwhite	990	991	978	945	944	899	885	821	795[b]	286	729[a]	676[a]	683[a]	—[d]
1944														
White	996	997	994	985	982	949	935	904	901[c]	338[a]	732[b]	577[c]	206[c]	—[d]
Nonwhite	992	993	983	953	950	908	887	827[a]	791[c]	291[a]	665[b]	497[c]	278[c]	—[d]

[a] 0.50 to 0.99 per cent of cohort enrolled in higher grade in 1960.   [b] 1.00 to 1.49 per cent of cohort enrolled in higher grade in 1960.   [c] 1.50 or more per cent of cohort enrolled in higher grade in 1960.   [d] Not calculated.

SOURCE: *U.S. Census of Population: 1960*, vol. I, part 1, Tables 168, 172, and 173.

tween grades five and seven. For the cohort whose members reached the age of six between 1936 and 1940, the deficit in the continuation ratio for nonwhites widened between successive grade levels to a maximum of ten percentage points between grades eleven and twelve.

Among both the Southern-born and persons born in the North and West, the disadvantage of the nonwhite with respect to schooling has lessened over time (Table 29). Nonwhite males who had been born in the South and reached school age shortly after 1900 completed an average of 2.8 fewer grades than their Southern-born white age-mates, but the difference averaged only 2.1 grades among Southern-born males who reached school age in the early 1930's. Differences for the corresponding cohorts amounted to 1.8 and 1.1 grades, respectively, among males born in the North and West. Convergence of the attainment level of nonwhites with the attainment level of whites appears to have proceeded as rapidly, in absolute terms, in the South as in the rest of the nation, although the color differential remains substantially greater among the Southern-born. The word "appears" is used advisedly, for there is no certainty that schooling occurred in the region of birth or that it is progression through Southern and non-Southern school systems which is being contrasted.

The handicap of the Southern-born nonwhite relative to the white born in the South is markedly more pronounced than the handicap of the non-Southern nonwhite relative to the non-Southern white at the lower levels of schooling. In the Southern population, for example, the elementary-completion rate remained twenty percentage points lower for nonwhites than for whites in the cohort reaching school age in the early 1930's; but the color differential had nearly disappeared among members of the same cohort born outside the South. In contrast, the color differential with respect to the continuation of high-school graduates into the colleges or the rate of graduation among college entrants has been no greater in the South than in the rest of the nation.

Ultimate educational attainment cannot yet be evaluated for more recent birth cohorts. Distributions by enrollment status and grades completed as of 1960, however, provide a fairly sound basis for estimating the ultimate percentage of elementary-school graduates for cohorts reaching school age in the late 1940's (Table 30). Whereas among whites there exists a "high-school dropout" problem, there exists an "elementary-school dropout" problem among nonwhites. The elementary-school dropout may pose the more serious problem. Not only is he ill-equipped to participate effectively in the nation's economic

TABLE 29. MEASURES OF SCHOOLING RECEIVED FOR MALES AGE SIX BETWEEN 1901 AND 1935, BY COLOR AND REGION OF BIRTH

Region, year cohort age six, and color	Mean grades completed	Percentage completing grade			Continuation ratio between grades per 1,000 completing lower grade					
		8	12	16	0–5	5–8	8–9	9–12	12–13	13–16
South										
1901–1910										
White	8.1	57.5	21.3	5.1	832	691	647	572	528	454
Nonwhite	5.3	25.4	6.9	1.4	528	481	558	488	499	421
1911–1920										
White	8.9	66.5	29.8	6.3	887	750	746	602	449	470
Nonwhite	6.3	36.0	10.9	2.1	653	550	636	479	417	460
1921–1930										
White	9.9	75.5	42.0	9.5	920	820	831	670	429	526
Nonwhite	7.6	50.9	18.2	2.9	775	657	738	484	369	436
1931–1936										
White	10.4	79.8	46.3	12.1	940	850	856	677	472	553
Nonwhite	8.3	59.9	22.6	3.6	839	714	786	479	381	420
Non-South										
1901–1910										
White	9.5	77.8	29.2	7.9	959	811	613	612	536	506
Nonwhite	7.7	55.6	18.4	3.8	804	692	613	539	450	461
1911–1920										
White	10.5	87.1	42.5	10.2	981	888	744	656	459	525
Nonwhite	9.0	71.4	30.2	5.0	897	796	740	572	360	457
1921–1930										
White	11.4	93.4	58.4	13.6	988	945	860	726	423	552
Nonwhite	10.0	85.6	46.3	6.9	950	901	860	630	334	448
1931–1936										
White	11.8	94.5	61.2	17.4	989	955	893	726	477	596
Nonwhite	10.7	89.3	47.7	8.2	962	928	878	608	389	444

SOURCE: *U.S. Census of Population: 1960*, Subject Report PC(2)–5B, Table 3.

and social life, but he also lacks the habits and skills that would facilitate learning outside the classroom. Yet, perhaps as many as an eighth of the nonwhite males now reaching their majority have completed fewer than eight grades of formal schooling. A twelfth of the nonwhite females may have equally little education. In contrast, no more than 4 per cent of the young whites lack an elementary-school education. The problem of the elementary-school dropout continues to be especially acute in the South.

Information about the distribution of school leavers in each cohort by age and grade might illuminate the so-called dropout problem. To interpret the distributions by enrollment status and grades completed for successive birth-year cohorts as readings on a single cohort as it progresses through the schools is tempting. Differences between these distributions then would provide estimates of school leavers by age and grade. A few attempts at reconciling the age-grade distributions of school leavers implied by increments to the not-enrolled population with the distributions implied by decrements to the enrolled population demonstrate the futility of inferring a cohort's progress through the schools from such statistics, however. (The difficulty can be illustrated by reference to distributions for white females in the cohorts reaching age six in 1948 and 1949 which are reported in Table 30. The number of cohort members who were not enrolled in school and had completed at least twelve grades increased from seven to 62 per thousand in the course of the year. These school leavers, numbering 55 per thousand, must have been drawn from the group of cohort members who were in school and had completed at least eleven grades a year earlier; but the in-school group who had completed at least eleven grades a year earlier numbered only 48 per thousand.)

A confounding of the effect of race with the effect of region on schooling has been documented earlier. The effect of race also is confounded with the effects of other background characteristics; but there is, at present, no possibility of assessing trend in the racial differential in schooling within other background strata. The obstacle is one of numbers, or dollars.

In a survey covering a random sample of the national population, only some 10 per cent of the respondents will be members of America's racial minorities. To assess trend, the nonwhite respondents must be classified into several cohorts defined by year of birth. To assess trend for cohort members sharing a common background, each cohort must be subclassified into strata defined by background. Sampling ratios of about one in 500 are required to ensure minimally adequate

TABLE 30. PERCENTAGE DISTRIBUTION BY ENROLLMENT STATUS AND GRADES COMPLETED FOR COHORTS AGE SIX BETWEEN 1945 AND 1949, BY SEX, COLOR, AND REGION

Sex, year cohort age six, color, and region	Not enrolled, by grades completed								Enrolled, by grades completed					
	0-4	5-7	8	9	10	11	12	13+	0-7	8	9	10	11	12+
Male														
1945														
White	1.6	4.0	5.9	6.0	7.0	5.3	34.0	6.9	0.7	0.3	0.6	0.8	2.8	24.0
Nonwhite	5.1	11.6	8.3	8.5	10.2	8.5	25.0	3.4	1.8	0.7	1.1	2.0	4.5	9.3
1947														
White	1.1	3.4	4.6	5.0	5.5	4.2	20.0	0.7	1.6	0.9	2.0	6.0	24.5	20.5
Nonwhite	3.7	9.0	6.6	7.0	7.2	5.2	12.0	0.4	5.0	3.3	5.5	10.3	17.9	6.7
1948														
White	0.9	2.9	3.9	4.2	4.1	2.6	3.8	0.1	2.5	2.4	7.0	26.1	37.5	1.9
Nonwhite	3.2	7.8	5.2	5.2	4.8	2.9	3.2	0.1	8.5	6.9	12.1	20.1	18.7	1.3
1949														
White	0.9	2.6	2.9	2.6	2.2	1.0	0.4	0.0	5.4	8.8	28.2	41.2	3.6	0.2
Nonwhite	2.8	6.1	3.5	3.2	2.3	1.0	0.6	0.0	16.4	14.6	23.1	22.1	4.0	0.2
Female														
1945														
White	1.1	2.7	4.6	5.8	7.8	6.1	43.4	9.0	0.4	0.2	0.3	0.4	2.0	16.2
Nonwhite	2.8	7.9	7.4	8.3	11.1	9.9	30.6	5.1	1.1	0.4	0.9	1.1	3.6	9.6
1947														
White	0.8	2.2	3.6	4.7	6.3	5.0	29.3	1.1	1.1	0.6	1.1	3.3	20.8	20.0
Nonwhite	2.1	6.0	5.8	6.7	9.2	7.1	17.8	0.7	3.4	2.0	3.6	7.9	18.0	9.4
1948														
White	0.7	1.9	3.0	3.9	5.0	3.4	6.1	0.1	1.7	1.3	4.1	22.8	43.8	2.2
Nonwhite	1.8	5.4	5.0	5.6	6.3	4.2	5.0	0.1	5.3	4.6	9.5	20.7	24.1	2.3
1949														
White	0.7	1.7	2.4	3.0	3.2	1.3	0.7	0.0	3.4	5.0	24.7	48.9	4.7	0.1
Nonwhite	1.5	4.3	3.8	4.1	3.7	1.6	1.0	0.0	10.1	11.0	23.4	28.9	6.1	0.2

SOUTH

Male

1947

White	1.7	6.4	6.1	6.0	5.9	4.1	17.8	0.6	2.2	1.3	2.7	7.0	22.8	15.4
Nonwhite	4.8	11.8	7.0	6.7	6.3	4.1	9.4	0.3	6.1	3.9	6.3	10.9	16.9	5.5

Female

1947

White	1.2	4.4	5.2	6.3	7.2	5.3	23.0	1.0	1.6	0.9	1.5	4.1	21.6	16.4
Nonwhite	2.5	7.8	6.2	6.8	8.5	6.3	13.8	0.5	4.0	2.6	4.4	9.1	18.4	9.0

NON-SOUTH

Male

1947

White	0.9	2.0	4.0	4.5	5.3	4.2	21.0	0.8	1.3	0.8	1.7	5.5	25.2	22.8
Nonwhite	1.8	4.4	5.9	7.5	8.9	7.1	16.4	0.8	3.1	2.1	4.1	9.3	19.7	8.8

Female

1947

White	0.6	1.3	3.0	4.1	5.9	4.9	31.8	1.2	0.9	0.5	1.0	2.9	20.4	21.5
Nonwhite	1.5	3.1	5.0	6.6	10.2	8.3	24.2	1.3	2.2	1.2	2.5	5.9	17.5	10.3

SOURCE: *U.S. Census of Population: 1960*, vol. I, part 1, Tables 168, 172, 240; and *Reports by States*, Table 102.

663

numbers of adult nonwhite respondents for such analyses, but the sampling ratio for the Current Population Survey conducted by the Bureau of the Census, and regarded as large in scale, is on the order of one in 1,700. Still higher sampling ratios are needed when the study population is made up of young persons whose distribution by enrollment status and grades completed is changing rapidly with each advance of a year in age. The one in 1,000 sample of records from the 1960 Census of Population made available by the Bureau of the Census for special analyses proves grossly inadequate to establish a firm benchmark for the nation's youth.

In the absence of information about schooling and social background from sufficiently large numbers of minority-group respondents, differences in background must be "held constant" statistically to evaluate the effect of race as such on schooling. One such analysis made allowance for the difference between white and nonwhite males in their distributions with respect to four aspects of social background: the family type; education and occupation of the family head; and the number of siblings. The difference in educational attainment that remains when these four factors have been "held constant" has been identified as the effect of "color" although compounded in it are the effects of unmeasured aspects of social background as well as abilities and aspirations. The residual difference, or the effect of "color," is estimated to be about two grades for the cohort reaching school age before World War I and about one year for the cohort reaching school age in the 1930's (Table 31). The disadvantage of the nonwhite with respect to progress through the schools that accrues from his color as such appears to have lessened over time. The conclusion cannot be stated unequivocally because of both the hypothetical nature of a calculation in which whites and nonwhites are matched with respect to background and the substantial number of potentially important but unmeasured factors.

GRADES COMPLETED AS AN INDICATOR OF EDUCATION

Inquiry into the possible meanings of the concept of "education" is not likely to lead to an uniquely apt statistical indicator of that concept. Education, like unemployment, is an elusive concept. Both terms are common in usage, yet defy precise definition. It is somewhat instructive to review the problem of measuring unemployment as it has come

TABLE 31.   GRADES COMPLETED BY NATIVE WHITE AND
NONWHITE MALES REACHING AGE SIX BETWEEN 1906
AND 1940, WITH ALTERNATIVE ESTIMATES OF THE
RESPECTIVE EFFECTS OF FAMILY BACKGROUND
AND "COLOR" ON SCHOOLING

Statistic	Year cohort age six		
	1906–20	1921–30	1931–40
Mean grades completed by			
White males	10.1	11.2	11.9
Nonwhite males	6.6	8.1	9.9
Difference in means, white less nonwhite	3.5	3.1	2.0
Difference in means due to family type, education and occupation of head, and number of siblings			
Estimate A	1.4	1.1	1.2
Estimate B	1.5	0.9	1.2
Estimate C	1.6	1.4	0.9
Residual difference in means due to "color"			
Estimate A	2.1	2.0	0.8
Estimate B	2.0	1.2	0.8
Estimate C	1.9	1.7	1.1

Estimate A: Effect of color estimated as partial regression coefficient in the regression of grades completed on color, family type, education and occupation of head, and number of siblings for all males.

Estimate B: Effect of color estimated by using regression of grades completed on family type, education and occupation of head, and number of siblings for white males with mean background composition of nonwhite males.

Estimate C: Effect of color estimated by using regression of grades completed on family type, education and occupation of head, and number of siblings for nonwhite males with mean background composition of white males.

SOURCE: Duncan, Otis Dudley, "Discrimination against Negroes," *Annals of the American Academy of Political and Social Science,* vol. 371, May, 1967, Table 3, p. 101.

to be understood over the past several decades. The pithy statement of the problem which follows captures the essential points.

> . . . it is important to remember that there are no unique "right" defini-
> tions. The test of a definition of unemployment—or of anything else—
> is its usefulness. A number of different possible definitions might be
> about equally useful. What matters is to get a definition that accords
> reasonably well with the common understanding of the term and one
> that is applied consistently from time to time and from one part of the
> economy to another. Given this consistency, we can develop the experi-
> ence that tells us whether or not unemployment is serious.[28]

Can a definition of education in terms of grades completed square with the common understanding of the term "education"? Most usages would include the notion that education involves a command of some valuable body of skills and facts. The criterion of a valuable skill or fact might be that its transmission warrants expenditure of public monies. The institutionalized form of such transmission is the regular school system, and, hence, the school curriculum tends to define the most highly valued body of knowledge. The school system is graded, with the content of the curriculum of successively higher grades incorporating increasingly higher orders of skills and facts. Accordingly, the number of grades completed indexes the amount of the valuable knowledge that has been mastered.

The number of grades completed is an imperfect measure of education, even if the rather narrow conception of education outlined above is accepted. Learning can occur outside the classroom as well as inside it, and in-school learning varies among those passing through the same sequence of graded classrooms. On the other hand, the number of grades completed is an item of information that can be secured rather inexpensively; that is amenable to independent checks on accuracy; that is irreversible over time for an individual; that has an established history of collection on a mass basis. Considerations of these two types must be weighed one against the other in evaluating the utility of grades completed as an indicator of education.

Relevant to the point of variability in measured intellectual development among individuals who have completed the same grade is the survey of educational opportunities referred to earlier. The importance of the survey findings is that they not only document variability in measured achievement among children attending the same grade, but also reveal noteworthy differences in mean measured achievement among grade-mates who differ in background. Widely commented on has been the finding that the mean measured achievement of Negro children falls short of the measured achievement of their white grade-mates at each grade level surveyed. Also to be observed in the survey results are persistent differentials within racial groups by place of residence and by parental education, however. Residence in the nonmetropolitan South or low parental educational attainment, for example, is a distinct handicap to the child's intellectual development. There can be no doubt that mastery of the valuable skills and facts varies in systematic ways among children who have progressed equally far through the school system.

Moreover, the survey results suggest that out-of-school learning is facilitated by the intellectual skills acquired through formal schooling. Included in the battery of tests administered to the secondary-school students were not only verbal and nonverbal achievement tests, but also a general-information test which probed "areas likely to have become known through out-of-school rather than curriculum activities."[29] Among the practical arts covered were tools, automobiles, and building for males, and food, sewing, and decorating for females. Natural sciences were represented by questions on aeronautics and space, chemistry, and health; the humanities and arts by questions on literature, music, and art; and social science by questions on history, government, and public affairs. The coefficients of correlation (reported in the *Supplemental Appendix to the Survey* . . .) between scores on the verbal and nonverbal achievement tests and the general-information test for twelfth-graders are summarized below.

	White	Nonwhite
Verbal and nonverbal achievement	.52	.57
Verbal achievement and general information	.77	.78
Nonverbal achievement and general information	.50	.57

It can be argued that the paper-and-pencil character of the out-of-school learning test introduces a bias or is culture-bound, but effective participation in American society has precisely this bias.

Among the items of information collected for students covered by the educational-opportunities survey were parental education, the type of family, and the number of siblings. The associations of measured intellectual development or mastery of general information with these indicators of social background for grade-mates are not unlike the associations between number of grades completed and the social-background characteristics for older Americans (Table 32). These indicators of background can be shown to influence in a similar direction both the relative numbers enrolled and the mean number of grades completed by the enrolled among age-mates in the school-age population.[30]

Can patterned variability in achievement within grade and patterned variability in the number of grades completed be reconciled in such a way that grades completed adequately indexes the command of valuable knowledge on the part of adults? If overlap in achievement between the less able children in successive grades is not great and if, at each grade level, it is the children of lesser ability who become school leavers, the distribution of adults by grades completed will be a more or less faithful representation of their distribution by ability or

TABLE 32. COEFFICIENTS OF CORRELATION BETWEEN SELECTED "EDUCATION" MEASURES AND FAMILY BACKGROUND CHARACTERISTICS, FOR THREE GROUPS OF STUDENTS IN 1965 AND TWO BIRTH COHORTS OF NATIVE MALES IN 1962

Group and "education" measure	Parental education[a]		Family type[b]		Number of siblings[c]	
	White	Negro[d]	White	Negro[d]	White	Negro[d]
First-graders, 1965						
Verbal achievement	.24	.21	.05	.01	-.14	-.09
Nonverbal achievement	.30	.23	.06	.02	-.10	-.08
Sixth-graders, 1965						
Verbal achievement	.31	.22	.11	.10	-.14	-.12
Nonverbal achievement	.21	.19	.09	.07	-.06	-.07
Twelfth-graders, 1965						
Verbal achievement	.33	.26	.07	.04	-.17	-.23
Nonverbal achievement	.22	.21	.06	.07	-.10	-.16
General information	.30	.24	.08	.05	-.18	-.20
Males, 20–26 in 1962[e]						
Grades completed	.47	.36	.08	.02	-.40	-.26
Males, 27–61 in 1962						
Grades completed	.41	.37	.09	.07	-.34	-.16

[a] Grades completed by head of the family in which respondent lived at age 16 for native males.
[b] At age 16 for adult males.
[c] Ultimate number of siblings underestimated more seriously the younger the respondent.
[d] Nonwhite for adult males.
[e] Excludes an appreciable number of males in armed forces or institutions.

SOURCE: *Supplemental Appendix to the Survey on Equality of Educational Opportunity*, Government Printing Office, Washington, 1966, and Duncan, Beverly, *Family Factors and School Dropout: 1920–1960*, University of Michigan, Ann Arbor, 1965, Table 3–2.

command of the valued knowledge. The coefficient of correlation between measured mental development and the number of grades completed among adults probably is on the order of .6, an estimate influenced heavily by the relation of scores on the Armed Forces Qualification Test to grades completed among males called for military service. No appreciable difference can be detected in the closeness of the association among whites and that among nonwhites. In evaluating the strength of this association, it is germane to note the similarity with the association between scores on the verbal and nonverbal components of the achievement test administered to students as part of the educational-opportunities survey.

Although the achievement of white students exceeds the achievement of their nonwhite grade-mates, differential attrition by grade apparently operates to minimize the white-nonwhite difference in ability among persons who terminate their schooling at the same grade level. The mean mental development of nonwhite adults does not differ substantially from that of white adults who have terminated their schooling at the same grade level.[31]

Still troublesome is whether increases in the average duration of schooling or the average number of grades completed by members of successive birth cohorts can be taken to mean that young American adults are more "educated" or able than older Americans. If a recently constructed achievement test were administered to a cross-section of American adults, the mean score of the young probably would exceed that of the old. No relation between birth cohort and innate ability need be posited to account for the difference. The content of valued knowledge changes over time; the acquisition of such knowledge occurs primarily in the schools; and the time that has elapsed since school-leaving grows shorter for each successive birth cohort.

There are, in fact, curious contradictions that arise between arguments that can be advanced to point up the inadequacy of grades completed as an indicator of education. One line of argument implies that a grades-completed measure overstates change over time in education. The position is taken that the holder of a high-school diploma is a more educated man if he is fifty years of age than if he is twenty years of age because high-school graduates are relatively fewer among the age-mates of the older man. Another line of argument, however, implies that a grades-completed measure understates gains in education. Increases over time in so-called school quality and the in-classroom time per grade have enhanced the educational value of a school year. Neither indictment seems a sufficient basis for recommending that the grades-completed measure be replaced by a new measure of education, at least in recurring surveys financed with public monies.

SOME FUTURE DATA NEEDS

What must be done to better gauge the trend of education in America? A more judicious arrangement of data collected under existing statistical programs must be assigned top priority. It is the progression of successive birth cohorts through the school system that generates the American stockpile of education. Results of the recurring surveys begin to take on meaning only when they are brought into juxtaposition for a cohort defined by year of birth.

Comparisons between birth cohorts with respect to the rate of school attendance at a given age or with respect to the cumulative schooling completed by a survey date are reported frequently in discussions of educational trends. Instances in point would be the difference between 1950 and 1960 attendance rates for sixteen-year-olds and the difference between mean grades completed by persons aged twenty-five to twenty-nine and the corresponding mean for the thirty-five to thirty-nine age group as of 1960. The most critical intercohort comparison for measuring change in education, however, contrasts the cumulative schooling completed by a given age. That is, are persons better educated now, in 1968, than a decade ago when they reach, say, their teens, their majority, or their fortieth birthday? The answer must be based on the following comparisons: grades (or years of schooling) completed by age thirteen for the cohorts born in 1945 and 1955; grades completed by age twenty-one for the cohorts born in 1937 and 1947; and grades completed by age forty for the cohorts born in 1918 and 1928.

The pressing need is not the collection of new items, but a new tabulation format for old items. Records now on file which include information about enrollment status, grades of school completed, and birth year (or age at the survey date which can be translated into birth year) must be re-examined with a view to compiling as complete an account as is possible on the progress of successive birth cohorts through the school system. As additional records including these items accumulate, the series for each birth cohort can be extended forward in time or made more detailed with respect to the past.

A second priority, far more costly than the first on a long-run basis, is an increase in the size of the sample surveyed periodically with respect to enrollment status and grades completed. On the assumption that information on these items continues to be collected as part of the Current Population Survey conducted by the Bureau of the Census, the incremental cost probably should not be attributed wholly to "education." Although the information collected on education becomes intelligible only in relation to other characteristics of the respondents, the usefulness of other survey items also is enhanced by the larger sample size. Analysis of the work status of out-of-school youth, for example, is limited by sample size in precisely the same way as analysis of their educational attainment.

In the substantive materials reviewed earlier, some of the analytical uses of statistics arranged by birth cohort and based on samples of adequate size have been illustrated. The thrust of analytical work with closely spaced readings on education should be directed increasingly to establishing covariation between measures of a cohort's progress through the schools and ongoing changes in the society at large.

NOTES

1. Ryder, N. B., "Notes on the Concept of a Population," *American Journal of Sociology,* vol. 69, 1964, pp. 447–463.
2. U.S. Bureau of the Census, *Census of the Population: 1910,* General Report and Analysis, Washington, 1910, p. 1187.
3. A more comprehensive account appears in Folger, John K., and Charles B. Nam, *Education of the American Population,* Washington, Government Printing Office, 1967.
4. U.S. Bureau of the Census, *Current Population Reports,* Series P-20, no. 12, February, 1948, and no. 19, July, 1948.
5. Reported in *U.S. Census of Population: 1960,* vol. I, part 1, p. L.
6. The results are reported in "Out-of-School Youth—Two Years Later," Special Labor Force Report No. 71, reprinted from *Monthly Labor Review,* August, 1966.
7. Eckland, Bruce K., "College Dropouts who Came Back," *Harvard Educational Review,* vol. 34, 1964, pp. 402–420.
8. U.S. Bureau of the Census, *Current Population Reports,* Series P-25, no. 359, February, 1967, and no. 365, May, 1967.
9. *Ibid.,* no. 359.
10. Anderson, C. Arnold, and Mary Jean Bowman, "Educational Distributions and Attainment Norms in the United States," *Proceedings of the World Population Conference, 1954,* vol. 4, 1954, pp. 931–941.
11. U.S. Bureau of the Census, *Current Population Reports,* Series P-20, no. 162, March, 1967.
12. See Morgan, James N. *et al., Income and Welfare in the United States,* McGraw-Hill, New York, 1962, Table 22–2.
13. Measures of the income distribution appear, among other places, in U.S. Bureau of the Census, *Historical Statistics of the United States,* Series G 100–104.

14. Bowman, Mary Jean, "Human Inequalities and Southern Underdevelopment," *Southern Economic Journal,* vol. 32, 1965, pp. 73–102.
15. *Ibid.,* p. 101.
16. *U.S. Census of Population: 1960,* Subject Report PC(2)-5A, Table 5.
17. Eckland, Bruce K., "Social Class and College Graduation: Some Misconceptions Corrected," *American Journal of Sociology,* vol. 70, 1964, pp. 36–50.
18. Duncan, Beverly, *Family Factors and School Dropout: 1920–1960,* Cooperative Research Project No. 2258, U.S. Office of Education, University of Michigan, Ann Arbor, 1965, Table 8–1.
19. U.S. Bureau of the Census, *Current Population Reports,* Series P-20, no. 15, May, 1948.
20. The resurvey results appear in U.S. Bureau of the Census, *Current Population Reports,* Series P-20, no. 45, October, 1953.
21. The survey and data derived from it are discussed at some length in Blau, Peter M., and Otis Dudley Duncan, *The American Occupational Structure,* John Wiley, New York, 1967; and Duncan, Beverly, *Family Factors and School Dropout, op. cit.*
22. Duncan, Beverly, *op. cit.,* Table 3–2.
23. *Ibid.,* Table 4–8.
24. *Ibid.,* chaps. 3, 4; and Duncan, Beverly, "Education and Social Background," *American Journal of Sociology,* vol. 72, 1967, pp. 363–372.
25. Duncan, Beverly, *Family Factors and School Dropout, op. cit.,* chap. 8.
26. The analysis is reported in Duncan, Otis Dudley, "Ability and Achievement," *Eugenics Quarterly,* vol. 15, March, 1968, pp. 1–11.
27. This point has been made previously by William H. Sewell, in his review of Coleman, James S. *et al., Equality of Educational Opportunity,* Government Printing Office, Washington, 1966, which appeared in the *American Sociological Review,* vol. 32, 1967, pp. 475–479.
28. Rees, Albert, "The Measurement of Unemployment," in *Studies in Unemployment,* Government Printing Office, Washington, 1960, pp. 18–19.
29. Coleman, James S. *et al., Equality of Educational Opportunity, op. cit.,* p. 583.
30. Duncan, Beverly, *Family Factors and School Dropout, op. cit.,* chap. 8.
31. The work on measured mental development and number of grades completed in the adult population was carried out by Otis Dudley Duncan and is reported, in part, in "Ability and Achievement," *op. cit.*

V. AGGREGATIVE FEATURES

13. SOCIAL STRATIFICATION AND MOBILITY

Problems in the Measurement of Trend

Otis Dudley Duncan

T HE SPATIOTEMPORAL frame of reference for this chapter is the United States since about the end of World War I. For the purpose of sketching movements in the state of opinion on the topic—the first task of the chapter—a further restriction is advisable. We will not miss much that is important in the literature of the interwar period if we take note only of Cooley's "Opportunity and Class" (1918)[1] and Sorokin's *Social Mobility* (1927).[2] The era of modern research begins with 1942, when Sibley's "Some Demographic Clues to Stratification"[3] was published. Cooley and Sorokin are of permanent value (or as near to being so as any sociological writing can be) for conceptual orientation, and are much more useful for the purpose of acquiring concepts suited to the study of specifically American social stratification than are the writings of Weber, Veblen, or Marx. Sibley initiates the characteristic contemporary emphasis on *measurement* as the method of resolving issues that ultimately turn on matters of fact.

The organization of the chapter is somewhat unbalanced. After a quick demonstration that sociologists' views on the character of stratification trends have been neither uniform nor consistent, the chapter turns to a highly compressed conceptual exposition intended to identify what should be the major foci of trend studies. Finally, in the longest primary subdivision of the paper, there is a detailed appraisal of our present capability to measure *one* of the kinds of trends thus identified. The chapter, therefore, is rather less compendious than the whole book that would have to be written to do the topic full justice.

THE TREND OF PROFESSIONAL OPINION

There is no better way to summarize Sibley's argument than to use his own words:

Not universal equality nor near-equality of status but a high rate of vertical mobility has been the most important demographic basis of this nation's tradition of classlessness. The long-existing favorable balance of vertical circulation of individuals in American society, i.e., the excess of upward over downward moves, has diminished and seems likely to be further reduced. Development of class consciousness will be likely to occur unless our social institutions are so readjusted as to produce a large amount of compensating up-and-down movement of individuals. The educational system, which is the chief American institution explicitly conceived as a mechanism for facilitating the ascent of talented individuals, must become more highly selective of individual merit if the loss of certain dwindling sources of upward mobility is to be offset. It must be admitted that there is no criterion of what would be exactly enough vertical mobility to prevent the formation of conscious and hostile classes in our nation, yet in relative terms, it can be shown that there is danger of actual circulation falling short of the critical amount.[4]

Sibley had no data on vertical mobility as such. He was able to point to net shifts in the occupational structure as presumptive evidence that much occupational mobility had occurred in the past. Moreover, he illustratively calculated that immigration, selective of predominantly unskilled persons, and differential fertility resulted in higher rates of recruitment to the bottom than to the top of the social structure, thus engendering upward movement. But if the latter two forces should wane in importance, and particularly if rapid economic growth should not be resumed after World War II, then Sibley foresaw a possibility that our "social arteries" would "become sclerotic."

The more systematic part of Sibley's paper was an analysis of the joint influence of family background and intelligence on educational attainment. After showing that the net importance of the former was far from negligible, particularly as concerns college attendance, Sibley remarked, "It is evident that the American educational system is far from being as effective as it might be in counteracting tendencies toward social stratification." The conclusion depended, of course, on the plausible assumption that educational attainment is a crucial step in occupational achievement.

In contrast to the disciplined conjectures offered in Sibley's paper, some of the professional literature of the subsequent years was more freely speculative. A psychological hypothesis was advanced by Havighurst,[5] who argued that by the end of World War II people had lost "the old belief in the possibility of social mobility for themselves and their children." He anticipated that in the postwar period there would be a tendency to be satisfied with "group mobility," illustrated by the gains made for workers by labor unions, and that "individual mobility will become less important to them." The hypothesis, though daring and unsubstantiated, was presented circumspectly: "It must be admitted that the evidence for decrease in the number of people with a strong drive for individual mobility is not completely convincing. We lack some of the facts." Indeed, almost all the facts were lacking. Havighurst contented himself with some quotations from essays written by a few school students in 1942–1943: "The writer was impressed, as he read the essays, with a surprising lack of evidence of personal ambition and drive for social mobility, which he would have expected from high school seniors in his own school days."

A few years later Hertzler argued in the same vein, at greater length and with a wider array of purported documentation.[6] His conclusion was grim:

> In general, there is evidence that the American Dream is becoming less real for many people. . . . In the main, we seem to be "settling" as a people. The strata are becoming more rigid; . . . Status is crystallizing. There is both a tendency toward restriction of access to the means of personal and family advancement, and an apparent reduction in the vertical mobility drive and psyche and ethos.

Hertzler's discussion began by recapitulating Sibley's arguments. It then proceeded by way of a review of various items of poll data to present the "grounds for thinking that the fundamental *psychology* underlying the American Dream of 'climbing to the top' is undergoing considerable change." Here, the orientation that Petersen was shortly to dub "nostalgic Americanism" seems to dominate any tendency to conform to canons of inference. There are absolutely no data on *trends* in this section of the article, yet the author does not hesitate to employ such phraseology (italics added) as "*more and more* people covet . . . peace of mind"; "stratum fixity in a labor union . . . is, *increasingly,* . . . sought after"; "*subsiding* of the climbing drive"; "workers *are becoming* 'security-minded' "; "*growing* sympathy with and belief in unionization"; "*waning* interest in long-time goals"; "*growing* feeling among people that they 'might not be able to make it' "; "*growing* complacency regarding status and role." In sum, without any evidence whatever about how things looked to the "predecessors," Hertzler tells us that "The heavens of achievement look quite different to many contemporaries than they did to their predecessors."

One more item from the "rigidification" literature also illustrates how easily proponents of this thesis fell into methodological traps. Hollingshead[7] evinced an awareness of the requirements for an inference on this matter in acknowledging that "an assay of trends is difficult because data are not in existence to enable the construction of a satisfactory profile of what the stratification system was during a base period and then to measure another period against the base." He showed less methodological sophistication in approaching the problem of occupational mobility. Here he was limited to a comparison of the 1910 and 1940 occupation distributions in New Haven. His comments on the data tended to minimize the rather substantial differences between the two distributions, but more serious was the introduction of the completely gratuitous postulate, "if the occupational structure is not expanding, particularly in the upper reaches, upward mobility will be restricted to a very small percentage of the population." In all the discussion of *net* changes in the occupational distribution there was not one iota of evidence for Hollingshead's conclusion that "movement into the higher positions in the status system is more difficult today than it was before World War I."

It is easy today to spot the weaknesses in the rigidification thesis that apparently enjoyed much currency between 1942 and 1952. At best (in Sibley's case) stratification trends were not directly measured but were inferred from data on the operation of presumed causes. At worst (in the method of "nostalgic Americanism") "trends" were manufactured out of whole cloth, perhaps by an exercise of the sociological imagination.

After about 1952 the rigidification thesis apparently lost ground. It was subject to several sharp attacks, and there was an increasing supply of relevant—though far from conclusive—data. During the past ten years, authors discussing trends have actually had at their disposal trend data, or have made highly self-conscious use of procedures designed to permit rigorous, if indirect, inferences of trends. A student of the sociology of knowledge might wish to entertain other hypotheses to account for a shift in the "mood" of the profession. Petersen did not hesitate to suggest that

> Whenever a conclusion is based on isolated facts torn from their social context, we do well to suspect that the choice of these facts was not haphazard but in line with some prejudice or ideology. In this case, two ideologies that seem to have little in common—nostalgic Americanism and Marxism—have cooperated to create and maintain "enlightened" illusions about the American class structure.[8]

Other critics[9] writing at about the same time elaborated some cogent themes that had hitherto not been sufficiently emphasized: First, that there is a desperate paucity of hard data suited to the measurement of trends; and second, that the effort to infer trends from the operation of presumed causes had been handicapped by the neglect of certain social forces operating to relax rather than to intensify rigidity.

Perhaps the most significant item of information to be injected into the discussion at this time was the startling finding reported by Rogoff from her analysis of marriage licenses issued in Marion County, Indiana: *"No significant changes took place in over-all mobility rates between 1910 and 1940."*[10] All subsequent commentary featured this result in the discussion. Subsequent investigators, appreciating the methodological elegance of Rogoff's research, were constrained to conform to much more exacting standards of inference than had previously been observed.

Lenski's[11] ingenious attempt to piece together a trend series from intercohort comparisons had some temporary value until an accumulation of national samples permitted a straightforward assessment of changes in the frequencies of movement between broad occupational categories (white-collar, manual, and farm). In accomplishing this assessment Jackson and Crockett "found scant evidence that the system of occupational inheritance is growing more rigid."[12] Their conclusion pertained specifically to the period 1945–1957. It shortly became possible to confirm it with data extending to 1962.[13]

It cannot be supposed that the rigidification thesis (the sociological counterpart to the economists' contemporaneous "stagnation" thesis?) has been finally laid to rest. For one thing, even if the earlier reading of trends has been shown to be defective and even if prognostications for the post-World War II period have turned out to be excessively glum, there is nothing about a trend—supposing it to have been reliably ascertained for some specific period—that guarantees its own continuation. Sorokin, above all others, had been tireless in his insistence that there is "no perpetual trend toward either an increase or a decrease of vertical mobility."[14]

It is true, moreover, that the decisive rejection of the rigidification thesis was accomplished by narrowing the scope of the issue to the question of what had been the trend in intergenerational occupational mobility. Several of the earlier discussions had already emphasized the multidimensional nature of social stratification; and there had been speculation as to shifts in the extent of social inequality, as distinguished from the ease of movement between strata. Thus, while the rigidification thesis in its original form is no longer actively espoused, there is much new talk about increasing "concentration of power" and increasing "inheritance of poverty." Unfortunately, the literature on these topics has not been very explicit on the question of measurement.

Hence to engage in a critique of it one would have to run a considerable risk of setting up straw men to be knocked down.

For present purposes, it is sufficient to acknowledge that the subject of "stratification trends" may well not be exhausted by even the most careful analysis of occupational mobility. In the next section of this chapter an attempt will be made to indicate just how comprehensive a full-blown effort to measure such trends would have to be. But then, in the final section, the material on occupational mobility is re-examined in detail, because it affords the most convenient opportunity to illustrate a host of technical but unavoidable problems that would confront any honest and serious effort to assay the trends in stratification.

STRATIFICATION CONCEPTS

One can share my strong operationalist bias without denying that it is a good idea to think about that which is to be measured before undertaking to measure it. A conceptual digression is included here not for its own sake but as a challenge to the ingenuity of the specialist in measurement.

Process and Product

Some emphasis is to be given to a distinction among functional differentiation, institutionalized inequality, and social stratification.

The very notion of society entails the concept of *differentiation*. A population is functionally differentiated when some of its members regularly do and are expected to do different things (perform different roles) than others. In human society, the division of labor is "occupational" in a broad sense; this implies that role differentiation is predominantly learned, conventional, and habitual. In infrahuman societies, the division of labor may be largely "morphological"—what an organism does depends on what kind of organism it is, as among polymorphic insects. (That age and sex, physical and mental capacities, and the like limit or condition human role differentiation is a complication of this distinction.)

Institutionalized *inequality* exists when, as a matter of more or less consistent practice, different roles are differently rewarded, when their performance confers status distinctions, or when different performances of a given type of role are differentially evaluated. What the rewards may be and how they are assigned are empirical contingencies to be investigated in particular cases, as is the structure of differentiation itself.

Social *stratification* refers to the persistence of positions in a hierarchy of inequality, either over the life time of a birth cohort of individuals or, more particularly, between generations. The definition implies that a stratified population is one in which there is intertemporal predictability (to a greater than chance extent) of an individual's status at one time, given his status (or that of his family of orientation) at some earlier time. Thus a society is stratified with respect to wealth if a wealthy family's offspring are discernibly more likely to be wealthy than are the offspring of a poor family. The rigidity of stratification, in this sense, is measured by the intergenerational correlation or coefficient of association. This concept is to be distinguished from the degree of inequality, which refers to the extent of differentiation on a relevant scale of rewards (or dispersion of the status distribution). A society might be highly—or even completely—stratified even though inequality is slight, as in the case of a wealthy and a poor class the difference in whose actual holdings is small but membership in which is virtually fixed at birth.

An explanation of the structure of differentiation lies beyond the scope of this discussion, which must be something less than an encyclopedia of sociology. Nor can we linger over the problem of how societies become differentiated. Two processes centered upon functional differentiation are, however, germane.

The first is the process of social metabolism, the recruitment of personnel to roles in a division of labor and the turnover of personnel in such roles, or (if one prefers) the allocation of people to tasks. Among the principal bases of allocation are age, sex, and the "capacities" and "dispositions" of individuals. Without speculating on how allocation on these bases might work in the limiting case of an unstratified society, we can indicate two things that happen as a consequence of stratification. First, position in a stratified hierarchy may be a basis for role allocation (e.g., noble birth may be a prerequisite to political office). Second, capacities and dispositions, insofar as they are produced or developed by training or socialization, may turn up in disproportionate frequencies in the several strata of the stratified hierarchy, given, for example, differential access to educational facilities. To the extent that the basis of capacities and dispositions is genetic, biosocial mechanisms of stratification may have a similar outcome. Both principles amount to the statement that the "qualifications"—however these may be defined, and whether they may be intrinsic or extrinsic qualities of the individuals concerned—for occupying various roles are not evenly distributed over strata in a stratified system.

The second process linked to differentiation is that of allocation of rewards. It would be possible to construct a formidable list of the mechanisms that may operate in this process: pricing of the services of role incumbents (wages and salaries), legal stipulations of perquisites and prerogatives, customary or conventional patterns of distribution, awards or prizes for performance to a set standard, and so on. Again, the point here is not to attempt a taxonomy of such mechanisms, but to indicate that stratification impinges upon the process of reward distribution. The general principle is that stratification may constitute a bias with respect to the operation of one or more reward mechanisms or devices for conferring status. Perhaps some categories in a stratified hierarchy are simply ineligible for certain kinds of rewards. Or the magnitude of reward for a given performance may be a function of stratum membership.

The account of processes linking differentiation, inequality, and stratification is completed by designating the classes of mechanisms by which social inequality is converted into social stratification: primarily, intergenerational transmission of status and, incidentally, continuity of status over the life span. The latter without the former would generate only a weak and transitory system of stratification; hence the emphasis on intergenerational transmission. In two respects, this concept is given a somewhat broader reference than is usual. First, although the most important case of intergenerational transmission concerns the nexus between achieved status and status of the family, *qua* family, of orientation, it seems economical to include under this rubric such ascribed statuses, derived via the family, as kinship or lineage, racial (as socially defined, of course), ethnic, cultural, or religious group membership. That some of these are not absolutely fixed does not alter the principle that they typically are transmitted intergenerationally. Second, the term "transmission" is not limited to ascription of the identical status of the family of orientation nor to inheritance of its precise position on a status scale. Any positive association or linkage, deterministic or probabilistic, between statuses in the two generations (parent and offspring) conforms with the idea of transmission advanced here. This stipulation eliminates, for example, the insoluble problem of estimating the absolute amount of "occupational inheritance" in a set of data on intergenerational occupational mobility. (It is insoluble because there is no final solution to the problem of the breadth and heterogeneity of categories in a classification of occupations.)

Mechanisms of Stratification

The process of stratification comprises all that is involved in the intergenerational transmission of status and the impact thereof on status achievement and the securing of rewards. There is interest in estimating the parameters of the process as of a given period of time, temporal variations (trends or fluctuations) in these parameters, and the alterations of structure to which these variations may give rise. Such parameters refer to quantitative aspects of any of the mechanisms by which the process operates. Identification of these mechanisms is a preliminary step. The listing that follows is not based on any systematic principle of classification; it is merely a culling from the current lore and observation in the literature of what is usually termed "social mobility."

Ascription. Perhaps the clearest case of intergenerational transmission is simple ascription: status is conferred at birth (or is perfectly predictable at that time) and is the same for the offspring as for the parent. In typological descriptions of a "caste" system it is stated that the son necessarily belongs to the same caste as the father, and neither of them can change his caste membership. In societies with sharply defined "racial" categories, racial status is conferred in this way. A similar principle operates in connections with titular rank, as in the case of "nobility." The estate system of stratification, as it is conventionally described, rests heavily on the principle of ascription, although changes of status are not entirely precluded.

There is some ambiguity about the mechanism of ascription as it operates in reference to what are called "ethnic" or "minority" statuses in the United States. Apart from the more strictly "racial" categories, ethnic groups in this country represent for the most part aggregates identifiable in terms of national origins or religious communities. Such identification, however, is tenuous to a degree in that assimilation and acculturation may render it vestigial. Thus, while the initial status is ascribed, it is not thereby entirely fixed. The situation is one of considerable empirical complexity as well as conceptual ambiguity.[15]

Inheritance. Another apparently clear form of transmission is inheritance of real property, wealth, and certain intangibles (such as the reputation of a "fine family"). Our understanding of how inheritance actually works, however, is extraordinarily poor. A normative prescription such as primogeniture breaks down in the not infrequent case that a man dies without heirs. Legal intervention in the form of estate taxes and the like has resulted in the invention of many disguised forms of inheritance. The capital value of a family name may be squandered before the fact by one who achieves the status of "black sheep."

Genetics. While social status as such is not transmitted by the genes, various personal qualities that serve as advantages or handicaps in status achievement are thought to have a genetic basis. What the relevant qualities are may well be a matter of social definition; thus strength, stamina, and visual acuity may be important traits for achievement in a hunting society while verbal intelligence is critical in a literate civilization. Yet in both cases one may postulate a hereditary basis for the capacity to develop the relevant skills, granted that the development thereof is a contingent matter in itself.

Socialization. Students of American society lay heavy stress on socialization. The circumstances of birth and rearing are thought to have much bearing upon the development of linguistic habits, motives, attitudes, aspirations, orientations, skills, and cognitive resources, which in turn are crucial for status achievement. The rubric socialization may be taken broadly to include not only the inculcation of behavior patterns by the family of orientation but also formal training in educational systems and acquisition of orientations from peer groups and the wider social milieu. Not all agencies of socialization, of course, need reinforce the effects of the others. Thus the school in American society is increasingly being called upon to remedy the effects of "cultural deprivation," i.e., undesirable or dysfunctional socialization by the family of orientation.

Access to Opportunities. The several strata may differ in resources and access to opportunities. Amounts of funds available for education and "improvement" are more or less proportional to income, as are resources to be used in acquiring information about job openings or in undertaking spatial mobility in response to such information. Among the initial conditions confronting an individual by virtue of the circumstances of his birth are his locations in space and time. These may be seen as constraints on access to opportunities. Temporal location (i.e., membership in a given birth cohort) is, of course, unalterable. Geographic mobility, however, may more or less neutralize the advantage or disadvantage of an initial spatial location.

Environments. The strata, similarly, differ in the environments in which they live. Differentials in personal safety, nutrition, health care, and the like may be reflected in persistent advantages or handicaps with respect to subsequent achievement.

Differential Association. The factors of segregation and differential association are perhaps best regarded as conditions influencing some of the foregoing mechanisms. They are, however, sufficiently important (presumably) to merit special mention, partly because they are subject to fairly direct measurement. A special instance of differential association, often studied though not so much in the context of stratification, is assortive mating. All these mechanisms can be viewed, for example, as constraints upon the field of socialization or as limits upon access to opportunities.

Although the foregoing list is probably incomplete, it is clear enough that our conceptual apparatus is better developed than our equipment for measurement. The goal of measurement is to devise models incorporating all the mechanisms of intergenerational transmission and to estimate their relative importance and interrelationships in particular populations. We have only crude and partial approximations, but enough has been done to indicate promising directions for further work.

The order in which the mechanisms of transmission were listed is somewhat suggestive. Evidently the task of social analysis is quite different, according to whether the investigator is concerned with a system with predominantly ascriptive principles or with one in which most statuses are achieved. Assuming that American society falls toward the latter pole, the analyst's task is somewhat like that of one who bets on the races. A stratified society which places stress on achievement is not unlike a race in which the runners differ not only in skill and ability, but also in respect to various advantages or handicaps. Some begin the race with heavy packs upon their backs and many obstacles in their course, while others enjoy freedom from such impediments. The race is rendered less predictable, too, in that these initial conditions may be modified as the contest progresses, not only in response to the success of the contestants up to a given point, but because the handicaps are varied somewhat randomly during the running. The outcome is hardly determinate when the race begins, but an informed bettor could nevertheless make money if his odds were accepted. From a normative standpoint, one can be concerned with whether the race is run fairly, given the rules, or whether the rules themselves should be changed.

The insistence that some notion of a *process* should be central to our concept of stratification may seem idiosyncratic, given the overwhelming emphasis on structural description in the recent American literature on the subject. There are, however, significant precedents for the emphasis that is urged here.

Cooley, for example, wrote: "All societies are more or less stratified into classes, based on differences in wealth, occupation, and enlightenment, which tend to be passed on from parents to children; and this stratification creates and perpetuates difference in opportunity."[16] What is suggested here is that "passing on from parents to children" be taken as the antecedent of "this stratification." "Classes," strata, or other like products of stratification exist insofar as there is more or less continuous and consistent operation of some such mechanisms as have been listed above.

The point of view taken here was expounded even more explicitly by Buckley, who was protesting against the prevalent confusion of social stratification with social inequality and social differentiation. In attempting to convey the force of the distinction, he wrote:

> . . . the distinction between stratification and differentiation . . . may perhaps be brought out more clearly by the consideration that a non-stratified society . . . containing no intergenerationally continuous strata: (1) would nevertheless be differentiated in terms of duties, rights, and perquisites, (2) might, without being inconsistent, recognize differential evaluation of roles (though not necessarily of perons), and (3) would still have the problem of training and selecting the new members for the various roles. The classlessness of the society would have nothing directly to do with its differentiation but would be manifested in the fact that a person's initial social position or milieu at birth would not be correlated with his adult social position, except perhaps to the very small extent that current fact and theory allow us to correlate validly the individual's biologically based capacities or talents with his biological background. . . . This is why the several recent empirical studies of *intergenerational* mobility, as distinct from career patterns *per se,* are crucial in establishing the fact and the extent of stratification.[17]

Similarly, Svalastoga, although his terminology is not free of the confusion that Buckley discerned, is quite clear as to the conceptual issue: "The permeability of a society, i.e., the degree to which positions are filled without respect to social origin or other characteristics determined at birth, is the most important single clue to its system of stratification."[18] Following this clue systematically, Svalastoga is led to a typology comprising five "models" of stratification: the egalitarian, caste, estate, class, and continuous models. The last is offered as the most relevant to contemporary Western industrial nations.

Forms of Inequality

The preceding discussion relied on the assumption that the analyst of stratification is clear in his own mind as to what are the relevant statuses, the intergenerational transmission of which constitutes stratification. He has, in other words, already made a commitment as to the "what" in the famous question, *Who Gets What, When, How?*[19] But it is not wholly obvious what that commitment should be. Indeed, much that passes for "stratification theory" consists in a rather unconvincing elaboration of distinctions among forms of inequality.

The present discussion requires no firm resolution of the ambiguities and obscurities that infest the literature on this topic. The presentation here is only illustrative of a range of possibilities. The reader might have preferred Svalastoga's[20] classification of "stratification criteria":

1. Social status or amount of deference enjoyed.
2. Political status or amount of power possessed.
3. Informational status or amount of skill or knowledge possessed.
4. Economic status or amount of wealth possessed.

A somewhat more elaborate set of distinctions is attempted in Figure 1. This particular scheme has been found unsatisfactory by several

FIGURE 1.   SOME SCALES OF REWARD OR STATUS

Item	Stock or state concept	Flow or incidence concept	Conventional rubric
1.	Wealth Assets Property	Income	"Economic" (production)
2.	Level of living Possessions	Expenditures Consumption Leisure	"Economic" (consumption)
3.	Prestige Honor Reputation, fame Esteem	Deference Recognition, awards Concern, care, love Moral evaluation	"Social"
4.	Education Knowledge Skill	Schooling Training	"Informational"
5.	Style of life Status symbols Manners Language	Psychic income Satisfaction Utility Diversion	"Cultural"
6.	Power Authority	Influence Decision-making	"Political"
7.	Legal status Freedom	Exercise rights, choice, participation Experience punish- ment, deprivation, sanctions	"Civic"
8.	Welfare	Life chances	(Composite, summation of 1-7)

critics (who shall remain anonymous but not unappreciated); the only certain thing about it is that it will require much revision.

One unusual feature of the classification merits further consideration in future work even if its presentation here is not entirely successful. This is the attempt to coordinate the two alternatives that appear to exist with respect to the treatment of the temporal dimension. On the one hand, a status variable may be conceived as a "stock" or a "state" that could in principle be inventoried or assayed at a particular moment in time. On the other hand, the variable may be definable only with regard to a "flow" that occurs over some finite interval of time or an "incidence" of events during such a period.

The distinction between stock and flow is conventional with regard to wealth and income (even though many sociologists seem unaware of the convention and its utility, indeed, necessity). Actually, it was the idea of making additional distinctions analogous to this one that inspired the arrangement of Figure 1. Wealth, conceived as a stock of productive (or potentially productive) assets, may by being employed as capital generate a stream of income. Conversely, a stream of income, insofar as it is diverted into saving or investment, may contribute to the growing stock of wealth.

It would not be wise to push this analogy too hard with regard to such concepts as "power" and "influence," especially in view of the extreme latitude in regard to the use of these terms on which the disciplines of social science insist. Nevertheless, the distinction between "state" and "incidence" approaches to measurement is germane here, as is obvious from the controversy that developed over the "reputational" (state) versus the "decision-making" (incidence) techniques of ascertaining who holds power in a community. As it turns out, the two techniques do not have to yield the same results, any more than there has to be a perfect correlation between wealth and income. This complication of life can hardly be welcome, even if we cannot wish it away, because our present techniques of model construction are ill-suited to the incorporation of fine distinctions concerning the way in which variables operate over time.

If we can only conjecture as to the ultimate import of the temporal distinction, it is much more evident what is at stake in the presentation of distinctions as to types of status. Sorokin pointed out:

> Not always are the wealthiest men at the apex of the political or occupational pyramid; and not always are the poor men the lowest in the political or the occupational gradations. This means that the intercorrelation among the three forms of stratification [read "inequality"] is

far from being perfect; the strata of each form do not coincide completely with one another. There is always a certain degree of overlapping among them. This fact does not permit us to analyze in a summary way all three fundamental forms of stratification. For the sake of a greater accuracy each form has to be studied separately.[21]

Or, as Spengler phrased the point with characteristic elegance, "Positions on diverse distribution curves cannot, in the absence of arbitrary assumptions, be added and converted into a single position."[22]

One consequence of the multiplicity of forms of inequality is to raise the issue of the degree of "rigidity" of a system of rewards and statuses. (This is to be distinguished from the rigidity of the *stratification* system, which refers to the degree to which status is intergenerationally transmitted.) The notion of rigidity with respect to social inequality is that the several reward or status variables may be more or less highly intercorrelated. If the correlation is high, the wealthy always have the most prestige, the greatest power, the most desirable style of life, and so on. If not, there is room for status discrepancy. The idea of rigidity, of course, resembles that of "status crystallization," much discussed in the stratification literature of the past decade and a half. High rigidity (or crystallization) would be generated if all rewards depended in the same way on a fixed set of positions in the division of labor, as the power, prestige, and income of the men in a military organization depend on grade and rank. If one believed—it is not suggested that anyone does or has cause to do so—that all rewards are a function of ownership of the means of production, he would also have to believe that there is great rigidity in the system of inequality (even if, by the way, there were no inheritance of property). There may be considerable rigidity in this sense, even if the extent of inequality is not great (a capitalistic society is not necessarily rich or highly differentiated by amount of riches).

The absence of "occupational status" from Figure 1 may seem surprising. Are we not accustomed to think of "socioeconomic status" in America as a vague composite of education, occupation, and income and "things like that," usually unspecified? But, of course, occupation is a *role,* and it is the rewards of pursuing roles, not the roles themselves, that appear in Figure 1. Occupations differ in regard to earnings (income), prestige, power, attractiveness of working conditions, and intrinsic appeal of job assignments, among other things. Indeed, it is the assumption that occupation is the source of many of the most important kinds of rewards that allows some sociologists to fix upon occupation as the key variable in the American stratification system. But this involves an ellipsis, albeit a harmless one for the most part. In the sequel there will be occasion to indulge in it so as to refer conveniently to "occupational status" and its intergenerational transmission. The danger in the ellipsis arises when we assume there is some natural "occupational scale," rather than one that arises only if occupations are ranked or graded in terms of one or more of the items listed here.

Measurement and Models

The foregoing discussion implies, or presupposes, a concept of "stratification system." Such a system comprises two analytically distinct components, both essential to the concept: (1) a set of one or more hierarchies of institutionalized inequality with respect to the statuses (rewards, evaluations, prerogatives) conferred on the basis of incumbency and performance of roles; (2) a pattern of intergenerational transmission of status or access to roles such that the position of an individual on a scale of inequality is associated to a nonnegligible degree with the position of his family of orientation.

On this point of view, there is some ambiguity about the statement that, for example, a given society is "highly stratified." This could mean one of several things: that there is a great range or dispersion of values of one or several status variables; that there are strong correlations between pairs of status variables; or that the coefficient of intergenerational status transmission is high. Empirically it may be true that one of these conditions is likely to be realized if and only if the others are also. But it is not logically necessary for them to go together. Cursory consideration of illustrative cases suggests, indeed, that they do not always do so. In any event, it is prudent to accept definitions that do not beg questions of fact. We, therefore, reach the following classification of the tasks of measurement in the area of stratification trends.

Degree of Inequality. With respect to each relevant status variable in a society, what is the extent or degree of inequality and how does this change over time? The best illustration here, because of the amount of careful and methodologically sophisticated effort that has gone into the problem, is the measurement of trends in the inequality of the income distribution.[23] Despite this careful work—or, really, because of it—we are not able to offer any simple and unequivocal summary statement as to trend. Much depends on the income concept that is used as well as the method accepted for measuring the inequality of its distribution. Although it would be entirely appropriate to do so in the present context, no attempt will be made to review the several alternative concepts of inequality; the relevant literature is voluminous.[24] As for the conundrums that bedevil the measurement of income per se, it is well that we have this example of an ostensibly simple operation that turns out to be very complex indeed.

It is unlikely that measurement of other status variables will prove to be simpler in the end. (See, for example, the discussions of measurement in the chapters on welfare and education in this volume.) Of course, for several kinds of status—most notoriously, perhaps, "power"—we simply do not have as yet even a plausible beginning on the task of measuring the variable and the inequality of its distribution. But if the analogy with income is worth anything, it may suggest that even casual talk about "concentration of power" might be more carefully disciplined by adhering to a distinction between the aggregate or average amount of power in a system and the inequality of the distribution of power. One sometimes has the strong impression that those deploring the alleged increase in concentration of power are mistaking an increase in the total amount of power in the society for a heightening of power inequality. In the case of income, a rise in the average seems to be a prerequisite for a decline in the concentration (the same need not necessarily be true of power, of course).

Rigidity of Inequality. The second task of measurement presupposes that there are two or more significant forms of inequality or status variables. The question is, then, to what extent are these intercorrelated, or what is the degree of rigidity of inequality or degree of status crystallization, and in what direction is the rigidity of inequality changing? In some respects, this problem may be somewhat simpler than the previous one, at least if one is willing to accept a measure of association that does not make strong assumptions concerning the metric of the variables being correlated. Thus, even with only a crude grading of degree of power—one for which a rigorously defined measure of dispersion or inequality would not be applicable—one could calculate the association of, say, power and wealth. If comparable data could be had for successive points in time, rudimentary inferences as to trend would be possible.

Although sociologists have given much attention to status crystallization during the past fifteen years especially, there is really little in the way of substantial opinion, let alone actual measurement, on the subject of trends. Hollingshead's article recorded his conclusion that "compartmentalization is becoming more rigid with the passage of time"; but it was not wholly clear from his discussion what patterns in his limited data he took to be critical in reaching this conclusion. Most of the work on status crystallization has been concerned with its consequences for personal orientations and behavior, as inferred from cross-sectional data; little has been done to ascertain the degree of crystallization in the society at a given point in time, not to mention changes therein over time.

Rigidity of Stratification. The third question addressed to the specialist in measurement concerns the degree of rigidity of stratification and the trend therein. It is assumed in this chapter that the question concerning the "stratification trend," if posed without further qualification, really refers to this third problem. Hence, it is this problem that has been chosen as a vehicle for the extended illustration of problems in trend measurement in the last section of this chapter.

The program implied by the foregoing classification would appear to be formidable enough and the increment to knowledge that would result from its realization substantial enough that we should not complicate it still further at this point. Nevertheless, it is well to remember that trends are merely the raw material of social analysis. The successful measurement of conceptually distinct trends will only heighten the demand for analysis that discloses their empirical interrelations. Having a notion of how this may be done, moreover, will affect the way we go about trend measurement in the first place. It will be urged here, as in a previous publication,[25] that the compilation of social indicators and the assessment of the trends they reveal should proceed at the same pace as the construction of models contrived with the intention of interpreting interrelationships among indicators.

Indeed, to the extent that plausible models of the whole process of stratification can be developed and means of estimating their relationships can be found, the problem of trend measurement can be restated as that of detecting changes in the parameters of the process. If, for example, we had models adequately taking into account the several "mechanisms" of stratification listed earlier, we should be interested in ascertaining shifts over time in the relative contribution of each mechanism to the outcome of the entire process. Given this way of looking at stratification trends, a program for trend measurement would specify that successive birth cohorts would be followed through their life cycles and observed periodically to establish whether significant differences emerge in comparisons of recent with earlier cohorts in respect to any of the parameters of a model.

FIGURE 2.   PATH DIAGRAM REPRESENTING DEPENDENCE
OF ACHIEVED STATUSES ON FAMILY BACKGROUND
AND INTELLIGENCE

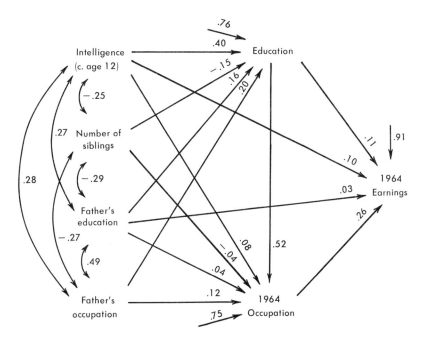

NOTE: Path coefficients estimated for white men 25 to 34 years old in 1964;
see source for details of estimates. Coefficients less than .02 in absolute value are
not shown.

SOURCE: Duncan, Otis Dudley, "Ability and Achievement," *Eugenics Quarterly,* March, 1968, pp. 1–11.

Just to illustrate the possibility envisaged here, Figure 2 displays
one model of the process of stratification that has emerged from recent
research.[26] The coefficients in this model have been estimated for only
one cohort: white men in the United States aged twenty-five to thirty-
four in 1964. (Actually, certain data used in making the estimates do
not pertain strictly to this particular cohort, so that the statement just
made is an idealization of our present statistical capability.) Waiving
questions of the adequacy of the particular model exhibited here, the
proposition advanced is that a fully developed program for measuring
stratification trends might well provide for the quinquennial estimation
of the parameters of such a model for five-year birth cohorts. To ac-

complish this with due regard to reliability of measurement and adequate control of sampling error would be no mean task; but the task is technologically feasible. If we seriously want to know the answer to such questions as "Are Social Classes in America Becoming More Rigid?"[27] and "Is America Still the Land of Opportunity?[28] we can hardly be satisfied with less.

Stratification and Class

The entire chapter to this point has skirted issues suggested by the concept of "class" or "social class." The last section of the paper will likewise eschew a confrontation with such issues. There are two main reasons for this bias in the treatment of the subject. First, the concept of "class" is often used in such a way that it means little more than the imposition of more or less arbitrary intervals on the scale of a status variable, as when poverty is defined as having an income below $3,000 per annum, whereupon the analyst imperceptibly insinuates "lower class" as a synonym for those "in poverty." An incredible amount of paper and ink has been wasted in presenting factitious solutions for the artificial problem of where "class boundaries" really belong. "Class" in the sense of a statistical "class interval" is merely a nominal category of greater or less analytical convenience. The virtually irresistible temptation to make something more of it is reason enough to forego employment of the term in a treatment of social stratification.

More significantly, the framework advanced here has deliberately omitted reference to "class" because that concept does open up a range of genuine problems requiring a different orientation and set of techniques from those suggested by the generally demographic approach to stratification exemplified in this chapter. These problems may be summarily identified as those relating to, first, accommodative relations between social strata; second, the growth of "class consciousness," or awareness of common or like interests on the part of people similarly situated in a stratification system, and third, the emergence therefrom of individual, mass, and collective action oriented to conflict over class interests. As the latter problem is followed up, it is seen to merge with more general problems concerning conflict, social movements, and social transformations that may indeed result in modifications of the stratification system as here defined—for example, in regard to the character of the division of labor itself, the bases and mechanisms of status conferment, the degree or pattern of intergenerational status transmission, or the mechanisms of role allocation.

The distinction between stratification and class implicit in these remarks conforms fairly well with the usage urged by Dahrendorf: "*Class* is always a category for the purposes of the analysis of the dynamics of social conflict and its structural roots, and as such it has to be separated strictly from *stratum* as a category for purposes of describing hierarchical systems at a given point of time."[29] Acceptance of such a distinction would not deny the possibility of important interactions between stratification systems and patterns of class relations—interactions that would become particularly salient given an interest in long-run sociopolitical evolution of societies and the dynamics of major social transformations. The kind of program for measuring stratification trends suggested in this chapter clearly should be complemented by parallel studies of "class trends" in American society; and these two kinds of complementary research should ultimately be synthesized in a more general theory of social and political change. These tasks are not only beyond the scope of this chapter and the competence of this writer; they constitute an agenda for the future of sociology rather than one on which substantial progress is currently being made.

MEASURING THE TREND IN SOCIAL STRATIFICATION

As has been indicated already, the detailed illustration of measurement problems will refer to only one segment of a program for measuring stratification trends. The point of departure is the assertion by Svalastoga that "the permeability of a society . . . is the most important single clue to its system of social stratification."[30]

Sociologists and social statisticians have been studying what Svalastoga calls "permeability" for some time, with varying degrees of effectiveness. The studies are usually presented as investigations of so-called "social mobility," most often "intergenerational occupational mobility." For several reasons, both methodological and substantive, I feel that Svalastoga's formulation conveys the emphasis I would prefer to the one usually placed on "mobility." In a society where most of the statuses that entitle a person to socially valued and distributed rewards are, in fact, achieved (rather than ascribed) statuses, the crucial question is what factors determine the level of achievement, not whether achievement involves a person in "mobility" from the status level of his social origins. Moreover, mobility statistics are treacherous, especially in a multivariate context. If you try to explain "mobility," it may easily turn out that your results are an uninterpretable compound of actual causal influences and artifactual regression effects. There is no need to expound this point here, as it has been dealt with elsewhere in detail.[31]

Several problems must be solved in order to arrive at an estimate of the past trend of social stratification in the United States or to propose a program for following the trend in the future. These may be listed summarily, by way of introduction; a more extended consideration of details will follow.

1. We require a conceptual orientation that will lead to criteria for the measurement of stratification.
2. Pertinent data must be located or created.
3. It must be established that the data for successive periods of time are sufficiently comparable, so that intertemporal differences can be taken to signify change rather than mere fluctuation in errors of measurement or variation in study design.
4. The intertemporal comparisons must be inspected for evidence of secular trend or other identifiable temporal pattern.

Concept and Measurement

A commitment on this problem is already implied in the opening lines of this section. The degree of stratification—or the degree of "rigidity" in the stratification system, if one prefers to think of it that way—refers to the extent to which the level of status achievement depends upon the level of social origin. If there is much intergenerational transmission of status, a society is highly stratified; if there is little, the degree of stratification is low. To reiterate, a society need not be highly stratified merely by virtue of the existence in it of much inequality of social rank. Rank may be highly differentiated, but if there is roughly equal access to unequally ranked positions, the society is not highly stratified, within the meaning of the term as it is used here.

Our problem, therefore, is to measure the relationship or association between achieved statuses and origin statuses. If for the moment we limit the problem to that of analyzing the conventional intergenerational occupational mobility table, the problem is to fix upon an indicator or indicators of the degree to which a son's occupational status depends upon that of the father.

Some analysts have chosen to emphasize the extent to which sons remain at the same status levels as their fathers, or experience so-called "occupational inheritance." This is a rather inadequate measure of what we want, even if the analysis is complicated by relating the observed inheritance to the amount expected on a null hypothesis of no association of statuses in the two generations. The main reason that this measure is inadequate is that the amount of "occupational inheritance" one can observe is strictly a function of the nature and number of occupational categories recognized in a given classification scheme. A second reason for rejecting this approach is that "inheritance" of either a fairly broadly defined occupational status or a relatively specific occupational title does not comprehend everything that we wish to understand by transmission of status between generations. The son's status may depend upon that of the father to a degree, even if the son ends up in a different classification. (I seriously doubt the generality of results that appear to imply the contrary.)[32]

While devotees of so-called nonparametric statistics may be tempted to turn to one of the measures of association that do not require the assumption of interval scaling, I believe a strong case can be made for treating the problem as one concerning the association of two quantitatively scaled variables: father's status and son's status. Surely we do not wish to go so far as to employ a measure that does not at least make use of what we know about the social grading of occupations. Indexes of association that assume only a nominal scale of measurement misrepresent the nature of the problem fully as much as an index that rests on an overly strong assumption of an interval scale. Moreover, it is significant to note the high degree of convergence of the several efforts at scaling occupations.[33] If we accept one of these scales for reasons of convenience, we can have some confidence that we are at worst dealing with a monotonic transformation of the "true" measure of occupational status (whatever that might be).

On the line of argument sketched here but amplified elsewhere,[34] I am led to the choice of classical regression statistics as the preferred method of measuring the intergenerational association of statuses. At least some of the assumptions of these statistics can be checked. Fears that the regression would turn out to be markedly nonlinear are found, for example, to be groundless.[35] For better or worse, therefore, it will be assumed in the sequel that most of what we want to learn from an intergenerational occupational mobility table can be summarized by the linear correlation and regression coefficients. Perhaps the most compelling reason for making this decision is the ease with which one then can proceed from the bivariate to the multivariate problem.

Data

Again taking occupational status as the type case, we can quickly indicate the deplorable state of affairs with respect to availability of data on intergenerational mobility. National data with any legitimate claim to adequacy have been in existence for no more than two decades. The renowned study of occupational prestige conducted by the National Opinion Research Center (NORC) in 1947 included questions on respondent's and father's occupation, and the statistics derived from this survey have been cited fairly frequently. Close inspection reveals, however, that either the use of a quota sample or anomalies in occupational coding, if not both, rendered the intergenerational mobility information highly suspect.[36]

Various national surveys conducted by the Survey Research Center (SRC) during the 1950's for other purposes incidentally included questions on father's occupation. The data becoming available in consequence have provided some useful indications of mobility patterns, but I have detected discrepancies in the distributions of fathers' occupations as given by SRC and the 1962 study of Occupational Changes in a Generation (OCG) for matched cohorts that are too large to attribute to chance. It appears that the SRC data are not sufficiently comparable with data collected and processed by the Bureau of the Census to warrant close comparisons. A sufficiently ambitious project, which would involve complete recoding of original schedules in SRC files, could provide valuable indications of the integenerational relationship for terminal dates such as 1952 and 1957. Indeed, a systematic canvass of the archives of national surveys taken in the past fifteen years would no doubt reveal enough information, if properly processed, to establish trend values for this recent period with reasonable confidence.

The current standard for surveys on this topic is the 1962 OCG study, executed by the Bureau of the Census as a supplement to the March, 1962, Current Population Survey. Here, for the first time, is a survey of intergenerational mobility of high technical quality that covers a sufficiently large sample to permit reliable estimates for important subpopulations as well as the national total. To some extent, as will be indicated, stratification trends can be studied by internal analysis of the OCG data. But this is evidently no substitute for the interperiod comparisons that are the basic stuff of trend analysis.

In default of national data for earlier periods, we turn perforce to the few substantial community surveys of sufficiently high quality to merit sustained attention. Rogoff's well-known analysis[37] of marriage license applications for periods centering approximately on 1940 and 1910 was based on records secured in Marion County, Indiana, of which Indianapolis is the principal urban center. Occupational coding was done with exceptional care, and the basic data were published in considerable detail. There is every reason to believe that the statistics compare favorably in quality with those derived from surveys.

The Six-Cities Study of Labor Mobility, carried out in 1951,[38] is a veritable mine of information for the selected populations covered in that study. Unfortunately, the preoccupation with labor mobility, at the expense of an interest in social stratification, meant that the data were underexploited from the point of view of our present interest, a deficiency that has, thus far, been only partially remedied by secondary analyses.

Finally, reference is made to the series of Detroit Area Study (DAS) projects that have included from time to time the requisite questions on occupational background.[39] The writer was associated with the 1966 project to the extent of ensuring that the occupation coding was sufficiently detailed and reliable to permit comparisons with the other sources mentioned.[40] The size of the sample is a rather important limitation of this source, as it is for the Six-Cities data, unless resort is made to the perhaps questionable tactic of aggregating the cities.

Comparability of Data

The first substantive presentation of statistics will concern the sets of data just reviewed: Rogoff's information for Marion County, 1910 and 1940; the Chicago data from the Six-Cities study for 1950, partially extended back to 1940 in virtue of the ten-year work histories that the study included; the 1962 national OCG data; and the 1966 DAS information for Detroit and environs. Unfortunately, resources have not been at hand for the reworking of materials in the SRC and possibly other data archives.

Several steps have been taken to secure comparability—or as close an approximation thereto as is possible—with respect to certain significant factors in social stratification. First, the calculations in Tables 1 and 2 are for white men only; except for the Marion County series, where small minorities of the sons were foreign-born, there is a further limitation to native white men. In all cases sons of farmers and farm laborers are excluded. Since the urban community studies must be very selective in their coverage of men with farm background—excluding in the nature of the case those remaining in farm occupations—this restriction is virtually dictated. While it leaves us with only a partial view of the past, it is a view that may be especially interesting as a benchmark for future trends, since in the future larger and larger proportions of the national population will have nonfarm origins. Finally, some care has been taken with the age classification, because the

TABLE 1. CORRELATION BETWEEN SON'S AND FATHER'S OCCUPATIONAL STATUS, FOR NATIVE WHITE MALES WITH NONFARM BACKGROUND: SELECTED DATES AND AREAS, 1910–1966

Line no.	Area and age group	Year						
		1966	1962	1950	1940	1930	1920	1910
(1)	Marion County, Indiana (marriage license applicants)	—	—	—	.385	—	—	.407
(2)	Detroit (1966); U.S. (1962), Chicago (1950 and 1940), by age	(Det.)	(U.S.)	(Chicago)				
	25–34	.272	.353	.293	.347			
	35–44	.286	.390	.314	.344			
	45–54	.409	.378	.300	.241			
	55–64	.296	.354	.301	—			
	25–64	.312	.371	.304				
(3)	U.S., urbanized areas, by size (men 25–64)							
	1,000,000 and over	—	.352	—	—	—	—	—
	250,000 to 1,000,000	—	.399	—	—	—	—	—
	50,000 to 250,000	—	.374	—	—	—	—	—
	U.S., other urban (men 25–64)	—	.357	—	—	—	—	—
(4)	Son's occupation in terms of first job, U.S. (age in 1962)	—	—	.371 (25–34)	.366 (35–44)	.387 (45–54)	.394 (55–64)	—

NOTES AND SOURCES: Line (1). Age distributions, in percentages, for 1940 and 1910 respectively are: Under 24, 36 and 40; 24 to 30, 37 and 36; 31 and over, 27 and 24. Data include foreign-born sons, 3 per cent in 1940 and 10 per cent in 1910. Original data from appendix tables, Rogoff, Natalie, *Recent Trends in Occupational Mobility*, Free Press, Glencoe, Ill., 1953; correlations computed in Duncan, Otis Dudley, "Methodological Issues in the Analysis of Social Mobility," *Social Structure and Mobility in Economic Development*, Smelser, N. J. and S. M. Lipset, editors, Aldine Publishing Co., Chicago, 1966, chap. II. Line (2). *Detroit:* Unpublished data from 1966 Detroit Area Study, directed by Howard Schuman and Edward O. Laumann; sample of 815 men aged 25–64 covers suburban territory as well as Detroit. *U.S.:* Occupational Changes in a Generation survey, U.S. Bureau of the Census, March, 1962; covered population includes a negligible number of nonwhites other than Negroes. *Chicago:* Data (for central city only) from "Six-Cities Survey of Labor Mobility," as analyzed in Duncan, Otis Dudley, and Robert W. Hodge, "Education and Occupational Mobility: A Regression Analysis," *American Journal of Sociology*, vol. 68, May, 1963, pp. 629–644. 1940 data are from retrospective reports for the same sample as the 1950 data, with age lagged 10 years. Sample for 1950 data includes 1,105 men 25–64 years old. Lines (3) and (4): OCG; includes nonwhites, except Negroes.

TABLE 2. REGRESSION OF SON'S ON FATHER'S OCCUPATIONAL STATUS, FOR NATIVE WHITE MALES WITH NONFARM BACKGROUND: SELECTED DATES AND AREAS, 1910–1966

Line no.	Area and age group	Year						
		1966	1962	1950	1940	1930	1920	1910
(1)	Marion County, Indiana (marriage license applicants)	—	—	—	.389	—	—	.381
(2)	Detroit (1966); U.S. (1962), Chicago (1950 and 1940), by age	(Det.)	(U.S.)	(Chicago)				
	25–34	.295	.396	.308	.349	—	—	—
	35–44	.275	.417	.307	.324	—	—	—
	45–54	.443	.401	.286	.230	—	—	—
	55–64	.269	.378	.282	—	—	—	—
	25–64	.316	.402	.298	—	—	—	—
(3)	U.S., urbanized areas, by size (men 25–64)							
	1,000,000 and over	—	.377	—	—	—	—	—
	250,000 to 1,000,000	—	.413	—	—	—	—	—
	50,000 to 250,000	—	.408	—	—	—	—	—
	U.S., other urban (men 25–64)	—	.393	—	—	—	—	—
(4)	Son's occupation in terms of first job, U.S. (age in 1962)	—	—	.390 (25–34)	.350 (35–44)	.370 (45–54)	.370 (55–64)	—

NOTES AND SOURCES: See Table 1.

701

Indiana data are limited to men of marriageable age. Discrepancies remain on this score, however, although it is not clear that they represent a serious impairment of comparability.

In regard to factors beyond direct control, some inferences are attempted in the hope of bolstering confidence in comparisons. The Detroit and Indianapolis data cover territory suburban to the respective central cities, while the Chicago data do not. Bearing in mind the selectivity of suburban migration in the postwar period, we may well entertain doubts as to the legitimacy of a comparison of Chicago with either of the other two cities. The 1962 OCG data, however, are available in a breakdown into central cities vs. suburbs of all urbanized areas of 1,000,000 or more population. The father-son correlation differs only in the third decimal place when the central cities are compared with the entirety of the urbanized areas. What happens is that the correlation is lower in the suburbs than in the central city, but the between-area component of the correlation for urbanized areas almost exactly compensates for this difference.

Another legitimate concern is the difference in city size between Detroit and Chicago, on the one hand, and Indianapolis on the other. Again, a breakdown of the OCG data by size of community (see Tables 1 and 2) provides an estimate of this effect, which we may possibly wish to consider as a correction in the comparison. The difference in the father-son correlation between the size class that includes Detroit and Chicago and the one containing Indianapolis is very close to the difference between the 1940 Chicago correlation for men twenty-five to thirty-four years old (which is the nearest approximation to the age range of the 1940 Indianapolis data) and the Indianapolis correlation.

Another factor that may be equally or more important than the respondent's age is the time reference of the inquiry on father's occupation. In the marriage license data, father's occupation presumably refers to the time at which the license is applied for; hence the fathers are comparatively advanced in age. In the Six-Cities data, the time reference is ambiguous, for the question stipulates "father's longest job." In the OCG and DAS data, the reference is to the father's occupation at the time the respondent was about sixteen years old. I believe this is the preferable form of the question for the purposes at hand, inasmuch as it provides a reading on social origin of the respondent that is proximate in time to the crucial decisions and contingencies that will have a large bearing upon his own occupational achievement. Nonetheless, we are quite uninformed as to the extent to which the other types of question may yield information comparable to this one. My own guess is that the distortion is slight, but I have fairly little evidence except the finding that over a ten-year period men's occupational statuses are sufficiently stable to produce an interannual correlation of .77 for men forty-five to fifty-four years old in the 1951 Chicago data.

Another source of noncomparability is that in the OCG data, in contrast to the other sources, the occupation of the family head other than the father was used in place of father's occupation, in the event that the respondent was not living with the father at age sixteen. In all the studies, there are appreciable proportions with father's occupation unknown. This proportion was doubtlessly increased in the Indianapolis data, in view of the fathers' advanced ages, if applicants made no report on deceased fathers.

Several of the problems of comparability already mentioned arise in rather acute form when we juxtapose line (4) of Tables 1 and 2 with the other lines. In line (4), the report on son's occupation pertains not to his occupation at the time of the 1962 survey but to the occupation he identified as his "first job" (after being instructed not to count part-time jobs during schooling, jobs held during school vacations, or military service). The time reference is rather nonspecific, since the age interval includes ten years; and the age at first job, averaging around eighteen, is also rather variable. The dates against which the coefficients for the four cohorts are shown are merely the approximate centers of rather extended periods over which the experience actually occurred. Nonetheless, intercohort comparisons here do provide a valid indication of trend, if the retrospective reports can be trusted, while intercohort comparisons of occupation in 1962, shown in line (2), do not, for in the latter case the cohorts are not even approximately equivalent in length of working force experience.

I have devoted more space to the possibility of errors arising from noncomparability than is usual in a discussion of trends. This is not because I believe that the present problem is one in which such problems are unusually severe—quite the contrary. The distressing truth is that we devote all too little concern to the *sine qua non* of comparative analysis: the demonstration that the materials being compared are indeed sufficiently comparable for the purpose at hand. Among other things, a livelier appreciation of the impact of errors produced by noncomparability could provide motivation for the strenuous efforts that are needed to effect comparability by standardization of study design and operational concepts.

Comparability: Structural Considerations

Further delaying comment on the possible inferences as to trend afforded by Tables 1 and 2, we should consider another kind of problem in comparability that is sometimes posed as a virtually insuperable obstacle to the drawing of such inferences. In view of the well-known changes in the occupational distribution of the labor force, the emergence of new jobs and obsolescence of old ones, changing skill and educational requirements for jobs with the same nominal titles, shifts in annual salaries and earnings rates due to unionization and other factors, changes in the demographic composition of occupational categories, and so on—in view of all these changes, is there any real meaning in the comparison of father-son correlations for periods separated by several decades? I am unable to cite a coherent published exposition of this line of criticism, but I have encountered it so often in informal communications that I am sure it is no straw man.

A preliminary separation of issues is required. In the first place, unquestionably the occupation structure, in the sense of the relative numbers in the several occupations, has changed markedly in the past several decades. The general nature of the changes is well known. If we were to focus our inquiry on *mobility,* unquestionably changes in occupation structure, in this sense, would have to be reckoned as a cause of the redistribution of opportunities for achievement—although, as I have had occasion to point out at length elsewhere, it is by no means obvious how we are to take structural change into account in analyzing mobility.[41]

Our interest here, however, is not in mobility as such. (The reader who is interested in this way of looking at social stratification is referred to careful reviews of the evidence appearing elsewhere.)[42] The concern here is, to reiterate, with the question of the extent to which a man's occupational achievement may depend on the level of occupational status that we identify as his origin. It is perfectly conceivable that occupational opportunities might expand, in the sense that relatively more high-status jobs are opening up, without there being a change in the intergenerational correlation. Indeed, this is presumably a part of the explanation for the mean shift between generations that we observe in a regression analysis—the average occupational status of sons is typically higher than that of fathers. (Another factor in this effect is that "fathers" are usually represented in a sample in proportion to the number of sons that they have, so that differential fertility induces a downward bias in the mean estimated for the "father's generation.") But the approach taken here places emphasis on the regression slope or correlation, not on the mean difference between generations.

If this stipulation is accepted, there remains the question of whether we are entitled to regard "occupational status" as a fixed attribute of an occupation title, so that, say, a physician or a plumber in 1930 had the same status as his counterpart in 1962.

The scale of occupational status used throughout the present analysis is one based on census information for 1950 and opinion-poll data for 1947. For each detailed census title, the scale score is a weighted average of the percentage of men in the occupation who were high-school graduates in 1950 and the percentage with 1949 incomes of $3,500 or more. The weights were chosen in such a way that, for a selection of 45 detailed occupations, they afforded optimal prediction of the percentage of respondents in a national poll who assigned the occupation an "excellent" or "good" rating.[43]

The issue, specifically, comes down to the question of whether occupational status, scaled in such a fashion, is sufficiently stable over time as to permit meaningful intertemporal comparisons of intergenerational correlations. Conclusive evidence on this point is not at hand, but strong presumptive evidence of stability can be adduced.

First, consider occupational prestige. Prestige studies have been made from time to time over a period of several decades. Robert Hodge, Paul Siegel, and Peter Rossi, the most prominent contemporary students of the subject, recently reviewed the accumulation of evidence and concluded, "There is . . . no evidence whatsoever of any substantial changes in the over-all structure of prestige."[44]

In the upper part of Figure 3, I have manipulated the data assembled by Hodge, Siegel, and Rossi to represent variation in occupational prestige scores over time as a simple causal chain which accounts for the correlations between the scores given to occupations in four studies conducted, respectively, in 1925, 1940, 1947, and 1963. The version of this chain given here differs slightly from one presented elsewhere.[45] Here I have, as it were, taken the earliest study as the benchmark and considered how subsequent readings of prestige have diverged from it. Hence the estimates of path coefficients for this diagram were obtained from the following equations:

$$p_{SC} = r_{SC};$$
$$p_{SC}p_{XS} = r_{XC}; \text{ hence } p_{XS} = r_{XC}/p_{SC};$$
$$p_{SC}p_{XS}p_{YX} = r_{XS}; \text{ hence } p_{YX} = r_{XS}/p_{SC}p_{XS}.$$

The assumption of this method of estimation is that the residuals (or

FIGURE 3. CAUSAL CHAINS REPRESENTING PERSISTENCE
OF PRESTIGE AND INCOME DIFFERENCES
BETWEEN OCCUPATIONS

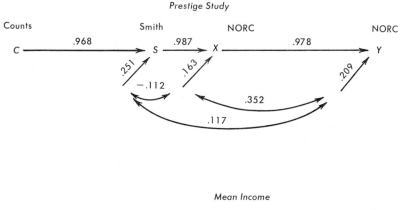

Prestige Study

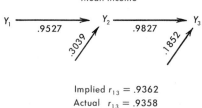

Mean Income

Implied r_{13} = .9362
Actual r_{13} = .9358

SOURCE: Derived from Hodge, Robert W., Paul M. Siegel, and Peter H. Rossi,
"Occupational Prestige in the United States, 1952–1963," *American Journal of
Sociology,* vol. 70, November, 1964, pp. 286–302; and Miller, Herman P., *Income Distribution in the United States,* A 1960 Census Monograph, Washington,
1966, Table C–6.

"disturbances") for variables S, X, and Y are uncorrelated with C, but
not necessarily with each other. In this rudimentary model, such disturbances are a compound of at least three factors: (1) unreliability of
measurement, which is presumably exceedingly small, inasmuch as
prestige scores are averages of ratings supplied by a large number of

respondents; (2) actual "shocks" to the prestige structure, such as might be occasioned by a relative downward shift in the reputed wages of an occupation or modifications in its public "image"; (3) differences in technique between studies. It has been found[46] that differences in techniques of collecting ratings and scoring them have a surprisingly small effect on the outcome, but it is relevant, nonetheless, that the two NORC studies represent a virtually exact replication, while the two earlier studies used techniques differing from each other as well as from NORC.

It is interesting to note how closely the path coefficients estimated for this model correspond to the simple correlations between adjacent sets of scores. Thus, by assumption, $r_{SC} = p_{SC}$; $r_{XS} = .982$ as compared with $p_{XS} = .987$; and $r_{YX} = .990$, while $p_{YX} = .978$. The model thus represents the exceedingly high correlation between the two NORC studies as due in part to the replication of technique, rather than to any lessening of the impact of random shocks to the prestige structure with the passage of time. The effect of similarity in technique is reflected in the positive correlation, .352, between the disturbances of Y and X. Neither of the other two correlations between disturbance terms, at an absolute value of about .1, is statistically significant, in wiew of the small number of occupations that can be compared between the respective studies.

Perhaps the most striking single datum in the collection of information summarized in Figure 3 is that the correlation between prestige scores in two studies separated by as much as thirty-eight years is no less than .934. We can state the import of this figure in the following way. Suppose that a sample of fifty-four-year-old men are reporting their own current occupations and the occupations their fathers held at the time the respondents were sixteen years old. Suppose further that both occupation reports are scored on a prestige scale constructed in the year of the survey and that the correlation between son's and father's occupation comes out as .40. We might then argue that if the fathers' occupations had been scored on a scale of prestige as of thirty-eight years ago, the correlation between the "true" value of father's occupation at that time and the value as we have scored it today would be .934. Hence, we should correct or adjust the father-son correlation to the extent of $.40/.934 = .4283$.

The essentially trivial nature of this adjustment is seen from two circumstances. First, in any practicable sample survey, the sampling error of an obtained correlation is likely to be at least .02 or .03. Second, we know from census reinterview and matching studies that occupation reports themselves are far from perfectly reliable. One estimate, for example, places the reliability coefficient at .861.[47] Hence, correcting an obtained correlation for attenuation by reporting error (assuming independence of the errors in reports of father's and son's occupation) would entail a larger adjustment than any reasonable correction for intergenerational shifts in the prestige value of occupations.

So much for prestige. Figure 3 also summarizes data on stability in the income positions of 118 occupations for which census data on mean wage and salary income have been assembled by Miller.[48] Again, the model of a simple causal chain seems appropriate. If we merely take the two correlations referring respectively to the decades 1939–1949 and 1949–1959 as the path coefficients, the correlation implied by the chain model for the twenty-year period is .9362 as compared with the observed value of .9358. On this evidence, we should conclude that income positions of occupations are slightly less stable than prestige scores. This comparison would only be warranted, however, if the same set of occupations were used in both cases. Inasmuch as the income data are much more representative of the entire occupation structure than are the prestige data—where ratings are available only for selected occupations—the alternative conclusion is that the income series reflect somewhat more accurately than the prestige series the actual stability of occupational status.

Finally, we may adduce one further finding. For 118 occupations Hodge computed the percentage of men who were high-school graduates in 1940 and 1950, and found the interannual correlation to be .97.[49] Hence, educational levels of occupations are much like prestige scores and income levels in regard to intertemporal stability.

The findings just reviewed are substantively significant in their own right. From the standpoint of the methodological issue that motivated their introduction here, these findings mean, in few words, that we are *not* measuring occupational status with a rubber yardstick. The implication of the disturbance terms, with path coefficients on the order of .2 or .3, and with relatively low intercorrelations of disturbances, is that in each period the occupational status structure is subject to a fairly small "random shock" and that such shocks cumulate over time. Hence the structure, if it continued to evolve under these conditions, would gradually drift away from its initial configuration to one which bore no resemblance thereto, in much the same way that a simple Markov process leads to a distribution over system states that does not depend on the initial distribution. Yet, on the estimates now available, this would take quite a long time. If the prestige structures separated by thirty-eight years are correlated to the extent of .934, those seventy-six years apart will still be correlated as highly as $(.934)^2 = .872$. We shall not be in too much trouble on this score if it ever becomes possible to compute reliable intergenerational correlations between grandfather and grandson.

Interpretation of Results

As the reader has guessed by now, this discussion mostly concerns how to measure stratification trends and not the results of such measurement. But we are, at last, ready to discuss the substance of Tables 1 and 2, though not without alluding to a few more technicalities in the process.

The first thing to note is that small changes or differences in father-son correlations are not always in the same direction as those in the regression coefficient for son's status on father's (compare Tables 1 and 2). For example, the correlations, taken literally, suggest a slight decline in stratification in Marion County between 1910 and 1940, while the regressions change in the opposite way. In neither case, of course, is the change large enough to be taken seriously, even if statistically significant.

The second point is that all our care in seeking to effectuate comparability cannot overcome the uncertainty inherent in the confounding of time changes with alterations in the spatial unit for which data happen to be available. It may be true, as one noted student of stratification once averred, that "All America dwells in Jonesville," but statisticians are still well-advised not to accept statistics for Jonesville, Indianapolis, Chicago, or Detroit as estimates of national parameters, or vice versa. Discounting the likelihood of any pronounced change over so short a period as 1962 to 1966 (especially inasmuch as we give evidence shortly of stability of national estimates between 1962 and 1964), it is plausible that the difference between U.S. in 1962 and Detroit in 1966 is due to the contribution of between-area covariation to the national correlation, inflating it by comparison with the correlation for one locality.

The same argument would allow us to suppose that national correlations in 1940 and 1910 might well have been higher than the corresponding figures for Indianapolis. This does not strictly follow, however. The only thing that is made reasonably sure by the algebra of covariance is that the *average* within-locality correlation will be lower than the national correlation. Perhaps Indianapolis was a locality with a higher correlation than the average locality. At any rate, it falls in a size group with a slightly higher correlation than the nation as a whole.

It would be easy to persuade me that, of all the six communities in the Six-Cities Study, Chicago is the one most likely to be comparable with Detroit. If we assumed that the two places are interchangeable, the data would suggest the most minute increase in stratification between 1950 and 1966, though one that is not consistently in evidence for all age groups. At present, however, there is simply no way to assess comparability; and even if there were, we are plagued by substantial sampling errors. An unpublished re-analysis of the data for all six cities,[50] makes it clear that time changes, 1940 to 1950, in the Six-Cities data are swamped by the variation in sample estimates between age groups and places.

Only lines (1) and (4) in the two tables, therefore, provide reasonably firm estimates on which to base a conclusion about trend. As already noted, the Indianapolis data suggest that no appreciable change occurred between 1910 and 1940. The national data on first jobs for successive cohorts indicate the same thing. (Once more it is pertinent that the correlation and regression coefficients do not tell precisely the same story about the differences between cohorts.) The national data on first jobs bring forward the evidence to a somewhat later date than is available for Indianapolis. Thus, the best information we have suggests that no change occurred in the rigidity of stratification in America between 1910 and 1950. (Remember, of course, that none of the conclusions of this chapter is taken to apply to groups explicitly excluded from the analysis, most notably, females and Negroes; relevant evidence for these groups is far weaker than for white males and essentially nothing can be said about trends within these classifications.)

I personally feel that the best guess we can make from the remaining data in the two tables is that the period of no trend in degree of stratification extends to 1966. This hunch had best be left as a hypothesis to be verified subsequently. The replication studies called for at the end of this paper could settle the matter, or at least would have a good chance of doing so.

Intercohort Comparisons

Although most of the preceding analysis concerns interperiod comparisons, one intercohort comparison of data collected cross-sectionally was included: the correlation of first job with father's occupation. Several other such comparisons will now be examined. Of course, we are here using a cross-sectional but retrospective data-collection procedure in an attempt to reconstruct the past in such a way that intercohort differences validly represent time changes in the experience of successive cohorts. We must be careful to discriminate between items for which this kind of inference is permissible, given confidence in the retrospective data, and those for which it is not. Efforts to infer mobility trends from cross-sectional age data on the contemporaneous experience of different cohorts[51] must be rejected.

Exercises in intercohort comparison will be limited to data from the OCG survey. This survey includes not only occupational data, but also information on educational attainment, which is extremely relevant to the problem of measuring stratification. Hence, Tables 3 and 4 present a selection of correlations taken to be either direct measures of the degree of stratification or of mechanisms involved in the process of stratification. By happenstance, correlations are available for two alternative age classifications. Hence, we are alerted to the possibility that inercohort differences may arise from essentially arbitrary choices as to the grouping of birth dates, given sampling variability in the basic data. Thus, the second line of Table 3 might suggest a slight increase in the father-son correlation with respect to educational attainment (an increase of .03 from the two oldest to the two younger cohorts); but the second line of Table 4, for an alternative age classification on very nearly the same population, betrays no such symptom of trend. In addition, Table 4 incorporates two series that just happen to be available for females. The idea is not to attempt any analysis of female achievement as such, but merely to call attention to the lack of synchronism in the fluctuations over cohorts for men and women. I interpret this to mean that such fluctuations in the correlation between education and father's occupation or between education and number of siblings are merely evidence of sampling variation rather than any indication of time-specific causes of variation in the degree or process of stratification.

Indeed, the very considerable amount of data compactly summarized in the two tables appear to tell a monotonously repetitive story: none of the series shows reliable and regular increases or decreases in the magnitudes of the correlations such as we should expect if stratification were steadily becoming more or less rigid in the United States during the period around World War I up to about a decade ago. It is possible that sufficiently circumspect analysis would succeed in identifying meaningful patterns in the fluctuations, of the sort, say, that could be attributed to the Great Depression or the impact of

TABLE 3. CORRELATIONS BETWEEN SELECTED STRATIFI-
CATION VARIABLES FOR NATIVE NON-NEGRO MEN 25
TO 64 YEARS OLD IN THE EXPERIENCED CIVILIAN
LABOR FORCE, TOTAL AND NONFARM BACK-
GROUND, BY AGE: MARCH, 1962

Population and variables	Age in 1962			
	25–34	35–44	45–54	55–64
All men				
Father's occupation, father's education	.49	.51	.45	.51
Education, father's education	.42	.42	.39	.39
Oldest brother's education, father's education	.44	.47	.45	.51
Education, father's occupation	.42	.44	.45	.39
Oldest brother's education, father's occupation	.41	.44	.36	.44
Education, oldest brother's education	.56	.54	.57	.53
Education, number of siblings	−.35	−.34	−.34	−.29
First job, father's education	.33	.34	.30	.31
First job, father's occupation	.39	.40	.42	.43
First job, number of siblings	−.29	−.26	−.24	−.24
First job, oldest brother's education	.38	.36	.33	.44
First job, education	.58	.53	.56	.56
Nonfarm background				
Father's occupation, father's education	.49	.53	.49	.53
Education, father's education	.40	.40	.37	.35
Oldest brother's education, father's education	.42	.45	.44	.50
Education, father's occupation	.41	.43	.45	.39
Oldest brother's education, father's occupation	.38	.44	.38	.48
Education, oldest brother's education	.54	.51	.54	.54
Education, number of siblings	−.33	−.33	−.30	−.28
First job, father's education	.31	.34	.31	.30
First job, father's occupation	.37	.37	.39	.39
First job, number of siblings	−.27	−.26	−.20	−.25
First job, oldest brother's education	.35	.34	.34	.47
First job, education	.59	.55	.56	.56

SOURCE: Unpublished tabulations from Occupational Changes in a Generation survey, U.S. Bureau of the Census, March, 1962.

World War II. The reader is at liberty to conjecture such interpretations, but after repeated inspection of these data, I find none that is wholly plausible. If a repetition of the OCG survey should find the same pattern of intercohort differences, giving us greater confidence in their reliability, then more effort might profitably go into this kind of interpretation. In the meanwhile, it is salutary to remember that the standard error of the correlations in Table 3 is usually of the order of

TABLE 4. CORRELATIONS BETWEEN SELECTED STRATIFICATION VARIABLES FOR SPECIFIED POPULATIONS OF MEN AND WOMEN, BY AGE: MARCH, 1962

Population and variables	Age in 1962						
	27–31	32–36	37–41	42–46	47–51	52–56	57–61
Native white civilian men							
Father's occupation, father's education	.45	.48	.50	.46	.44	.42	.50
Education, father's education	.40	.39	.42	.39	.39	.42	.42
Education, father's occupation	.41	.43	.47	.40	.46	.39	.44
Education, number of siblings	–.36	–.30	–.36	–.31	–.34	–.34	–.25
White women, married, spouse present							
Education, father's occupation	.40	.35	.37	.39	.35	.30	.41
Education, number of siblings	–.31	–.33	–.30	–.28	–.25	–.21	–.30

SOURCE: Data for men from Duncan, Beverly, *Family Factors and School Dropout: 1920–1960*, Cooperative Research Project No. 2258, U.S. Office of Education, University of Michigan, Ann Arbor, 1965, Tables 3–2 and 3–3; data for women from unpublished OCG tabulations for wives of men in OCG sample.

.02 or .03, not to mention the errors arising from varying fractions of nonresponse to particular questions.

In summary: *no trend*. The OCG data permit estimates of some parameters of the process of stratification that are astonishingly near to being invariant over the experiences of successive cohorts completing their schooling and entering the labor market during the period, roughly, 1920–1955.

In the case of one of the correlations, that between father's education and fathers' occupation, we have a somewhat different measure, that of the extent to which the occupational achievement of mature men depends on their prior educational attainment. This too appears to be nearly constant over time. However, there is an intergenerational difference which indicates the contrary. For all the four cohorts of OCG respondents themselves, the education-occupation correlation is in the range .56 to .64, appreciably higher than the corresponding correlation for "fathers." The comparison is strained, however, because "fathers" in a retrospective intergenerational study do not represent a real cohort, but rather a curious aggregate of men appearing in the sample in proportion to the number of sons they happen to have. Even the inference that educational attainment has been an increasingly important factor in occupational achievement, therefore, had best be regarded as tentative, even though it is compatible with various stray bits of evidence and received opinion. (There is no question, of course, that the occupational structure has been educationally "upgraded," but that is not the issue in the present discussion, which has to do with differential occupational achievement among the members of a cohort.)

PROSPECTS FOR TREND ANALYSES

The exercise in temporal comparisons summarized here is somewhat reminiscent of the experience others have had with international comparisons of occupational mobility.[52] Some differences between nations appear in the raw data, but the more careful the attempt to ensure real comparability, the less certain the differences seem to be. Such differences as do withstand scrutiny from a technical standpoint are not easily or convincingly explained on empirical or theoretical grounds. The simple fact may be that we are, in comparative studies and trend analysis, extending our research techniques into a region in which they cannot yield trustworthy results. So little effort has gone into calibration and standardization of technique that we cannot be sure what the marginal return to a *serious* effort to achieve comparability would be.

I am able, however, to report a single (more or less unplanned) effort at pure replication with respect to the subject matter at hand. The OCG survey already referred to was carried out by the Bureau of the Census in March, 1962. Two and one-half years later, in October, 1964, the Bureau carried out a survey for another purpose that included some items parallel to those in OCG. The two surveys not only shared a common technique of sampling; the administration of the questionnaires was handled in much the same way. We can inspect a set of correlations from the two studies computed for very nearly comparable populations: native non-Negro men twenty-five to thirty-four years old in 1962, and all white men twenty-five to thirty-four in 1964. There is, of course, an approximately 75 per cent overlap of the two cohorts in the population, although the two samples are quite distinct. Table 5 shows the correlations for items treated in closely similar

TABLE 5.   INTERCORRELATIONS OF STRATIFICATION VARIABLES IN TWO SURVEYS: ABOVE DIAGONAL, 1962 OCG; BELOW DIAGONAL, 1964 CPS-NORC

	Variable (see stub)			
Variable	V	X	U	Y
Father's education (V)	—	.491	.420	.349
Father's occupation (X)	.487	—	.419	.388
Respondent's education (U)	.407	.429	—	.644
Respondent's occupation (Y)	.336	.391	.637	—

NOTE: 1962 data for native non-Negro men 25–34 years old in experienced civilian labor force; 1964 data for white men 25–34 years old. 1962 data from OCG supplement to March, 1962, Current Population Survey; 1964 data from supplement to October, 1964, Current Population Survey, tabulated by National Opinion Research Center.

fashion in the two surveys. It is gratifying to observe that the largest difference between the two sets of correlations does not exceed .013 in absolute magnitude. If we assume that there should have been no appreciable real change during this brief interval of time and that the uncontrolled impairments to comparability are really negligible, these findings may stand as a demonstration of the reproducibility of correlation estimates secured with the technique being used. Actually, we might have expected some larger differences on the basis of sampling errors alone, although the effect of constancy in sample *design* would be to reduce such errors.

Inverting the proposition, we are now in a position to argue that any real change in degree of stratification, or in correlations between variables implicated in the process of stratification, provided the change is large enough to be interesting, can be detected by repeated surveys, provided there is rigorous standardization of concepts, scales, and survey techniques. Thus, I would urge that high priority be given to a replication of the OCG survey in 1972 (to take advantage of the convenience of a ten-year interval). In all relevant particulars, the survey should repeat the procedures used ten years earlier. This would not preclude experimentation with new questions, alternative measures of occupational status, and so forth, provided that these are handled as additions to the replication and not as substitutes for it. Such additions in the case of the 1964 repetition evidently did not impair comparability. If, by 1972, for example, it appears desirable to experiment with a new scale of occupational status, this can be done along with the repetition of the use of the old one, at the relatively small cost of dual recoding.

Second priority, in a program to measure stratification trends, might well be given to a 1971 replication of the Six-Cities Survey of Labor Mobility. Again, a mere "re-study" without *serious* intent to replicate would merely result in "interesting" data, not in trend measurement. Even with every effort to replicate, the comparison might yield somewhat equivocal findings, given the modest sample sizes used in 1951. However, if at least four of the original six cities were covered again, the problem of sampling errors should be manageable.

A third proposal would depend on the feasibility of recovering and recoding schedules in data archives, to capitalize on the various ad hoc measurements of intergenerational mobility that have been made in connection with studies on other topics. Several points would have to be established: that the original data are of sufficiently high quality to merit lavish attention; that sampling and field procedures came up to a sufficiently high standard; and that the data archives contain enough auxiliary information not elsewhere available to present unique opportunities for analysis. Should the verdict be positive on all these counts, it would then be pertinent to ascertain whether future replication studies, designed for comparability with archival data, would stand a chance to render useful estimates of trend.

Finally, if there should be interest in the long-term historical trend, it would be possible to explore the possibilities in repeating and extending Rogoff's *tour de force*. I have no informed opinion as to the outcome of feasibility studies along this line and suspect that, in any event, higher priority will be given to studies that monitor future trends rather than those concerned with the more and more remote past. There is, nevertheless, much concern these days with measurement problems in historical investigations, and it would be premature to discount the possibilities.

NOTES

1. Cooley, C. H., *Social Process,* Charles Scribner's Sons, New York, 1918, chap. 8.
2. Sorokin, Pitirim, *Social Mobility,* Harper & Bros., New York, 1927.
3. Sibley, Elbridge, "Some Demographic Clues to Stratification," *American Sociological Review,* vol. 7, June, 1942, pp. 322–330.
4. *Ibid.,* p. 322.
5. Havighurst, Robert J., "The Influence of Recent Social Changes on the Desire for Social Mobility in the United States," in Bryson, Lyman, *et al.,* editors, *Conflicts of Power in Modern Culture, Seventh Symposium,* Harper & Bros., New York, 1947.
6. Hertzler, J. O., "Some Tendencies Toward a Closed Class System in the United States," *Social Forces,* vol. 30, March, 1952, pp. 313–323.
7. Hollingshead, August B., "Trends in Social Stratification: A Case Study," *American Sociological Review,* vol. 17, December, 1952, pp. 679–686.
8. Petersen, William, "Is America Still the Land of Opportunity?" *Commentary,* vol. 16, November, 1953, pp. 477–486 (quoted at p. 482).
9. Sjoberg, Gideon, "Are Social Classes in America Becoming More Rigid?" *American Sociological Review,* vol. 16, December, 1951, pp. 775–783; Chinoy, Ely, "Social Mobility Trends in the United States," *American Sociological Review,* vol. 20, April, 1955, pp. 180–186.
10. Rogoff, Natalie, *Recent Trends in Occupational Mobility,* Free Press, Glencoe, Ill., 1953, p. 49.
11. Lenski, Gerhard E., "Trends in Inter-Generational Occupational Mobility in the United States," *American Sociological Review,* vol. 23, October, 1958, pp. 514–523.
12. Jackson, Elton F., and Harry J. Crockett, Jr., "Occupational Mobility in the United States: A Point Estimate and Trend Comparison," *American Sociological Review,* vol. 29, February, 1964, pp. 5–15.
13. Duncan, Otis Dudley, "The Trend of Occupational Mobility in the United States," *American Sociological Review,* vol. 30, August, 1965, pp. 491–498; Blau, Peter M., and Otis Dudley Duncan, *The American Occupational Structure,* Wiley, New York, 1967, chap. 3.
14. Sorokin, Pitirim, *Social Mobility, op. cit.,* p. 160 *et passim.*
15. Schnore, Leo F., "Social Mobility in Demographic Perspective," *American Sociological Review,* vol. 26, June, 1961, pp. 407–423.
16. Cooley, C. H., *Social Process, op. cit.,* p. 78.
17. Buckley, Walter, "Social Stratification and the Functional Theory of Social Differentiation," *American Sociological Review,* vol. 23, August, 1958, pp. 369–375 (quoted at pp. 372–373).
18. Svalastoga, Kaare, *Social Differentiation,* David McKay Co., New York, 1965, p. 70.

19. The subtitle of Harold D. Lasswell's *Politics,* McGraw-Hill, New York, 1936.
20. Svalastoga, Kaare, *Social Differentiation, op. cit.,* p. 16.
21. Sorokin, Pitirim, *Social Mobility, op. cit.,* p. 12.
22. Spengler, Joseph J., "Changes in Income Distribution and Social Stratification: A Note," *American Journal of Sociology,* vol. 59, November, 1953, pp. 247–259 (quotation at p. 247).
23. *Ibid.;* Miller, Herman P., *Income Distribution in the United States,* A 1960 Census Monograph, Government Printing Office, Washington, 1966, chap. 1.
24. Alker, H. R., Jr., and B. M. Russett, "On Measuring Inequality," *Behavioral Science,* vol. 9, July, 1964, pp. 207–218; Bowman, Mary Jean, "A Graphical Analysis of Personal Income Distribution in the United States," *American Economic Review,* vol. 35, September, 1945, pp. 607–628; Yntema, Dwight B., "Measures of the Inequality in the Personal Distribution of Wealth or Income," *Journal of the American Statistical Association,* vol. 28, December, 1933, pp. 423–433.
25. Duncan, Otis Dudley, "Discrimination against Negroes," *Annals of the American Academy of Political and Social Science,* vol. 371, May, 1967, pp. 85–103.
26. Duncan, Otis Dudley, "Ability and Achievement," *Eugenics Quarterly,* vol. 15, March, 1968, pp. 1–11. (The model is given here in a slightly different form from that appearing in the source publication.)
27. Sjoberg, Gideon, *op. cit.*
28. Petersen, William, *op. cit.*
29. Dahrendorf, Ralf, *Class and Class Conflict in Industrial Society,* Stanford University Press, Stanford, 1959; as quoted in Lasswell, Thomas E., *Class and Stratum,* Houghton Mifflin Co., Boston, 1965, pp. 477–478.
30. Svalastoga, Kaare, *loc. cit.*
31. Duncan, Otis Dudley, and Robert W. Hodge, "Education and Occupational Mobility: A Regression Analysis," *American Journal of Sociology,* vol. 68, May, 1963, pp. 629–644, esp. pp. 638–640; Blau, Peter M., and Otis Dudley Duncan, *The American Occupational Structure, op. cit.,* chap. V.
32. White, Harrison C., "Cause and Effect in Social Mobility Tables," *Behavioral Science,* vol. 8, January, 1963, pp. 14–27; Goodman, Leo A., "On the Statistical Analysis of Mobility Tables," *American Journal of Sociology,* vol. 70, March, 1965, pp. 564–585.
33. Duncan, Otis Dudley, "Methodological Issues in the Analysis of Social Mobility," in Smelser, N. J., and S. M. Lipset, editors, *Social Structure and Mobility in Economic Development,* Aldine Publishing Co., Chicago, 1966.
34. *Ibid.*
35. Blau and Duncan, *op. cit.,* chap. IV.
36. *Ibid.,* chap III.
37. Rogoff, Natalie, *Recent Trends in Occupational Mobility,* Free Press, Glencoe, Ill., 1953.
38. Palmer, Gladys L., *Labor Mobility in Six Cities,* Social Science Research Council, New York, 1954.
39. For example, Curtis, Richard F., "Income and Occupational Mobility," *American Sociological Review,* vol. 25, October, 1960, pp. 727–730.
40. The 1966 DAS was under the direction of Professors Edward O. Laumann and Howard Schuman. I am grateful to them for the opportunity to make use of the data in Tables 1 and 2 in advance of the investigators' own reports on the project.
41. Duncan, Otis Dudley, "Methodological Issues . . . ," *op. cit.*
42. Blau and Duncan, *op. cit.,* chap. III; Duncan, Otis Dudley, "The Trend of Occupational Mobility in the United States," *American Sociological Review,*

vol. 30, August, 1965, pp. 491–498; Jackson, Elton F., and Harry J. Crockett, Jr., "Occupational Mobility in the United States," *op. cit.*

43. Duncan, Otis Dudley, "A Socioeconomic Index for All Occupations," in Reiss, Albert J., Jr., and others, *Occupations and Social Status,* Free Press of Glencoe, New York, 1961, chap. VI.

44. Hodge, Robert W., Paul M. Siegel, and Peter H. Rossi, "Occupational Prestige in the United States, 1925–63," *American Journal of Sociology,* vol. 70, November, 1964, pp. 286–302 (quoted from p. 298).

45. Duncan, Otis Dudley, "Path Analysis: Sociological Examples," *American Journal of Sociology,* vol. 72, July, 1966, pp. 1–16.

46. In work in progress by the authors cited in note 44.

47. Siegel, Paul M., and Robert W. Hodge, "A Causal Approach to the Study of Measurement Error," in Blalock, Hubert M., Jr., and Ann B. Blalock, editors, *Methodology in Social Research,* McGraw-Hill, New York, 1968, Table 2.2.

48. Miller, Herman P., *Income Distribution in the United States, op. cit.,* Table C-6.

49. Hodge, Robert W., "Occupational Composition and Status Crystallization," M.A. Thesis, University of Chicago, 1961.

50. Lane, Angela, "Occupational Mobility in Six Cities," unpublished M.A. Research Paper, University of Chicago, 1967.

51. Glass, David V., editor, *Social Mobility in Britain,* Free Press, Glencoe, Ill., 1954, p. 187; Blau, Peter M., "Inferring Mobility Trends from a Single Study," *Population Studies,* vol. 16, July, 1962, pp. 79–85.

52. Miller, S. M., "Comparative Social Mobility," *Current Sociology,* vol. 9, no. 1; Svalastoga, Kaare, "Social Mobility: The Western European Model," *Acta Sociologica,* vol. 9, 1965, pp. 175–182.

14. WELFARE AND ITS MEASUREMENT

Ida C. Merriam

CONCEPTS AND MEASURES

WELFARE IS A summing-up concept—appropriately placed at the end of a volume on social change. Growth in population, changes in technology, in work and play, in family relations and social organization (or disorganization) all have welfare aspects. A large part of the meaning of welfare is to be found in the issues surrounding the questions "how much," "what quality," "for whom," that must be asked with respect to each separate component of social life and social change. But this cannot be the total meaning. For these parts are interacting and potentially conflicting. And the human mind—no matter how sophisticated—persists in wanting to know whether conditions in general are better or worse, while the policymaker must ask which emphasis or which choice will contribute most to the general welfare.

Whether welfare in this general sense can ever be measured is highly doubtful. Like positive health, welfare may be impossible to define in operational or policy terms. Indeed, at this level of abstraction, the two concepts are almost indistinguishable. Without fundamentally changing the concept, the term "welfare" could be substituted for the word "health" in the World Health Organization definition of positive health: "Health (read Welfare) is a state of complete physical, mental and social well-being and not merely the absence of disease and illness" to which one might add a final phrase, such as "or the absence of poverty and social disorganization." This is not to say that the idea of welfare has no meaning. But because the meaning is value-laden and complex, the social scientist can hope to discover only symbolic indicators and proxy measures.

Measurement is feasible and significant along two main axes. One is the axis of productivity and abundance. An increasing quantity and quality of all the elements that make up the level of living is a basic aspect of welfare. Whatever caveats there may be with respect to the negative effects of overindulgence, closely scheduled activities, loss of

721

open spaces, and other accompaniments of technology and economic growth, there is no doubt that the net result thus far has been a gain in individual welfare. It is possible that failure to control international conflict and population growth may reverse the balance. Other negative effects—environmental pollution, for example—may be more easily corrected, in part from the products of further growth. Nevertheless, the Gross National Product and its derivative per capita personal income remain among the basic measures that can serve as proxy welfare indicators.

The second major axis—and perhaps the most distinctive for an approach to the measurement of welfare—is that of distribution. From whatever reference point, and in whatever specific context the idea of welfare is introduced, it carries an overtone of equity and social justice. The general concept of fairness in the distribution of whatever goods, services, or life chances the society can offer seems to have an almost universal acceptance as a goal if not in practice. Notions as to what is fair and just obviously differ among individuals in different circumstances, among societies in different stages of economic and political development and over time. But the preference for an equitable society is deeply rooted.

The two axes—abundance and distribution—intersect at many points. As has frequently been observed, inequalities of wealth and power are greatest in poor and partially developed economies. Increasing productivity and modern technology make possible a more equitable and less concentrated distribution. And at least at certain stages of economic growth, they also require mass consumption. Even in a highly developed economy, economic growth generally contributes more to distributional welfare than would any conceivable redistribution of the existing aggregate output of the economy. In the expanding economy of the 1940's in the U.S., all groups shared in the general gains; but the young, the old, women, and unskilled workers shared to a much greater extent than the average. General growth was an equalizing factor. In the decade of the 1950's, on the other hand, growing unemployment hit hardest among the younger workers and among those with the lowest incomes. The general slowdown in the economy meant the end of a trend toward lesser inequality.

In a longer historical perspective, the relationship between economic growth and changes in the distribution of income may take on a different form and involve somewhat different institutional forces in later as compared with earlier stages of economic development. Industrial expansion and agricultural progress, which result in an increased supply of basic consumer goods at lower prices, translate directly into improvements in the living conditions of those at the bottom of the income scale and to a lessening of inequality. In the later stages of technological development and particularly with the dominance of large urban concentrations of population, the translation is accompanied by more constraints and depends in much greater measure on social action and governmental intervention. The actions taken by government (or foundations or large businesses) with respect to urban housing and transportation, environmental sanitation, and the availability of medical services, for example, increasingly affect the distribution of the products of economic growth. At the level of economic development of the U.S. today, the direction of future economic growth is critical, and equality and inequality become issues that must be faced explicitly and in an increasing number of contexts.

Distribution may also become a more important issue as the general level of living expands. Wants and aspirations respond to what is seen to be possible. Equity, in whatever way it is perceived by the current generation, becomes a condition of political and social stability.

Equity, of course, does not necessarily mean equality. Some inequality is necessary to provide economic incentives to produce, although our knowledge as to the effects of different types of incentive or disincentive (earnings differentials, progressive taxation, power relationships, status and symbolic rewards) is limited. And while there is a fairly general concern that the trend toward a less unequal distribution of income in the United States appears to have come to a standstill in the past two decades, there is certainly no consensus as to how far a shift in the direction of equality "should" go—either from the point of view of fairness of rewards or optimum motivation. Tibor Scitovsky notes that "We have yet to devise machinery whereby consumers or citizens could express their preferences between a small addition to income and a slight easing of conscience over the inequality of man."[1] It is possible, however, to measure distributional elements without complete agreement on a definition of equity.

If we are not sure as to the desirable shape of the total distribution curve, we can perhaps come closer to agreement on certain cut-off points or negative welfare indicators. The current interest in poverty measures is an example of this approach, and one which will be discussed in some detail later in this chapter. This idea of a boundary zone between acceptable—indeed desirable—variations in status and functioning and conditions which social policy should not accept can be applied in many different areas. Some unrest, some family disorganization, some school dropouts, some poor health, some unemployment, some crime are inevitable, and inevitably greater in a society undergoing rapid change, but there is a point or line at which one can say this is "too much"—i.e., this is a sign that corrective social action will have net positive effects. As in so many of the problems with which social scientists deal, every individual may have his own firmly held ideas—in this case, as to where the balance tips. These ideas may be among the data which the social scientist has to build into his models. It seems reasonable to assume that there are tipping points that may themselves change over time, but that it is part of the task of analysis to help locate them. Such points may then help to define a social minimum that becomes part of an operational definition of welfare.

The idea of a social minimum has a long history, both in philosophical discourse and in reform movements. The relation of this concept to the general concept of equity may be particularly relevant to currently important issues of social policy. Kenneth Boulding has suggested that the concept of social justice encompasses two different ideas. One he calls disalienation—the idea that no one should be alienated from the society in which he lives, that everyone should enjoy equality before the law, and religious and racial equality. The second idea is that of desert—in a just society each individual will get what he deserves. One way in which society reconciles these two dimensions of justice is by establishment of a social minimum, with individual desert given play above this minimum.[2] This formulation leaves open the question of how individual desert is defined or determined. It is possible that conflicts over the valuation of individual merit or individual contributions to society will be less sharp when there is a general conviction that those at the bottom are assured at least of the necessities of life.

So long as necessities mean largely subsistence needs, the distinction between a social minimum concept and a measure of the over-all degree of inequality can be fairly clear-cut. As the general wealth of a society and the goods and services which are perceived as necessities increase, the distinction becomes somewhat blurred. The higher the poverty level in absolute terms, the more critical becomes the question of the distribution of real income both below and just above the level. The social minimum which gains solid public and political support at any given time will certainly be related to and largely bounded by the existing distributional patterns in the middle-income levels.

The general level of income and welfare affects distributional problems in another way. To the extent that necessities consist primarily of food, clothing, and other items produced and effectively distributed by the private market economy, the measurement of income inequality can focus on money income. The value of home-produced food and services was a more important qualifier of money income as a measure of welfare at the turn of the century than today. (The qualification continues to affect international comparisons, particularly between more and less developed countries.) A more significant factor in the measurement of distribution and welfare today is the increasing number of goods and services—of current necessities—that can be generally available and equitably distributed only as a result of public action. One can exaggerate the extent of change. Education has for well over a century been regarded as a necessity that must be publicly provided, but this consensus was not arrived at without sharp social conflict. Eminent domain has always played a part in the distribution of land and capital. Research and technology, however, have made certain basic services —notably medical care—much more expensive as well as much more important. At the same time the growth of population and the pressure of people into cities have made goods that were once "free"—clean air, quiet, and privacy—obtainable only at a price. Public services and governmental decisions thus become more important in the evaluation of equity and in the range of social policies relating to welfare.

PROBLEMS OF MEASUREMENT

Defining What Is Distributed

The argument up to this point has been intentionally cast in general terms. The thesis is that in an industrialized country like the United States the level and distribution of income provide the most useful over-all measure of welfare that has yet been devised. The question of what is meant by income and to whom it is distributed (the individual or a defined family group) as well as the reference period, have been largely avoided. They must be faced before one can begin looking for trend data or outlining a theoretical framework in which to place the available data.

The relevant literature is so voluminous[3]—and the unsolved questions so numerous—that it is difficult to know how to get a hold on the problem. It might help to start with some didactic propositions.

If the basic purpose is to measure change in over-all welfare, we must look for an indicator that lends itself to repeated use and to the provision of meaningful trend data. An indicator in this context is not intended to mean one series of figures. It does mean an interrelated set of measures, not just a congeries of statistical data. Several different methods of summarizing the income distribution measures may be appropriate and desirable. The basic measures should be usable as a classificatory scheme for the analysis of the distributional effects of all the components of economic and social change. Supplementary measures will be needed for specific analytic purposes. They may lead to refinements in the basic measure or simply to better understanding of its limitations and its meaning.

Money Income. From this perspective, perhaps one can turn to the obvious starting point—current money income—and ask how useful for an analysis of welfare is the distribution of money income alone. I would argue that it is considerably more useful than much current discussion implies, largely because of the degree to which it is related to other factors that affect the way people are able to live and their control over their life situation.

Recent attention to the problems of the poor has highlighted the fact that ability to use income may in some circumstances be almost as important for the level of living as the amount of income itself. The availability of credit at reasonable terms, access to decent housing, knowledge of where to buy and what to buy can stretch dollars while slum conditions shrink them. As in a number of other relationships, however, there appears to be a high correlation between the amount of money income and the ability to use it effectively. Efforts to improve the purchasing power of the poor through better access to the market and lessened discrimination of all kinds are highly desirable. In the end, the amount of money income may prove to be the critical factor.

From time to time, the suggestion has been made that distributional equity should be measured in terms of consumption rather than income. Quite aside from problems of measurement over time, current consumption is not a good measure of the distribution of welfare, because there is no satisfactory way to take account of individual tastes and choices. For certain types of consumption, notably food, it has been possible to develop accepted standards of minimum adequacy. Housing is another area in which actual physical condition—that is, consumption—may be a more reliable indicator of a level of living than income, at minimum or below minimum levels. But the minimum is only one part of the concept of equity and welfare.

The extent to which the distribution of money income may be accepted as a valid indicator of welfare can be better assessed after considering what kinds of correctives one might want to make were it feasible to do so. Most important are various types of nonmoney income and assets and wealth. The latter brings in the question of the time-scale over which income, however defined, is measured.

Nonmoney Income. Considerable attention has been devoted to the definition of nonmoney equivalents of money income. At an earlier period one of the obvious and important factors in any comparison of farm and nonfarm incomes was the value of home-grown food or home-produced clothing. Trends over time are affected by the treatment of such items. While their importance is declining as agriculture becomes a quantitatively less important occupation and the money economy extends to the farm, they cannot be entirely disregarded. Of a different character is the imputed value of the use of owner-occupied dwellings or of consumer durables. The latter concept approaches a wealth-income measure. It is important for certain kinds of economic analysis, but may not be essential for a welfare-distribution indicator because of the relation between current money income levels and the quantity and value of durables possessed.

The U.S. National Income Accounts include the estimated value of wages in kind and the estimated net rental value of owner-occupied homes in the income total. Hence distributions of family income derived from the National Income Accounts accept this definition. Most household survey data, on the other hand, attempt no such imputations and measure essentially money income.

While the National Income Accounts include an estimate for wages in kind (primarily the value of meals or company-owned housing provided by the employer) they have not attempted to measure certain other forms of private compensation that may be of growing importance. Expense accounts, help in the purchase of a home, stock bonuses, advanced education and training, private pension plans—all benefit disproportionately the higher-income groups. Our knowledge as to the aggregate value and distributional effect of such forms of compensation is very limited. This is an area where much more work is needed.

Nonmoney income is by its very nature a highly circumscribed type of income—it may increase the level of consumption of a particular category, but it is not available for other uses. The welfare significance of nonmoney income is probably quite different at low than at high money income levels where adequate choice is already assured.

Public Expenditures. The growing importance of public expenditures and their close tie to social welfare policy make it desirable to look specifically at this sector. A sizable part of current government expenditures goes for transfer payments. In cash transfers, society is distributing money income. Such payments are included in all estimates of money income. For various analytic purposes it is important to know what proportion of personal income arises out of various types of income-maintenance or income-support programs. On the consumption side, however, this is money like any other money, which can be spent as the individual chooses—within the constraints imposed by his personal circumstances and the total amount of income available to him.

Most if not all transfer payments have a specific distributional purpose. The largest of the existing programs, the national system of Old-Age, Survivors, Disability and Health Insurance (OASDHI), involves primarily a lifetime distribution of income to assure continuing income flows during periods when the head of the family is out of the labor force. Because the retired aged, the disabled and their families, and younger survivors constitute a sizable proportion of the total population, it also has a significant effect on the current distribution of income. The other existing large transfer payments, public assistance and veterans pensions (but not veterans compensation), are entirely oriented to current income.

Society has decided that certain goods and services must be made available through mechanisms other than those of the marketplace. Some, like education and, increasingly, medical care, are regarded as being so essential that no one can be left without the opportunity (and even the obligation) to acquire them. The benefits of such consumption extend beyond the individual to society as a whole. Others involve a kind of stand-by collective benefit—such as parks, open spaces, libraries, museums, opera, and theater—for all of which there may be user charges, but for which the return to the initial capital investment is diffuse. Public utilities such as urban transportation, water supplies and sewerage systems, and, increasingly, pure air, may involve public subsidy as well as use of the police power or the power of eminent domain. Even general law and order may have distributional elements.

The distribution by money income classes of the value of, or of expenditures for, publicly provided services involves a large number of theoretical as well as empirical problems. Public education is intended to be available for all. The value (cost) of the services may, however, vary greatly from school to school and neighborhood to neighborhood, with the lesser value too often associated with poor neighborhoods and families. On the other hand, the imputed addition to income will be proportionately greater the lower the family income, although the ability to take advantage of the service may be much less. Similar problems of quality and use arise in relation to health services, whether provided or paid for by public funds. Recent findings that educational success depends more on family and cultural background than on the quantity or quality of schooling provided raise a question as to whether a "correction" of the money income distribution to take account of the redistributive effect (downward) of public education really improves the value of the measure as a welfare indicator. This is not to say that society and social scientists should not be vitally concerned with the relative expenditures on education and on health for different groups in the population. Nor is it to question the importance of sophisticated analyses of the net effect of taxes and public expenditures on different income classes. It does suggest that the distribution of money incomes is itself a very meaningful measure. At least at the lower end of the income scale, what is needed may be not correction through the addition of assumed values for nonmoney income, so much as interpretation through reference to other analytic data.

If this is accepted for public expenditures that have a direct social welfare purpose, it is even more true of general community services. For such services there may be no conceptual gain (for welfare analysis) from attempts to distribute either availability or use across all income classes. These are the areas either where individual choice (of modes of transportation or recreation, for example) should play a major part or where the benefit derived (e.g., pure air) is not divisible. This is not to say that society should not be concerned with such questions as the general character of the urban environment, or whether public transportation is really available to the poor, or whether police and fire protection is adequate in all neighborhoods. These are in a sense subissues, which may help us understand and interpret more general measures. They probably have considerable bearing on the question of the optimum degree of equality, and the most appropriate level of the social minimum. But our knowledge of interrelationships is still too limited to indicate how they should be weighted into an over-all distributional index.

A general measure of the distribution of government expenditures would have to include also the subsidies to special groups—the merchant marine, the oil industry, farmers or the special credit or other advantages resulting from loan guarantees and subsidized interest rates —for suburban housing or higher education, for example. In the case of loan guarantees there may be virtually no net cost to the government; the aggregate cost of subsidies can be estimated. An attempt to trace the distributional effects of some of these benefits leads into even more controversial areas of economic theory than those skirted earlier. For many the general direction of the effect, however, is clearly to shift the income distribution toward the higher income levels.

"Total Income." One general observation may be worth making with respect to all attempts to develop an inclusive income figure. All such attempts involve imputations that rest on more or less arbitrary assumptions as to dollar values and as to incidence. The inclusion of items which are fairly equally distributed among money income classes automatically makes the distribution of total income less unequal.

Furthermore, as Dorothy Brady pointed out in one of the early analyses of income size distribution, an individual or family whose income is 80 per cent nonmoney and a family with the same total income all in the form of money are simply not in the same situation or welfare category.[4] To put the point another way, the school child who can get a school lunch if he declares himself needy may consume the same food as the child who buys his lunch, but he does not feel himself to be in the same position.

Assets and Wealth. To what extent must the distribution of assets and wealth be included in a welfare analysis? Possession of wealth affects the level at which people live in several different ways. The stock can give rise to a flow of income in money or in kind. (The most important asset for most families is an owned home.) It can have a significant effect on the sense of security and the freedom of action of the individual. And in large enough amounts it can represent power and control of the future well beyond the lifetime of the owner. Richard Titmuss has elaborated and given substance to this aspect of the problem.[5]

Ownership of wealth and particular forms of wealth also have different meanings in a dynamic growth economy than in a more static society. Small—or even fairly large—amounts of assets can lose their value as a result of inflation or economic depression. Physical assets—such as an owned home—can appreciate in value or be destroyed in the path of urban renewal or highway construction. To assign a present value to small or medium-sized stocks of wealth involves hazardous predictions of the future course of economic development. It may be safer—in terms of probabilities—to assume long-term accretion in value the larger the aggregation of wealth, although the type of wealth is also a factor.

The importance of social insurance derives not only from the transfer of income from the economically active to the economically inactive years (or generations), but from the ability of the system to assure a continuing income with a stable or increasing purchasing power. It represents for the middle- and lower-income groups some of the security of wealth. While Social Security benefit levels are as low as they are today, the analogy may seem painfully strained. In terms of the potential of the institutional mechanism, it is valid.

The question of security (i.e., continuity) of income is another aspect of the relation of income to welfare that calls for separate analysis. For the present we can do little more than note the probable direction of corrections or interpretations of the money-income distribution that such analysis would suggest.

Looking only at the current value of assets or wealth, there have been enough studies to give a fairly clear picture of the situation. By and large, there is a high correlation between current income and asset holding. In other words, the poor have little in the way of assets—and almost no liquid assets. For the near-poor and middle-income groups, the value of an owned home is likely to be the major asset. About 60 per cent of all persons or couples sixty-five and over own their homes and in more than four-fifths of the cases it is mortgage-free.[6] When one asks how Social Security beneficiaries can possibly get along on monthly benefits of $60, $70, even the current average of $86 ($130 for a couple), a large part of the answer appears to be that an owned home—their major lifetime savings—provides shelter, even though it may not be suitable and even though it may be allowed to run down and depreciate with the years.

There are some individuals with very limited current incomes and large asset holdings (income from assets is, of course, included in total income).

The Recipient Unit

Both conceptually and statistically the unit of reference or of count can significantly affect the apparent distribution of income. In terms of welfare, the individual is the ultimate referent. But the well-being of the individual is dependent on a network of social relations.

In analyzing the distribution of income and of welfare, the structure of individual earned income is an important subsystem. For more general analysis the unit of count is usually either the family or the spending unit, but attention must then be given to demographic changes and family patterns. The age at which young persons leave home and at which new families are formed are affected both by employment opportunities and by existing family incomes. In turn they affect any measure of the inequality of family incomes. Changes in family composition through marriage, divorce or separation, birth, and death introduce confusion into any measure of family income over time. Adults, primarily aged persons, may live with children or relatives other than the spouse, because they have no economic alternative. An increase in income can lead to an undoubling of families and thus to a change in the distribution of family income of a different kind than might be expected. It seems clear, for example, that the Social Security program has led to an increase in very low-income households by making it possible for more aged persons to live in their own homes rather than with their children. In this case the increased inequality in the income distribution may have a positive value, since aged persons would appear to place a high value on independent living. A decrease in inequality as a result of more adequate benefits might have a still greater value.

One of the major determinants of family income is the number of adult workers. Employment of the wife and adult children moves many families well up the income scale. Since these are presumably desired family groupings, the summation of incomes does not present the same conceptual issues as in the case of "extra" aged persons. Changes in the extent to which married women work in paid employment do affect trends in family income distribution, however. Here again, the relationship is not simple or static. The relative number of families in the population is affected by the availability of opportunities for employment by wives and children. When these are numerous the formation of new families will be encouraged; when and where employment levels are low, family formation is retarded.

The Time Dimension

The conventional time period for measurement of income is a year. The cycle of the seasons, the measurement of man's aging, and a host of social customs confirm the practice. In practical data-collection terms, the income-tax year further defines the twelve months selected.

Income, however, may fluctuate both within a year or between years. The time period chosen to define "current" income smoothes out or averages fluctuations within the period, but accentuates fluctuations between periods. There is no way of avoiding this effect. An important task of analysis is to measure the variability of income and to assess its effects.

Irregularity of employment produces one type of variability—usually but not necessarily associated with low annual income. Variability of returns to self-employment—the writer, the artist, the farmer—or to investment may be associated with almost any level of living.

Of a different character are changes in income over a lifetime. Even abstracting from the effect of changes in the value of money or in earnings levels, there is usually some progression in individual earnings and in family income. From less skilled to more skilled and more responsible jobs, from one to more than one earner in the family or vice versa, and then to a falling off in earnings and finally to the usually lower level of retirement income. There are probably several distinguishable patterns of life-cycle earnings. The familiar curve, rising to a plateau in late middle age and then dropping off slightly until retirement when the drop is sharper, is certainly one common pattern. There may be another for certain professional groups where the rise is slower but from a higher base and more continuous. And for some with inadequate training and opportunities that are limited by discrimination, there may be no upward curve at all. (See discussion of age and income in the next section.)

Low current income clearly has a different significance for welfare if it represents a temporary situation rather than a permanent condition. There is a considerable body of economic theory and analysis relating to the differential meaning and effects on spending-saving patterns and family welfare of "permanent" and transitory income. The time dimension for such analysis is the medium long run—longer than a year, shorter than a lifetime. The lag in adjustment of consumption to longer-term changes in income levels has been studied.

It is, however, easier to recognize the significance of the distinction between reasonably "permanent" and variable income than it is to separate the two, particularly in trend data. We need more longitudinal family income data to increase our understanding of this aspect of distribution as related to welfare.

TRENDS IN THE LEVEL AND DISTRIBUTION OF INCOME

Rising average levels of living in the U.S. in recent decades have been visible enough to have become a part of the background interpretation of our society. Aggregate personal income as measured in the National Income Accounts increased from $14 billion in 1897–1901 to $584 billion in 1966; or more than fortyfold. Since population increased about 2.6 times over this period, personal income per capita was only 15.5 times as great in 1966 as at the turn of the century and in constant dollars four times greater. On the average those of us living today have four times as much in the way of goods and services as did those living in 1900. Detailed income data for single years and for various family and personal characteristics are shown in Reference Tables A–H at the end of the chapter.

That the goods and services are different and the conditions of living changed in character may affect the nature of the social problems and the economic and political issues that are dominant today. Whatever qualifications are introduced, the increase in the general level of living is unarguable.

How total income and increases in the total have been shared— whether inequality is increasing or decreasing—is more difficult to measure. A first approximation can be drawn from the figures in Table 1. These are derived from two somewhat different series—the Office of Business Economics (OBE) estimates for the period 1929–1962 of the distribution of personal income as calculated in the National Income Accounts, and estimates for 1947 to date based on the Current Population Survey (CPS) of the Bureau of the Census. The definitions of income in the two series are somewhat different (see notes, Reference Table B). The aggregate income in the family personal income series is larger than that in the CPS series for two main reasons. All survey data tend to miss certain types of income—such as irregular income, self-employment, and investment income—some found most often among low-income groups and some among high-income groups. The OBE series adjusts reported data upward to take account of this fact. In addition, and more important in relation to distribution, it includes an estimate of the value of certain nonmoney income such as wages in kind, the value of food and fuel produced and consumed on farms, the net imputed rental value of owner-occupied homes and imputed interest. The inclusion of the imputed rental value of an owned home, in particular, increases the share of the lowest two-fifths of the population. Farmers and older people are the groups most likely to own their homes. They also typically have low cash incomes. Particularly for these groups, inclusion of an imputed rental value in income may give a somewhat exaggerated impression of their consumption potential.

The OBE is in the process of revising this series and carrying it forward. As of the present, for years after 1962, one has to look at the data on money income from the CPS. The CPS ordinarily reports on

TABLE 1. DISTRIBUTION OF PERSONAL AND MONEY INCOME: MEAN INCOME AND SHARE OF AGGREGATE RECEIVED BY EACH FIFTH AND TOP 5 PER CENT OF FAMILIES AND UNRELATED INDIVIDUALS, SELECTED YEARS, 1929–1966

Year and Income	Mean Income Before Tax (Current Dollars)	Percentage Distribution of Aggregate Income					
		Lowest Fifth	Second Fifth	Middle Fifth	Fourth Fifth	Highest Fifth	Top 5 Per Cent
Personal Income							
Families and unrelated individual							
1929	$2,335	12.5		13.8	19.3	54.4	30.0
1935–36	1,631	4.1	9.2	14.1	20.9	51.7	26.5
1944	3,614	4.9	10.9	16.2	22.2	45.8	20.7
1947	4,126	5.0	11.0	16.0	22.0	46.0	20.9
1957	6,238	4.7	11.1	16.3	22.4	45.5	20.2
1962	7,262	4.6	10.9	16.3	22.7	45.5	19.6
Money Income							
Families and unrelated individuals							
1947	3,224	3.5	10.5	16.7	23.5	45.8	19.0
1957	4,861	3.4	10.8	17.9	24.8	43.1	16.7
1962	6,049	3.5	10.3	17.3	24.5	44.3	17.3
1966	7,425	3.7	10.5	17.4	24.6	43.8	16.8
Families							
1947	3,566	5.1	11.8	16.7	23.2	43.3	17.5
1957	5,483	5.0	12.6	18.1	23.7	40.5	15.8
1962	6,811	5.1	12.0	17.3	23.8	41.7	16.3
1966	8,423	5.4	12.3	17.7	23.7	41.0	15.3
Unrelated individuals							
1947	1,692	2.9	5.4	11.5	21.3	58.9	33.3
1957	2,253	2.9	7.2	13.6	25.3	51.0	19.7
1962	2,800	3.3	7.3	12.5	24.1	52.8	21.3
1966	3,490	2.8	7.5	13.2	23.8	52.7	22.5

SOURCE: Personal income: Reference Table B; Money income: Reference Table C, and Henson, Mary F., "Trends in the Income of Families and Persons in the U.S., 1947–64," Technical Report No. 17, U.S. Bureau of the Census, Washington, 1967.

the money income of families (two or more related persons living together) and of unrelated individuals separately. The average income level of unrelated individuals is considerably less than half that of families and the distribution considerably more unequal. To provide a bridge between the OBE and CPS data, the Bureau of the Census kindly prepared special tabulations showing the distribution of the aggregate money income of families and individuals combined (Reference Table C).

In spite of the differences in definition, the trends in income distribution shown in these series are consistent. Special studies of the changes in the share of income of the top 1 per cent or 5 per cent of income receivers, based on income tax returns, make it possible to extend estimates for these portions of the distribution back to 1913.[7]

The over-all picture is one of a moderate decrease in the share of total income received by the very top income groups from 1913 through World War I, and an increase in their share during the 1920's. With the depression of the 1930's there came a sharp drop in the share of the top 5 per cent, and a rise in the share of the lowest fifth. World War II brought an even more marked rise in the share of the lowest fifth. Since the mid-1940's there has been little observable change in the over-all distribution of income. It is still too soon to tell whether an apparent slight increase in the share of the lowest 20 per cent of families in the past few years represents a real trend.

In concentrating on the stability of the shares received by different groups, one should not overlook the fact that the real income of all groups was increasing. The income which placed a family in the lowest 20 per cent of income receivers in 1935–1936 was $560; by 1966 it was close to $3,400. Even when corrected for price changes, this represents a significant improvement in levels of living.

The over-all income curve represents the merging of a number of different curves. There is the dominant pattern of wage and salary income; but this breaks down into very different patterns for men and women, for full-time and part-time workers, for different racial groups, occupations and regions of the country. Self-employment income, while smaller in the aggregate, tends to be concentrated at the upper end of the income curve. The grouping of individuals into families produces its own pattern of distribution. Changes in the relationships over time in the income patterns of important subgroups may help explain the general pattern of income distribution as well as point up issues for social policy.

Trends in Relative Income Level

A continuous series of income data for many subgroups in the population is available for years since 1947 from the Current Population Survey. Because it is both readily available and continuing, most of the tables and much of the analysis that follows relies on that source.[8] Additional statistical series and special studies are also drawn upon for further explanation or greater depth of analysis.

Both the receipt, and more important, the spending of income are shaped by the family and household groupings in which individuals live. When one is concerned with consumption patterns or levels of living, the income classifier that is generally most relevant is family income—including one-person as well as multiperson families. Most income, however, is earned by individuals. To understand the economic factors that determine family income, it is useful to start with an analysis of trends in individual income. Changes both in size of income and in the number and characteristics of income receivers are significant.

Employment and Occupation. The most important determinant of the income position of a group is whether or not its members are employed and whether full-time or part-time. Within the structure of earnings there are marked differences in the level of earnings and also in the spread or dispersion of earnings for different occupations. Detailed analyses of changes since 1939 made by Herman Miller[9] suggest a high degree of stability in the relative income positions (by rank) of occupations from farm laborers and foremen up to professional and managerial workers. From 1939 to 1949, however, the lower-paid jobs made relatively greater gains than the higher-paid, with a resultant narrowing of the differentials between occupations and for most occupations a decline in the share of aggregate income going to the top 20 per cent. These were years of decreasing inequality in the over-all income distribution. From 1950 to 1960, higher-paid jobs made, if anything, slightly greater gains than lower.

Comparisons of average income and the degree of inequality of incomes in one occupation as compared with another is more important for labor-market and productivity analysis than for measures of welfare except insofar as there are significant barriers to entry or advancement in the higher-paid and more stable occupations. The opening up of jobs in occupations hitherto closed to women or nonwhites or other special groups can have a significant effect on the absolute and relative incomes of those groups without having an immediately measurable effect on the over-all distribution.

On the other hand, the shift from agriculture to industrial occupations has over an even longer period been a dominant factor in rising levels of income and a factor making for greater equality over-all. Farm incomes have been and remain not only lower than nonfarm incomes on the average but more unequally distributed.

Incomes of Men and Women. Most women for part of their adult lives depend on someone else—usually a husband—for at least partial support while they concentrate on running a home and raising a family. However, the available data on income of persons do not reflect this dependency: they attribute to an individual only the earnings and other income received directly by that individual. Income received jointly by husband and wife, or only by the husband but shared by other family members, for example, is not generally allocated among them in the recorded statistics but attributed to only one person. The distinction is important because, unlike data for families of two or more or one-person households—i.e., unrelated individuals—income data for persons are generally shown only for income recipients. Thus, women who are not themselves working or receiving direct payments from other sources are counted as having no income and are not represented in the series.

Changing social forces resulting in a greater tendency for women to work at least part of the year throughout longer periods in their lives and the spread of social insurance to provide some income for both women and men in their old age cause a seeming downward shift in the income status of women relative to that of men. Actually, in one sense women are better off than they used to be because more of them now have some money of their own and so are in some degree economically independent.

In the past twenty years, the average income of women having any income has declined relative to that of men. In 1947, the median income of all women fourteen and over (with any income) was **46 per** cent of the median for all men fourteen and over. By 1957, the ratio had dropped to 33 and by 1966, to 31 per cent. The trend actually started earlier. In 1939, the median wage and salary income of women was 59 per cent that of men; by 1949, this ratio had dropped to 49 and by 1959, to 36. One reason is the increasing proportion of all women with income of their own who are married and working less than full-time.

But a more important reason is the fact that because of OASDHI so many more aged women now have some money of their own. The maturing of the Social Security program during these twenty years has seen the percentage of women sixty-five and over receiving a benefit check increase markedly from a rate only 70 per cent that prevailing among aged men in 1947, to a rate 2 per cent higher than that for men in 1966. In parallel fashion, the proportion of aged women having income from any source increased from fewer than one in two to better than four in five, a greater rise than in any other age group. Accordingly, in 1966, one in five women receiving income was age sixty-five or older compared with one in eight in 1947. Among men, the proportion of recipients who were aged rose too, but in lesser degree: in 1947, one in eleven of all male income recipients was aged; by 1966, the number was one in eight.

The figures in Table 2 show for aged men and women and for persons of all ages fourteen or older the changing percentage receiving any income.

TABLE 2. PERCENTAGES OF AGED PERSONS AND ALL PERSONS AGED 14 AND OVER RECEIVING ANY INCOME, SELECTED YEARS, 1947–1966

Age group	1947	1953	1957	1964	1966
Total aged 14 or over		(percentages)			
Men	89	91	92	91	92
Women	34	46	53	60	61
Age 65 or over					
Men, all sources	84	92	95	98	99
OASDHI	14	38	59	78	83
Women, all sources	47	59	72	82	83[a]
OASDHI	9	30	49	74	85[a]

[a] Slight discrepancy because data come from different sources. An aged husband and wife receiving joint benefit checks would be counted as two OASDHI beneficiaries, but census income data could show wife with zero income if she did not state that part of the check was hers.

SOURCE: Derived from Current Population Survey, Series P-60, and unpublished data from the Social Security Administration.

Age and Income. Income generally increases with age up to a point and then declines again. The extent of the differences and the age at which income peaks are different for different groups.

For all men, median income is highest in the age group thirty-five to forty-four and declines thereafter. However, those with lowest incomes reach their peak on the age cycle before the age of forty, while the incomes of those in the highest income groups do not decline before age sixty. Among women with some income, peak incomes in recent years have occurred in the forty-five to fifty-four year age group at all income levels.[10]

These general relationships have changed relatively little in the past two decades. A comparison of the ratio of median income for five-year age groups to the median of all males or all females over the period 1947 to 1966 shows considerable stability for most groups. For fourteen to nineteen year-olds among both men and women, however, both the absolute and relative income levels declined over these two decades. More years at school and a consequent later entry into the labor force, with some increase in unemployment among teenagers are reflected in these figures. There was also a decline, though not as marked, in the relative income position of the twenty- to twenty-four-year-old men.

The other instance of a change large enough and persistent enough to suggest a definite trend was in the relative income position of women fifty-five to sixty-four. The median income of women in this age group increased considerably faster than that of other women (the ratio of the median for this age group to the total for all females was .95 in 1947 and 1.35 in 1966).

A closer look at changes in the income position of different age groups since 1941 provides hints as to some of the forces that have been at work and their effect on the over-all income distribution during this period. Using data for 1941 from the special studies of family spending and saving in wartime carried out by the Department of Labor and the Department of Agriculture in 1942, and census data for 1951 and 1961, Dorothy Brady analyzed the changes over time in the income position of different age groups.[11] Table 3 shows the relative changes in the upper income limits of the lowest and next to the highest income classes for different age groups that occurred between 1941 and 1951, between 1951 and 1961 and between 1961 and 1966 (the latest year available). In the earlier decade, income increased most rapidly for the younger age groups among both men and women and for those in the lowest quintile. For men up to age fifty-five the income limit for the lowest income group was more than three times as high as the same relative position in 1941. Between 1951 and 1961, however, with the exception of those aged sixty-five and over, the income of the lowest fifth increased substantially less than that of the other income classes, and particularly at the younger ages. For women the increase in income for those in the lowest relative income position was even

TABLE 3.   CHANGES IN THE INCOMES OF PERSONS,
1941–1966: RATIOS OF SELECTED PERCENTILES
OF INCOME IN 1951 COMPARED TO 1941, IN
1961 COMPARED TO 1951 AND IN 1966
COMPARED TO 1961, BY AGE GROUP

Sex and Ratio	20–24	25–34	35–44	45–54	55–64	65 and over
Men						
Ratio of first quintiles						
1951 to 1941	3.4	3.2	3.1	3.1	2.6	1.7
1961 to 1951	0.9	1.3	1.5	1.5	1.7	2.0
1966 to 1961	1.3	1.4	1.3	1.4	1.2	1.3
Ratio of fourth (top) quintiles						
1951 to 1941	2.5	2.1	2.1	2.1	2.3	2.3
1961 to 1951	1.4	1.6	1.6	1.6	1.7	1.3
1966 to 1961	1.3	1.3	1.3	1.3	1.2	1.2
Women						
Ratio of first quintiles						
1951 to 1941	4.9	5.3	5.0	2.4	4.1	1.6
1961 to 1951	0.9	0.9	1.2	1.4	1.3	2.3
1966 to 1961	1.3	1.3	1.4	1.5	1.5	1.3
Ratio of fourth (top) quintiles						
1951 to 1941	2.6	2.8	3.0	2.6	3.5	1.4
1961 to 1951	1.4	1.4	1.5	1.6	1.5	1.6
1966 to 1961	1.2	1.2	1.2	1.2	1.3	1.3

SOURCE: Brady, Dorothy, "Age and the Income Distribution," Research Report No. 8, Social Security Administration, Washington, D.C., 1965, Table 1; and unpublished census data.

greater during the war years than for men and similarly was less for low than high income groups from 1951 to 1961. Between 1961 and 1966, the relative increase in income was nearly the same for all age groups, except women aged forty-five to sixty-four who showed a greater gain, particularly at the lowest income levels.

These relationships confirm the general impression of increasing equality of income during the war years and a reversal of this trend or at least a stability in the distribution of income in the subsequent period. They also show very clearly the effect of improvements in Social Security benefits after 1950.

They confirm the decline in the relative income position of younger men suggested by the comparison of median incomes. In 1951 the first quintile income of twenty to twenty-four-year-old men was 47 per cent of the corresponding income of thirty- to thirty-five-year-olds; in 1961 it was 30 per cent and in 1966 only 28 per cent. The relationship of the second quintiles was reduced proportionately about as much in the decade 1951 to 1961, from 58 to 41, and remained at 40 per cent in 1966.

Within age groups, except for the age group under twenty-five, there is an increase in inequality of incomes with age, particularly for men. There has been little change in this pattern in recent years. Differential advancement in occupations involving different degrees of skill, as well as income from accumulated assets explains part of the variation among age groups, but the major factor appears to be differences in the extent of full year work. James Morgan computed the Gini ratio for all men and men who worked fifty weeks or more in 1959 as reported in the CPS and also for all heads of families and heads who worked a full year in 1957 from the University of Michigan Survey Research data. Both showed clearly that part-year earnings have a major effect on the degree of inequality, with such earnings largely concentrated among the young and those over fifty-five.[12]

Morgan noted further that the number of weeks worked during a year appears to be closely associated with the level of formal education. The impact of education on changes in income with age is a result of a combination of greater unemployment among those with less education and more advancement among those with more education.

Changes in the dispersion of income—the relative degree of inequality—for different age groups are indicated perhaps more clearly by the ratio of the income limits of the first, second and third income quintiles to the fourth. This comparison, as well as the ratio of the 95th percentile to the fourth quintile is shown in Table 4.

Here also it is clear that during the decade of the 1940's, the relative income position of the lowest income groups, except men sixty-five years of age or older, was improving. By 1961 the ratios, particularly for the younger age groups, were reversing toward the 1941 position. By 1966 there had been an improvement in the middle age groups, but not in the position of the twenty- to twenty-four-year-olds.

The increasingly unfavorable income position of the younger age groups points to a danger that inequalities in the income distribution will be perpetuated over the next twenty years as these cohorts age unless expanding opportunities provide a corrective.

For those over age sixty-five, and to some extent those aged sixty to sixty-four, changes in income and income shares are now the result of social insurance and other income maintenance programs almost to a

TABLE 4. CHANGES IN THE DISPERSION OF INCOMES OF
MEN AND WOMEN: RATIOS OF SELECTED PERCENTILES
OF INCOME TO THE FOURTH QUINTILE, 1941,
1951, 1961, AND 1966

	Age Group and Comparison					
Sex and Years	20–24	25–34	35–44	45–54	55–64	65 and over
Men	Ratio of first to fourth quintile					
1941	.23	.32	.31	.26	.23	.23
1951	.31	.49	.45	.38	.26	.16
1961	.22	.41	.41	.35	.27	.25
1966	.22	.46	.42	.39	.27	.26
	Ratio of second to fourth quintile					
1941	.50	.53	.56	.54	.40	.38
1951	.54	.68	.64	.58	.52	.30
1961	.45	.62	.61	.58	.50	.39
1966	.44	.65	.61	.58	.52	.41
	Ratio of third to fourth quintile					
1941	.72	.76	.76	.75	.66	.65
1951	.78	.81	.79	.75	.74	.50
1961	.71	.79	.77	.76	.71	.59
1966	.70	.80	.76	.74	.72	.60
	Ratio of 95th percentile to fourth quintile					
1941	1.42	1.34	1.38	1.40	1.47	1.98
1951	1.35	1.41	1.58	1.64	1.71	1.96
1961	1.44	1.63	1.70	1.89	1.84	2.55
1966	1.37	1.44	1.72	1.86	1.90	2.12
Women	Ratio of first to fourth quintile					
1941	.10	.09	.12	.17	.13	.19
1951	.20	.18	.17	.16	.15	.22
1961	.13	.12	.13	.14	.13	.31
1966	.14	.13	.15	.17	.15	.31
	Ratio of second to fourth quintile					
1941	.30	.30	.29	.29	.34	.36
1951	.47	.45	.41	.35	.32	.43
1961	.35	.34	.35	.37	.30	.47
1966	.37	.38	.41	.42	.32	.46
	Ratio of third to fourth quintile					
1941	.63	.60	.55	.55	.55	.58
1951	.70	.66	.66	.68	.59	.70
1961	.64	.64	.66	.64	.56	.62
1966	.69	.68	.67	.66	.64	.64
	Ratio of 95th percentile to fourth quintile					
1941	1.36	1.63	1.90	1.82	1.85	2.14
1951	1.28	1.33	1.44	1.45	1.67	2.30
1961	1.37	1.52	1.45	1.56	1.68	2.07
1966	1.39	1.47	1.48	1.54	1.63	2.43

SOURCE: See Table 3.

greater extent than changes in employment. The larger increase between 1951 and 1961 in the income of those aged sixty-five and over compared with younger persons in the lowest income quintile has been remarked. For middle-income groups the relative position of those sixty-five and over compared less favorably with that of men in their working years.

For the top 5 per cent of income receivers, those sixty-five and over are the most favored age group. It is of interest, also, that among women the sixty-five and over group is in a generally more favorable income position than the younger ages. It would appear that there is less inequality in the social insurance benefits and other payments received by aged women than in the earned incomes of women who work varying amounts of time.

Income of Whites and Nonwhites. The generally lower earnings and income levels of nonwhites as compared with whites is well known. Here is an area where improvement could be significant even before the change was large enough to have much effect on the over-all income distribution curve.

In 1948, the median money income of nonwhite males ($1,765) was a little over half that of white males ($3,258). By 1966, both groups had money incomes about two-thirds larger ($2,961 and $5,364), but the level for nonwhite men was still only a little over half that of white men. For nonwhite women and for nonwhite compared with white families the picture was more encouraging. The ratio of nonwhite to white median incomes for several different groups in selected years is shown in Table 5.

TABLE 5.   RATIO OF NONWHITE TO WHITE MEDIAN INCOMES FOR SELECTED GROUPS AND YEARS, 1947–1966

Groups	1947	1953	1957	1964	1966
Males 14 and over[a]	.54[c]	.55	.47	.57	.55
Females 14 and over[a]	.49[c]	.59	.62	.70	.76
Families[b]	.51	.56	.54	.56	.60
Unrelated individuals[b]	.72	.80	.67	.69	.73

[a] Median for those with income only.
[b] Includes families and individuals with zero income.
[c] 1948 (1947 not available).

Source: Henson, Mary F., "Trends in the Income of Families and Persons in the U.S., 1947–64," Technical Report No. 17, U.S. Bureau of the Census, Washington, 1967; and "Income in 1966 of Families and Persons in the U.S.," Current Population Survey, Series P-60, no. 53, December 28, 1967.

The shift in the position of nonwhite women is striking. At the end of the period the median income of nonwhite women was above that of white women in all regions except the South, where it remained little more than half that of white women. In 1953, when such regional data first became available, the median income of nonwhite women was about 80 to 85 per cent that of white women in the North and a little less than 50 per cent in the South.

It would appear that nonwhite women in the North and West have been shifting into higher-paid occupations. Nonwhite women are also more apt to work full time than are white women. In the country as a whole, full-time employment among nonwhite females has been increasing to a greater extent than part-time work while the opposite has occurred among white women.

The incomes of nonwhite men are relatively the highest as compared with the incomes of white men when they are young and when they are old. They are relatively high at the young ages because for nonwhites income does not rise in the middle years to the same extent as for whites. They are relatively high after age sixty-five because Social Security benefits are relatively more adequate—that is, replace a larger proportion of previous earnings—for persons with low earnings. The relative income position of nonwhite women is most favorable in the ages from twenty-five to forty-four and after sixty-five. Indeed in these ages they are approaching equality with white women.

These relationships are summarized in Table 6 for the year 1959 (from the 1960 Census; these breakdowns are not available from the CPS).

In interpreting these differences several factors are important. The longer hours worked by nonwhite women have been noted. Nonwhite men on the other hand experience more unemployment or part-time employment than do white men. The importance of full-year work in relation to income levels was pointed out earlier. Nonwhites, both men and women, are generally employed in the low-paying occupations— those requiring little skill and having little future. Beyond this there is some indication that even within the same occupations there may be significant differentials in pay and in the opportunity to advance.

In an analysis which takes account of the effects of family background, education, mental ability, number of siblings, and occupation, Otis Dudley Duncan concludes that at least one-third of the difference in average income (for 1961) of Negroes and whites "arises because Negro and white men in the same line of work, with the same amount of formal schooling, with equal ability, from families of the same size

TABLE 6.   PERCENTAGE OF NONWHITE MEN AND WOMEN
IN INCOME QUINTILES FOR THEIR AGE GROUPS, 1959

Sex and income rank	20–24	25–34	35–44	45–54	55–64	65 and over
Nonwhite men						
Number per 1,000 persons	110	106	97	93	89	79
Percent	100	100	100	100	100	100
In lowest fifth	33	48	51	48	43	37
In second fifth	24	26	27	28	29	26
In third fifth	22	14	14	15	18	18
In fourth fifth	13	8	6	7	8	13
In upper fifth	7	4	3	3	3	7
Nonwhite women						
Number per 1,000 persons	122	164	140	118	101	77
Percent	100	100	100	100	100	100
In lowest fifth	31	25	28	35	32	25
In second fifth	29	25	27	30	31	25
In third fifth	20	24	22	18	21	25
In fourth fifth	11	15	14	11	11	16
In upper fifth	9	11	10	7	6	9

SOURCE: Brady, Dorothy, "Age and the Income Distribution," *op. cit.,* Table
A6, p. 60.

and the same socioeconomic level simply do not draw the same wages
and salaries."[13]

Regional Variations in Income Levels. There is an interacting set of
relations between the income levels of different population groups and
of the several regions of the country. In general, incomes in the South
are substantially lower than those in other parts of the country. The
median income of men aged fourteen and over for the U.S. as a whole
was $5,306 in 1966; in the South it was $4,025 or only three-fourths as
much. The ratio of median income for the four census regions to the
U.S. median has changed relatively little since 1953, the first year for
which such data are available, as shown in Table 7.

As noted earlier, for the U.S. as a whole, the median income of nonwhite men is a little over half (.55 in 1966) that of white men. In the
South the median for nonwhite men in 1966 was only 49 per cent that
for whites whereas in the other three regions it was about three-fourths
that of white males. There has been no significant change in these relationships since 1953.

For females, on the other hand, as was noted earlier there has been
a significant relative increase in the incomes of nonwhite women in all
regions except the South. Table 8 gives the ratio of nonwhite to white

TABLE 7. RATIO OF REGIONAL TO U.S. MEDIAN INCOME,
SELECTED YEARS, 1953–1966

	1953	1959	1964	1966
Males 14 and over				
Northeast	1.08	1.11	1.10	1.09
North Central	1.10	1.08	1.09	1.08
South	.73	.73	.76	.76
West	1.09	1.15	1.14	1.13
Females 14 and over				
Northeast	1.29	1.29	1.26	1.22
North Central	1.01	.97	.99	.97
South	.78	.75	.81	.85
West	.97	1.09	1.06	1.07

SOURCE: See Table 5.

median incomes for females aged fourteen and over in the four regions.

Over a longer time span, there has been an increasing convergence in the income levels in the different regions of the country. In an interesting comparison of changes in the spatial distribution of income in the U.S. and changes in the national size distribution, Eugene Smolensky has analyzed the factors underlying changes in the dispersion of state per capita incomes and of income shares over the period 1919–1948.[14] There was a marked similarity in trend in the two measures: in the period of the 1920's when income inequality was increasing, so were the differences in state per capita income; in the 1940's when incomes were becoming more equal, state per capita incomes also tended to converge.

Smolensky isolates the factors that appear to have been responsible for these changes. The major force affecting both the size distribution and the regional distribution was the shift out of agriculture. Interestingly, he finds that the shift into manufacturing played a negligible part

TABLE 8. RATIO OF NONWHITE TO WHITE MEDIAN
INCOMES FOR FEMALES AGED 14 AND OVER BY
REGION, SELECTED YEARS, 1953–1966

Region	1953	1959	1964	1966
U.S.	.594	.621	.702	.761
Northeast	.834	1.005	1.087	1.194
North Central	.869	1.123	1.002	1.126
South	.482	.438	.530	.571
West	n.a.	1.060	1.258	1.076

SOURCE: See Table 5.

in the reduction of regional income differentials, but the shift into service industries—trade, finance, professions and government—was a major factor.

Family Income Distribution. The changes that have been occurring in the employment and relative income position of older women, nonwhite women at all ages and younger men and women suggest something of what has been happening with respect to family income.

Over the past two decades the number of unrelated individuals has been increasing at a faster rate than the number of families. This is in part due to the undoubling of families that occurs in prosperous times, in part to the independence that Social Security benefits have brought to many older persons who would formerly have been forced to live with their children. There has been an increase also in the number of aged couples living by themselves. The independence has in many cases been at the price of very low income levels. The effect of these changes has no doubt been in the direction of greater inequality in the total distribution.

On the other hand, the increasing employment of women has been a factor tending toward greater equality in family incomes. Because most people live as members of families, the trend in the over-all distribution of income of families has not been very different than that of all families and individuals combined (see Table 1).

For families as for individuals one can analyze differences in the level and distribution of income by age and sex of the head, by number of earners, by size of family, region and other characteristics. Some of these relationships have remained fairly stable over the past two decades, others have shown a definite trend. The ratio of the median income of families of different types in selected years since 1947 indicates some general patterns (Table 9):

TABLE 9. SELECTED RATIOS OF MEDIAN FAMILY
INCOME, SELECTED YEARS, 1947–1966

Ratios	1947	1957	1964	1966
Nonwhite to white	.51	.54	.56	.60
Female to male head	.72	.54	.50	.51
Heads 65 and over to all	.60	.50	.51	.49

SOURCE: See Table 5.

The improvement in the position of Negro families is clear. When the comparison is made between nonwhite and white heads of families who worked year-round full-time, median income for nonwhites is 68 per cent that of whites in 1966, as compared with 60 per cent for all families. White families with a head who was a year-round full-time worker had a median income 15 per cent higher than that of all white families; for nonwhite families the difference was 30 per cent. These figures suggest again the greater extent to which income of nonwhites is pulled down by part-time or part-year employment and by the fact that a larger proportion of nonwhite families have a female head.

Total family income is, of course, related to the number of earners in the family. In recent years median income has increased with each increase in size of family from two through five persons, then decreased. Above five, additional persons in the family are more likely to be children under eighteen. The median income of families with four children in 1966 was lower than that of families with three children and additional children reduced the median level still further.

The extent to which the employment of married women has added to family income can be inferred from the proportion of husband-wife families at each income level in which the wife was in the paid labor force (Table 10). Among husband-wife families in the lowest 20 per

TABLE 10. PERCENTAGE OF HUSBAND-WIFE FAMILIES WITH WIFE IN PAID LABOR FORCE, SELECTED YEARS, 1949–1966

Income rank	1949	1957	1959	1964	1966
Lowest fifth	10.3	11.9	11.8	11.8	12.5
Second fifth	15.2	19.5	19.2	23.3	24.3
Third fifth	15.7	22.3	23.6	28.6	30.5
Fourth fifth	24.8	32.2	32.4	38.1	40.6
Highest fifth	27.2	38.2	36.9	41.6	45.6
Top 5 per cent	18.4	29.3	24.8	35.0	38.4

SOURCE: Reference Table G.

cent of families ranked by income, there has been little increase since 1949 in the proportion in which the wife works. In each year for which we have data, moreover, the proportion of working wives is greater in each successive income quintile and drops off only in the top 5 per cent.

If families with working wives are underrepresented among families with low incomes, families with heads aged sixty-five and over, families headed by a woman and nonwhite families are overrepresented. In 1966, for example, families headed by an aged person accounted for 14 per cent of all families, but for 37 per cent of families in the lowest fifth and 6 per cent in the top fifth. Similarly families headed by a woman represented 11 per cent of all families, but 25 per cent of those in the lowest fifth and 3 per cent of those in the top fifth. Nonwhite families made up 10 per cent of all families in 1966, twice as large a proportion of the lowest fifth and 4 per cent of the highest fifth.

The proportion of all families in the lowest fifth who are headed by an aged person or a woman has increased significantly since 1947 (Table 11). The improvement in the relative position of nonwhite fam-

TABLE 11.   SELECTED FAMILY TYPES AS PERCENTAGES OF ALL FAMILIES IN LOWEST INCOME FIFTH, SELECTED YEARS, 1947–1966

Type of family	1947	1957	1964	1966
	(percentages)			
With head aged 65 and over	26	32	34	37
With female head	18	22	24	25
Nonwhite	22	22	21	21

SOURCE: See Reference Table G.

ilies between 1947 and 1966 was somewhat greater than the above figures alone would suggest. In 1947, nonwhite families formed only 9 instead of 10 per cent of all families. Hence in 1947 there were 2.4 times as many nonwhite families in the lowest income group as their proportion in the population, while by 1966 the ratio had dropped to 2.1.

Another way of looking at the same relationships is to compare the proportion of all families of a given type who are in the lowest income quintile. As compared with 20 per cent of all families in the lowest fifth, the percentages for specific type families are shown in Table 12. Nonwhites were overrepresented in the lowest income group in 1966, but

TABLE 12.   PERCENTAGES OF ALL FAMILIES OF GIVEN TYPE IN LOWEST INCOME FIFTH, SELECTED YEARS, 1947–1966

Type of family	1947	1957	1966
White families	17.2	17.3	17.6
Nonwhite families	48.9	46.1	41.2
Head aged 65 and over	45.6	50.1	52.1
Female head	36.4	46.5	47.7
Male head, wife in paid labor force	n.a.	9.6	8.1

SOURCE: See Reference Table G.

to a considerably lesser extent than in 1947. The relative position of families with an aged or a female head, however, had worsened.

Trends in Poverty

As the general level of income and the over-all degree of inequality change, the characteristics of the families and individuals in the lowest fifth of the income ranks can also be expected to change. There will, of course, always be a lowest fifth. The important questions for policy are whether the share of aggregate income going to the lowest 20 per cent of income receivers can and should be increased and whether or not certain kinds of families are found in disproportionate numbers in the lowest group.

In general parlance the term "disproportionate" carries a vague overtone of ethical judgment. Everyone would recognize that certain differences are to be expected and raise no real questions of social policy. The young husband-wife family just starting out on a career would be expected to show up with greater frequency in the lower income ranks. Persons with irregular and fluctuating income will be overrepresented, in any given year, in both the low and the high income groups. Neither situation may raise any serious welfare or equity problems—although irregular income resulting from continuing part-year unemployment is a problem. On the other hand, the continuing large overrepresentation of nonwhites and the now larger and increasing overrepresentation of families headed by aged persons and by women at the bottom of the income ladder raise evident social policy issues.

Any attempt to distinguish between acceptable and unacceptable degrees of disparity or concentration of particular groups in the lowest income levels leads toward some concept of minimum need and some recognition of variations in need among different types of families.

Since the latter part of the nineteenth century, the conceptual tool that has most often been used to arrive at such judgments is the family budget—a listing and pricing of the items of consumption regarded as necessary for minimum subsistence or for adequacy. The development of objective standards of nutritional "needs" and at least minimum standards for housing has provided one basis for such budgets. Most of the early budgets attempted to define a subsistence standard. With rising levels of living the concept of a social minimum, enough for comfort and decency, became more common.[15] As early as 1909 the Bureau of Labor Statistics developed budgets for cotton-mill workers in the South and in Fall River, Massachusetts, that defined two living levels—minimum and fair. The WPA budgets of the 1930's also used two levels and the BLS is again in 1968 planning to develop a lower level budget as well as the "modest but adequate" budget that has become standard in recent years—and a higher level also.

The fact that the lowest fifth of all families (measured by family income) receive only 5 per cent of aggregate family income may take on a somewhat different coloring depending on the presumed adequacy of the income they get to meet minimum needs. On the other hand, the repeated revisions of measures of minimum need as the general level of living goes up is evidence of the way in which the concept of fair shares permeates the budget approach.

It would be of some interest to see how the amount regarded as necessary for either subsistence or for decent living related to the existing income distribution of the period. Most budgets tie so closely to an individual place and specifically defined family type that comparisons with per capita income or other generalized averages are not very meaningful and it is only in recent years that the data have been available that would make it possible to estimate the incomes of families like the assumed budget family. The most recent BLS four-person family budget at a moderate level, for example, is for a family with an employed husband aged thirty-eight, a nonworking wife, a boy of thirteen, and a girl of eight. The amount needed by such a family in Autumn, 1966, to meet the budget standards was $9,191 in all cities—ranging from $11,190 to $7,855 in the areas for which the budget is priced. The BLS estimates that for families like those for whom the budget was computed, the mean income was about $11,000. A comparable figure for median income is unfortunately not available. Estimates from the CPS indicate the range within which it would fall. In 1966, the median income of four-person families with a head who worked year round was $8,960; in about a third of these families, however, the wife as well as the husband was employed. For families (of all sizes) with a male head who worked year round and a wife who was not in the labor force, the median family income was $8,168. The median income of all men who worked year round full-time was $6,955 and for those in nonfarm employment, $7,095.

A comparison of family budgets for New York City for different years beginning with 1914, with annual earnings of workers in manufacturing shows the budgets in all years to be somewhat higher than the average earnings of production workers generally. In Table 13 published family budgets for New York City are related to estimates of the annual earnings of production workers (weekly earnings times 52).

TABLE 13. FAMILY BUDGETS RELATED TO ESTIMATES OF
ANNUAL EARNINGS OF PRODUCTION WORKERS,
NEW YORK CITY, SELECTED YEARS, 1914–1966[a]

Year and Budget	Annual Earnings of a Worker on Manufacturing Payroll (1)	Family Budget (Four-Person Family) (2)	Ratio: (2) / (1)
1914 New York Factory Commission	$ 624.62	$ 1,062.23	1.701
1918 New York Minimum Comfort	1,093.66	1,408.40	1.288
1920 New York City Labor Bureau	1,488.34	2,106.14	1.415
1935 New York WPA Maintenance	1,138.85	1,375.13	1.207
1947 BLS New York City Workers	2,780.44	3,347.00	1.204
1951 BLS New York City Workers	3,374.80	4,083.00	1.210
1954 New York City Family Budget Standard	3,718.00	4,221.88	1.136
1966 New York City Family Budget Standard	5,790.20	5,980.00	1.033
1966 BLS New York City Workers			
All	5,790.20	10,195.00	1.761
Renters	5,790.20	9,075.00	1.567

[a] Data on earnings for all U.S. from 1914 through 1935 were increased by 10
per cent in order—it is believed—to approximate more closely the New York
level than would the United States average. Data for New York were available
for the later period. The earlier budgets were adjusted roughly to a four-person
family.

Earlier studies in England as well as current budget studies for countries at various stages of economic development generally show minimum budgets at a lower level relative to prevailing wages.[16]

There have been a number of official and unofficial studies in the
past two decades that have attempted to identify the low-income groups
in our population. A 1949 Report of the Joint Economic Committee
assembled estimates of the number of low-income families defined as
those with less than $2,000 a year income for urban families and
$1,000 for farm families. "The cash income levels chosen—were se-
lected only to designate an income group for intensive study. An important consideration in making the choice was to use amounts which
would be realistic in even the lowest cost areas of the country. It is
improbable that there will be more than a minor proportion of families

able to purchase all their requirements with incomes below these amounts."[17] The Report estimated that in 1948 one-third of all families and individuals in the United States received incomes under $2,000. In 1948, $2,000 was about mid-way between the upper limit of the lowest fifth ($1,655) and of the second fifth ($2,721) of family incomes.

In 1955, the Joint Economic Committee again assembled information on the low-income population, and again used $2,000 as the measure of low income. Estimates were also made on the basis of constant (1948) dollars. On this latter basis there was little change in the number and a small decrease in the proportion of "low income" families.[18]

In its 1964 report, the Council of Economic Advisers used $3,000 as the poverty line for families and $1,500 for unrelated individuals, basing the choice of the amount for families on the lower of two indexes developed by the Social Security Administration (SSA) for a nonfarm family of four. It was estimated that 20 per cent of all families had money income of less than $3,000 in 1962. The dividing line between the first and second 20 per cent of families ranked by income was $3,018 in 1962.

In 1965, the SSA having refined and expanded the budgets to include minimum cost standards for all sizes and types of families, the Council adopted the lower of the two SSA measures as the working delineator of poverty. The SSA poverty index, discussed in more detail below, adjusted annually for price change has been used since as the working definition of poverty. Trend data on this basis extend back to 1959. In subsequent reports for somewhat longer historical trend data (from 1947) the Council of Economic Advisers has retained the $3,000 and $1,500 measures, with the amounts adjusted for earlier years to reflect price changes.

Variable Measures of Need. If one wants to introduce a concept of need, and equity as related to need, it is necessary to go beyond a distinction between families and individuals. $3,000 will provide a very different level of living for a family of seven than for a family of two. Some earlier studies had taken account of this by using a figure of $1,500 for the first person plus $500 for each additional person in a family up to some specified amount. The poverty and low-income indexes developed by the Social Security Administration incorporate variations based more specifically on family composition as well as size, age of the head, and farm-nonfarm residence.[19]

The gross number and proportion of the population counted as poor by any measure will reflect primarily the level of living used as the basis. The level of the Social Security Administration poverty index for a nonfarm family of four averaged $3,130 for 1962 incomes. For single individuals it was $1,580 for those under sixty-five and $1,470 for those over sixty-five. It is not surprising therefore that the total count of the poor was about the same using the more refined and variable index as the $3,000 measure.

The poverty level is a stringent level. It is based on a food budget that the Department of Agriculture defines as adequate for short periods and on an emergency basis only, and it allows only twice the amount of the food budget to cover all other family expenditures. The SSA has also developed a "low-income index" at a level about a third higher. In 1966, this low-income index was about 25 per cent above the upper limit of incomes for families in the lowest income fifth.

It is when we look at the detailed characteristics of the families and individuals classified as poor (or near-poor) that the differences between the two types of poverty measure appear. When differential need is taken into account, and the income limit or cut-off point varied to provide some approximation of equivalent levels of living, the poverty or low-income group will include a much higher proportion of large families and of children under eighteen and a smaller proportion of aged persons. Because Negro families are, on the average, larger than white families, the percentage of nonwhite is also greater than when a single figure is used for all family sizes.

A comparison of families in the lowest fifth of income receivers with families below a variable poverty line shows some of the same contrasts. The general magnitude of these differences is indicated in the comparison in Table 14 for 1964 incomes.

It is worth noting that when families are grouped by such characteristics as male and female head, without reference to the size of the family or age of the head, the differences in the proportion shown as poor or in the lowest income fifth are small. The figures in Table 15 are also for 1964 incomes.

Incidence of Poverty. The disproportionate representation of certain groups in the lowest income fifth was noted earlier. One can express this same relationship by saying that the risk of being poor is greater for some groups than for others. Comparable data for the years 1959–1967 based on the SSA poverty and low-income indexes make possible analyses of the changing incidence and volume of poverty among many subgroups as well as the noninstitutional population as a whole.

TABLE 14.   COMPARISON OF FAMILIES IN LOWEST INCOME
FIFTH AND THOSE BELOW VARIABLE POVERTY LINE, 1964

Type of Family	Families in Lowest Income Fifth	Poor Families	Low-Income (Poor and Near-Poor) Families
Total families (in thousands)	9,567	6,832	10,665
		(percentages)	
All family sizes	100.0	100.0	100.0
2 persons	52.6	32.4	33.8
3–5 persons	36.2	41.3	41.5
6 persons	4.3	8.6	8.6
7 or more persons	6.8	17.7	16.2
All families	100.0	100.0	100.0
No children under 18	53.6	33.4	34.9
1 or 2 children	26.8	27.3	28.6
3 or 4 children	12.6	22.8	21.7
5 or more children	7.0	16.6	14.8
All families	100.0	100.0	100.0
Head 14–24	8.7	8.3	8.6
Head 25–44	27.7	41.0	40.8
Head 45–64	29.7	28.9	27.7
Head 65 and over	34.0	21.9	23.0
All families	100.0	100.0	100.0
White	78.9	72.5	77.2
Nonwhite	21.1	27.5	22.8

SOURCE: Henson, Mary F., "Trends in the Income of Families and Persons in
the U.S., 1947–64," Technical Report No. 17, U.S. Bureau of the Census, Washington, 1967; and unpublished data from the Social Security Administration.

TABLE 15.   COMPARISON OF FAMILIES IN LOWEST INCOME
FIFTH AND THOSE BELOW VARIABLE POVERTY LINE,
BY FAMILY TYPE, 1964

Type of family	Families in Lowest Income Fifth	Poor Families	Low-Income (Poor and Near-Poor) Families
		(percentages)	
All family types	100.0	100.0	100.0
Male head	75.6	73.2	77.8
Married-wife present	72.0	69.9	74.9
Wife in labor force	11.8	11.8	13.6
Wife not in labor force	60.2	58.0	61.3
Other marital status	3.6	3.3	2.9
Female head	24.4	26.8	22.2

SOURCE: See Table 14.

TABLE 18. NUMBER AND PERCENTAGE DECLINE OF
PERSONS IN POOR OR LOW-INCOME CATEGORIES,
1959 AND 1966

Item	1959	1966	Percentage Decrease
Number of persons (in millions)			
Poor	38.9	29.7	24
Near-poor	15.8	15.2	4
Low income	54.7	44.8	18
Percentage			
Poor	22.1	15.3	31
Near-poor	9.0	7.8	13
Low income	31.1	23.1	26

SOURCE: Reference Table H.

TABLE 19. PERCENTAGE DECLINE IN POOR OR
LOW-INCOME CATEGORIES, BY COLOR, 1959 AND 1966

Item	1959	1966	Percentage Decrease
Percentage poor			
White	18.0	11.9	34
Nonwhite	54.6	40.6	28
Percentage low-income			
White	26.7	19.1	28
Nonwhite	65.4	53.0	19

SOURCE: Reference Table H.

The incidence of poverty was higher in both years for persons aged sixty-five and over than for any other age group (Table 20).

Regional and Geographic Distribution of the Poor and Near Poor. The proportion of the poor and low-income groups found in different regions of the country is, as noted earlier, similar to that of families in the lowest income fifth. The distributions for 1964 are shown in Table 21.

Even more interest attaches to the question of the extent to which poor persons are concentrated in central cities or in rural areas. For 1964 and 1966 special tabulations are available from which it was possible to derive the incidence of poverty in metropolitan and nonmetropolitan areas, in central cities and suburbs and for persons on farms and (1966) rural nonfarm areas.

As compared with 15 per cent of the total population poor in 1966, the poor constituted 16 per cent of those in central cities, 9 per cent of

TABLE 20.   INCIDENCE OF POVERTY, BY AGE GROUP AND FAMILY STATUS, 1959 AND 1966

Age group and family status	Number Poor in Millions		Percentage Poor	
	1959	1966	1959	1966
All ages	38.9	29.7	22.1	15.3
Children under 18[a]	16.6	12.5	26.1	17.9
In families with male head	12.6	8.0	21.7	12.9
In families with female head	4.0	4.5	72.6	60.6
Persons 18–64[b]	16.4	11.9	16.9	11.2
Persons 65 and over	5.9	5.4	37.2	29.9
In families	3.4	2.7	28.4	20.5
Unrelated individuals	2.5	2.7	68.1	55.3

[a] Never-married children in families.
[b] Includes ever-married persons under age 18.

SOURCE: Orshansky, Mollie, "Counting the Poor: Before and After Federal Income Support Programs," in *Old-Age Assurance*, submitted to Subcommittee on Fiscal Policy of U.S. Joint Economic Committee, 1968, Part II, pp. 177–231.

TABLE 21.   PROPORTION OF POOR AND LOW-INCOME GROUPS, BY REGION, 1964

Region	Families in Lowest Income Fifth	Poor Families	Low-Income Families
		(in millions)	
Total families	9,567	6,832	10,665
		(percentages)	
All regions	100.0	100.0	100.0
Northeast	17.7	16.2	18.1
North Central	25.1	23.1	23.4
South	44.0	48.2	45.3
West	13.2	12.6	13.3

SOURCE: See Table 14.

those in the suburbs, 23 per cent both of those on farms and in rural nonfarm areas and 19 per cent of those in smaller cities and towns (population of 2,500 or over and not in metropolitan areas). (See Table 22.)

Again, it is important to distinguish between incidence—the risk of poverty for a particular group—and the number of poor persons. Of the 29.8 million poor persons in 1966, more than a third lived in central cities and close to half of all poor nonwhites were in central cities (Table 23).

TABLE 22. INCIDENCE OF POVERTY: PERCENTAGE OF
PERSONS IN HOUSEHOLDS BELOW THE SOCIAL
SECURITY ADMINISTRATION POVERTY LEVEL,
BY COLOR AND RESIDENCE, 1964 AND 1966

Color and type of residence	1964	1966
All persons	*18.0*	*15.4*
White	14.1	12.0
Nonwhite	47.4	40.7
Metropolitan areas	*13.5*	*12.1*
Central cities	17.2	16.2
White	12.0	11.7
Nonwhite	38.0	33.0
Suburbs	10.0	8.6
White	8.7	7.6
Nonwhite	31.6	28.2
Nonmetropolitan areas	*26.0*	*21.4*
Farm	32.9	22.5
White	26.4	16.3
Nonwhite	75.4	70.1
Other, total	*24.4*	*21.2*
Rural nonfarm	n.a.	23.1
White	n.a.	19.0
Nonwhite	n.a.	56.3
Urban	n.a.	18.7
White	n.a.	14.2
Nonwhite	n.a.	58.0

NOTE: This table includes as poor some children aged 6 to 13 who lived as
unrelated individuals in families to no member of which they were related.
Other tables exclude these children because the Bureau of the Census does not
normally collect data from unrelated individuals aged 14.

SOURCE: Orshansky, Mollie, "The Poor in City and Suburb, 1964," *Social
Security Bulletin,* December, 1966, pp. 22–37; and Table 20.

Persons Poor on Basis of Own Income. The poverty and low-income
estimates presented thus far—and those used in official estimates of
poverty—relate to the noninstitutional population and measure poverty
on the basis of total family income. A considerable number of older
persons and some young families have incomes well below the poverty
line but are living in families with total income above that line, although not necessarily much above. A large proportion of such families are themselves below the low-income line.

In 1966, there were 2.7 million persons aged sixty five and over
living alone and with incomes below the poverty level. Another 2.7
million aged persons lived in poor families, giving a total of 5.4 million
noninstitutionalized aged persons who were living below the poverty

TABLE 23.   NUMBER OF PERSONS IN POOR HOUSEHOLD,
BY RESIDENCE, 1966

Residence	Number of Persons in Poor Households		
	Total	White	Nonwhite
	(in millions)		
United States	29.8	20.4	9.4
Central cities	9.4	5.4	4.0
Suburbs	5.8	4.8	.9
Farm	2.4	1.6	.9
Rural nonfarm	7.4	5.4	2.0
Small cities[a]	4.8	3.2	1.5

[a] Urban nonmetropolitan areas.
NOTE: See Table 22.
SOURCE: See Table 20.

level. If one wants to know how many older persons could afford to live alone if they wanted to do so, however, the income of the aged individual or aged couple is the relevant measure. In 1966 there were 1.6 million aged persons whose own income was below the poverty line but who were living in households whose total income was above the line. (There are also some aged persons with enough income of their own to put them above the poverty line who share a household with relatives so poor that the total family income is below the poverty line. The number of such cases is much smaller, however.) Adding these persons and those in institutions, one gets a total count of poor aged persons in the United States in 1966 of 7.7 million. For the purpose of estimating the probable effect of income-maintenance payments, it is the larger figure which is likely to be more meaningful.

Changing the Poverty Line. An acceptable social minimum is obviously related to the general level of affluence of a society. In a dynamic economy it must therefore change over time. It is easy to reach agreement that what was an appropriate poverty measure in 1900 or 1933 is no longer relevant. It is also possible to get agreement that an acceptable social minimum in 1985 will be different from the poverty level of 1967. But it is very difficult to find a satisfactory method of gradually moving the level up from its present to a hypothetical future position. The difficulty is not simply that of measuring progress in a war with an ever-escalating goal. There are other conceptual problems involved.

The problems take on a somewhat different cast if one conceives of the poverty index as a statistical measure with its important characteristic, the income-equivalency factor, or if one attempts to use it for direct program eligibility purposes. I am discussing it here as a welfare indicator—the purpose for which it was originally devised. In this context it can, of course, define a social policy goal—the goal of bringing every family up to the defined minimum. The basic question is whether the normative standard should move up proportionately with rising per capita income or by some lesser or greater amount.

The issues involved go in part to the question of optimum allocation of resources at different levels of GNP. They relate to the relative growth of public expenditures for services and for particular types of services. The weights for equivalencies may change as the absolute level of per capita income rises.

Thus far, the poverty and low-income indexes have been adjusted only for price changes. There would seem no question that the logic of a standard based on minimum food consumption needs requires a purchasing power—not a fixed dollar—measure. The change in the average poverty cut-off point for a family of four has been from $3,060 in 1959 to $3,335 in 1966. Clearly this adjustment thus far has had minor quantitative effect; its importance has been conceptual.

There has been considerable discussion of the desirability of other and more fundamental changes in the SSA poverty and low-income indexes. As now calculated, they rest on an assumption that families generally should not have to spend more than one-third of their total income on food (the proportion is somewhat smaller for one- and two-person families whose housing costs per capita are generally larger). This relationship, which is normative, but derives from analyses of consumer behavior, might well change as the general level of income rises. Richer families have more income for other things. It has been suggested also that explicit account might be taken of other items of consumption than food.

While further refinements in the index are desirable, particularly to the extent that they illuminate some of the interrelationships involved, it is worth noting that fairly substantial changes would be required to change the general picture as to who the disadvantaged groups are. The 1949 Joint Economic Committee study, using a very gross measure, listed the poverty groups as the farm poor, the aged, nonearners, unskilled workers, nonwhites, broken families, the poorly educated, and the disabled. The same groups appear in all the poverty and low-income lists and in analyses of income shares, although their proportions vary as does the total number of persons counted as poor.

One method of adjusting the poverty index over time that has attracted considerable attention was suggested by Victor Fuchs.[20] He proposes that poverty be defined as family income less than half the median family income in any year. He is apparently more concerned with having an automatic adjustment of the index than with the level, since he has also said that the standard might be one-fourth or one-third of the median family income. Such a relative measure presumes or postulates a desired degree of inequality that would not vary with the growth of GNP. Intuitively there seems no reason to think that the degree of inequality that is regarded as optimum will remain fixed any more than a standard based on some kind of minimum budget.

Technically there are other difficulties with the measure. Fuchs recognizes that it would need to be varied by family size, but does not indicate how this would be done. The simple use of calculated medians for different family groups—even if adequate data for the purpose were available—would not suffice. Large families, particularly those with children, have lower incomes than smaller families. Hence to use the median, or a fraction of it, for such families would be to accept their present relative position. (The median family income in 1966 of families with two children was $7,945; the poverty cut-off calculated by the SSA for such families was $3,335. For families with six or more children, however, the actual median income was $6,014 while the poverty cut-off point was $5,430.) One could vary the median (by half or a third) for all families in relation to the ratio of equivalent levels of living inherent in the SSA poverty index. Alternatively, of course, one could adjust the poverty and low-income cut-off points in relation to the percentage change in median family, or per capita, income from year to year.

For trend data, there is a very real question as to how frequently and by what amounts the level of a poverty index should be raised. Obviously, as income levels rise, the number of persons with incomes below any given level will fall. By holding the poverty measure constant (in real dollars), one can see more readily which groups are moving up relative to others. Changing the level year-by-year might emphasize that goals should not lag behind resources. On the other hand, it would tend to blur changing relationships of subgroups.

A point worth keeping in mind is that the level of the cut-off point can emphasize or obscure differences in the incidence of "poverty" for subgroups. This is simply another way of saying that some people are poor but others are very, very poor. An example may illustrate the point. The incidence of poverty among nonwhites in 1966 was 3.4 times that of whites. If one moves up to the low-income level, the incidence for nonwhites was 2.7 times that of whites. If one moves down the income scale the situation of nonwhites is relatively worse. In 1964, for example, the income deficit (the amount by which income was less than the poverty line) was less than $500 for a third of the white families and one-tenth of the nonwhites; it was $2,000 or more for 16 per cent of the white and for 26 per cent of the nonwhite families.

One is led back to an appreciation of the importance of income distribution. (Similar differences, of course, occur when one looks at income distribution in terms of tenths rather than fifths of the population.) A poverty line is one convenient way of summarizing the income distribution. Whatever changes are made over time in the minimum standard, it would seem desirable to have at least two levels of cut-off points—similar to the SSA poverty and low-income lines—in all years.

Summarizing the Distribution

Very early in the history of income distribution analysis, attempts were made to develop summary statistical measures of the degree of inequality in the entire distribution in order to facilitate time-to-time and place-to-place comparisons. The best known and most frequently used are the Lorenz curve and the Gini ratio or index of concentration. The curve is a plotting of the cumulative proportion of units arrayed in order from the smallest incomes to the largest against the cumulative share of aggregate income accounted for by these units. The Gini ratio is a measure of the area falling between the income curve and a straight line diagonal. Perfect equality would result in points along the diagonal; the area between the curve and the diagonal can thus provide an index of inequality. The ratio is expressed as a percentage of 1; the smaller the figure, the closer does the distribution it is measuring approach equality.

This measure and several of its variations have been criticized on grounds of the unreality of an assumption of either perfect equality or perfect inequality and the statistical consequences of this assumption. It has also been frequently pointed out that such measures are very insensitive to small changes in the income distribution. On the other hand, it is independent of the absolute amount or level of income.

The usefulness of any such single measure of concentration or dispersion lies primarily in the possibility it offers of testing the effect on over all inequality of a great variety of actual or hypothetical variations in income patterns.

The Gini ratio has been used at a few points in this chapter to illustrate specific relationships. Gini ratios year by year 1947–1966 for all families and unrelated individuals, white and nonwhite families, white and nonwhite unrelated individuals and men and women (income of persons) are shown in Reference Tables C–F at the end of the chapter. A few general observations may be worth making.

Over time, the trends in the Gini ratio for any group will of course parallel the changes in the shares of aggregate income going to the lowest, next lowest, etc., fifth of the group. The drop in the Gini ratio for all families and individuals from .417 in 1947 to .402 in 1966 summarizes the total decrease in inequality that also resulted in a rise in the share of the lowest fifth between those years from 3.5 to 3.7 and a decline in the highest fifth from 45.8 to 43.8.

The Gini ratio can also summarize quickly the fact that there is more inequality in the distribution of money incomes of nonwhite than of white families (in 1966, the ratios were .385 and .343 respectively) and far greater inequality for unrelated individuals than for families.

Another indication of the effect of family groupings in reducing income inequalities can be seen in a comparison of the Gini ratios for family income and adult unit income. The adult unit count includes as separate units single individuals and secondary households living in families, usually because their own income is low. In their detailed analyses of income and wealth in the U.S. in 1959, James Morgan and his colleagues calculated the Gini ratio for family money income to be .385 and that for adult units .448.[21]

Morgan also calculated the effect of federal income taxes; in 1959 inequality in family income was reduced from .385 (total family money income) to .355 (income after federal income tax). Taking account of imputed rent and nonmoney transfers including food and housing provided by relatives brought the Gini ratio down a little further—to .346.

When the differential needs of different-sized families were taken into account, the over-all measure of inequality was further reduced to .309. As Morgan points out, many low-income families are small and many large families are headed by a middle-aged person at his earnings peak. The same relationships are involved as those which reduce the count of aged persons in poverty and increase the number of large families counted poor when one changes from a uniform to a variable measure of poverty. The shifts which result in a lesser degree of inequality on a family welfare-needs basis than on a straight family-income basis affect primarily the lower and middle segments of the income curve. In Morgan's calculations for 1959 income, they were large enough to have a somewhat greater effect on the over-all measure of inequality than the allowance for federal income taxes.

Distribution of Other Income

To what extent are the inequalities in the distribution of money income and its insufficiency for some 15 per cent of the total population offset or reinforced by the availability of income in kind or by other institutional factors?

Nonmoney Income. Home-grown food, while of decreasing importance compared with earlier years, adds to the consumption of some families, primarily farm families. As noted earlier, the poverty index incorporates an adjustment to reflect the availability of home-produced food for farm families. Morgan and his colleagues found that in 1959, home-grown food added only $40 a year on the average to the money income of families. There was relatively little variation by income class but such production was concentrated in farm families. The BLS Consumer Expenditure Survey for 1960–1961 covering both urban and rural families, shows essentially the same picture; the average value of home-produced food for all families in the survey was $44; for those with money incomes of under $1,000, the average value was $53; for families with money income of $15,000 and over, the average value of home-produced food was $25 for the year.

Morgan also estimated the amount of real income from home improvements made by family members. These averaged $140, ranging from $22 for those with gross disposable incomes of $500–999 to $367 for those with incomes of $10,000–14,999 and $277 for incomes above $15,000. Morgan comments: "Clearly considerations other than rational comparisons of employment opportunities must have been involved since these upper income units must have better earning opportunities in their jobs, and it is doubtful that they have more manual skills."[22] Home production including both food and maintenance and repair work added about 3 to 4 per cent to gross disposable income. It did not, however, tend to offset differences in money income or to make the distribution of "welfare" any more equal.

More significant as an addition to welfare is the use value of owner-occupied homes. Home ownership is particularly important for one low-income group—the aged. In a survey of aged persons made in 1963, about two-thirds of the married couples reported some equity in a home, with the median amount of equity being $10,000. Only about a third of nonmarried aged men and women reported any equity in a home and the amounts were smaller. In general, those with low incomes were less likely to have any equity in a home and the amounts were much smaller than those with high money incomes.[23]

The Federal Reserve Board survey of the assets and wealth of the civilian noninstitutional population at the end of 1962 found that 57 per cent of all consumer units had equities in owned homes and 42 per cent of these units owned their homes free of mortgage debt. The rate of home ownership was relatively high in the lower-income brackets, largely because of the concentration of older families in these income brackets. Forty per cent of consumer units with incomes of less than $3,000 owned their homes and three-fourths of the group had no mortgage debt.[24] Inclusion of the rental value of an owned home in income thus increases the percentage share of the lower income groups and makes for greater equality in the over-all distribution.

Assets. To what extent are inequalities in the income distribution offset by asset holdings? To the extent that assets yield monetary returns these are, of course, included in current income. The question is usually raised in relation to proposals for income supplementation for low-income groups and reflects a conviction that families should convert assets to current income if additional income is needed.

From this point of view, an owned home may have little conversion value. The sale of an old home, particularly in the modest price ranges, is likely to yield less than the cost of rental housing. Liquid assets, which could be used to supplement current income, are held in significant amounts by middle- and high-income, not by low-income families.

The Federal Reserve Board study found that almost 80 per cent of the population had some liquid assets (defined to include savings and checking accounts and U.S. savings bonds). However, for 30 per cent of the population these amounted to less than $500; and only 25 per cent had as much as $2,000. Investment assets (stocks and other marketable securities, mortgage assets, investment real estate, business investments not managed by the unit and company savings plans) were even more heavily concentrated among those with large incomes. The distribution of total net worth was similar to that of money income, highly concentrated in the upper income groups. Only 1 per cent of families with income of less than $3,000 had net worth of as much as $50,000; of those with incomes of $100,000 and over, 93 per cent had a net worth of more than $500,000 and 37 per cent had more than $1,000,000.

The question is often raised as to why this group, particularly older persons, should not use up their assets to supplement their current incomes. If one thinks in terms of modest amounts of savings, the question almost answers itself. The aged still face contingencies for which it is reasonable to retain some reserve. Medicare has removed a part—but only a part—of the threat of heavy medical care costs. Assets once used up are not replaceable when earnings have ceased. And the probability of rising prices could well lead a prudent man to question the wisdom of converting all his assets into fixed dollar annuities. Nevertheless, it is instructive to calculate what would be added to current income if assets were so used.

Such an analysis of potential income from assets was made on the basis of data from the SSA 1963 Survey of the Aged. Assets were assumed to be capable of earning a 4 per cent annual rate of return. The principal and appropriate interest amounts were divided over the expected remaining years of the unit's life (based on its age in 1963) in equal annual sums so that the assets would be exhausted at the end of the period. The annual amount computed in this way was added to current money income less the income actually received from assets.

If all assets other than equity in a home could have been converted to income prorated over the expected life of the holder in this way, the median income of the entire aged group would have been increased by about 10 per cent. The increases would have been larger for those with the higher money incomes. More than three-fourths of those with incomes of less than $3,000 did not have asset holdings great enough to place their potential income in a higher $1,000 income bracket than that in which their actual income fell.

The Federal Reserve Board study made a somewhat different calculation for consumer units of all ages with incomes below the poverty line. Equity in an owned home was assigned a use value of 4 per cent a year and liquid and investment assets were assumed to be used up over varying periods from one to five years. Allowance for home equity would have brought 6 per cent of the units above the poverty line. Allowance for home equity plus use of liquid assets would have kept 13 per cent of the units above poverty for five years or more—half of these units were headed by persons aged sixty-five and over. Another 8 per cent would have been kept above the poverty line for between one and four years. Sixty-one per cent of the total group, however, had no liquid or investment assets and for another thirteen per cent the amounts were too small to make up their income deficiency for as much as a year.

As suggested earlier, a more significant aspect of assets and wealth than the potential supplementation of low incomes is the control over the future and the security, the ability to adjust to economic and social change which they give. It is clear that a wealth income measure, however wealth was defined, would show greater inequality than a current income measure. This is true if one includes some measure of human wealth—i.e., education, training, good health. Inequalities in current income have a cumulative effect that is not easily counteracted.

Public Expenditures

With the growth of technology, increasing affluence, an expanding population and the appearance of large conurbations, it is inevitable that collective goods and services should become more important. The general functions of maintenance of law and order and national defense become more highly organized. The provision of public utilities— water, sewage disposal, air pollution control—transportation, housing and city planning, recreation and cultural activities require larger amounts of resources and depend increasingly on governmental action. Public education in this country has a long history, but the scope of publicly supported education has been vastly expanded as research and advanced training have become an indispensable factor in further economic growth. An organized system of income maintenance for the nonearning segment of the population is an economic necessity in modern society. And a variety of health, welfare, and manpower services are increasingly called for and provided in all economically developed countries.

What can be said about the effect of government activities on the distribution of real income? In fiscal 1967, public expenditures amounted to about 30 per cent of the Gross National Product and tax revenues were only slightly less. What groups in society are benefited the most?

There is no objective basis on which to allocate the benefits of general governmental services. Some have argued that the citizens of a country should share equally in the benefits of law and order, military defense, space exploration, etc. Others would distribute these expenditures more nearly in relation to the distribution of property. Two recent studies which have attempted to measure the net redistributive effect of all government activities will be discussed later.

There are certain government activities which have an explicitly redistributive or broad social welfare purpose. Such expenditures have grown at a rapid rate in the past three decades and now amount to more than $100 billion a year or more than 13 per cent of the GNP. While we have less information than would be desirable on the distribution of these expenditures by income class, rough estimates can be made with some degree of reliability.

Cash Transfer Payments. The cash benefits and payments under Social Security, public assistance, veterans and related programs are included in the money income of individuals and families. Though this income is already accounted for, it is useful to look a little more closely at its effect on the total distribution.

Total cash transfer payments under public programs in fiscal 1967 were $46 billion or 7.5 per cent of aggregate personal income. OASDHI benefits represented half and all social insurance benefits (OASDHI, unemployment insurance, cash sickness in four states, workmen's compensation, and special systems for railroad workers and public employees) more than three-fourths of the total. Veterans and public assistance programs made up less than a fourth of the total.[25]

Social insurance benefits are designed to provide a continuing source of income when earnings are interrupted or cease. Since they are also designed to provide a lesser amount than the individual was earning, they go to a large extent to persons in the lower income groups. By the nature of the programs they go also to aged persons, disabled, unemployed, and one group of families headed by a woman (survivor families)—all family types that are found in large numbers among the poor and low-income groups.

Most of the 5.4 million persons sixty-five and over shown as poor in 1966, in the estimates cited earlier, were receiving OASDHI benefits. At least as many aged persons, however, were above the poverty level because of their benefits. Even those below the poverty line were less far below than aged persons who were not receiving benefits. We have less adequate data relating to disabled and younger survivor beneficiaries; but it is clear that for these groups also the social insurance benefit does now or could represent the difference between poverty and a more acceptable level of living. With the increases in social security benefits resulting from the 1967 amendments, it is estimated that about 10 million beneficiaries have incomes above the poverty level only because of these benefits.

Special questions on the CPS for 1966 provided information on the amount of family income in 1965 that came from OASDHI benefits, from public assistance and from all other public programs as a group. The data have obvious limitations. Respondents in a survey do not always identify correctly the program from which they are receiving benefits. In addition, the grouping of individuals into families on the basis of the situation at the time of interview (March, 1966) and the reporting of income for the previous year may result in more ambiguities when one is concerned with particular sources of income than with total income.

Nevertheless, certain relationships stand out clearly. Had it not been for public income payments, the number of households with income below the poverty line in 1965 would have been 15.9 million (26 per cent of all households) rather than the 11.2 million (19 per cent) shown as poor in the poverty series. The Social Security program alone kept 3½ million households out of poverty. While most of these were headed by a person aged sixty-five and over, almost 700,000 were headed by a younger person.

All public transfer payments combined prevented poverty for about one in three of the households headed by a person under age sixty-five who received such payments and for about one in two aged households. As one would expect, however, since such payments go primarily to families without current income from earnings, the proportion of aged families receiving such public transfer payments was much larger— six out of seven households—compared with younger families, where one in five households received some public income support.[26]

Private employee benefit plans paid out cash benefits—pensions, group life, voluntary sickness insurance, paid sick leave—of $7 billion in fiscal 1967. By and large these payments go to the middle- and upper-income groups. It is primarily the better organized and better paid workers who are covered by such plans; sick pay and supplementary unemployment benefits go to workers only temporarily out of the labor force, those who receive private pensions supplementing Social Security are generally not in the lowest income groups and the private pensions going to the high-paid executives can be very large.

Morgan found that money transfers substantially increased the degree of equality in the total income distribution in 1959. For money income other than transfer income, the Gini ratio for families was .419; with money transfers included the ratio dropped to .385. For adult units, the ratios were respectively .485 and .448.[27]

Cash transfer payments under public programs are redistributive even after taking account of the contributions or taxes used to finance the benefits. Public assistance payments go only to very low-income groups and are financed in large measure from federal general revenues. Social insurance benefits go to persons who are no longer earning and in general have reduced incomes while the contributions are paid by persons who are currently at work and by their employers. Whatever assumptions are made as to the incidence of the employer tax— whether one assumes it is born by employees in the form of lower wages or by consumers in higher prices or in part by reduced profits— the net effect of Social Security is to add most to low and medium incomes. A recent analysis measures the degree of progressivity for families grouped not by income but by a welfare ratio which takes into account equivalent levels of income for families of varying size. By this measure also, when taxes are set off against benefits the net benefit as a proportion of income is greater for families with the lowest welfare ratio for all the cash transfer programs.[28]

Health Services. An increasing proportion not only of the costs of health research, medical facilities construction, and public health environmental sanitation activities, but also of personal health care services in the U.S. has in recent years been financed from public funds. In fiscal 1967, 30 per cent of the $41.5 billion spent for personal health care came from public funds, as compared with 9 per cent in 1929. The new program of health insurance for the aged was primarily responsible for the increase in the public share from 22 per cent in fiscal 1966, but vendor medical payments under medical assistance and increased funds for maternal and child health services and medical care financed through the Office of Economic Opportunity also played a part.

Public expenditures for personal health care are made through a variety of programs, with federal funds of increasing importance, as the figures in Table 24 illustrate.

There are no data that offer a really satisfactory basis for distributing all public expenditures for personal health care by income class. A rough estimate of the proportion going for services to the poor can be made. All public assistance vendor medical payments, all OEO medical care expenditures, and essentially all maternal and child health services as well as a substantial proportion of medical costs under vocational rehabilitation go to persons who have passed a fairly stringent means test and can safely be classified as low income if not desperately poor. It is roughly estimated that about 30 per cent of the medical care benefits under Medicare—health insurance for the aged—go to persons with money incomes below the SAA poverty line.

About 50 per cent of the expenditures in municipal hospitals and state mental institutions are estimated to be for the poor and 55 per cent of the Veterans Administration hospital and medical care ex-

TABLE 24.   PUBLIC EXPENDITURES FOR PERSONAL
HEALTH CARE, 1949–1950 AND 1966–1967

	1949–50		1966–67	
Type of Expenditure	Amount, in Billions	Federal Funds, in Percentage	Amount, in Billions	Federal Funds, in Percentage
Total	*$2.1*	*47*	*$12.6*	*61*
OASDHI (health insurance for the aged)	—	—	3.2	100
Temporary disability insurance (medical benefits)	ᵃ	0	.1	0
Workmen's compensation (medical benefits)	.2	3	.7	2
Public assistance (vendor medical payments)	.1	0	2.3	49
General hospital and medical care	.9	5	2.8	6
Defense Department hospital and medical care	.3	100	1.6	100
Military dependents' medical care	—	—	.1	100
Maternal and child health services	ᵃ	67	.3	42
School health (educational agencies)	ᵃ	0	.1	0
Veterans' hospital and medical care	6	100	1.2	100
Medical vocational rehabilitation	ᵃ	69	.1	75
OEO health and medical care	—	—	.1	100

ᵃ Less than 50 million.

SOURCE: Based on Social Security Administration, "Public and Private Expenditures for Health and Medical Care, Fiscal Years 1929–67," Research and Statistics Note No. 21, Washington, 1967.

penditures are assumed to be for persons with cash incomes below the poverty or at least below the low-income line. For lack of data and to be on the conservative side, all of the following program expenditures were allocated to the nonpoor: medical benefits under temporary disability insurance and workmen's compensation, Defense Department medical and hospital care, and military dependents' medical care and school health expenditures.

On this basis one could say that roughly $6 billion or 46 per cent of all public expenditures for personal health care in fiscal 1967 paid for care received by poor persons. In fiscal 1966, the year before Medicare, $4 billion paid for health services for the poor, but this represented a larger proportion—49 per cent—of public personal health care expenditures. This decrease in the proportion of the personal health care dollar going to the poor in fiscal 1967 was due to the large Medicare outlay—now about one-fourth of the total public personal health care expenditure. The larger part of Medicare outlays paid for services for aged persons with incomes above the poverty line, in many cases because their cash Social Security benefits had moved them out of the poverty group. Many of these persons were still below the low-income line.

The proportion of all public personal health care expenditures that benefit persons with very low incomes is still considerably larger than in 1950 or even in 1960 (Table 25).

TABLE 25. PROPORTION OF ALL PUBLIC PERSONAL
HEALTH CARE EXPENDITURES BENEFITING POOR
PERSONS, SELECTED YEARS, 1929–1967

| | | Public Expenditures for Personal Health Care | | |
| | Total Personal Health Care Expenditures | | For Poor Persons | |
Fiscal Years		Total	Amount	Per Cent of Total Public
1929	$ 3.3	$ .3	$ .1	30
1940	3.5	.5	.2	36
1950	10.6	2.1	.8	39
1960	23.4	4.9	2.0	42
1966	36.8	8.1	4.0	49
1967	41.5	12.6	5.8	46

SOURCE: Merriam, Ida C., "Social Welfare Expenditures, 1929–67," *Social Security Bulletin,* December, 1967, pp. 3–16; and Social Security Administration, "Public and Private Expenditures for Health and Medical Care, Fiscal Years 1929–67," Research and Statistics Note No. 21, Washington, 1967.

The question of quality of services is unanswered by these figures. There is, of course, great variation in the quality of services received by persons who pay for care privately. The intent of the newer public programs is to assure equally high if not higher quality care to those (poor and nonpoor) entitled to services paid for from public funds. Evaluation of the extent to which this intent is being realized is beyond the scope of this chapter. From the point of view of income supplementation, however, it seems clear that public expenditures for personal medical care represent an increasingly significant addition to the consumption potential of lower-income families. Expenditures for personal health services now represent about 78 per cent of all public health expenditures (in this definition, sewage and waste disposal and water supplies are not included). No attempt has been made to distribute by income class expenditures for medical research, general public health activities or medical facilities construction. The question of redistribution—i.e., the source of the public funds so used—is discussed briefly below.

The Medicare program reflects a recognition that the cost of medical care is increasingly beyond the means of all but the wealthiest group in the population unless the cost can be averaged over periods of health and illness, and that for low-income groups like the aged even average costs may be more than they can pay out of current income. Direct payment for service at the time it is received, which accounted for 89 per cent of such expenditures in 1929 and 68 per cent in 1950, covered only 46 per cent in 1967. Thus more than half of all personal health care is now covered by third-party payments. About 56 per cent of third-party payments in 1967 were made under the public programs already discussed. About 90 per cent of the remainder represented payments under private health insurance obtained as a result of employment and largely paid for by employers.

For the future, the important question may be how health services can best be organized and health manpower and facilities expanded so that they can be available to all through whatever method or combination of methods they are paid for.

Public Education. To what extent does publicly provided education supplement the incomes of those in very low-, middle- and high-income brackets? Here again, one has to distinguish between the distributional effects of expenditures and the relative quality of services. Neither is easily measured. One of the most sophisticated and elaborate analyses was that carried out by Morgan and his associates in the Michigan study.

In this study, relating to 1959 incomes and expenditures, average public school expenditures per pupil were estimated for 133 separate areas and the benefits from public education received by each family in the sample determined by multiplying the per capita expenditure in its area by the number of children in the family who attended public school. The resulting benefits were then compared with money income, gross disposable income (defined to include nonmoney income such as the estimated rental value of owned homes) and the family welfare ratio (a measure of the relation of gross disposable income and needs).

For all three measures the ratio of educational benefits to income was greater the lower the income. "Even the average dollar amounts of benefits per family are greater for those with the lower levels of economic welfare. These are large families with more children in school. The benefits of free public education appear to go largely to those who would find it hardest to pay for them."[29] The analysis did show a difference in the expenditure per child in schools attended primarily by children of high income families (6 per cent above average) and those attended by children of very low-income families (13 per cent below average). The authors note also that the quality of education per dollar spent may be greater than these figures would indicate. An evaluation of the quality of education—whether for the poor or the rich—obviously requires a different approach.

Morgan and his colleagues also analyzed the burden of the property tax, still the major source of state and local school revenues. They concluded that the tax is not regressive when renters are included in the analysis and account is taken, in assessing ability to pay, of the imputed rental income of the owners' equity in his home, of federal income tax liability, and of family size and structure. These findings reinforce their conclusion that "free public education is a powerful redistributive force, both in the short run for the parents and later through its effect on the future earnings of the pupils," and that "nonwhites benefit more both absolutely and relatively from free public education."[30]

Public expenditures for higher education, on the other hand, probably benefit disporportionately families in the middle and higher income groups. The sons and daughters of these families are much more likely to go to college and graduate school. A recent study of expenditures for higher education under federal programs enacted in the past few years indicates, however, that these newer programs are benefiting primarily students from poor families, as was intended.[31]

Other Social Welfare Expenditures. Cash transfers and expenditures for health and education make up about 95 per cent of all social welfare expenditures included in the SSA series. A number of the remaining social service programs are directed primarily to low-income groups—child welfare, vocational rehabilitation, school lunch, institutional care and the newer manpower training and OEO community action programs. The addition to current real income is not large. What their impact on future income distribution may be is impossible to evaluate at this time.

The problem of housing deserves separate mention. Where and what kind of housing can be built is more and more a matter of collective decision. Discrimination in access to housing is one of the more difficult forms of discrimination to eliminate and yet central to many others. Public subsidies for housing represent only one aspect of social intervention in this area. Expenditures for public housing or rent subsidies—which go only to low-income groups—have been much smaller in the aggregate than the tax subsidies afforded to home owners through allowances for mortgage interest and real estate taxes as deductions on the federal income tax. Higher money incomes enable families to improve their housing as well as other forms of consumption. Where money income is inadequate, we are still searching for the public program or programs that can most effectively assure that housing needs are met. The problems are interwoven with the many other factors that affect the quality of urban life.

Redistributional Effects of Government Programs. To assess the extent of the benefit which the various income groups derive from public expenditures, one has to ask what groups give up the income—that is, pay the taxes or contributions—necessary to finance the transfer payments or the services.

For some purposes, one may want to measure the effect of tax payments—independent of the benefits they finance—on the level of living of the lowest and middle-income groups. Family budgets usually include an amount to cover direct taxes the family would have to pay. Indirect taxes are reflected in large measure in the prices of the items that make up the budget total. Neither the poverty or low-income level cut-off points discussed earlier include any allowances for direct taxes. Most families at the poverty level would pay no income tax, although many of them would pay Social Security and property taxes. Most families at the low-income level would pay federal income taxes. Both sets of income cut-off points must therefore be regarded as implicitly covering more than current consumption needs, at least under present tax policies.

Economists are far from agreement on the real impact of many types of taxes. A business tax or an employment tax, for example, may be passed on to consumers in the form of higher prices or back to employees in the form of lower wages than would otherwise have been paid. By and large the federal tax system, because of the weight of the federal income tax, is generally progressive—that is, those with higher incomes pay somewhat higher rates of tax. The total tax system, however, with sales, excise and property taxes included, is probably more nearly U-shaped, taking relatively more from the lowest than from a fairly wide range of middle income groups and again relatively more from those in income levels above $10,000 or $15,000, though there is very little information as to the degree of progression at really high income levels.

Two recent studies have attempted to measure the net redistributive effects of all (federal, state, and local) government activities. Working with different sets of data and using different assumptions with regard to tax incidence and the distribution of the benefits of general government expenditures, W. I. Gillespie[32] and George Bishop[33] nevertheless reach very similar over-all conclusions. (For his standard case, Gillespie allocates general expenditure proportionately to income, Bishop half on the basis of number of families and half on the basis of family income.) Both find that the lowest income groups receive substantial net benefits, that the middle-income groups about pay their own way and that families with incomes of $10,000–15,000 and over contribute more than they receive. Gillespie's figures related to 1960, Bishop's to 1961. Both show substantial net benefits to families with incomes under $2,000 and lesser but still significant redistribution through the $3,000–3,999 family income class. Significant excess contributions begin with the $10,000 and over class on Gillespie's method of calculation and $15,000 and over on Bishop's.

Since 1961 there have been important changes both in expenditure programs and in taxes. With further study, it should also be possible to develop better bases for allocating various types of expenditures to income classes. The general picture of net redistribution from high to low-income groups with a middle group paying about what it receives might remain. The boundaries of low, middle, and high will certainly change, as may the extent of redistribution.

DIRECTIONS FOR FUTURE RESEARCH

This chapter has selected one measure of changes in welfare and briefly summarized some of the major trends that are revealed by existing statistics. Before turning to the question of directions for future research and analysis, it might be well to state explicitly some of the dimensions of welfare that have been deliberately omitted from this discussion.

Omissions in this Analysis

Except in the emphasis on equality as a coordinate goal, the question of social policy has been largely by-passed. Acceptance of reduction in inequality as a goal does seem to me to imply the selection of methods of combatting poverty that rest wherever possible on universalist and integrative policies.

There has been no attempt to quantify and only the briefest reference to the social costs of economic growth. The crowding, the loss of privacy, the noise, the excitement and the cultural variety of life in a big city weigh differently in the balances of different individuals. Perhaps the best one can say is that opportunities for individual choice and the ability to take protective measures are likely to be as unequally distributed as is money income.

Other social costs, such as occupational diseases and accidents, air and water pollution can be assigned dollar values (or disvalues) in the aggregate and may perhaps some day be worked into a set of national accounts.

Considerable attention has been given in recent years to leisure time as a measure of welfare. Certainly the reduction in average hours of work has to be balanced against the increase in average hours required to get to and from work. There also needs to be included in the equation the differential availability of transportation (dramatized by the situation in Watts, but a reality in every big city) and the pressures on the low-paid worker to take a second job.

Differential opportunities to spend income effectively were only briefly touched upon. Both private merchandising practices and public program limitations are involved. The frequently noted differential use of services such as health services may have much to do with the quality of services actually available to the poor and the opportunity cost involved in taking the time to get them.

Specific aspects of welfare can be measured in outcome terms— morbidity rates, rates of higher education, adequacy of housing, etc. Other chapters in this volume deal with some of these aspects, and with consumption in general. The value of income is, of course, the consumption and the security it makes possible. This discussion has dealt with the potentialities rather than with their specific actualization.

Two other dimensions of welfare have also been put aside—the cultural and aesthetic use of resources, and the international problems both of war and peace and of wealth and poverty among peoples and nations.

Future Studies and Analyses

One direction for future analysis is suggested by this list of omissions and the interactions it implies.

Within the limits set by this chapter, there is much to be done. Some of the analyses would require new data collection efforts. There are, however, existing masses of data that await and that warrant analysis.

Reference has already been made to several areas where knowledge is lacking or very limited. While much more can be done through cohort analysis of existing data, there is a place for longitudinal studies of particular individuals and families. Such studies in themselves might not tell us why some people move out of poverty—or into it—but they would give us a better idea than we have now as to what kind of people change circumstances.

Longitudinal studies are expensive and they require a long-term research commitment. With more attention and more funds for social science research, it should become possible to get additional support for such studies. A few longitudinal studies now under way will provide some relevant data. A series of five-year studies designed to focus on problems of employability of older men, middle-aged women, and persons entering the labor force is being supported by the Department of Labor. A longitudinal study of the retirement history of workers aged fifty-eight to sixty-three at time of first interview, which is just getting under way and which the Social Security Administration plans to continue for at least ten years, will focus on changing retirement incomes in relation to the individual's income during his working years.

Regional variations in income and their relation to variations in costs and in standards of living pose many questions for analysis. To what extent and in what ways are regional differences in median income and in income shares associated with different demographic characteristics of the population and the industrial structure of the region at a given time. To what extent can changes be accounted for by differential rates of economic growth and by population movement? How do the differences among major regions in income levels compare with the differences in all regions between central city, suburb and rural areas.

The question is frequently raised with respect to measures of minimum income, such as a subsistence budget or a poverty index, as to whether the minimum should vary by size of city or by region. If one could be sure one was measuring only differences in the cost of an equivalent level of living, one might for some purposes want to introduce such variations. But the danger is great that one will become involved in a circular process. If lower apparent costs for lower levels of living—caused by inadequacies in current income—are incorporated in a reduced measure of need, our measures will have accepted and may help perpetuate income differentials that are not justified or desired.

There will always be room for improvement in measures of poverty. One can assume that "improvements" which win general acceptance will grow out of more detailed analyses of the relation between income and consumption and better understanding of the causal connections between poverty, discrimination, and other aspects of individual and social life and change.

At the upper end of the income scale, mention has been made of the need for more data and more analyses relating to the distributional effects of private employee benefit plans and of nonwage compensation such as expense accounts and various forms of consumption of very high income groups that is paid for by the employing organization and does not show up as individual income.

Studies of redistribution, which have suffered from a lack of empirical data, will become increasingly possible and useful as a result of data links now in process (in particular the linkage of CPS, IRS, and SSA data).

Another area in which much more research is needed is how to measure and evaluate public preferences for collective goods. A substantial start on such studies has been made at the University of Michigan Survey Research Center, but the area is large and difficult.

The importance of these newer areas should not be allowed to interrupt the continued development and improvement of data on money income and its distribution—from which we can continue to infer a great deal about the welfare of the United States.

NOTES

1. Scitovsky, Tibor, *Papers on Welfare and Growth,* Stanford University Press, Stanford, Calif., 1964.
2. Boulding, Kenneth, *Principles of Economic Policy,* Prentice-Hall, Englewood Cliffs, N.J., 1958; and "Social Justice in Social Dynamics," in Braudt, Richard B., ed., *Social Justice,* Prentice-Hall, Englewood Cliffs, N.J., 1962.
3. See, for example, the reports of the National Conference on Research in National Income and Wealth, *Studies on Income and Wealth,* National Bureau of Economic Research, New York, 1937–   . Volumes 3 (1939), 5 (1943),

13 (1951), 15 (1952), and 33 (forthcoming) deal specifically with size of income distribution. See also Goldsmith, Selma, *et al.*, "Size Distribution of Income Since the Mid-Thirties," *Review of Economics and Statistics,* no. 36, February, 1954.

4. Brady, Dorothy, *Research on Size Distribution,* vol. 13 (1951) in *Studies on Income and Wealth, op. cit.*

5. Titmuss, Richard M., *Income Distribution and Social Change,* Allen & Unwin, London, 1962; and *Commitment to Welfare,* Allen & Unwin, London, 1968, Part III, "Issues of Redistribution in Social Policy."

6. Projector, Dorothy S., and Gertrude S. Weiss, *Survey of Financial Characteristics of Consumers,* Federal Reserve Board, Washington, August, 1966.

7. Kuznets, Simon, *Shares of Upper Income Groups in Income and Savings,* National Bureau of Economic Research, New York, 1950.

8. Henson, Mary F., "Trends in the Income of Families and Persons in the U.S., 1947–64," Technical Report No. 17, U.S. Bureau of the Census, Washington, 1967; and "Income in 1966 of Families and Persons in the U.S.," *Current Population Reports,* Series P-60, no. 53, December, 1967.

9. Miller, Herman P., "Income Distribution in the United States," A 1960 Census Monograph, U.S. Department of Commerce, Washington, 1966.

10. Brady, Dorothy D., "Age and the Income Distribution," Research Report No. 8, Social Security Administration, Washington, 1965.

11. *Ibid.*

12. Morgan, James, "The Anatomy of Income Distribution," *Review of Economics and Statistics,* vol. 44, August, 1962, p. 270.

13. Duncan, Otis Dudley, "Inheritance of Poverty or Inheritance of Race?" in a forthcoming book on poverty in America edited by Daniel Moynihan to be published by Basic Books.

14. Smolensky, Eugene, "Interrelationship among Income Distributions," *Review of Economics and Statistics,* vol. 45, no. 2, May, 1963, pp. 197–206.

15. Lamale, Helen, "Changes in Concepts of Income Adequacy over the Last Century," *American Economic Review,* vol. 48, no. 2, May, 1958, pp. 291–299.

16. Franklin, N. N., "The Concept and Measurement of Minimum Living Standards," *International Labour Review,* vol. 95, no. 4, April, 1967; also see Abel-Smith, Brian, and Peter Townsend, "The Poor and the Poorest," Occasional Papers on Social Administration No. 17.

17. U.S. Congress Joint Committee on the Economic Report, Subcommittee on Low-Income Families, *Low-Income Families and Economic Stability,* 81st Congress, 2nd session, 1950, and materials assembled by the Subcommittee on Low-Income Families, 81st Congress, 1st session, 1949.

18. U.S. Congress Joint Committee on the Economic Report, Subcommittee on Low-Income Families, *Characteristics of the Low-Income Population and Related Federal Programs,* 84th Congress, 1st session, 1955.

19. Orshansky, Mollie, "Counting the Poor: Another Look at the Poverty Profile," *Social Security Bulletin,* January, 1965, pp. 3–29; "Who's Who Among the Poor: A Demographic View of Poverty," *Social Security Bulletin,* July, 1965, pp. 3–32; "More About the Poor in 1964," *Social Security Bulletin,* May, 1966, pp. 3–38.

20. Fuchs, Victor, "Redefining Poverty," *The Pubic Interest,* no. 8, Summer, 1967, pp. 88–95.

21. Morgan, James, M. H. David, W. J. Cohen, and H. E. Brazer, *Income and Welfare in the United States,* McGraw-Hill, New York, 1962.

22. *Ibid.,* p. 105. See also Morgan, James, Ismael A. Sirageldin, and Nancy Baerwaldt, *Productive Americans,* University of Michigan, Survey Research Center Monograph 43, 1966.

23. Epstein, Lenore, and Janet H. Murray, "The Aged Population of the United States: The 1963 Social Security Survey of the Aged," Research Report No. 19, Social Security Administration, Washington, 1967.
24. Projector, Dorothy S., and Gertrude S. Weiss, *Survey of Financial Characteristics of Consumers,* Federal Reserve Board, Washington, August, 1966.
25. Merriam, Ida C., "Social Welfare Expenditures, 1929–67," *Social Security Bulletin,* December, 1967, pp. 3–16.
26. Orshansky, Mollie, "Counting the Poor: Before and After Federal Income-Support Programs," in *Old-Age Income Assurance,* a compendium of papers on Problems and Policy Issues in the Public and Private Pension System, submitted to the Subcommittee on Fiscal Policy of the U.S. Joint Economic Committee, 1968, Part II, pp. 177–231.
27. Morgan, J., *et al., Income and Welfare in the United States, op. cit.,* p. 315.
28. Bridges, Benjamin, "Current Redistributional Effect of Old-Age Income Assurance Programs," in *Old-Age Income Assurance, op. cit.,* Part II, pp. 95–176.
29. Morgan, J., *et al., Income and Welfare in the United States, op. cit.,* pp. 303–304.
30. *Ibid.,* p. 308.
31. Froomkin, Joseph, *Students and Building,* An Analysis of Selected Federal Programs for Higher Education, Planning Paper 68-2, Office of Education, Washington, 1968.
32. Gillespie, W. Irwin, "Effect of Public Expenditures on the Distribution of Income," in *Essays in Fiscal Federalism,* Richard Musgrave, ed., Brookings Institution, Washington, 1965.
33. Bishop, George, *Tax Burdens and Benefits of Government Expenditures by Income Class, 1961 and 1965,* Tax Foundation, New York, 1967.

REFERENCE TABLES

TABLE A.   TOTAL PERSONAL INCOME AND PER CAPITA
PERSONAL INCOME IN CURRENT AND CONSTANT
1967 DOLLARS, 1897–1967

Year	Personal Income (in Millions)	Per Capita Personal Income	
		Current Dollars	1967 Dollars[a]
1897–1901	$ 14,300	$ 191	$ 841
1902–06	20,200	246	976
1907–11	26,700	295	1,073
1912–16	33,700	341	1,104
1917–21	62,500	592	1,165
1919	65,000	619	1,209
1920	73,400	689	1,178
1921	62,100	572	1,149
1922	62,000	563	1,188
1923	71,500	639	1,323
1924	73,200	641	1,341
1925	75,000	647	1,323
1926	79,500	677	1,384
1927	79,600	669	1,400
1928	79,800	662	1,371
1929	85,905	705	1,460
1930	77,015	625	1,333
1931	65,896	531	1,267
1932	50,150	401	1,084
1933	47,004	374	1,054
1934	53,966	427	1,124
1935	60,405	474	1,222
1936	68,602	535	1,368
1937	74,118	575	1,416
1938	68,346	526	1,318
1939	72,769	555	1,409
1940	78,285	590	1,482
1941	95,972	717	1,683
1942	122,901	908	1,896
1943	151,297	1,102	2,103
1944	165,276	1,190	2,156
1945	171,113	1,218	2,129
1946	178,730	1,259	2,044
1947	191,266	1,322	1,941
1948	210,216	1,428	1,986
1949	207,154	1,383	1,937
1950	227,619	1,495	2,062
1951	255,595	1,650	2,132
1952	272,455	1,729	2,186

Year	Personal Income (in Millions)	Per Capita Personal Income	
		Current Dollars	1967 Dollars[a]
1953	$288,163	$1,799	$2,243
1954	290,136	1,780	2,200
1955	310,889	1,874	2,311
1956	333,006	1,972	2,379
1957	351,101	2,041	2,390
1958	361,174	2,065	2,363
1959	383,528	2,157	2,437
1960	400,953	2,219	2,468
1961	416,814	2,268	2,498
1962	442,617	2,371	2,586
1963	465,487	2,457	2,650
1964	497,462	2,589	2,757
1965	537,760	2,764	2,909
1966	584,005	2,966	3,042
1967	626,400	3,146	3,146

[a] Based on implicit price deflators for personal consumption expenditures (1958 = 100) from *Survey of Current Business;* adjustment to 1967 prices by the Office of Research and Statistics, Social Security Administration.

SOURCE: Personal income from *Survey of Current Business,* Office of Business Economics, Department of Commerce; population data for per capita personal income from *Current Population Reports,* Series P-25, U.S. Bureau of the Census.

TABLE B. FAMILY PERSONAL INCOME:[a] MEAN INCOME, INCOME AT SELECTED POSITIONS, AND PERCENTAGE SHARE RECEIVED BY EACH FIFTH AND TOP 5 PER CENT OF FAMILIES AND UNRELATED INDIVIDUALS, SELECTED YEARS, 1929–1962

Year	Mean Income Before Tax	Income at Selected Positions[b] (Upper Limit of Each Fifth)					Percentage Distribution of Aggregate Income					
		Lowest	Second	Middle	Fourth	Top 5 Per Cent	Lowest Fifth	Second Fifth	Middle Fifth	Fourth Fifth	Highest Fifth	Top 5 Per Cent
		(In current dollars)										
1929	$2,335	—	$1,340	$1,860	$2,810	$ 5,690		12.5	13.8	19.3	54.4	30.0
1935–36	1,631	$ 560	930	1,380	2,120	3,910	4.1	9.2	14.1	20.9	51.7	26.5
1941	2,209	740	1,370	2,040	2,940	5,010	4.1	9.5	15.3	22.3	48.8	24.0
1944	3,614	1,510	2,450	3,410	4,800	8,240	4.9	10.9	16.2	22.2	45.8	20.7
1946	3,940	1,660	2,680	3,650	5,130	9,180	5.0	11.1	16.0	21.8	46.1	21.3
1947	4,126	1,730	2,800	3,830	5,470	9,560	5.0	11.0	16.0	22.0	46.0	20.9
1950	4,444	1,810	3,020	4,160	5,850	10,200	4.8	10.9	16.1	22.1	46.1	21.4
1951	4,904	2,090	3,420	4,680	6,450	11,100	5.0	11.3	16.5	22.3	44.9	20.7
1952	5,122	2,170	3,610	4,910	6,760	11,480	4.9	11.4	16.6	22.4	44.7	20.5
1953	5,389	2,260	3,770	5,180	7,160	12,320	4.9	11.3	16.6	22.5	44.7	19.9
1954	5,356	2,200	3,700	5,120	7,100	12,350	4.8	11.1	16.4	22.5	45.2	20.3
1955	5,640	2,390	3,920	5,370	7,410	13,070	4.8	11.3	16.4	22.3	45.2	20.3
1956	6,007	2,540	4,170	5,680	7,960	13,960	4.8	11.3	16.3	22.3	45.3	20.2
1957	6,238	2,590	4,280	5,940	8,320	14,580	4.7	11.1	16.3	22.4	45.5	20.2

TABLE B (cont.)

Year	Mean Income Before Tax	Income at Selected Positions[b] — Upper Limit of Each Fifth				Top 5 Per Cent	Percentage Distribution of Aggregate Income					
		Lowest	Second	Middle	Fourth		Lowest Fifth	Second Fifth	Middle Fifth	Fourth Fifth	Highest Fifth	Top 5 Per Cent
1958	$6,284	$2,610	$4,290	$5,970	$8,450	$14,700	4.7	11.0	16.3	22.5	45.5	20.0
1959	6,615	2,690	4,500	6,320	8,910	15,740	4.6	10.9	16.3	22.6	45.6	20.0
1960	6,819	2,770	4,660	6,530	9,270	16,240	4.6	10.9	16.4	22.7	45.4	19.6
1961	6,930	2,790	4,710	6,650	9,460	16,460	4.6	10.9	16.3	22.7	45.5	19.6
1962	7,262	2,940	4,950	6,960	9,900	17,230	4.6	10.9	16.3	22.7	45.5	19.6

[a] Family personal income represents the current income received by families and unrelated individuals from all sources, including wage and salary receipts (net of social insurance contributions), other labor income, proprietors' and rental income, dividends, personal interest income, and transfer payments. In addition to monetary income flows family income includes certain nonmoney items such as wages in kind, the value of food and fuel produced and consumed on farms, the net imputed rental value of owner-occupied homes, and imputed interest. Excludes the income received by institutional residents (including military personnel not living with their families), or retained by nonprofit institutions, private trust, pension, and welfare funds. The aggregate income covered in this table is smaller than the total income shown in Table A, because of these exclusions. The aggregate income in this table on the other hand, is larger than the income covered in Table C because of the inclusion of nonmoney income.

For further discussion of the definitions and basis of the estimates of personal income of the Office of Business Economics (OBE), Department of Commerce, as given in Tables A and B, and the income estimates based on the Current Population Survey (Tables C–H), see *Historical Statistics of the United States, Colonial Times to 1957*, Chapter G, General Notes, and Miller, Herman P., "Income Distribution in the United States," Appendix A, a 1960 Census Monograph, U.S. Bureau of the Census.

[b] Rounded to nearest $10.

SOURCE: U.S. Bureau of the Census, *Historical Statistics of the United States, Colonial Times to 1957*; and *Continuation to 1962 and Revisions*—Series G 120, G 113–117, G 100–105.

TABLE C. TOTAL MONEY INCOME OF FAMILIES AND UNRELATED INDIVIDUALS: GINI RATIO, MEAN INCOME, INCOME AT SELECTED POSITIONS, AND PERCENTAGE SHARE RECEIVED BY EACH FIFTH AND TOP 5 PER CENT, 1947–1966

Year	Gini Ratio	Mean Income	Income at Selected Positions						Percentage Distribution of Aggregate Income					
			Upper Limit of Each Fifth				Top 5 Per Cent	Lowest Fifth	Second Fifth	Middle Fifth	Fourth Fifth	Highest Fifth	Top 5 Per Cent
			Lowest	Second	Middle	Fourth							
			(In current dollars)										
1947	.417	$3,224	$1,138	$2,211	$3,190	$4,568	$7,773	3.5	10.5	16.7	23.5	45.8	19.0
1948	.408	3,298	1,156	2,324	3,334	4,726	7,874	3.5	10.7	17.2	23.9	44.7	17.9
1949	.414	3,194	1,060	2,239	3,245	4,652	7,643	3.2	10.5	17.2	24.1	45.0	17.9
1950	.414	3,411	1,114	2,409	3,460	4,939	8,104	3.1	10.5	17.4	24.1	44.9	18.0
1951	.400	3,804	1,393	2,777	3,897	5,483	8,642	3.4	11.1	17.6	24.1	43.7	17.6
1952	.411	4,016	1,406	2,863	4,047	5,725	8,990	3.4	10.8	17.2	24.0	44.6	18.7
1953	.407	4,252	1,440	3,066	4,399	6,138	9,760	3.2	10.7	17.6	24.5	44.0	17.5
1954	.415	4,200	1,342	2,967	4,339	6,170	9,904	3.1	10.3	17.4	24.6	44.6	17.7
1955	.411	4,466	1,475	3,179	4,598	6,498	10,141	3.3	10.5	17.4	24.5	44.3	18.0
1956	.404	4,793	1,649	3,453	4,981	6,953	10,926	3.4	10.7	17.6	24.5	43.8	17.4
1957	.397	4,861	1,679	3,555	5,150	7,082	10,989	3.4	10.8	17.9	24.8	43.1	16.7
1958	.401	5,040	1,744	3,638	5,291	7,341	11,654	3.5	10.7	17.7	24.7	43.5	16.9
1959	.408	5,431	1,842	3,831	5,635	7,878	12,572	3.4	10.4	17.5	24.5	44.2	17.6
1960	.411	5,686	1,921	3,987	5,830	8,234	13,106	3.4	10.4	17.4	24.3	44.5	18.0
1961	.419	5,855	1,913	4,014	5,958	8,526	13,891	3.3	10.1	17.1	24.4	45.2	18.3
1962	.408	6,049	2,027	4,225	6,226	8,869	14,189	3.5	10.3	17.3	24.5	44.3	17.3
1963	.407	6,304	2,122	4,416	6,538	9,278	14,620	3.5	10.4	17.4	24.7	44.0	17.1
1964	.406	6,568	2,246	4,555	6,808	9,735	15,722	3.5	10.3	17.3	24.7	44.1	17.1
1965	.404	6,945	2,384	4,888	7,199	10,179	17,533	3.6	10.5	17.4	24.6	44.0	17.1
1966	.402	7,425	2,549	5,243	7,674	10,826	19,243	3.7	10.5	17.4	24.6	43.8	16.8

SOURCE: Unpublished data from Current Population Survey, provided by U.S. Bureau of Census.

TABLE D. TOTAL MONEY INCOME OF PERSONS AGED 14 AND OVER BY SEX AND AGE: GINI RATIO, MEAN INCOME, INCOME AT SELECTED POSITIONS, AND PERCENTAGE SHARE RECEIVED BY EACH FIFTH AND TOP 5 PER CENT, SELECTED YEARS, 1947–1966

Year, Sex, and Age	Gini Ratio	Mean Income	Income at Selected Positions					Percentage Distribution of Aggregate Income					
			Upper Limit of Each Fifth				Top 5 Per Cent	Lowest Fifth	Second Fifth	Middle Fifth	Fourth Fifth	Highest Fifth	Top 5 Per Cent
			Lowest	Second	Middle	Fourth							
1947			*(In current dollars)*										
Men	.413	$2,636	$939	$1,860	$2,587	$3,489	$5,853	3.7	10.7	16.9	22.6	46.1	21.3
14 to 19	.431	746	199	397	719	1,296	2,048	6.6	6.5	13.3	25.2	48.5	16.2
20 to 24	.323	1,641	758	1,296	1,828	2,416	3,315	5.8	12.5	18.9	25.3	37.6	12.1
25 to 34	.304	2,704	1,461	2,183	2,769	3,484	5,126	6.7	14.0	18.1	22.6	38.6	15.7
35 to 44	.372	3,344	1,628	2,457	3,198	4,164	7,281	5.6	12.3	17.2	21.5	43.5	20.4
45 to 54	.406	3,329	1,464	2,323	3,077	4,090	7,602	4.8	11.8	16.1	21.0	46.3	22.8
55 to 64	.408	2,795	1,090	2,014	2,722	3,674	6,235	4.2	11.1	16.9	22.5	45.3	21.0
65 and over	.597	1,906	369	757	1,329	2,354	5,279	2.6	6.0	9.9	19.0	62.6	37.2
Women	.452	1,290	333	757	1,329	1,967	2,968	3.8	7.7	15.6	24.8	48.1	20.7
14 to 19	.415	686	189	379	668	1,203	1,855	7.1	7.1	12.7	26.0	47.1	15.1
20 to 24	.349	1,226	427	955	1,463	1,895	2,442	4.0	10.7	19.5	27.7	38.1	12.3
25 to 34	.376	1,321	444	944	1,492	2,040	2,821	3.7	10.3	17.9	27.1	41.0	14.5
35 to 44	.395	1,465	449	1,033	1,622	2,246	3,381	3.3	9.9	18.5	25.9	42.4	15.5
45 to 54	.438	1,517	394	965	1,619	2,308	3,420	3.2	8.0	17.4	25.5	45.8	18.9
55 to 64	.473	1,290	301	687	1,282	2,047	3,413	3.8	6.5	14.9	25.1	49.7	20.9
65 and over	.587	1,057	213	425	723	1,201	2,845	4.6	4.6	10.9	16.1	63.8	39.0

TABLE D (cont.)

Year, Sex, and Age	Gini Ratio	Mean In-come	Income at Selected Positions					Percentage Distribution of Aggregate Income					
			Upper Limit of Each Fifth				Top 5 Per Cent	Lowest Fifth	Second Fifth	Middle Fifth	Fourth Fifth	Highest Fifth	Top 5 Per Cent
			Lowest	Second	Middle	Fourth							
		(In current dollars)											
1953													
Men	*.406*	*$3,549*	*$1,145*	*$2,624*	*$3,737*	*$5,039*	*$7,744*	*3.1*	*10.8*	*18.1*	*24.4*	*43.7.*	*18.4*
14 to 19	.496	803	180	360	615	1,307	2,771	6.1	6.1	9.2	21.8	56.9	20.8
20 to 24	.363	2,285	959	1,656	2,441	3,461	5,012	4.4	11.7	17.4	25.9	40.6	14.2
25 to 34	.283	3,909	2,300	3,306	4,119	5,189	7,064	7.0	14.6	19.0	23.6	35.8	13.3
35 to 44	.316	4,435	2,480	3,538	4,436	5,795	9,109	6.4	13.9	17.8	23.0	38.9	15.4
45 to 54	.372	4,382	2,090	3,308	4,318	5,681	8,920	4.9	12.4	17.4	22.7	42.6	19.7
55 to 64	.412	3,796	1,439	2,777	3,737	4,913	8,216	3.7	11.4	17.2	22.4	45.3	21.2
65 and over	.580	2,217	506	885	1,534	3,029	5,770	2.3	6.6	10.2	19.8	61.0	33.4
Women	*.471*	*1,583*	*375*	*840*	*1,621*	*2,606*	*3,885*	*3.1*	*7.3*	*14.7*	*26.5*	*48.4*	*18.8*
14 to 19	.455	686	175	349	564	1,085	2,223	7.1	7.1	9.5	23.0	53.2	19.1
20 to 24	.363	1,595	502	1,190	1,931	2,563	3,333	3.2	10.9	19.2	28.3	38.5	11.3
25 to 34	.421	1,840	480	1,162	2,073	3,012	4,048	2.7	8.8	17.7	27.3	43.6	15.5
35 to 44	.410	1,812	502	1,203	2,016	2,924	4,084	2.8	9.6	17.4	26.6	43.6	15.4
45 to 54	.442	1,968	476	1,219	2,154	3,056	4,298	2.5	8.6	17.2	25.9	45.8	18.7
55 to 64	.468	1,602	431	879	1,550	2,483	4,305	3.1	8.3	14.4	24.7	49.6	19.8
65 and over	.537	1,071	260	521	796	1,278	2,990	4.6	5.5	13.7	16.6	59.7	34.1

TABLE D (cont.)

Year, Sex, and Age	Gini Ratio	Mean Income	Income at Selected Positions					Percentage Distribution of Aggregate Income					
			Upper Limit of Each Fifth				Top 5 Per Cent	Lowest Fifth	Second Fifth	Middle Fifth	Fourth Fifth	Highest Fifth	Top 5 Per Cent
			Lowest	Second	Middle	Fourth							
			(In current dollars)										
1957													
Men	*.421*	*$4,068*	*$1,203*	*$2,936*	*$4,333*	*$5,820*	*$9,063*	*2.9*	*10.0*	*18.0*	*24.7*	*44.4*	*18.7*
14 to 19	.477	678	164	328	491	974	2,363	7.2	7.2	7.2	21.4	57.0	23.6
20 to 24	.358	2,614	1,051	1,989	2,919	4,061	5,626	4.3	11.3	18.5	26.7	39.3	12.6
25 to 34	.285	4,552	2,658	3,925	4,857	5,969	8,628	6.9	14.6	19.3	23.4	35.9	12.6
35 to 44	.334	5,300	2,955	4,224	5,297	6,735	10,442	6.0	13.8	18.1	22.1	40.0	17.2
45 to 54	.389	5,227	2,313	3,918	5,125	6,726	11,313	4.4	12.0	17.4	22.2	43.9	20.0
55 to 64	.417	4,295	1,477	3,022	4,305	5,842	9,651	3.4	10.6	17.1	23.2	45.6	20.9
65 and over	.482	2,233	707	1,146	1,809	3,255	6,053	4.5	7.9	12.7	21.3	53.5	23.9
Women	*.486*	*1,713*	*370*	*848*	*1,694*	*2,963*	*4,512*	*2.8*	*6.6*	*14.0*	*26.2*	*50.3*	*18.6*
14 to 19	.494	690	155	310	465	1,080	2,482	7.1	7.1	7.1	19.8	59.0	22.5
20 to 24	.386	1,776	538	1,229	2,078	2,974	3,837	3.1	10.0	18.4	27.6	40.9	12.2
25 to 34	.428	1,969	444	1,220	2,225	3,362	4,597	2.5	8.1	17.4	28.1	43.9	14.2
35 to 44	.470	2,187	474	1,318	2,242	3,385	4,956	2.2	8.1	16.3	25.2	48.1	20.7
45 to 54	.429	2,121	507	1,354	2,289	3,446	5,269	2.4	8.6	17.2	26.7	45.1	15.5
55 to 64	.486	1,884	432	945	1,814	3,144	5,336	2.6	7.0	14.4	25.5	50.4	18.9
65 and over	.466	1,054	330	618	864	1,351	2,979	4.6	9.2	13.9	18.7	53.5	27.0

TABLE D (cont.)

Year, Sex, and Age	Gini Ratio	Mean Income	Income at Selected Positions					Percentage Distribution of Aggregate Income					
			Upper Limit of Each Fifth				Top 5 Per Cent	Lowest Fifth	Second Fifth	Middle Fifth	Fourth Fifth	Highest Fifth	Top 5 Per Cent
			Lowest	Second	Middle	Fourth							
			(In current dollars)										
1964													
Men	*.429*	*$5,329*	*$1,446*	*$3,586*	*$5,634*	*$7,808*	*$12,841*	*2.6*	*9.5*	*17.5*	*24.8*	*45.7*	*18.6*
14 to 19	.514	773	169	339	524	1,108	2,832	6.3	6.3	7.3	20.5	59.5	26.4
20 to 24	.391	3,172	1,015	2,289	3,535	5,042	6,868	3.3	10.3	18.5	26.9	41.0	13.5
25 to 34	.294	6,073	3,454	5,065	6,418	8,092	11,616	6.9	14.2	19.0	23.6	36.3	13.3
35 to 44	.321	7,211	3,905	5,746	7,249	9,524	15,298	6.4	13.6	18.1	22.7	39.2	15.2
45 to 54	.350	6,914	3,382	5,342	6,837	9,197	15,663	5.4	13.0	17.3	22.8	41.5	16.7
55 to 64	.418	5,884	2,016	4,070	5,876	8,188	14,133	3.6	10.5	16.7	23.7	45.6	19.1
65 and over	.534	3,534	1,100	1,642	2,386	4,230	10,316	4.3	7.6	11.3	17.6	59.2	33.1
Women	*.506*	*2,205*	*451*	*1,001*	*2,086*	*3,712*	*5,984*	*2.2*	*6.4*	*13.6*	*25.8*	*52.1*	*20.6*
14 to 19	.496	679	154	307	461	933	2,654	7.2	7.2	7.2	18.5	59.9	25.1
20 to 24	.421	2,165	523	1,355	2,484	3,697	5,033	2.4	8.4	17.5	28.8	42.8	13.4
25 to 34	.452	2,420	485	1,422	2,658	4,170	5,864	2.0	7.6	16.8	28.2	45.4	15.2
35 to 44	.442	2,659	578	1,639	2,933	4,345	6,521	2.2	8.1	16.9	27.1	45.7	16.1
45 to 54	.437	2,857	751	1,860	2,984	4,598	7,170	2.6	8.9	16.7	26.2	45.6	16.0
55 to 64	.487	2,599	592	1,310	2,547	4,315	7,162	2.5	7.0	14.5	25.7	50.3	18.9
65 and over	.487	1,556	568	824	1,153	1,832	4,451	4.9	9.4	11.8	17.9	56.0	30.1

TABLE D (cont.)

Year, Sex, and Age	Gini Ratio	Mean Income	Income at Selected Positions					Percentage Distribution of Aggregate Income					
			Upper Limit of Each Fifth				Top 5 Per Cent	Lowest Fifth	Second Fifth	Middle Fifth	Fourth Fifth	Highest Fifth	Top 5 Per Cent
			Lowest	Second	Middle	Fourth							
			(In current dollars)										
1966													
Men	.434	$6,005	$1,657	$4,097	$6,330	$8,760	$14,127	2.6	9.5	17.5	24.7	45.7	18.9
14 to 19	.531	941	198	397	721	1,378	3,320	2.1	6.3	11.2	21.0	59.4	26.5
20 to 24	.383	3,722	1,269	2,604	4,116	5,859	8,031	3.7	10.4	18.0	26.7	41.2	13.9
25 to 34	.278	6,886	4,099	5,826	7,194	8,971	12,954	7.5	14.6	18.9	23.3	35.7	12.8
35 to 44	.314	8,193	4,529	6,493	8,174	10,707	18,437	6.9	13.7	17.8	22.7	38.9	15.2
45 to 54	.361	8,169	4,046	6,100	7,790	10,469	19,481	5.7	12.7	17.0	21.9	42.7	18.9
55 to 64	.414	6,857	2,464	4,816	6,639	9,267	17,616	3.8	10.8	16.8	22.6	46.0	20.1
65 and over	.490	3,427	1,154	1,780	2,615	4,356	9,255	4.5	8.5	12.7	19.4	54.9	27.9
Women	.492	2,400	508	1,169	2,327	4,064	6,602	2.1	6.8	14.0	26.2	50.8	19.0
14 to 19	.520	798	169	338	526	1,209	3,028	2.1	6.4	10.6	20.7	60.2	25.0
20 to 24	.424	2,363	561	1,484	2,736	3,974	5,515	2.3	8.3	17.9	28.2	43.3	14.1
25 to 34	.443	2,763	596	1,714	3,113	4,561	6,684	2.0	8.1	17.3	27.4	45.2	15.6
35 to 44	.432	2,964	738	1,971	3,231	4,805	7,131	2.2	8.9	17.6	26.5	44.8	15.6
45 to 54	.432	3,206	874	2,110	3,369	5,077	7,797	2.6	9.1	17.2	26.0	45.2	16.5
55 to 64	.473	2,906	701	1,502	2,985	4,678	7,639	2.4	7.4	15.3	25.8	49.1	18.8
65 and over	.463	1,633	619	913	1,291	2,005	4,879	4.6	9.4	13.4	19.2	53.4	26.2

SOURCE: Data for 1947, 1953, 1957, and 1964 from Henson, Mary F., "Trends in the Income of Families and Persons in the United States, 1947–1964," Technical Paper No. 17, U.S. Bureau of the Census, Table 36; data for 1966, unpublished data furnished by U.S. Bureau of the Census.

TABLE E. TOTAL MONEY INCOME OF FAMILIES BY COLOR OF HEAD: GINI RATIO, MEAN INCOME, INCOME AT SELECTED POSITIONS, AND PERCENTAGE SHARE RECEIVED BY EACH FIFTH AND TOP 5 PER CENT, 1947–1966

Year and Color of Head	Gini Ratio	Mean Income	Income at Selected Positions (Upper Limit of Each Fifth) (In current dollars)					Percentage Distribution of Aggregate Income					
			Lowest	Second	Middle	Fourth	Top 5 Per Cent	Lowest Fifth	Second Fifth	Middle Fifth	Fourth Fifth	Highest Fifth	Top 5 Per Cent
White													
1947	.363	$3,718	$1,756	$2,714	$3,603	$5,072	$8,383	5.5	12.2	16.9	22.8	42.6	17.4
1948	.361	3,842	1,844	2,877	3,785	5,256	8,581	5.4	12.4	17.3	23.1	41.9	16.9
1949	.367	3,729	1,715	2,784	3,699	5,199	8,330	5.0	12.3	17.3	23.4	42.0	16.6
1950	.372	3,991	1,836	3,025	3,961	5,502	8,877	4.9	12.3	17.2	23.5	42.1	17.3
1951	.352	4,398	2,154	3,368	4,370	5,944	9,339	5.5	12.7	17.5	23.0	41.3	16.6
1952	.359	4,722	2,282	3,559	4,708	6,325	9,793	5.3	12.6	17.4	23.1	41.6	17.6
1953	.353	4,916	2,354	3,824	5,048	6,778	10,495	5.0	12.8	18.0	23.6	40.6	15.7
1954	.359	4,909	2,235	3,741	4,984	6,796	10,703	4.9	12.4	17.5	23.8	41.4	16.2
1955	.358	5,228	2,465	4,005	5,306	7,104	10,917	5.1	12.6	17.9	23.3	41.1	16.7
1956	.347	5,619	2,729	4,324	5,698	7,638	11,874	5.4	12.8	17.9	23.4	40.6	16.2
1957	.345	5,719	2,813	4,467	5,829	7,747	11,854	5.5	12.9	18.1	23.5	40.1	15.7
1958	.340	5,911	2,874	4,577	5,996	7,965	12,500	5.6	12.8	17.6	23.5	40.5	15.6
1959	.349	6,367	3,028	4,900	6,437	8,693	13,540	5.5	12.5	17.9	23.2	40.8	16.1
1960	.357	6,676	3,105	5,083	6,697	9,079	14,203	5.3	12.4	17.5	23.3	41.5	16.8
1961	.364	6,933	3,146	5,157	6,917	9,446	15,367	5.2	12.2	17.1	23.3	42.2	17.3
1962	.350	7,112	3,331	5,381	7,148	9,833	15,839	5.5	12.5	17.5	23.4	41.2	15.9
1963	.348	7,420	3,484	5,628	7,548	10,286	16,856	5.5	12.6	17.7	23.6	40.7	15.4
1964	.349	7,732	3,610	5,867	7,875	10,702	18,273	5.6	12.3	17.7	23.8	40.6	15.0
1965	.347	8,200	3,881	6,239	8,285	11,170	19,911	5.6	12.5	17.7	23.4	40.8	15.5
1966	.343	8,749	4,193	6,671	8,870	11,940	21,115	5.7	12.6	17.7	23.5	40.5	15.1

TABLE E (cont.)

Year and Color of Head	Gini Ratio	Mean Income	Income at Selected Positions					Percentage Distribution of Aggregate Income					
			Upper Limit of Each Fifth				Top 5 Per Cent	Lowest Fifth	Second Fifth	Middle Fifth	Fourth Fifth	Highest Fifth	Top 5 Per Cent
			Lowest	Second	Middle	Fourth							
Nonwhite													
1947	.406	$2,016	$ 760	$1,319	$1,927	$2,937	$ 5,398	4.8	10.2	15.7	23.6	45.8	17.0
1948	.406	2,104	771	1,402	2,148	3,144	5,215	4.3	10.1	16.9	24.4	44.3	16.6
1949	.415	1,965	660	1,303	2,023	2,918	4,921	3.8	9.9	16.6	24.6	45.1	17.1
1950	.402	2,128	723	1,479	2,254	3,178	5,200	3.8	9.7	17.9	25.1	43.4	16.6
1951	.405	2,368	827	1,625	2,458	3,577	5,568	3.8	10.3	16.9	25.3	43.8	16.1
1952	.365	2,639	1,122	1,945	2,733	3,622	6,019	5.0	11.4	16.9	23.7	41.9	16.0
1953	.393	2,890	1,038	2,033	2,992	4,378	7,117	3.9	10.7	17.0	25.1	43.4	15.2
1954	.402	2,758	929	1,848	2,990	4,183	6,685	3.6	10.0	17.2	25.8	43.4	15.5
1955	.388	2,890	1,043	2,013	3,129	4,423	6,733	4.0	10.3	17.8	25.5	42.4	14.3
1956	.396	3,073	1,092	2,127	3,213	4,661	7,340	3.9	10.5	17.2	25.3	43.1	15.0
1957	.405	3,241	1,078	2,193	3,427	5,087	7,813	3.6	10.2	16.9	26.0	43.3	15.0
1958	.417	3,351	1,169	2,172	3,433	5,033	8,141	4.0	9.9	16.2	25.0	44.9	17.0
1959	.414	3,523	1,215	2,257	3,559	5,387	8,627	4.1	9.5	16.5	25.3	44.7	16.2
1960	.410	3,913	1,323	2,515	3,959	6,046	9,951	3.9	9.6	16.4	25.4	44.7	16.2
1961	.414	4,031	1,409	2,489	3,988	6,045	10,353	4.0	9.6	15.9	24.5	46.0	17.4
1962	.403	4,020	1,487	2,713	4,019	5,959	10,114	4.2	10.6	16.6	24.2	44.5	16.3
1963	.403	4,340	1,655	2,806	4,294	6,517	10,462	4.4	10.2	16.1	24.6	44.7	17.2
1964	.399	4,772	1,866	3,155	4,696	7,060	11,492	4.5	10.5	16.2	24.3	44.6	16.7
1965	.388	4,903	1,949	3,308	4,915	7,427	11,813	4.6	10.7	16.5	24.7	43.5	15.5
1966	.385	5,526	2,175	3,724	5,637	8,299	12,907	4.7	10.7	16.8	24.9	42.9	15.4

NOTE: These figures are estimates derived from a sample survey of households (Current Population Survey) and, therefore, are subject to sampling variability. Moreover, as in all field surveys of income, the figures are subject to errors of response and nonreporting. See Table B, footnote a, for references to discussion of definitions and coverage of different income series.

SOURCE: 1947–1962, data from Henson, Mary F., "Trends in the Income of Families and Persons in the United States, 1947–1964," Technical Paper No. 17, U.S. Bureau of Census, Table 23; 1965–66, unpublished data from U.S. Bureau of the Census.

TABLE F. TOTAL MONEY INCOME OF UNRELATED INDIVIDUALS BY COLOR: GINI RATIO, MEAN INCOME, INCOME AT SELECTED POSITIONS, AND PERCENTAGE SHARE RECEIVED BY EACH FIFTH AND TOP 5 PER CENT, 1947–1966

Year and Color	Gini Ratio	Mean Income	Income at Selected Positions — Upper Limit of Each Fifth (In current dollars)				Top 5 Per Cent	Percentage Distribution of Aggregate Income — Lowest Fifth	Second Fifth	Middle Fifth	Fourth Fifth	Highest Fifth	Top 5 Per Cent
			Lowest	Second	Middle	Fourth							
White													
1947	.574	$1,798	$325	$751	$1,445	$2,400	$4,117	2.7	5.3	11.3	21.3	59.4	34.2
1948	.481	1,542	377	804	1,442	2,464	4,045	3.2	7.5	13.4	25.1	50.9	20.6
1949	.475	1,612	382	832	1,596	2,623	4,253	3.0	7.3	14.0	26.1	49.6	19.4
1950	.484	1,658	378	819	1,635	2,809	4,276	2.9	7.0	13.5	26.6	49.9	19.4
1951	.476	1,789	408	868	1,866	3,106	4,584	2.7	7.0	14.1	27.5	48.6	17.9
1952	.479	2,071	527	1,054	2,061	3,309	5,121	2.7	7.5	14.8	25.5	49.5	20.7
1953	.522	2,227	478	966	2,101	3,310	5,439	2.2	6.4	13.6	23.8	53.9	26.2
1954	.489	1,975	491	932	1,854	3,238	5,454	2.5	7.4	13.4	25.5	51.2	20.2
1955	.516	2,206	530	996	1,960	3,386	5,643	2.5	6.6	13.0	24.1	53.6	24.9
1956	.488	2,196	570	1,044	1,986	3,658	5,752	3.0	7.1	13.3	25.6	51.0	20.4
1957	.482	2,381	599	1,177	2,209	3,954	6,446	2.9	7.2	13.6	25.2	51.1	19.9
1958	.506	2,481	586	1,178	2,261	4,033	6,781	2.6	7.0	13.1	25.2	52.1	21.4
1959	.515	2,600	599	1,233	2,300	4,155	6,868	2.6	6.9	12.9	24.2	53.4	23.4
1960	.487	2,705	679	1,328	2,565	4,414	6,966	3.0	7.1	13.8	25.7	50.5	20.3
1961	.506	2,900	708	1,380	2,529	4,582	7,694	2.9	6.8	13.1	24.2	53.0	23.1
1962	.488	2,956	793	1,411	2,559	4,863	8,117	3.3	7.2	12.9	24.5	52.1	20.9
1963	.502	3,003	752	1,429	2,561	4,969	8,418	2.7	7.2	12.8	24.8	52.6	20.8
1964	.506	3,272	812	1,484	2,917	5,191	8,663	2.6	6.9	13.0	24.7	52.8	22.9
1965	.486	3,379	916	1,674	3,139	5,497	9,201	2.7	7.6	13.6	25.1	51.0	20.3
1966	.498	3,638	1,032	1,753	3,217	5,644	10,028	2.8	7.4	13.2	23.8	52.7	22.7

TABLE F (cont.)

Year and Color	Gini Ratio	Mean Income	Income at Selected Positions					Percentage Distribution of Aggregate Income					
			Upper Limit of Each Fifth				Top 5 Per Cent	Lowest Fifth	Second Fifth	Middle Fifth	Fourth Fifth	Highest Fifth	Top 5 Per Cent
			Lowest	Second	Middle	Fourth							
Nonwhite													
1947	.447	$ 980	$258	$ 527	$ 965	$1,548	$2,683	5.0	5.8	14.9	25.5	48.7	18.7
1948	.448	1,056	286	597	981	1,748	3,098	4.6	7.2	13.9	25.8	48.6	16.7
1949	.423	1,054	301	629	1,019	1,793	2,798	4.6	8.0	14.6	26.8	46.1	15.3
1950	.475	1,172	277	589	1,078	2,047	3,353	4.2	6.0	13.6	25.8	50.4	18.0
1951	.446	1,259	311	688	1,393	2,091	3,047	3.9	7.0	14.7	27.9	46.5	17.1
1952	.445	1,359	378	813	1,318	2,144	3,462	3.6	8.6	15.3	24.3	48.2	19.1
1953	.419	1,504	467	884	1,535	2,565	3,449	3.2	9.4	15.1	27.5	44.7	15.0
1954	.525	1,489	347	697	1,166	2,239	3,723	3.3	7.1	11.1	23.0	55.6	26.7
1955	.459	1,322	350	732	1,255	2,215	3,454	3.7	8.0	13.9	25.5	48.9	18.3
1956	.462	1,616	437	834	1,652	2,596	4,329	3.0	8.3	13.8	26.2	48.7	17.6
1957	.453	1,559	482	833	1,438	2,641	4,183	3.1	9.2	13.0	26.0	48.6	16.4
1958	.472	1,603	430	842	1,436	2,714	4,336	3.0	8.2	13.1	25.6	50.0	18.4
1959	.480	1,637	435	837	1,500	2,688	4,696	3.0	8.1	12.9	24.8	51.2	19.1
1960	.490	1,798	507	855	1,467	2,974	5,320	2.9	8.1	11.6	24.5	52.8	18.8
1961	.503	1,875	468	890	1,490	3,156	5,665	2.6	7.5	11.9	24.0	54.0	21.2
1962	.479	1,886	570	976	1,563	2,870	5,676	3.5	7.8	13.5	22.1	53.1	21.6
1963	.499	1,979	468	973	1,714	3,183	5,712	2.5	7.1	13.4	23.8	53.2	20.9
1964	.485	2,205	540	1,128	2,026	3,729	6,567	2.6	7.7	13.2	24.9	51.6	17.9
1965	.471	2,406	635	1,275	2,205	4,163	6,677	2.6	8.0	13.9	25.4	50.1	17.3
1966	.472	2,500	673	1,316	2,339	4,149	6,981	2.7	8.1	14.0	25.0	50.3	17.9

SOURCE. See Table E.

TABLE G. PERCENTAGE DISTRIBUTION OF ALL FAMILIES AND OF LOWEST FIFTH OF FAMILIES RANKED BY SIZE OF MONEY INCOME BY SELECTED CHARACTERISTICS, SELECTED YEARS, 1947–1966

Characteristics	All Families				Lowest Fifth Ranked by Size of Money Income				Per Cent of All Families in Lowest Fifth			
	1947	1957	1964	1966	1947	1957	1964	1966	1947	1957	1964	1966
Number (in thousands)	37,237	43,696	47,835	48,922	7,447	8,739	9,567	9,784	—	—	—	—
Color of head												
Total per cent	100.0	100.0	100.0	100.0	100.0	100.0	100.0	100.0	20.0	20.0	20.0	20.0
White	91.2	90.5	90.0	90.0	78.5	78.1	78.9	79.4	17.2	17.3	17.5	17.6
Nonwhite	8.8	9.5	10.0	10.0	21.5	21.9	21.1	20.6	48.9	46.1	42.2	41.2
Region												
Total per cent	100.0	100.0	100.0	100.0	100.0	100.0	100.0	100.0	20.0	20.0	20.0	20.0
Northeast	n.a.	26.2	25.2	24.6	n.a.	16.8	17.7	18.9	n.a.	12.8	14.0	15.4
North Central		28.8	28.1	27.8		25.0	25.1	23.4		17.4	17.9	16.8
South		30.4	30.4	30.6		47.9	44.0	43.9		31.5	28.9	28.7
West		14.6	16.3	17.0		10.3	13.2	13.8		14.1	16.2	16.2
Region and color												
Total per cent	100.0	100.0	100.0	100.0	100.0	100.0	100.0	100.0	20.0	20.0	20.0	20.0
Northeast												
White	n.a.	24.7	23.4	22.9	n.a.	14.6	15.3	16.3	n.a.	11.8	13.1	14.2
Nonwhite		1.5	1.8	1.7		2.2	2.4	2.6		29.3	26.7	30.1
North Central												
White		26.8	26.2	25.7		22.1	22.2	20.4		16.5	16.9	15.9
Nonwhite		2.0	1.9	2.1		2.9	2.9	3.0		29.0	30.5	28.6
South												
White		25.3	25.4	25.8		32.4	29.7	30.8		25.6	23.4	23.9
Nonwhite		5.1	5.0	4.8		15.5	14.3	13.1		60.8	57.2	54.6
West												
White		13.7	15.0	15.5		9.0	11.7	11.9		13.1	15.6	15.3
Nonwhite		0.9	1.3	1.4		1.3	1.5	1.9		28.9	23.1	27.2

TABLE G (cont.)

Characteristics	All Families				Lowest Fifth Ranked by Size of Money Income				Per Cent of All Families in Lowest Fifth			
	1947	1957	1964	1966	1947	1957	1964	1966	1947	1957	1964	1966
Age of head												
Total per cent	100.0	100.0	100.0	100.0	100.0	100.0	100.0	100.0	20.0	20.0	20.0	20.0
14 to 24	5.0	5.2	6.1	6.2	6.5	6.2	8.7	8.7	26.0	23.8	28.5	28.1
25 to 34	22.8	22.1	19.4	19.5	17.4	12.9	13.7	13.1	15.3	11.7	14.1	13.4
35 to 44	24.0	24.1	23.3	22.7	17.5	14.6	14.0	12.6	14.6	12.1	12.0	11.1
45 to 54	20.7	21.2	21.6	21.7	15.9	17.5	13.8	13.6	15.4	16.5	12.8	12.5
55 to 64	16.0	14.5	15.6	15.7	16.6	16.4	15.9	14.9	20.8	22.6	20.4	19.0
65 and over	11.5	12.9	14.0	14.2	26.2	32.3	34.0	37.0	45.6	50.1	48.6	52.1
Type of family												
Total per cent	100.0	100.0	100.0	100.0	100.0	100.0	100.0	100.0	20.0	20.0	20.0	20.0
Male head	90.1	90.6	89.8	89.4	81.8	78.2	75.6	74.7	18.2	17.3	16.8	16.7
Married, wife present	86.8	88.0	87.3	86.9	77.5	74.4	72.0	71.3	17.9	16.9	16.5	16.4
Wife in paid labor force	n.a.	24.7	28.7	30.7	n.a.	11.9	11.8	12.5	n.a.	9.6	8.2	8.1
Wife not in paid labor force	n.a.	63.3	58.6	56.3	n.a.	62.5	60.2	58.8	n.a.	19.7	20.5	20.9
Other marital status	3.3	2.6	2.5	2.4	4.3	3.8	3.6	3.4	26.1	29.2	28.8	28.4
Female head	10.0	9.4	10.2	10.6	18.2	21.9	24.4	25.3	36.4	46.5	47.8	47.7

SOURCE: Data for 1947, 1957, 1964 from Henson, Mary F., "Trends in the Income of Families and Persons in the United States, 1947–64," Technical Paper No. 17, U.S. Bureau of the Census, Tables A and C; data for 1966 from unpublished data provided by U.S. Bureau of the Census.

801

TABLE H. THE POOR AND NEAR POOR: NUMBER AND PERCENTAGE OF PERSONS IN HOUSEHOLDS BELOW SOCIAL SECURITY ADMINISTRATION POVERTY LEVEL AND BELOW LOW-INCOME LEVEL, BY FAMILY STATUS AND COLOR OF HEAD, 1959, 1964, AND 1966

(numbers in thousands)

Family Status and Color of Head	1959					1966				
	Total	Poor		Poor and Near-Poor		Total	Poor		Poor and Near-Poor	
		Number	Per Cent	Number	Per Cent		Number	Per Cent	Number	Per Cent
All persons	176,479	38,940	22.1	54,746	31.0	193,415	29,657	15.3	44,807	23.2
In families	165,777	33,864	20.4	49,124	29.6	181,048	24,836	13.7	39,205	21.7
Head	45,062	8,281	18.4	12,040	26.7	48,922	6,086	12.4	9,640	19.7
Male	40,559	6,352	15.7	9,741	24.0	43,750	4,276	9.8	7,337	16.8
Female	4,503	1,929	42.8	2,299	51.1	5,171	1,810	35.0	2,302	44.5
Children under age 18	63,745	16,637	26.1	22,604	35.5	69,771	12,539	18.0	19,176	27.5
Other family members	56,970	8,946	15.7	14,480	25.4	62,355	6,211	10.0	10,389	16.7
Unrelated individuals	10,702	5,076	47.4	5,622	52.5	12,367	4,821	39.0	5,602	45.3
Under age 65	7,068	2,603	36.8	2,929	41.4	7,489	2,124	28.4	2,436	32.5
Men	3,145	924	29.4	1,065	33.9	3,279	712	21.7	858	26.2
Women	3,923	1,679	42.8	1,864	47.5	4,210	1,412	33.5	1,578	37.5
Aged 65 and over	3,631	2,473	68.1	2,693	74.2	4,878	2,697	55.3	3,166	64.9
Men	1,070	641	59.9	731	68.3	1,285	565	44.0	700	54.5
Women	2,561	1,832	71.5	1,962	76.6	3,593	2,132	59.3	2,466	68.6

TABLE H (cont.)

(numbers in thousands)

Family Status and Color of Head	1959					1966				
	Total	Poor		Poor and Near-Poor		Total	Poor		Poor and Near-Poor	
		Number	Per Cent	Number	Per Cent		Number	Per Cent	Number	Per Cent
White persons	156,869	28,231	18.0	41,917	26.7	170,384	20,313	11.9	32,591	19.1
In families	147,714	24,072	16.3	37,290	25.2	159,598	16,287	10.2	27,888	17.5
Head	40,828	6,183	15.1	9,483	23.2	44,016	4,375	9.9	7,343	16.7
Male	37,277	4,932	13.2	7,933	21.3	40,006	3,264	8.2	5,850	14.6
Female	3,544	1,251	35.3	1,550	43.7	4,010	1,111	27.7	1,493	37.2
Children under age 18	55,017	11,067	20.1	17,154	31.2	59,578	7,526	12.6	12,748	21.4
Other family members	51,869	6,822	13.1	10,653	20.5	56,004	4,386	7.8	7,797	13.9
Unrelated individuals	9,155	4,159	45.4	4,627	50.5	10,786	4,026	37.3	4,703	43.6
Under age 65	5,810	1,913	32.9	2,166	37.3	6,296	1,626	25.8	1,867	29.7
Men	2,481	611	24.6	716	28.9	2,688	540	20.1	650	24.2
Women	3,329	1,302	39.1	1,450	43.6	3,608	1,086	30.1	1,217	33.7
Aged 65 and over	3,344	2,246	67.2	2,461	73.6	4,490	2,400	53.5	2,836	63.2
Men	943	550	58.3	637	67.6	1,132	467	41.3	581	51.3
Women	2,401	1,696	70.6	1,824	76.0	3,358	1,933	57.6	2,255	67.2

TABLE H (cont.)

Family Status and Color of Head	1959					1966				
	Total	Poor		Poor and Near-Poor		Total	Poor		Poor and Near-Poor	
		Number	Per Cent	Number	Per Cent		Number	Per Cent	Number	Per Cent
	(numbers in thousands)									
Nonwhite persons	*19,610*	*10,709*	*54.6*	*12,829*	*65.4*	*23,034*	*9,345*	*40.6*	*12,218*	*53.0*
In families	18,063	9,792	54.2	11,834	65.5	21,450	8,549	39.9	11,317	52.8
Head	4,234	2,098	49.6	2,557	60.4	4,905	1,711	34.9	2,297	46.8
Male	3,285	1,420	43.2	1,808	55.0	3,744	1,012	27.0	1,488	39.7
Female	949	678	71.4	749	78.9	1,161	699	60.2	810	69.8
Children under age 18	8,728	5,570	63.8	6,577	75.4	10,193	5,014	49.2	6,427	63.1
Other family members	5,101	2,124	41.7	2,700	52.9	6,352	1,824	28.7	2,593	40.8
Unrelated individuals	1,547	917	59.3	995	64.3	1,584	796	50.3	901	56.9
Under age 65	1,258	690	54.8	763	60.7	1,196	499	41.7	571	47.7
Men	664	313	47.1	349	52.6	592	172	29.1	209	35.3
Women	594	377	63.5	414	69.7	604	327	54.1	362	59.9
Aged 65 and over	288	227	78.8	232	80.6	388	297	76.5	330	85.1
Men	128	91	71.1	94	73.4	152	98	64.5	119	78.3
Women	160	136	85.0	138	86.3	236	199	84.3	211	89.4

SOURCE: Derived by the Social Security Administration from special tabulations by the U.S. Bureau of the Census from the Current Population Surveys for March, 1960 and 1967.

INDEX

INDEX